Platinum Edition

Using

MICROSOFT®

Using

Windows® 98

Ed Bott and Ron Person

Platinum Edition Using Windows 98

International Standard Book Number: 0-7897-1489-2

Library of Congress Catalog Card Number: 98-84642

Printed in the United States of America

First Printing: *June, 1998*

00 99 98   4   3   2   1

Trademarks

All terms mentioned in this book that are known to be trademarks or service marks have been appropriately capitalized. Que Corporation cannot attest to the accuracy of this information. Use of a term in this book should not be regarded as affecting the validity of any trademark or service mark.

Contents at a Glance

Table of Contents

9 Working with Disks and Drives 135

III Working with Applications

VI | Windows Internet Services

VII | Windows Network Services

VIII | Appendixes

Credits

EXECUTIVE EDITOR
Jeff Koch

ACQUISITIONS EDITOR
Jane Brownlow

DEVELOPMENT EDITORS
Mark Cierzniak
Jim Minatel

MANAGING EDITOR
Sarah Kearns

PROJECT EDITOR
Christopher Morris

COPY EDITORS
Sydney Jones
Audra McFarland
June Waldman

TECHNICAL EDITORS
Rob Bogue
Kyle Bryant
Ron Ellenbecker
Walter Glenn
Henry Wolin

SOFTWARE DEVELOPMENT SPECIALIST
Jack Belbot

BOOK DESIGNERS
Ruth Harvey
Kim Scott

COVER DESIGNER
Dan Armstrong
Ruth Harvey

PRODUCTION TEAM
Laura Knox
Nicole Ritch
Lisa Stumpf
Pamela Woolf

INDEXER
Cheryl Jackson

Composed in *Century Old Style* and *ITC Franklin Gothic* by Que Corporation.

To Judy, for her love and patience, and to Katy and Bianca, who have taught me the meaning of happiness
—Ed Bott

About the Authors

Dean Andrews is a freelance writer living in Boston. After receiving a bachelor's degree in computer science from the University of California at Berkeley, he worked as a software developer at IBM and was a systems consultant to small businesses in the San Francisco Bay area. In 1991, he joined the computer press and has worked on staff at *InfoWorld*, as a Senior Test Developer, and *PC World*, as the Manager of Usability Testing. Now, as a freelance writer, he frequently contributes to a variety of publications including *PC World*, *Macworld*, and *Boston.com*, the on-line hub of the *Boston Globe*. Mr. Andrews also is a contributing author in *Peter Norton's Guide to Upgrading and Repairing PCs* and *Windows 98 Installation and Configuration Handbook*.

Ty Belknap has been in the computer industry for over six years, working as a hardware technician, technical support advisor, and software support engineer. He helped launch the Windows 95 help desk for Microsoft, and vowed to "never do it again." He currently is a support engineer for a government agency in Washington state. He is spending his free time obtaining his MCSE, and currently holds MCPs in Windows 95 and Networking Essentials. Ty can be reached by email at **wrldbuld@blarg.net**.

Ed Bott is a best-selling author and award-winning computer journalist with more than 10 years' experience in the personal computer industry. As senior contributing editor of *PC Computing*, he is responsible for the magazine's extensive coverage of Windows 95, Windows 98, Windows NT, and Microsoft Office. From 1991 until 1993, he was editor of *PC Computing*, and for three years before that he was managing editor of *PC World* magazine. Ed has written numerous books for Que Publishing, including the "User Friendly" editions of *Using Windows 95* and *Using Microsoft Office 97*.

Ed is a two-time winner of the Computer Press Award, most recently for *PC Computing*'s annual Windows SuperGuide, a collection of tips, tricks and advice, for users of Windows 95 and Windows NT. He lives in Redmond, Washington, with his wife, Judy Merrill, and two incredibly smart and affectionate cats, Katy and Bianca.

Kyle Bryant, Microsoft MVP for NT and Operating Systems, is the owner of a Dallas-based PC network integration firm and has over 15 years' experience in the personal computer industry. He was an early advocate of the Microsoft Windows platform and continues to follow Windows technology developments under Windows 95, Windows 98, and Windows NT.

Phil Callihan is the WAN Administrator at the National Center for Manufacturing Sciences (NCMS), a research and development consortium based in Ann Arbor, Michigan. Phil has six years' of experience with Microsoft products and holds both the MSCE and MCT certifications from Microsoft. In addition to his employment at NCMS, he works as a consultant and performs training in Microsoft Networking and Internet technologies. He is a 1993 graduate of the University of Michigan. Phil lives in Ann Arbor, Michigan with his wife, Lisa, and their dog, Tribble. Phil can be reached on the Internet at **philc@ncms.org** and on his home page (**http://mis.ncms.org/philc/phil.htm**).

Michael Desmond is a senior associate editor at *PC World* magazine and author of *Peter Norton's Guide to Upgrading and Repairing PCs*. He is also president of the Computer Press Assocation, an organization of working editors, writers, and producers covering computing issues and the computer industry. He is a contributor to both the *Special* and *Platinum Editions* of *Using Windows 98*, and was co-author of *Platinum Edition: Using Windows 95*. Michael lives in Vermont with his wife, Anne, and two sons, Kevin and Patrick.

Christopher Gagnon is a network analyst and consultant with an Atlanta-based software development firm. He has worked with Digital Equipment Corporation, IBM, and several practice management firms in the healthcare industry. He has served as network administrator on several occasions and knows only too well the politics and technical nuances of this unique environment. When he's not reading trade magazines and technical manuals, he enjoys playing his didgeridoo, chasing his cat, and reading about theoretical physics. He currently resides in the Atlanta suburb of Roswell, Georgia, with his wife, Keshly, and their daughter, Paige.

Theresa Hadden, MCSE, MCT, has over 10 years of system administration experience using Novell, UNIX, and Windows NT. She is currently teaching in the MCSE program at a local college where she teaches core courses and Internet products, both in the classroom and via the Internet. In addition, she does consulting for organizations with Windows NT and Novell networks. She is actively involved in the design and implementation of online courses, which includes instructor access using audio conferencing via the Internet. She is the mother of two sons and lives in New Mexico.

Jerry Honeycutt provides business-related technical leadership to the Internet community and software development industry. He has served companies such as The Travelers, IBM, Nielsen North America, IRM, Howard Systems International, and NCR. Jerry has participated in the industry since before the days of Microsoft Windows 1.0, and is completely hooked on Windows 95 and the Internet.

Jerry is the author of *Using the Internet with Windows 95, Windows 95 Registry & Customization Handbook, Special Edition Using the Windows 95 Registry, VBScript by Example, Special Edition Using the Internet 3E, Using the Internet 2E*, and *Windows NT and Windows 95 Registry and Customization Handbook* published by Que. He has been printed in *Computer Language* magazine and is a regular speaker at the Windows World and Comdex trade shows on topics related to software development, Windows 95, and the Internet.

Feel free to contact Jerry on the Internet at **jerry@honeycutt.com** or visit his web site at **http://rampages.onramp.net/~jerry**.

Dennis Jones's first desktop computer was a North Star Horizon, which in 1981 began his long fascination with microcomputers. He is co-author of Que's *Special Edition Using Microsoft FrontPage 98*, and has contributed to several other Que titles. He is a freelance technical writer, software trainer, writing instructor, and also a published novelist. He lives near Ottawa, Canada.

Grant King is a software developer, author, and attorney who lives in Atlanta with his wife, Nancy, and daughter, Elizabeth. He has been either the lead author or a contributing author on several books and articles relating to 32-bit Windows operating systems and software development. He also maintains *The Windows Mill*, a web site devoted to news about Windows 95, Windows 98, and Windows NT. Grant received his B.A. from The University of the South and his J.D. from Georgia State University College of Law where he graduated *magna cum laude*. His email address is **ggking3@mindspring.com**.

Curtis Knight is a senior quality assurance analyst, technical writer, and technical editor. Curtis lives in Vancouver, Washington. By day he works in Symantec Corporation's Beaverton, Oregon, development site. At night he is a freelance writer and technical editor for Macmillan Computer Publishing.

Curtis's overall computer industry experience includes MIS, technical support, data recovery, quality assurance, technical writing, and technical editing. Like most computer professionals, he is his family's personal computer consultant. He is currently training his 11-year-old son to take over the family consulting responsibilities.

Dan Logan is an award-winning freelance writer, book publisher, technical writer, and journalist from Cambria, California. He has contributed to a number of computer books, including Que's *Using PCs*. He has also published a regional book, *The Computer Resource Guide: San Luis Obispo and Santa Maria*, and is publisher of a regional web site and newsletter called the *Tri-tip Computer News* (**http://www.thegrid.net/dlogan**). Dan's articles have appeared in more than 40 magazines and newspapers, including the *Los Angeles Times* and *San Francisco Chronicle*. He is on the board of directors of Softec, the Central Coast Software and Technology Association.

Larry Passo is a principal systems engineer for QuickStart Technologies, a Microsoft Solution Provider Partner and Authorized Technical Education Center, at their headquarters in Newport Beach, California. With over 20 years of experience in the computer industry as a software developer, design engineer, and network specialist, Larry holds certifications as both a Microsoft Certified Systems Engineer and Microsoft Certified Trainer. He provides advanced-level consulting and training for a variety of Microsoft operating systems and the Microsoft BackOffice family of products, and is a Contributing Writer for *Microsoft Certified Professional* magazine. Larry and his wife, Debra, live in Irvine, California.

Ron Person has written more than 20 books for Que Corporation, including the best-selling original editions of *Special Edition Using Microsoft Word 97* and *Special Edition Using Microsoft Excel 97*. He was lead author for the original editions of the best-selling *Special Edition Using Windows 95* and *Platinum Edition Using Windows 95*. He has an M.S. in physics from Ohio State University and an M.B.A. from Hardin-Simmons University. Ron was one of Microsoft's original Consulting Partners and Microsoft Solution Providers.

James Portanova, CNE, is a self-employed computer programmer and consultant who has earned a CTIA A+ certified technician rating. He owns Network Consulting Services, which specifies, installs, configures, maintains, and troubleshoots Local Area Networks for small- to medium-sized business and professional clients. He also is the owner of Hot Properties Software, the programming and reselling arm of his business.

James earned a B.A. in English and philosophy from Adelphi University in Garden City, NY, in 1976. He is the author of the 1996 "Career Focus" feature article for *LAN Times*. James is currently involved in completing the requirements for the MCSE+Internet track.

Paul Sanna has been using PCs for almost 10 years, and he has been using Windows NT since its first Beta program. Paul is a project manager in the development department of Hyperion Software, Stamford, CT, where he works on the company's line of client/server financial accounting software. He has co-authored three books on Windows 95, *Understanding Windows 95, Inside Windows 95* (New Riders), and *The Windows Installation and Configuration Handbook* (Que). Paul has a degree in English from Boston University. He lives in Bethel, CT, with his wife, Andrea, his twin daughters, Rachel, and Allison, and their new sister, Victoria. He can be reached on the Internet at **psanna@ix.netcom.com**.

Rob Tidrow is a writer, web-site designer, trainer, and president of Tidrow Communications, Inc., a firm specializing in content creation and delivery. Rob has authored or co-authored over 25 books on a wide variety of computer topics, including Windows 95, Netscape Communicator 4, Windows NT, and Microsoft Internet Information Server 4.0. He authored *Windows 95 Registry Troubleshooting, Windows NT Registry Troubleshooting*, and *Implementing and Supporting Windows 95*, all published by New Riders, and *Windows 95 Installation and Configuration Handbook*, published by Que. You can reach him on the Internet at **rtidrow@iquest.net**.

Keith Underdahl is an electronic publishing specialist for Ages Software in Albany, Oregon, where he produces electronic versions of classic texts on CD-ROM. Keith is also a prolific author and personal computing consultant, and has served as technical editor on numerous titles from Que. When he is not goofing off with computers, Keith is a road tester and regular contributor to *Street Bike*, a motorcycle magazine serving the western United States.

Robert Voss is an independent software trainer with extensive experience training in Windows 95, Microsoft Word, and Microsoft Excel. Bob has worked with Ron Person on several of Que's bestselling books, including *Special Edition Using Word 6 for Windows, Special Edition Using Microsoft Excel 97*, and the *Using Windows 95* books.

Robert Ward is best known as the founder of the *C/C++ Users Journal, Windows Developers Journal*, and *System Administrator*. In addition to writing numerous technical articles for these and other magazines he has also authored *Debugging C* (Que) and co-authored *Windows Custom Controls*. He has worked as a consulting digital engineer and was named Professor of the Year while teaching computer science at McPherson College.

John West is a Managing Consultant at IntelliNet Corporation (**www.intelli.net**), based in Atlanta. IntelliNet is a Microsoft Solution Provider Partner and ATEC, specializing in infrastructure planning, deployment, and support. John is an MCSE, MCSD, MCT, and CNE. When he's not designing large NT-based network deployments, he enjoys creating web sites with ASP and programming with Visual Basic. He likes to write programs that help administer and monitor the networks he's implementing. To relax, he enjoys boating at Lake Lanier and hanging out with his friends from church. Contact John at **johnw@intelli.net**.

Craig Zacker has been employed as a network administrator, a technical writer and editor, a webmaster, a technical support engineer and supervisor, a courseware developer, and a freelance network consultant. He now spends most of his time tinkering with computers and writing about them. His previous credits for Que include *Special Edition Using NetWare 4.1, Platinum Edition Using Windows 95, Windows NT 4.0 Workstation Advanced Technical Reference*, and *Upgrading and Repairing Networks*, among others. He can be reached at **craigz@tiac.net**.

Acknowledgments

A book of this size and scope doesn't just happen overnight. It takes a hard-working team of professionals to put all the pieces together. Literally dozens of people—co-authors, editors, designers, proofreaders, technical reviewers, and others—had a hand in the making of this book. It's impossible to thank them all personally, but a few deserve special thanks for special efforts.

It was a pleasure to work with Development Editor Mark Cierzniak, who succeeded at the unenviable job of keeping the entire team focused on a single objective. Thanks, too, to Executive Editor Jeff Koch for his leadership and astute insights into Windows 98 (and for several pounds of excellent coffee, which arrived just in the nick of time), and to Acquisitions Editor Jane Brownlow, who managed the tight editorial schedule with grace and good humor.

Technical Editors Robert Bogue, Ron Ellenbecker, Kyle Bryant, Walter Glenn, and Henly Wolin checked the manuscript for accuracy and added valuable insights in several key chapters. Behind the scenes, Copy Editor Audra McFarland did a marvelous job of smoothing the rough edges so that this book is easier to read, and Project Editor Chris Morris made sure all the pieces wound up on all the right pages.

I owe a special debt to the many beta testers of Windows 98, who shared their insights and discoveries freely (and occasionally sacrificed their PCs for the cause). And I couldn't have written this book without the unwavering support of Paul Somerson of *PC Computing*, who challenged me years ago to become a Windows expert.

Finally, a very big thank you to Claudette Moore and Debbie McKenna of Moore Literary Agency, for handling all the boring but essential business details so I could concentrate on Windows 98.

Ed Bott

Introduction

In this chapter

As an upgrade to the best-selling software package in history, Windows 98 has a tough act to follow. The original release of Windows 95 revolutionized the computer industry, and today Windows is the undisputed standard for personal computing. It's virtually impossible to buy a PC without Windows, and there are thousands of productivity programs, utilities, and games that assume your PC is running Windows.

Windows 98 doesn't look dramatically different from its predecessor, but under the hood it's packed with changes that make computing and communication easier. The same is true with this book: *Platinum Edition Using Windows 98* adheres to the same high standards as its best-selling predecessors, but between the covers the content is all new for Windows 98. Microsoft has produced a major upgrade to Windows 95, and we've produced a brand-new volume designed to help you work effortlessly and productively with its new features and capabilities.

It doesn't matter how you use Windows 98 and Internet Explorer 4.0. If your family shares a home computer for work and play, you'll find plenty of help here. If you dial in to a local Internet service provider, we can help you make smoother, faster connections. We've also included detailed information that can help you integrate your computer into a business network, whether your business is a simple storefront or a far-flung multinational corporation. This book includes all the content you'll find in the best-selling *Special Edition Using Windows 98,* plus six all-new chapters, two new appendixes, and dozens of expert-level tips and updates throughout the book. All of this new material is aimed exclusively at the needs of advanced users and network administrators.

How to Use This Book

This book was designed and written expressly for intermediate and advanced Windows users who understand the importance of keeping up with advances in technology. *Platinum Edition Using Windows 98* contains detailed information about every aspect of Windows 98, including setup, customization, troubleshooting, and networking. You'll find complete coverage of Internet Explorer here as well, from basic web browsing to advanced security topics. And *Platinum Edition Using Windows 98* also includes step-by-step instructions on how to find and install online updates.

Platinum Edition Using Windows 98 is a comprehensive reference that makes it easy for you to accomplish any task quickly and effectively. To help organize this enormous breadth of coverage, we've divided the book into eight parts, beginning with the essentials and progressing to more specialized or advanced subjects.

Part I: Getting Started

This part covers the absolute essentials of Windows 98 and Internet Explorer 4.0. Pay particular attention to Chapter 1, "What's New in Windows 98?," which includes an overview of significant new features in Windows 98, including Internet Explorer 4.0. You will find the basics of starting and quitting Windows as well as controlling the operating system to help you accomplish your tasks. Windows 98 also includes a new HTML-based help system; you'll find details about the changes in Chapter 4, "Getting Help."

Part II: Working with Files and Folders

Windows 98 completely replaces the original Windows Explorer with a single browser that lets you manage files, folders, and web pages in the same window. Read Chapter 5, "An Overview of the Windows Desktop Update," for step-by-step instructions on how to configure the new Windows interface, including the controversial Active Desktop. This section also introduces Windows 98's new set of file-management tools. You'll learn basic and advanced techniques for working with programs, files, and folders, whether they're stored on a local disk or on a corporate network. You'll also find detailed information to help you customize the new Explorer and manage associations between data files and programs.

When Windows 95 was released, gigabyte-class hard drives were an expensive novelty. Today, even entry-level PCs include several gigabytes of storage. The most efficient way to partition and format large hard drives is to use the FAT32 file system, and Windows 98 includes a utility that can safely convert existing drives to FAT32. Chapter 9, "Working with Disks and Drives," explains this important new feature.

Part III: Working with Applications

There are literally tens of thousands of applications available for Windows 98. Collectively, they give you the power to organize your thoughts, communicate with other people, run a business of any size, and even create your own custom applications. This section covers the essentials of installing, running, and managing applications—including 32-bit Windows programs as well as older 16-bit Windows and MS-DOS programs. You'll also find details about applets included with Windows itself. And you'll learn how to make any application work well with local and network printers.

Part IV: Managing your System

Exclusively in *Platinum Edition Using Windows 98*, you'll find in-depth instructions for safely editing the Windows Registry (see Chapter 20, "Advanced Registry Hacks," for a treasure trove of advanced tips and techniques). Windows 98 also lets you automate routine tasks using VBScript and JavaScript. In the past, scripts written in these languages would only run in a browser window; Chapter 21 shows how to use the Windows Scripting Host to run these mini-programs by simply clicking an icon.

Part V: Configuring and Customizing Windows

Windows owes a large measure of its enormous popularity to its impressive flexibility. This section exhaustively details how you can modify Windows 98 to suit your personal preferences. Add new hardware, reconfigure existing peripherals, set multimedia options, and troubleshoot your system. Customize the Windows desktop, Start menu, and taskbar. Change the colors, fonts, and background images to make Windows more visually appealing. Reset the many system-level options that help define how Windows works, from which keyboard layout and language you prefer to which sounds play in response to system events. Understanding and configuring power management features are also explained.

Part VI: Windows Internet Services

In just a few years, the Internet has evolved into a crucial source of information for tens of millions of people, and increasingly it's a major force in banking, commerce, and stock trading. This comprehensive section details all of Windows 98's Internet-related features. It covers every aspect of Internet connectivity, from setting up a dial-up connection to configuring TCP/IP options to downloading files from FTP servers. If you've got questions about the World Wide Web, email, newsgroups, or Internet security, you'll find the answers here.

This section also covers Windows 98's Personal Web Server, which lets you turn any Windows 98 PC into a full-featured web host for use on a corporate network; it's also ideal for staging a personal web site that you plan to upload to an Internet service provider.

Part VII: Windows Network Services

Even a two-person office can benefit from Windows' capability to communicate and share files over a network. In this section, we cover the full range of network topics: setting up a simple workgroup; sharing resources on a small network; setting up Windows 98 as a client on larger networks with Novell NetWare and Windows NT servers. Chapter 41, "Windows 98 Network Administration," is exclusive to *Platinum Edition Using Windows 98*.

Part VII: Appendixes

If you're upgrading from Windows 95, look here for details on how to install Windows 98 (on one system or throughout an entire department) and how to find and install the most recent patches and updates.

Special Features in the Book

Que has over a decade of experience writing and developing the most successful computer books available. With that experience, we've learned what special features help readers the most. Look for these special features throughout the book to enhance your learning experience.

Note   Notes present interesting or useful information that isn't necessarily essential to the discussion. This secondary track of information enhances your understanding of Windows, but you can safely skip notes and not be in danger of missing crucial information. Notes look like this:

N O T E   Be careful not to add too much to your taskbar. If you do, you might find yourself spending more time searching your taskbar than it would take to just browse to the file, application, or shortcut the old-fashioned way.

To gain maximum benefit from toolbars and Quick Launch, implement them only for those programs you use frequently. If you access a file or program once a week or less, think twice before establishing a toolbar or Quick Launch icon.

Tip   Tips present short advice on quick or often overlooked procedures. These include shortcuts that save you time. A Tip looks like this:

TIP   Select multiple items on the desktop by clicking the desktop and dragging the selection rectangle that displays so that it surrounds the items. Release to select all objects within the rectangle.

Caution   Cautions serve to warn you about potential problems that a procedure might cause, unexpected results, and mistakes to avoid.

CAUTION

When the Task Scheduler brings up the Backup utility, you have to run the proper backup job. The Task Scheduler only runs the Backup utility; it doesn't perform the actual backup.

Troubleshooting   No matter how carefully you follow the steps in the book, you eventually come across something that just doesn't work the way you think it should. Troubleshooting sections anticipate these common errors or hidden pitfalls and present solutions. A Troubleshooting section looks like this:

TROUBLESHOOTING

When I use the Windows Setup feature to add new components, it adds those components, but it also removes other components. Why? If you clear a check box for a component that was checked, this tells Windows to remove the component when you run Windows Setup rather than to not install it. This can be confusing the first time you run Setup again to add new components. Leave those components that are already installed checked unless you want to uninstall them.

Cross References   Throughout the book, you see references to other sections and pages in the book (like the one that follows this paragraph). These cross references point you to related topics and discussions in other parts of the book. They also point to Internet references where you can find out additional information about topics.

▶ **See** "Creating Custom Web Views," **p. 130**

▶ **See** "Managing Buttons on a Toolbar," **p. 435**

Conventions

In addition to these special features, several conventions are used in this book to make it easier to read and understand. These conventions include the following.

Underlined Hot Keys, or Mnemonics   In this book, hot keys appear underlined as they appear onscreen. In Windows, many menus, commands, buttons, and other options have these hot keys. To use a hot key shortcut, press Alt and the key for the underlined character. For example, to choose the Properties button, press Alt and then R.

Shortcut Key Combinations   In this book, shortcut key combinations are joined with plus signs (+). For example, Ctrl+V means hold down the Ctrl key and then press the V key.

Menu Commands   Instructions for choosing menu commands have this form:

Choose File, New.

This example means open the File menu and select New, which is one way to open a new file.

Instructions involving the Windows 98 Start menu are an exception. When you are to choose something through the Start menu, the form is as follows:

Open the Start menu and choose Programs, Accessories, WordPad.

In this case, you open the WordPad word processing accessory. Notice that in the Start menu you simply drag the mouse pointer and point at the option or command you want to choose (even through a whole series of submenus); you don't need to click anything.

This book also has the certain typeface enhancements to indicate special text, as described in the following table.

Typeface	Description
Italic	Italic is used to indicate terms and variables in commands or addresses.
Boldface	Bold is used to indicate text you type, as well as Internet addresses and other locators in the online world.
MYFILE.DOC	Filenames and directories are set in all caps to distinguish them from regular text, as in MYFILE.DOC.
`Monospace`	Mono indicates screen messages, code listings, and command samples.
Underline	Underline indicates keyboard hot keys. For example, to choose the Properties button, press Alt and then R.

Getting Started

What's New in Windows 98?

by Ed Bott

In this chapter

Faster, Smarter, Easier: Architectural Improvements in Windows 98

If you were to walk up to a computer running Windows 98, you'd be hard-pressed to distinguish between it and a PC running Windows 95 with Internet Explorer 4.0. When you work with Windows 98 for even a few minutes, though, you'll *feel* the difference.

Only three years passed between the first release of Windows 95 and the debut of Windows 98, but it might as well have been a millennium as far as personal computers are concerned. CPUs are up to 10 times faster and cost one-third what they did three years ago. Gigabytes of storage and gobs of RAM are commonplace. Practically everyone has email. There are literally tens of thousands of applications that let you work and play on a Windows PC.

And, of course, there's the Internet. In 1995, the World Wide Web was still brand new, and the Internet was a gathering place for hard-core techies. Today, you can't pass a billboard or switch on a television without seeing a web address, and the Internet has become the defining technology of our time.

Taken together, those two changes define Windows 98. Because Internet Explorer 4.0 is tightly integrated into Windows 98, you won't need to install any additional software to access the World Wide Web. And Windows 98 also does a superb job of getting the most out of all the new types of hardware and software that have sprung up since 1995. Yes, this is an upgrade to Windows 95, but the list of significant improvements seems endless:

- Windows 98 is the ultimate maintenance release. It includes more than 150 updates, bug fixes, and usability tweaks to the original Windows 95 code. These were originally included in service packs and downloadable patches from Microsoft. Even the unsupported-but-indispensable Power Toys collection is brand-new for this release. (You'll find full details of TweakUI and other utilities in Appendix C, "Using Power Toys.")

- In all, Windows 98 contains drivers for more than 1,200 new devices, and virtually all of them support Plug and Play for simplified setup. Some categories of hardware supported in Windows 98 didn't even exist when Windows 95 first hit store shelves. Most significant of all are peripherals that use the Universal Serial Bus (USB).

  You can plug just about any type of device into a USB port, including mice, keyboards, modems, scanners, digital cameras, speakers, telephones, and more. The technology makes your PC incredibly more flexible and does away with the need for serial and parallel ports, IRQs, and other configuration hassles. See Chapter 26, "Adding New Hardware," and Chapter 27, "Configuring Hardware," for details about how to install new device drivers and configure peripherals.

- Whether you upgrade an existing copy of Windows 95 or install Windows 98 on a new PC, you'll notice significant changes in this operating system. The new Setup program is dramatically streamlined compared with its Windows 95 equivalent. You answer a few questions at the start, and then—because it's capable of restarting automatically—the Setup program runs unattended. If you're responsible for installing the software on multiple PCs, use Windows 98's batch installation tools to streamline the process as much as possible.

See Appendix A, "Installing Windows 98," for detailed instructions on upgrading to Windows 98 and making sure you have the most recent version.

■ Windows 98 is generally faster overall, although you may notice that some tasks take longer than they would on the same system running Windows 95. In particular, startup and shutdown should go more quickly, especially on new systems. Most of the key system files, including networking components like Windows Sockets services and TCP/IP, have also been tuned for performance. And on large networks you'll notice completely new options, including support for Point-to-Point Tunneling Protocol and NetWare Directory Services.

■ One of the most significant weaknesses in the original retail release of Windows 95 was its dependence on the old 16-bit FAT format. That restriction becomes particularly painful when you add a hard drive greater than 2G, because FAT16 forces you to create multiple partitions that waste huge amounts of space. Microsoft fixed those problems with the introduction of the FAT32 disk format in OEM Service Release 2 of Windows 95. Windows 98 adds a major new tool that you need when upgrading: a utility that quickly converts your existing data to the new format.

■ Notebook users will see improved power-management features, enhancements in the way Windows works with PC Cards, and support for the latest infrared devices.

■ And if you have a dial-up Internet connection, you'll find substantial improvements in the Dial-Up Networking features, including a simplified wizard for creating connections and support for *multilink* connections, which use two phone lines for faster data transfers.

▶ **See** "Converting a FAT16 Drive to FAT32," **p. 154**
▶ **See** "Special Features for Notebook Users," **p. 1043**
▶ **See** "Establishing a Dial-Up Internet Connection," **p. 567**

How Windows and the Web Work Together

If you've grown accustomed to the Windows 95 interface, you'll see some changes in Windows 98. The Windows Desktop Update, first introduced with Internet Explorer 4.0 and standard in Windows 98, adds hundreds of improvements to the tools and techniques you use to manage files, folders, and programs in Windows. Most of the changes are simple refinements, but if you're willing to turn on some of the new options, you can radically change the way Windows works. For a full description of the changes to the Windows interface, including its many options, see Chapter 5, "An Overview of the Windows Desktop Update."

You'll notice a new Quick Launch toolbar just to the right of the Start button, for example. You can add your own shortcuts here to make it easier to get started with your favorite programs. The Start menu is also improved. Most notably, you can now reorganize items on the Programs menu by dragging them directly from one place to another.

Windows 95 offered the Windows Explorer for file management and a separate Internet Explorer for web browsing. Internet Explorer 4.0 brought the two Explorers into a single window, and Windows 98 incorporates that feature. If you prefer to browse files and folders using the single-click navigation techniques of Internet Explorer, you can configure Windows to work that way. And you can view any or all your folders using HTML templates so that they look and act like web pages.

 TIP Why would you want to treat your files like web pages? See Chapter 8, "Managing Files Using Web View," for a description of some of the benefits.

When you use Windows 98, you'll have ready access to the web. There's a new Favorites option on the Start menu, which lets you jump quickly to your favorite web sites. And if you turn on the Active Desktop, you can embed live HTML components (such as news or stock-quote tickers) or even entire web pages on the Windows desktop.

In a corporate setting, the Active Desktop can be a mixed blessing because of its ability to consume network bandwidth and the inevitable instabilities it adds to Windows. Fortunately, it's possible to disable virtually all the "active" features in Windows 98.

▶ **See** "Web Subscriptions and the Active Desktop," **p. 677**

A New Way to Explore the Internet

If you've used Netscape Navigator or previous versions of Internet Explorer, you're already familiar with the basic concepts of web browsing. Windows 98 includes the full suite of Internet applications Microsoft introduced with Internet Explorer 4.0. There's much more than just a web browser.

Internet Explorer 4.0: Offline Browsing and Web Subscriptions

The single biggest objection to the Internet (at least for users with ordinary dial-up connections) is that it's too slow. IE4 addresses that concern by letting you set up web subscriptions, which you can use to download individual pages or entire web sites at regular intervals. Then, when you tell IE4 you'd like to work offline, you can browse the stored pages without dialing up and waiting for them to download.

You'll find it easier to find information on the Internet with IE4, and its tools enable you to organize that information more intelligently, too.

Corporate network administrators and individual users concerned with protecting PCs and servers from unauthorized access can fine-tune Internet Explorer's security settings. You can completely disable ActiveX controls and Java applets, for example, or shut down the browser's ability to run scripts. You can also define security zones that allow greater capabilities for pages on the corporate intranet than for those on the Internet. See Chapter 30, "Web Browsing with Internet Explorer 4.0," and Chapter 32, "Internet Security," for more details.

Stay in Touch with Outlook Express Mail and News

With Windows 98, Microsoft officially replaces the Windows 95-vintage Exchange Inbox with a new Internet-standard email program called Outlook Express. The new mail client software is easy to set up, easy to use, and easy to customize. If you receive large volumes of email, you'll appreciate the Inbox Assistant, which lets you define rules the software can use to automatically manage messages for you. Outlook Express also acts as a reader for accessing Internet news servers, like those that offer support for Microsoft products.

▶ **See** "Using Outlook Express," **p. 701**

Web Editing and Publishing Tools

Windows 98 won't let you set up a web site that can compete with Yahoo!, but it does include basic tools you can use to create web pages. FrontPage Express is a graphical web-page editor that incorporates a subset of the features in Microsoft's award-winning FrontPage program.

Windows 98 also includes Personal Web Server software that lets users host a simple web site on a desktop PC. To publish HTML pages to any web server, use the built-in Web Publishing Wizard. Of course, you wouldn't want to use this software to run a commercial web site, but it's an ideal way to add intranet capabilities to a corporate network. It's also a useful tool for developing and testing web sites before posting the pages on a full-strength web server.

Chapter 37, "Using the Microsoft Personal Web Services," offers complete instructions for setting up a web server on a Windows 98 PC, configuring it for intranet access, and posting pages to the server. You'll learn more about Windows 98's web-page authoring capabilities in Chapter 36, "Creating Web Pages with FrontPage Express."

An Operating System That Maintains Itself

Maintaining the health of your PC is like visiting the dentist: Even highly motivated PC users do irksome maintenance chores less often than they should. Windows 98 can't supply extra motivation, but it does include software that automates some of the more unpleasant tasks. Most notable is the Tune-Up Wizard, which regularly scans local hard disks for errors, defragments disks, and cleans up unneeded files—all without requiring any work from you.

And if you've ever tried to troubleshoot a hardware or software problem using Windows 95, you've probably experienced information overload. With Windows 98, you'll find a new System Information tool that consolidates a wealth of data—about system resources, hardware, components, and running tasks—in a single location. This well-organized window is also a launching pad for other troubleshooting tools, such as the System File Checker (which undoes the damage when a crucial file becomes corrupted) and the Registry Checker (which automatically backs up your database of system settings for quick recovery in the event of trouble). And whenever Microsoft issues a Windows patch, you can install it automatically by clicking the Windows Update icon. (See Chapter 16, "Maintaining and Troubleshooting Your System.")

Previous versions of Windows offered no way to recover from such system disasters as a hard disk crash. Windows 98, however, includes a new, easier-to-use Backup program. If you use

Backup in conjunction with the new System Recovery utility, you can completely restore a system's configuration if necessary. Chapter 18, "Backing Up Your Data," offers step-by-step instructions for using these new features.

The preferred way of adjusting most Windows settings is to use the Control Panel. Sometimes, however, you have no alternative but to edit the Windows Registry directly. Navigating through the six main Registry keys can be a daunting process, and if you make a mistake, the results are potentially disastrous. For a comprehensive overview of safe and effective ways to use the Registry Editor, see Chapter 19, "Working with the Windows Registry."

Windows 98 at Home

If you've installed Windows 98 at home, you're probably expecting your PC to work hard and play hard. For game players, there's DirectX5 technology and MMX support, two technologies that make multimedia more appealing. In addition, the broadcast architecture components let you watch TV on your PC (if you have compatible hardware, of course).

▶ **See** "Setting Up Windows 98 Multimedia," **p. 473**

Are you concerned about setting up a single PC that every member of the family can use? The Family Logon option lets you create custom desktops for everyone, and you can use IE4's Content Advisor to block access to web sites that contain violence, pornography, or other material you deem undesirable.

Windows 98 in the Office

In a corporate setting, you're most likely to be concerned with getting Windows 98 to work smoothly with an existing network. From an administrator's viewpoint, Windows 98 doesn't look dramatically different from Windows 95—although it's smoother in operation. You'll find support for many more network cards, for example, and you'll find it easier to connect with Windows NT or NetWare networks. Windows 98 also makes it easier to configure a TCP/IP connection (the default protocol in Windows 98), eliminating the sometimes tortuous steps that Windows 95 required. See Chapter 38, "Configuring Windows Network Components," and Chapter 42, "Setting Up a Simple Windows Network" for more details on basic network setup.

How do you manage Windows 98 PCs on a network? The operating system includes a collection of tools, services, and utilities that let network administrators view and edit the Windows Registry, inspect system configurations, and perform other essential administrative tasks from a distance. Chapter 41, "Windows 98 Network Administration," offers a complete set of tips and techniques intended especially for administrators of corporate networks. ●

CHAPTER 2

Starting and Quitting Windows 98

by Ron Person and Kyle Bryant

In this chapter

Starting Windows

After Windows 98 is installed on a system, the system typically boots directly into the Windows 98 environment. If your system requires real-mode drivers, you might see a text screen as the drivers load. Also, if your Windows system has multiple configurations installed—to enable you to work with different hardware configurations, for example—a text screen prompts you to choose between the configurations. After you make your choice, Windows starts.

 For a faster startup, press the Esc key during startup of Windows 98 to bypass the Windows 98 logo. To permanently bypass the logo, edit the MSDOS.SYS text file located in the root folder of the boot drive by adding **LOGO=0** to the Options section. To see the logo on startup, change the 0 to 1. Note: MSDOS.SYS is a hidden read-only system file; you'll have to change the file attributes to enable editing.

Logging On to Windows

When Windows starts, it might display an Enter Network (or Windows) Password dialog box that contains your username and a field for your password. Windows uses this dialog box information for several purposes:

- Windows matches the name against a user profile. The user profile tells Windows which configuration of desktop and software settings to use.

- If your system is connected to a network, Windows logs you into the network using the name and the password provided. (An additional field might be displayed in the dialog box for a Windows NT Domain or other server name.)

After login is complete, the Windows 98 desktop appears. When you initially start Windows, it displays a Welcome to Windows 98 screen. Close this screen by clicking the Close icon in the top-right corner. You will be asked if you want the Windows Welcome screen to be displayed each time. Most people elect not to display the Welcome screen again. However, the Welcome screen is actually an executable file, welcome.exe, that is located in the main Windows folder. Execute the program if you need to run Welcome again.

Starting Windows with Your Custom User Profile or Network Password

Windows can assign unique Windows environment settings and network capabilities to each user. For example, if your system is shared by multiple users, you might want to shut down Windows and log on as a different user. In those cases you don't have to completely shut down Windows. To log on as a different user without shutting down, follow these steps:

1. Click Start, Log Off *User Name*. Click Yes in response to the question Are You Sure You Want to Log Off?

2. An Enter Windows (or Network) Password dialog box appears. Enter the new User Name and Password.

NOTE If your Windows 98 system is configured with multiple user profiles, you might not be able to visually tell which desktop you are currently using. To enable at-a-glance identification, create a unique folder on the desktop of each user profile and name the folder to indicate the login name (for example, "This is Mary's Desktop"). ■

▶ **See** "Choosing Your Primary Network Logon," **p. 878**

Disabling the Enter Network (Windows) Dialog Box

If you have no need to change user profiles or you want to log on to your network without being prompted by the Enter Network (or Windows) dialog box, you can disable the dialog box by following these steps:

1. Right-click Network Neighborhood and select Properties.

2. Change the Primary Network Logon to Windows Logon.

3. When you're prompted to restart, elect *not* to restart your system.

4. Open the Control Panel, click the Passwords icon, and select the User Profiles tab. Select the option All Users of This Computer Use the Same Preferences and Desktop Settings.

5. Click the Change Passwords tab, and then click the Password button. Change the password to a blank password.

6. Restart your system.

Controlling Programs and Documents When Windows Starts

You can define how Windows applications and documents open on startup. By defining which applications and documents automatically open and whether windows are full-screen or windowed, you can set up a system that's easier for less-experienced computer users to use.

Running Programs and Opening Documents

Windows starts all program or document files or shortcuts located in the Windows StartUp folder at system startup. Use the Find, Files or Folders command to locate the folder path location to the StartUp folder. Then, from Windows Explorer, drag and drop or copy and paste entries into the StartUp folder.

You can also add entries to the StartUp folder by creating shortcuts to programs, data files, or folders. To do so, right-click the taskbar and select Properties to open the Taskbar Properties dialog box. Select the Start Menu Programs tab, shown in Figure 2.1, and then click the Add button to start the Create Shortcut Wizard.

NOTE If you frequently change the programs, documents, or folders that you want to execute at system startup, make the StartUp folder accessible as a shortcut on the desktop so you can easily edit or modify its contents. ■

FIG. 2.1
Use the Start Menu Programs tab to specify programs to run at system startup.

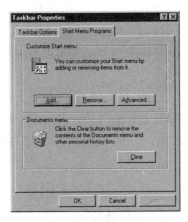

If you want folders to open on your desktop when Windows starts, drag the folder icon into the StartUp folder.

▶ **See** "Using Shortcuts," **p. 94**

Specifying How Programs, Documents, and Folders Are Displayed

You can control whether programs, documents, or folders start in a normal window, are minimized, or are maximized. To control how these items appear when Windows starts, follow these steps:

1. Open the StartUp folder and select the shortcut entry you want to modify.

2. Display the entry's Properties dialog box and choose the Shortcut tab, shown in Figure 2.2.

3. Open the Run drop-down list and select one of the three options: Normal window, Minimized, or Maximized.

FIG. 2.2
Use the Shortcut Properties dialog box to specify how a program or document will appear on startup.

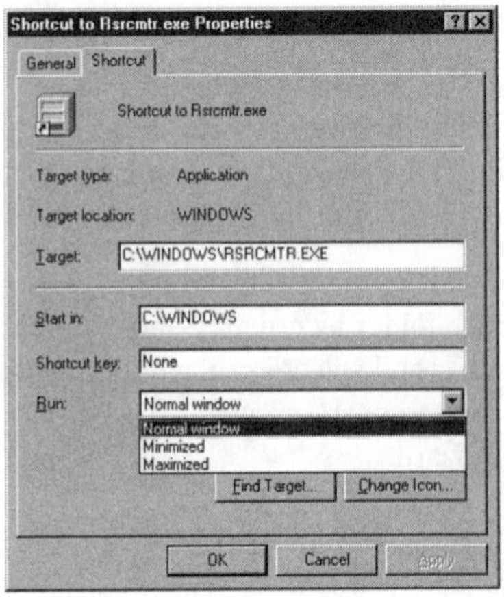

TROUBLESHOOTING

After I place some entries in the StartUp folder, Windows fails to start correctly. To check to see if
the entries in the StartUp folder are indeed causing the problem, hold down the Shift key during initial
Windows login. (If you hold down the Shift key during initial system boot, Windows goes into safe
mode.) Pressing the Shift key prevents applications in StartUp from executing. If Windows starts
correctly, a problem exists with one of the entries in the StartUp folder. Remove entries from the
StartUp folder one at a time until you locate the offending entry.

▶ **See** "Using Windows Explorer to View Files and Folders," **p. 72**

Part

I

Ch

2

Protecting Yourself with a Startup Disk

A startup disk can help you recover data from your hard disk when Windows will not start. The
startup disk starts your system in DOS mode even when Windows will not start.

During Windows 98 installation, you had the opportunity to create a startup disk. In case you
didn't take advantage of that opportunity, you can create a startup disk at any time. Open the
Control Panel and click the Add/Remove Programs icon. Then select the Startup Disk tab to
create a new startup disk.

Make at least two copies of your startup disk. Be sure to test each disk for proper operation
immediately after you create it (confirm that the disks start your system as intended). Then
keep one disk accessible to your work area and store the other disk in a safe remote location.

CAUTION

A startup disk created for a FAT16 version of Windows 98 will not give you access to the data on a hard
drive formatted for FAT32. If you did not create a startup disk with the appropriate FAT system, you might be
able to use a startup disk created from another similar system formatted with the correct FAT version.

The startup disk does not start your system in Windows. It starts the system in DOS but provides access to your floppy and hard drive(s). New in Windows 98 is limited support for CD-
ROM drives. Whether or not you will have access to your CD-ROM drive after a startup disk
boot is a CD-ROM hardware compatibility issue. Review the supplied system drivers contained
on your startup disk.

To start your system using the startup disk, insert it in the booting drive and reboot the system. The system should restart to the DOS A: prompt. You can then use internal DOS commands to copy files to and from the hard drive, replace corrupted Windows files, and perform
other common tasks. Set a path statement in the Windows environment to utilize external DOS
commands available from the \Windows\Command folder.

Before you test for CD-ROM availability, remember that upon booting from a Windows 98
startup disk, by default Windows 98 creates a RAM drive and assigns the first available drive

letter after your hard drive to the RAM drive. (The RAM drive would typically be assigned to drive D:.) The drive designation of your CD-ROM might have changed after the startup disk boot because any previously assigned network drives are no longer available.

For example, in normal Windows 98 mode, your CD-ROM might have been assigned to drive G:. Assuming that you have one hard drive in your system, after a startup disk boot, you might find that your CD-ROM is now assigned to drive E:—the next drive letter available after the RAM drive.

 If you have the available hard disk space and you have determined, as just outlined, that your particular system does not provide CD-ROM support under a startup disk boot, you might want to copy all the Windows 98 CAB files from your Windows installation CD-ROM onto your hard disk so that you'll always have access to the Windows installation and driver files. After booting from the startup disk, go to the appropriate folder and run SETUP. When you install new hardware, point Windows to this folder when it asks for a Windows 98 file location.

Starting Windows After Technical Problems Occur

It's guaranteed that Windows will fail occasionally. These failures and their recovery are handled more automatically in Windows 98.

Checking for Drive Errors with ScanDisk

If Windows gets shut down incorrectly or detects errors on your hard disk, it automatically runs ScanDisk, a program that checks for invalid filenames, file and folder name length errors, magnetic surface errors on the drive, and more. If you start your system and ScanDisk begins running, usually your best option is to let it finish.

If you want to control ScanDisk parameters, you can open the MSDOS.SYS file and edit the AutoScan line in the [Options] section to change ScanDisk's startup behavior. You can use any of the following parameters:

ScanDisk Mode	Behavior
AutoScan=0	Disables ScanDisk on startup.
AutoScan=1	Windows startup pauses, giving you a chance to stop it. If you do not stop it, ScanDisk runs automatically. (This is the default.)
AutoScan=2	ScanDisk runs automatically when needed without pausing to allow for user intervention.

Starting Windows in Safe Mode or an Alternative Mode

If Windows has difficulty starting, you will want to start it in one of its diagnostic modes. In most troubleshooting situations, you will want to start in safe mode. In safe mode, Windows uses basic default settings that restart Windows with minimal functionality. For example, if a video adapter driver is incorrect or becomes corrupted, Windows will restart in safe mode using a default driver (standard VGA) that provides minimum functionality. In this case, safe mode gives you access to the Windows graphical user interface in order to review Control Panel or Device Manager settings.

When Windows starts in safe mode, a message informs you that Windows is running in safe mode and that some of your devices might not be available. The words Safe mode appear at each corner of the screen.

The default safe mode settings use a generic VGA monitor driver, the standard Microsoft mouse driver, and the minimum device drivers necessary to start Windows. When you start Windows with the default settings, you cannot access CD-ROM drives, printers, modems, or other external hardware devices. One of the safe modes allows networking devices to function.

For help on troubleshooting hardware and driver problems, refer to the section "Troubleshooting Common Problems" in Chapter 16 or sections in the appropriate chapters on installing hardware drivers.

To start Windows in a different mode, follow these steps:

1. Turn on the system.

2. Hold down the Ctrl key as soon as the memory test is complete. Continue holding down the Ctrl key until the Windows 98 Startup Menu appears.

3. The Windows 98 Startup Menu displays different starting modes. If you do not press a key within 30 seconds, Windows will continue startup with the default selection. Press either the up or down arrow key to prevent automatic startup.

4. The Microsoft Windows 98 Startup Menu offers choices that reflect the configuration of your system. You might see some or all of the following choices:

> Normal
>
> Logged (\BOOTLOG.TXT)
>
> Safe mode
>
> Safe mode with network support
>
> Step-by-step confirmation
>
> Command prompt only
>
> Safe mode command prompt only
>
> Previous version of MS-DOS
>
> Select the mode in which you want to start, and then press Enter.

To skip the Windows 98 Startup Menu and start directly in a mode, start your system and hold down one of the key combinations listed in the following table while Windows is starting.

Part

I

Ch

2

Operating Mode	Key Combination	Actions
Windows 98 in safe mode without networking	F5	Loads HIMEM.SYS and IFSHLP.SYS, loads DoubleSpace or DriveSpace if present, and then runs Windows 98 WIN.COM. Starts in safe mode.
Windows 98 in safe mode with minimum network functions	F6	Loads HIMEM.SYS and IFSHLP.SYS. Processes the Registry, loads COMMAND.COM, loads DoubleSpace or DriveSpace if present, runs Windows 98 WIN.COM, loads network drivers, and runs NETSTART.BAT.
DOS command prompt	Shift+F5	Loads COMMAND.COM.
Step-by-Step	Shift+F8	Gives you Yes or No choices for each Windows 98 startup action (such as loading drivers).

▶ **See** "Keeping Windows 98 Up-to-Date," **p. 292**

▶ **See** "Using the Add New Hardware Wizard," **p. 526**

Using Step-by-Step Mode to Interactively Test Startup

Interactively test each action in the boot process by following the procedure described in the preceding section and selecting Step-by-Step Confirmation. As Windows loads each item, it displays a message onscreen saying so. You must press Y (Yes) or N (No) for each action. This enables you to boot Windows 98 but bypass suspect drivers by responding with N.

 If you install Windows 98 as an upgrade over a previous version of Windows, Windows 98 typically inherits the previous version's configuration; for example, entries in AUTOEXEC.BAT and CONFIG.SYS will be retained. A useful preliminary troubleshooting technique is to rename AUTOEXEC.BAT and CONFIG.SYS to non-operational names and then reboot to see if the problem still exists. Unlike in Windows 3.x installations, many Win98 systems do not require AUTOEXEC.BAT or CONFIG.SYS files.

Managing Windows After an Application Failure

Windows 98 continuously polls applications to see if they are running and responding. When an application fails to respond, Windows 98 displays a dialog box in which you can click the End Task button to close the application. If you do that, however, you lose all changes you've made to data in the application since the last time you saved. Click Cancel to return to the application.

If the application misuses memory or has a fatal error that causes the application to fail, other applications usually will not be involved. When an application fails to respond—for example, if clicks or keystrokes get no response—press Ctrl+Alt+Delete to display the Close Program dialog box.

The problem application or component might show the message [Not responding]. To continue working in Windows with your other applications, you must shut down this application. Select the application or component and click End Task. If you click Shut Down or press Ctrl+Alt+Delete again, all applications and Windows 98 will shut down. Usually a second End Task confirmation dialog box appears a few seconds after the initial End Task command is executed. Click End Task again. The process of shutting down the application or component might take several more seconds.

Part

I

Ch

2

Dual Booting with Windows NT

You can run Windows 98 on a multi-boot system in the same way you could with previous versions of Windows, Windows NT, and DOS. However, you have to take into account certain considerations involving the FAT32 file system that might have been installed with Windows 98 or Windows 95 OSR2.

You cannot multi-boot to another operating system if drive C: is a FAT32 file system. Other file systems can't access files on a partition formatted as FAT32. Older operating systems, such as DOS and previous versions of Windows and Windows NT, do not recognize the FAT32 file system.

If you want to use Windows 98 in a multi-boot system, format drive C: as a FAT16 file system. You can have other partitions that are formatted in FAT32, but DOS and versions of Windows or Windows NT prior to release 5.0 will not recognize files on the FAT32 partition.

▶ **See** "Choosing a File System," **p. 148**

▶ **See** "Converting a FAT16 Drive to FAT32," **p. 154**

Shutting Down Windows

Windows now has multiple ways to turn off your system. To shut down your system, click Start, Shut Down, and then click one of the following choices:

Stand By	Conserves power and restores applications, documents, and settings quickly when restarting.
Shut Down	Turns off power and prompts you to save documents.
Restart	Reboots and restarts Windows.
Restart in MS-DOS Mode	Shuts down Windows and restarts with a DOS prompt.

You can also use the keyboard shortcut Ctrl+Shift to perform a Windows-only restart (without a cold boot).

If you prefer to shut down by clicking on a desktop icon, create a one-line DOS batch file with Close on Exit Properties as follows:

```
C:\WINDOWS\RUNDLL32.EXE user.exe,ExitWindows
```

This batch file example assumes that your main Windows folder is c:\Windows. If you are using a non-standard installation, edit the folder path as necessary. Give the batch file an appropriate name, such as Shut Down or Power Down PC. Save the batch file on your desktop or create a shortcut to the desktop from the folder of your choice. Then you can click on the icon to shut down your system. You could also use a timer program such as Windows 98 Scheduled Tasks to execute the batch file to shut down your system at a scheduled time. ●

CHAPTER 3

Navigating and Controlling Windows

by Ron Person

Basic Elements of the Windows 98 Interface

It's important that you know the name and function of each graphical element in a Windows screen, because each element causes some effect when clicked.

Figure 3.1 shows a Windows desktop containing multiple application windows. The figure identifies the parts of a typical Windows 98 screen.

FIG. 3.1
To run Windows effectively you need to know the elements in the Windows screen.

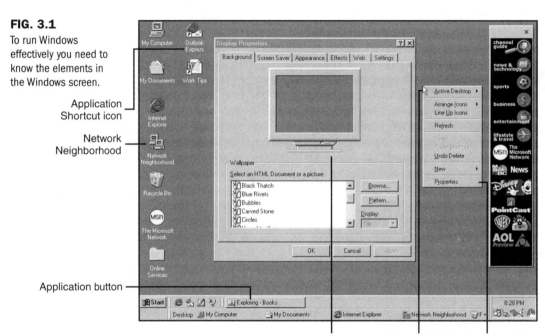

Program and Document Shortcut Icons

You can place shortcut icons on the desktop that point to program or document files. Clicking an icon starts the program or opens the document in the appropriate application. By modifying the shortcut's properties, you can control how the program's window opens.

▶ **See** "Using Shortcuts," **p. 94**

Folder Icons

Clicking a shortcut icon that points to a folder will open the folder into a window. A folder shortcut also acts as conduit to the actual folder. For example, dragging a file from the Windows Explorer and dropping it onto a folder shortcut places that file into the folder the shortcut points to.

▶ **See** "Using Shortcuts," **p.94**

Desktop

The Windows Desktop covers the entire screen and lies under all icons, windows, and objects. It is the container for shortcut icons, taskbar, desktop toolbars, and program windows. When the desktop displays active content such as a Web site or Channel bars, it is known as the Active Desktop.

▶ **See** "Creating Custom Web Views," **p. 130**

▶ **See** "Managing Buttons on a Toolbar," **p. 435**

Active Desktop

The Windows desktop becomes the Active Desktop when it displays active content such as Web components or links to Web data or an active channel. It can contain hyperlinks that open programs, documents, or Web sites. It also can display information that frequently updates through an Internet or intranet connection.

▶ **See** "Classic or Web? Choosing a Navigation Style," **p. 62**

▶ **See** "Customizing the Windows Desktop," **p. 441**

▶ **See** "Adding Web Content to the Active Desktop?" **p. 678**

My Computer

The My Computer shortcut gives you access to all the resources in your computer, hard drives, CD-ROMs, Control Panel, printers, and so forth. The My Computer window displays the same resources as the left pane of the Windows Explorer.

▶ **See** "Two Views of Windows Explorer," **p. 70**

Network Neighborhood

If you are connected to a network, click Network Neighborhood to open an Explorer Window displaying all your network resources. You can connect or disconnect from network drives, find computers on the network, or use network resources such as shared folders and files.

▶ **See** "Using Network Neighborhood to View Shared Resources," **p. 116**

Start

Click Start to display a menu of programs, documents, and Windows tools. All Windows features are available through Start or from one of its submenus. Start is displayed at the left end of a horizontal taskbar or the top of a vertical taskbar.

▶ **See** "Adding and Removing Programs in the Start Menu," **p. 436**

Part

I

Ch

3

Taskbar

The taskbar is easily accessed to show you all programs currently open and running. Click a program button in the taskbar to activate the Window containing that program. The taskbar is movable and can be relocated or resized to anywhere onscreen. You can hide the taskbar so that it displays only when the pointer touches the screen edge containing the taskbar.

▶ **See** "Resizing the Taskbar," **p. 429**

Channel Guide

The channel guide is displayed both on the Active Desktop and in Internet Explorer. It gives you easy access to specialized Web sites that can send information to your browser at pre-defined times. Web sites that use a channel include a navigation map that enables you to find information more quickly.

▶ **See** "Managing the Channel Bar," **p. 695**

Desktop Toolbars

Desktop toolbars give you quick access to frequently used programs, documents, folders, and hyperlinks; clicking a button on a toolbar opens that program, document, folder, or Web site. Toolbars are more accessible than desktop shortcuts because you can move and resize them as well as hide them against the side of a screen. When you move the mouse pointer against that side of the screen, the toolbar is displayed, ready for use.

▶ **See** "Managing Buttons on a Toolbar," **p. 435**

Shortcut Menus

Shortcut menus display menus that contain the most appropriate actions for the item on which you right-click. This is a real time-saving feature.

Property Sheets

Resources in Windows such as the desktop, printers, shortcut icons, disks, folders, and so forth have associated property sheets. These property sheets display fixed and changeable characteristics (properties) about the item. Display property sheets through a menu selection or by right-clicking the item and then clicking Properties.

Using the Mouse

Nearly all actions in Windows and Windows programs can be controlled with the mouse. Most people, after they become familiar with Windows, use a combination of mouse actions, reserving a few keystroke combinations for frequently repeated commands.

CAUTION

Windows 98 can be configured to use the web style single-click with a mouse rather than the classic style double-click to complete some Windows actions. Learn about these two styles in the following sections.

Dragging Items with a Mouse

Dragging with a mouse selects multiple text characters or moves graphic objects such as windows. Dragging is the same whether you have single- or double-click selected. Place the mouse pointer over a movable object, such as a file icon; then press and hold down the left mouse button. Continue holding the button down as you move the mouse. The object will move with the mouse pointer. When you have positioned the object where you want it, release the mouse button to drop the object.

 Select multiple items on the desktop by clicking on the desktop and dragging the selection rectangle that displays so that it surrounds the items. Release to select all objects within the rectangle.

Right-Clicking to Display Shortcut Menus

Most objects in Windows and Windows programs have a shortcut menu associated with them. This shortcut menu contains frequently used commands appropriate to the selected item. For example, the shortcut menu that displays when you right-click selected text includes the commands Cut, Copy, and Paste.

In some situations, such as dragging a file onto the desktop, you can drag using the right mouse button. When you release the right mouse button, a shortcut menu will display that gives you the choices of Move Here, Copy Here, and Create Shortcut(s) Here.

 Hold the Shift key down as you right-click a file or folder to get a menu listing every available command.

Activating with Classic Style (Double-Click Methods)

When Windows is configured in classic style, a single-click selects an item, such as a file, folder, or shortcut, and a double-click activates it. You can select adjacent (contiguous) items by clicking the first file in a list and then holding the Shift key as you click the last file you want selected. All files between the first click and Shift+click are selected. To select multiple nonadjacent files, click the first file; then hold the Ctrl key down as you click additional files in the same folder. Ctrl+click a selected file to deselect it.

▶ **See** "Classic or Web? Choosing a Navigation Style," **p. 62**

Part
I

Ch
3

Activating with Web Style (Single-Click Method)

Changing Windows 98 to use a web style of navigation makes the mouse work on the desktop or in Windows and Internet Explorer as it does on web pages. A single click activates an item. For example, a single-click on a desktop icon opens the icon's program or document.

N O T E If you have just switched to the web style, you might find yourself occasionally opening more files and folders than you want. What you might find occurring while in web style is that you open a folder in the Explorer's right pane the old way, with a double-click, only to find that you've activated a program or document. What has happened is that the first click opened the folder and the second click activated a file or program. ▪

To select a single desktop item, or a file or folder in Explorer, move the pointer over the item and pause. The focus, highlighting, will move to that item.

To select multiple adjacent items on the desktop or in the Explorer, move the pointer over the first item and pause until it is selected. Do not click. Hold down the Shift key and move the pointer smoothly until it is over the last item you want selected; then pause. All items between the first and last will be selected.

To select nonadjacent items on the desktop or in Explorer, move the pointer over the first item and pause until it is selected. Do not click. Hold down the Ctrl key and smoothly move the pointer over the next item to select and pause until that item is selected (see Figure 3.2). Continue the process of holding the Ctrl key, moving and pausing until each nonadjacent item is selected.

FIG. 3.2
Select nonadjacent items by pausing the pointer over items as you hold down Ctrl.

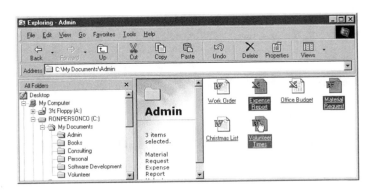

Activate or run multiple selected items by right-clicking one of the items and selecting Open or another appropriate command from the shortcut menu.

▶ **See** "Classic or Web? Choosing a Navigation Style," **p. 62**

Using the Microsoft Intellipoint Mouse

Microsoft's Intellipoint mouse was released coincidentally with the release of Office 97. This new mouse has a small wheel between the left and right mouse buttons. Rolling the wheel with your index finger enables you to scroll without using scroll bars, pan in any direction, zoom documents using different magnifications, expand/collapse outlines, and drill down or up in worksheet data. The features available depend on the program.

CAUTION

Only programs designed to work with the Intellipoint mouse take advantage of its features.

Holding down the Intellipoint mouse's wheel button, located between the mouse buttons, in combination with the Ctrl or Shift keys gives you access to additional features and commands, listed in Table 3.1.

Part

I

Ch

3

Table 3.1   Intellipoint Mouse Actions

Roll wheel	Scroll up in a window by rolling the wheel forward. Scroll down in a window by rolling the wheel down.
Drag wheel	Pan any direction in a window by holding down the wheel button as you move the mouse in any direction. The entire document moves in any direction.
Ctrl+wheel roll	Zoom a document to greater or lesser magnification by holding down the Ctrl key as you roll the wheel forward or backward.
Shift+wheel roll	Expand or collapse data structures like outlines or worksheet drill-downs by holding down the Shift key as you roll the wheel forward or backward.

Using the Keyboard

Table 3.2 shows the keyboard shortcuts that can save you time as you become proficient in Windows. A few of these keystrokes, such as F1 for Help, Alt+Tab to switch between applications, and F2 to edit selected text should be part of everyone's skill set. Some keyboards, such as the Microsoft Natural Keyboard, include a *Windows* and an *application* key that give quick access to certain predefined functions.

Table 3.2   Universal Windows Shortcut Keys

Topic	Description	Key Combination
Close, Program	Exit active program	Alt+F4
Close, Document Window	Close the active document window	Ctrl+F4
Help	Display Windows Help	Windows+F1
Help	Display Help for the selected item in a dialog box	F1
Menu, Document's System	Display document system menu to control program window	Alt+hyphen
Menu, Program	Activate menu bar	F10
Menu, Program's System	Display program system menu to control program window	Alt+Spacebar
Menu, Select Menu	Select from the active menu bar the menu containing the underlined letter	Alt+*underlined letter*
Menu, Shortcut	Display shortcut menu for selected item	Shift+F10 or Application key
Menu, Start	Display Start menu	Ctrl+Esc or Windows
Command, Cut	Cut selected item	Ctrl+X
Command, Copy	Copy selected item	Ctrl+C
Command, Paste	Paste item from Clipboard at current insertion point	Ctrl+V
Command, Delete	Delete selected item	Delete key
Command, Delete	Delete selected item from desktop without Recycle Bin	Shift+Delete
Command, Find: All Files	Displays Find: All Files dialog box when desktop active	F3 or Windows+F
Command, Find: Computer	Displays Find: Computer dialog box when desktop active	Ctrl+Windows+F

Topic	Description	Key Combination
Command, Minimize	Minimize all windows	Windows+M
Command, Minimize or Restore	Minimize or restore all windows	Windows+D
Command, Properties	Display Properties of selected item on desktop	Alt+Enter
Command, Refresh	Refresh all window contents	F5
Command, Rename	Rename selected item	F2
Command, Run	Display Run dialog box	Windows+R
Command, Select All	Selects all items when Desktop active	Ctrl+A
Command, System Properties	Display System Properties dialog box	Windows+Break
Command, Undo	Undo last effect of last command	Ctrl+Z
Command, Undo Minimize	Undo minimizing all windows	Shift+Windows+M
Switch, Document Window	Activate the next document window	Ctrl+F6
Switch, Program Window	Activate the next application window	Alt+Tab
Switch, Program	Activate Taskbar and cycle through buttons	Windows+Tab

Part

I

Ch

3

Using Menus and Dialog Boxes

The Windows system of graphical menus and dialog boxes reduces the learning curve and increases skill retention. Menus are displayed in the same location in all programs, and they display groups of commands by functional category. Dialog boxes present a unified way of defining an object's properties or modifying a command's operation. The operating techniques for menus and dialog boxes are the same for all Windows applications.

Choosing Menus and Commands

The menu bar, located directly under the title bar of a program, displays the menu names. Windows programs use the same menu headings for common functions (such as File, Edit, Window, and Help), which makes it easier for you to learn new applications. To open a menu, click its name with the left mouse button, or press Alt and then the underlined letter in the menu name.

Menu items, also known as commands, are displayed on each menu. Point to any menu item to select it. Click to activate the menu item or type the letter underlined in the submenu item name. If there is an arrow to the side of the menu item, a submenu will open. Click the menu item to keep the submenu open or move over the submenu item and click to activate that command. Menu items followed by an ellipsis (…) will display a dialog box giving you additional options.

Using Common Dialog Boxes to Open and Save Documents

Most programs designed for Windows 95 and Windows 98 have a few dialog boxes in common. The two most frequently used common dialog boxes are Save As and Open. Figure 3.3 shows an Open dialog box from WordPad. The Save As dialog box is very similar.

Navigating and managing files and folders within the work area of the Open or Save As dialog box is identical to working within an Explorer window. For example, you can drag and drop files or folders, use Ctrl+drag to copy, rename files or folders, right-click for an appropriate shortcut menu, and so forth.

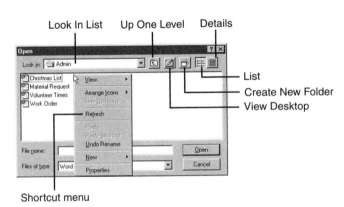

FIG. 3.3

Save As and Open dialog boxes, common to many programs, have many features built in.

Navigating between folders, as well as moving or copying files between folders, uses the same techniques in the common Open and Save As dialog boxes as the techniques used in Explorer windows. Table 3.3 lists the methods of manipulating folders.

Table 3.3 Navigating, Moving, and Copying in Common Dialog Boxes

Change drives or folders	Click Look In list
Open a folder	Activate folder
Go up a folder	Click Up One Level button or press Backspace
Create a new folder	Click Create New Folder button
Rename file or folder	Select, F2
Move file or folder	Drag
Copy file or folder	Ctrl+drag
Create shortcut	Right drag, Create Shortcut(s) Here

> **TIP** While in a common Save As or Open dialog box, press F4 to display the Save In or Look In lists. Press F5 to refresh the file and folder contents of the dialog boxes.

Within the Open or Save As dialog box, you can create a new folder in the currently displayed folder by clicking the Create New Folder button at the top of the dialog box. The folder will be displayed with its name selected. Type a new name over the selection and press Enter.

Rename a file or folder by selecting it and then pressing F2. Edit the name; then press Enter. To delete files or folders, select those you want to delete; then press Delete. Respond Yes when prompted if you want to send the file or folder to the Recycle Bin.

Selecting Options from Dialog Boxes

Use the controls in dialog boxes to change properties or the effect of a command. Figure 3.4 shows the Font dialog box from WordPad. Figure 3.5 shows the Word 6 tab from the Options dialog box in WordPad.

FIG. 3.4
Changing selections in a dialog box changes properties or the effect of a command.

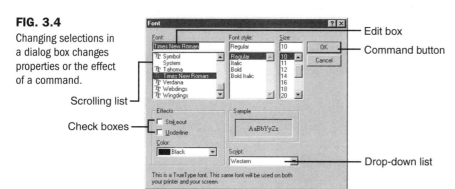

FIG. 3.5
You can select one
option button from a
group, but you can
select any number of
check boxes.

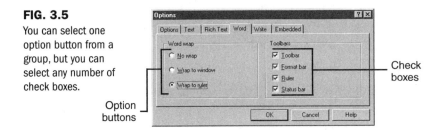

Option
buttons

Check
boxes

Using the Mouse in Dialog Boxes In the majority of cases it seems that only one or two items are changed in a dialog box. In that case a mouse is efficient for selecting the control and clicking OK. Table 3.4 shows mouse actions in a dialog box.

Table 3.4 Dialog Box Mouse Actions

Control Type	Effect	Mouse Action
Check box	Change check box	Click
Option buttons	Select one from group others	Click to select and clear
Edit Box	Edit text or number	Click and drag to select, type
Scrolling List	Scrolls list, then selects item in list	Click or drag scroll bar, click
Drop-down list	Select from drop-down list	Click down arrow, click item in list
Command button	Choose command button	Click

Using the Keyboard in Dialog Boxes If you need to change many settings in a dialog box or using a mouse is not possible, use one of these keyboard methods. If it's too much to remember all these keystrokes, just remember Ctrl+Tab to move between tabs in a dialog box and Alt+*underlined letter* to select or clear a control. Table 3.5 shows keystrokes for operating a dialog box.

Table 3.5 Dialog Box Keys

Effect	Keystroke
Move to next control	Tab
Move to previous control	Shift+Tab
Select next tab	Ctrl+Tab
Select previous tab	Shift+Ctrl+Tab

Effect	Keystroke
Acts the same as a click on the current control	Spacebar
Choose active button	Enter
Cancel dialog box	Esc
Select or clear control	Alt+*underlined letter*

 TIP You can Cut, Copy, and Paste between dialog boxes or between dialog boxes and applications. Select the text; then press Ctrl+X to cut or Ctrl+C to copy. Press Ctrl+V to insert text from the Clipboard.

Controlling the Size and Position of Windows

Part

I

Ch

3

The taskbar's shortcut menu enables you to quickly arrange windows on the desktop. Right-click a gray area of the taskbar; then click one of the following commands to arrange all open windows:

Cascade Windows	Arrange windows in an overlapping cascade from top to bottom, left to right.
Tile Windows Horizontally	Arrange windows in horizontal strips across the full screen width. Screen height is divided evenly between windows.
Tile Windows Vertically	Arrange windows in vertical strips from screen top to bottom. Screen width is divided evenly between windows.
Undo Tile	Restore all windows to their previous locations.

Quickly clear the desktop of windows by right-clicking a gray area of the taskbar and then clicking Minimize All Windows.

To quickly arrange your desktop so you can work in two program windows that evenly divide the screen, right-click a gray area of the taskbar; then click Minimize All Windows. Now display only the two programs in which you want to work by clicking their buttons in the taskbar. Finally, right-click a gray area of the taskbar; then click Tile Windows Horizontally or Tile Windows Vertically.

Move a window by dragging its title. Change the size of windows by dragging a window's edge or corner.

Move a desktop icon by dragging the icon. When you manually move desktop icons, they might not exactly align. If you want to align them, right-click the desktop; then click Arrange

Icons. From the submenu, click one of the choices for how you want them aligned on the desk: by N̲ame, by T̲ype, by Si̲ze, or by D̲ate. If you want desktop icons to automatically align themselves whenever they are moved, click A̲uto Arrange on the submenu.

Changing Settings and Properties

Nearly every item on the Windows desktop or within a program's contents has associated properties. Properties are characteristics inherent to an item. A property sheet for each item enables you to view and change properties. To display an item's property sheet, right-click an item; then click P̲roperties on the shortcut menu. A property sheet similar to the Display Properties sheet in Figure 3.6 displays. Change properties by selecting, editing, or clearing entries and then clicking OK.

FIG. 3.6
Property sheets enable you to view and change an item's properties.

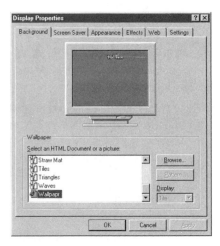

Using the Start Menu

The Start menu is the starting place for many of the tasks that you want to accomplish in Windows. You can open the Start menu at any time, from within any program, with one mouse click. From the Start menu, you can start programs, open recently used documents, customize the look and feel of Windows, find files and folders, get Help, and shut down your computer.

TROUBLESHOOTING

The windows of some programs written for older versions of Windows covers the taskbar so it is difficult to switch between applications or click the Start button. Even when you can't see the taskbar, you can switch between applications by holding down the Alt key and pressing Tab. A bar is displayed with icons for each application. Press Tab until the application you want is selected; then release both keys.

To simultaneously display the taskbar and open the Start menu, press Ctrl+Esc.

Starting a Program

To start a program using the Start menu, click Start. Point to Programs. The Program menu then is displayed to the right. Point to the program that you want to start, as shown in Figure 3.7, and click. You can keep any of these menus open by clicking once on the menu. If you do not do this, the menu will close when the pointer moves outside the menu.

If the program you want to start is not displayed in the Start menu, point to an appropriate folder on the Start menu to see the programs within the folder.

 T I P If you have moved the taskbar, you might not see the taskbar and Start button at the bottom of your screen. If you see a gray line at one edge of the screen, move the pointer to that edge to display the taskbar.

FIG. 3.7
Open the menu that contains the program that you want to start and then click the program.

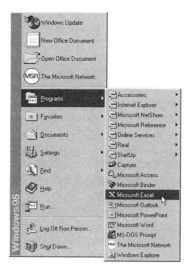

When you open a program, a button for the program appears in the taskbar. These buttons tell you which programs are open. Quickly activate the window for one of these programs by clicking on its button.

▶ **See** "Adding and Removing Programs in the Start Menu," **p. 436**

Opening a Recently Used Document

Clicking the Documents command on the Start menu displays your most recently opened documents. When you choose this command, the Documents submenu is displayed with a listing of the files that you have worked on recently. To open a document in this list, simply click on it. Windows then automatically starts the associated application, if it is not already running, and opens the document.

After a while, the listing in the Documents menu can become quite long and contain documents that you no longer are working with. To clear the list, right-click a blank area of the taskbar and choose Properties. Select the Start Menu Programs tab on the Taskbar Properties dialog box; then click the Clear button.

Using the Taskbar

The taskbar resides at an edge of the screen, usually the bottom, and displays all programs currently open and running. Switch between programs by clicking a program button on the taskbar.

 T I P Press Alt+Tab to cycle between programs without using the mouse or taskbar.

Using Toolbars

Toolbars give you quick access to applications and other resources. They reside on the taskbar. There are four default toolbars, but you can create your own custom toolbars that contain buttons for programs, files, folder, and hyperlinks. Figure 3.8 shows the four built-in toolbars.

FIG. 3.8
The taskbar and built-in toolbars are displayed in this order: Quick Launch, Taskbar, Desktop, Address and Links.

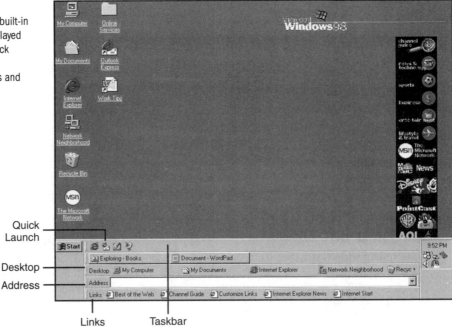

To display a built-in toolbar, right-click in a gray area of the taskbar or a toolbar, click Toolbars, and then click the name of the toolbar. To remove a toolbar, right-click the toolbar title; then click Close. You cannot close the taskbar. The different toolbars are described in Table 3.6.

Table 3.6	Built-In Toolbar Descriptions
Toolbar	**Description**
Address	Displays hyperlinks you enter to web or local items
Link	Displays hyperlinks to web sites: Best of the Web, Microsoft, Product News, Today's Links, and Web Gallery
Desktop	Displays a button for each item on the desktop
Quick Launch	Shows Desktop, displays Channels, launches Internet Explorer, Mail

Move a toolbar by dragging the move handle at its left corner. Dragging a toolbar to midscreen creates a toolbar window. To resize and manipulate these, use normal window techniques.

▶ **See** "Managing Buttons on a Toolbar," **p. 435**

 T I P A quick way to open a window onto a folder is to click Start, Run. When the Run dialog box is displayed, type the path of the folder in the Open edit box and click OK.

Working with Applications

Windows enables you to run more than one program at the same time. Each program is displayed in its own window or as an item on the taskbar. The term *active* is used to describe the window that receives input. This is usually the topmost program window. The active window's title bar will be a different color than that of inactive windows.

Figure 3.9 shows two program windows. The active window contains multiple documents. The taskbar at the bottom of the screen displays the programs that are running. The button for the active program is highlighted on the taskbar.

▶ **See** "Installing Windows Applications," **p. 173**

Scrolling in a Document

Document windows containing contents larger than the window display scroll bars. A vertical scroll bar displays along the right edge and a horizontal scroll bar along the bottom edge.

In most programs you can move through document contents using the mouse with the actions shown in Table 3.7.

Part
I

Ch
3

FIG. 3.9

This active program window contains multiple document windows.

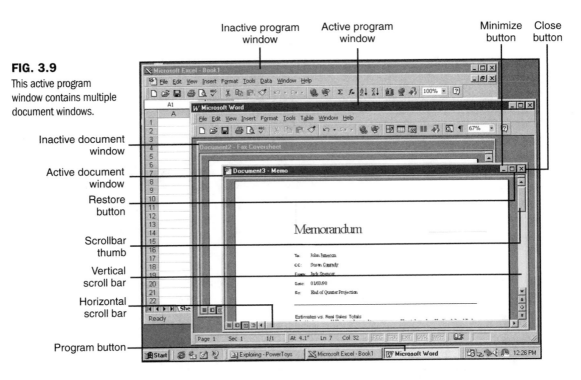

Inactive program window — Active program window — Minimize button — Close button

Inactive document window

Active document window

Restore button

Scrollbar thumb

Vertical scroll bar

Horizontal scroll bar

Program button

Table 3.7 Scrolling with Mouse Actions

Movement	Mouse Action
Scroll by smallest increments	Click arrowheads at ends of scrollbar
Scroll by screenful	Click in scrollbar
Scroll to edge of document	Drag thumb in scroll bar to appropriate end of scrollbar

In most programs you can move through document contents using the keyboard with the actions shown in Table 3.8.

Table 3.8 Scrolling with Keystrokes

Movement	Keystroke
Scroll by up/down by line	up/down arrow key
Scroll left/right by character	right/left arrow key
Scroll left/right by word	Ctrl+right/left arrow key
Scroll to beginning of line	Home
Scroll to end of line	End
Scroll up/down by screenful	Page Up/Page Down

Selecting Text and Objects

Select text by dragging across the text. Select words by double-clicking the word.

Select objects by clicking on them. On the Windows desktop and in most programs you can select multiple items by clicking on the first object and then holding Shift or Ctrl as you click other objects.

Select multiple adjacent objects on the desktop by dragging the pointer diagonally across the objects you want to select. A selection rectangle is displayed as you drag. Objects within or touching the selection rectangle will be selected when you release the mouse button.

Select text with the keyboard by holding down the Shift key as you move. Select words by holding the Shift and Ctrl key as you press an arrow key.

Using Simple Editing Techniques

Edit text with a mouse by clicking within text to position the insertion point and then typing. Replace text by selecting it and then typing.

Edit text with the keyboard by moving the insertion point to where you want to insert text and then typing. Replace text by selecting it and then typing. Delete selected text by pressing the Delete key.

Part
I
Ch
3

Copying and Moving

Use menu commands or mouse actions to copy or move selected items. Cut a selected item from its current location by clicking Edit, Cut (Ctrl+X). Copy a selected item by clicking Edit, Copy (Ctrl+C). Paste the cut or copied item by moving the insertion point where you want the item and then clicking Edit, Paste (Ctrl+V).

To move a selected item using the mouse, drag the selected item to its new location; then release. To copy a selected item, hold down the Ctrl key as you drag the item.

▶ **See** "Understanding the Data-Sharing Capabilities of Windows 98," **p. 196**

Switching Between Document Windows

Activate a document window by clicking on a portion of the window. If you cannot see the inactive window to click on it, then click Window, and click on the document name you want active. In some programs you can cycle between document windows by pressing Ctrl+F6.

Closing a Document Window

Close a document window by first activating the document and then clicking File, Close or clicking the Close button for the document window. If the document has been modified since the last time it was saved, you will be prompted if you want to save the document. If you click Yes, the document will be saved with its current name.

Quitting Windows Applications

Most Windows applications use the same procedure for quitting. To quit a Windows application, follow these steps:

1. Activate the application by clicking the application's window or by pressing Alt+Tab until the application's window is active.
2. Click File, Exit or click the Close button for the program window.

If the application contains documents that you have modified since the last time that you saved them, the application prompts you to save your changes before the application quits.

Working with the Active Desktop

The Active Desktop in Windows 98 can change the way you work and think. Instead of working from a Windows desktop containing static folders and icons, you can work from the Webtop, a desktop that displays dynamic information changing to meet your needs. The Active Desktop can show you static or changing information from your local PC, your network, or the web.

The Active Desktop is one of the most important aspects of the Webtop metaphor. In Windows 95 the desktop displays static information such as shortcut icons to start programs or open folders as well as a picture or pattern as a background. The Active Desktop that is available in Windows 98 makes your desktop a display and work area for constantly changing information. For example, your Active Desktop can contain live web pages, ActiveX components, and Java applets. This enables you to see changes to information that might be important to your work and life, such as currency or stock market changes as well as local weather or news bulletins specific to your interests.

You can turn the Active Desktop on or off and customize it to fit your needs. You can use any HTML page as your Active Desktop. This means your Active Desktop can display information such as the following:

- any graphic or text that will display in a web page
- Web links to favorite sites such as finance, sports, lifestyle, or weather
- continually updating web pages from favorite sites
- information pushed to your active desktop from Channel vendors
- ActiveX components or Java applets that run as applications in the Active Desktop
- Help information or company bulletins that change frequently

▶ **See** "Customizing the Windows Display," **p. 438**

▶ **See** "Displaying Objects on the Active Desktop," **p. 680**

▶ **See** "Using an HTML Page as Your Desktop," **p. 679**

▶ **See** "Using Subscriptions to Download Web Pages," **p. 683**

Getting Help

by Ron Person

Beginners and experts alike occasionally need help operating Windows or one of its applications. The Help system in Windows 98 is new, but you will find it very easy to use. It includes access to help files on your local drive, links to resources on the web, access to Microsoft support engineers, and a Windows Update Manager that keeps your software and drivers current. This chapter also contains a brief description of the WinHelp system used in Windows 95 and earlier Windows applications.

Understanding Help

Windows 98 Help uses the new HTML Help engine created by Microsoft. The HTML Help engine displays HTML pages containing help information. With this help engine, Windows 98 can look locally, on your network, or on the Internet for help files or other types of assistance programs. Although HTML Help displays HTML pages, you will not find a large collection of HTML Help files on your system. The HTML Help engine accesses HTML files that have been compressed into one or more files, thereby preserving disk space.

Windows applications existing when Windows 98 was released use the WinHelp system that was available in Windows 95. You'll find a brief description on how to operate help systems based on WinHelp later in this chapter.

Getting Help from Windows Help Files

You start Windows 98 Help by clicking Start, Help. Figure 4.1 shows the Help window that appears. The help shown uses the HTML Help engine.

FIG. 4.1
Windows 98 Help uses the HTML Help engine to produce clean and simple displays.

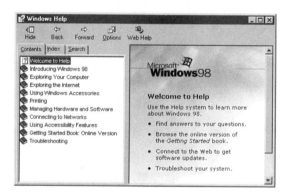

N O T E   To start Help from within a Windows application, you can press the F1 key. Windows then displays help information for the active application or window. ▪

Navigating the Contents Pane

The Contents tab, the left pane shown in Figure 4.1, lists Windows 98 help topics by category. The Contents pane of the Help window displays the books and pages with their topic titles. The right pane displays the contents of the page that's selected in the left pane.

Categories in the left pane appear as books. You can open a book to see additional categories or help pages it contains. Figure 4.2 shows the Contents tab with a book expanded to multiple levels and a page selected from the book. To expand or close a book, click in the left pane on the book or its topic title.

FIG. 4.2

Expand books to see their topical contents.

Help Hide (Show) Button

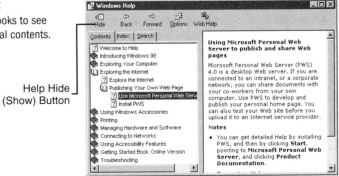

You can change the widths of the panes by dragging the vertical bar between the panes to the left or right. To completely hide the left pane, click the Hide button in the toolbar. While the topic list is hidden, the Hide button is replaced by a Show button. Click the Show button to redisplay the topic list pane.

Part I

Ch 4

Jumping to a Related Help Topic

Some help topics contain hyperlinks to related topics. These hyperlinks appear underlined as you would expect in a web browser. To display a page of related information or a list of related topics, click the hyperlink. To return to the original page, click the Back button located on the toolbar.

Searching by Topic on the Index Page

If you aren't sure of how to describe the topic on which you need help, use the Index tab. The Index tab, shown in Figure 4.3, enables you to find the help you need by scanning for appropriate words or phrases. The Index tab is visible when the left pane is shown.

Suppose you want to find information on a feature called NetWatcher. As you can see in the figure, you would type the word *netwatcher* and then click Display. A Topics Found window appears showing all topics containing this key word. Choose one of the topics listed, such as "Using Net Watcher to Monitor Shared Resource Use." In the right pane, the Help system displays how to use NetWatcher to monitor shared resources.

You can search through the list by scrolling or by typing a key word or phrase in the edit box at the top of the list. When you find a word or phrase that seems to be appropriate, click on it.

FIG. 4.3

The Index tab displays phrases describing helpful topics.

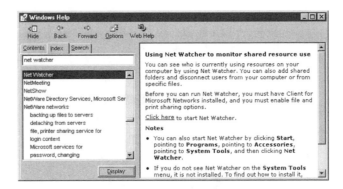

In some cases, when you click Display, the Topics Found window appears, showing a list of subcategories that further differentiate your choice. Just choose the topic most related to what you want. Help will appear in the right pane of the Help window.

If you aren't sure what you are looking for, scroll through the index looking for related topics. Choose a related topic, and then check the right pane to see if the topic contains a hyperlink to a more specific topic that fits your needs.

Getting Help on the Active Dialog Box

If you are faced with a dialog box or window that contains an item you need help with, look for a question mark (?) button in the upper-right corner of the dialog box or window. Click the question mark button, and then click the item in the dialog box or window about which you want information. A pop-up window like that shown in Figure 4.4 shows you information about the item. When you finish reading the information, click to close the pop-up window.

FIG. 4.4

Pop-up help describes specific items or areas in dialog boxes and window.

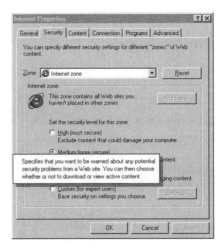

Finding Help with a Keyword

If you know a word that describes the topic you need help on, click the Search tab. To find all topics that contain your word, type the word in the text box at the top of the right pane, and then click List Topics. Help displays a list of topics that contain this word, as shown in Figure 4.5.

Multiple topics will probably appear in the Topic list. Click the topic that looks most helpful, and then click Display to see the help information in the right pane.

FIG. 4.5

Save time by using the Search tab to quickly find topics.

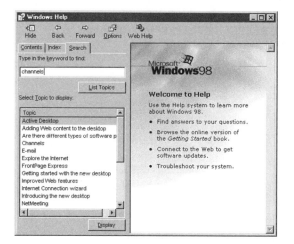

Printing a Help Topic

If you have a large display area, it's possible and convenient to display the application in which you are working and the Help window side by side. However, if your display area is smaller or if you want to create a written reminder, you might want to print a page of help so you can refer to it as you work.

To print any displayed page, either right-click the topic shown in the Contents pane and choose Print, or click in the right pane and choose Print.

N O T E Some of the handiest information that you can print or copy from help is an application's shortcut keys. If you didn't get a shortcut keystroke template for your application, look in the application's help contents for a topic similar to Keyboard Shortcuts. Copy these topics by selecting them and pressing Ctrl+C. Then paste (Ctrl+V) them into a word processor, reorganize them, and print them. Alternatively, you can print the topics directly from Help. You can then copy the contents at a reduced size and paste them onto 3-by-5 cards. ▪

Part

I

Ch

4

Using Windows 95 Help

Windows 95 and applications designed for Windows 95 use the WinHelp engine to create a Help system that appears slightly different from that of Windows 98's HTML Help. Even if you use Windows 98, you will probably continue to see and use Help based on the WinHelp engine because it is used with Windows 95–compatible applications. Figure 4.6 shows the Windows 95 Help system's Contents tab for Microsoft Word 97. It is similar to the Contents tab in Windows 98 Help. However, Windows 95 Help has only a single pane. The Index and Search tabs function similarly to those in HTML Help, but they also disappear when you select a help selection.

FIG. 4.6

Windows 95-based Help systems appear similar to that of Windows 98, but the tabs and topics disappear and are replaced by specific help contents you choose.

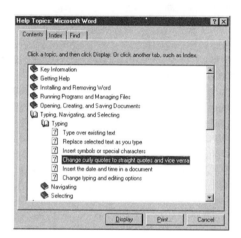

If you compare Figure 4.1 with Figure 4.6, you see that the HTML Help in Figure 4.1 displays the procedural steps or help information in a window to the side of the help topic. Because the Contents or Index list in Windows 98 Help remains open in the left pane, it's easy for you to see the context of a procedure and see related help. However, in Windows 95 Help, the Contents, Index, and Search tabs disappear when a Help window appears.

Another significant difference between the two types of help is that Windows 98 Help is displayed in a browser. Therefore, it runs scripting languages, supports Dynamic HTML, and contains links to Internet and intranet sites. This enables Windows 98 Help to be more active and to link users to current information and downloadable files.

Adding Custom Notes to Help Topics

You can annotate your own notes to help topics in Windows 95 Help. You might want to use annotations to describe a topic in greater detail, to document information related to tasks you do, or to add a function-related tip. When a Windows 95 help topic has an annotation, a paper clip icon appears next to it.

To create an annotation, follow these steps:

1. Display the topic that you want to annotate.
2. Click the Options button and then choose Annotate. The Annotate dialog box, a small notepad, appears.
3. Type the notes that you want to save regarding this Help topic.
4. Click the Save button.

To read the annotation to a topic, just click the paper clip icon. To remove an annotation, click the paper clip icon and then choose Delete from the Annotate dialog box.

Copying Help Information to Another Application

You can create a collection of help topics from Windows 95 Help by copying the help information and pasting the data into another Windows application such as a word processor document file.

▶ **See** "Cutting, Copying, and Pasting Data," **p. 198**

To copy the contents of a Windows 95 Help window, click the Options button, and then click Copy. Then paste the data into another application by using normal Windows paste procedures.

 To copy portions of text in the help screens of Windows 98 or Windows 95 Help windows, drag across the text to select it, and then press Ctrl+C. Paste it into the new location using the paste procedure appropriate to the receiving application.

Part
I
Ch
4

Finding Help on the Web

The web offers a wide range of resources that are available to help you with Windows 98. Windows 98 has built-in links to some of these resources. To display these links, click Start, and choose Programs, Accessories, Welcome to Windows. You will see links to numerous resources, including Microsoft's web site and Microsoft Technical Support.

Using the Microsoft Support Page

If you have an Internet browser installed, you can connect to the Windows Support web page shown in Figure 4.7. Click the Support Online hyperlink to display the Microsoft Technical Support page shown in Figure 4.8. From this page, you can search for support or answers by product and by keyword. This page also displays tabs that link you to frequently asked questions, phone numbers, and support options. If you want to go there directly in your browser, enter the following URL for Microsoft's Support page:

`www.microsoft.com/support`

FIG. 4.7
Microsoft's Support page contains links to help, tips, and troubleshooting for Microsoft products.

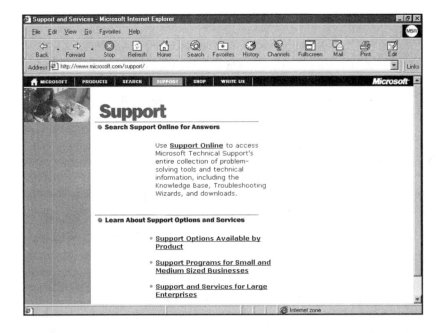

FIG. 4.8
FAQs (Frequently Asked Questions) often hold the answers to most questions.

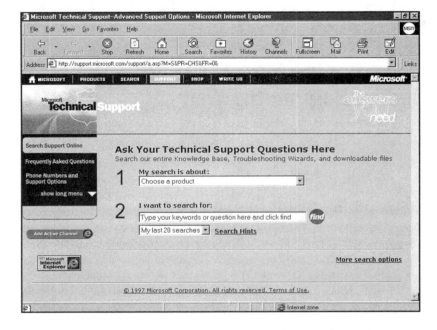

Within the Windows Support page, you will find many hyperlinks to helpful resources. Some of the most valuable resources are covered in the other sections of this book.

▶ **See** "What Is Internet Explorer 4.0?," **p. 600**

▶ **See** "Navigating Internet Explorer," **p. 605**

Looking for FAQs

Frequently Asked Questions (FAQs) are lists maintained on bulletin boards or web sites that contain the most frequently asked questions about the site's topic. In most cases involving generic problems, you should look through the FAQ lists on Microsoft's Support page before you do a search through the Knowledge Base. To access Windows FAQs from the Support page, go to the main support page at www.microsoft.com/support and click the Frequently Asked Questions link. A page similar to Figure 4.9 appears. Select the product and topic you want, and then click the Find button.

FIG. 4.9
A Frequently Asked Questions list contains answers to the site's most common questions.

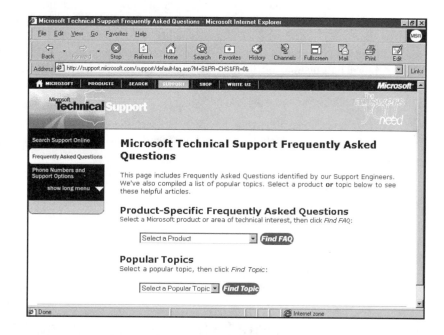

Reporting Problems to Online Support Engineers

Sometimes you try and try only to finally realize that you're not getting closer to solving the computer problem you face. That's when it's time to call in the professionals. For a fee, you can submit a technical problem to Microsoft's technical support engineers. To do this, go to the Microsoft Support web page and click the Phone Numbers and Support options. Follow the steps provided to register for online support. Microsoft gives no-charge support for 90 days. After that period, you can subscribe to fee-based support options.

Consulting the Hardware Compatibility List

If you have difficulty getting Windows 98 to recognize or properly run a hardware device, you will probably want to examine the Hardware Compatibility List (HCL). It contains a list of computer systems and peripherals that have been tested by the Microsoft Windows Hardware Quality Labs. To see this list, access the Microsoft Support Web page and select Windows 98 from the My Search Is About list. In the I Want to Search For box, type **Hardware Compatibility List**. Then click the Find button to access a page containing hardware compatibility information.

Getting Answers from TechNet

One of the most valuable resources of technical knowledge on Windows and Windows applications is TechNet. TechNet is a compilation of troubleshooting procedures, technical papers, product descriptions, product announcements, drivers, and so on. TechNet is a paid subscription service that sends you three CDs each month containing more than 150,000 pages of technical information, fourteen Resource Kits, Service Packs, the KnowledgeBase, and the software library containing the latest drivers and patches. It also includes a full-text search engine to help you find what you need.

To learn more about subscribing to TechNet, click the Web Resources link on the Windows 98 Help page, and then click the TechNet hyperlink on the Windows Support Web page.

To subscribe to the TechNet CD-ROM, contact them at:

Microsoft TechNet
One Microsoft Way
Redmond, WA 98052-6399
FAX: (206) 936-7329, Attn: TechNet
Voice: (800) 344-2121
Internet: technet@microsoft.com
Web: www.microsoft.com/technet

Getting Peer Support Through Newsgroups

Newsgroups provide you with an online area in which you can post technical questions and get responses from your peers. As you can see from the few newsgroups listed in the left pane of Figure 4.10, newsgroups cover a wide range of topics including Microsoft's products. You can access newsgroups with most Internet newsreader software. You must configure your newsreader for Microsoft's news server at msnews.microsoft.com. If you are using Internet Explorer 4, the newsgroup reader was configured for Microsoft's news service when you installed Internet Explorer 4 and Windows 98.

FIG. 4.10
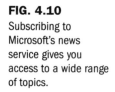
Subscribing to Microsoft's news service gives you access to a wide range of topics.

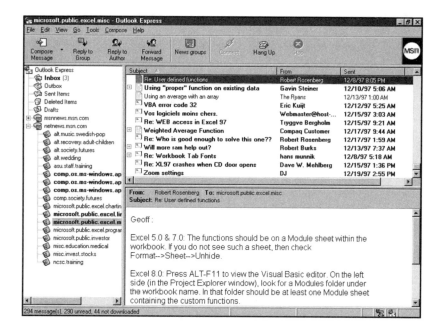

Newsgroups are monitored by Most Valuable Professionals (MVPs). These professional consultants and trainers are very conscientious and hard working. They are volunteers and are paid only in professional recognition and their desire to help others, so help them out. Be careful of advice you receive from respondents you are not familiar with. While they mean well, they might not be well informed.

▶ **See** "Setting Default Mail and News Clients," **p. 620**

Finding Help, Support, and Resources

Even though local and online help is readily accessible, you might find it more comforting to talk with a person who guides you through troubleshooting. Or maybe you find books to be a less expensive yet very informative way of learning.

Part

I

Ch

4

Getting Telephone Support

For customer service and product upgrade information, call (800) 426-9400. At the time this book was published, Microsoft offered three methods of support for Windows with live support personnel. These numbers and support levels are outlined here:

Description	Type	Telephone
Support for 90 days from your first support call.	Free. Initial 90-day support.	(425) 635-7000
$35 charge to a credit card until the specific problem is resolved. Make sure you keep the charge code ID and incident ID assigned by Microsoft.	$35 per incident charged to a credit card.	(800) 936-5700
$35 charge to a telephone number until the specific problem is resolved. Incident ID is assigned by Microsoft.	$35 per incident charged to telephone.	(900) 555-2000

This support is available Monday through Friday, 6:00am to 6:00pm Pacific time, excluding holidays.

You also can get help on Windows via a FAX that lists the most frequently asked questions and their answers. To get answers from FastTips, call (800) 936-4200.

Microsoft also supports a stable of service providers who can give you or your company help on Windows. These service providers are:

Name	Description	Support Options	Telephone
Sitel	Technical services.	Wide range of services available.	800-363-5448
Corporate Software	Corporate support	Windows 95 support and training.	(617) 440-1000
Unisys Corporation	Support for home users and businesses.	$35 per incident $2.95 per minute Prepaid callbacks.	(900) 555-5454 (800) 757-8324 (800) 863-0436

Consultants and Training

Microsoft Certified Solution Providers and Certified Trainers are consultants and trainers certified by Microsoft to work with or train on Microsoft products. They are independent consultants who have met the strict qualifying requirements imposed by Microsoft.

You can find the Microsoft Certified Solution Providers and training centers in your area by calling (800) SOL-PROV.

Que is the publisher of *Platinum Edition Using Windows 98*, and of the *Special Edition Using* series of books. To order books or catalogs or to get additional information, please call Macmillan Computer Publishing at:

(317) 581-3500
(800) 428-5331

Or point your browser to:

`http://www.mcp.com/`

Part
I

Ch
4

Working with Files and Folders

An Overview of the Windows Desktop Update

by Ed Bott

In this chapter

Introducing the Windows Desktop Update

When Microsoft first introduced Internet Explorer 4.0, they didn't just offer a web browser: The complete IE4 package included an optional component called the Windows Desktop Update, which made radical changes to the interface that debuted in the original version of Windows 95.

With Windows 98, the Windows Desktop Update is no longer an option, but instead is an integral part of the new operating system. If you're familiar with the original Windows 95 interface and haven't previously used IE4, you'll notice the following interface changes when you install Windows 98:

- An enhanced taskbar, which includes a new Quick Launch toolbar and changes the way taskbar buttons work.
- An enhanced Start menu, with a new menu item for Web Favorites, new options on the Find menu, and the capability to edit or rearrange program shortcuts directly.
- New folder and desktop options, including a choice of single-click or double-click navigation.
- Many, many small improvements to the original Windows interface, which collectively make file management more productive.
- The Web View option, with which you can display the contents of drives and folders as part of a customizable web page.
- The optional Active Desktop setting, which enables you to add web pages and HTML components to the Windows desktop.

N O T E Because the names are so similar, it's easy to confuse the Windows Desktop Update and the Active Desktop. In fact, even some Microsoft marketing pieces use the two names interchangeably. The two are not the same, however; in fact, the Active Desktop is one small part of the Windows Desktop Update. You'll find detailed information about the Active Desktop in Chapter 33, "Web Subscriptions and the Active Desktop."

Classic or Web? Choosing a Navigation Style

With the Windows Desktop Update installed, you have several important interface choices to make. To see the available options, open My Computer or an Explorer window and choose View, Folder Options. Click the General tab to see the dialog box shown in Figure 5.1.

FIG. 5.1

Choose your interface: the Classic Windows 95 style, one that resembles a web browser, or one that combines the two.

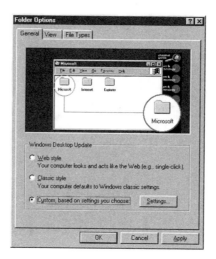

TROUBLESHOOTING

I've opened Explorer, but I can't find the Folder Options choice on the View menu. You're probably viewing a web page in the Explorer window, in which case the View menu offers an Internet Options choice instead. Click in the Address bar, type **C:**, and press Enter. The Folder Options command should now appear on the View menu.

Choose one of the following three interface options:

- *Web Style.* This style sets the Windows desktop and folder options to resemble your web browser. Icons are underlined, like hyperlinks on a web page. You point at icons to select them and single-click to open folders and launch programs.

- *Classic Style.* This resembles the original Windows 95 interface. As in Windows 95, you single-click to select icons and double-click to open folders and launch programs.

- *Custom, Based on Settings You Choose.* With the Custom option, you can mix and match interface options. After you choose this option, click the Settings button to choose from four options in the Custom Settings dialog box, shown in Figure 5.2.

▶ **See** "Using an HTML Page as Your Desktop," **p. 679**

The following sections provide details on the options in the Custom Settings dialog box.

Part

II

Ch

5

FIG. 5.2
Choose any combination of these options to create your own custom interface.

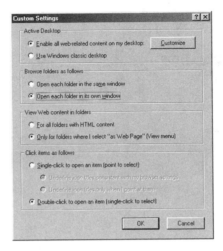

 TIP   Although the Custom Settings dialog box looks daunting, it actually follows a simple organization. Each of the four options includes two choices. If you choose the top item in each list, you end up with web style; choose the bottom option in all four cases, and you end up with classic style.

Turning on the Active Desktop

Choosing the option labeled Enable All Web-Related Content on My Desktop has the same effect as checking the Active Desktop's View As Web Page option: It turns on the Active Desktop. Clicking the Customize button takes you to the web tab of the Display Properties dialog box. Choosing Use Windows Classic Desktop turns off the Active Desktop.

For a full discussion of your Active Desktop options, see Chapter 33.

Choosing a Browsing Style

In the classic style Windows interface (Open Each Folder in Its Own Window), the original window remains open when you display the contents of a new drive or folder. If you drill down through multiple folders and subfolders, you'll end up with a screen full of windows. Choose the web style interface (Open Each Folder in the Same Window) to display the contents of each new drive or folder in the same window you started with, replacing the contents that were there previously.

▶ **See** "Two Views of Windows Explorer," **p. 70**

Viewing Web Content in Folders

Thanks to the Windows Desktop Update, Explorer lets you view any folder as a web page, using a standard folder template or a custom HTML page you create. web view adds a banner to the top left side of the folder window and an info pane below it; the file list appears on the right side of the window. Choose the top option (For All Folders with HTML Content) to use web view with all folders; choose the bottom option (Only for Folders Where I Select "as Web Page" [View Menu]) if you want to selectively turn on web view.

For a full discussion of web view, including details on how to create your own custom HTML folder templates, see Chapter 8, "Managing Files Using Web View."

Single-Click or Double-Click?

The most important interface choice you'll make is how you use the mouse to select icons and open folders or launch programs. By default, Windows 98 takes a conservative approach, preserving the familiar double-click style introduced in the original Windows 95 interface. To change this option, choose Web Style or open the Custom Settings dialog box and choose Single-click to Open an Item (Point to Select). The first time you choose this option, you'll see the Single-click warning dialog box shown in Figure 5.3.

FIG. 5.3
Because the single-click interface is a radical change, Windows asks you to confirm your choice when you first select it.

Why the warning? Because when you choose the web style interface, you change the way Windows handles some of its most basic tasks. Table 5.1 offers a side-by-side comparison of how you deal with files and folders using the two navigation styles.

Table 5.1   Web Style Versus Classic Style

Task	Web Style	Classic Style
Select an icon	Point to the icon.	Click the icon.
Open an icon	Click the icon.	Double-click the icon.
Select a group of adjacent icons	Point to the first icon, press and hold down the Shift key, and point to the last icon.	Click the first icon, press and hold down the Shift key, and click the last icon.
Select multiple icons	Hold down the Ctrl key and point to individual icons.	Hold down the Ctrl key and click individual icons.
Drag and drop	Point to an icon, press and hold down the mouse button, and drag icon to a new location (same as classic style).	Point to an icon, press and hold down the mouse button, and drag icon to a new location.

TROUBLESHOOTING

I've chosen the single-click option, but Windows ignores me when I adjust the option to underline icons only when I point at them. When you choose the single-click option in the Custom Settings dialog box, you also have the choice to underline all icon titles (as Internet Explorer does) or to underline icons only when you point at them. If you've selected the top choice in all four sections of the Custom Settings dialog box, Windows shifts your choice to web style and ignores your underlining preferences. The only way to force Explorer to accept this change is to select the bottom (classic) choice in one of the first three sections of this dialog box.

Customizing Other Folder Options

Installing the Windows Desktop Update adds an assorted group of advanced folder options as well. To adjust these settings, choose View, Folder Options, and then click the View tab of the Folder Options dialog box. The advanced folder options are listed at the bottom of the dialog box, as shown in Figure 5.4. Table 5.2 outlines the effects of each of these settings.

FIG. 5.4

These are the default settings for advanced folder options.

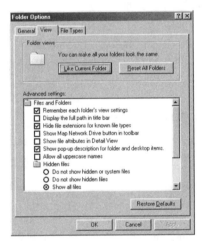

Table 5.2   Advanced Folder Options

Option	Effect When Checked
Remember Each Folder's View Settings	Saves the icon view of folder windows; also saves size and position when you use multi-window browsing option. Does not apply to two-pane Explorer windows.
Display the Full Path in Title Bar	Shows full DOS-style path (e.g., C:\Windows\System) in folder windows. This is handy when comparing subfolders with identical names in different parts of the Explorer tree.

Option	Effect When Checked
Hide File Extensions for Known File Types	Uncheck this box to show all file extensions, even when the file type is registered.
Show Map Network Drive Button in Toolbar	Adds two buttons to the Standard toolbar. Check this option if you regularly assign drive letters to shared network folders.
Show File Attributes in Detail View	Adds a column at the far right of Details view.
Show Pop-Up Description for Folder and Desktop Items	Displays ScreenTips when you point to My Computer and other desktop items; experienced users should not check this box.
Allow All Uppercase Names	Normally, Windows capitalizes only the first letter of all filenames (e.g., Abc). Remove the check from this box to allow file and folder names to consist of all uppercase letters (such as ABC).
Hidden Files	Choose whether to display hidden and/or system files.

▶ **See** "Changing the Way a Folder's Contents Appear," **p. 76**

▶ **See** "Associating Files with Programs," **p. 102**

Part

II

Ch

5

Managing Files with My Computer and the Windows Explorer

by Ed Bott

Two Views of Windows Explorer

The most basic building block of Windows is the icon. Every object you work with—including files and folders, drives and network servers, programs, printers, and shortcuts to web pages—has its own icon. Program icons are as distinctive as product logos; data files use standard icons that help you group related files easily; system objects use icons that are intended to illustrate their main function. And they're all organized into folders and subfolders in a strict hierarchy.

Most often when you view or manage icons and folders, you use a program called the Windows Explorer in one of its two views. Right-click a drive or folder icon, and shortcut menus let you choose between the two faces of Explorer: Click Open, and the contents of the drive or folder you selected appear in a simple window; choose Explore, and you see a more complex view, with one pane that shows all the resources available to you and another that displays the selected folder's contents. When you open the My Computer icon, you're using the simpler version of Explorer; when you choose Windows Explorer from the Start menu, you open the same program, with a handful of additional menus and some advanced options.

Once they learn how Explorer works, most Windows users incorporate both views into their working style.

Viewing Resources in My Computer

For a simple, uncluttered view of all the resources on your computer, find the My Computer icon on the desktop and open it. The resulting window looks something like the one shown in Figure 6.1.

FIG. 6.1
The My Computer window offers a simple way to view local resources, including drives, printers, and other hardware.

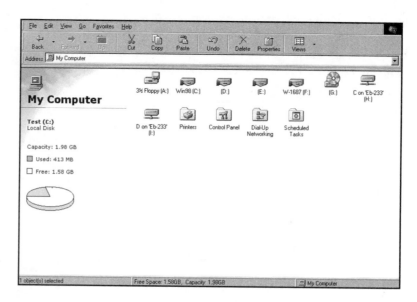

Microsoft's interface designers created My Computer as the primary file management interface for novice users, but even Windows experts will find it ideally suited for some file management tasks. Because the My Computer window displays the amount of free disk space, for example, it's a convenient way to see at a glance how much total storage is available on your system.

 TIP To see the maximum amount of information about drives in the My Computer window, choose View, Details. Click the Free Space heading to sort drives in order of available storage space.

Browsing the Contents of a Folder

Unlike the Windows Explorer, which shows you the outline-style hierarchy of all drives and folders on your system, starting with the My Computer window shows you the contents of one folder at a time. To view the contents of drives and folders from the My Computer window, open a drive icon, then a folder within that drive, then a folder within that folder. Keep drilling down in this fashion until you find the folder you're looking for.

The two easiest ways to go back up through the hierarchy of folders are to press the Backspace key and to click the Up button on the Standard toolbar. (If the toolbar is hidden, choose View, Toolbars, Standard Buttons to make it visible.)

What happens to the current folder window when you open a drive or folder icon from the My Computer window? If you've chosen the Web style interface, the contents of the folder you selected replace the contents of the current window, so you're always working with a single window. If you've selected the Classic style interface, on the other hand, the My Computer window remains open and a new drive or folder window appears. For each folder you open, you see a new folder window (see Figure 6.2).

FIG. 6.2
Opening a folder window shows this simple view of the folder's contents.

Up button—

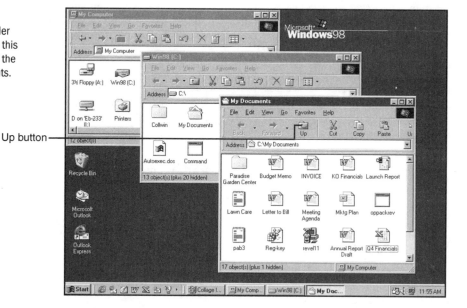

Part

II

Ch

6

The multiple-window option (Classic style) creates unnecessary and confusing clutter when you delve several folders deep. But sometimes you want to open two or more windows at once so you can move or copy icons from one folder to another. Windows lets you specify whether each new folder will use the same window or will open in a separate window. To adjust the default behavior of folder windows, you use the Custom settings in the Windows Desktop Update.

▶ **See** "Customizing Other Folder Options," **p. 66**

The settings you choose in the Folder Options dialog box will determine whether new folder windows replace the current window or open a new one. You can also hold down the Ctrl key and double-click on a folder or drive icon to override the default setting at any time. If the default is the single-window option, this procedure will open a new window; if your default is to open a new window, this technique will replace the contents of the current window. Note that this option requires you to hold down Ctrl and double-click even if you've chosen the Web style single-click option.

N O T E   When you view the contents of a floppy disk, Windows does not automatically update the display when you change disks. Likewise, if another user adds, renames, or deletes files in a shared network folder, these changes do not automatically appear in an open window on your system. Under these conditions, you need to *refresh* the display to see the most up-to-date contents. In the Windows Explorer, point to the icon for the drive or folder and click to refresh the window. Alternatively, you can choose View, Refresh or press F5. ▣

Using Windows Explorer to View Files and Folders

When you right-click on a drive or folder icon and choose Explore from the shortcut menu, Windows opens the two-paned view of Explorer, which comprises a tree-style All Folders pane on the left and a contents pane on the right. The title bar contains the word *Exploring,* followed by the currently selected drive or folder. As Figure 6.3 shows, the left pane includes every available resource, including local and network drives, system folders, and even Internet shortcuts.

T I P   Here are some common ways to open the Windows Explorer. Open the Start menu and choose Programs, Windows Explorer. Right-click on the Start button or the My Computer icon and choose Explore. Type **Explorer** in the Run dialog box or at an MS-DOS prompt. Create a shortcut on the desktop or on the Quick Launch bar.

As noted earlier, the two-paned Explorer uses the same program code as the single-pane folder window, adding only the All Folders pane. When you use the Explore command to open a new window, you can show or hide the All Folders pane by choosing View, Explorer Bar, All Folders. This technique lets you quickly switch between Internet pages, folder windows, and Explorer windows. Curiously, if you start with a folder window onscreen or if you start by opening an Internet shortcut, the All Folders pane is not available.

FIG. 6.3
The Windows Explorer provides these two panes in which you can quickly navigate through local, network, and Internet resources.

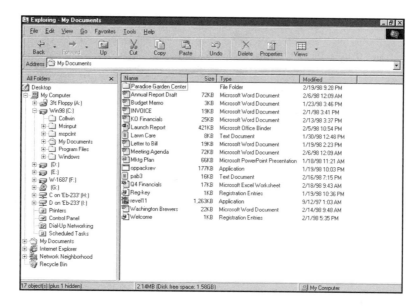

Understanding the Explorer Hierarchy

When you use the two-pane Explorer view, it's easy to see the organization of drives, folders, and system resources in the left-hand All Folders bar. If the Address bar is visible, you can see a compact version of the same tree in a folder window. Click the arrow at the right of the Address bar to see a drop-down list like the one shown in Figure 6.4.

FIG. 6.4
The Address bar lets you jump to different drives or system folders even when the All Folders pane is hidden.

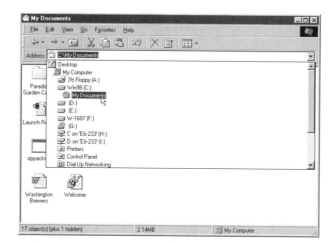

Part
II

Ch
6

If you've used MS-DOS or earlier versions of Windows, the hierarchy of a local drive is easy to understand: Each drive can contain one or more folders, starting with the root folder. Windows and Windows applications create folders to store program and data files, and you can create folders within folders to keep your files organized. In the case of data and program files, folders and subfolders are directly equivalent to MS-DOS directories and subdirectories.

But Windows also uses folders to display objects that do not correspond to directories on a hard disk. Look at the All Folders pane or the drop-down list in the Address bar, and you'll see that Explorer organizes available resources using a consistent hierarchy. The Desktop icon is always at the top of the list. It includes the following objects:

- *My Computer* displays icons for all local drives, any shared network drives that have been mapped to a drive letter, and the Printers, Control Panel, Scheduled Tasks, and Dial-Up Networking folders.

- *Network Neighborhood* shows icons for all servers and workstations in your network.

- *Internet Explorer* displays shortcuts for web pages you've added to the Active Desktop, as well as pages you've browsed recently.

- *Recycle Bin* shows files you've deleted recently.

- *My Documents* points to the folder where you store personal documents. On a single-user system, this is C:\My Documents by default; on a system where you've set up multiple user profiles, this folder will be elsewhere.

- Any folders you create on the desktop appear at the bottom of the All Folders pane and the drop-down Address list.

 If you have set up custom profiles for individual users of your computer, you can create folders, files, and shortcuts that appear on the desktop or Start menu. You'll find the All Users folder within the Windows folder; any objects you create in the Desktop or Start Menu folders here will be visible to anyone who logs on to the computer.

Using Explorer Menus and Toolbars

When you browse files and folders using Explorer, you have access to a consistent set of menus and toolbar buttons. When you select system folders, additional menu choices and buttons appear to reflect special options available in those folders. For example, when you view the contents of the Subscriptions folder, two new toolbar buttons let you update subscriptions, and Briefcase folders add menu choices and toolbar buttons that let you synchronize files.

▶ **See** "Using the Briefcase to Keep Files in Sync," **p. 1050**

Navigating Through the Explorer Hierarchy

With the help of the Windows Explorer, it's easy to display the contents of any drive or folder. When you click on an icon in the All Folders pane, the contents of that folder appear in the right-hand pane.

By default, each branch of the tree-style listing in the All Folders pane is collapsed when you first open the two-pane Explorer view; all you see are the top-level icons for drives and system folders. A plus sign to the left of an icon means there are additional folders beneath it. Click the plus sign to expand that branch and see additional folders. When you expand the folder listing, the plus sign turns to a minus sign. Click the minus sign to collapse that branch again. Figure 6.5 shows a typical display, with the contents of the Accessories folder visible in the right-hand pane.

FIG. 6.5

Click the plus sign to expand a branch of the tree; click the minus sign to collapse the list again.

TROUBLESHOOTING

I see a plus sign to the left of a drive icon, but when I click the icon, the plus sign disappears.
Windows is behaving exactly as designed. When you first open the two-pane Explorer view, Windows checks the contents of all local hard drives and adds the plus sign if it detects subfolders. However, it does not automatically check for subfolders on removable drives (such as floppy disks) or network connections because doing so might slow down the performance of your system. Instead, it places the plus sign next to each of those icons and waits until you select the icon to see whether there really are any subfolders. If there are none, it removes the plus sign, as you've seen.

To display the contents of a different folder, select its icon in the All Folders pane. As you move from folder to folder, you can use the Back and Forward buttons to quickly return to folders you visited previously.

You can also use the keyboard to navigate through file and folder listings in Explorer. Here's a partial listing of useful keyboard shortcuts:

■ Use the Tab key (or F6) to move from pane to pane. When you press Tab, the selection moves from the All Folders pane to the Contents pane, then to the Address bar, then back to the All Folders pane, and so on.

■ When the focus is in the All Folders pane, you can press the up and down arrows to move through the list of folders without expanding collapsed branches. The contents of the selected icon automatically appear in the right-hand pane as you move through the list.

■ To move to the parent of the currently selected folder, press the Backspace key.

■ To expand a collapsed folder, select its icon and press the right-arrow key or the plus (+) key on the numeric keypad. Use the minus (–) key on the numeric keypad to collapse a branch.

■ To quickly move to the Address bar and open the drop-down list of top-level icons, press F4.

■ Press the star (*) key on the numeric keypad to expand all branches of the currently selected icon.

> **CAUTION**
>
> Be careful when using the * key shortcut! Pressing the * key when the Desktop or Network Neighborhood icon is selected might cause extremely long delays as Explorer checks the contents of every available network drive.

Changing the Way a Folder's Contents Appear

Display options let you control how icons appear in an Explorer window. You can choose the size, arrangement, and order of icons, and you can also specify whether Explorer should show or hide system files. All of the options described in this section work the same in folder windows or in the right-hand contents pane of Windows Explorer.

Icons, List, or Details: Choosing a View

Windows lets you choose from four icon arrangements when displaying the contents of a folder. Each view has advantages and disadvantages under given circumstances. To apply a new view to the folder currently displayed, choose View, and then select one of the following choices:

■ *Large Icons* view displays full-size icons (32 pixels on each side), which help you easily distinguish between different types of icons. A label appears along the bottom of each icon. You can position icons anywhere within the folder. This view is most practical for folders that contain few icons, such as My Computer; it's an impractical choice when you want to find a small number of files in a folder that contains hundreds of icons.

■ *Small Icons* view displays icons that are one-fourth the size of those in the Large Icons view (making them 16 pixels on each side). A label appears to the right of each icon.

Initially, Small Icons view arranges icons in rows from left to right, but you can move the icons anywhere within the folder. This view is useful when you want to select a large number of icons in one motion.

- *List* view uses the same size icons and labels that Small Icons view does. In List view, however, Windows arranges icons in columns, starting at the top left of the contents window; when the column reaches the bottom of the window, Windows starts a new column to the right. You cannot rearrange the position of icons in this view.

- *Details* view enables you to see the maximum information about objects in any window. From left to right, each row in this view includes the file's icon, name, size, and type and the date the file was last modified. Note that these details change slightly for different types of windows; the My Computer window, for example, shows the total size and amount of free space in the last two columns. You cannot move or reposition icons in Details view.

TIP The Views button on the Standard toolbar lets you cycle through all four views for the current folder. Each time you click, the view changes to the next option. Alternatively, you can use the drop-down arrow at the right of the Views button to choose a view.

Arranging File and Folder Icons

When you use either Large Icons or Small Icons view, Windows lets you move icons anywhere within the folder. You can cluster your favorite icons in one location and move the others to a far corner, for example, or just rearrange the order in which the icons appear. Two options let you control the arrangement of icons within a folder.

If you prefer to have all your icons lined up neatly at all times, choose <u>V</u>iew, Arrange <u>I</u>cons, <u>A</u>uto Arrange. A check mark appears next to this menu choice to indicate that it is in use with the current folder. You can still move icons into any order you want, but other icons will shift position to make room for the icons you move. When you resize a folder window with this option turned on, the rows of icons will automatically reposition so that you can see them properly within the window.

If you prefer to arrange icons yourself but you want them to snap into position along an imaginary grid, rearrange the icons and then choose <u>V</u>iew, Line <u>U</u>p Icons. This option allows you to leave empty spaces within the folder window. If you resize the window, some icons may no longer be visible; you'll need to use the scroll bars to view them.

Part
II

Ch

6

CAUTION

These icon-arranging options apply to the Windows desktop as well. Right-click on any empty desktop area and choose Line <u>U</u>p Icons to straighten up the display of icons on the desktop. Avoid checking the <u>A</u>uto Arrange option on the Windows desktop, however. Most users prefer to position desktop icons in predictable locations; letting Windows automatically arrange desktop icons lines them up in columns, from top to bottom and left to right, without regard for wallpaper and Active Desktop items. That can make it difficult to work with desktop icons.

Sorting Files and Folders

Windows lets you sort the contents of any folder using one of four menu choices. These options work the same in folder windows and in the contents pane of an Explorer window.

To sort files within a folder, follow these steps:

1. Display the contents of the folder.

2. Choose View, Arrange Icons, or right-click in any empty space within the contents pane and choose Arrange Icons from the shortcut menu.

3. Choose one of the following options from the submenu:

   By Name. Sorts in ascending alphabetical order by filename, with folders grouped at the top of the list.

   By Type. Sorts in ascending alphabetical order by file type (note that this does not sort by file extension; Windows uses the registered name of the File Type to determine sort order).

   By Size. Sorts folders first in ascending alphabetical order by name, then arranges files by size, with smallest files at the top of the list.

   By Date. Sorts folders by date in descending order, then sorts files the same way; in both cases, newest files appear at top of list.

By far the easiest way to sort files and folders is to switch to Details view. When you click on the column headings in Details view, Windows sorts the folder's contents by the column you selected. Click again to sort in reverse order—something you cannot do in any other view.

Saving Folder Display Options

When you use the two-pane Windows Explorer, the view options you choose apply to all folders you display in the contents pane. If you choose Large Icons view for one folder, all folders will be displayed in that view until you choose a different view.

When you use folder windows, however, Windows lets you save separate view options for each folder. As you move from folder to folder, the view changes to reflect the settings you last used. If you prefer to set all folder windows to a single view, follow these steps:

1. Open any folder window and choose View. Select Large Icons, Small Icons, List, or Details. If you want to use Web View for all folders, choose View, As Web Page.

2. Choose View, Folder Options, and click on the View tab. You'll see the dialog box shown in Figure 6.6.

3. In the Folder Views area, click the button labeled Like Current Folder.

4. When you see the confirmation dialog box, click Yes.

5. Click OK to save your changes.

Note that using this option does not save the sort order for windows, nor does it save toolbar settings.

FIG. 6.6
Choose a view you
want to use for all
folder windows.

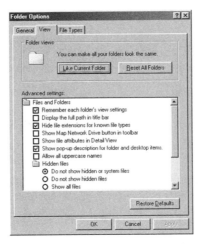

To restore folder windows to their default view settings, choose View, Folder Options, click the View tab, and click the button labeled Reset All Folders. This restores the My Computer, Control Panel, Fonts, and other system folders to their default, Large Icons view.

Displaying or Hiding Certain File Types

You can set four special attributes for all files and folders you create under MS-DOS or Windows. Using these settings, you can prevent inadvertent damage to important files. To see the assigned attributes for a given file or folder, select its icon and choose Properties from the shortcut menu. Click the General tab to see the current settings for the following four attributes:

Attribute	Description
Read-only	Prevents changes to files and folders. Note that setting a folder's read-only attribute does not prevent changes to the files within that folder.
Hidden	Prevents the display of files using Windows Explorer or the MS-DOS DIR command.
Archive	Marks files that have been changed since they were last backed up. The MS-DOS XCOPY command and most backup programs use the Archive attributes to perform partial backups.
System	Prevents the display of files and folders required by the system.

N O T E Windows 98 sets the read-only attribute on a number of system folders, including the Windows and My Documents folders.

For the most part, Windows and Windows applications adjust file attributes automatically. The one reason you might want to manually adjust file attributes is to set a crucial workgroup file as read-only.

Part
II

Ch
6

CAUTION

Setting the Read-only or System attribute for an object doesn't make it impossible to delete that file or folder; it only adds a warning dialog box to the process. If the file is truly important, make sure you have a backup copy stored in a safe location.

Windows hides a tremendous number of files by default. Why? To prevent accidental changes or deletions that can cause the system to stop working properly. Look at the left-hand side of the status bar in any Explorer window to see how many hidden files are in the current folder.

If you're confident that you can work with hidden and system files without causing your computer to crash, you can adjust Explorer's options to display those files. Follow these steps:

1. Open Windows Explorer or any folder window and choose View, Folder Options.

2. Click on the View tab, shown in Figure 6.7. In the Advanced Settings box, find the entry labeled Hidden Files.

3. Select the Show all files option, as shown in Figure 6.7.

FIG. 6.7

Use this option to make hidden and system files visible.

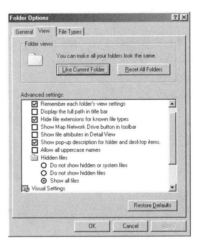

4. Click OK to save your changes and close the Folder Options dialog box.

If you choose to make hidden files visible, you'll be able to easily distinguish them in Explorer windows. In Explorer, they appear as grayed-out icons. (You might have to press F5 or choose View, Refresh to make these files appear.)

CAUTION

There's generally a good reason why Windows sets some files as hidden or system. If you need to change that attribute, just do it temporarily (to edit MSDOS.SYS, for example). Then be sure to change the attribute back when you're finished.

If you use the menus or the Ctrl+A keyboard shortcut to select all files in a folder that contains hidden files, you'll see a warning message like the one shown in Figure 6.8. There is no way to manage hidden files from Explorer unless you make them visible.

FIG. 6.8
Before you can select all the files in this folder, you must make hidden files visible.

You can use Explorer to change the Read-only, Hidden, and Archive attributes of a file or folder. To do so, right-click on the icon, choose Properties, and check or uncheck the appropriate box. Explorer will not allow you to change a file's System attribute, however. If you must perform that task, open an MS-DOS Prompt window and issue the command **ATTRIB –S *filename***. For more information about the ATTRIB command, type **ATTRIB /?** at the MS-DOS prompt.

 T I P Do you want to see information about file attributes every time you switch to Details view? Open Explorer and choose View, Folder Options. Then click the View tab and scroll through the list of Advanced Settings. Check the option labeled Show File Attributes in Details View and click OK.

Viewing Files as Thumbnail Images

Under most circumstances, the View menu lets you choose from only four icon arrangements. If you want, however, you can choose to enable a fifth view option, which displays each file and folder in a box four times the size of the icons in Large Icons view. Within the boxes, you'll see thumbnail images of graphics files, HTML documents, and other compatible file types, as shown in Figure 6.9.

FIG. 6.9
Thumbnails view displays miniature images of compatible file types in an Explorer window. If the file type doesn't support thumbnails, you'll see the icon.

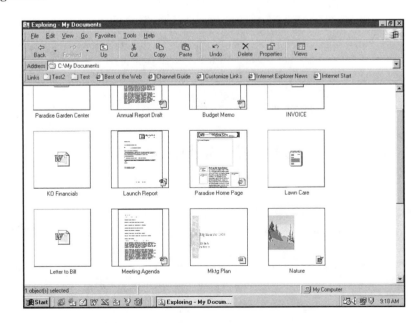

Part
II

Ch
6

N O T E Don't confuse Thumbnails view with the thumbnail viewer included in the default Web view template. In Web view, only one file at a time appears in the thumbnail viewer; Thumbnails view previews all the files in the current folder. Because Thumbnails view and Web view use the same program code to display miniature images, you cannot use the two views together. ▪

Before you can choose this option from the pull-down View menu in an Explorer window, you must specifically enable Thumbnails view for that folder. Follow these steps:

1. Right-click the folder icon and choose Properties.
2. Check the box labeled Enable Thumbnail View, and then click OK.
3. Display the contents of the folder using Windows Explorer. Pull down the View menu and choose Thumbnails. Compatible file types in the folder appear as miniature versions of the actual images in the right pane.

CAUTION

It might be tempting to enable Thumbnails view for every folder, but resist the temptation unless you really need to use the feature. To display thumbnails, Windows must create an index file (called Thumbs.db) in each folder where you enable this option. These index files take up a lot of space—a megabyte or more in a folder filled with graphics. Not only will you incur a noticeable delay as Windows creates and updates the index files, you will also have to deal with performance delays.

The following file types will display as miniature images in Thumbnails view:

- ▪ BMP (Windows bitmap files)
- ▪ GIF (Graphics Interchange Format files)
- ▪ JPG, JPEG (Joint Photographics Export Group files)
- ▪ HTM, HTML (Hypertext Markup Language files)

If you use Office 97, some (but not all) Office documents will also appear as miniature images in a folder where Thumbnails view is enabled. To see these files as thumbnails, you must first open the document in the Office program that created it and choose File, Properties. Then click the Summary tab and check the box labeled Save Preview Picture. For files that cannot be displayed in Thumbnails view, Windows displays the default icon.

Customizing Explorer's Appearance

Like most parts of Windows, Explorer contains a wide array of customization options.

Changing the Width of Panes

To change the proportions of the two panes when using Windows Explorer, point to the vertical dividing line between the panes. When the pointer changes to a two-headed arrow, click and drag in either direction. Release the mouse button when the panes are the desired sizes.

Changing the Width of Columns

In Details view, Windows uses columns to display information about files, folders, and system objects. To change the width of columns, point to the dividing line between column headings. When the pointer changes to a two-headed arrow, click and drag in either direction. You can also double-click on the dividing line to the right of a column heading to automatically resize that column to match the widest entry it contains.

TROUBLESHOOTING

One or more columns are missing when I switch to Details view. You might have resized a column to zero width, which makes it disappear from view. To restore the default column widths, click anywhere in the contents pane, hold down the Ctrl key, and press the + key on the numeric keypad.

Showing and Hiding the Status Bar

The status bar shows important information about the number and size of objects in the current folder, and it works the same in folder windows and in the two-pane Explorer view. To show or hide this screen element, choose View, Status Bar. A check mark next to the menu choice means the status bar should appear at the bottom of the window.

Showing and Hiding Toolbars

By default, the Address bar and the Standard Buttons toolbar (with text labels) appear when you open the two-pane version of Explorer. You can use both screen elements with folder windows as well. To show or hide either element, choose View, Toolbars, and check or uncheck the Standard Buttons and Address Bar menu choices.

There's no way to customize the buttons on these toolbars, but if you want maximum room to work with files and folders, you can hide the text labels on the Standard Buttons toolbar. To do so, choose View, Toolbars, and then remove the check mark from the Text Labels menu choice. Figure 6.10 shows a screen in which the toolbar buttons' text labels are not displayed.

FIG. 6.10
To conserve Explorer space, hide the text labels that normally appear under the toolbar buttons.

Opening Explorer at Specific Folders or Files

The full two-pane Explorer view can be overwhelming, particularly when you just want to reorganize files among a handful of subfolders in a single location. The solution is to create shortcuts for each task. It's possible to launch a copy of Explorer that opens at the location where you want to work. Even better is to restrict the display of objects in the left-hand pane so that it includes only the drives or folders with which you want to work.

If you create a shortcut with only the command **explorer**, you'll open the default two-pane Windows Explorer, with all resources visible in the All Folders pane. To reduce the clutter, you'll need to use command-line switches along with the Explorer command. Specifically, follow the command with the /e switch to force it to open in two-pane mode (use /n to specify a single-pane window instead). Normally, Explorer uses Desktop as the root of the All Folders pane, but you can specify any drive or folder to fill this role. When you do, the display becomes much less confusing. Use the /root, *object* switch to restrict the scope of the All Folders pane to the object you specify. In place of *object*, substitute the name of a network server (in UNC format), a local drive, or a folder.

ON THE WEB

For a detailed explanation of all the options you can use when creating an Explorer shortcut, read the Microsoft Knowledge Base article "Command-Line Switches for Windows Explorer." You'll find it at

http://premium.microsoft.com/support/kb/articles/q130/5/10.asp

To open a two-pane Explorer window that includes only files and folders on drive C:, for example, follow these steps:

1. Right-click on any empty desktop space and choose <u>N</u>ew, <u>S</u>hortcut. The Create Shortcut Wizard appears.

2. In the <u>C</u>ommand Line text box, enter the following command (spacing and punctuation are crucial):

   explorer /e,/root,c:

3. Click <u>N</u>ext, and then name the shortcut **Explore Drive C**.

4. Click Finish. The shortcut appears on the desktop.

5. Open the shortcut to verify that it works. You can move or copy the shortcut to another location if you want.

Managing Files and Folders

Although many Windows applications offer basic file management functions, Explorer is the tool you'll use most often to organize your files. Regardless of which view you choose, Explorer allows you to create new folders, copy and move files between folders, delete files, and rename files.

Selecting Files and Folders

Before you can perform any action on an object, you must select the object. The procedures for selecting files, folders, and other icons vary, depending on the folder and desktop options you've chosen. If you've chosen the Classic style (double-click) interface, you click on an icon to select it. If you've chosen the Web style (single-click) interface, on the other hand, simply point to a file to select it. Objects change color to indicate that you've selected them.

T I P Use the Display Properties dialog box to adjust the color of selected items.

▶ **See** "Customizing the Windows Desktop," **p. 441**

To select multiple icons that are adjacent to one another in a folder window or on the desktop, select the first icon, hold down the Shift key, and then select the last icon. All the icons between the two will be selected as well. To select multiple icons that are not adjacent to one another, select the first one, hold down the Ctrl key, and select all additional icons. To deselect an icon, continue holding down the Ctrl key and select it again.

You can also use marquee selection to quickly select a group of adjacent files using the mouse. Using this technique, you draw an imaginary rectangle around the group of files (see Figure 6.11). Specifically, point to one corner of the rectangle, and then hold down the left mouse button and drag the selection to the opposite corner. This technique works regardless of which icon view you've selected.

FIG. 6.11
As you draw this rectangle around a group of icons, watch the dotted line. All icons within the box are selected.

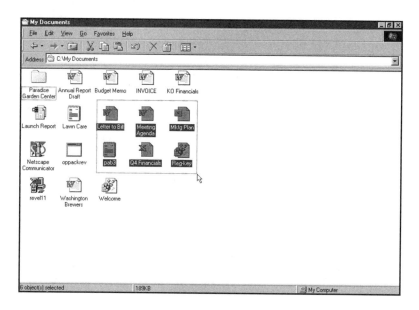

Part
II

Ch
6

You can also select multiple icons using the keyboard. In a two-pane Explorer window, press Tab to move the focus into the right-hand contents pane. Then use the arrow keys to move through the list to the first item you want to select. To select a group of adjacent icons, hold down the Shift key and use the arrow keys to move through the list. To use the keyboard to select a group of icons that are not adjacent to one another, select the first file, and then hold down the Ctrl key and use the arrow keys to move through the list; press the Spacebar for each file you want to select.

To quickly select all the files in a folder, choose Edit, Select All (or press Ctrl+A). To deselect all current selections, click on any empty space or on another object in the folder window or on the desktop.

 There's a lightning-fast way to select all but a few icons within a folder. This technique comes in handy when you want to archive or delete most of the files in a folder yet keep a small number of items. Select the objects you plan to keep, and then choose Edit, Invert Selection. You can now use any of the standard Windows techniques to move, copy, or delete the selected objects.

Renaming a File

To rename a file or folder, first select its icon. Then use any of the following options to select the name for editing:

- Press the F2 key.
- Choose File, Rename.
- Right-click the icon and choose Rename from the shortcut menu.

When the label text is selected, type the new name. To save the name you enter, press Enter or click on any empty space on the desktop or in a folder window.

Renaming Multiple Files

There is no way to rename more than one file at a time using Explorer. To accomplish this task, you must open an MS-DOS Prompt window and use the REN (Rename) command.

To rename multiple files with long filenames, use this procedure:

1. Open the Start menu and choose Programs, MS-DOS Prompt.
2. At the MS-DOS prompt, type **CD** ***pathname*** to switch to the directory that contains the files you want to rename. You might have to repeat the command a few times to reach the correct drive and directory.
3. Type **REN** ***oldname.ext newname.ext***. If either name contains a space, enclose the name and extension in quotation marks. Press Enter.
4. Use the ? wildcard character to match any single letter in the filename; use the * wildcard to substitute for any group of characters. For example, if you start with the following group of files:

    05 Sales Forecast.xls

    06 Sales Forecast.xls

    07 Sales Forecast.xls

    08 Sales Forecast.xls

Enter this command at the MS-DOS prompt to rename them in one operation:

REN "?? Sales*.*" "?? Mrktg*.*"

The result will be four files named as follows:

05 Mrktg Forecast.xls

06 Mrktg Forecast.xls

07 Mrktg Forecast.xls

08 Mrktg Forecast.xls

Creating New Folders

To create a new folder, follow these steps:

1. Select the icon for the drive or folder in which you plan to create the new folder.

2. Right-click on the icon or on any empty space in the contents pane and choose New, Folder.

3. The new folder has a generic name; to replace it with a more meaningful name, just start typing. When you've finished, press Enter to record the new name.

N O T E When naming folders, you must follow the same rules that govern long filenames.

▶ **See** "Working with Long Filenames," **p. 113** ▪

Moving and Copying Files and Folders

With Explorer, the easiest way to move and copy files is not always the surest. When you select one or more objects and drag them from one location to another, the results can vary dramatically. The exact effect depends on the location and the type of file. When you drag and drop files using Explorer, one of three things happens:

- When you drag an object from one location to another on the same logical volume, Explorer *moves* the object. On local drives, each logical volume uses the same drive letter, so dragging a group of icons from C:\Windows\Temp to the Windows desktop moves them to the new location.

- When you drag an object from one logical volume to another, Explorer *copies* the file. If you drag a group of icons from C:\Data and drop them on the icon for a floppy disk (A:) or a shared network folder, Explorer leaves the original files untouched and creates copies in the new location.

- When you drag a program file from one location to another, regardless of location, Explorer *creates a shortcut*, leaving the original file untouched.

Part
II

Ch
6

There are solid logical reasons for this default behavior, but the results can be confusing to novice users. Even experienced Windows users can sometimes stumble over these rules. For example, if you drag multiple program icons from a folder onto the desktop, Explorer will create a group of shortcuts, but if you select even one icon that isn't a program, Windows moves or copies instead.

The best way to predict what Explorer will do when you drag and drop icons is to examine the mouse pointer before you release the mouse button. If you see a plus sign just to the right of the pointer (see Figure 6.12), you can expect a copy; a small arrow next to the pointer means you'll get a shortcut; and a plain pointer means you're about to move the selected objects. If the pointer you see doesn't match the result you intended, press Esc before releasing the mouse button to abort the procedure.

FIG. 6.12
The small plus sign next to the mouse pointer means you're about to make a copy of this icon.

For maximum control over the results of drag-and-drop operations, select one or more objects and hold down the right mouse button as you drag. When you release the button, Windows pops up a shortcut menu like the one shown in Figure 6.13. The default action appears in bold type, but you can choose any of the three actions, or you can cancel the whole operation if you prefer.

FIG. 6.13
When you hold down the right mouse button while dragging files, Windows lets you choose the result you prefer from a shortcut menu like this.

Dragging and Dropping Files Between Folders   The easiest way to move or copy files between folders is to open two folder windows and arrange them side by side. Follow this procedure to let Windows position two folder windows automatically:

1. Minimize or close all open windows. The easiest way to accomplish this task is to click the Show Desktop button on the Quick Launch toolbar.
2. Open both folder windows so that they're visible on the desktop.
3. Right-click any empty space on the taskbar and choose Tile Windows Vertically from the shortcut menu. Windows will arrange both windows so that each occupies exactly half the display.

If you inadvertently left an extra window open on the desktop before attempting this procedure, right-click an empty space on the taskbar, choose Undo Tile, and try again.

To move or copy files from one folder window to another, select the icon or icons and drag them to any empty space in the destination folder.

TIP To quickly copy one or more files to a floppy disk, select the icon(s) in an Explorer window, right-click, and choose Send To from the shortcut menu. Then choose the floppy drive from the submenu.

▶ **See** "Customizing the Send To Menu," **p. 112**

Dragging and Dropping Files in Explorer View   To move or copy files using the two-pane Explorer view, follow these steps:

1. Open Windows Explorer. In the left-hand All Folders pane, select the icon for the folder that contains the files you want to move or copy.

2. In the right-hand contents pane, select the icon or icons you want to move or copy.

3. Hold down the right mouse button and drag the icon(s) over the top of the folder icon in the left-hand pane. If the icon for the destination folder is not visible, let the mouse pointer hover over the parent icon for a second or two; the branch will expand automatically.

4. When the pointer is over the icon for the destination folder, release the mouse button.

5. Choose the appropriate action—Move, Copy, or Create Shortcut(s)—from the menu that appears.

Using Cut, Copy, and Paste   Explorer offers one final option for moving and copying files that doesn't involve dragging and dropping. Use the Windows Clipboard to cut, copy, and paste files between folders and drives in exactly the same way you copy text and graphics between documents. These techniques work equally well in Explorer windows, in folder windows, in email messages, and on the Windows desktop.

To copy, move, or create shortcuts using the Clipboard, follow this procedure:

1. Select the file or files.

2. To copy a file from one folder to another, use the Copy command; to move a file, use the Cut command. Any of the following mouse or keyboard techniques will work:
   - Choose Edit, Copy or Edit, Cut.
   - Right-click on the selected icon and choose Copy or Cut.
   - Press Ctrl+C (Copy) or Ctrl+X (Cut).
   - Click the Copy or Cut button on the Explorer toolbar.

3. Display the contents of the destination folder and use any of the following commands to complete the move or copy:
   - Choose Edit, Paste.
   - Right-click on the folder icon or in the contents pane and choose Paste.

Part

II

Ch

6

- Right-click on the folder icon or in the contents pane and press Ctrl+V.
- Click the Paste button on the Explorer toolbar.

Copying Disks

It's impractical to copy an entire hard disk or CD-ROM, but it's ridiculously easy to copy a floppy disk. Windows includes a utility that handles the whole process in two passes—one for the source (original) disk and the second for the destination (copy) disk.

To copy a floppy, make sure you have a formatted disk that's the same size as the original you plan to copy. Then follow these steps:

1. Insert the original disk in the floppy drive.
2. Open the My Computer window or Windows Explorer, right-click on the floppy drive icon (normally A:), and choose Copy Disk.

    If you have only one drive that handles the selected disk format, the same drive letter will appear in the Copy From and Copy To areas of the dialog box. If you have more than one such drive, select the destination drive in the Copy To box; if this is a different drive, insert the destination disk in that drive.

3. The Copy Disk dialog box (see Figure 6.14) appears. Click Start, and Windows reads the entire contents of the disk into memory.

FIG. 6.14

Follow the prompts to duplicate a floppy disk.

4. If you're copying from one physical drive to another, Windows handles the operation in one pass. On most systems, where there is only a single floppy drive, you'll see a prompt when the Copy From phase is complete. Remove the original disk, insert the destination disk into the drive, and click OK.
5. Windows transfers the stored data to the destination disk; if the disk requires formatting, that is done automatically. When the copy is completed, you'll see a message at the bottom of the Copy Disk dialog box.
6. To copy another floppy, remove the destination disk, insert another source disk, and repeat steps 3 through 5. When you've finished, click Close.

CAUTION

Windows automatically erases any data on a destination disk without prompting you. That can be disastrous if the destination disk contains important data. If you store important files on floppy disks, always use the write-protect tab to prevent accidental erasure.

Deleting Files and Folders

To delete one or more files or folders, select the icons and then use any of the following techniques:

- Press the Delete key.
- Choose File, Delete from Explorer's menu bar.
- Right-click and choose Delete.
- Drag the icon(s) and drop them on the Recycle Bin icon.
- To delete files completely without using the Recycle Bin, hold down the Shift key and press the Delete key, or right-click and choose Delete.

Normally, when you delete one or more files or folders, Windows displays a Confirm File Delete dialog box. You can turn off the dialog box that asks whether you're sure you want to send the files to the Recycle Bin. However, when you bypass the Recycle Bin, you must deal with the dialog box shown in Figure 6.15.

FIG. 6.15
When you bypass the Recycle Bin, Windows forces you to deal with this dialog box.

> **CAUTION**
> When you delete a folder, you also delete all files and subfolders within that folder. Check the contents carefully before you trash an entire folder.

Undoing Changes

In Windows, you can undo the last three actions you perform when working with the Windows Explorer. If you inadvertently delete a file, move it to the wrong location, or make a mistake when renaming a file or folder, click the Undo button on the Standard Buttons toolbar or press Ctrl+Z.

It's not always easy to tell exactly what Undo will accomplish, and there's no Redo option to restore your original action, either. Within an Explorer window, look at the top of the Edit menu to see what Windows can undo. Likely choices include Undo Delete, Undo Move, and Undo Rename.

Part
II

Ch
6

 Although it's not obvious, the Undo shortcuts also work if you make a mistake on the Windows Desktop. If you inadvertently move or delete a desktop file by mistake, press Ctrl+Z immediately to recover.

Using the Recycle Bin

The Windows Recycle Bin can't prevent every file management disaster, but it can help you recover if you accidentally delete a crucial file. When you delete a local file using the Windows Explorer, it doesn't actually disappear; instead, the Recycle Bin intercepts it and stores it. The file remains there until you empty the Recycle Bin or until it is displaced by a newer deleted file. As long as that file remains in the Recycle Bin, you can recover it intact.

CAUTION

The Recycle Bin is far from perfect, and every Windows user should be aware of its limitations. If you use a network connection to delete files on another computer, or if you delete files on a floppy disk or other removable medium, those files are not saved in the Recycle Bin. Likewise, using the DEL command from an MS-DOS Prompt window removes the files permanently, without storing safe copies in the Recycle Bin. And if you overwrite a file with another file of the same name, the old file does not go into the Recycle Bin. If these limitations disturb you, check out Norton Utilities and other third-party programs, which can expand the capabilities of the Recycle Bin to cover some of these situations.

Recovering a Deleted File   To recover a deleted file, open the Recycle Bin (you'll find its icon on the desktop). Browse its contents until you find the file or files you're looking for. To return the file to its original location, right-click and choose Restore from the shortcut menu. To restore the file to another location, such as the Windows desktop, drag the icon or icons to the location where you want to restore them.

Changing the Size of the Recycle Bin   By default, the Recycle Bin sets aside 10 percent of the space on every local hard disk for storing deleted files. If your hard disk is nearly full, that may be too much; on the other hand, if you have ample disk space, you may want to reserve more space for the Recycle Bin. On systems with more than one drive, you can choose different Recycle Bin settings for each drive.

To adjust the Recycle Bin's appetite, follow these steps:

1. Right-click on the Recycle Bin icon and choose Properties from the shortcut menu. The Recycle Bin Properties dialog box appears (see Figure 6.16).

2. Each drive will have its own tab in the dialog box. Use the option at the top of the Global tab to specify whether you want to configure the drives independently or use one setting for all drives.

3. Use the slider control on the Global tab to change the percentage of disk space reserved for the Recycle Bin (adjust this setting on each of the dialog boxes for individual drives). You can choose any setting between 0% and 100%, but the most realistic settings are between 3% and 20%.

4. To stop using the Recycle Bin completely, check the box labeled Do Not Move Files to the Recycle Bin.

FIG. 6.16
The default setting is to use 10% of hard disk space for storing deleted files. Use this dialog box to adjust this setting.

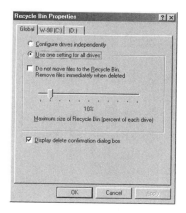

5. To avoid seeing the confirmation dialog box every time you move a file to the Recycle Bin, clear the check mark from the box labeled Display Delete Confirmation Dialog Box.

6. Click OK to save your changes and close the dialog box.

Emptying the Recycle Bin   Under normal circumstances, you shouldn't need to delete the Recycle Bin. When it fills up, Windows automatically deletes the oldest files to make room for new files you delete. If you run short of hard disk space—when installing a new program, for example—you may need to clear out the Recycle Bin to make room. To delete all files from the Recycle Bin, right-click on its icon and choose Empty Recycle Bin.

Previewing a Document with Quick View

Even the most compulsive file-naming system can't tell you exactly what's in every file on your hard drive. Using Windows Explorer, you can examine a file's name, type, size, and the date it was last modified. But to see the contents of a file, you'll need to open it with its associated application—or use Windows' Quick View utility to peek inside.

To view the contents of a file, right-click on the file and choose Quick View. A Quick View window like the one shown in Figure 6.17 appears.

N O T E   Quick View isn't installed as part of the Typical Windows setup option. To install this utility, use the procedures described in Chapter 2. ■

▶ **See** "Keeping Windows 98 Up-to-Date," **p. 292**

Although Quick View is useful, it's far from perfect. It supports only a limited number of file types, for example, and you can't copy the file's contents to the Windows Clipboard or print the file. The version of Quick View included with Windows 98 lets you view simple text and graphics files and those created by some word processing programs; unlike its Windows 95 predecessor, it allows you to view files created by Office 97 applications.

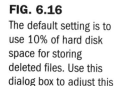

FIG. 6.17
Use the Quick View utility to see the contents of a file without opening it.

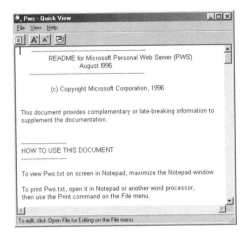

ON THE WEB

If you use Quick View regularly, consider purchasing the full commercial version from its developer: Inso software. Quick View Plus adds support for hundreds of file types. It also enables you to copy text and graphics to the Windows Clipboard or send a file directly to a printer without having to open the application. For more details, go to

`http://www.inso.com`

Using Shortcuts

The files you use most often are scattered across your hard disk in a number of folders. When you set up a new program, its files go in their own folders, and you organize data files using whatever system makes the most sense—by project, date, or department, for example. If you had to root through folders and subfolders every time you wanted to open a document or launch a program, you'd hardly have any time to get work done.

So how do you maintain an orderly filing system and still keep programs and documents close at hand? The solution is to use *shortcuts*. As the name implies, a shortcut is a pointer file that allows you to access a file without moving the file or creating a copy of it. You can create a shortcut for almost any object in Windows, including programs, data files, folders, drives, Dial-Up Networking connections, printers, and web pages. Windows uses shortcuts extensively: Every item in the Programs folder on your Start menu is a shortcut, for example, and every time you save a web address to your Favorites folder, you create an Internet shortcut. Learning how to create and manage shortcuts is a crucial step in mastering Windows.

How Shortcuts Work

Shortcuts are small files that contain all the information Windows needs to create a link to a *target file*. The shortcut uses the same icon as the target file, with one crucial difference: a small arrow in the lower-right corner that identifies the icon as a shortcut instead of an original.

When you right-click on a shortcut, the available menu choices are the same as if you had right-clicked on the target file. Opening the shortcut has the same effect as opening the target file.

Shortcuts are a tremendous productivity aid. If you have a document file stored six subfolders deep, for example, you can create a shortcut icon and store it on the desktop so it's always accessible. The target file remains in its original location.

You can create many shortcuts to the same file. For your favorite programs, you might create shortcuts on the desktop, on the Start menu, and on the Quick Launch bar. Each shortcut takes up a negligible amount of disk space (typically no more than 500 bytes), even if the original file occupies several megabytes of disk space.

What happens when you attempt to launch the target file using its shortcut icon? Windows is intelligent enough to re-establish the link to the target file even if you've moved or renamed the original; to do so, it follows these steps:

1. Windows looks at the static location (the file name and path) whether the file is stored locally or on a network.

2. If that file no longer exists, Windows checks to see whether you've renamed the file, looking in the same folder for a file with the same date and time stamp but a different name.

3. If that search fails, Windows checks to see whether you moved the file, looking in all subfolders of the target folder and then searching the entire drive. (On a network location, the search extends to the highest parent directory to which you have access rights.) If you have moved the target file to a different drive, Windows won't find it, and the shortcut will break.

4. If Windows can't find the target file, it tries to identify the nearest matching file and displays a dialog box like the one shown in Figure 6.18. Confirm the choice if it's correct; otherwise, choose No, and then delete the shortcut and re-create it using the correct file.

FIG. 6.18

If Windows can't locate the target file for a shortcut, it will suggest the closest matching file.

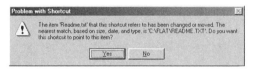

▶ **See** "Using Internet Shortcuts," **p. 634**

Creating a New Shortcut

The easiest way to create a new shortcut is with the help of the Create Shortcut Wizard. Follow these steps:

1. Right-click on an empty space on the Windows desktop and choose New, Shortcut. The Create Shortcut dialog box, shown in Figure 6.19, appears.

Part

II

Ch

6

FIG. 6.19
Creating a new shortcut
is a two-step process
with this wizard.

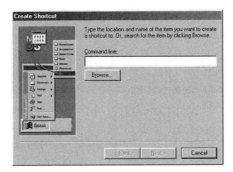

2. Click the Browse button and select the document or program file from the Browse list.
   To create a shortcut to a drive or folder, you must type its name directly in the Command
   Line text box. Include the full path if necessary. Then click Next.

3. Give the shortcut a descriptive name and click Finish. Test the shortcut to make sure it
   works correctly.

You can also create a shortcut from an icon. Select the icon in an Explorer window, hold down
the right mouse button, and drag the icon to the desktop or another folder. Choose Create
Shortcut(s) Here from the pop–up menu.

Renaming a Shortcut

To modify the name that appears under a shortcut icon, right-click the icon and choose
Rename. (This technique works with shortcuts on the Programs menu and Quick Launch
folder as well.) The pointer changes to an I-beam and the entire name becomes selected. Begin
typing to completely replace the name, or click to position the insertion point where you want
to add or change text. After you edit the name, press Enter or click on an empty portion of the
desktop or taskbar to register the change. Note that changing the name of a shortcut does not
affect the target file.

Deleting a Shortcut

To delete a shortcut, use any of the techniques described earlier in this chapter. When you
delete a shortcut, you remove only the link to the target file. The target file itself remains intact
in its original location.

Setting the Properties for a Shortcut Icon

To change the appearance and behavior of a shortcut icon, right-click on the shortcut icon and
choose Properties. The General tab of the properties sheet includes basic information, such as
the shortcut's name and when it was created. Click the Shortcut tab to change the link between the shortcut and its target file. Using the options on the Shortcut tab (see Figure 6.20),
you can make the following adjustments:

- To associate a different file with the shortcut, click in the Target box and type the filename, including its full path.

- To specify a startup folder, click in the Start In box and enter the name of the folder, including its full path. (This setting is most useful for programs.)

- To define a keyboard shortcut, click in the Shortcut Key box, and then press the specific key combination you want to use. The shortcut key must consist of a letter or a number plus any two of the following three keys: Ctrl, Alt, and Shift. (If you simply press a letter or number, Windows defaults to Ctrl+Alt+*key*.) You can also use any function key (F1 through F12) with or without the Ctrl, Alt, and Shift keys. You cannot use Esc, Enter, Tab, the Spacebar, Print Screen, or Backspace. To clear the Shortcut Key box, click in the box and press the Spacebar.

CAUTION

Shortcut keys you create take precedence over other access keys in Windows. Be careful that you don't inadvertently redefine a system-wide key combination or one that you use in other Windows applications.

- Indicate whether you want the document or application to run minimized, maximized, or in a window.

- Change the icon that appears with the shortcut.

FIG. 6.20
The shortcut's properties sheet lets you change the target file, startup folder, shortcut key, and icon used by a shortcut.

Using Shortcuts with Mapped Drives

An important caution applies whenever you create a shortcut that points to a resource on a mapped network drive. If you later change the drive or computer to which the mapped drive letter refers, your shortcut might fail to work; worse, it could access the original file or folder and create a new drive mapping to a different letter without warning you. This problem is an unintended consequence of a Windows feature that existed in Windows 95 and continues to plague users in Windows 98.

▶ **See** "Using Explorer with Shared Resources on a Network," **p. 116**

Here's how the problem might affect your organization. Say you've mapped the drive letter S: to a shared folder called Data on a server called Research. When you create a shortcut that points to S:\, opening that shortcut opens the folder \\Research\Data, just as you would expect.

Now imagine that your work moves out of the research labs and into production. As a result, you move your old files to a shared folder called Files on a server named Production. Because you don't want to change all the shortcuts or retrain the workers in your department, you decide to change the network mapping so that the drive letter S: now points to \\Production\Files.

If you open a Windows application and type the letter S: in a File Open dialog box, it correctly displays the contents of the shared Files folder. Likewise, if you select S: from the drop-down drive list in an Explorer window, you'll see the correct file listing. But if you open the shortcut that refers to S:, it will open the shared resource that S: referred to when the shortcut was created—in this case, \\Research\Data. And it will spontaneously create a new drive mapping (to an arbitrary letter such as J: or Q:).

The problem arises because Windows stores the UNC name of the resource along with the original shortcut and uses that information instead of the current drive mapping. The solution? Don't use mapped drive letters with Windows shortcuts. If your organization insists on using shortcuts that refer to mapped drive letters, create DOS batch files to open the shared resources. A one-line batch file containing the command Start S:, for example, will always open the resource currently mapped to S:.

 TIP When you create a shortcut that runs an MS-DOS batch file, Windows opens a command window every time the batch file runs. You need to adjust the shortcut's settings to close this window automatically. To do so, right-click the shortcut icon, choose Properties, click the Program tab, and check the box labeled Close on Exit.

You can also choose to modify individual shortcuts using a tool called Shortcut.exe, which removes UNC path information from each shortcut. For more information about this utility, search the Microsoft Knowledge Base for article Q150215, "Disabling Automatic Network Shortcut Resolution."

Creating Shortcuts to Virtual Folders

When is a folder not a folder? Windows 98 includes a variety of *virtual folders* that behave like ordinary folders but have a few crucial differences. Virtual folders—including My Computer, Network Neighborhood, Control Panel, Dial-Up Networking, and Printers—aren't actually storage locations on a disk. Instead, they represent data that's stored in the Windows Registry. You can't move files into a virtual folder, but you can create shortcuts to icons within a virtual folder.

When you right-click an icon in a virtual folder, you'll see Create Shortcut on the menu. If you choose that option, however, you'll see the error message shown in Figure 6.21. Click OK to create a shortcut on the desktop. That shortcut will work just as you would expect it to, and you can move it to the Start menu, the Quick Launch toolbar, or another file folder.

FIG. 6.21

If you try to create a shortcut within a virtual folder, Windows displays this error message. Click OK to create a shortcut on the desktop, and then you can move it to any location.

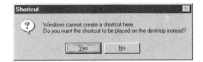

Part

II

Ch

6

Advanced File Management Techniques

by Ed Bott

Associating Files with Programs

When you attempt to open an icon, Windows checks the file's extension against a database of registered file types to determine what action it should take. A registered file type can have multiple actions (open and print, for example), all of which are available on the right-click shortcut menus. Windows uses the default action when you launch the icon. If Windows does not recognize the file type, it offers a dialog box and lets you choose which application to use with the file you've selected.

File extensions have been around since the very first version of DOS. Beginning with the first release of Windows 95, Microsoft began tracking file types as well. File types are inextricably linked to file extensions, but the relationship isn't always easy to understand. Here are the essential facts you need to know:

- File types typically have friendly names (HTML Document), while extensions are typically three or four letters (.HTM or .HTML).

- File types are listed in their own column when you choose Details view in the Windows Explorer. You can also inspect a file's properties to see which file type is associated with it. Extensions for registered file types are hidden by default; extensions for unregistered file types are always visible in the Explorer list.

- Every file type has an associated icon, which appears when you view files of that type in the Windows Explorer or a folder window.

- Every unique file extension is associated with one and only one file type. After you install Microsoft Word, for example, Windows associates the .DOC extension with the Microsoft Word Document file type.

- A file type, on the other hand, can be associated with multiple extensions. The HTML Document file type works with both .HTM and .HTML extensions, for example, and files of the JPEG Image file type can end with the extension .JPE, .JPEG, or .JPG.

- As the previous examples illustrate, a file extension can be more than three letters long.

- Windows common dialog boxes (File Open and File Save As) include a drop-down list that lets you choose a file type; Windows adds the default extension for the file type automatically when you save a document.

- A Windows filename can contain more than one period. Windows defines the extension as all characters that appear after the last period in the filename.

Most application programs handle the details of registering file types and associations when you install them. Creating a file type manually and editing an existing file type are cumbersome and difficult processes best reserved for expert users as a last resort.

▶ **See** "Managing File Associations," **p. 179**

TROUBLESHOOTING

My document appears to have the correct extension, but when I try to open it, the wrong application launches. You or another user tried to add or change the file extension manually by adding a period and the extension. The associated program added its own (hidden) extension as well, resulting in a file name such as Letter.doc.rtf. To see the full name, including extensions, choose View, Folder Options, click the View tab, and remove the check mark from the box next to the option labeled Hide File Extensions for Known File Types. The file extension is now visible and editable. Be sure to restore this option after you repair the problem filename.

Viewing File Associations

To see a list of all registered file types, open the Windows Explorer or any folder window (including My Computer). Choose View, Folder Options, and click the File Types tab. You'll see a list like the one in Figure 7.1.

FIG. 7.1
Use this list of registered file types to see which applications are associated with the various file types.

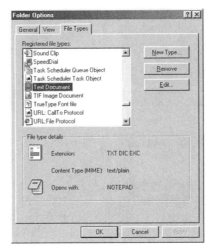

The list is arranged in alphabetical order by file type. As you scroll through the list, note that the details in the dialog box change. For each entry in the list, you can view the registered file extensions, MIME details, and the name of the associated application.

CAUTION

Multipurpose Internet Mail Extensions (MIME) are the standards that define how browsers and mail software should handle file attachments. Do not adjust these settings in the File Types dialog box unless you are certain the changes will produce the correct result. Unnecessary tinkering with these settings can cause your mail and web pages to be unreadable.

Part
II

Ch
7

Changing File Associations

Windows allows you to associate only one program with each action for each file type. In most cases, if two applications claim the right to edit or open a given file type, the one you installed most recently will claim that file type as its own. If a newly installed program "hijacks" a file type in that way, you might want to restore the association with the older application. You have two options for accomplishing this goal:

■ *Reinstall the original program.* The setup process typically edits the Windows Registry and adjusts file associations. If the setup program was written correctly, you will not lose any custom settings or data.

■ *Edit the file type directly,* changing the associated program to the one you prefer. To do so, follow these steps:

1. Open the Windows Explorer or any folder window (including My Computer) and choose View, Folder Options. Click on the File Types tab.

2. Select the file type you want to change and click the Edit button. The Edit File Type dialog box appears (see Figure 7.2).

FIG. 7.2

Use caution when manually editing file types. Entering a wrong setting in this dialog box can hinder your ability to work with common document types.

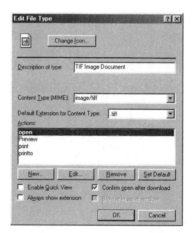

3. Select an entry from the Actions list—the default action is in bold type—and click the Edit button. The dialog box shown in Figure 7.3 appears.

FIG. 7.3

Change the program listed here to adjust how Windows works with a given file type.

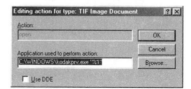

CAUTION

Note that some actions require Dynamic Data Exchange (DDE), an extremely complex process that passes information between programs; if you see these options listed, exit this dialog box and don't attempt to edit the action by hand.

4. Click the <u>B</u>rowse button. In the dialog box that appears, find and select the executable (.EXE) file for the program you want to use with the selected action, and then click <u>O</u>pen.

5. The filename you selected now appears in the App<u>l</u>ication Used to Perform Action text box. Click OK to close the Editing Action dialog box and save your change.

6. Repeat steps 3 through 5 for other actions you want to change. When you finish, click OK to close the Edit File Type dialog box, and click OK again to close the Folder Options dialog box.

Three options in the Edit File Type dialog box are worth noting here:

■ *<u>S</u>et Default.* Choose an action and click the <u>S</u>et Default button to make that action the default action for the file type. The previous default action will still appear as a choice on right-click shortcut menus.

■ *Enable <u>Q</u>uick View.* Check this box to control whether you see a Quick View choice on the shortcut menu for the selected file type.

▶ **See** "Previewing a Document with Quick View," **p. 93**

■ *Al<u>w</u>ays Show Extension.* Check this box to display the file's extension in all Explorer and folder windows. This setting is useful if you regularly change the extensions of certain types of documents (such as .RTF documents created by Office 97) but don't want to clutter the Explorer window with other extensions.

CAUTION

It's possible to completely eliminate a file type or an action associated with a file type. Generally, however, such a drastic step is not recommended. The settings for each file type take up a trivial amount of space in the Windows Registry, and removing a file type can cause installed programs to fail.

Using an Alternate Program to Open a Registered File Type

You might have several programs at your disposal with which you can view or edit a particular type of file. For example, FrontPage Express and Microsoft Word both allow you to edit HTML files. Unfortunately, Windows forces you to associate one and only one program with

Part

II

Ch

7

the default action for each registered file type. However, you can override that default decision at any time and choose which program you want to use for a given file icon. To do so, follow these steps:

1. Select the document icon, hold down the Shift key, and right-click. The shortcut menu that appears includes a new Open With choice that's not found on the default menu.

2. Choose Open With from the shortcut menu, and the dialog box shown in Figure 7.4 appears.

FIG. 7.4

Use this dialog box to open a document with the application of your choice instead of the default program.

3. Scroll through the list and find the program you want to use. Note that the list shows only the short names of executable files (Winword, for example), not the long names of the applications (Microsoft Word).

4. If the program appears in the list, select its entry. If you can't find its entry, click the Other button and browse for the program's executable file, then click Open.

5. Before you click OK, note the check box labeled Always Use This Program to Open This Type of File. By default, this box is unchecked. Do *not* add a check mark unless you want to change the program associated with the Open action for this type of file.

6. Click OK to open the document.

Opening an Unrecognized File Type

When you attempt to open the icon for an unrecognized file type, Windows displays an Open With dialog box similar to the one shown in Figure 7.4. There are two crucial differences between this dialog box and the one that appears when you hold down the Shift key and click a recognized file type. These differences are designed to enable you to quickly create a new file type for the unrecognized type.

- This Open With dialog box includes a text box at the top. Enter the name of the new file type there.

- By default, the box labeled Always Use This Program to Open This Type of File is checked. Remove this check mark if you don't want to create a new file type.

If you accidentally create a new file type by using this dialog box, it's easy to remove that file type. Open the Folder Options dialog box, click the File Types tab, select the newly created file type, and click the Remove button.

Finding Files

A hard disk with a capacity measured in gigabytes can hold tens of thousands of files in hundreds or even thousands of folders. So you shouldn't be surprised if you occasionally lose track of one or more of those files. Fortunately, Windows includes a handy utility that lets you hunt down misplaced files, even if you can't remember the file's exact name. You can search for a portion of the name, or you can search for some other detail, such as the size and type of the file, the date it was created, or a fragment of text within the file.

Finding a File or Folder by Name

To begin searching for a file on a local disk or on a shared network drive, click the Start button and choose Find, Files or Folders. (If the Windows Explorer is open, choose Tools, Find, Files or Folders.) You'll see a dialog box like the one in Figure 7.5.

FIG. 7.5
Use the Find utility to search for any file—anywhere on your computer or across a network.

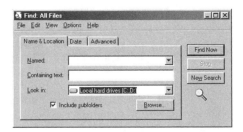

The most common type of search is to look for a file when you remember all or part of the name. Here's how:

1. Click in the box labeled Named and enter all or part of the filename. (The file extension is not necessary.)

 DOS-style wildcards (* and ?) are not required in the Named box, but they can be extremely useful in helping you reduce the number of matches. For example, if you enter the letter *b*, Windows will return all files that include that letter anywhere in the name. On the other hand, a search for *b** will find only files that begin with *b*, and a search for *b???.** will return only files that begin with the letter *b* and contain exactly four characters, not counting the extension.

2. Tell Windows which drives and folders you want to look in. If you opened Find from the Windows Explorer, the Look In box includes the name of the currently selected drive or folder; if not, this entry shows the location you specified when you last used Find. Enter

a folder name directly (C:\Data, for example), or click the Browse button to choose a folder name from a dialog box, or use the drop-down list to select any of the following default locations:

The Windows desktop

The My Documents folder

Document Folders, which includes My Documents and the Desktop folder

Any local drive

Any mapped network drive

All local hard drives

My Computer (searches all local hard drives as well as floppy and CD-ROM drives)

 You can specify multiple locations in the Look In box. Enter the full path, including the drive letter or UNC-style server and share name, for each location. Separate the entries in this list with semicolons.

3. To search in all subfolders of the location you selected, place a check mark in the box labeled Include Subfolders.

4. Click Find Now to begin searching.

The more details you provide, the more restrictive the results will be. But don't provide too much information, or there's a good chance that you'll miss the file you're looking for, especially if the spelling of the filename is even slightly different from what you enter.

Windows compares the text you enter in the Named box with the name of every file and folder in the specified location, returning a result if that string of characters appears anywhere in a filename. For example, if you enter **"log"** as the search parameter, Windows will turn up all files that contain the words *log, logo, catalog,* or *technology* (see Figure 7.6). A search's results appear in a pane at the bottom of the Find dialog box.

By default, the results list appears in Details view. However, you can right-click in the results pane and use the shortcut menu to change to a different view. You can also click on the column headings to sort results by name, size, type, the date the files were last modified, or the folder in which the files are stored. Click again to sort in reverse order.

 After you complete a Find, look at the status bar at the bottom of the window. The message Monitoring New Items means that Windows continues to watch your actions and will update the results list automatically if you create, rename, move, or delete files that match the specified criteria.

Advanced Search Techniques

The Find utility is fast and extremely effective, even when you haven't the vaguest idea what the target file is named. Advanced options let you search by using other criteria.

FIG. 7.6

The Find utility returns all filenames that include the characters you enter. Click on any column heading to sort the results.

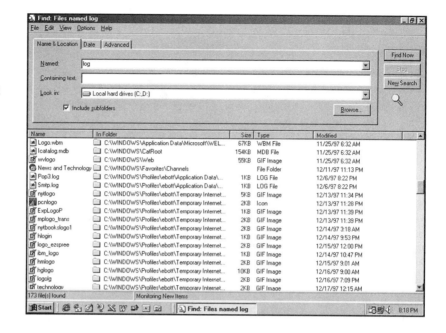

If you have a general idea of when you created a file or when you last edited it, click the Date tab and narrow the search by date. Spinners let you specify ranges of dates by day or month. To find all files you worked with yesterday or today, for example, click the Find all files option, choose Modified from the drop-down list, and choose the option During the Previous 1 Day(s). You can also specify a range of dates, as illustrated in Figure 7.7.

FIG. 7.7

Narrow your search by entering a range of dates.

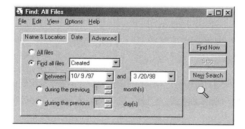

You can type dates into this dialog box, but it's far easier to use the built-in calendar controls that appear when you click drop-down arrows in date boxes (see Figure 7.8). On the calendar that appears, click the month heading to produce a menu of months; click the year to reveal a spinner control that lets you quickly adjust the year.

Click the Advanced tab to search for files by type and by size. On this tab (shown in Figure 7.9), you can select only registered file types. Because it requires you to enter size parameters in kilobytes, be sure to multiply by 1,000 when specifying megabytes.

Part

II

Ch

7

FIG. 7.8

This calendar appears automatically when you click the drop-down arrow.

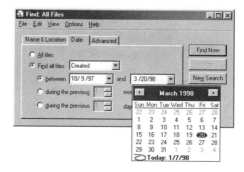

FIG. 7.9

This set of search criteria lets you hunt down large graphics files.

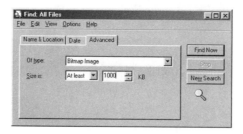

TIP Use the Find utility to organize and archive files. For example, you can search for all Microsoft Word files modified more than six months ago and then move the results to a backup location on the network. Or you might use advanced Find parameters to search for files larger than 1MB in size. If you leave all boxes blank and check the Include Subfolders option, the resulting list will include all files on your computer, up to a maximum of 10,000. You can then sort that list to find files of a certain type or size.

With the help of the Find utility, you can also search for text within files. Obviously, it won't do you much good to search for common words like "the," but if you remember a specific phrase that appears in a lost document, you can have Windows track down all files that contain that phrase. To look for a draft of your company's annual report, for example, click the Name & Location tab and enter **annual report** in the Containing Text box. Click the Find Now button to begin searching. Note that text searches can take a very long time, especially on large hard disks or across a network.

TIP Combine the settings from the Find dialog box to narrow your search for a specific file. For example, you might order Windows to search for a Microsoft Word document that contains the phrase "annual report" and was last modified in February, 1998. With those specifics, you have a good chance of finding the file you're looking for, even if you can't remember what you named it.

If the search didn't find the file you were looking for, modify the criteria and click the Find Now button again. Or, to clear all criteria and start from scratch, click the New Search button.

Managing Files from the Find Window

Because the Find dialog box is actually a specially modified version of the Windows Explorer, you can use the results pane for virtually any file management task. Right-click on any icon to display a shortcut menu that includes file management options, or drag items from the results pane and drop them anywhere—in a folder window, the Windows Explorer, the desktop, or an email message.

Use the File menu or right-click for these choices:

- Open
- Quick View
- Send To
- Cut and Copy (available only from the shortcut menu)
- Create Shortcut
- Delete
- Rename
- Properties

The Find utility includes an extremely powerful feature that's so well hidden even many Windows experts don't know it exists. Select any file in the results pane and choose File, Open Containing Folder. This choice, available only from the main menu and not from the right-click shortcut menus, opens a window displaying the full contents of the folder that contains the file you selected in the Find Results pane.

Saving and Reusing a Search

If you find yourself performing the same search regularly, save the search criteria as an icon so you can reuse it later. To save a search and use it later, follow these steps:

1. After you've completed your search, choose File, Save Search. You won't be prompted for a name or location; instead, Windows automatically creates a Saved Search icon on the desktop.

2. Close the Find window and locate the new Saved Search icon on the desktop. The icon will have a descriptive name drawn from the title bar of the search. Rename the icon if you want. You can also copy or move the icon to any other location, including the Start menu.

3. To reuse a saved search, double-click its icon and click the Find Now button.

> **CAUTION**
>
> When you reuse a saved search, the results are not up to date. The Options menu in the Find dialog box includes a Save Results menu item, but checking this option might not produce the effect you expect. Save Results keeps the search results pane open, displaying the names of the files you found. The next time you use that saved search, the results pane will reappear, but the contents will not reflect files you've added, deleted, or renamed since the last time you used the search. To update the list, you must click the Find Now button.

Part
II

Ch
7

Working with Compressed Files

File compression utilities make it possible to pack large files into small spaces. Therefore, they enable you to store large numbers of files in a single archive. Windows 98 users will typically encounter compressed files in one of two formats:

- *CAB.* Setup files for Windows 98 and other Microsoft products are stored in Cabinet format; you can recognize these files by the .CAB extension. Microsoft's Setup program processes cabinet files automatically, without requiring any utilities.
- *ZIP.* The Zip compression format is a widely used standard for distributing files over the Internet. Windows does not include support for Zip files.

The Windows Explorer treats cabinet files as though they were folders. You can open a cabinet file, browse its contents, and copy files by opening a cabinet file. Windows also includes a command-line utility with which you can pull one or more compressed files out of a cabinet. This capability is useful when Windows won't boot and you need to replace a lost or corrupted system file in order to reinstall or repair Windows. The Extract tool also lets you list the files in a cabinet so you can determine the exact location of the file you're looking for. To see detailed instructions on this command, go to an MS-DOS prompt, type **EXTRACT /?**, and press Enter.

ON THE WEB

Although many utilities let you work with Zip files, the best by far is WinZip, from Nico Mak Computing. Download the shareware version from

`http://www.winzip.com`

Customizing the Send To Menu

Whenever you right-click on a file or folder, one of the choices on the shortcut menu is Send To. Selecting this option opens a submenu containing destinations to which you can send the selected icon with one click. The result is the same as if you had selected the file and dropped it directly on a shortcut. This is an extremely handy way to move files around without having to open Explorer windows.

All the entries on the Send To submenu are shortcuts stored in the \Windows\SendTo folder. When you first install Windows 98, the Send To menu includes a relatively small number of destinations: your default floppy drive, the Windows desktop, and the My Documents folder. Programs like Microsoft Outlook, Microsoft Fax, and the Web Publishing Wizard add shortcuts to this list, as does the Windows PowerToys collection.

It's simple to add new shortcuts in the SendTo folder. When you do, the new shortcuts immediately show up on the Send To menu. You can add shortcuts to local or network folders, printers, applications (such as Notepad or WordPad), or drives. You can even create a cascading menu by creating a subfolder in the SendTo folder and then creating shortcuts in that subfolder.

To customize the Send To menu, follow these steps:

1. Open the Start menu, choose Run, type **sendto**, and press Enter. The \Windows\SendTo folder opens.

2. Right-click on any empty space in the SendTo folder and choose New, Shortcut. Use the Shortcut Wizard to create the shortcut you want to add.

   If you prefer, you can hold down the right mouse button, drag icons into the SendTo folder, and then choose Create Shortcut(s) Here.

3. Give each shortcut a name that will be self-explanatory on the Send To menu.

4. Repeat this process for any other shortcuts you want to add.

When you finish, select an icon, right-click, and choose Send To. You'll see an expanded menu like the one in Figure 7.10. It should include all the shortcuts you just added.

FIG. 7.10
When you customize the Send To menu, you increase your one-click file management options.

Customizing the Send To menu can result in some unexpected side effects. If you plan to use this technique, be aware of these facts:

- All shortcuts follow the Explorer rules for moving and copying. When you "send" an icon to a shortcut on the same logical volume, you move that file; if the target is on a different drive, such as your floppy drive, you'll copy the file instead.

- You can select multiple files and then choose Send To, but the results might not be what you expect. In particular, sending multiple files to a program shortcut might not work.

- If you add a program shortcut to the SendTo folder and then use it to open a file whose name contains a space, you might see an error message, or the program might open the file using its short name instead.

Working with Long Filenames

Windows allows you to create names for files and folders by using up to 255 characters. Legal filenames can contain spaces and most special characters, including periods, commas, semicolons, parentheses, brackets ([]), and dollar signs. However, you are not allowed to use the following characters when naming a file or folder:

: ' " \ / * ? ¦

How Windows Generates Short Filenames

Because Windows 98 maintains backward compatibility with older operating systems and applications, the file system automatically generates short filenames from long names you create. Although this process happens in the background, it's important to understand how the rules work.

When you save a file using Windows 98 or a 32-bit Windows application, Windows checks the filename you enter. If the name is a legal MS-DOS name (with no spaces or other forbidden characters), has no more than 8 characters in the name, and has no more than 3 characters in the extension, the short filename is the same as the long filename. If the long filename contains spaces or other illegal characters, or if it is longer than 8 characters, Windows uses performs the following actions to create a short filename:

1. Removes all spaces and other illegal characters, as well as all periods except the rightmost one.

2. Truncates the long filename to six characters, if necessary, and appends a tilde (~) followed by a single-digit number. If this procedure duplicates an existing filename, Windows increases the number by one: ~1, ~2, ~3, and so on. If necessary, it truncates the long filename to five characters, followed by a tilde and a two-digit numeric tail.

3. Truncates the file extension to the first three characters. If the long filename does not include a period, the short filename will have no extension.

4. Changes all lowercase letters to capital letters.

> **CAUTION**
>
> Several books and computer magazines have published details for adjusting a Registry setting (NameNumericTail) that controls the way in which Windows automatically generates short filenames from the long filenames you create. Do not make this Registry change! The result can seriously affect the operation of some Windows accessories that depend on the Program Files folder. For more details on this problem, go to http://support.microsoft.com and search for Knowledge Base article Q148594.

There is no way for the user to change the automatically generated short filename. To see the MS-DOS-compatible name for any file, right-click its icon, choose Properties, and click the General tab.

Using Long Filenames with Older Windows and DOS Programs

If you use 16-bit Windows programs, you will not be able to see long filenames in common dialog boxes such as File Open and File Save As. Instead, you'll see the truncated short version of all filenames. You'll see the same results if you use the old-style Windows File Manager (see Figure 7.11).

Through a process called *tunneling*, Windows allows you to preserve long filenames even when you edit them by using older programs. If you create a file and give it a long name by using Windows or a 32-bit Windows program, and you then edit the file by using a 16-bit program and save the file to the same short filename, Windows will preserve the long filename.

FIG. 7.11

When you view files using 16-bit Windows programs, you see only the short filenames, not their long equivalents.

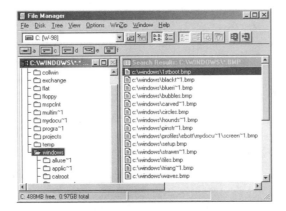

Working with Long Filenames at an MS-DOS Prompt

When you open an MS-DOS Prompt session within Windows 98, Windows recognizes long filenames and allows you to work with them directly. By default, directory listings display the DOS-compatible short name at left and the long name at right, as shown in Figure 7.12.

FIG. 7.12

Enter DIR in an MS-DOS Prompt session to see long and short filenames.

When managing files from an MS-DOS prompt, you can use either the long or short version. If you want to display, rename, copy, or move a file using a long filename that contains one or more spaces, you must enclose the entire name and path in quotation marks.

Working with Long Filenames in Mixed Environments

If you work on a network in a mixed Windows environment (in which some users are running 16-bit Windows applications on Windows 95/98 and some are running Windows NT 4.0), the potential for confusion with long and short filenames is enormous. When using 16-bit Windows applications, users see only the short filenames; the short filenames are also visible if you boot a Windows 98 machine in MS-DOS mode or if you copy files to a machine that is running DOS or Windows 3.x.

Like Windows 95 and Windows 98, Windows NT 4.0 also automatically generates short filenames when you save a file, but it uses a slightly different algorithm for creating short names. Under NT 4.0, the rules are the same as those in Windows 95 and 98 for the first four filenames in a series. Beginning with the fifth name, however, NT switches to a confusing new scheme that starts with only the first *two* letters of the long filename. To assign the rest of the short name, NT mathematically manipulates the remaining letters in the long filename.

Each time you move or copy files between NT and Win95 PCs, the operating system on the destination machine generates a new short filename. Thus, a file with a short name under Windows 98 of Letter~5.doc might become Lefaff~1.doc.

Worse, NT's file-naming algorithm is case-sensitive, unlike that in Windows 95 and 98. So moving files might cause them to be renamed in an order that appears arbitrary unless you know exactly what happened. Users who copy files from a Windows 95 or 98 workstation to a Windows NT server and then try to access them through the File Open dialog box of a 16-bit Windows application will have no way of knowing which file is which, short of blindly opening each one.

In mixed environments where some users will regularly encounter shared files with automatically generated short filenames, your best bet is to avoid long filenames completely. Devise an MS-DOS-compatible file-naming scheme that requires all filenames to be of eight characters or less.

Using Explorer with Shared Resources on a Network

The Windows Explorer lets you view and manage files and folders across a network, provided you have a working network connection and sufficient permissions. Use the Network Neighborhood to view all available network resources or to map shared resources to drive letters to make them easier to work with. If you know the exact name of the shared resource, you can enter it directly into any Windows common dialog box.

Using Network Neighborhood to View Shared Resources

Icons for other computers, including Windows workstations and network servers, appear in the Network Neighborhood. You'll typically see some or all of the following icon types when you open the Network Neighborhood:

- Windows workstations
- Windows NT servers
- NetWare and other servers
- Windows workgroups (which in turn contain icons for other workstations)

When you open a computer icon in Network Neighborhood, you see all the named shares available on that computer. These may be individual drives, folders, printers, or fax modems. Before you can browse shared files and folders or print to a shared printer, you must have permission to use that resource.

To connect with a shared resource, follow these steps:

1. Open the Windows Explorer and click Network Neighborhood.

2. Click the plus sign to the left of the computer name; available shares appear in a list below the computer icon, as in Figure 7.13.

FIG. 7.13

The Network Neighborhood displays all shared resources available on other workstations and servers.

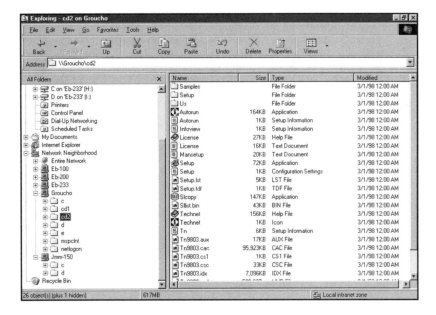

3. Select a share name from the list, and its contents appear in the right-hand pane.

4. Open a document, launch an application, or perform any other file management task as though you were working with a local file or folder.

For more information about sharing resources on your computer with other network users, see Chapter 43, "Sharing Network Resources."

TROUBLESHOOTING

When I attempt to connect to a shared drive or folder on a Windows NT server, I'm asked to supply a password for \\servername\IPC$. What's the problem? Your computer has successfully created an interprocess communication (IPC) connection with the Windows NT resource, but your username and password are not recognized by the NT domain controller. You must log off and log on again using an account that is valid on the domain.

Opening Shared Folders with UNC Names

In Windows programs and in the Start menu's Run dialog box, you can specify any file by entering its Universal Naming Convention (UNC) path name. To use a UNC name, you must follow this syntax:

```
\\computername\sharename\path
```

For example, if a coworker whose computer is named BillG has created a shared folder named Budget and has given you permission to access that folder, you can browse his shared files by entering \\Billg\Budget in the File Open dialog box and pressing Enter. You can also create a shortcut to a shared network drive or folder using the UNC name of the resource.

Mapping a Network Drive

Drive mapping, as the name implies, lets you assign a virtual drive letter to a shared network resource. When you map a network drive, you refer to it using the drive letter, just as though it were a local drive on your own computer.

There are two reasons why you might want to map drive letters. First, it makes working with files more convenient; instead of browsing through the Network Neighborhood, you can simply choose a drive letter from the Drives drop-down list in a common dialog box. Second, some older programs (and even some components of Windows 98) do not allow you to browse network resources directly; in such cases, the only way to access a shared file or folder is to first map it to a drive letter.

To map a shared drive or folder, follow these steps:

1. Open the Network Neighborhood in a folder window or the Windows Explorer, and then open the server or workstation icon to display available shared resources on that computer.

2. Right-click the share icon and choose Map Network Drive from the shortcut menu. The Map Network Drive dialog box shown in Figure 7.14 appears.

FIG. 7.14

Mapping a shared folder to a drive letter is the only way to use network resources with some programs.

3. Select an available drive letter from the Drive drop-down list.

4. If you want Windows to automatically reestablish the drive mapping every time you start your computer, check the box labeled Reconnect at Logon. If you want the mapping to be temporary, remove the check from this box.

5. Click OK to map the drive to the selected letter. The mapped drive letter will be available in all common dialog boxes. You can also display its contents directly by typing the drive letter and a colon in the Run dialog box (available via the Start menu).

N O T E All mapped drives appear in the My Computer window alongside the icons for local drives. The label for a mapped drive includes the share name, server name, and drive letter. ▓

To remove a drive mapping, follow these steps:

1. Right-click the Network Neighborhood icon and choose <u>D</u>isconnect Network Drive. A list of mapped drives appears.
2. Choose the mapped drive from the <u>D</u>rive list.
3. Click OK to disconnect. You will not see a confirmation dialog before disconnecting.

Finding a Computer on Your Network

Large networks can include hundreds of computers across different domains and workgroups. On large networks, just opening the Network Neighborhood and displaying all the icons in it can take minutes. To find a specific computer without browsing through the entire network, follow these steps:

1. Click the Start button and choose <u>F</u>ind, <u>C</u>omputer. The Find Computer dialog box appears (see Figure 7.15).

FIG. 7.15
To avoid long delays when you open the Network Neighborhood, search for a computer name instead.

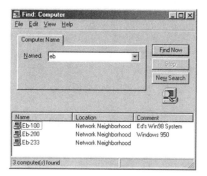

2. In the <u>N</u>amed box, enter all or part of the computer name you're searching for.
3. Click the F<u>i</u>nd Now button. A list of matching computer names appears in the Results pane at the bottom of the dialog box.

 T I P Right-click a computer name and choose P<u>r</u>operties to see more information about the computer, including the name of the workgroup or domain it belongs to and the operating system it uses.

Managing Files from an MS-DOS Prompt

You can do certain things from an MS-DOS prompt that you can't do any other way, and for some people an MS-DOS session is the most efficient way to work. By using the DIR command and MS-DOS wildcards, for example, you can quickly display a filtered list of files within a given folder and redirect the output to a text file. In addition, the MS-DOS prompt offers the only way to quickly rename a group of files using wildcards, and it's the fastest way to change the extension (and thus the file type) of some types of documents without having to adjust Windows Explorer preferences.

N O T E   MS-DOS commands are not case-sensitive. Although the examples given here follow standard MS-DOS conventions and list commands and switches in all caps, you can enter any such command using lowercase letters.   ■

Starting an MS-DOS Prompt Session

To open an MS-DOS Prompt session within Windows, open the Start menu and choose Programs, MS-DOS Prompt.

Note that an MS-DOS Prompt session behaves differently from the command prompt that appears when you restart your computer in MS-DOS mode. Here are some key differences:

- The MS-DOS Prompt session allows you to work with long filenames. In MS-DOS mode, you see only the short 8.3-style names. In addition, some MS-DOS commands, such as XCOPY, behave differently under Windows and from MS-DOS mode.

- The MS-DOS Prompt session can run in a window or in full-screen mode. When you start in MS-DOS mode, on the other hand, you are limited to full-screen display.

- All network resources are available to an MS-DOS Prompt session; accessing those resources in MS-DOS mode requires that you load real-mode network drivers.

- You can launch any Windows or MS-DOS program or batch file from the MS-DOS Prompt window. When you restart in MS-DOS mode, you can run MS-DOS programs only.

T I P   To switch between a windowed MS-DOS Prompt and a full-screen display, press Alt+Enter.

To close an MS-DOS Prompt window, type **EXIT** at the prompt and press Enter.

Using the Windows Clipboard with the MS-DOS Prompt

You must use a special set of procedures for copying text to and from an MS-DOS Prompt window. These procedures are particularly useful when you need to copy a lengthy filename, complete with its full path. Follow these steps:

1. Open an MS-DOS Prompt window. If the MS-DOS Prompt session opens in full-screen mode, press Alt+Enter to force it into a window.

2. Click the Control-menu icon at the far left end of the title bar to open the pull-down Control menu shown in Figure 7.16.

3. Choose the Edit command, and a cascading menu appears to the right.

4. To copy part or all of the screen, choose Mark. This switches the mouse pointer into Mark mode, which enables you to select any rectangular portion of the MS-DOS screen.

FIG. 7.16

Use this pull-down menu to cut, copy, and paste text between an MS-DOS window and the Windows Clipboard.

5. Mark the section you want to copy, and then press Enter. Whatever you marked is copied to the Windows Clipboard; you can paste it into the MS-DOS window or into any Windows program.

6. To paste text from the Clipboard into your MS-DOS window, position the insertion point where you want it in your DOS screen. Click the Control-menu icon on the title bar and choose Edit, Paste from the pull-down menu.

▶ See "Using the Windows Clipboard," p. 198

Using UNC Path Names in an MS-DOS Prompt Window

In Windows programs and in the Start menu's Run dialog box, you can specify any file by using its Universal Naming Convention (UNC) path name. In an MS-DOS Prompt window, however, UNC names are not recognized. To list or manage shared files across the network from an MS-DOS Prompt session, you must first map the share to a drive letter. Use the procedures outlined earlier in this chapter to do so.

To map a drive letter at the MS-DOS prompt, type **NET USE** *driveletter:* *\\servername* *sharename* (substitute the appropriate drive letter, server name, and share name). For more details about this command, type **NET USE /?** and press Enter.

Advanced Techniques for Working at an MS-DOS Prompt

Some file management tasks can be performed only from an MS-DOS Prompt window (or with the help of a third-party utility). For example, if you want to see a list of hidden folders on a given system, open an MS-DOS window, log onto C:\, and issue the command DIR /AHD. If you want to duplicate the directory structure from one machine to another without copying any files, use XCOPY with the /T and /E switches.

Windows 98 stores all external MS-DOS commands (FORMAT, FDISK, and XCOPY, for example) in the Windows\Command folder. Internal commands, shown in Table 7.1, are embedded in COMMAND.COM, the command interpreter that loads whenever you open an MS-DOS Prompt window.

Part

II

Ch

7

Table 7.1   Internal Commands Available in an MS-DOS Prompt Window

For Use in MS-DOS Batch Files

CALL	FOR	GOTO
IF	LFNFOR	LOADHIGH
REM	PAUSE	SHIFT

For Use in Setting the MS-DOS Environment

BREAK	CHCP	CLS
CTTY	DATE	ECHO
EXIT	PATH	PROMPT
SET	TIME	VER

For Working with Files and Disks

CD	CHDIR	COPY
RD	RMDIR	DEL
DIR	ERASE	LOCK
MD	MKDIR	REN
TYPE	UNLOCK	VERIFY
VOL		

In Windows 98, internal and external MS-DOS commands are poorly documented; for full details about command syntax, you'll need to find other references. Fortunately, only a handful of the MS-DOS commands in Windows 98 have changed since MS-DOS 6.0, so even a classic reference like Que's *Using MS-DOS 6.0* will be surprisingly helpful for Windows 98 users. The following tips will help advanced users work more efficiently within an MS-DOS Prompt window:

- Rudimentary Help information is available for all MS-DOS commands, both internal and external. From an MS-DOS prompt, type the name of the command followed by the /? switch. For example, typing **DIR /?** and **XCOPY /?** displays all available switches for those two useful commands.

- If you use the DIR command to view file listings, use the /P switch to pause after each screen of information.

- To see the results of other commands that fill more than one screen, use the pipe symbol (|) and the MORE command to display results one screenful at a time. For example, typing **XCOPY /? | MORE** lets you read the entire listing of command-line switches for XCOPY; without this switch, the first part of the help text will scroll off the screen before you can read it.

■ To capture the output of any MS-DOS command in a text file, use the redirection symbol (>) followed by the name of the file. For example, to capture an alphabetical list of all executable files in the Windows folder and its subfolder, use this command (substitute any legal filename, complete with the path, for *filename*):

```
DIR C:\WINDOWS\*.EXE /S /ON > filename
```

To view the results of the command, use the redirection symbol in reverse along with the MORE command. For example, using the full name of the text file you just created, type the following command at the MS-DOS prompt and press Enter:

```
MORE < filename
```

■ You can launch any Windows program or open a folder window from an MS-DOS Prompt with the help of the START command. For example, the command START C:\WINDOWS opens a folder window and displays the contents of your Windows folder. The command START *filename* opens the file you specify using its associated program. (Type START /? to see all switches for this command.)

■ When you drag the icon for a file or folder from an Explorer window into an MS-DOS Prompt window, the file or folder name appears at the end of the current command line, just as if you had typed it.

■ To significantly improve the usability of the MS-DOS Prompt, run the DOSKEY program. This utility keeps a history of commands you've issued and allows you to recall previous commands using the arrow keys or one of several function-key shortcuts; it also lets you edit the current command line, and you can define simple one-line batch files called *macros* that work whenever DOSKEY is loaded. Enter **DOSKEY /?** to see a list of its features. To run DOSKEY automatically every time you open an MS-DOS Prompt window, create a simple batch file that includes the command C:\WINDOWS\COMMAND\DOSKEY.COM. Display the properties sheet for the MS-DOS Prompt command, and then enter the name of that batch file on the Program tab in the box labeled Batch File.

CHAPTER 8

Managing Files Using Web View

by Ed Bott

In this chapter

What Is Web View?

Windows 98 incorporates a single Explorer window that lets you shift effortlessly between local files and pages on the web. So why not take the next step and view your files and folders as web pages?

Ordinarily, Explorer displays files, folders, and other system objects as icons in a window. You can choose between large and small icons, and you can arrange them in a list or in a column-oriented Details view. A separate web view option, independent of the icon arrangement you've chosen, lets you add web-style information panels around the display of icons.

When you turn on web view, Explorer uses HTML templates to customize your view of files and folders. You see more information at a glance, and for a modest investment of programming time, you can even create custom views that make it easier for other users to navigate through folders. With web view turned on, an ordinary folder display changes to resemble the one in Figure 8.1.

FIG. 8.1
When you choose web view, Explorer displays extra information about the current folder and files within it.

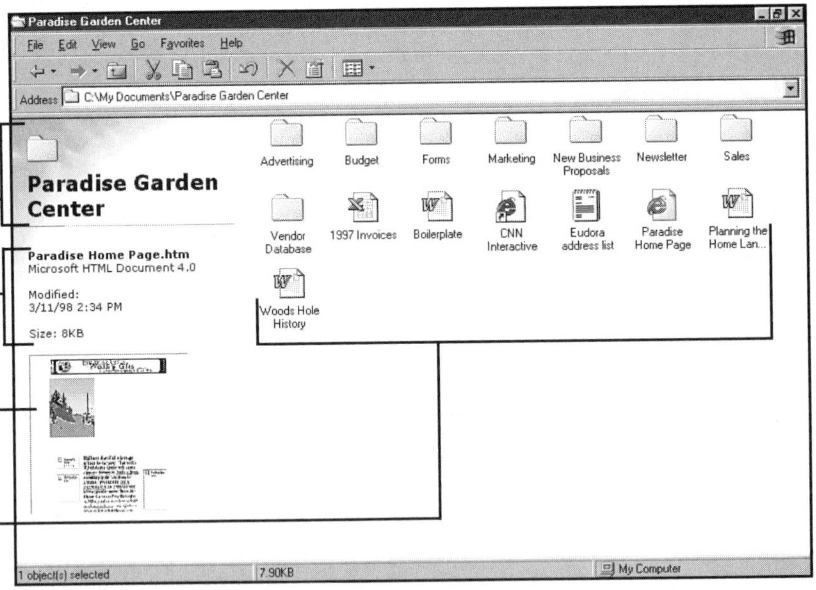

The default web view includes four standard elements:

- A banner identifies the title of the current folder.
- An info panel displays details about the folder and the currently selected file(s).
- Thumbnail images of certain file types appear below the contents pane, making it easier to identify the file's contents at a glance.
- The file list is contained in an ActiveX control embedded within the folder window.

Web view works in folder windows and in the contents pane of a two-pane Explorer window.

Using Web View with Folders

If you've selected web style navigation, web view is turned on for all folders by default. If you've selected classic style navigation, web view is disabled for all folders by default. With custom settings, you can choose whether to enable or disable web view by default.

▶ **See** "Classic or Web? Choosing a Navigation Style," **p. 62**

Regardless of the global settings, you can turn web view on or off for any folder. The web view menu choice is a toggle: If web view is on, choose <u>V</u>iew, As <u>W</u>eb Page to restore the current folder window to a normal Explorer view.

Setting this option for one folder window does not have any effect on other folder windows. However, if you turn on web view using the two-pane Explorer view, your preferences apply to all folders you view in the current Explorer window.

Displaying Thumbnails and File Information

When you choose web view and select any file, the info panel at the left side of the window displays that file's name, its file type, the date it was last modified, and its size. If you select a folder icon, the info panel shows the name only.

When you select multiple files, the info panel displays a different set of details. You'll see a count of the number of items you've selected, the total combined size of the selected files (useful if you're planning to move or copy files to another folder), and a column listing the name of each selected file (see Figure 8.2).

FIG. 8.2
When you select multiple documents in web view, you see these summary details in the info pane.

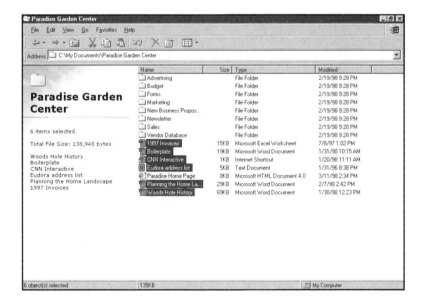

Below the info panel, the default web view template includes a thumbnail image of certain file types. Only a handful of file formats appear as thumbnails in web view. Those that do include Document files; Bitmap, GIF, and JPEG images; and web pages in HTML format (if the page is stored locally or in your browser's cache). If you create a document with one of the applications in the Standard edition of Microsoft Office 97, you can see detailed information about the file, along with a thumbnail image of the document.

TIP   If you're an Office 97 user, taking advantage of web view requires some extra effort. By default, Word and Excel files do not display thumbnail images unless you choose File, Properties, click the Summary tab, and check the box labeled Save Preview Picture. Similarly, the info panel displays the name of the author and other file properties, but only if you go out of your way to add that information in the Summary dialog box.

Can you turn on thumbnails for a given file type? Unfortunately, the answer is no. In theory, any application can add thumbnail support if the developer integrates its file formats with the WebViewFolderContents object; that's the ActiveX control that adds web view capabilities to the Windows Explorer. If an application includes this feature, it should appear automatically, without extra effort on your part.

TROUBLESHOOTING

I've turned on web view, but I can't see a thumbnail view in some folders. The folder window you're using may be too small. Maximize the folder and see if thumbnails appear. When you restore the drive or folder to a window, try resizing it, watching the changes in web view as it decreases in size. The banner along the top becomes more compact, and the thumbnail viewer goes away when the window reaches a certain size.

Using Web View with System Folders

A handful of system folders use custom web view templates. When you display the My Computer folder in web view, for example, you'll see a display like the one in Figure 8.3.

N O T E   Although it's easy to forget this fact, the Windows desktop is just another Explorer folder, minus the window borders, menus, and toolbars. When you turn on the Active Desktop and display web content on the desktop, you've actually told Windows to display the desktop folder in web view. IE4 automatically generates a custom web view template, called DESKTOP.HTT, every time you customize your Active Desktop settings. Although it's theoretically possible to find this template and edit it manually, doing so is not recommended. ◼

Other system folders have custom web view templates, including the Control Panel and Printers folders. Table 8.1 lists the built-in web view templates you'll find in a typical Windows 98 installation. All of these templates are stored in the Windows\Web folder.

FIG. 8.3
You'll see detailed drive
information when you
turn on web view in the
My Computer folder.

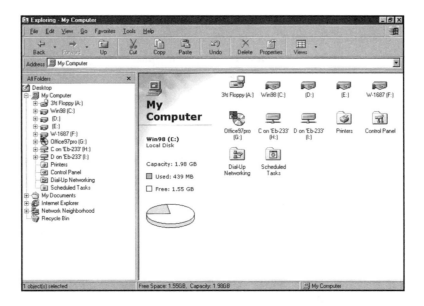

Table 8.1   Built-in Web View Templates

Template File	Description
CONTROLP.HTT	Displays help text in the Info panel when you select individual Control Panel icons. Includes hyperlinks to two Microsoft web pages.
FOLDER.HTT	The default template Windows uses when you customize web view options for a folder. Editing this file does not change folders you have already customized.
DESKMOVR.HTT	Provides support for Active Desktop objects. Do not edit this file.
MYCOMP.HTT	Displays information about selected local and network drives in My Computer; also displays help text for system folders.
PRINTERS.HTT	Offers instructions for setting up a new printer; selecting the printer icon displays the number of messages in print queue.
SAFEMODE.HTT	Contains information and troubleshooting links for resolving problems when Active Desktop crashes.
DIALUP.HTT	Displays information to help you use the Dial-Up Networking folder.
NETHOOD.HTT	Provides an explanation of the contents of the Network Neighborhood.
RECYCLE.HTT	Includes JavaScript links that let you empty the Recycle Bin or restore all its contents at once.
SCHEDULE.HTT	Explains how the Scheduled Tasks folder works.

CAUTION

Before editing any of the default templates in the Windows\Web folder, be sure to create backup copies so you can recover the original HTML files if you want to start over.

Creating Custom Web Views

There's no particular magic to web view. When you display a folder's contents and choose View, As Web Page, you instruct Explorer to look in the current folder for two files:

- *DESKTOP.INI* lists shell objects that allow the folder to interpret HTML code and display files in a defined region within the folder. It also includes pointers to custom HTML templates and/or background images for the folder. If this file does not exist in the current folder, Explorer uses default settings.

- *FOLDER.HTT* is a HyperText template file that defines scripts, objects, and HTML code that allow files to be displayed. If this file does not exist in the current folder, Explorer uses the default file in the Windows\Web folder. You can customize this template file, and you can use a file with a different name by specifying it in DESKTOP.INI.

Windows also includes a wizard that lets you customize the look of a folder by editing the web view template.

CAUTION

There's no way to force users to open a folder using web view. If you've designed a custom web page to help other users of your PC navigate in a particular folder or to simplify file access for coworkers on a network, your work will only pay off if they choose to use web view. If they access the custom folder using a version of Windows that does not include the Windows Desktop Update, they cannot view your changes.

Using the Web View Wizard

To customize the appearance of a folder in web view, choose View, Customize This Folder. That action launches the wizard that appears in Figure 8.4. Note that, as wizards go, this one is fairly crude.

When you choose the option Create or Edit an HTML Document, the wizard launches Notepad and loads the HyperText template specified in DESKTOP.INI. If this is the first time you've used the wizard in a given folder, it copies the FOLDER.HTT template file from the Windows\Web folder. When you finish editing the file in Notepad, you can close the Customize This Folder dialog box and return to the folder to see your changes.

The second option, Choose a Background Picture, enables you to add a background graphic behind the file list control on the web view folder. You can use any file in any standard graphic format, including Bitmap, JPEG, or GIF. To see how this works, start the Customize This Folder Wizard and follow these steps:

FIG. 8.4
Use this wizard to edit the web view template or add a background graphic to a folder.

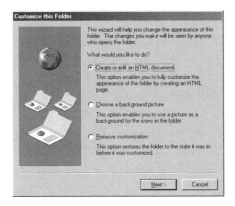

1. Select Choose a Background Picture. Click the Next button.

2. The next dialog box (see Figure 8.5) displays a list of graphics files from the \Windows folder. Click the Browse button to choose a different folder, if necessary.

FIG. 8.5
Choose a background image to appear behind the file list control in web view. Pick a light image that won't obscure icons.

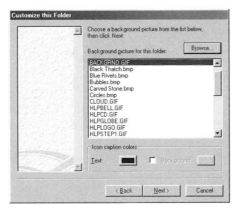

3. As you click on graphics files in the list, the contents of the file appear in the preview window at the left of the dialog box. If the graphic is small, Windows tiles the image to fill the preview box.

4. When you've selected an appropriate graphic file, click the Text button to choose a contrasting color for icon labels that will appear on top of the graphic. You might also want to check the Background check box and adjust the color that is to appear behind the icon labels.

5. Click Next to record your changes, then click Finish to close the wizard. You might have to press F5 to refresh the folder's contents and see your changes.

 TIP If you must use a graphic behind the file list control, choose a light image, preferably in a shade of gray. Dark or detailed images such as photographs can make it difficult to see icons in the file list.

Editing a HyperText Template

To edit a HyperText template, you need to be fluent in HTML—and you won't be able to fall back on the WYSIWYG editor in FrontPage Express. By default, when you choose to customize the HyperText template file for a folder, Windows dumps you into the most rudimentary HTML editor imaginable: Notepad.

▶ **See** "Using Notepad," **p. 262**

Some sections of FOLDER.HTT are strictly for web experts. Don't edit the scripts that display file information, for example, unless you're sure you know what you're doing. But even an inexperienced editor can safely add hyperlinks to the default folder template.

N O T E   Future updates to Windows and Internet Explorer might include more complex templates for customizing folders. In that case, you might need to adjust the instructions that follow to deal with the revised HTML code. ▪

The default folder template includes a section where you can add your own hypertext links to web pages or files. (Open Control Panel and turn on web view to see examples of these links.) To customize this section, use the Customize This Folder Wizard to open FOLDER.HTT for editing in Notepad. Then follow these steps:

1. Choose <u>S</u>earch and enter the following text in the Fi<u>n</u>d What text box: **A FEW LINKS OF YOUR OWN**.

   Then click Fi<u>n</u>d Next.

2. The HTML code in this section includes two sample URLs. Replace the two sample URLs with your own link, and replace the link text ("Custom Link 1" and "Custom Link 2") with your own label.

3. To create additional links, copy the two lines that follow the first sample link, and paste them below the second sample. Repeat for any additional links, and then customize as in step 2.

4. Delete the comment tags above and below the links to make them visible in web view. When you finish, the code should look like the sample shown in Figure 8.6.

5. Close Notepad, saving the file with the default name. Then press F5 to refresh the folder view and see the links in place.

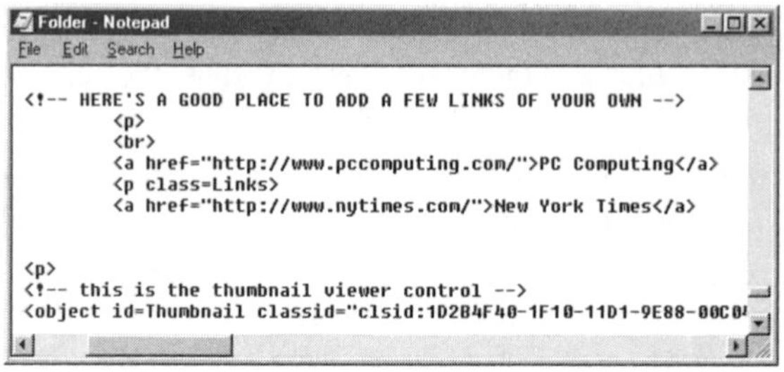

FIG. 8.6

Edit the HyperText template to add links that appear in web view. Note that links can include web pages, folders, or filenames.

Removing Custom Web View Settings

If you've customized a folder's web view template and you're not happy with the results, use the wizard to delete your changes and start over. The procedure is simple:

1. Choose View, Customize This Folder.

2. Select the Remove Customization option, and then click the Next button.

3. A dialog box appears, warning you that you're about to delete FOLDER.HTT and remove custom settings from DESKTOP.INI. Click Next to continue.

4. Click Finish to close the wizard. You'll see the default web view settings for the current folder.

Advanced Customization Options

There's no limit to the amount of customization a skilled HTML author can perform. As you learned earlier, you can create your own HyperText template file, giving it any name. Store it in the folder you want to customize, and then open DESKTOP.INI and enter the name of your custom HTML file after the PersistentMoniker= entry.

TIP

Remember, both DESKTOP.INI and FOLDER.HTT are hidden files. To edit either one without using the wizard, you may need to adjust Explorer's options to show hidden files.

▶ **See** "Changing the Way a Folder's Contents Appear," **p. 76**

Although most users will specify an HTML file in DESKTOP.INI, you have the option of calling out a web page in this file. This option is not officially supported, but it works just the same. You can point a folder to a page on the Internet or your intranet. The effect is a bit baffling: Although the Address bar displays the name of the folder, the Explorer window shows the web page listed in DESKTOP.INI.

To use the file list control in a custom web page, open the default FOLDER.HTT file and copy the file list code to the Clipboard. Then paste it into your custom HTML document. Look for this block of code:

```
<object
classid="clsid:1820FED0-473E-11D0-A96C-00C04FD705A2">
</object>
```

You also might have to add a Position statement to place the control where you want it to appear on the page.

ON THE WEB

For ideas on how to create useful custom web view pages, check out the following article on the Microsoft SiteBuilder Network:

http://www.microsoft.com/workshop/prog/ie4/folders.htm

Working with Disks and Drives

by Craig Zacker and Kyle Bryant

In this chapter

One of the oldest relics of DOS that has been retained in Windows 98 is the way that the operating system handles its local disk storage. The file allocation table (FAT) file system and the use of drive letters to represent the disk drives installed in the computer are unchanged from earlier versions of DOS.

However, Windows 98 has not stood idle in this respect. The capacity of hard disk drives has grown faster than virtually any other area of computing technology. Also, there is now a whole new breed of storage devices, such as CD-ROM and removable cartridge drives, that are rapidly becoming standard equipment on new systems. Windows 98 supports today's large capacity drives, as well as a wide range of other storage devices.

Windows 98 and Local Media

The steady rise in capacity and sophistication of the local storage devices in the typical PC has forced operating systems to change in order to keep up with the technology. Most new systems today are equipped with a CD-ROM drive in addition to the standard floppy and hard disk drives. Many are also shipping with a removable cartridge drive, usually an Iomega Zip drive, as standard equipment.

In addition, the capacity of the typical hard disk drive has skyrocketed to the point at which drives holding from two to eight gigabytes or more are common, even on entry-level machines. Windows 98 supports a wide array of storage devices, and yet it maintains the familiar drive access paradigms at the Windows command line and in the graphical interface.

Floppy Drives

The floppy disk drive was the original storage medium for the personal computer. At one time, most users ran their applications directly from floppies, and if they were lucky, they had a second floppy drive to store their data. Today, as a software distribution medium, the floppy disk is virtually obsolete because of its limited capacity and the size of current applications.

As a case in point, the core Windows 98 installation files would require more than 70 floppy disks, and even that number would be higher if Microsoft didn't use a special format (CAB) to store 1.7 megabytes on each disk. When compared to a single CD-ROM that can store much more data and be produced much more cheaply, the choice is obvious.

As demonstrated by Microsoft, the physical disk can be formatted to a greater capacity, but the format is a proprietary read-only one that is designed primarily to inhibit the copying of disks. IBM introduced a 2.88 megabyte floppy disk drive standard in 1991, but like some other IBM innovations, it never caught on with other manufacturers to any significant extent.

All DOS and Windows operating systems reserve the drive letters A: and B: for floppy disk drives. Today, floppy drives serve primarily as an alternative boot device in case of a hard drive failure. Most systems are configured to boot from the floppy if a disk is present in the drive. This is why the Windows 98 installation process strongly recommends that you create an emergency startup disk.

▶ **See** "Installing Windows 98," **p. 967** for more information on startup disk issues.

Hard Disk Drives

Hard disk drives are, of course, the core of a PC's data storage subsystem. Hard drives usually offer the greatest capacity and the highest speed of any storage medium in the machine. To keep up with ever larger applications and data files, hard drives have had to become faster and more capacious at an incredible rate. At the same time, the price of hard disk storage has plummeted: A one gigabyte drive that sold for $2,000 in the early 1990s can now be had for less than $150.

This need for increasingly larger hard drives has resulted in serious inefficiencies when they are used with legacy file systems such as FAT16, which was originally developed for use with DOS. Windows 98 addresses these problems with a new file system, FAT32, that makes it possible to use large hard disk drives more efficiently.

The large capacity of today's drives and the limitations imposed by existing file systems often make it necessary for users to divide hard disk drives into separate partitions. A *partition* is a portion of a hard disk that is devoted to exclusive use by a specific file system. When you create multiple partitions on a single disk and all are compatible with Windows 98, the operating system mounts each one using a different drive letter.

N O T E A hard disk storage device consists of the disk itself, which takes the form of a stack of platters, and the drive that spins the platters and moves the heads to the appropriate position. However, common terminology among DOS and Windows users also uses the word drive to refer to a logical drive, represented by a letter that the operating system assigns to a partition as it is mounted. Thus, you may hear the physical device referred to as a hard disk or a hard drive, but although there is only one mechanical drive in the unit, there may in fact be several partitions and, therefore, several logical drives. The first logical drive designation in a sequence of drives is usually referred to as Drive 0, followed by Drive 1, Drive 2, and so on.

You can also create partitions for different file systems on the same disk. You can, for example, create one FAT32 partition for use with Windows 98 and another NTFS partition for use with Windows NT. However, to access a partition, you must load an operating system that supports its file system. In this example, each operating system will be able to access its own partition, but not the other partition because Windows NT doesn't support FAT32 and Windows 98 doesn't support NTFS. If you used FAT16 instead of FAT32, however, Windows NT could access both partitions.

N O T E Windows NT 5 is expected to provide support for the FAT32 file system.

When a partition is not supported by an operating system, it is effectively invisible. In the example just presented, each operating system mounts its own partition as the C: drive, no matter where each partition is physically located on the disk. Each operating system has its own function or utility for creating partitions on hard drives. NetWare, OS/2, and other operating systems all have their own file systems.

CD-ROM Drives

In a very short time, the CD-ROM drive has become a common part of the average PC configuration. Because most applications and operating systems are now distributed on CD, a CD-ROM drive is essential on a standalone system. On business networks, CD-ROM drives tend to be less prevalent because software can be installed and distributed over the network.

Originally, CD-ROM drives required SCSI (Small Computer System Interface) subsystems, which made them more costly and difficult to configure. However, the adoption of the EIDE (Enhanced Integrated Drive Electronics) interface has enabled CD-ROM drives to share the same host adapter used by the EIDE hard drives that are typically used in desktop PCs.

For a CD-ROM drive to operate on an EIDE interface, the device must be supported by the system BIOS, just like the hard disk and floppy drives. This support makes it possible for the CD-ROM to be used as a boot device, simplifying the installation of operating systems onto new systems.

N O T E   For older systems that do not have BIOS support for EIDE devices, you can purchase an expansion card that effectively replaces the system BIOS and permits the connect of additional devices such as CD-ROM drives.

When Windows 98 detects a CD-ROM drive on the system during the installation process, it mounts the disk using the next available drive letter after the floppy drive and hard disk partitions. You can access files on the CD-ROM using Windows Explorer or the My Computer window just as you would those on a floppy or a hard drive—except of course that the CD-ROM is a read-only medium.

N O T E   Writeable CD-ROM drives are now available at reasonable prices, along with software that enables you to write to the disk by dragging and dropping files in Windows Explorer. These are known as write-once/read-many, or WORM, devices. In addition, a new breed of rewriteable CD-ROM drives are now on the market, but the disks that they create generally are not readable by standard read-only drives.

Removable Cartridge Drives

Although the technology has been available for many years, rewriteable, removable, magneto-optical cartridge drives are now becoming increasingly popular options on desktop PCs. Many desktop systems aimed at the home consumer market now include a cartridge drive as standard equipment.

The Iomega Zip drive is rapidly becoming a *de facto* standard for removable data storage. To their advantage, the drive and the media are both inexpensive, their proliferation makes it easy for users to exchange files, and their 100 megabyte capacity makes them a more practical alternative than floppy disks.

Iomega also produces higher capacity cartridge drives, such as the Jaz drive, available in both one gigabyte and two gigabyte versions. The capabilities of these devices rival those of hard drives in speed and flexibility. Cartridge drives can use either the EIDE or SCSI interface to connect to the system. There are also slower models that connect through the computer's parallel port, which makes it very easy to move the drive from system to system.

Like the other drive types discussed in this section, Windows 98 mounts cartridge drives using a standard drive letter. Larger capacity drives, such as the Jaz, even support the creation of multiple partitions, enabling you to use them just like hard disk drives.

However, using multiple partitions on removable media can cause a rearrangement of the system's assigned drive letters, depending on how many partitions exist on a particular cartridge. The drive letter of a CD-ROM mounted after a removable drive, for example, changes depending on the number of DOS partitions on the cartridge that is currently loaded. You can avoid this problem by configuring Windows 98 to permanently assign drive letters to specific devices. To do this, open the System Control Panel and select the Device Manager tab. Open the Properties dialog box for the removable device, click the Settings tab, and select a range of drive letters. After you reboot the system, those letters will not be assigned to another device.

DVD Drives

Various manufacturers continue to develop new types of storage devices for use with PCs, hoping to see them come into popular use and become a standard in the way the Zip drive has. The most promising of these is the DVD drive.

Originally named the Digital Video Disk, the acronym is now often called the Digital Versatile Disk because of its adaptation to use on computers. The DVD medium looks just like a CD-ROM except that it is double-sided, and each side can have two separate layers. By adjusting the focus of the laser that reads the disk, the device can read a separate data stream on each of the layers on each side. This increases the potential capacity of the disk enormously.

DVD was originally intended as a read-only video transport medium. It used MPEG-2 compression to store more than two hours of video, plus high-quality audio and other material on a single disk. Movies are already becoming available on DVD, and many PC vendors are offering the drives on their high-end systems.

As a data storage medium, DVD has great potential for use in the PC world, but it's still too early to gauge its success. There is not yet a ratified standard for the technology, and a recordable version of DVD is currently in development, which could end up replacing the read-only version in general use. Investing in DVD technology today might be akin to the old days of investing in 1X CD-ROM drives.

Understanding Disk Partitions

To view, create, and manage a disk drive's DOS partition table in Windows 98, you still use FDISK. FDISK is a command-line utility inherited from DOS that has changed little in appearance over the years. The primary difference in the Windows 98 version of FDISK is its capability to create partitions by using the new FAT32 file system.

N O T E FAT32 was actually introduced in the OEM Service Release 2 of Windows 95, but Windows 98 fully integrates it into the operating system by enabling you to convert existing FAT16 partitions to FAT32. ▨

Under Windows 98, no matter which of the FAT file systems you use, the partitions that FDISK creates on a disk drive are referred to as DOS partitions. FDISK creates a partition table on the drive in the *master partition boot sector,* which is the first sector on the drive. This table lists the locations of the other *partition boot sectors* on the drive. Each partition boot sector precedes the section of the disk that has been allocated for that partition.

Each partition boot sector contains information that defines the size and nature of a particular partition. The partition boot sectors and the master partition boot sector are strictly DOS conventions. Other non-DOS file systems create their own partitions and have their own methods of allocating space on a drive.

N O T E All Windows 98 hard disks and some types of removable disks have a master partition boot sector and one or more partition boot sectors. Floppy disks, however, do not have these and, as a result, cannot contain multiple partitions. ▨

Since DOS 3.3, it has been possible to create multiple DOS partitions on a single hard disk. The first partition that you create is called the *primary DOS partition*, and any others are called *extended DOS partitions*. In contrast, some other file systems (such as NetWare's) allow you to create only one partition of that type per disk.

As long as it has sufficient capacity, you can use one hard disk drive to boot several different operating systems, each of which uses its own file system. You can create DOS partitions of any size, leaving unallocated space on the disk, and then use the partitioning utility from another operating system to create partitions for a different file system in that empty space.

Each area of a hard disk that is allocated as a DOS partition by the partition boot sectors begins with a *DOS volume boot sector*. After you make a particular DOS partition *active* (or bootable) with FDISK and you install the DOS, Windows 95, or Windows 98 system files on it, the system BIOS passes control of the machine to that partition's DOS volume boot sector each time the system restarts. When this happens, the code in the DOS volume boot sector runs and attempts to load the system file IO.SYS from the root directory of the partition. If IO.SYS cannot be found, the boot fails. To view a complete summary of a hard disk's allocated file structure including numbers of files and directories, use the DOS Directory (DIR) command with the /A /S and /V command-line switches.

N O T E Because floppy disks have no partition boot sectors, the DOS volume boot sector is always placed on the first sectors of the disk. That enables the floppy to function as a boot device just like a hard drive. It is the system BIOS that determines whether control of the machine should pass to the floppy drive or to the active partition on the hard disk. ▨

Using FDISK

To create DOS partitions on a hard disk, you must run the FDISK utility from the DOS command prompt. You can run FDISK from a Windows 98 DOS session, but only if you do not intend to work with the currently active partition. Obviously, if you destroy the partition containing the system files and operating system the computer is currently using, the system will halt as soon as you exit FDISK.

After you create a partition, exit FDISK, and reboot the system, you will find that the system has assigned the new partition a drive letter. You can switch to that drive letter from the DOS prompt but you cannot read from it or write to it because the drive has not yet been formatted. You must use the FORMAT utility from the command line, the Windows Explorer, or My Computer to format the drive before you can use it to store data.

In most cases, it is best to run FDISK from a boot floppy, so that you can continue to access the machine even if there are no partitions on the hard disk. You can create a Windows 98 startup disk by launching Add/Remove Programs from the Control Panel and selecting the Startup Disk tab (see Figure 9.1).

Part
II

Ch
9

FIG. 9.1

A Windows 98 startup disk contains all the tools you need to boot the system and partition and to format its hard disks.

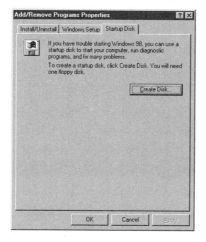

The Windows 98 startup disk includes the system files needed to boot the computer to the DOS prompt, as well as the FDISK and FORMAT utilities you need to prepare the hard disk for a full Windows 98 installation.

If your system contains a hard disk drive with a capacity greater than 512 megabytes, you see the following message when you run FDISK:

```
Your computer has a disk larger than 512 MB. This version of Windows
includes improved support for large disks, resulting in more efficient
use of disk space on large drives, and allowing disks over 2 GB to be
formatted as a single drive.
```

```
IMPORTANT: If you enable large disk support and create any new drives on this
disk, you will not be able to access the new drive(s) using other operating
systems, including some versions of Windows 95 and Windows NT, as well as
earlier versions of Windows and MS-DOS. In addition, disk utilities that
were not designed explicitly for the FAT32 file system will not be able
to work with this disk. If you need to access this disk with other operating
systems or older disk utilities, do not enable large drive support.

Do you wish to enable large disk support (Y/N)...........? [N]
```

Your response to this question determines whether or not FDISK will create FAT32 partitions on your hard disks. Under normal circumstances, drives with a capacity of less than 512 megabytes cannot use FAT32. On the other hand, if you have a large capacity drive and want to create a partition larger than two gigabytes in size, you must use FAT32. Otherwise, see "Choosing a File System," later in this chapter, for information that can help you decide whether or not you should use FAT32. This initial screen is the only indicator that the Windows 98 version of FDISK provides support for FAT32. The screens that follow are the same, whether or not you enable large disk support.

The main FDISK screen appears, displaying the following information:

```
                        Microsoft Windows 98
                        Fixed Disk Setup Program
                (C)Copyright Microsoft Corp. 1983 - 1998

                            FDISK Options

Current fixed disk drive: 1

Choose one of the following:

1. Create DOS partition or Logical DOS Drive
2. Set active partition
3. Delete partition or Logical DOS Drive
4. Display partition information
5. Change current fixed disk drive

Enter choice: [1]
```

The following sections provide details about each of FDISK's available options.

Creating Partitions

When you select the Create DOS Partition or Logical DOS Drive option, FDISK presents the following options for creating a new partition on the selected hard disk:

```
Create DOS Partition or Logical DOS Drive

  Current fixed disk drive: 1

  Choose one of the following:

  1. Create Primary DOS Partition
  2. Create Extended DOS Partition
  3. Create Logical DOS Drive(s) in the Extended DOS Partition

  Enter choice: [1]
```

If the disk currently has no DOS partitions, you must first create a primary DOS partition. If the disk does already have a primary DOS partition and there is still unallocated space, you can create an extended DOS partition. Finally, if the disk already has an extended DOS partition and you want to divide it into two drive letters, you can create logical DOS drives in the extended partition.

When you create a new partition, FDISK first asks you if you want to use all of the space available on the disk and make the partition active. This enables you to create the most common partition configuration in one step. If you say no, you are prompted to specify the size of the new partition in megabytes. Alternatively, you can specify a size using a percentage of the free space available by including the percent symbol ("%") after the value.

FDISK also prompts you to specify a volume label for the partition. This label can contain up to eleven numbers or letters used to identify the partition. The Windows Explorer and the My Computer window display the volume label along with the drive letter for each local drive on the system.

Making a Partition Active

After you create a partition on your system's first or only hard disk, you will most likely want to make that partition active so the system can boot from it. When you choose the Set Active Partition option, you are prompted to select the partition that will hold the system boot files. Only one DOS partition on your computer can be active at any given time.

Making a partition active does not in itself make the disk bootable. It only means that the BIOS will turn over control of the system to that partition at boot time. To make the disk bootable, you must also place the system boot files on that partition by formatting the drive with the system files option or by using the SYS utility.

Deleting Partitions

If you select the Delete Partition or Logical DOS Drive option from FDISK's main screen, you'll see a list of the partitions and logical drives on the selected disk. This list includes all the DOS partition types, as well as partitions created by other file systems (which are identified as non-DOS partitions).

Deleting a partition is always a big step that should cause you to stop and carefully consider your actions. Deleting a partition destroys all the data that is currently stored there and, in the case of an active partition, the system boot files as well. FDISK repeatedly prompts you to confirm your actions before it deletes the partition, including a requirement that you enter the volume name of the partition to be deleted. This virtually ensures that entering a random series of accidental keystrokes cannot cause you to lose your data.

Obviously, you must back up any important data before you delete the partition where it resides. It is also important to be sure that you have a means of booting your system after the partition is gone. If you delete the active partition, you must have a boot floppy disk, such as a Windows 98 startup disk, to restart the system.

If you find yourself in a situation in which you must boot from the startup disk, keep in mind that you might still have access to your CD-ROM drive. Whether or not you do depends upon your CD-ROM drive and the limited driver support provided by Windows 98. Review the CD-ROM drivers on your startup disk and try a test startup disk boot to determine whether or not your hardware is compatible. Note that Windows 98 loads a RAM drive as part of the startup disk boot sequence. This might cause the usual drive designation letter of your CD-ROM to change.

> **CAUTION**
>
> Many of the personal computers sold today use a small non-DOS partition to store a configuration program for the system BIOS. This program is activated when you press a particular key combination during the system boot process (the exact key combination varies depending on the BIOS manufacturer). Be sure not to delete this partition unless you are certain that you have the configuration program on some other medium. Otherwise, you might be unable to access the information in the BIOS.

Displaying Partition Information

When you choose the Display Partition Information option, you see a list of all the partitions on the selected disk. The list should look similar to this one:

```
Display Partition Information

Current fixed disk drive: 1

Partition  Status   Type    Volume Label  Mbytes   System   Usage
   C: 1       A     PRI DOS  DRIVE1          2014    FAT32    100%

Total disk space is  2014 Mbytes (1 Mbyte = 1048576 bytes)
```

This example shows that fixed disk drive 1 contains a single 2,014 megabyte partition that constitutes 100% of the space on the disk. It is a primary DOS partition that has been set as active and will use the FAT32 file system. FDISK has assigned this partition the drive letter C: and the volume label DRIVE1.

FDISK is a program that many people look upon with fear and trepidation because of the catastrophic damage that can result from accidental or improper use. The Display Partition Information option is totally safe, however, because this screen contains no controls that can affect the state of the disk.

Changing the Current Fixed Disk Drive

FDISK offers the Change Current Fixed Disk Drive option on its main screen only when it detects more than one supported disk drive in the system. FDISK can address only one drive at a time and defaults to the first drive in the system BIOS. To manage the partitions on the system's other disks, you must first use this option to select the desired drive.

Selecting the option displays a list similar to the following that outlines the disk drives in the system along with their disk numbers, partitions, drive letters, sizes, and the percentage of the disk occupied by each:

```
Change Current Fixed Disk Drive

   Disk   Drv   Mbytes   Free   Usage
    1             2014           100%
          C:      2014
    2             2014      2    100%
          D:      2012
```

To change to another disk, you select it by specifying the disk number shown in the Disk column. Once you have selected another disk drive, it becomes the default for all of FDISK's other functions until you change it or exit the program. Most of the other screens contain a line that specifies the number of the disk that the program is currently addressing.

Formatting Disks

When you create one or more DOS partitions on a hard disk, you must format them before you can use them to store data. The formatting process divides a partition into clusters. A *cluster* is a logical unit that represents the smallest amount of disk space that can be allocated at one time. A disk formatting program determines the size of the clusters to be created based on the size of the partition and creates an entry in the FAT for each cluster. Windows 98 includes the character-based real-mode FORMAT program inherited from DOS, as well as protected-mode GUI alternatives in the Windows Explorer and the My Computer window.

 TIP You must reboot your system after you create a partition but before you format it. The Windows 98 version of FDISK does not reboot the system automatically after it creates a partition.

Formatting from the Command Line

The Windows 98 FORMAT.EXE program operates from the DOS command line and provides more options than the GUI formatting utility. The program includes all the switches from the previous versions of the utility included with the DOS operating system, although many of them are obsolete unless you use the older floppy disk types. Despite its similarity to previous versions, however, it is imperative that you use the Windows 98 FORMAT program on disks with FAT32 partitions.

The syntax for FORMAT is as follows:

```
FORMAT drive: [/V:label][/S][/B][/Q][/C]
```

These are the switches:

drive:	The variable *drive* is replaced by the drive letter of the disk to be formatted.
/V[:label]	The /V switch specifies the volume label that is to be assigned to the disk being formatted, where *label* is replaced by a string of up to eleven characters.

/S The /S switch causes the program to write the system boot files to the specified disk after the formatting process.

/B The /B switch causes the program to reserve sufficient space on the formatted disk for the later addition of system boot files.

/Q The /Q switch causes the program to perform a quick format on the selected disk by overwriting its FAT table. This removes all of the existing files on the disk, but does not check the clusters for damage. You can perform a quick format only on a disk that has already been formatted.

/C The /C switch causes the program to test the clusters on the disk that have already been marked as "bad" by a previous format.

In most cases, no switches are needed with FORMAT except for a drive letter and possibly /S to create a boot disk. Other switches for FORMAT, that are now seldom needed, are appended to the syntax in this order:

```
[/F:size][/T:tracks][/N:sectors][/1][/4][/8]
```

Those switches function as described here:

/F:size The /F switch specifies capacity of the floppy disk to be formatted, where *size* is replaced by a value in kilobytes or megabytes, such as 160, 180, 320, 360, 720, 1.2, 1.44, or 2.88. This switch is not needed when formatting standard 1.44 megabyte 3.5-inch floppies.

/T:tracks The /T switch enables you to specify the number of tracks on each side of the floppy disk to be formatted.

/N:sectors The /N switch enables you to specify the number of sectors on each track of the floppy disk to be formatted.

/1 The /1 switch causes the program to format one side of a floppy disk.

/4 The /4 switch causes the program to format a 5.25-inch 360K floppy disk in a 1.2 megabyte high-density drive.

/8 The /8 switch causes the program to format a floppy disk with eight sectors per track.

An undocumented switch for the Windows 98 version of FORMAT is /Z:*n*, which enables you to specify the cluster size used to format a given partition. When you run FORMAT with the /Z:*n* switch, where *n* multiplied by 512 represents the cluster size in bytes, you can override the cluster size that is normally determined by the size of the partition. The /U switch is also undocumented under Windows 98, and although it is still allowed, it has no relevant meaning and can be ignored.

CAUTION

The /Z switch is a powerful option that is not recommended for use on production systems without extensive testing. The switch does not override the 65,536 cluster limit on FAT16 drives, so it should generally be used only with FAT32. Specifying a smaller than normal cluster size may lessen the amount of disk space wasted by partially filled clusters, but it can also create enormously large FATs that severely affect the performance of the file system.

Part

II

Ch

9

GUI Formatting

Windows 98 also includes a GUI-based formatting utility that's accessible as a drive letter under Windows Explorer or My Computer. Figure 9.2 shows the GUI display.

FIG. 9.2
The Windows 98 GUI disk formatting utility provides access to the same major options found in the command line FORMAT program.

In the Format dialog box, you can select the capacity of the disk to be formatted and the type of format (quick, full, full with system files, or system files only). You can also specify a volume label for the disk. The utility will not allow you to format the hard disk drive where the Windows 98 operating system files are stored and will prompt you to confirm your actions before it destroys any files on a disk that has already been formatted.

Creating a Bootable Disk

When you elect to include the system files during a format by using the /S switch with the FORMAT program or by activating the Copy System Files check box in the Format dialog box, the following boot files are written to the disk after the formatting process is complete:

- *IO.SYS.* Primary Windows 98 boot file
- *MSDOS.SYS.* Windows 98 operating system configuration file
- *DRVSPACE.BIN.* DriveSpace compression support file
- *COMMAND.COM.* Windows 98 command processor

The first three files are flagged with the system attribute, which you must remove before you can delete them. COMMAND.COM functions as a normal executable and is launched whenever you open a DOS session from the Windows 98 GUI. Together, these four files occupy 393,728 bytes, which is a substantial amount of space on a floppy disk. Unlike the boot sector and the FATs, which reside outside the disk area that is visible to the operating system, the system boot files are visible and can be manipulated by conventional means. However, such manipulation can damage the disk's capability to boot the system.

During boot time, the system BIOS in nearly all PCs is configured to check the first floppy drive for the presence of a disk containing system boot files. Therefore, you can use any floppy disk containing those files to boot the system by inserting it into the A: drive. On a hard disk drive, however, the mere presence of the system boot files on the disk is not sufficient to boot the system. You must also configure the partition containing those files to be active, as detailed in the section, "Making a Partition Active," earlier in this chapter.

Choosing a File System

In addition to its partition boot sector and its DOS volume boot sector, each DOS partition also contains two copies of its *file allocation table*, or FAT. The FAT is a matrix that correlates the files and folders stored in the partition with their physical locations on the hard disk. Two consecutive copies of the FAT are stored in the disk area before each partition. Like the boot sectors, the FATs are stored outside the disk area that is visible to the file system.

N O T E   Although the data structures that comprise a partition's boot sectors and FAT tables cannot be displayed or manipulated by the standard Windows 98 file management utilities like Windows Explorer, they are not inaccessible. Many products on the market address disk devices directly instead of through the file system. These products, called *disk editors* or *sector editors*, enable the direct manipulation of data in a disk's boot sectors and FATs. In many cases, professionals use them in a last ditch effort to recover the data on a drive that has already been damaged by an attempt to manually repair a FAT. ■

When files are written to a disk, they do not necessarily occupy a contiguous space equivalent to the size of the file. Instead, the files are broken up into *clusters* of a given size (sometimes called *allocation units*), which may be scattered all over the partition. As a result, the FAT is not a list of files and their locations as much as it is a list of the clusters in the partition and their contents. Whenever you access a file on a given partition, Windows 98 accesses the directory entry for that file, which contains the starting cluster. This cluster points to the entry in the FAT representing the next cluster in the chain. Each successive cluster then points to the next until the entire file is read.

Each entry in the FAT is a 12-, 16-, or 32-bit hexadecimal number, the size of which is determined by the FDISK program—even though FORMAT actually creates the entries. All floppy disks and hard disk volumes under 16 megabytes in size use 12-bit FAT entries. Hard disks and removables with volumes that are 16 megabytes or larger typically use 16-bit entries, but a volume larger than 512 megabytes can now use Windows 98's FAT32 file system and 32-bit FAT entries.

The size of the clusters on a given partition is determined during its creation by the size of the partition that you specify in the FDISK program. The intent is to strike a balance between the number of clusters listed in the FAT and the size of those clusters. This need for balance is the source of the FAT file system's biggest problem—a problem that is addressed by the new FAT32 file system. FAT32 does not completely resolve the problem, but it does provide a greater flexibility of solutions.

Part

II

Ch

9

Obviously, the smaller the clusters used on a partition, the more clusters that partition can hold. The more clusters there are on a partition, the larger the FAT table must be and the longer it takes for the operating system to search the table for the information it needs to access a file. On the contrary, when you create larger clusters, the FAT table becomes smaller and more manageable, but you also increase the amount of disk space wasted by clusters that are only partially filled.

Cluster Size and Slack Space

A file can be of almost any size, but when Windows 98 writes it to disk, it splits the file into a series of uniform clusters. The result is that the last cluster is almost never an exact fit. The end of the file is written to the last cluster and the remainder of that cluster stays empty (see Figure 9.3). This slack space is wasted as long as the file remains on the disk.

FIG. 9.3
Because the FAT file system divides the disk into clusters of a uniform size, disk space is wasted whenever a cluster is not completely filled with data.

135 KB File

25 KB Wasted

32 KB Clusters

How much partition space is wasted is determined by the relationship between the size of the clusters and the size of the files. If, for example, you have large files and small clusters, relatively little space is wasted. However, the combination of small files and large clusters (a more common occurrence) produces the exact opposite effect. When you store a large number of 10KB files on a partition with 32KB clusters, more than two thirds of the allocated disk space is wasted.

FAT16 and Hard Disk Expansion

Although the problem of disk space being wasted by partially filled clusters has existed as long as the FAT file system has, it was exacerbated to an alarming degree by the ever-increasing capacity of the typical hard disk drive. As disks and the partitions on them grow larger, the cluster size must also grow to prevent the FAT from becoming too big. FDISK uses the following cluster sizes for FAT16 partitions of various sizes:

Partition Size	Cluster Size
128MB	2KB
256MB	4KB
512MB	8KB
1GB	16KB
2GB	32KB

Because the FAT16 file system can only support a maximum of 65,526 clusters, the largest partition it can support is just under two gigabytes. (65,526 32-kilobyte clusters equals 2,096,832 kilobytes or 2,047.6875 megabytes.)

CAUTION

FDISK uses the literal definitions of kilobyte and megabyte. That is, one kilobyte equals 1,024 bytes, and one megabyte equals 1,024 kilobytes or 1,048,576 bytes. Some hardware vendors have been known to make their drive capacities seem larger by defining a kilobyte as 1,000 bytes and a megabyte as 1,000 kilobytes or 1,000,000 bytes. Be sure to take this into account when you are trying to create partitions with a particular cluster size.

Introducing FAT32

When you purchase a new PC today, it is not uncommon for the machine to be equipped with a hard disk drive holding six or eight gigabytes or more. The primary reason for FAT32's existence is to prevent users from having to divide a device that large into three or more separate partitions. FAT32 can support drives holding up to two terabytes of data (1 terabyte equals 1,024 gigabytes) and single files up to nearly four gigabytes, so it is likely to remain a viable tool for some time to come.

At the same time, FAT32 eliminates the file allocation table's 65,536 cluster limit, making it possible to use smaller clusters than FAT16 partitions of the same size can use. This results in many more clusters and a larger FAT, but FAT32 can also dramatically reduce the amount of space wasted by partially filled clusters. FAT32 partitions of various sizes use the following default cluster sizes:

Partition Size	Cluster Size
less than 260MB	512 bytes
260MB–8GB	4KB
8GB–16GB	8KB
16GB–32GB	16KB
greater than 32GB	32KB

Thus, with most of the hard disk drives on the market today, you can create a single FAT32 partition that uses 4KB clusters. The FAT for a two gigabyte drive would therefore contain 524,288 entries using FAT32, as opposed to 65,536 entries with FAT16. In many cases, converting from FAT16 to FAT32 on a large drive creates up to approximately 40% extra disk space. According to Microsoft, this enables programs to run up to 50% faster, and your system will use fewer system resources. Of course, however, results will vary depending on the sizes of the files.

Duplicate FATs

FAT32 also includes other improvements besides larger partitions and smaller clusters. Since its inception, the FAT file system has always used two identical file allocation tables for each partition. The two FATs are written consecutively in a contiguous area of the disk just before the beginning of the partition itself. During normal operations, the operating system updates the second FAT by copying data from the first on a regular basis.

FAT16, however, takes very little advantage of this redundancy. A FAT16 file system will use the second copy of the FAT if damaged disk sectors prevent access to the first copy, but it does not access the second copy of the data if the first simply becomes corrupted. In fact, the file system is far more likely to continue to update the second FAT, overwriting it with the corrupted data from the first copy. Some third-party disk utilities can take advantage of the second FAT and use it to repair the first, but only if they perform the repair operation before the second FAT has been damaged, too.

FAT32 takes greater advantage of the two FAT copies. In any situation in which the file system finds the data in the primary copy of the FAT to be unreadable, it switches to the secondary FAT, which then becomes the primary. This is in direct contrast to FAT16, in which the first FAT is always the primary. In addition, FAT32 provides greater control over the FAT mirroring process. The file system can temporarily disable the process by which the data from one FAT is replicated to the other.

The modification in the behavior of the FATs results in a greater degree of fault tolerance—without the need to interrupt system operations and apply third-party utilities.

FAT32 and Small Partitions

Despite the first entry in the cluster size table (shown earlier, in the section "Introducing FAT32"), the Windows 98 FDISK utility in its default configuration will not create FAT32 partitions smaller than 512 megabytes. Indeed, when it detects a drive smaller than 512MB, it does not even present the option to enable support for large drives.

However, certain third-party products on the market, such as Partition Magic 3.0 (www.powerquest.com), make it possible to convert FAT16 partitions smaller than 512MB to FAT32. In addition, an undocumented switch for FDISK enables you to create new FAT32 partitions smaller than 512MB. By running FDISK with the /FPRMT parameter, you can specify a FAT32 partition size smaller than 512MB.

> **CAUTION**
>
> FDISK's /FPRMT parameter is undocumented. Experiment with it at your own risk. It should not generally be used on disks containing vital data. Because hard disk drives smaller than 512 megabytes are becoming an increasingly rare sight, the compatibility of these drives with FAT32 should not be a major issue. In addition, because a 512MB drive with a FAT16 partition already uses 8KB clusters, the savings realized by FAT32 will not be significant.

FAT32 Tools

After you enable large disk support in FDISK, the rest of the program functions identically with both FAT16 and FAT32 partitions. To verify that a partition you have created is using FAT32, you can either use the Display Partition Information option on FDISK's main screen or right-click a drive letter in Windows Explorer or My Computer window and choose Properties from the context menu. In either case, the display should show the selected drive as using the FAT32 file system (see Figure 9.4).

FIG. 9.4

The Properties dialog box for a hard disk drive identifies the file system that has been used to create the partition.

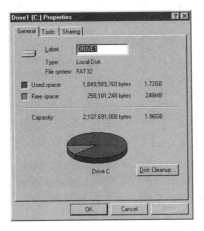

Because FAT32 operates at the file system level, it does not have compatibility problems with most applications (whether they are shrink-wrapped or custom written). The sole exception to this is a type of applications that address the storage devices directly, such as disk utilities and some antivirus products.

> **CAUTION**
>
> Disk tools designed for use with the FAT16 file system, such as sector editors, disk repair tools, and defragmenters, should absolutely not be used on FAT32 drives. They can potentially cause serious damage to the partition, including data loss.

Windows 98 includes new versions of ScanDisk and Defrag, in both real and protected mode, that are designed to work with FAT32. If you are familiar with the functionality of ScanDisk, you'll easily understand how converting a FAT16 drive to FAT32 affects the program's diagnostic process. Whereas the examination of the FATs on a FAT16 drive takes only a few seconds, the larger tables on a FAT32 drive of the same size take longer because of the greater number of entries.

While the Windows 98 disk utilities are certainly adequate, many users have come to rely on the greater functionality provided by third-party disk repair and utility products. Most manufacturers of these tools have by now released versions of their products that support FAT32 drives. Be sure, however, to verify that a disk utility supports FAT32 before you actually use it. The damage you could cause might be irreparable.

Part
II

Ch
9

FAT32 Drawbacks

The primary drawback of FAT32 is unquestionably its incompatibility with previous versions of the DOS and Windows operating systems. FAT32 was originally released as part of the OEM Service Release 2 of Windows 95, but the original Windows 95 release cannot access FAT32 partitions. Likewise, all previous DOS versions and all current versions of Windows NT are incompatible with FAT32. A FAT32 drive will not be able to serve as a boot device for a Windows NT system.

Because of this incompatibility, you cannot configure a system to dual boot Windows 98 and Windows NT or Windows 3.1 using a FAT32 drive to store both operating systems. You can, however, create separate partitions for the two file systems and boot each one from its own drive.

Here is a list of other issues you should consider before making the decision to convert to FAT32:

- Once you convert your hard drive to FAT32, you cannot return to FAT16 unless you repartition and reformat the drive.
- Most disk compression software, including Microsoft's DriveSpace, is not compatible with FAT32.
- If you convert a removable disk and use it with other operating systems that are not FAT32-compatible, those other systems cannot read the disk.
- If your system's BIOS supports power management hibernation, FAT32 might turn off the feature.
- If, during the Windows 98 installation routine, you initially opted to save the Windows 95 system files for subsequent uninstallation purposes, you will no longer be able to uninstall Windows 98 and return your system to Windows 95.

CAUTION

Using Drive Converter to format a removable disk as FAT32 might void your removable disk's manufacturer warranty. Check with your removable disk manufacturer before proceeding.

Converting a FAT16 Drive to FAT32

When Microsoft first released the FAT32 file system as part of the Windows 95 OEM Service Release 2 product, the only way to use it was to delete the existing partitions on a disk drive and create new ones. Obviously, this resulted in the loss of all the data and, therefore, the need for a complete backup and restore procedure. Windows 98 remedies this problem by providing a FAT32 conversion wizard, known as Drive Converter (FAT32), that enables you to preserve your data while gaining the advantages of the new file system. To access the wizard, you can launch the Drive Converter program from the Start menu's Programs, Accessories, System Tools program group, or you can execute CVT1.EXE from the Run dialog box (Start, Run).

The wizard provides you with information about the new file system and the possible consequences of the conversion. After you select a drive to be converted (see Figure 9.5), the wizard scans the drive for applications that might cause problems with FAT32 and then gives you the chance to remove them before proceeding. The wizard also gives you the opportunity to back up your data with Microsoft Backup, and it warns you repeatedly about the consequences of your actions, requesting your confirmation before proceeding.

▶ **See** "Backing Up Files," **p. 345**

FIG. 9.5
Windows 98's FAT32 converter implements the new file system on selected drives without the need for repartitioning or reformatting.

The actual conversion is a DOS process. After you complete the wizard's information and configuration screens, it reboots your system to the DOS prompt. Because the converter must manipulate the existing data on the drive as it creates new clusters, the process can take many times longer than it would to partition and format an empty drive. The length of the conversion process is, of course, dependent on the number and size of the files on your drive, as well as the speed of the device itself. It is not uncommon for a FAT32 conversion to take a considerable amount of time.

> **CAUTION**
> You should take whatever steps are possible to ensure that the conversion process runs from start to finish without interruption. A power failure during the operation might not be avoidable, but you can use common-sense precautions (like connecting the system to a UPS if possible and not converting your disks during a thunderstorm) to lessen the chances.

Copying Disks

When you have partitioned and formatted your disks, you can use the standard Windows 98 disk tools to store and manage your files, regardless of which file system you have elected to use. From the drive letter icons in Windows Explorer or My Computer, you can copy files, directories, and entire disks by dragging and dropping them onto other drives or directories.

By default, when you drag a file or directory to another location on the same drive, Windows 98 moves it, deleting the file or directory from its original location. When you drag a file to a location on another drive, Windows 98 copies it, leaving the original in place.

In addition to the Windows 98 graphical file management tools, you can also use the traditional DOS COPY and XCOPY programs. COPY is an internal DOS command that's designed to copy one or more files to a new location on the same or a different drive. XCOPY is also a holdover from DOS, but it is an external program that's used to copy entire directory trees.

Part
II
Ch
9

The syntax for COPY is as follows:

```
COPY [/A:[[-]rhsda] /C /E /H /K /M /N /P /Q /R /S /T /U /V /X /Z]
➥source[+]...[destination]
```

These are the parameters and switches:

source	The *source* variable is replaced with one or more filenames. Standard DOS wildcards are permitted. If the filenames are separated by plus signs (+), the files are joined into a single destination file.
destination	The *destination* variable is replaced with the name of the file, directory, or DOS device to which the *source* is to be copied. When the destination is omitted, the source is copied to the current default directory.
/A:[-]rhsda	Copies the source files flagged with the attributes specified after the / A:. If /A is used but no attributes are specified, all files are copied, regardless of attributes.
/C	Copies a file only if a duplicate file in the destination directory is older than the source file.
/E	Suppresses the display of non-fatal error messages during the copy process.
/H	Copies files flagged with the hidden and system attributes. Normally, COPY ignores files with these attributes.
/K	Causes the copied files to retain the DOS read-only attribute if it is present in the source files.
/M	Copies only files that are flagged with the archive attribute.
/N	Parses the COPY command for testing purposes without actually performing the copy.
/P	Prompts the user for confirmation of each file copied.

/Q	Suppresses the display of filenames and totals during the copy process.
/R	Prompts the user for a confirmation before overwriting files in the destination directory. (By default, COPY silently overwrites files.)
/S	Parses the subdirectories of the source for files to be copied, creating identical subdirectories at the destination as needed.
/T	Displays the total number of files that have been copied, but suppresses the display of individual filenames during the copy process
/U	Copies files that are newer than files of the same name in the destination directory as well as files that don't exist at the destination at all. The /C switch does not copy files that don't exist at the destination.
/V	Verifies that the data copied to the destination directory is readable.
/X	Removes the archive attribute from the source files after they are successfully copied.
/Z	Causes COPY to overwrite a read-only file of the same name in the destination directory.

The syntax for XCOPY is as follows:

```
XCOPY source [destination] [/A /C /D[:date] /E /F /H /I /K /L /M /N /P /Q /R /S /
➡T /U /W /Y /-Y
```

source	The *source* variable is replaced with the name of the file or directory to be copied. Standard DOS wildcards are permitted.
destination	The *destination* variable is replaced with the name of the file or directory to which the source is to be copied.
/A	Copies only the source files that are flagged with the archive attribute, without changing the attribute at the source.
/C	Continues the copy process after encountering errors.
/D[:date]	Copies only the files with a date more recent than that specified by the *date* variable. If no date is specified, only source files newer than the destination files are copied.
/E	Creates all subdirectories found at the source to the destination directory, even empty ones.
/F	Displays the complete path names of files and directories as they are copied.
/H	Copies files flagged with the hidden and system attributes, in addition to all other files.
/I	Assumes that a nonexistent destination is a directory when copying multiple files. By default, XCOPY prompts the user to identify a nonexistent destination as a file or directory.
/K	Maintains the attributes of the source files in the destination directory.

/L	Parses the XCOPY command and displays the files to be copied without actually performing the operation.
/M	Copies only the source files that are flagged with the archive attribute, and then removes the attribute at the source.
/N	Copies files to the destination using DOS 8.3 filenames.
/P	Prompts the user for a confirmation before copying each file.
/Q	Suppresses the display of filenames during the copy process.
/R	Overwrites destination files flagged with the read-only attribute.
/S	Copies all subdirectories of the source to the destination, except empty ones.
/T	Creates the directory structure of the source in the destination directory but does *not* copy files or empty directories.
/U	Overwrites older files in the destination directory.
/W	Prompts the user to press a key before beginning the copy process.
/Y	Overwrites files that already exist in the destination directory without confirmation.
/-Y	Prompts the user for a confirmation before overwriting files that already exist in the destination directory.

Understanding Disk Compression

Windows 98 includes DriveSpace 3, a disk compression product that can increase the capacity of your disk drives by 50% to 100%. As with many of Windows 98's optional features, however, you should carefully consider whether using DriveSpace on your system is a good idea.

Unlike static compression programs such as PKZIP, DriveSpace compresses files automatically as they are saved to your drive and then decompresses them on-the-fly when you request access to them. Naturally, this introduces an additional level of processing overhead that can diminish the overall performance of your system.

Compression programs function by scanning files for redundant bit patterns and replacing them with codes that take up less space than the patterns themselves. The degree of compression the program achieves is based on the nature of the files being compressed. If, for example, you apply DriveSpace to a drive that contains mostly ZIP and GIF files, you will see little gain because these file formats are already compressed and cannot be reduced any further.

Bitmap and database files, on the other hand, contain a large number of redundant bit patterns and often can be reduced to one-fifth their original size or smaller. Executables and dynamic link libraries typically fall between these two extremes, compressing at a ratio of approximately 2:1.

DriveSpace also can save disk space, even when you choose to create a new drive without actually compressing the files. Instead of using the standard FAT16 cluster size, which can be as large as 32KB, DriveSpace breaks files down into 512-byte pieces in order to minimize the wasted space caused by partially filled clusters.

DriveSpace 3 is a new version of the DriveSpace program that was included in Windows 95. Originally released as part of the Windows 95 Plus! product, this new version can create compressed volumes up to two gigabytes in size, while the Windows 95 version of DriveSpace was limited to 512 megabyte volumes.

To Compress or Not to Compress

Dynamic compression technology has been around for several years, and at one time, it was a sound method for improving the economy of PC data storage. Today its value has lessened—for several reasons. First, the price of hard disk storage has plummeted in recent years, to the point at which a new two gigabyte drive can be had for one-tenth the price of a slower model five years ago. Therefore, it might be more economical to simply purchase additional storage for your system instead of reducing your productivity by adding compression.

Second, you can improve the storage efficiency of your hard disk drives without the aid of compression by using the FAT32 file system included with Windows 98. The additional available disk space you realize with FAT32 will not be as great as what you could achieve with DriveSpace, but even a fast system will exhibit degraded performance under DriveSpace.

If system performance is of paramount importance to you, you might find the performance penalty suffered under DriveSpace to be unacceptable. Carefully consider your other alternatives (converting to FAT32 or adding a new hard drive to your system) before you make the decision to use compression.

> **CAUTION**
> DriveSpace compression is not compatible with the FAT32 file system. If you have any plans to use FAT32, you should not apply DriveSpace compression to your drives.

Finally, like FAT32, DriveSpace renders the data on your compressed drives inaccessible to operating systems that do not support the technology. If you ever plan to boot your system with other operating systems, carefully consider whether you will need access to the files on the drives you plan to compress.

N O T E   DriveSpace 3 can read disks that have been compressed with the earlier DriveSpace versions included with MS-DOS 6.22 and Windows 95, as well as disks that use the DoubleSpace technology that was part of earlier MS-DOS versions. If you want, you can upgrade these older drives to DriveSpace 3 in order to take advantage of its additional features. However, it's a one-way compatibility: The earlier compression products cannot read disks compressed with DriveSpace 3. ■

How DriveSpace 3 Disk Compression Works

When you compress the C: drive on your system with DriveSpace, you end up with a C: drive that can hold 50% to 100% more data. But what you are seeing is not really a drive at all. During the compression process, DriveSpace creates a file on your drive called DRVSPACE.000. This file is called a *compressed volume file*, or CVF. It is the CVF that actually contains your compressed data.

When you view the contents of your C: drive after the compression process is complete, you are actually viewing the contents of the CVF, which exists as a file on your physical disk drive that's flagged with the read-only, hidden, and system attributes. You will also find that DriveSpace has added another drive letter to your system. This new drive is your original disk, now called the *host drive*, with all of its data migrated to the DRVSPACE.000 file. In essence, DriveSpace has created a new virtual drive on your system and then switched the drive letters so that your data appears to be in the same place it always was.

You do not have to compress your entire drive when using DriveSpace. You can specify a part of the free space on the disk and create a new compressed drive out of that space. You can create several smaller compressed drives this way. Each one has its own CVF, called DRVSPPACE.001, DRVSPACE.002, and so forth.

 T I P | If possible, avoid compressing your Windows 98 boot drive; compress another partition instead in order to store infrequently used data or archive files. This lessens the DriveSpace performance penalty.

You can also use DriveSpace to compress floppy disks, and the process is essentially the same as that for a hard disk drive. A new drive letter appears on the system, representing the host drive for the floppy. You continue to access the floppy disk using the A: or B: drive letter as before, but that is actually a view of the CVF. The floppy can hold more data as a result of the compression, but it cannot be read by a system that doesn't have DriveSpace3 installed.

When the compression process begins, DriveSpace creates the CVF file and begins compressing the files already stored on the disk. By moving newly compressed files to the CVF until it is full, the program clears space on the host drive, which it uses to increase the size of the CVF. The process then repeats until all the files have been compressed and migrated. The smaller the amount of free space on the drive when the compression process begins, the more times the CVF has to be expanded, and the longer it takes to complete the entire operation.

It is not possible to compress a drive that does not have any free space because DriveSpace must have room to work. A 1.44 megabyte floppy, for example, must have at least 512 kilobytes of free space in order to be compressed.

N O T E You can compress floppy disks and removable cartridges just like any other disks. However, when you insert a compressed disk into the drive after the system has been booted, you must mount the drive before you can access its files. To mount a drive, highlight the drive letter in the main DriveSpace window and select the Advanced, Mount command. You can dismount the disk in the same way. ▪

Compressing an Entire Drive

To compress a drive, you launch the DriveSpace application from the Start menu's Programs, Accessories, System Tools program group. Figure 9.6 shows the DriveSpace 3 screen. This window lists the drives in your system, shows their compression status, and enables you to perform most compression operations. The display also includes any host drives created by previous compression operations. If a host drive is left with less than two megabytes of uncompressed free space after the compression process is complete, it is hidden from view from Windows Explorer and My Computer.

FIG. 9.6

The DriveSpace 3 dialog box is the main control center for compression operations.

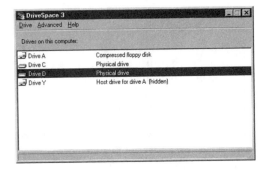

When you select a drive for compression, DriveSpace launches a wizard that walks you through the process. The wizard shows you the current state of the drive and the estimated amount of free space that will result from the compression process (see Figure 9.7).

FIG. 9.7

DriveSpace graphically displays the estimated results of performing the compression process.

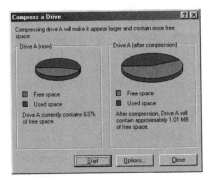

If you click the Options button, you can select the drive letter that will be assigned to the host drive, the amount of free space to be left on the host drive, and whether it should be visible in the Windows 98 file management utilities.

CAUTION

When you compress an entire drive, it is recommended that you leave the host drive letter invisible. It is possible to manipulate the CVF like any other file on the disk, but in this case, you are essentially dealing with all your files in one package. If you were to damage the CVF, change its attributes, or accidentally delete it, you could lose all your data.

Because DriveSpace cannot create compressed volumes larger than two gigabytes in size, it takes a different tack when faced with a hard disk drive larger than one gigabyte. Because the program estimates a compression ratio of 2:1, it compresses one gigabyte of the space on the drive, expecting to create a compressed volume of approximately two gigabytes. The compressed volume will contain most of the existing data on the disk, and DriveSpace creates a new host drive containing free, uncompressed space.

For example, as you can see in Figure 9.8, a two gigabyte D: drive with 91.56 megabytes free is converted to a two gigabyte compressed drive (also called D:) that contains all the original data from the disk. The free space on the compressed drive only increases to 127.81 megabytes, but the host drive, X:, is left with 987.25 megabytes of free uncompressed space. You can then take that free space on the host drive and create another compressed volume that increases the total capacity of the two gigabyte hard disk drive to nearly four gigabytes.

FIG. 9.8

When compressing hard disk drives larger than one gigabyte, DriveSpace compresses as much of the data as possible and leaves the remaining space uncompressed on the host drive.

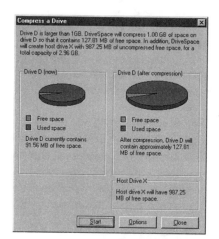

If you attempt to compress your system's boot drive or the drive on which Windows 98 is installed, DriveSpace takes steps to ensure that access to the system is still possible after the compression process and that Windows 98 performance is not too severely affected. As you pass through the screens of the compression wizard, DriveSpace gives you the opportunity to create or update a startup disk for your system because the compression process requires a reboot that might not be possible with your hard drive in its interim state.

> **CAUTION**
>
> Before beginning the compression process, DriveSpace also gives you the opportunity to back up your drive using Microsoft Backup. Whether you use this program or not, always be sure to have a viable backup before beginning a major disk operation.
>
> Ensure that all applications are closed before you begin the compression routine, and do not interrupt DriveSpace while the compression process is running.

Compressing Part of a Drive

DriveSpace 3 also adds a Compression tab to the Properties dialog box of every local drive on your computer (see Figure 9.9). From this dialog box, you can launch a full compression of the drive (which is the same operation discussed earlier in "Compressing an Entire Drive"), or you can create a new compressed drive from the free space left on the disk. Another way to access this feature is to highlight an uncompressed drive with free space on it in the DriveSpace program and then select the Advanced, Create Empty command.

FIG. 9.9

The Properties dialog box of every local drive has a Compression tab that displays its compression status and enables you to initiate compression operations.

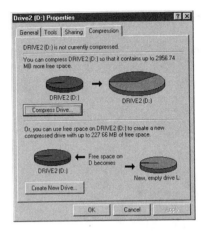

The process of creating a new compressed drive is far less involved and invasive than that of compressing the existing files. In the Create New Compressed Drive dialog box (see Figure 9.10), you specify the letter to be used for the new drive, the amount of uncompressed space to use, and the source drive for that uncompressed space. DriveSpace displays the estimated capacity of the new drive and, on your approval, creates the new CVF.

FIG. 9.10

You can create new compressed volumes out of your free space by using the drive's Properties dialog box.

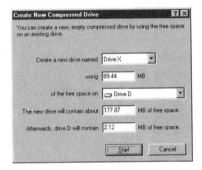

When you create a new compressed drive, no swapping of drive letters is necessary because the host drive still contains other data that must be accessed as before. The new CVF appears as an extra drive letter on your system, which you can access like any other disk drive.

Changing the Settings for a Compressed Drive

You can view the current status of compressed drives on your system and manage their properties using the DriveSpace utility. When you double-click on a compressed drive, a dialog box like that shown in Figure 9.11 appears, displaying the disk's used space, free space, and compression ratios.

FIG. 9.11

The DriveSpace utility can display the status of any currently mounted compressed drive.

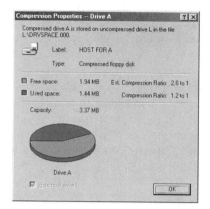

Changing Compression Ratios   When you are dealing with disk compression, statistics such as disk capacity are always estimates because there is no way to know what the compression ratio for a given file will be until it is actually compressed. The status displays in Windows 98's various file management utilities often include an indicator of a disk's remaining free space, however. DriveSpace defaults to a 2:1 ratio in its estimates of a compressed disk's capacity. You can adjust this ratio to achieve a more realistic estimate based on the actual compression ratio of the files already on the disk and your own understanding of the types of files you will be storing on the drive.

Select the Change Ratio command from DriveSpace's Advanced menu, and you see a dialog box like that shown in Figure 9.12. This dialog box shows the current actual compression ratio of the files on the disk. Beneath this is a slider showing the current estimated ratio, which is 2:1 by default. If you plan to store more of the same types of files that are already on the disk, you can adjust this figure to equal the actual ratio, and Windows 98 will adjust the estimates displayed elsewhere in the operating system. If you plan to store files you know to be highly compressible or not highly compressible, you can adjust the value accordingly. Setting the ratio to 1:1 displays the actual free space that will remain available on the drive if you choose to store files that cannot be compressed at all.

FIG. 9.12

The Compression Ratio dialog box enables you to correct Windows 98's estimates of a compressed drive's free space.

N O T E It is important to understand that the Change Ratio feature does not adjust the degree to which your files are compressed, it only enables you to make Windows 98's estimates of the compressed drive's capacity more realistic. ■

Adjusting Free Space After DriveSpace creates a compressed volume, free space is usually left on both the new and the host drives. You can adjust this free space as needed, moving it to either drive, as long as the compressed drive does not exceed two gigabytes. To do so, choose a drive letter in the DriveSpace program and select Adjust Free Space from the Drive menu9. The Adjust Free Space dialog box (see Figure 9.13) contains a slider that enables you to move space from one drive to another, changing the pie charts to display the correct proportion.

FIG. 9.13
DriveSpace's Adjust Free Space feature enables you to move the remaining drive space between a compressed volume and its host drive.

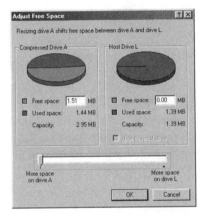

Changing Drive Letters Sometimes the additional drive letters that DriveSpace creates can be confusing, especially when they are hidden and you want to use one of those letters for a network drive or some other device. You can change the letter assigned to a host drive or an empty drive by highlighting it in the DriveSpace program and selecting Change Letter from the Advanced menu.

Using the Compression Agent to Improve Performance

DriveSpace provides three levels of compression that trade off disk space for system performance. By default, DriveSpace uses Standard compression. However, you can configure the system to use HiPack compression whenever new files are written to a compressed drive. To achieve the maximum possible compression, called UltraPack, you must use another utility called the Windows 98 Compression Agent.

The Compression Agent lets you initiate compression events on-demand and choose the level of compression that it should apply to your drive. Unlike DriveSpace itself, Compression Agent does not automatically compress files on-the-fly. Instead, it takes existing compressed drives and compresses them further when you specifically instruct it to do so.

You can use Compression Agent in any of several different ways—to suit your work habits. You can, for example, set DriveSpace to use standard compression or even no compression, to minimize system performance degradation, and to run a nightly Compression Agent job to UltraPack your files after you finish working by using the Task Scheduler.

You can also configure the agent to UltraPack only the files that you have not accessed within a specified number of days. This keeps your seldom-used files at maximum compression while speeding up access to those you use frequently.

When you display the Compression page in any compressed drive's Properties dialog box, you can see a summary of the compressed files on your disk, the type of compression used, and the compression ratios achieved by each one, as shown in Figure 9.14.

Part

II

Ch

9

FIG. 9.14

A single compressed disk can contain Standard, HighPack, and UltraPack files.

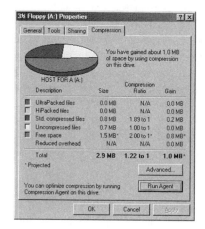

To use the Compression Agent, launch the program from the Start menu's Programs, Accessories, System Tools program group. Click the Settings button to see the dialog box shown in Figure 9.15. You can select the degree of compression desired, and you can access other screens that enable you to apply specific compression rules to individual files and execute compression events based on the current amount of free space on the disk.

FIG. 9.15

You can use the Compression Agent to customize your system's compression behavior to your needs.

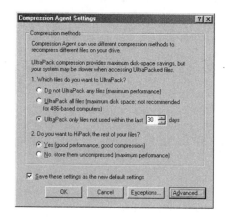

Uncompressing a DriveSpace Volume

DriveSpace enables you to return the files in a compressed volume to their uncompressed state and delete the CVF. To do this, you highlight a drive in the DriveSpace program and select Uncompress from the Drive menu. The program displays a screen showing how much uncompressed free space will be left on the drive after the process.

Unfortunately, you will in all likelihood have more data on the compressed drive than will fit on the same drive in its uncompressed state. The program informs you if this situation arises, letting you know how much data you must remove before the process can proceed.

Deleting a Compressed Drive

Do not confuse the process of deleting a compressed drive with that of uncompressing it. When you highlight a drive in the DriveSpace program and select Delete from the Advanced menu, the program deletes the CVF from the host drive, destroying its data and freeing up all the disk space that it previously occupied. As always, the DriveSpace program warns you of the impending data loss and requires your confirmation before it proceeds. You should only use this feature if you do not need the data on the compressed volume or if you have already backed it up to another medium.

Using a CD-ROM Drive

CD-ROM drives have become an important component of personal computers. Most software is now distributed on CD-ROMs, and their large capacity makes them ideal for use with games and multimedia titles that require large amounts of disk space but do not warrant permanent storage on a hard disk drive. Chapter 24, "Setting Up Windows Multimedia," provides more information on using Windows 98's multimedia features with CD-ROMs.

Autoplay

Windows 98's autoplay feature enables software developers to create CD-ROMs that automatically launch a program when they are mounted by the file system. The program can initiate the installation process for a new application or load a multimedia program that is designed to run directly from the CD-ROM.

Autoplay is made possible by the 32-bit, protected-mode device drivers that Windows 98 uses to support CD-ROMs. These drivers enable the operating system to detect the insertion of a disk into the drive. Real-mode drivers loaded from the CONFIG.SYS file do not have this capability.

When Windows 98 detects that you have inserted a disk into the CD-ROM drive, it mounts the disk in the file system and searches for a file called AUTORUN.INF in the root directory. This file specifies the program to be launched and the icon to be used to represent the program in Windows. A typical AUTORUN.INF file looks like this:

```
[autorun]
open=filename.exe
icon=filename.ico
```

The open= directive specifies an executable file on the CD-ROM, and the icon= directive specifies an icon file.

In your working environment, you might find that the autoplay feature is more of an intrusion than a help. To disable this feature, open Device Manager's System Properties dialog box for your CD-ROM drive, click the Settings tab, and clear the Auto Insert Notification check box.

Running Software from a CD-ROM

In many cases, you can save disk space on your hard drives by running applications directly from a CD-ROM. Other applications, such as games and multimedia titles, require that you do this. Some applications, such as Microsoft Office, have installation options that enable you to select how much of the software is copied to the hard disk and how much should be executed directly from the CD.

Running a program from a CD-ROM is always slower than running it from a hard disk, and you are, of course, limited to running a single application in this manner (unless your system has multiple CD-ROM drives). In some cases, however, the conservation of disk space is worth the delay. This is particularly true if an application enables you to control which software components run from the CD. For example, you might be able to install the core program files of a word processor to your hard disk but run less frequently used modules (such as the spell checker) from the CD-ROM.

Improving CD-ROM Performance

If your CD-ROM drive uses the EIDE interface, Windows 98 includes a feature that might be able to speed up your CD-ROM and overall system performance. In your drive's Properties dialog box in the System Control Panel, click the Settings tab and see if the DMA check box is available. If you can check this box and it remains checked after you reboot the system, you are using Windows 98's bus mastering IDE controller drivers.

Direct memory access (DMA), also called bus mastering, is a technique by which a device performs data transfers without utilizing the services of the main system processor. If you turn on this feature for your EIDE CD-ROM or hard disk drives, the system does not use any CPU time for drive access requests. While bus mastering may not produce a noticeable increase in the data transfer rate for the device, it can result in a general improvement in system performance because of the reduced load on the CPU. ●

P A R T

III

Working with Applications

CHAPTER 10

Installing and Managing Applications

by Bob Voss

In this chapter

Understanding How Windows Runs Applications

Windows applications fall into one of two general categories: 32-bit applications (designed for Windows NT, Windows 95, and Windows 98) and 16-bit applications (designed for Windows 3.x and lower versions). This chapter discusses how Windows 98 runs these programs. The last part of the chapter describes how to work with MS-DOS applications in Windows 98.

Support for 32-Bit Windows Applications

Many of the benefits of using Windows 98 result from its support of 32-bit applications. The following list outlines the benefits of Windows 98:

- Support for long filenames (up to 255 characters).

- Each 32-bit application runs in its own isolated memory space, which protects other applications and the operating system if an application crashes.

- Preemptive multitasking prevents a poorly written or "hung" application from locking up other applications and the operating system.

- Multithreading allows more efficient scheduling of CPU time.

▶ **See** "Working with Long Filenames," **p. 113**

Support for MS-DOS and 16-Bit Windows Applications

Windows 98 can run applications designed specifically for Windows 95 and Windows 98, as well as most older 16-bit Windows 3.x applications and MS-DOS-based applications. Windows 98 does not require the traditional CONFIG.SYS, AUTOEXEC.BAT, and INI files for configuration information. However, for backward compatibility, Windows 98 can use settings from INI files and can maintain its own versions of CONFIG.SYS and AUTOEXEC.BAT in order to support the loading of real-mode device drivers.

What the "Designed for Windows" Logo Really Means

The "Designed for Windows 95" logo program has evolved into the "Designed for Windows NT and Windows 98" logo program. In the early days of the Windows logo program, the requirements were relatively permissive, but the program has continually been reevaluated and revised. Microsoft has added many new requirements to better serve users who are looking for software that is designed to take full advantage of the Windows 98 and Windows NT operating environments and that is fully compatible with other Windows applications. To acquire the logo, an application must be submitted for testing by an independent third-party testing firm (VeriTest).

The basic concept behind the logo program is that it provides users with a means for selecting software that has been tested for compatibility and functionality on both the Windows 98 and Windows NT 5.0 platforms. The application must conform to a series of criteria to ensure that it takes full advantage of the Windows 98/Windows NT technology and that it is compatible with other Windows software. For in-depth information about and specifications for the logo program, and to download the "Designed for Windows Logo" handbook, visit the following web site:

`http://www.microsoft.com/windows/thirdparty/winlogo/`

> **CAUTION**
> Beware of software that claims to be "Windows-compatible" and that displays a logo to this effect. Be sure your applications have the genuine "Designed for Windows NT and Windows 98" logo.

Installing Windows Applications

Most Windows 98 (and Windows 95) applications can be installed easily using the setup programs that come with them. Installing MS-DOS-based applications is a different matter, however, and is often not as simple. That topic is covered in the later section "Working with MS-DOS Applications."

▶ **See** "Adding and Removing Programs in the Start Menu," **p. 436**

Part
III

Ch
10

Installing Windows 95 and Windows 98 Applications

The basic technique for installing Windows 95 and Windows 98 applications consists of running the Setup (or Install) program for the application and following the prompts. The Setup program takes care of all the details of installing the application. You can start the Setup program by using the Run command on the Start menu.

Another way to install an application is to use the Install Programs Wizard, which is accessible via the Add/Remove Programs icon in the Control Panel. The Add/Remove Programs dialog box provides a common starting point for adding and removing Windows applications and Windows system components and accessories.

To use the Install Programs Wizard to install a Windows application, follow these steps:

1. Open the Start menu and choose Settings, Control Panel.
2. In the Control Panel window, click the Add/Remove Programs icon to open the Add/Remove Programs Properties sheet, shown in Figure 10.1.
3. Choose Install to start the Install Program Wizard.
4. When the Install Program from Floppy Disk or CD-ROM dialog box appears, insert the first floppy disk or compact disc in the appropriate drive and choose Next.

   The wizard searches the disk's root directory for an installation program (usually named SETUP.EXE or INSTALL.EXE) and displays the command line in the Run Installation Program dialog box.
5. If the wizard fails to find the setup program (perhaps because it is in a subdirectory) or if you want to run a different setup program (perhaps from a network drive), you can choose Browse and select a different file in the Browse dialog box. Choose Open to insert the selected filename in the wizard.

FIG. 10.1
Use the Add/Remove
Programs Properties
dialog box to add and
remove applications.

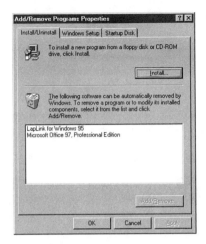

6. When the correct command line for the setup program appears in the Run Installation
   Program dialog box, choose Finish to start the setup program and begin the application
   installation.

Installing 16-Bit Windows Applications

Windows 98 features full backward compatibility with 16-bit Windows 3.x applications, enabling
you to install and use them in Windows 98 without modification.

If you encounter a compatibility problem when trying to run a legacy application (an older
application designed for a previous version of MS-DOS or Windows) in Windows 98, check
with the application's developer for a patch or workaround for the problem. In some cases, the
only solution is to upgrade to a newer Windows 95 or Windows 98 version of the application.

You install 16-bit Windows 3.x applications in Windows 98 the same way you install them in
Windows 3.x. You simply insert the first disk of the program's installation disks in your floppy
disk or CD-ROM drive, run the Setup program by using the Run command on the Start menu,
and then follow the prompts and instructions.

CAUTION

Save a copy of your AUTOEXEC.BAT and CONFIG.SYS files before you install any new MS-DOS or Windows
3.x application. After you install a Windows 3.x or MS-DOS application, it is a good idea to check your
AUTOEXEC.BAT files to see if any unnecessary programs or configuration lines were added. For example,
some applications add a line that loads SHARE.EXE or SMARTDRV.EXE, neither of which is needed in
Windows 98. Not only do these programs waste memory, but you might have problems with your system if
they are loaded.

Of course, the setup program for a legacy application will be tailored to Windows 3.x instead of Windows 98. For example, the installation program will probably offer to create Program Manager groups and update INI files. Windows 98 intercepts Program Manager updates and automatically converts them to Start menu shortcuts. Windows 98 also transfers WIN.INI and SYSTEM.INI entries into the Registry.

What If There Is No Setup Program?

You might occasionally encounter a Windows application that does not include a setup program. Installation for small utilities, for example, usually consists of copying a couple of files to your hard drive and adding a shortcut to your Start menu to launch the application. You'll probably find instructions for installing such applications in an accompanying manual or README file.

Organizing the Programs Menu

When you install an application, the installation process creates a new item on the Programs menu. Although this item appears automatically, you can modify it. For example, items on the Programs menu can be removed, rearranged, or renamed. While you can modify the Programs menu using the same procedure you do to customize the Start menu (described in Chapter 17, "System Information Utility"), you will have greater flexibility if you use the technique described here to directly modify the folders and shortcuts on which the Programs menu is based.

The Programs menu reflects the contents of a Programs folder. You can find this folder under Windows\Start Menu if you are the only person using the computer or if everyone who uses your computer shares the same Start menu and program groups. If the computer has multiple user profiles and the individual users do not share the same Start menu and program groups, the appropriate Programs folder for a specific user is found under Windows\Profiles\ *username*\Start Menu.

A simple way to make sure you are modifying the correct Programs menu is to log in to Windows with the user name whose Programs menu you want to change. Right-click in the gray area of the taskbar and choose Properties. Select the Start Menu Programs tab, and then click the Advanced button. This displays an Explorer window that is restricted to the appropriate Start menu. You can modify and reorganize the Start menu or Programs menu items by modifying folders and shortcuts in this Explorer window.

To work on just the Programs menu, open and select the Programs folder in the left Explorer pane. The folder hierarchy and shortcut names you see displayed in the right pane are those that make up the Programs menu. Use normal Explorer techniques to modify the folders and files in the right pane, and your changes will then be reflected in the Programs menu.

You can create new submenus under the Programs menu by creating new folders in the right pane. Drag and drop program shortcuts into these folders to organize them. Delete folders you do not want, but make sure you first remove shortcut icons you want to retain.

Windows sorts the folder and shortcut names in alphanumeric order and displays them on the Programs menu accordingly. You can reorder files and folders by renaming them. To change the name of an item on the Programs menu, select the folder or file, press F2, and then edit the existing name or type a new one. To reorganize the Programs menu, change the names to achieve the sort order you want. For example, if you want Microsoft Word to appear in the menu before Microsoft Excel and you want their names shortened, change the shortcut names to *1 Word* and *2 Excel*. You can also start shortcut names with special characters such as !, _, and $, which are listed before shortcuts that start with a letter or a number.

Configuring Windows 98 for Unique User Desktops

If you have multiple users on the same Windows 98 computer, you can configure it so that each user has his or her own unique desktop. To see if all users on your computer share the same Start menu and program groups, you set up user profiles. Follow these steps:

1. Open the Control Panel and click on the Passwords icon.

2. In the Passwords Properties dialog box, select the User Profiles tab (see Figure 10.2).

3. Look in the User profile settings area. If the option labeled Include Start menu and Program groups in user settings is selected, each user on your computer has his or her own selection of program group icons. Note that this option is available only if you first select the option button at the top of the dialog box labeled Users can customize their preferences and desktop settings.

FIG. 10.2
You configure Windows 98 for unique user desktops by setting up user profiles.

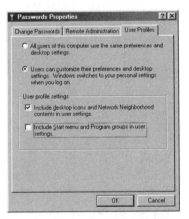

Working with Program Shortcuts

In Chapter 6, "Managing Files with My Computer and the Windows Explorer," you learned how to create shortcuts to your files and programs. In this section, you'll learn some more advanced techniques for working with shortcuts.

Starting Programs on Startup

If you routinely keep certain programs open because you use them throughout the day, you can have Windows 98 start those programs automatically when you start Windows. To do this, you simply create a shortcut for the program in a special folder call the StartUp folder. The StartUp folder is located in the Programs folder on the Start menu.

To create a shortcut for a program in the StartUp folder, follow these steps:

1. Open the Start menu and choose <u>S</u>ettings and then <u>T</u>askbar & Start Menu.

2. Select the Start Menu Programs tab.

3. Choose <u>A</u>dd, and then click B<u>r</u>owse.

4. In the Browse dialog box (see Figure 10.3), locate the program you want to add to the StartUp folder. Select the program and choose <u>O</u>pen (or double-click the program).

Part

III

Ch

10

FIG. 10.3
Use the Browse dialog box to locate the program that you want to add to the StartUp folder.

5. You're returned to the Create Shortcut dialog box, where the pathname for the selected program appears in the <u>C</u>ommand Line text box. Click Next.

6. Select the StartUp folder in the Select Program Folder dialog box (see Figure 10.4).

FIG. 10.4
Select the StartUp folder as the destination for the shortcut.

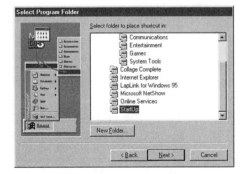

7. In the text box, type the name you want to appear in the StartUp menu. Then choose Finish.

8. Click OK to close the Taskbar Properties dialog box.

Now, whenever you start Windows, any application(s) you added to the StartUp menu will be started automatically.

Specifying How a Shortcut Starts a Program

Once you have created a shortcut for an application, you can customize the shortcut using its properties sheet. For example, if you create a shortcut for an application in the StartUp folder (as just described), you can specify whether the application is started in a normal window, in a maximized window, or minimized as an icon on the taskbar. You can also add command-line parameters to the command line for the application, specify a folder for the application to start in, and assign a shortcut key with which you can start the application from the keyboard.

To customize a shortcut, follow these steps:

1. Open My Computer or Windows Explorer and locate the shortcut.

2. Right-click the shortcut and choose Properties from the shortcut menu.

3. Select the Shortcut tab (see Figure 10.5).

FIG. 10.5
You can customize a shortcut using the Short-cut tab in the shortcut's properties sheet.

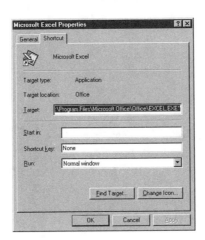

4. To add a parameter to a command line, click in the Target text box, press End to move to the end of the command line, and enter a space. Then type in the command-line param-eter you want to add.

   For example, to start an application and open a document within that application, type the path and filename for the document you want to open at the end of the application's command line (as shown in Figure 10.6).

5. In the Start in text box, specify a folder for the application to start from. With some applications, you need to start the application in a folder that contains files related to the application.

6. In the Shortcut key text box, assign a keyboard shortcut for starting the application. Keyboard shortcuts use a combination of Ctrl+Alt+*character*. You cannot use the Esc, Enter, Tab, Spacebar, Print Screen, or Backspace keys.

FIG. 10.6

You can add command-
line parameters to the
command line for an
application's shortcut.

N O T E Shortcut keys defined in a Windows application take precedence over shortcut keys
defined for a shortcut. Be sure to use a unique keyboard shortcut.

7. Specify whether you want the application to run in a normal window, in a maximized
   window, or minimized as an icon.

8. Click OK.

Managing File Associations

Recall that in Windows 3.x you could associate a file extension with an application. For
example, you could associate the DOC extension (which Microsoft Word adds to files) to
Word so that when you chose a file with the DOC extension, the file would be opened in Word.

In Windows 98, you can define a *file type*, which is associated with a file extension, and then
associate any number of *actions* with the file type. Again using Word as an example, you can
define the Microsoft Word Document file type and then define one or more actions associated
with that file type. The default action can be executed by choosing a file with a DOC extension
in Windows Explorer or in a folder window or by right-clicking a DOC file and choosing the
default action from the top of the shortcut menu that appears.

Other actions that you define and associate with a file type will also appear in the shortcut
menu when you right-click a file of that type. When Microsoft Word for Windows is installed,
for example, the Print command is automatically associated with the Word Document file type,
so you can right-click a Word file and choose Print from the shortcut menu. The document will
be opened in Word and printed, and then the document and Word will be closed.

How Applications Register File Types

All file types and their actions are registered in the HKEY_CLASSES_ROOT key of the Windows Registry. If you are experienced at working in the Registry using REGEDIT, you can add
and edit file types directly in the Registry.

CAUTION

Use extreme caution when directly modifying the Windows Registry. Make sure you carefully back up the Windows Registry before you begin and that you know what you are doing.

▶ **See** "Understanding the Windows Registry," **p. 354**

Registering a New File Type

Many applications automatically register a file type when you install the application. In some cases, however, you might want to register a file type for an extension that is not already associated with an application.

To register a new file type, follow these steps:

1. In the Explorer, choose <u>V</u>iew, Folder <u>O</u>ptions.

2. Click the File Types tab of the Options dialog box (see Figure 10.7).

FIG. 10.7

Register and modify file types on the File Types tab of the Options dialog box.

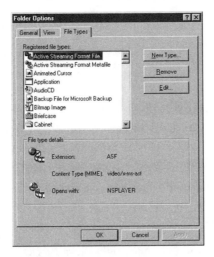

3. Click the <u>N</u>ew Type button.

4. Enter a description of the file type in the <u>D</u>escription of type text box. This description will appear in the Registered file <u>t</u>ypes list on the File Types tab of the Options dialog box. For example, if you want to be able to use Microsoft Word to open WordPerfect files, which use the extension WPD, you could use the description WordPerfect Document, as shown in Figure 10.8.

5. Enter the file extension to be associated with this file type in the Asso<u>c</u>iated extension text box. This is the three-letter file extension associated with MS-DOS-based files. In this example, you would enter WPD.

FIG. 10.8

Enter the information for a new file type in the Add New File Type dialog box.

6. Select the type of file from the Content Type (MIME) list. This list shows all the installed applications in the Registry.

7. If you want to specify an action to be performed on this file type by its associated program, or if you want to add a shortcut menu item for this file type, skip step 8 and continue with the next procedure to specify an action.

8. Click OK twice.

N O T E MIME (Multipurpose Internet Mail Extensions) is a standard for defining different types of file attachments for email delivered over the Internet. The goal of MIME is to allow multiple types of data, such as text, video and audio files, and application files, to be gathered into an email message and transferred successfully from sender to recipient, even if those two people are using different email applications. ■

You can specify the action that will occur when a file of a particular file type is chosen. The action you specify will also appear as an item on the file type's shortcut menu and on the File menu when that file is selected. This procedure begins with either the Add New File Type or Edit File Type dialog box open. To create actions for a new file type, follow the preceding procedure through step 7 and then continue with this procedure. To edit an existing file type, select the file type from the Registered file types list and click Edit.

To simultaneously specify actions for the file type and create shortcut menu items, follow this procedure:

1. In the New Action dialog box, click New to add a new action to the file type. (The action is actually a custom command that appears on the shortcut menu when you right-click the file.)

2. Type an action, such as **Open in Word**, in the Actions text box. What you type will appear as an item on the shortcut menu for this file type. You can type anything, but commands usually start with a verb. If you want the command to have an accelerator key, precede that letter with an ampersand (&).

Part

III

Ch

10

3. In the Application used to perform action text box, enter or select the application to be used to perform the action. If you do not know the application's path, use the Browse button to select the application. Figure 10.9 shows the completed New Action dialog box.

N O T E Some applications have command-line switches you can append to the end of the command line to control how the application behaves. See the documentation or online Help for your application to find out what command-line switches are available. ▣

FIG. 10.9
Designate a shortcut menu action and the program used to perform that action in the New Action dialog box.

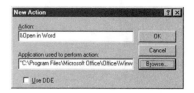

4. Select the Use DDE check box if the program uses DDE (Dynamic Data Exchange), and then add the DDE statements for this action. (This is rarely used.)

 T I P See the next section for more information on using DDE statements to communicate with an application.

5. Click OK.

6. If more than one action is listed in the Actions box, select the one you want to be the default action and click the Set Default button. (The default action is the one that is automatically performed when you choose a file of this type in Explorer or a folder window.)

7. Select the check boxes for any or all of the following options you want enabled for this file type:

    Enable Quick View. Quick View allows you to view a file without opening it

    Always Show Extension. Always displays the MS-DOS extension, even when the Hide File Extension option has been enabled.

    Confirm Open After Download. Instructs Windows to request confirmation before opening files after downloading them from the Internet.

8. Click Close twice.

▶ **See** "Previewing a Document with Quick View," **p. 93**

Understanding DDE Settings

If the application you use to create a file type and define an action uses DDE (Dynamic Data Exchange), you can use DDE statements to exercise more control over the actions that are carried out by the application. DDE statements are messages that are passed to the application to tell it what actions to carry out.

Figure 10.10 illustrates the use of DDE statements in the definition of the Print action for the Microsoft Excel Worksheet type. The first DDE statement (in the DDE Message text box) is the command passed to Microsoft Excel to specify what action the program should take when the Print command is selected from the shortcut menu for an Excel worksheet:

```
[open("%1")][print()][close()]
```

This DDE statement tells Excel to open the selected file, print the file with the default print options, and close the worksheet.

FIG. 10.10

You can use DDE statements to control the actions associated with a registered file type.

The entry in the Application box is the string used to start a DDE exchange with the specified program. If this box is left empty, the command that appears in the Application used to perform action text box is used.

The following DDE statement appears in the DDE Application Not Running box:

```
[open("%1")][print()][quit()]
```

This statement starts Excel, prints the selected file, and then exits Excel.

These two simple examples illustrate how useful the DDE statements can be. By specifying two different statements in the DDE Message and DDE Applications Not Running boxes, you can control how Excel will react when you select the Print command from the shortcut menu. If Excel is already open, the file you select is opened in that session of Excel (that is, another session of Excel is not started), the file is printed, and then the file is closed. The running session of Excel is not terminated. On the other hand, when Excel is not already open and you select the Print command, Excel is started, the selected file is opened and printed, and then Excel is shut down.

Changing the Icon for a File Type or Other Object

You can change the icon used to designate a file type, drive, folder, or other object on your computer. To change the icon used for a particular file type or object, follow these steps:

1. In the Explorer, choose View, Folder Options.

2. Choose the File Types tab to display the File Types page of the Options dialog box (refer to Figure 10.7).

3. In the Registered file types list, select the file type or other object whose icon you want to change.

4. Choose the Edit button.

5. Choose the Change Icon button to display the Change Icon dialog box, shown in Figure 10.11.

6. Select a new icon from the Current icon scrolling list.

   The name of the file containing the icons currently shown is listed in the File name text box. You can use the Browse button to search for a new file containing different icons. Figure 10.11 shows the selection of icons in the Moricons.dll file, which is located in the Windows folder on your hard drive.

7. Click OK and then click Close two times.

FIG. 10.11
Use the Change Icon dialog box to select a new icon for a file type or other type of object.

Working with MS-DOS Applications

Although Windows 98 is designed to shield the user from the often-confusing world of the command line, AUTOEXEC.BAT, CONFIG.SYS, and memory-management practices, it offers surprisingly rich support for users who still desire or need to work in the MS-DOS environment. Windows 98 offers extensive control over MS-DOS application environments, allowing you to fine-tune your MS-DOS sessions to optimize performance.

Many MS-DOS applications will run under Windows 98 without any modifications. In some cases, you will need to modify the setup for the application for it to run in Windows. For applications that won't run at all under Windows 98, a special mode helps you run them quickly and easily from within Windows and then automatically returns you to your Windows session when you're finished.

Installing and Uninstalling MS-DOS Applications

Installing MS-DOS applications is a straightforward procedure. Simply locate and run the installation program for the application. The installation program creates a folder for the application and copies the files to it. In addition, it performs the additional operating system configuration chores that may be necessary for successful operation. You might have to handle some of the steps yourself. In the program folder, look for the documentation file that details the manual program installation process. Often this is a simple text file labeled README.TXT or INSTALL.TXT.

You can also run the installation program for an MS-DOS application from the MS-DOS prompt. Running the installation program from an MS-DOS prompt is just like doing so on a machine that's running only MS-DOS. Follow these steps to begin:

1. Open a new MS-DOS session from the Start menu.

2. At the MS-DOS prompt, enter the command to start the installation program (for example, **a:\install.exe**) and press Enter.

3. When the installation program finishes, close the MS-DOS session manually or run the application if you want.

Some MS-DOS applications don't have installation programs at all. This is most common with shareware applications or small utility programs.

To install your application manually, follow these simple steps:

1. Open a new MS-DOS session from the Start menu.

2. At the MS-DOS prompt, enter the command to create a folder for your program (such as **md c:\myprog**) and press Enter.

3. Enter the command to copy the program to the new folder, such as **xcopy a:*.* c:\myprog**. MS-DOS copies the files to the new folder.

N O T E If the files that you want to copy to the new folder include any subfolders, you must use the following command, or the subfolders will not be copied:

xcopy a:*. c:\myprog /s*

The /s option for the xcopy program causes subfolders to be copied. ▨

You might need to alter the preceding routine slightly if your application comes as a compressed archive (such as a ZIP or an ARJ file). Usually all this means is an additional step for decompression after the files are copied.

Configuring Your MS-DOS Application

Your MS-DOS applications are very likely to run fine without any reconfiguration. Preset configurations for the most popular MS-DOS applications are stored in Windows, and in many cases, these configurations will work perfectly. However, in those cases where your application doesn't run properly (or at all), you can modify many settings using the properties sheet to control how your MS-DOS application runs. To display the properties sheet, click the Properties button in the toolbar of the MS-DOS window. The next sections provide details on the tabs of this properties sheet.

Part
III

Ch
10

General Properties   The General properties page is primarily informational, with minimal controls other than file attributes (see Figure 10.12).

FIG. 10.12
The General properties page gives you most of the basic information about the file and easy access to control of the file attributes. Context-sensitive help on any of the properties pages is available at any time by clicking the ? button.

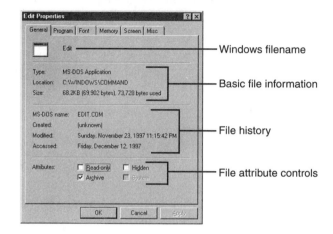

Windows filename

Basic file information

File history

File attribute controls

The only real controls in the General properties page are the file attribute settings. These are used mainly to protect documents (by setting the read-only attribute), and you shouldn't alter them unless you have a specific reason.

Program Properties   The Program properties page gives you control over the basic environment your application starts with (see Figure 10.13).

FIG. 10.13
The Program properties page allows you to alter the variables used to name and start the application.

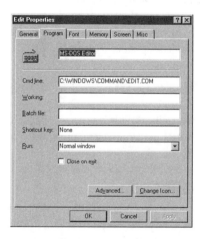

You can click the Advanced button on the Program properties page to open the Advanced Program Settings dialog box, shown in Figure 10.14.

FIG. 10.14
The Advanced Program Settings dialog box enables you to define the precise mode and environment for your MS-DOS session.

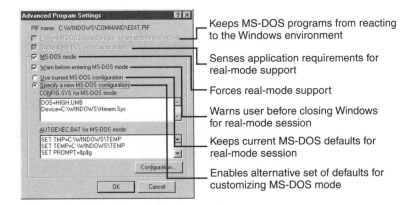

Keeps MS-DOS programs from reacting to the Windows environment

Senses application requirements for real-mode support

Forces real-mode support

Warns user before closing Windows for real-mode session

Keeps current MS-DOS defaults for real-mode session

Enables alternative set of defaults for customizing MS-DOS mode

If you need to run your application in MS-DOS mode, you enable it here. You can even set up custom CONFIG.SYS and AUTOEXEC.BAT values for your session. If you click Specify a new MS-DOS configuration, you can edit the special CONFIG.SYS and AUTOEXEC.BAT values right in this dialog box.

If you click the Configuration button, you see the dialog box shown in Figure 10.15.

FIG. 10.15
The Select MS-DOS Configuration Options dialog box lets you control expanded memory, disk caching, disk access, and command-line editing.

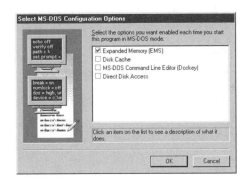

You should not alter any of the settings in the Advanced dialog box unless your MS-DOS application simply won't run in a standard session with the default settings. For that matter, don't even enable MS-DOS mode unless your application demands it.

▶ **See** "Using MS-DOS Mode," **p. 190**

Font Properties   The Font an file attributes (see Figure 10.16). It works just like the Font list control on the MS-DOS session toolbar.

Memory Properties   The Memory properties page makes simple work of the traditional maze of MS-DOS memory management (see Figure 10.17). With a few mouse clicks, you can configure your application memory precisely as needed.

FIG. 10.16
The Font properties page lets you choose the font type and size, and it gives you both a window and font preview.

FIG. 10.17
The Memory properties page vastly simplifies the formerly arcane topic of memory management.

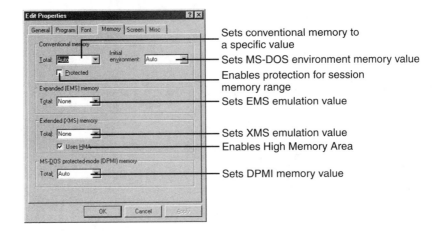

Sets conventional memory to a specific value

Sets MS-DOS environment memory value

Enables protection for session memory range

Sets EMS emulation value

Sets XMS emulation value

Enables High Memory Area

Sets DPMI memory value

If your application works without your altering these values, *do not change them.* If your application doesn't work with the default settings, first consult the documentation for your application to determine what the appropriate settings are. *Then* you can alter the values in this dialog box. Proceeding in any other way—unless you have considerable experience with the techniques involved—can severely inhibit the performance of your system.

Screen Properties   The Screen properties page lets you control the appearance of the MS-DOS session (see Figure 10.18).

You might find that certain MS-DOS programs (especially those running in Graphics mode) respond poorly to the video emulation used in the windowed mode. If so, try defeating the performance defaults by clearing the Fast ROM e̲mulation and Dynamic m̲emory allocation options. Fast ROM e̲mulation tells the Windows 98 display driver to mimic the video hardware to help display MS-DOS programs faster. Dynamic m̲emory allocation releases display memory to other programs when the MS-DOS session isn't using it. If you experience strange display problems with your MS-DOS programs, try changing these settings. You can also solve poor graphics performance by executing the poorly behaving MS-DOS application in full-screen mode.

FIG. 10.18

The Screen properties page gives you control of the size, type, and performance of the MS-DOS interface.

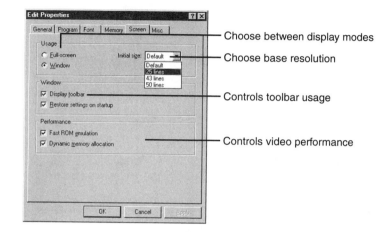

Choose between display modes

Choose base resolution

Controls toolbar usage

Controls video performance

Part
III

Ch
10

N O T E When an MS-DOS application is open, you can rapidly toggle it between full-screen and window operation by pressing Alt+Enter. ■

Miscellaneous Properties   The Misc properties page covers the remaining configuration items that don't fit under the other categories (see Figure 10.19).

FIG. 10.19

The Misc properties page controls screen saver, mouse, background operation, program termination, shortcut key, and editing options.

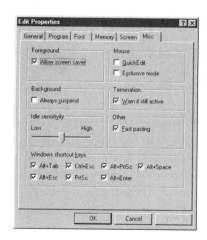

This properties page offers the following controls:

- *Allow screen saver* lets your default Windows screen saver operate even if your MS-DOS session has the foreground.

- *Always suspend* freezes your MS-DOS application when you bring another application (whether it's MS-DOS or Windows) to the foreground. If you have an application that must perform time-sensitive operations (such as a communications program), be sure to disable this option.

- *Idle sensitivity* tells your MS-DOS program to yield the system to other applications if it really isn't doing anything important. A word processor, for example, won't have a problem letting go of the system clock when you're not using it; you can set its idle sensitivity to High. A communications program, however, might need to respond quickly, so you want to set its idle sensitivity to Low.

- The *Mouse* controls enable QuickEdit mode (letting you mark text using just the mouse) and Exclusive mode (in which the MS-DOS application has control of the mouse cursor when the application is in the foreground, even if you try to move the mouse out of the MS-DOS window).

- The *Warn if still active* item in the Termination box tells Windows to notify you before the MS-DOS session is closed. It's really best to leave this enabled, unless you are absolutely certain that the MS-DOS program will never, ever have open data files when you close it.

- The *Fast pasting* setting simply tells Windows that your MS-DOS program can handle a raw data stream dump from the Windows Clipboard. Some MS-DOS programs clog at full speed, so if you find that when you paste to your MS-DOS application you consistently lose characters, turn this one off.

- *Windows shortcut keys* allows you to override the standard quick navigation aids built into the Windows environment, just for your MS-DOS session. (Some MS-DOS programs think they can get away with using the same keys, and something has to give—Windows!). By default, Windows "owns" these shortcuts, but you can lend them to your MS-DOS application by clearing this option.

Using MS-DOS Mode

Although you will be able to run most MS-DOS applications without any difficulty from within Windows, you might run into problems with certain poorly designed MS-DOS applications that demand total control over system resources and that access hardware directly.

Windows 98 accommodates a poorly behaved application to the best of its ability via *MS-DOS mode*. This mode is the equivalent of the Real mode that is present in older versions of Windows, but it does offer some improvements.

MS-DOS mode works by giving the errant MS-DOS application the entire system for the duration of the session. Windows removes itself from memory, leaving only a small "stub" loader in preparation for when regaining control of your system.

Before you decide to enable MS-DOS mode for an application, try these other options:

■ Confirm that you've optimized the MS-DOS session settings for that application. Check the program's documentation for special memory requirements or other unusual needs. You might be able to adjust Windows' MS-DOS support to make the application work in a standard MS-DOS session.

■ Try running the application in full-screen mode (which you switch to by pressing Alt+Enter).

If either of the preceding methods works, you will have a faster, more convenient alternative that allows you the full benefit of Windows' multitasking and other features—all of which disappear during an MS-DOS mode session.

Whenever possible, Windows 98 determines that an application needs to run in MS-DOS mode and closes down all other applications and switches to this mode automatically. Unless you specify otherwise, you'll be warned when Windows is about to switch to MS-DOS mode.

If you try to run an application that gives you an error message telling you that you can't run it in Windows, you should manually configure the application to run in MS-DOS mode. Follow these steps:

1. If you haven't created a shortcut for the application, create one now. You can only modify the settings of an MS-DOS application using a shortcut.
2. Right-click the shortcut for the application and choose Properties.
3. Select the Program tab, and then click Advanced to display the Advanced Program Settings dialog box.
4. Select the Prevent MS-DOS-Based Programs from Detecting Windows option.
5. Click OK.

Click the shortcut icon to try running the application. If the application still doesn't run, follow these steps:

1. Open the Advanced Program Settings dialog box, as described in steps 2 and 3 of the preceding procedure.
2. Select the MS-DOS Mode option.
3. Click OK.

Try running the application again. If it still doesn't run, you have to modify the configuration for MS-DOS mode. To do so, follow these steps:

1. Open the Advanced Program Settings dialog box.
2. Select the Specify a New MS-DOS Configuration option. The dialog box shown in Figure 10.20 appears. In this dialog box, you can override the default settings for the MS-DOS mode session.
3. In the CONFIG.SYS for MS-DOS mode and AUTOEXEC.BAT for MS-DOS mode windows, modify the lines as needed to allow this application to run.

FIG. 10.20
Windows allows you to override the default settings for MS-DOS mode support. You can even run a different CONFIG.SYS and AUTOEXEC.BAT file for each application.

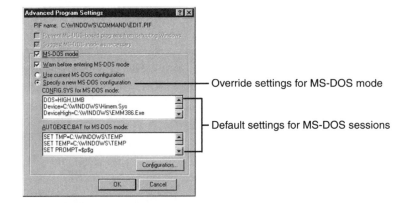

— Override settings for MS-DOS mode

— Default settings for MS-DOS sessions

The changes you make here affect only this application. In this way, you can individually customize each application that must run in MS-DOS mode.

4. If necessary, click the Configuration button. Then select from the options in the Select MS-DOS Configuration Options dialog box and click OK. Be aware, however, that when you choose from among the options in this dialog box, you remove the entries that already appear in the CONFIG.SYS and AUTOEXEC.BAT text boxes.

CAUTION
Use the Direct Disk Access option with great care. It is possible for an MS-DOS application to destroy long filename support when you select this option.

5. Click OK twice to close the dialog boxes.

Removing Applications

When you install a Windows application, not only does the installation program copy the application's files into its own folder, but in most cases it copies numerous other support files into the Windows folder and modifies the Windows Registry file. For this reason, uninstalling an application can be a complex procedure. Fortunately, many application setup programs now offer an uninstall option to automate the process in case you need to remove the application from your system. The Add/Remove Programs properties sheet has an uninstall feature that can help with this process.

Uninstalling Applications Automatically

To uninstall an application automatically, start by opening the Control Panel and choosing the Add/Remove Programs icon to open the Add/Remove Programs Properties sheet—the same sheet you used to install the application (see Figure 10.21). Only applications that provide uninstall programs specifically designed to work with Windows 98 appear in the list of applications that Windows 98 can remove automatically.

FIG. 10.21

From the Add/Remove Programs Properties sheet, you can remove applications as well as install them.

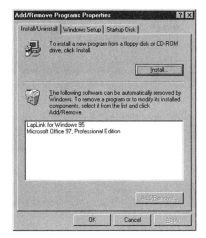

To remove an application, select it from the list of applications in the lower portion of the dialog box and choose Add/Remove. After you confirm that you want to remove the program, Windows runs the selected application's uninstall program.

Removing MS-DOS Applications

If you decide to remove an MS-DOS application from your computer, follow these steps:

1. Locate the application folder in Windows Explorer or My Computer.
2. Check to make sure there are no data files (or subfolders) in the folder.
3. Drag the folder to the Recycle Bin icon or press Delete, and then choose Yes.

▶ **See** "Deleting Files and Folders," **p. 91**

CHAPTER 11

Sharing Data Between Applications

by Bob Voss and Keith Underdahl

In this chapter

Understanding the Data-Sharing Capabilities of Windows 98

Windows 98 enables you to share data between different applications in a variety of ways. These range from simple cut-and-paste operations to advanced linking and embedding of various objects. Which method you use will depend not only on your specific needs at the time, but also on the applications you are using.

Compound Documents and the Windows Clipboard

The simplest level of data sharing is done using cut-and-paste or copy-and-paste. When you select a piece of data such as text or an image and use an <u>E</u>dit, Cu<u>t</u> or <u>E</u>dit, <u>C</u>opy menu command, the object is placed in an area of Windows called the Clipboard. It can then be pasted into virtually any applet or application. In theory, this is like using scissors and glue to paste together a school newspaper or a Mother's Day card.

The Clipboard's strength lies in its versatility. It handles any kind of data that Windows can interpret, which can then be pasted into various types of documents. This allows the creation of *compound documents*, which can hold text, pictures, spreadsheet data, and more (see Figure 11.1). Of course, you need to keep in mind that although the Clipboard can hold many kinds of data, not all data can be pasted into all applications. For instance, you cannot paste an image into a Notepad document because Notepad won't support it. And while text can usually be pasted anywhere, you might lose some formatting (bold, superscript, and so on) in the pasting process.

FIG. 11.1

This compound document contains several different kinds of data.

A potential drawback, however, is that all applications might not be able to edit all types of data. For instance, suppose you have pasted a picture into a word processing document. Later you realize that you need to resize the picture, or perhaps you need to convert it from color to black and white. If the word processing program doesn't have image-editing capabilities (it probably doesn't), your only solution might be to manually remove the image and open it with another program that *can* edit it. And when you finished editing it, you would have to paste it back into the word processor, which might require repositioning text, moving things around, and so forth.

Understanding Object Linking and Embedding

As wonderful as the Windows Clipboard is, it still presents certain limitations. What if you want to create a document containing two types of data that change frequently? Enter *Dynamic Data Exchange* (DDE), a protocol developed by Microsoft many years ago to address this problem. This allows the data object to be accessible to the program it was created in (the *server* application), as well as to many other programs (*client* applications) at the same time.

For instance, suppose you are responsible for publishing a monthly training report for your company. You might track training hours for each employee using an Excel worksheet (see Figure 11.2), but you need to use this data in the monthly report that you publish with a word processor.

Part
III

Ch
11

FIG. 11.2

This worksheet tracks data that must be input into the monthly training report.

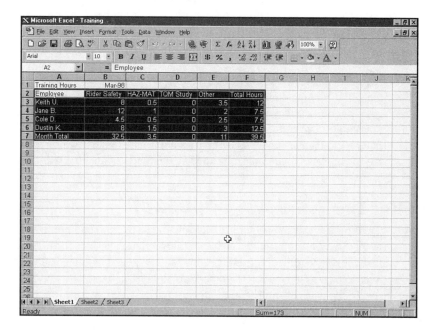

In the published report, most of the text stays the same from month to month, and the only real changes occur in the actual training numbers. Thus, copying and pasting data from the worksheet would be inefficient, because you would have to re-paste the data every time you prepared the report. With the data sharing technology called *Object Linking and Embedding* (OLE), you can link the data to the other application for quick, efficient updating of the data.

An extension of the object linking concept is object embedding. Embedding allows you to edit a data object without leaving the client application. For example, suppose you want to edit an image you embedded into a word processing document. Clicking on the image enables you to use controls from Paint (or another image editor) to edit the object within the word processor.

OLE technology extends to Internet documents as well. To an ever-increasing extent, cybersurfers expect web content to be both interactive and up-to-the-minute. ActiveX controls, for instance, utilize the OLE concept to automate functions and link applications. This allows web sites to be truly interactive, as they ask for user input, launch browser plug-ins, and more. ActiveX controls are also used by the new Windows 98 Help system, which is HTML-based. This allows Windows Help to link with other applications to better illustrate its topics.

JavaScript or ActiveX?

JavaScript and VBScript (the scripting used to enable ActiveX controls) are different languages that serve the same purpose. JavaScript is similar to the programming language Java and is provided by Netscape. On the other hand, Microsoft has championed VBScript, an offshoot of its own Visual Basic.

Given this, you can easily surmise that JavaScript works better with Netscape Navigator, and VBScript works best with Internet Explorer. With the right plug-ins, however, a Netscape user can still take advantage of ActiveX controls. One such plug-in is ScriptActive from NCompass, which is available online at `http://www.ncompasslabs.com/`.

A good example of this might be a web site that provides information about your company, including current stock market and other financial information. If you created the web page by simply copying and pasting data from the Clipboard into the HTML document, the data would not remain current for very long (unless, of course, you are willing to sit in front of the computer and manually update it 24 hours a day!). The better solution is to implement an OLE-based control that automatically updates the market data on a regular basis.

Using the Windows Clipboard

The simplest way to exchange data from one location to another, whether it is within an application or between applications, is to use the Windows 98 Clipboard. The Clipboard is an application you use to temporarily store data that you are exchanging from one location to another. You *cut* or *copy* data to the Clipboard and then *paste* the data from the Clipboard into a document. The data remains in the Clipboard until you cut or copy new data to the Clipboard or remove it manually, so you can paste the data into a document as many times as you like.

Cutting, Copying, and Pasting Data

The most common method for transferring data using the Clipboard is to use the menu commands that are found in most Windows applications. The Cut, Copy, and Paste commands are usually found in the Edit menu. Note the distinction between cutting and copying. When you cut data from a document, that original data is *moved* to the Clipboard and no longer appears in its original location. When you copy data from a document, a copy of the data is placed on the Clipboard, and the original data remains intact where it was.

N O T E Remember, material remains on the Clipboard only until the next piece of data is placed there. If you have cut a piece of data and you plan to paste it somewhere, make sure you remember to paste it, or the data might be lost. You might be able to correct such an error with the Edit, Undo command in the application you cut it from. See "Saving the Contents of the Clipboard," later in this chapter, for more information. ▪

To cut or copy data from one location to another, follow these steps:

1. Select the data in the source document that you want to cut or copy to another document (or another location in the same document).

2. Choose Edit, Cut to cut (move) the data to the Clipboard.

   or

   Choose Edit, Copy to copy the data to the Clipboard.

   The data is placed in the Windows Clipboard. Normally the Clipboard is invisible, but you can view its contents by choosing Start, Programs, Accessories, System Tools, Clipboard Viewer. As you can see in Figure 11.3, the training data worksheet you saw in Figure 11.2 has been copied to the Clipboard and is ready to be pasted into the training report.

FIG. 11.3

An Excel worksheet has been copied to the Windows Clipboard.

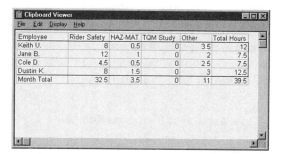

3. Place the insertion point at the point in the destination document where you want to paste the data.

   If you are working with a document in another application, open that application and the destination document and place the insertion point where you want the data.

4. Choose Edit, Paste or press Ctrl+V to paste the data from the Clipboard into the destination document. Figure 11.4 shows data from an Excel worksheet pasted into a Word document.

Many applications have Cut, Copy, and Paste buttons on a toolbar that you can use instead of the menu commands. Your application might also have shortcut menus that you can display by right-clicking the selected text. The shortcut menu has the Cut, Copy, and Paste commands.

FIG. 11.4
A data table from an
Excel worksheet has
been pasted into a Word
document.

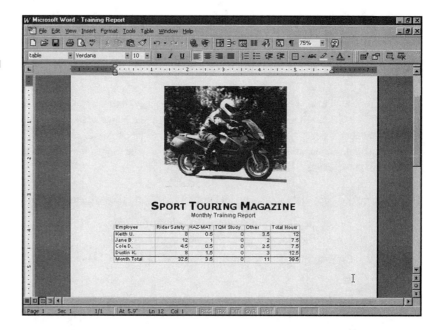

Using Keyboard Shortcuts

The mouse pointer was truly a revolution when it was first introduced to PCs nearly two decades ago. It makes the graphic user interface possible and has made computers more accessible to millions. However, some advanced users find that they can save some time by using keyboard shortcuts instead of the mouse for certain tasks.

Fortunately, some common keyboard shortcuts allow you to forgo the mouse at certain times. For our purposes here, the most important ones for you to know are the keyboard shortcuts for Cut, Copy, and Paste, which are listed in Table 11.1.

Table 11.1 Cut, Copy, and Paste Keyboard Shortcuts

Action	Shortcut Keys
Cut	Ctrl+X or Shift+Delete
Copy	Ctrl+C or Ctrl+Insert
Paste	Ctrl+V or Shift+Insert

You can use these in place of toolbar buttons or menu commands in virtually any Windows application. In fact, these shortcuts even work in applet windows and dialog boxes that don't have any buttons or menus. You can take better advantage of these keyboard shortcuts if you also know how to select objects using the keyboard. To select an area, move your cursor to the beginning of the data and press and hold the Shift key. Then use the arrow keys on the keyboard to extend the highlight to the end of the selection and release the Shift key.

 If you are using keyboard shortcuts to select text, try pressing Ctrl+Shift as you move the cursor. You'll notice that if you press the left or right arrow keys in combination with Ctrl+Shift, the cursor moves to the next word instead of just the next character. Press Ctrl+Shift+Up Arrow or Ctrl+Shift+Down Arrow to extend the highlight to the beginning or end of the current paragraph.

Using Drag and Drop to Copy Information

A second method for exchanging information is to use the mouse to drag and drop selected information, which can be text, graphics, or data, from one location to another. When you drag and drop information, the information is not stored in the Clipboard. The information is copied directly from one location to another. In this section, you learn how to drag and drop information within an application.

To use the drag-and-drop method, you must be working with an application that supports it. The applications in the Microsoft Office suite support it, for example, as does WordPad. Check the documentation or online Help for your application to find out if it supports drag and drop.

To copy information with drag and drop, follow these steps:

1. Open the application and then the document that contains the text you want to copy. Arrange the windows on your desktop so that you can see each one.

 If you have multiple displays enabled on your computer, open the applications so that each one is viewable on a separate monitor. You can then drag objects from one screen to another as if they were on one giant desktop.

2. Select the text you want to copy.
3. To *copy* the text, position the mouse pointer over the selected area and drag the text. The mouse pointer changes as you drag, and a plus sign (+) appears next to the pointer.
4. Drag the text to the position in the document where you want to place it. The vertical bar indicates the position of the new text.
5. Release the mouse button to complete the copy procedure, and the text appears in the new location.

Copying Information to a Dialog Box

Cutting, copying, and pasting information to and from dialog boxes can be tricky because there usually aren't toolbar buttons or menu commands for these procedures. Fortunately, you can easily use the keyboard shortcuts for cutting, copying, and pasting to a dialog box. For instance, suppose you are composing a web page and need to create a hyperlink. You can use your web browser to find the target web site, and then you can copy the URL from the Location box to the Clipboard. Then, when you create the hyperlink in your HTML editor, a dialog box asks you for an URL for the hyperlink (see Figure 11.5). Just press Tab to move the cursor to the correct text box and press Ctrl+V to paste in the URL.

To copy information into a dialog box, follow these steps:

1. Select the information that you want to copy into the dialog box.

2. Choose Edit, Copy or press Ctrl+C.

3. Open the dialog box into which you want to copy the information.

4. Place the insertion point in the text box into which you want to copy the data.

5. Press Ctrl+V to insert the text from the Clipboard. Figure 11.5 shows the Create Hyperlink dialog box in Microsoft FrontPage Express, in which a target URL has been pasted into the URL text box.

FIG. 11.5

Ctrl+V pastes the URL from the Clipboard into this dialog box.

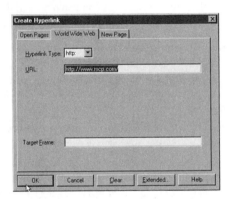

When you are in a dialog box, you can't use the Edit menu or the toolbar buttons, which is why you need to make use of the keyboard shortcuts. You can reverse the previous procedure to copy data from a dialog box into a document: Select the data in the dialog box, press Ctrl+C to copy it to the Clipboard, and then use the menu, keyboard, or toolbar technique to paste the information into a document.

Capturing Screens with the Clipboard

Windows has the built-in capability to capture screens. You won't have as many editing options as you would with many of the screen-capturing applications that are available. But if your needs are simple, you can use the Clipboard to capture an image of your screen. The captured image is stored in the Clipboard in bitmap format. To capture the entire screen and paste it into a document, follow these steps:

1. Set up the screen to appear as you want it in the screen image.

2. Press Print Screen to capture the entire screen using the screen resolution currently set for the display. The screen image is stored in the Clipboard.

To capture just the contents of the active window, press Alt+Print Screen or Shift+Print Screen, depending on your keyboard.

3. Open the document in which you want to insert the image and place the insertion point where you want the image to appear.

4. Choose <u>E</u>dit, <u>P</u>aste or press Ctrl+V. Windows 98 pastes the screen image into the document in bitmap format.

 TIP For best results, first paste the screen into an image editor, such as the Paint applet that accompanies Windows 98. You can use the editor to crop or touch up the image or to change some properties of the image before you paste it into your final document.

Viewing and Changing Clipboard Data

You can view the contents of the Clipboard using the Clipboard Viewer. To open the Clipboard Viewer, choose Start, <u>P</u>rograms, Accessories, System Tools, Clipboard Viewer. The last data that you cut or copied to the Clipboard appears in the Clipboard Viewer. If the Clipboard Viewer isn't listed in your System Tools menu, start the Add/Remove Programs utility from the Control Panel and install the Clipboard Viewer using the Windows Setup tab.

Controlling File Formats

The Clipboard viewer stores information in a variety of formats to help ensure compatibility over a wide array of applications. You can easily view the available formats for a given object by performing the following steps:

1. Open the Clipboard Viewer

2. On the menu bar, click <u>D</u>isplay. A menu appears, showing all available formats for the object currently in the Clipboard (see Figure 11.6).

3. To change the format of the object, make a selection from this menu.

FIG. 11.6
The Display menu lists the various formats that this object can be stored in.

Part
III
Ch
11

What formats are available will depend on the type of data that is currently in the Clipboard. The options shown in Figure 11.6 apply to most images, but text and other data types might offer many more options. The most common of these options include the following:

- *Text.* Displays the contents in unformatted text using the current Windows system font.
- *Rich Text Format.* Displays the contents in RTF (Rich Text Format). RTF retains character formatting, such as fonts and font styles.
- *Original Equipment Manufacturer Text.* Displays the contents in the unformatted OEM character set. You usually use this option when you copy text from the Clipboard to DOS applications.

If you paste an object into a document using the Paste Special command, you will see a dialog box similar to that shown in Figure 11.7. In this dialog box, you can make similar choices regarding the format of the object to be pasted, but notice that the choices are now more limited (namely, Palette is no longer available). This box lists only the formats compatible with the given application—not all formats available to the Clipboard. Before clicking OK, make sure the correct file format is selected. Otherwise, you might not be able to edit the embedded object using the techniques discussed later in this chapter.

FIG. 11.7

You might be able to choose formats in the Paste Special dialog box as well.

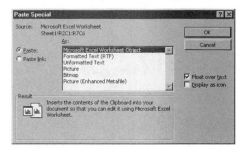

Saving the Contents of the Clipboard

Data you copy to the Clipboard is lost when you cut or copy new data or shut down Windows. If you want to reuse that data at a later time, you can save the contents of the Clipboard as a file. To save data that's in the Clipboard Viewer, follow these steps:

1. In the Clipboard Viewer, choose File, Save As to open the Save As dialog box.
2. Type a filename in the File Name text box (the Clipboard Viewer automatically appends the .CLP extension). By default, .CLP files are saved in the Windows folder of your hard drive.
3. Click OK.

To open a Clipboard file that you have saved, follow these steps:

1. In the Clipboard Viewer, choose File, Open to open the Open dialog box.
2. In the File Name list box, select the file you want to open. If necessary, select the file location from the Folders list box.
3. Click OK.

If you currently have something stored in the Clipboard, the Clear Clipboard message appears, asking if you want to clear the contents of the Clipboard. Choose <u>Y</u>es to replace the current contents with the data in the .CLP file. Choose <u>N</u>o if you don't want to clear the contents of the Clipboard.

N O T E Microsoft provides a number of useful tools in the Windows 98 Resource Kit, which is available for download from http://www.microsoft.com/. One of the tools in the kit is called ClipTray, which allows you to quickly view and edit Clipboard contents. When you install ClipTray, it adds an icon to the system tray next to the time. Click that icon to open ClipTray. ▒

Exchanging Data Between Windows and DOS

You are not limited to sharing data between Windows applications. If you are still using DOS applications in the Windows environment, you can exchange information, including text and graphics, using the Clipboard. You can transfer data from Windows to DOS, from DOS to Windows, and between DOS applications. You can even transfer text from the MS-DOS command prompt to a document.

To exchange data from a DOS application to a Windows application, follow these steps:

1. Open the DOS application. The DOS application should be in a window, not full-screen.
2. Open the Control menu of the DOS window and choose <u>E</u>dit, Mar<u>k</u>, or click the Mark button on the toolbar. A blinking cursor appears in the upper-left corner of the DOS window, indicating that you are in the marking mode.
3. Click in the location where you want to start marking, hold down the left mouse button, and drag a box around the text or graphics that you want to copy.

   or

   To mark the text using the keyboard, hold down the Shift key and use the arrow keys to mark the text.
4. Choose <u>E</u>dit, <u>C</u>opy, or press Enter, or click the Copy button on the toolbar. The selection is copied to the Clipboard.
5. Open the document in the Windows application in which you want to insert the Clipboard contents.
6. Place the insertion point where you want to insert the Clipboard contents.
7. Choose <u>E</u>dit, <u>P</u>aste, or press Ctrl+C, or click the Copy button on the toolbar.

Figure 11.8 shows a block of text selected in the MS-DOS Editor. In Figure 11.9, the selected text from the MS-DOS Editor document has been pasted into a Word document.

You can also copy data from a Windows application into a DOS application. However, any formatting that has been applied to the Windows data will be lost when it is pasted into the DOS application. Also, keep in mind that you will not be able to transfer some types of data (such as graphics) into MS-DOS applications.

Part
III

Ch
11

FIG. 11.8

You can mark text in a DOS application and copy it to the Clipboard using the commands on the Control menu or the tools on the toolbar.

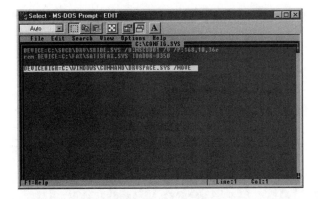

FIG. 11.9

This text has been copied from the MS-DOS Editor.

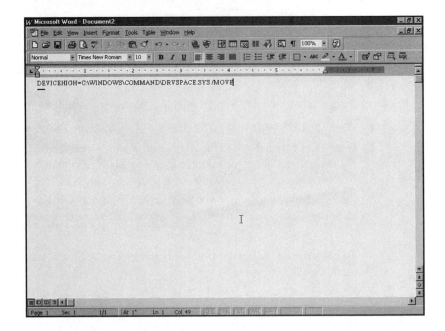

To copy data from a Windows application to a DOS application, follow these steps:

1. In the Windows application, open the document that contains the information you want to copy.

2. Select the information and choose Edit, Copy, or press Ctrl+C, or click the Copy button on the toolbar. The selection is copied to the Clipboard.

3. Open the DOS application. The DOS application should be in a window, not full-screen.

4. Place the cursor in the location where you want to insert the contents of the Clipboard.

5. Open the Control menu and choose Edit, Paste, or click the Paste button on the toolbar. The contents of the Clipboard is inserted into the DOS document.

Using Embedded Objects

In this section you will learn how to create compound documents that use embedded objects. Compound documents are documents you create using multiple types of data pulled in from various applications. The technology used to create compound documents is Microsoft's object linking and embedding (OLE).

The basic building blocks of a compound document are *objects*. Objects can be embedded into the *container* or *client* application, which contains one or more embedded objects. For example, you can embed a graphics object from a graphics application and a data table from an Excel worksheet into a Word document, which acts as the container for the objects. An application that supplies an object is referred to as a *server* application. The server application provides OLE services to the client application.

The major benefit of a document created using embedded objects over one created using simple copy-and-paste techniques that involve the Clipboard is that you can edit embedded objects without leaving the client application. If you use copy and paste, you have to edit the information in the source application and repeat the copy-and-paste procedure to update the client. In an OLE compound document, you simply double-click the object you want to edit, and the menus and toolbars of the object's original application temporarily replace those of the client application. Figure 11.10 shows an Excel object in a Word document. Notice that the Word menus and toolbars have been replaced with Excel's menus and toolbars so you can edit the object *in place*. When you finish editing the object, you click outside the object to restore the client application's menus and toolbars.

Part

III

Ch

11

In some cases, when you double-click an object, the source application of the object opens in a separate window instead of the source's menu and toolbars appearing over those of the client. In such cases, you edit the object in its original application and then return to the compound document.

Embedded objects can be updated dynamically whenever the source data changes. One of the main benefits of using OLE applications is that you can take advantage of the strengths of several applications, each of which excels at what it does, to create a single document. For example, you can use your favorite graphics application to produce the graphics for a document, use your spreadsheet application to analyze and summarize your data, and use your word processor to create a professional-looking document. OLE enables you to pull all these pieces together into one document and then edit and update information as needed.

It is important to understand the differences between linking and embedding data. When you link information, the information is stored in the source document. The destination document contains only the code needed to locate the information in the source document. Conversely, embedded information is actually stored in the destination document, and the OLE code points to the source *application* instead of the source *file*. This enables you to access the source application's tools for editing.

FIG. 11.10
You can edit an Excel
chart in Word by using
OLE capabilities.

You're still in Word...

...but these are Excel
menus and tools.

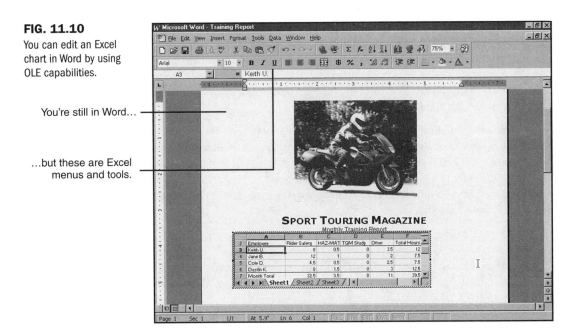

Embedding Information in Your Documents

You can embed information from one document into another using either the menu commands
or drag and drop. When you use the menu commands, you have the option of linking or not
linking the object with its source. When you drag and drop an object, the object is not linked to
its source.

N O T E   If you have linked or embedded an object into a word processor such as Microsoft Word,
you will probably need to look at the document in Page Layout View to see the object. You
can change the view by clicking the View menu and choosing an option. ▧

To embed an object from one document to another using the menu commands, follow these
steps:

1. Select the information in the source document.
2. Choose Edit, Copy or press Ctrl+C.
3. Open the destination application and document.
4. Choose Edit, Paste Special to display the Paste Special dialog box.
5. Select the object from the As list.
6. Select either the Paste or Paste Link option.

   If you select Paste, the object is embedded but *is not* linked to the source document.
   When you double-click the object, the menus and toolbars for the source application
   appear, allowing you to edit in place.

If you select Paste L̲ink, the object *is* linked to the source document. When you double-click the object, the original document opens and the information you linked is selected. See "Linking Data" later in this chapter.

7. Click OK, and the information is inserted into the destination document as an object, as shown in Figure 11.11.

FIG. 11.11
A Microsoft Excel table inserted as an object in a Word document. Notice the handles around the object when it is selected.

When you click the embedded object, square handles appear at the corners and ends, surrounding the object. You can drag these handles to resize the object.

You can sometimes also embed an object using drag and drop. Some OLE-compliant applications support drag and drop, enabling you to drag an object from one application and drop it in another application.

To drag and drop information from one application to another, follow these steps:

1. Open the source and destination applications and arrange their windows side by side.

2. In the source document, select the information you want to embed.

3. To *copy* the object from the source to the destination, drag the selected object and drop it at the desired location in the destination document.

N O T E Drag and drop will not work with some applications. For instance, you will not be able to drag a table or group of cells from an Excel worksheet because the dragging operation will simply select more cells within Excel instead of copying the existing selection. If drag and drop doesn't work for you, simply use the menu or toolbar commands for copying data. ▪

When you drag and drop information from one application to another, you do not have the option of linking the embedded object to its source. Use the menu method just described to link an embedded object.

If the application you want to drop an object in is minimized or is hidden by other applications, you can drag the object over the application's button on the taskbar and pause for a few seconds. The application window then appears. In the application window, drop the object at the desired location.

N O T E When you drag and drop information from one application to another, it is embedded as an object in the destination document if the data types for the two applications are different. If the data type is the same, the information is inserted in its native format. When you drag and drop a graphic to a Word document, for example, it is inserted as an object. When you drag a text selection from Word to Excel, on the other hand, it is inserted as straight text because a cell can accept text. To insert a text selection as an object, you must use the Edit, Copy and Edit, Paste Special commands. ▨

Inserting a File into a Document

In some cases, you might want to import an entire file from one application into another application instead of just copying and pasting part of a document. Many Windows applications have built-in *file converters* that enable you to convert a file of one format into the format of the application in which you are working. In many cases, the file converter preserves the formatting of the original document. For example, you can import a WordPerfect document into Word for Windows and preserve many of the formatting enhancements.

To open and convert a file from one application into another application, follow these steps:

1. Open the application into which you want to import the file.
2. Choose File, Open and locate the folder in which the file you want to convert is stored.

   You might have to choose All Files from the Files of Type (or equivalent) list box because the file you are converting probably doesn't use the same filename extension as files created by your application.
3. From the list of files, select the file you want to convert.
4. Click Open.

If the application has the correct conversion filter, the file is converted and opened in the application. You might need to fix some of the formatting if it was lost in the conversion process. If your application was unable to convert the file, you might not have installed the necessary converter when you installed the application. Check the documentation for your application to see what converters are included, and then run the Setup program again if necessary to install the required converter.

Rich text format (RTF) files have become the common language for exchanging files between word processors. You can preserve much of the formatting you apply to a document if you save it as an RTF file. If you don't have the correct converter for exchanging a file from one application to another, try turning the document into an RTF file and importing it into the receiving application.

Linking Data

The two techniques that you have learned so far place static copies of selected data in a new location. There is no link between the data in the source and destination locations.

A more sophisticated way to exchange data in Windows 98 is through linking. Before the arrival of the OLE standard, DDE (Dynamic Data Exchange) was the technology used to link data. Now OLE offers both linking and embedding. With OLE, you can create links from one document or file to another document or file. These links can be formed between documents that are created in the same application (such as Word) or documents that are created in different applications (such as Word and Excel). After you establish a link, you can update the linked information automatically by editing the original source information. This means you can use data in various places but update it in only one place.

You can set up a *link* only between two applications (or two documents) that supports OLE. The application that requests data is called the *client* application. The other application, called the *server* application, responds to the client application's request by supplying the requested data. When you change the data in the server application, Windows 98 automatically changes the data in the client application. The advantage to exchanging data by links is that data is kept up-to-date in both the client and server applications.

One example of how you can use data linking is to create a report in Microsoft Word that includes a data table linked to a worksheet in Excel. As you update the data in the Excel worksheet, the table in the Word report document is automatically updated as well, so your reports will always reflect the latest data. Using this approach, you don't have to create a new report each time your data changes. Figure 11.12 shows a data table in Excel that is linked to a document in Word (which is shown in Figure 11.13). The difference between the table in Figure 11.13 and the one shown in Figure 11.4 is that this table is linked to the data in the Excel worksheet; when you change the data in the Excel worksheet, the table in the Word document is automatically updated.

Windows 98 provides two ways to use linking: interactively and through a macro language. The simplest way to link data uses the copy and paste techniques you learned earlier in this chapter with a few important differences. Instead of the Paste command, you use either the Paste Special or Paste Link command. These commands enable you to set up the link between the source and destination documents.

The second method involves creating a macro in the application's macro language to automate data transfer or to store data in a programming variable that can then be used by another Office application. This method isn't discussed in this book. See *Special Edition Using Visual*

Part
III

Ch
11

Basic for Applications, published by Que, for more information on creating links using a macro language.

FIG. 11.12

Data from an Excel spreadsheet can be linked to a Word document.

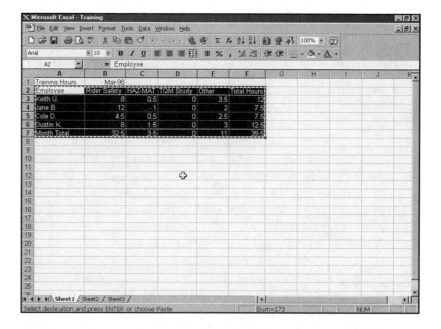

FIG. 11.13

Any changes you make in the Excel worksheet will be reflected in the table in the Word document.

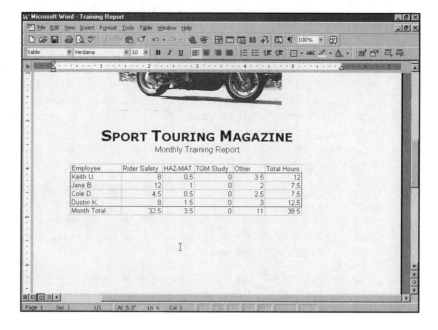

To set up a link between two applications, follow these steps:

1. Open the source document and select the data you want to link to a destination document (refer to Figure 11.12).

2. Choose Edit, Copy or press Ctrl+C to copy the selected data to the Clipboard.

3. In the destination application, open the document to which you want to link the data.

4. Choose Edit, Paste Special, and the Paste Special dialog box appears. Figure 11.14 shows the Paste Special dialog box in Microsoft Word.

FIG. 11.14

Use the Paste Special dialog box to set up the link between the source and destination documents.

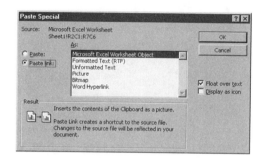

5. Select the Paste Link option. If you don't select this option, the data will be embedded into the destination document without linking.

6. Depending on the type of data you are working with, make an appropriate selection in the As dialog box. For example, if you were pasting data from an Excel worksheet into a Word document, you would select the Microsoft Excel Worksheet (XLS) option.

7. Click OK. The data is inserted into the destination document. (Refer to Figure 11.13, which shows the Excel data from Figure 11.12 inserted into a Word document.)

After a link is established, anytime you change data in the source document, the data is automatically updated in the destination document. Figure 11.15 shows the Excel worksheet from Figure 11.12 with some of the data changed. Figure 11.16 shows the table in the Word document from Figure 11.13 as it reflects these changes.

Part **III**

Ch **11**

Why Can't I Link Some Files?

In some cases, the Paste Link option will not be available in the Paste Special dialog box. This is because the original file format of the object (before it was copied to the Clipboard) is not compatible with the client application. For instance, suppose you want to paste a JPEG image from a web site or image editor into a Microsoft Word document. When you copy it to the Clipboard, it is copied as a bitmap image, which can then be embedded in the word processor. While you may be able to paste JPEG images into Word, you will not be able to link them.

If you want to edit the embedded image, you can double-click it to open the basic image-editing controls from Paint within Word. However, if you perform more advanced editing on the original JPEG in a program such as Photoshop, you will have to re-embed or re-paste the image after you are done.

FIG. 11.15
The data from the Excel worksheet in Figure 11.12 has been changed.

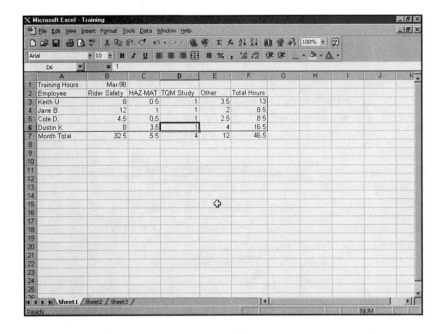

FIG. 11.16
The table in the Word document is automatically updated to reflect the changes in the Excel worksheet.

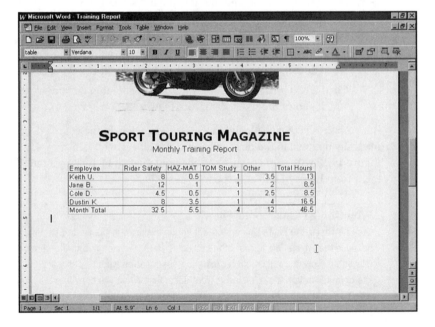

CAUTION

If you change the name or path of your client or server document, you must re-establish your links. You should make a habit of changing or creating file names and directories for your documents before you create links. Otherwise, your data links will be broken, and your data will no longer be updated automatically.

Inserting a New Object into Your Document

If you want to use the features of another application in your compound documents, you can choose Insert, Object and select an application from the provided list. Many applications support this feature, including the standard Microsoft Office applications, the applications that come with Windows 98 (such as Paint and WordPad), and many other Windows 98 applications.

Some Windows applications come with small applets that can only be used from within the main application. Microsoft Office 97 comes with several smaller applications that support OLE, as you can see in Table 11.2. When you install Microsoft Office on your system, these applications are installed in a centralized location that allows many Office applications to access them easily. The WordPad application, which comes with Windows 98, can embed many types of objects, some of which are listed in the table.

Table 11.2   Office 97 Applications That Support OLE

Application	Use
Microsoft Clip Gallery	Inserts clip-art pictures
Microsoft Map	Inserts a map showing different levels associated with data
Microsoft Equation	Creates mathematical expressions
Microsoft Graph	Inserts charts from data in a Word table
Microsoft Organization Chart	Creates organizational charts
Microsoft Word Picture	Inserts a picture and the tools associated with the Word drawing toolbar
Microsoft WordArt	Creates logos and other special text effects

You can quickly and easily check your system information to find out what OLE-compatible objects are currently registered on your system. Open the System Information applet by clicking the Start button and choosing Programs, Accessories, System Tools, System Information. In the left pane of the window, click the plus sign (+) next to Software Environment, and then click the plus sign (+) next to OLE Registration. Then click on INI File to display the OLE objects available on your system (see Figure 11.17).

FIG. 11.17

The System Information applet lists OLE objects available on your system.

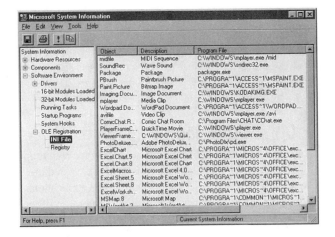

To insert an object from another application into a document, follow these steps:

1. In the destination document, place the insertion point where you want to insert the object.

2. Choose Insert, Object. The Object dialog box appears (see Figure 11.18).

FIG. 11.18

The Insert Object dialog box lists applications you can use to insert objects in a document.

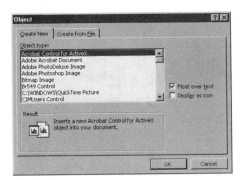

3. Select the Create New tab, and then select an application from the Object Type list.

4. If you want to display the object as an icon, select the Display as Icon check box.

5. Click OK. Depending on the applications you are working with, either a separate window for the application appears within the document, or the menu bar and toolbars change to those of the source application (as shown in Figure 11.19). In this figure, notice that although the title bar displays "Microsoft Word," the menu and toolbars are those of Excel. Likewise, the object displays the worksheet and scrollbars of Excel.

6. Create the object using the application's menus and toolbars.

7. When you finish creating the object, return to the document in one of two ways:

If a separate window appeared for the application, choose File, Exit, or click the window's Close (X) button.

FIG. 11.19

Some applications permit in-place editing: The menu bar and toolbars for the source application appear when you insert an object from that application.

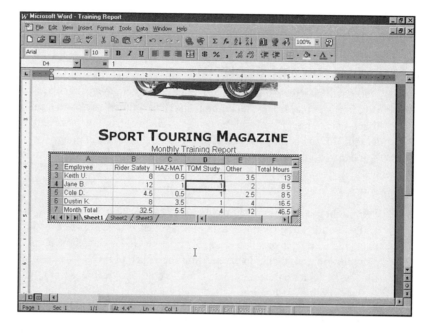

If in-place editing was enabled, click outside the object to restore the destination application's menus and toolbars.

Editing an Embedded Object

Regardless of which method you use to embed information into your document, you can edit the embedded object with the tools of the source application. To edit the object, follow these steps:

1. Click the object. Handles appear around the object, and the status bar tells you to double-click the object.

2. Double-click the object. Depending on the source and destination applications, either a separate window for the program appears or the current window's toolbar and menu bar change to those of the source application.

3. Edit the object using the source application's toolbar and menus.

4. When you finish editing the object, exit the object. If you launched a separate window for the application, choose File, Exit. If you stayed in your destination document, click outside the object.

Using OLE to Create Linked Shortcuts

Windows 98 gives you a variety of tools to make your work simpler and more efficient. In addition to the various uses we have already discussed, OLE allows you to create time-saving links in your documents. You can use links (or shortcuts) to move around within documents or to

Part
III

Ch
11

specific locations on documents of other applications. In addition, OLE allows you to create "scraps" of information that you can reuse as often as you want.

Creating Document Shortcuts

Document shortcuts enable you to quickly navigate to a particular location in a document. You can, for example, create a document shortcut on the desktop to a cell in an Excel worksheet so that you can open Excel and the target worksheet from the shortcut, and the cell will be selected. You can create a shortcut to a location or selection in any OLE-compliant application. You can keep these shortcuts on the desktop, or you can place them in a folder on the desktop if you don't want to clutter your desktop with shortcuts. Using folders to store your document shortcuts also can help you organize them.

You might use document shortcuts to save time, for example, if you are working in a document and you find you're spending a lot of time navigating from one location to another. To reduce navigation, you can create document shortcuts to key locations in the document so that you can move to a particular location using the shortcut for that location. You can then collect all the shortcuts for a document into a folder so that it becomes a computerized table of contents that streamlines navigation.

To create a document shortcut, follow these steps:

1. Make a selection in the document (select worksheet cells, text, graphics, and so on).
2. Drag and drop the selection onto the desktop using the right mouse button.
3. From the shortcut menu that appears when you release the mouse button, choose Create Document Shortcut Here.

When you choose a desktop shortcut, the document opens to the original selection. You can move the shortcut to a folder that you create on the desktop.

N O T E Not all OLE-compliant applications allow you to create document shortcuts using drag and drop. In such cases, you can create a document shortcut by making a selection, choosing Edit, Copy, right-clicking the desktop, and choosing Paste Shortcut from the menu. ■

Creating Document Scraps

You also can create document scraps on your desktop. *Scraps* are pieces of information from any OLE document that you store on your desktop or in a folder. At any time, you can drag a scrap into a document in any OLE application to insert it as an embedded object. You can use the scrap as many times as you like and in as many documents as you like. You might find scraps useful if you have certain bits of information that get used on a regular basis. For instance, you might use a scrap of your company logo in memos, faxes, reports, and various other documents.

To create a scrap, follow these steps:

1. Select the information from which you want to create a scrap.
2. Drag the selection to the desktop or to a folder.

A scrap consisting of the selected information is created. If you choose the scrap, the information in the scrap is displayed in the application in which it was created. You can drag and drop the scrap into any OLE document to embed it as an object in the document.

Use scraps to create pseudo-post-it notes on your desktop. If you want to save a bit of information on your desktop so you won't forget it, open WordPad (open the Start menu and choose Programs, Accessories, WordPad), type the note, select the text, and drag it to the desktop. You don't have to save the WordPad file. The name of the scrap that appears on the desktop is taken from the first sentence of the scrap text. However, you can rename the scrap to give it a more useful name. To read the note, simply choose the scrap.

Another way to use scraps to increase your productivity is to store boilerplate text that you use over and over again as scraps. Suppose, for example, that you have several standard paragraphs you use repeatedly in contracts. You can create a scrap for each of these paragraphs. Then whenever you are creating a new contract and you need one of the paragraphs, you can drag a copy of the scrap into your document. You could also create a scrap that contains the same information as your .sig (signature) file in your email client. This way you can quickly attach your "virtual signature" to any OLE document. To keep your desktop from getting cluttered with scraps, organize them in folders that you create on your desktop.

TIP

You can drag a copy of a desktop scrap into an email message created using Outlook Express, which is OLE-compliant. This is a very handy way to quickly send text from a document or cells from a worksheet to a client or coworker. See Chapter 34, "Using Outlook Express," to learn how to use Outlook Express to send email.

Creating Web Links in Documents

In Chapter 30, "Web Browsing with Internet Explorer 4.0," you'll learn how to create shortcuts on your desktop to sites on the Internet. This is useful if you routinely access certain sites and want to be able to access them more quickly by double-clicking a shortcut. You also can embed these shortcuts into any OLE document so that you can access these sites from within the document. Imagine distributing a document to your colleagues loaded with shortcuts to useful sites on the Internet. All they have to do is open the document and choose the shortcuts.

To embed an Internet shortcut in a document, drag and drop the shortcut from the desktop into the document. You can then choose that shortcut to sign on to the Internet and go directly to that site.

Some applications, such as Microsoft Word 97, allow you to create web links from within the program. Look for a button on the application's toolbar called "Create Hyperlink." If the button is available, create a hyperlink using the following procedure:

1. Highlight the text or object to which you want to connect the hyperlink.
2. Click the Create Hyperlink button on the toolbar or choose Insert, Hyperlink.

3. The Create Hyperlink dialog box appears. Type the URL or file location into the Link to File… text box.

4. Click OK.

The area you highlighted for the hyperlink will now appear in a different color (probably blue), as shown in Figure 11.20. Hold the mouse pointer over the link, but don't click it. Notice that a help bubble appears next to the pointer, showing the target address of the link. You can link to web sites using this method, or you can link to other file locations on your computer or network. Anyone who clicks on the link will instantly be taken to whatever location you listed when you first created the hyperlink.

N O T E   If the object you highlighted for creating your hyperlink contains text, you might have to reformat the text after the link is created. This is not a problem, but it's a good idea to keep the linked text a different color from that in the rest of your document. This will ensure that readers know it's a link.

FIG. 11.20
Some text in this training report now contains a hyperlink to a web site.

CHAPTER 12

Printing

by Grant King

In this chapter

Using the Printers Folder

One of the most basic uses for a computer is to print out documents. Although as a society we are moving toward the goal of decreasing the amount of paper we generate, in many cases you will still find the need to print material from your computer to preserve it or share it with other people. Whether you need to print letters, graphs, pictures, or other such items, to do this you must install a printer on your computer and understand some of the basics of managing any printers used by your computer. This chapter shows you how to make full use of the printing features found in Windows 98.

The printer settings for your computer are stored in the Printers folder. The usual way to access the Printers folder is to click on the Start button, select Settings, and then choose Printers. This opens the Printers folder, as shown in Figure 12.1.

FIG. 12.1

The Printers folder provides a central place from which to manage all your local and network printers. Note in this example that the HP LaserJet 5 is a network printer and is also shown as the default printer.

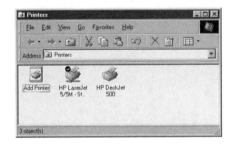

You can also access the Printers folder by any of the following methods:

- Selecting Printers from the Control Panel
- Opening My Computer and choosing Printers
- Clicking on Printers in the left pane of the Windows NT Explorer

The Printers folder contains icons for adding a printer as well as for any printers you have installed on your computer. If you have any other devices or software that use a printer driver, such as a fax modem, an icon representing the printer driver for that device also appears in this folder.

Default Printer

While you may have more than one printer installed on your computer, only one of these printers can be defined as your default printer, although you can change this default setting at any time. When a printer is set as the default printer, it is the printer that is automatically selected each time you print a document.

You can easily tell which printer is set as the default by looking at the printer icons found within the Printers folder. As you saw in Figure 12.1, the default printer has a check mark in the upper-left portion of its icon.

When you install the first printer on your computer, it is automatically installed as the default printer. Unless you change the default setting, the first printer you install on your computer remains as the default, even if you later add additional printers to the Printers folder.

If you want to select a different printer as the default, right-click on that printer's icon in the Printer Folder and choose Set as Default. The check mark moves to the selected printer's icon, and that printer is now set as the default printer.

Printer Properties

A printer's properties are the detailed settings for that particular printer. These properties are contained in the Properties page for each printer. You can access a printer's Properties page by either of the following methods from within the Printers folder:

- Right-clicking on the printer's icon and choosing Properties
- Clicking on the printer's icon with the left mouse button and then selecting Properties from the File pull-down menu

Because the Properties page for a printer is directly related to the functions exposed through the printer's driver, the Properties page looks somewhat different from printer to printer. Thus, the Properties page for your printer might appear differently than that shown in Figure 12.2.

FIG. 12.2

The Properties page for a printer contains multiple tabs, each containing various options you can set for that printer.

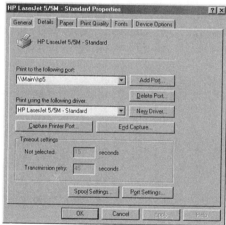

Part

III

Ch

12

Installing a Local Printer

For installation purposes, Windows 98 distinguishes between local and network printers. A local printer is one that is physically connected to your computer via a cable, whereas a network computer is physically attached to another computer but is available for use by your computer through your network connection.

Before you attempt to set up a local printer on your computer, you first need to make sure that you can connect to that printer from your computer. Some of the things you need to check are

- What port the printer needs to be plugged into
- If the printer is physically connected to the computer properly
- If the printer is turned on; otherwise, Windows 98 won't be able to detect the printer
- The exact make and model of that printer; for example, HP DeskJet 500

Plug and Play

In an effort to make it easier for you to install printers and other hardware on your computer, Microsoft has worked with hardware manufacturers to develop the Plug and Play standard. Through the use of Plug and Play support, Windows 98 can automatically detect hardware attached to your computer and install the appropriate drivers without any intervention on your part.

Assuming that your printer is Plug and Play–compliant, installing your printer is as easy as turning on your attached printer and booting into Windows 98. Plug and Play can install your printer either during the Windows 98 installation process or at any time thereafter when you want to add a printer.

In either event, when Windows 98 loads, it should automatically detect that the printer has been added to your computer. It then brings up a dialog box that informs you of this fact. After Windows 98 has identified the printer, it attempts to install the correct driver for that printer. At this point, it might prompt you to insert the Windows 98 CD-ROM. After you have done that, it looks for that driver on that disk. If the driver did not come with Windows 98 or if you have an updated driver that you want to install instead, simply insert the driver disk from your hardware manufacturer into a disk drive and direct Windows 98 to that drive.

In order for this process to work properly, you have to make sure that the printer you want to add complies with the Plug and Play standard. If you are purchasing the printer in a store, look for the "Designed for Windows 98" logo on the printer box. If the box bears this logo, this indicates that the printer has undergone hardware compatibility testing to make sure that it is fully compatible with Windows 98, including Plug and Play. Because Plug and Play was also supported in Windows 95, the printer should also be fully compatible with Windows 98 if the logo indicates that the printer was designed for Windows 95.

If your printer is an older model or if it came packaged with your computer, you might not be able to tell whether it supports Plug and Play. If Windows 98 does not automatically recognize your printer, you need to manually add it to your computer configuration through the Add Printer Wizard.

Using the Add Printer Wizard

If your printer does not support Plug and Play, you can manually install the printer on your computer through the use of the Add Printer Wizard. Open the Printers folder and double-click on the Add Printer icon. After the Add Printer Wizard window appears, click on the Next button to begin using the wizard.

Select the radio button for Local Printer and click the Next button (see Figure 12.3). You are then asked to choose the manufacturer and printer model for your printer. First select the manufacturer by scrolling down to the name (or abbreviation) for your printer's manufacturer in the left window of this page of the wizard. Select that name by clicking on it, and a list of all available printers from that manufacturer appears in the right window. Select your printer's model by clicking on its name in the right window.

FIG. 12.3

The Add Printer Wizard walks you through the steps needed to set up a printer on your computer.

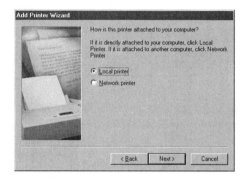

 T I P When the Add Printer Wizard prompts you to choose a printer manufacturer and model, you can quickly skip to your hardware manufacturer's printer listings by pressing the first letter of the manufacturer's name. Thus, if you press the letter E, the list scrolls down and selects Epson, thereby automatically opening the available printer selections for Epson printers from which you can choose.

Part
III

Ch
12

Unless your printer is a very recent model, it is very likely that Windows 98 already has a driver for your printer. In fact, Windows 98 includes drivers for over 1,000 different printers. However, if your printer does not appear to be among the printers listed, you need to click on the Have Disk button and insert a disk containing your printer's drivers into the floppy disk or CD-ROM drive. These drivers should have been supplied to you on disk when you bought your computer. After you indicate the drive on which Windows 98 should look, it then reads the disk you have inserted and lists any available printer drivers found on that disk. Note that the driver might be in a subdirectory on the disk, so you should check the documentation that came with your printer if you are unable to locate the driver. In the event that you are still unable to locate the driver, you need to contact the printer's manufacturer to obtain a Windows 98 driver for your printer (a Windows 95 driver should also work).

After you have selected the correct manufacturer and printer model for your printer, click on the Next button. You are then asked to choose the port on which you want to install the printer (see Figure 12.4). This is the hardware port to which you have attached the printer to your computer. In most cases, the correct port is LPT1, although you might need to check with your computer's manufacturer or the documentation that came with your computer to determine which port you should select.

FIG. 12.4

To install the printer correctly, you need to select the port to which your printer is attached.

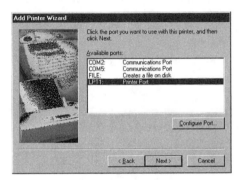

As part of the process of selecting a port, you can also configure the port, such as by having Windows 98 check the status of the port each time before it prints. If you want to change these settings, click on the Configure Port button found on this page of the Add Printer Wizard.

After selecting a port for your printer, you are then asked to choose a name for the printer (see Figure 12.5). In most cases, the default, which is usually the brand and model number, will suffice. However, if you plan to share this computer with other people on a network, you might want a more descriptive name, such as "7th Floor Laser Printer."

FIG. 12.5

You need to provide a name for your printer that distinguishes it from other printers on your computer or the network.

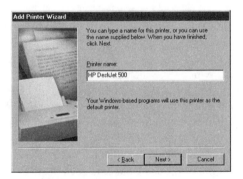

You then come to the last page of the Add Printer Wizard, where you are asked if you want to print a test page. Microsoft recommends that you print a test page when you install a printer. If you have not installed this printer on your computer before, this is a good opportunity to make sure that everything is working correctly. Simply choose the Yes radio button, which is selected by default, and a test page prints as soon as your printer has been installed.

After you click on the Finish button, Windows 98 installs and configures the printer for use on your computer. Unless the drivers for this printer have previously been added to your computer, such as if you previously installed this type of printer, a dialog box appears asking you to insert the Windows 98 CD-ROM. After you put the CD-ROM into the drive and click on the OK button, the printer driver and any other necessary files are copied to your computer. After this process has ended, an icon for your printer appears in the Printers folder. If this is the only printer installed on your computer, it is automatically selected as the default printer.

If you made it through all of these steps without incident, you are finished. Congratulations! You have just successfully installed your printer in Windows 98. If you need to install a network printer, you will find that the steps needed to make that installation are virtually the same as installing a local printer.

Setting Up a Network Printer

Setting up a network printer in Windows 98 can be as easy as connecting to a local printer, thanks in part to Microsoft's Point and Print process. This process usually allows you to automatically install the correct network printer driver without having to have the Windows 98 CD-ROM or other disk containing the printer driver. Through Point and Print, when you use the Add Printer Wizard to add a network printer, Windows 98 is often able to download the printer driver from the computer or server to which the printer is attached.

Before attempting to set up a network printer on your computer, you first need to know how to connect to the printer. Some of the information you need to know is

- The name that the printer and its attached computer or server (if applicable) uses on the network
- If the printer is set up for sharing over the network
- The exact model of that printer; for example, HP LaserJet 5

Connecting to the Network

To install a network printer on your computer, you first need to be connected to the network. If you have not already established a network connection with your computer, refer to Chapter 43, "Sharing Network Resources," before attempting to connect to and install a network printer. You might also need to check with your network administrator to make sure that you have been given permission to access that printer, because the printer may refuse your connection if you do not have permission.

While being connected to your network, open the Printers folder and double-click on the Add Printer icon. The Add Printer Wizard then appears. Select the radio button for Network Printer and click the Next button.

You are then asked to supply the location of the printer on the network. If you already know the name of the printer and its attached computer on the network, you can simply type it into the field on this screen, as shown in Figure 12.6. Note that you need to supply the UNC (Universal

Part

III

Ch

12

Naming Convention) path for the location of the printer, such as *computername**printername* where *computername* is the name of the computer to which the printer is attached, and *printername* is the name of the printer. Thus, in Figure 12.6, Main is the name of the computer on the network to which the printer hp5 is attached.

FIG. 12.6

You need to tell the Add Printer Wizard the location of the computer that you want to install on the network.

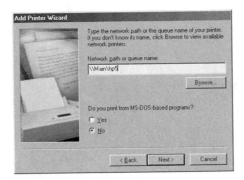

If you are not sure of the exact name of the computer and printer on the network, click on the Browse button. This brings up a separate window (see Figure 12.7) that lists all other computers on the network that have shared printers.

FIG. 12.7

The Browse window allows you to select from all available shared printers on the network.

Click on the plus sign to the left of any computer listed in this window to expand the view to show all shared printers attached to that computer. Click on the OK button after you have selected the printer you want to add.

N O T E You can choose to install only a single printer each time you run the Add Printer Wizard. If you want to install more than one printer on your computer, you have to add them one at a time. After you have added the first printer, you can then add additional printers one by one. This applies to both local and network printers.

Before you move on to the next window in the Add Printer Wizard, be sure to check the correct radio button indicating if you want to print from MS-DOS–based programs. If you select yes and click on the Next button, the next window of the wizard requests that you capture a printer port for these MS-DOS programs. Even though this shared network printer is not physically attached to your computer, MS-DOS programs often need to believe that they are printing to a local port. By choosing a port to capture for this purpose, when MS-DOS programs attempt to print to this port, Windows 98 redirects the print job to the network printer automatically.

As with local printers, the Add Printer Wizard asks you if you want to print a test page. Select the Yes radio button if you want to see if your connection to the network printer is working properly. After you have decided if you want to print a test page, press the Finish button to install the printer on your computer.

After you have selected the network printer you want to install and have finished with the Add Printer Wizard, Windows 98 then connects to that printer to determine its exact type. After it has determined the make and model of the printer, Windows 98 then sees if you already have a correct version of that printer's driver available on your computer. If you do, the printer should install correctly, and you will be done adding this printer to your Printers folder. In most cases, however, Windows 98 either downloads the correct driver to your computer or you are prompted to insert a disk containing the driver into one of your disk drives.

To address both of these situations, we begin by looking at what happens when Windows 98 is able to download the printer driver to your computer.

 TIP Although you can use the Add Printer Wizard to add a printer to your computer, an easier way is to open Network Neighborhood and browse for the printer (you will probably first have to double-click on the icon for the computer to which the printer is attached). After you have found the printer, right-click on the printer's icon and choose Install. This opens the Add Printer Wizard but skips several windows, thus making it easier and quicker to add a network printer.

Point and Print

After you have finished using the Add Printer Wizard, Windows 98 attempts to install the printer driver from the computer to which the printer is attached (if applicable). In many cases, if the shared printer is set up correctly on the computer to which it is attached, Windows 98 can download the printer driver from that computer and install it on your computer. This feature is known as Point and Print.

Assuming that this process works correctly on your computer, you should see a dialog box telling you that Windows 98 has found the proper driver on the remote computer and is installing the driver on your computer. After this has finished, you can connect to and use that printer.

In order for the Point and Print feature to work properly, the computer to which the shared printer is attached must be running Windows 98, Windows NT Server, or be a Novell NetWare server. Note, however, that this feature does not always work properly, and as such you may still have to install the printer driver from either the Windows 98 CD-ROM or the printer driver disk supplied by your printer manufacturer.

Installing Printer Drivers from Disk

If you are unable to install the driver for your printer through the Point and Print feature described in the previous section, you will need to use the Windows 98 CD-ROM or another disk with the appropriate driver in order to provide Windows 98 with the printer driver. After Windows 98 installs the printer driver, an icon for the printer appears in your Printers folder.

Printing from Applications

After you have installed one or more printers on your computer, you then can print from within any application. In Windows 98, when you print from a Windows application, you can change a number of the printer's configurations within the application itself for the print job you are processing. Windows 98 also includes a print spooler that allows you to get back to work while the operating system processes the print job in the background.

Changing Configurations

In most Windows applications, you can print the document you are working on by pressing a toolbar button or by selecting Print from the File pull-down menu. After you tell the application to print the document, you likely are presented with a window that allows you to change any needed settings for that print job. Note that although you don't always see this window when you choose a Print button on a toolbar, you should usually see a Print window if you use the pull-down menu.

Figure 12.8 shows the Print window as it appears in the WordPad application that comes with Windows 98. This window shows the relevant information on the selected printer, such as the printer's name and its current status. If you want to change from the default printer to a different printer, just choose the other printer that you want from the drop-down box next to Name. Instead of printing the entire document, you can also choose to select only one or more pages for printing by entering that information into the Print range frame.

FIG. 12.8

When printing from within applications, you can change your printer settings to best match the needs of your print job.

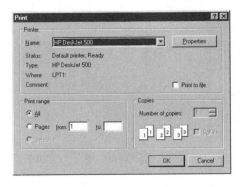

If you click the Properties button, a separate window appears that contains much of the same properties settings available for this printer in the Printers folder. From this window, you can set the printer resolution, change the paper size, alter the way the document is printed (such as from portrait to landscape), and other properties settings. After you have made any wanted changes to the printer settings, click on the OK button to return to the main Print window and print the document.

Note that the Print window includes an option to print to a file rather than to the selected printer. If you choose this option by selecting the Print to File check box, this does not save the file as a text file, but rather saves the printer output into a data file as opposed to sending it to the printer right away. Unless you want to save this raw printer data for some reason, you probably do not want to use this Print to File feature. If you want to save the file rather than print it, you should choose either Save or Save As from the File pull-down menu.

Spooling

Windows 98 includes a 32-bit print spooler that supports preemptive multithreading and multitasking, thereby allowing you to get back to work more quickly after you initiate a print job. Before print spoolers were incorporated into the operating system, when you printed a document in an application, you often had to wait until the entire document had been printed before you could return to work in that application. However, with Windows 98, when you tell an application to print a document, the print spooler takes over and accepts the print job in place of the actual printing device to which you have directed the document.

Thus, the print spooler effectively acts as a middleman that receives the print job on behalf of the printer and temporarily stores it on your hard disk. After the application has finished sending either part or all of the print job to the spooler (depending on what print spooler options you have chosen for your printer), the application is then freed up to continue with other work, and the print spooler begins feeding the print job data to the printer in the background.

By default, the print spooler begins feeding print data to the printer after it has received the first page of data from the application. However, if you want to return control to the application more quickly, you can adjust the print spooler properties so that it does not begin printing until the entire document has been received by the spooler. To change these and other print spooler settings, you need to reconfigure the properties for each printer on which you want to make these changes. To do this, right-click on the printer's icon in the Printers folder and choose Properties. Then select the Details tab and choose the Spool Settings button.

In this window (see Figure 12.9), you can change the default settings by instructing Windows 98 to wait until the last page is spooled before sending the document to the printer. This shortens the time it takes to return control back to the application that is printing the document. Alternatively, if you are having printing problems and want to see if the print spooler is causing the problem, select the related radio button to have all applications print directly to the printer. However, choosing this option will probably prevent you from working in the application until the printer has finished printing the document.

Part

III

Ch

12

FIG. 12.9

You can change the Spool Settings for the print spooler on a printer if you want to return control to an application more quickly or if you need to troubleshoot printing problems.

In this same window, you also see that you can choose between the *EMF* (*enhanced metafile printing*) and RAW spool data formats. Normally you want to use the default setting for your printer to help ensure error-free printing. EMF usually returns control back to the application more quickly than using the RAW data format because the latter must be generated by the printer driver. If the default for your printer is RAW, try using EMF to speed up the printing process in your application. However, because some applications do not support EMF, if you experience problems, you should switch back to the RAW format.

After a print job has been sent to the spooler, a printer icon appears in the system tray indicating that Windows 98 is processing the print job. If you click on this icon, a window opens for that printer from which you can get additional information about the status of the print job. For more information about managing print jobs through this printer window, see the next section.

Managing Print Jobs

Through the process of sending documents to your local or network printer, instances will arise when you need to cancel a print job or simply find out what other documents are waiting to be printed. If you want to view the status of a printer, you can open the printer window for that device. If you are in the process of printing a document from your computer, you can click on the printer icon in the system tray to bring up the window for that printer. You can also open that printer's window by double-clicking on its icon in the Printers folder. Note that while the former method might display only print jobs created by your computer, the latter method should display all pending print jobs, including those from any other users on your network.

When you open a printer window, all of the documents currently pending for that printer are displayed (see Figure 12.10). The pending print jobs are shown in their order in the print queue. The print job at the top of the print queue is the document currently being printed. Any documents below that are printed in descending order.

By right-clicking on any of your pending print jobs, you can choose to either pause or cancel that job. When you pause a print job, it is skipped over when its place in the queue comes up. While you can exercise control over your own documents, usually you cannot pause or cancel other people's print jobs unless you have administrative privileges on that printer.

FIG. 12.10

The printer window shows all print jobs currently pending on a printer and allows you to delete or pause any of your pending jobs.

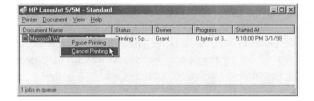

In addition to pausing or canceling print jobs, you can elect to purge all pending documents by selecting that option from the Printer pull-down menu, subject to the security restrictions discussed earlier regarding other user's documents. You can also change any of the properties for the selected printer by choosing Properties from the Printer pull-down menu.

Special Printing Considerations

While we have already discussed most of the main printing features found in Windows 98, a number of other areas are worth considering. In this section, we look at how to print

- By dragging and dropping a file onto a printer's icon
- A file from any disk drive through the Windows Explorer
- Frames in HTML documents viewed in Internet Explorer
- From within MS-DOS applications
- Documents containing color graphics
- When your printer is unavailable
- With multiple types of paper configurations

Drag and Drop Printing

While you normally print a document from within an application in which you are working, it is also possible to print a document without being in an application. This is done by dragging and dropping the document onto a printer icon. One of the ways to do this is to create a shortcut for one or more of your installed printers on your desktop. After you have done this, you can print documents by just dragging them from the desktop or any window and dropping them onto the printer shortcut.

To create a desktop shortcut for one of your installed printers, open the Printers folder. With either your left or right mouse button, select the printer's icon from the folder and drag it to the desktop. When you release the mouse button, a shortcut for the printer is created. If you prefer not to create a desktop shortcut for the printer, you can drag and drop documents onto the printer's icon in the Printers folder.

When you drag a document onto a printer's icon and drop it, Windows 98 opens the related application, prints the document within the program, and then closes that application. Because Windows 98 looks for a program that has previously been associated with that type of file in

Part
III

Ch
12

order for it to open an application and print the document, you need to have previously installed a program on your computer that is registered for handling that file type. Thus, if you want to print a document created in Microsoft Excel, you need to have Excel loaded on your computer because Windows 98 looks for an application associated with that file extension (in this case, files having an .XLS or other Excel-related extension).

Printing Files from Disk

In addition to printing files by dragging and dropping them onto printer icons, you can also print them directly from disk. In most cases, this is the quickest way to print a document without having to open the application yourself.

To print a file directly from disk, simply select the file from within the Windows Explorer. The file can be located on any floppy drive, hard drive, or network drive to which you have access. Right-click on the file and choose Print. The printing process is identical to that in drag and drop printing. Thus, Windows 98 opens the application associated with that type of file, prints the file within that application, and then closes the application automatically.

Printing Frames in Internet Explorer

While the print window that appears when you are printing from an application normally appears consistent from program to program, one difference occurs when you print a document from within Internet Explorer that contains multiple frames. When a web page contains multiple frames, it means that, although it appears to be a single page, it is actually made up of multiple pages that appear within a single frameset. Each of these frames is a separate document that can be printed out through your computer.

When you print a page containing multiple frames, the print window appears with additional options not found when printing from other applications (see Figure 12.11). From this window, you can select to print the selected frame (which usually is the main, or largest, frame), to print all of the frames individually, or to print the frameset as it appears on your screen. You can also select the option to either print all linked documents, in which case Internet Explorer prints all pages for which hyperlinks appear on the page you are printing. Alternatively, you can print a table containing links for these documents.

For further information on printing within Internet Explorer, see Chapter 31, "Finding, Organizing, and Saving Web-Based Information."

Printing from MS-DOS Applications

While most of the applications you run on your computer are likely written for Windows, you might have a few MS-DOS applications from which you will need to print. Windows 98 fully supports printing from MS-DOS applications, although you do not get the full benefits found in printing from Windows applications, such as EMF spooling. All print jobs created by MS-DOS applications are intercepted by the 32-bit print spooler prior to being sent to the printer, resulting in a quicker return of control back to the application.

FIG. 12.11

When printing an HTML document containing multiple frames, you are provided with several options regarding which frames you want to print.

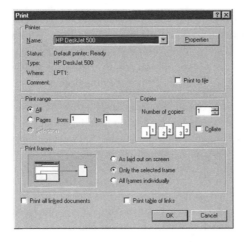

Printing in Color

One of the problems encountered when printing color graphics is that the color displayed on your monitor might not match the color generated by the printer. To help alleviate this problem, Microsoft has included support for *Image Color Matching* (*ICM*) in Windows 98. While Windows 95 supports ICM 1.0, Windows 98 supports the newer ICM 2.0, which includes a number of technical improvements. The end result is a better correlation between the colors as they appear on your monitor and those generated by your color printer. Because ICM is supported on multiple platforms, the images you create in Windows 98 applications should appear virtually the same on computers that are running other ICM 2.0–compliant operating systems.

Offline Printing

If you use a laptop computer, or if your printer is only available via a network connection, you are a good candidate for using the offline printing feature found in Windows 98. With a laptop computer, there may be many times when you are not physically connected to your printer, such as when you are working on a document while on a long flight. Similarly, if you work in a networked environment, there likely will be times that you cannot print due to problems connecting to the printer over the network. As its name implies, offline printing allows you to generate print jobs when you are not connected to a printer and allows you to have them printed at a later time.

N O T E Offline printing works only for portable and networked computers and also requires the use of the print spooler supplied with Windows 98. If you have configured the printer not to use print spooling, you have to enable this feature in order to put your printer into offline mode. Because offline printing is not supported for local printers, if you want to stop printing on a local printer, right-click on the printer's icon in the Printers folder and choose the Pause Printing command. ▪

Part
III

Ch
12

To use offline printing, open the Printers folder and select the printer you want to use offline. Right-click on the printer's icon and choose Use Printer Offline, at which point a check mark appears next to this choice. Any print jobs you generate are held in the queue until you instruct Windows 98 to actually print these jobs. When you want to print out the stored jobs, right-click on the printer's icon and deselect the Use Printer Offline option.

If your laptop is configured to be used with a docking station, when you boot your computer Windows 98 automatically selects offline printing if it detects that you are not connected to the docking station. If you later boot your laptop while being docked, the offline printing feature is turned off, and any stored print jobs are sent to your printer.

Managing Paper

By changing the properties for a printer, you can select the paper size, the paper tray the printer should use, and other such settings as determined by the capabilities of your printer. The properties can be changed at any time either from the Printers folder or from within any application.

To change the printer paper properties from within an application, select Print from the File pull-down menu and then click on the Properties button. You can also access these properties by right-clicking on the printer's icon in the Printers folder and choosing Properties. In either event, a properties page similar to that shown in Figure 12.12 appears (this example is from the WordPad application).

FIG. 12.12

You can change a printer's paper configurations to best match the needs of the document you are printing.

After the properties page appears, click on the Paper tab. From here you can select the size of the paper on which you are printing as well as the layout of the print job—that is, landscape or portrait. If your printer has multiple trays, an envelope holder, or other paper sources, you can also change the paper source on this part of the printer's properties page. As mentioned previously, because the properties page appears differently from printer to printer, the display for your printer will likely appear somewhat differently than that shown in Figure 12.12.

Configuring a Printer for Multiple Uses

With Windows 98, you can set up multiple virtual printers, each of which points to a single physical printer. This allows you to create one configuration for high-quality graphics printing, one for landscape (as opposed to portrait) printing, or any other configurations you want. Each of these can be saved as a separate printer even though each points to a single printing device.

To have the operating system configure additional printers for this purpose, use the Add Printer Wizard to go through the same process that you used to install the printer previously, but this time give the printer a slightly different name. Thus, you might name one printer "High graphics" and another "Landscape."

When you install each of these printers, the Add Printer Wizard tells you that a driver for this type of printer is already installed on your computer. It asks whether you want to keep the existing driver or install this new one. Unless you have a version of the driver on a disk that is newer than the Windows 98 CD-ROM, choose to keep the existing driver.

After you have finished using the Add Printer Wizard, a new icon appears for this printer. Right-click on its icon and choose Properties. Configure the printer according to its new name. Thus, for the Landscape printer example earlier, select the option to use landscape printing rather than portrait.

After you have configured your new virtual printers, they also are available for use within your applications. Thus, when you have a print job that you want to have printed in landscape format, choose the Landscape printer rather than choosing your main printer. This gives you a quick and easy way to print in this format without having to change the printer's properties each time.

Removing Printers

Although the focus of this chapter has involved installing and managing printers, you might need to remove installed printers and related devices from your computer. For example, if you buy a new printer and give the old one away, there would probably be no reason to keep the old printer's driver installed on your computer.

To remove a printer and its related drivers from your computer, open the Printers folder. Right-click on the printer's icon and choose Delete. Windows 98 then asks you to confirm that you want to remove that printer from your computer. Click on the Yes button, and the printer is then removed from your computer.

During the process of removing the printer, a dialog box appears asking whether you also want to remove the files that were used by that printer. The files to which Windows 98 is referring are the printer's driver and any other related files needed for use by that particular printer. If you think that you might use that printer in the future, you can choose No to keep these files on your computer. By doing so, you will not need to install the files from the Windows 98 CD-ROM the next time you add the printer to your computer. Otherwise, choose Yes to remove all the files associated with this printer from your computer. After this process has completed, the printer's icon is removed from the Printers folder.

Part
III

Ch
12

Troubleshooting Printer Problems

The Help files that come with Windows 98 include a number of Troubleshooters, which are wizard-like guides to help you solve common print errors that might occur. If you experience a printing problem in Windows 98 and are not able to fix it on your own, you should try the Print Troubleshooter before seeking technical support.

To start the Print Troubleshooter, click on the Start button and select Help. After the Help window opens, double-click on the Troubleshooting book icon and then again on the Windows 98 Troubleshooters icon. This expands to show a list of Troubleshooters from which you can select. Click on Print in this listing to open the Windows 98 Print Troubleshooter in the right pane of this window, as shown in Figure 12.13.

FIG. 12.13

The Print Troubleshooter can help solve many of the most common printing problems in Windows 98.

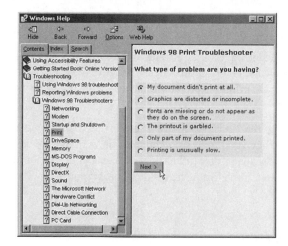

To use the Troubleshooter, select the radio button for the type of problem that is closest to that which you are experiencing. Then press the Next button and proceed through the steps that are designed to help solve your problem. If there is no Troubleshooter for your particular problem, or if the Troubleshooter does not fully solve the problem, you might need to contact either your printer manufacturer or Microsoft, such as by using the Windows Update tool, located off of the Start button. ●

CHAPTER 13

Using Windows Accessories

by Bob Voss

In this chapter

Windows 98 comes with several accessory applications, ranging from very simple applications, such as Calculator and Notepad, to more powerful applications such as WordPad (a word processor) and HyperTerminal (a communications tool). Table 13.1 describes the accessories that come with Windows 98 and tells you where to look to find out more about them. In this chapter, you will learn how to use the Calculator, HyperTerminal, and Phone Dialer.

Table 13.1　Windows 98 Accessories

Accessory	Description
Calculator	Used to perform calculations onscreen as on a desktop calculator. (Covered in this chapter.)
Imaging	Used to view, annotate, print, manage, store, and share images that have been created from faxes, scanned documents, or computerized images. (Covered in Chapter 15, "Using Paint and Imaging.")
Notepad	A simple text editor that you can use to create and edit text files. (Covered in Chapter 14, "Using Notepad and WordPad.")
Paint	An easy-to-learn graphics application that you can use to create and modify graphics images. (Covered in Chapter 15, "Using Paint and Imaging.")
WordPad	A word processing application used to enter, edit, and format documents. (Covered in Chapter 14, "Using Notepad and WordPad.")
Character Map	Used to insert special characters in your documents. (Covered in Chapter 23, "Working with Fonts.")
Dial-Up Networking	Used to connect your computer to another computer or a network using your modem. (Covered in Chapter 44, "Remote Access with Dial-Up Networking.")
Direct Cable Connection	Used to connect to another computer using a cable. (Covered in Appendix E, "Special Features for Notebook Users.")
HyperTerminal	A communications application used to work online with your computer. (Covered in this chapter.)
Phone Dialer	A tool for storing and automatically dialing phone numbers from your computer. (Covered in this chapter.)
CD Player	Used to play music CDs on your computer. (Covered in Chapter 24, "Setting Up Windows 98 Multimedia.")
DVD Player	Used to play DVD discs from your DVD drive. (Covered in Chapter 25, "Using Windows 98 to Play Games and Watch TV.")
Media Player	Used to play multimedia files (video, audio, and animation). (Covered in Chapter 24, "Setting Up Windows 98 Multimedia.")

Accessory	Description
Sound Recorder	Used to record digital sound files on your computer. (Covered in Chapter 24, "Setting Up Windows 98 Multimedia.")
Games	Four games—FreeCell, Hearts, Minesweeper, and Solitaire—for your entertainment. (Discussed briefly in this chapter.)

Adding Windows Accessories

The Add/Remove Programs icon in Control Panel enables you to install and remove Windows components and accessories, as well as applications. If you opted not to install a particular Windows 98 accessory when you installed Windows but you change your mind later, you can use the Windows Setup feature to add or remove a Windows component. To do so, follow these steps:

1. Open the Start menu and choose Settings, Control Panel.

2. Open the Add/Remove Programs Properties sheet using the Add/Remove Programs icon.

3. Select the Windows Setup tab to display a list of Windows components as shown in Figure 13.1.

FIG. 13.1
The Windows Setup tab of the Add/Remove Programs Properties sheet lets you add and remove parts of Windows.

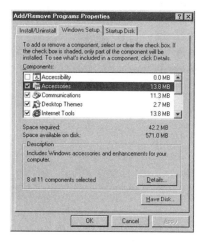

Part
III

Ch
13

In the Components list box, a check mark next to an item indicates that the component is already installed on your system. If the check box is gray, the Windows component is composed of more than one sub-component, and some (but not all) of the sub-components are currently installed. For instance, in Figure 13.2, only some of the sub-components (Calculator and Games) of the Accessories component are installed. To see what's included in a component, choose Details.

4. Select a component in the Components list box. The Description box in the lower portion of the dialog box displays a description of that component and tells you how many of the available sub-components are selected.

5. If the component you selected consists of more than one sub-component, choose Details to open a dialog box listing the sub-components. (For example, Figure 13.2 shows the Accessories dialog box listing the sub-components of the main Accessories component.) In some cases, a sub-component will have additional sub-components, which you can view by choosing Details again.

FIG. 13.2

The Accessories dialog box lists a component's parts. By choosing Details, you can narrow your selections.

6. Mark a component for installation or removal by clicking the check box beside that item in the Components list. Adding a check mark to a blank check box marks that item for installation. Conversely, clearing a checked box instructs Windows to uninstall that component.

7. If you're selecting sub-components in a dialog box you opened by choosing a Details button, click OK to close that dialog box and return to the Add/Remove Programs Properties sheet.

8. When the check marks in the Components lists specify the components that you want composing your Windows system, choose Apply in the Add/Remove Programs Properties sheet. You'll need to supply the Windows Setup disks or CD when prompted.

TROUBLESHOOTING

When I use the Windows Setup feature to add new components, it adds those components, but it also removes other components. Why? If you clear a check box for a component that was checked, this tells Windows to remove the component when you run Windows Setup rather than to not install it. This can be confusing the first time you run Setup again to add new components. Leave those components that are already installed checked unless you want to uninstall them.

Calculating with Calculator

Like a calculator you keep in a desk drawer, the Windows Calculator is small but saves you time by performing all the calculations common to a standard calculator. The Windows Calculator, however, has added advantages: You can keep this calculator onscreen alongside other applications, and you can copy numbers between the Calculator and other applications.

The Standard Windows Calculator, shown in Figure 13.3, works so much like a pocket calculator that you need little help getting started. The Calculator's *keypad*, the onscreen representation, contains familiar number *keys*, along with memory and simple math keys. A display window just above the keypad shows the numbers you enter and the results of calculations. If your computational needs are more advanced, you can choose a different view of the calculator, the Scientific view (see Figure 13.4).

FIG. 13.3
The Standard
Calculator.

FIG. 13.4
The Scientific
Calculator.

Part

III

Ch

13

To display the Calculator, open the Start menu and choose Programs, Accessories, Calculator. The Calculator opens in the same view (Standard or Scientific) in which it was displayed the last time it was used.

To close the Calculator, click the Close button in the title bar. If you use the Calculator frequently, however, don't close it; click the Minimize button to minimize the Calculator to a button on the taskbar.

The Calculator has only three menus: Edit, View, and Help. The Edit menu contains two simple commands for copying and pasting; the View menu switches between the Standard and Scientific views; and the Help menu is the same as in all Windows accessories.

Operating the Calculator

To use the Calculator with the mouse, just click the appropriate numbers and sign keys, like you would press buttons on a desk calculator. Numbers appear in the display window as you select them, and the results appear after the calculations are performed.

To enter numbers from the keyboard, use either the numbers across the top of the keyboard or those on the numeric keypad (you must first press the NumLock key if the NumLock feature is not enabled). To calculate, press the keys on the keyboard that match the Calculator keys. Table 13.2 shows the Calculator keys for the keyboard.

Table 13.2 Keyboard Equivalents for the Calculator

Calculator Key	Function	Keyboard Key
MC	Clear memory	Ctrl+L
MR	Display memory	Ctrl+R
M+	Add to memory	Ctrl+P
MS	Store value in memory	Ctrl+M
CE	Delete displayed value	Del
Back	Delete last digit in displayed value	Backspace
+/−	Change sign	F9
/	Divide	/
*	Multiply	*
−	Subtract	−
+	Add	+
sqrt	Square root	@
%	Percent	%
1/x	Calculate reciprocal	R
C	Clear	Esc
=	Equals	= or Enter

N O T E To calculate a percentage, treat the % key like an equal sign. For example, to calculate 15 percent of 80, type **80*15%**. After you press the % key, the Calculator displays the result (in this case, 12).

You can use the Calculator's memory to total the results of several calculations. The memory holds a single number, which starts as zero. You can add to, display, or clear this number, or you can store another number in memory.

Copying Numbers Between the Calculator and Other Applications

When working with many numbers or complex numbers, you make fewer mistakes if you copy the Calculator results into other applications instead of retyping the result. To copy a number from the Calculator into another application, follow these steps:

1. In the Calculator display window, perform the math calculations required to display the number.
2. Choose Edit, Copy, or press Ctrl+C.
3. Activate the application in which you want to place the calculated number.
4. Position the insertion point in the newly opened application where you want the number copied.
5. From the newly opened application, choose Edit, Paste, or press Ctrl+V.

You can also copy and paste a number from another application into the Calculator, perform calculations with the number, and then copy the result back into the application. A number pasted into the Calculator erases the number currently shown in the display window.

To copy a number from another application into the Calculator, select the number in the application and choose Edit, Copy. Then activate the Calculator and choose Edit, Paste.

If you paste a formula in the Calculator, you can choose the equal (=) button to see the result. For example, if you copy *5+5* from WordPad, paste the calculation into the Calculator, and then choose the = key, the resulting number 10 appears. If you paste a function, such as @ for square root, the Calculator performs the function on the number displayed. If, for example, you copy @ from a letter in WordPad and paste it into Calculator when the display shows the number 25, the result 5 appears.

Numbers and most operators (such as + and –) work fine when pasted into the Calculator display, but the Calculator interprets some characters as commands. The following chart lists the characters the Calculator interprets as commands:

Character	Interpreted As
:c	Clears memory.
:e	Lets you enter scientific notation in decimal mode; also the number E in hexadecimal mode.
:m	Stores the current value in memory.
:p	Adds the displayed value to the number in memory.
:q	Clears the current calculation.
:r	Displays the value in memory.
\	Works like the Dat button (in the Scientific calculator).

Using the Scientific Calculator

If you have ever written an equation wider than a sheet of paper, you're a good candidate for using the Scientific Calculator. The Scientific Calculator is a special view of the Calculator.

To display the Scientific Calculator, activate the Calculator and choose View, Scientific.

The Scientific Calculator works the same as the Standard Calculator but adds many advanced functions. You can work in one of four number systems: hexadecimal, decimal, octal, or binary. You can perform statistical calculations, such as averages and statistical deviations. You also can calculate sines, cosines, tangents, powers, logarithms, squares, and cubes. These specialized functions aren't described here but are well documented in the Calculator's Help command.

▶ **See** "Getting Help from Windows Help Files," **p. 46**

Using HyperTerminal

HyperTerminal is a Windows accessory that enables you to connect your computer to another PC or online service. HyperTerminal is a full-featured communications tool that greatly simplifies getting online. With HyperTerminal, you can connect to a friend's computer, a university, an Internet service provider, or even CompuServe.

Before the existence of graphical interfaces to online services such as CompuServe and The Microsoft Network, most communications tools were character oriented. For example, students all over the world used terminal emulation programs to connect to their schools' computers. They typically used VT100 terminal emulation, to make their PCs behave like any other display terminal on the system.

If you can use the graphical communications tools mentioned here, why do you need a character-oriented tool such as HyperTerminal? The reason is that most bulletin boards, Internet shell accounts, and university connections are still character oriented. Most bulletin boards do not provide a graphical interface like The Microsoft Network. HyperTerminal does the following:

- Makes the focal point of your activities the connections you create (documents), which allows you to dial or configure a connection without loading HyperTerminal first.
- Automatically detects the terminal-emulation mode and communications parameters of the remote computer.
- Fully integrates with TAPI and the centralized modem configuration, which provides Windows 98 applications a single interface to your modem for dialing, answering, configuration, and more.
- Supports several popular terminal-emulation modes and file transfer protocols, such as VT100, VT52, and Kermit.
- Enables you to greatly customize each of your connections.

What You Can and Can't Do with HyperTerminal

HyperTerminal is a communications tool with many uses. The following list describes many tasks you can perform with HyperTerminal:

- Connect to another computer and exchange files.

- Connect to an online service (such as CompuServe) that supports one of HyperTerminal's terminal-emulation modes.

- Connect to a school's computer using VT100.

- Connect to an Internet service provider using a shell account and even access the World Wide Web using Lynx.

Although HyperTerminal is a useful communications tool, it is not the only tool you will need for your communications activities. The following list describes some activities you can't do and refers you to other chapters in this book:

- *Connect to another network.* If you need to connect your computer to another network, use Dial-Up Networking as described in Chapter 29, " Establishing a Dial-Up Internet Connection."

- *Graphically connect to the Internet and World Wide Web.* While many service providers provide Lynx, a character-oriented web browsing tool, you'll need a graphical browsing tool to take full advantage of the web. See Chapter 30, "Web Browsing with Internet Explorer 4.0."

▶ **See** "Connecting to a Remote Access Server," **p. 950**

Creating a New Connection

When you installed Windows, you were given the option of installing HyperTerminal as one of your accessories. If you did not install HyperTerminal or if you removed it from the Start menu, you can install it at any time by selecting Install/Remove Applications from Control Panel. To load HyperTerminal, open the Start menu and choose <u>P</u>rograms, Accessories, HyperTerminal. If you have not yet configured your modem, Windows prompts you to set it up the first time you run HyperTerminal.

Figure 13.5 shows the HyperTerminal folder. By default, each connection that you create appears in this folder as an icon.

▶ **See** "Configuring a Modem," **p. 550**

Part

III

Ch

FIG. 13.5
Choose Hypertrm to create a new HyperTerminal connection, or choose another icon to open an existing connection.

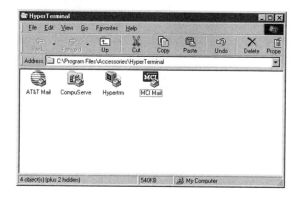

Before you can connect with HyperTerminal, you need to create a new connection. To do so, follow these steps:

1. Choose the Hypertrm icon in the HyperTerminal folder.

   If HyperTerminal is already loaded, choose <u>F</u>ile, <u>N</u>ew, or click the New button on the toolbar. HyperTerminal prompts you for a new connection description.

2. In the Connection Description dialog box, shown in Figure 13.6, type a descriptive name for your new connection, select an icon, and click OK. HyperTerminal then displays the Phone Number dialog box.

FIG. 13.6

Create a new connec-
tion and select an icon
to help you easily
identify it later.

3. Type the phone number for your new connection. Then verify the country code, area code, and modem choice, and click OK. HyperTerminal displays the Connect dialog box, shown in Figure 13.7.

FIG. 13.7

After you set up the
connection, simply
choose Dial to begin.

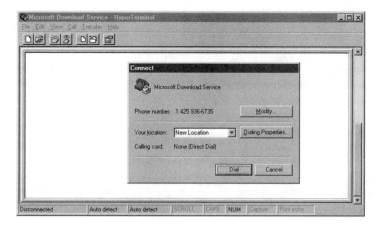

4. Select your location (usually Default Location) and choose Dial if you want to establish your new connection. You can choose <u>D</u>ialing Properties to change the default location, the outside line access, and other dialing properties.

Figure 13.8 shows the entire HyperTerminal window with a session in progress. Most of HyperTerminal's features are available on the toolbar. To see what a toolbar button's function is, hold the mouse pointer over the tool for a few seconds, and a tooltip appears.

FIG. 13.8
After establishing a connection to the remote computer, you interact with it just like a display terminal on the system. Click the scroll bar to review previously displayed text.

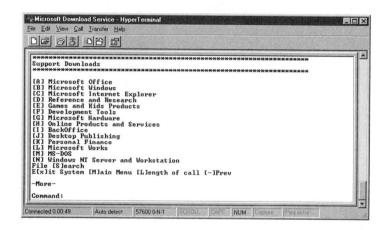

To save your new connection, choose File, Save As. HyperTerminal prompts you for a file name. If you want your connections to show up in the HyperTerminal folder, accept the default path. If you quit HyperTerminal without saving your new connection, HyperTerminal prompts you for a file name.

TROUBLESHOOTING

I connected to the service fine, but all I see onscreen is garbage—usually at the bottom of the screen. Choose File, Properties to display the properties sheet for your connection. Then click the Settings tab and set Emulation to Auto Detect. HyperTerminal automatically determines which terminal emulation your service uses.

To hang up, choose Call, Disconnect, or click the Disconnect button on the toolbar.

Using an Existing Connection

The next time you want to use the connection you previously created, it appears in the HyperTerminal folder. To establish this connection, choose the icon in the folder and click Dial.

If HyperTerminal is already running, choose File, Open, or click the Open button on the toolbar.

Changing a Connection Setup

It is easy to change the properties for a connection after you create it. You can change the connection's icon, name, country code, area code, phone number, and modem in the connection's properties sheet (see Figure 13.9).

Part
III

Ch
13

FIG. 13.9

Change the icon, name, phone number, and modem to use for this connection. Click OK to permanently save your settings.

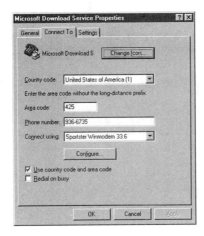

To change the properties of your connection, follow these steps:

1. Choose File, Properties, or click the Properties button on the toolbar.

   You can change the HyperTerminal Properties sheet without even running HyperTerminal. To do so, right-click the connection you want to change in the HyperTerminal folder, and then choose Properties.

2. Choose Change Icon, select another icon from the list, and change the connection name.

3. Select a country code.

4. Type the area code and phone number. (If you select the default location when you dial, Windows will not dial the area code if it matches your default area code.)

5. Select a modem. Windows displays the modems you currently have installed or enables you to go directly to the port. If you go directly to the port, you can bypass the Windows 98 modem configuration so you can control the modem directly. For normal use, select a configured modem so that you can take advantage of centralized modem configuration.

6. Click OK to save your settings.

Configuring the Connection Settings

The Settings tab of the properties sheet enables you to change the terminal properties of HyperTerminal. For example, you can change the terminal-emulation mode. Figure 13.10 shows the Settings tab of this sheet. Table 13.3 describes each terminal emulation available in HyperTerminal.

FIG. 13.10

Use the Settings tab of the properties sheet to change the terminal emulation and other useful settings.

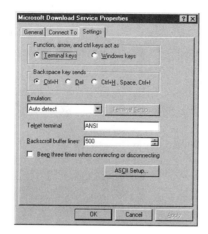

Table 13.3 Terminal Emulation Supported by HyperTerminal

Protocol	Description
ANSI	A popular generic terminal emulation supported by most UNIX systems that provides full-screen emulation.
Auto Detect	A system that automatically determines which terminal emulation the remote computer is using.
Minitel	An emulation primarily used in France.
TTY	Actually, the absence of any terminal emulation. TTY simply displays all the characters it receives on the display.
Viewdata	An emulation primarily used in the United Kingdom.
VT100	The workhorse of terminal emulations. Many remote systems such as UNIX use this.
VT52	A predecessor to VT100 that provides full-screen terminal emulation on remote systems that support it.

To change the settings for this connection, follow these steps:

1. Choose File, Properties, or click the Properties button on the toolbar. (Alternatively, right-click a connection document in the HyperTerminal folder and choose Properties.)

2. On the Settings tab, choose Terminal Keys or Windows Keys.

   Terminal keys sends function Keys F1 through F12 and arrow Keys to the remote computer instead of acting on them in Windows; Windows Keys causes Windows to act on those function keys. For example, if you choose Terminal Keys and press F1, the key is sent to the host, and the host responds to it. If you choose Windows Keys and press F1, Windows responds to the key by displaying Help.

3. In the Backspace Key Sends box, select <u>D</u>el or Ctrl+<u>H</u>, Ctrl+}. This selection determines which character is sent to the remote computer when you press the Backspace key.

4. Set <u>E</u>mulation to the terminal emulation you want. HyperTerminal must be using the same terminal emulation the host computer is using.

   If you set <u>E</u>mulation to Auto Detect, HyperTerminal automatically determines what emulation the host is using and configures itself appropriately. Use this setting for normal situations.

5. Enter the number of lines you want in the <u>B</u>ackscroll Buffer Lines box. In the HyperTerminal main window, the current screen is displayed with a white background. If you press Page Up or use the scroll bar to scroll backward, you see previously displayed text with a gray background. The default value for <u>B</u>ackscroll Buffer Lines is 500 lines, which allows you to review about 20 screens and doesn't consume a large amount of memory.

6. Turn on Bee<u>p</u> Three Times When Connecting or Disconnecting if you want to be notified when you are making or breaking a connection.

7. Optionally, click the AS<u>C</u>II Setup button and set the options for how text files are to be sent and received. Figure 13.11 shows the ASCII Setup dialog box, and Table 13.4 describes what each option does.

FIG. 13.11

Use the ASCII Setup dialog box to configure how ASCII files will be sent and received. For example, you can choose to send line feeds with line ends.

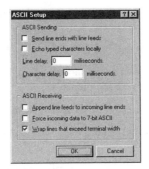

Table 13.4   ASCII Setup Options

Option	Description
<u>S</u>end Line Ends with Line Feeds	Attaches a line feed to the end of every line that HyperTerminal sends. Turn on this option if the remote computer requires it or if you turned on <u>E</u>cho Typed Characters Locally. Pressing Enter moves you to the beginning of the current line instead of starting a new line.

Option	Description
Echo Typed Characters Locally	Displays each character you type on the keyboard instead of depending on the host to echo each character. Turn on this option if you can't see the characters you type. If you see each character twice (ssuucchh aass tthhiiss), turn off this option.
Line Delay	Sets how much time to delay between lines. Increasing the amount of time between lines allows the remote computer time to get ready for the next line. Increase this setting in increments of 100 milliseconds if the remote computer frequently loses portions of each line.
Character Delay	Sets how much time to delay between characters. Increasing the amount of time between characters allows the remote computer time to get ready for the next character. Increase this setting in increments of 5 milliseconds if the remote computer randomly loses characters.
Append Line Feeds to Incoming Line Ends	Attaches a line feed to lines received. Turn on this option if the lines you receive from the host computer are displayed one on top of another.
Force Incoming Data to 7-bit ASCII	Changes 8-bit characters to 7-bit. Turn on this option if HyperTerminal displays unrecognizable symbols. This option forces HyperTerminal to stick with readable characters.
Wrap Lines That Exceed Terminal Width	Turns word wrapping on or off. Turn on this option if you want lines that are longer than the terminal width to be continued on the following line.

Exchanging Files with the Remote Computer

You can easily exchange files with another computer using HyperTerminal. For example, you may want to download a program update from the bulletin board of your favorite software vendor. You also can download public domain software from a variety of bulletin board systems (BBSs) around the country.

> **CAUTION**
>
> Before running a program downloaded from a remote computer, run it through a virus scan program to make sure that it's not infected. Otherwise, severe and irreparable damage may occur to your programs and data files if you download a virus.

Part
III

Ch

13

You might be asked to upload a data file to a vendor's bulletin board so that the vendor can help you fix a problem. HyperTerminal can also upload files.

Downloading Files

Before you begin downloading a file, you must make sure that you have a connection with a host computer, as described in the previous section "Using an Existing Connection."

The procedure for starting a download varies between bulletin boards and other host computers; follow the instructions given to you online. When you do start, you'll have to make a note of the file transfer protocol you select on the host. HyperTerminal supports several popular file transfer protocols, described in Table 13.5.

Table 13.5   File Transfer Protocols Supported by HyperTerminal

Protocol	Description
Xmodem	Xmodem is an error-correcting protocol supported by virtually every communications program and online service. It is slower than the other protocols.
1K Xmodem	1K Xmodem is faster than Xmodem, transferring files in 1,024-byte blocks as opposed to the slower 128-byte blocks in regular Xmodem. Otherwise, they are similar.
Ymodem	Many bulletin board systems offer Ymodem, which is another name for 1K Xmodem.
Ymodem-G	Similar to Ymodem, Ymodem-G implements hardware error control. It is more reliable than the first three protocols. However, to use Ymodem-G, your hardware must support hardware error control.
Zmodem	Zmodem is preferred by most bulletin board users because it is the fastest protocol of those listed. Zmodem is reliable, too, because it continues a valid download even if it's interrupted and because it adjusts its block sizes during the download to accommodate bad telephone lines. Zmodem has two other features that make it stand out from the rest. First, the host can initiate the download (you do nothing beyond step 1). Second, you can download multiple files at one time using Zmodem. The host computer initiates a download for each file you select.
Kermit	Kermit is extremely slow and should not be used if one of the other protocols is available. Kermit is a protocol left over from VAX computers and mainframes.

To download a file from a host computer, follow these steps:

1. Start the download process on the bulletin board or host computer as you are instructed online. Remember to note which file transfer protocol you select.

2. If you selected Zmodem as the protocol, you are done. The host computer initiates the file transfer with HyperTerminal.

   If you selected any other protocol, choose Transfer, Receive File, or click the Receive toolbar button. The Receive File dialog box appears (see Figure 13.12).

3. Enter a folder name, or choose Browse to select a folder from a dialog box. Then select a protocol to use for downloading the file. The protocol you use should match the protocol you chose (or the system chose for you) on the host computer.

FIG. 13.12

Tell HyperTerminal where you want to store the file, and then click Receive to begin the download.

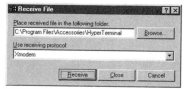

4. Click Receive, type a filename, and click OK. HyperTerminal starts your download. Figure 13.13 shows the dialog box that displays the status of your download. (You might see a different dialog box depending on the protocol you chose.)

FIG. 13.13

This dialog box shows the status of your download, including the filename and time elapsed. The dialog box might be different depending on which protocol you used for the download.

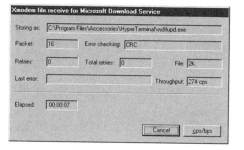

Uploading Binary Files

You can upload both binary and text files. Binary files include bitmaps, programs, and word processing documents that contain more than just readable text. For example, a program file contains code and program data that is not readable. On the other hand, text files contain characters that are easy to read. This section describes how to upload a binary file. To learn how to upload text files, see "Uploading Text Files," later in this chapter.

Before you begin uploading a binary file, you must establish the connection to the host computer as outlined in "Using an Existing Connection." Then, to upload a binary file to a host computer, follow these steps:

1. Initiate the upload on the bulletin board or host computer by following the onscreen instructions. The host displays a message indicating that it's waiting for you to start uploading.

Part

III

Ch

13

N O T E   If you are using Zmodem, you might not need to start the upload on the host computer. Zmodem can initiate the upload on the host for you. To try initiating the upload from your computer, skip step 1. However, if the host computer doesn't understand how to initiate an upload this way, you will have to start over from step 1. ■

2. Choose Transfer, Send File, or click the Send button on the toolbar. HyperTerminal displays a dialog box similar to the one shown in Figure 13.12 in the previous section, "Downloading Files."

3. Enter a filename, or choose Browse to select a file from a dialog box.

4. Select a protocol to use for uploading the file. The protocol you use should match the protocol you chose (or the system chose for you) on the host computer.

5. HyperTerminal starts the upload to the host computer. It shows the status of your upload in a dialog box similar to the one shown earlier in Figure 13.13.

TROUBLESHOOTING

I'm trying to use Ymodem-G as the transfer protocol, but it doesn't work. Your modem probably doesn't support hardware error control. Try using Ymodem instead.

After reviewing the preceding suggestions, I still can't download or upload a file. Make sure that you are selecting the exact same transfer protocol the host computer is using. If you continue to have difficulty, contact the sysop (system operator) of the remote computer.

Uploading Text Files

Before you begin uploading a text file, make sure you're connected to a host computer, as described in the earlier section "Using an Existing Connection." Then, to upload a text file to a host computer, follow these steps:

1. Start the upload on the bulletin board or host computer. The host displays a message indicating that it's waiting for you to start the upload.

2. Choose Transfer, Send Text File. HyperTerminal prompts you for a text filename.

CAUTION

Don't try to upload a binary file using this procedure. You might think that the file transfers okay, but the remote computer will receive a file with garbage in it.

3. Enter a file name, or click Browse to select a file from a dialog box.

4. Click Open. HyperTerminal starts uploading the text file to the host computer. Note that you do not see a dialog box showing the status of the upload.

N O T E HyperTerminal was developed by Hilgraeve Inc. for Microsoft Windows 98. They also produce a full-featured communications application called HyperACCESS. To find out more about HyperACCESS and to download a trial version of the software, visit their web site at:

http://www.hilgraeve.com ▓

Working with Phone Dialer

Phone Dialer is a handy accessory built into Windows 98 that remembers up to eight phone numbers and that you can use as a speed dialer. Although this may seem a bit redundant if you already have a speed dialer built into your existing phone, this one is very easy to program and change, and it can do the more intricate dialing needed to navigate voice-mail systems and make credit card calls. It can even keep a log of your outgoing and incoming calls. To access the Phone Dialer, open the Start menu and choose Programs, Accessories, Phone Dialer (see Figure 13.14).

FIG. 13.14
Use Phone Dialer to make calls with your modem.

Adding Phone Dialer Entries

When you first start Phone Dialer, it doesn't have any speed dial entries set. Your first task is to add names and phone numbers to the eight blank dial memories. Choose any blank entry and enter the name and number you would like to save (see Figure 13.15). You can choose a button by clicking it or by pressing Alt+ the number that appears next to the button.

FIG. 13.15
You can enter a short name for each Phone Dialer entry.

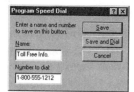

Both the Save and the Save and Dial buttons are now available. You can click the Save and Dial button to immediately dial the number of your new entry, or you can use the Save button to program your speed dial entry and exit the dialog box.

T I P If you want to enter a phone number that contains letters (555-FOOD or 1-800-555-SNOW), put quotation marks (") around the letters, as in 1-800-555-"SNOW".

After you have entered and saved your number, choosing the speed dial entry immediately starts the phone dialing process and opens the dialog box shown in Figure 13.16. While waiting for your call to be answered, you can type a description of the call as you would like it to appear in the phone log.

FIG. 13.16

Enter a log entry while the phone is dialing.

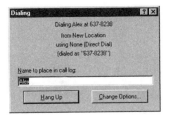

Choose the Hang Up button if you want to abort the call immediately. The Change Options button gives you a chance to stop the call and redial with a number you type into the Number to Redial field. This allows you to specify exactly what you want the modem to dial, ignoring any properties (such as your calling card number) set in the Dialing Properties sheet. After typing your number, choose the Redial button to dial your new entry. If you choose the Dialing Properties button, any changes you made in the Number to Redial text box are discarded, and your original speed dial number appears with your current Dialing Properties applied to it.

Using Complex Phone Number Sequences

The convenience of voice-mail has produced an annoying side effect: All those voice menus prompting you to "Press one to leave a message, Press two to talk with an operator" can drive you crazy and waste a lot of your time. Likewise, credit cards and various long distance carriers require us to use dozens of numbers and procedures to make connections. However, a few built-in extras in your modem can handle things like credit card dialing, long-distance service connections, and navigation through many voice-mail hierarchies:

- To wait for the prompts within a voice-mail system, you can use the comma (,) to insert a two second pause within your dialing sequence. Use more than one comma for a longer pause.

- If you need to wait for a secondary dial tone, enter the letter W.

- If you need to wait for silence on the line, you can insert the @ sign.

■ If you are making a credit card call and need to wait for the tone from your long distance carrier, insert a dollar sign ($) followed by your card number.

■ You can use the * and # characters within the phone number to make those voice-mail menu selections.

For example, let's say you want to make a personal long-distance call from your office and charge it to your AT&T calling card. You know that your company's long distance carrier is MCI, so you'll have to access the AT&T network to get the cheapest rates. Here's how to build your Phone Dialer sequence:

1. Type a **9** followed by a **W** to access the outside line and wait for the dial tone.

2. Type the AT&T network access code, **10"ATT"**, followed by a zero (**0**) to start the credit card call.

3. Type the phone number you're trying to reach, such as **(205)-555-3161**

4. To wait for AT&T to give their signal for you to enter your calling card number, type **$**.

5. Type in your credit card number, such as **314-555-2222-4321**.

Together, all these pieces of your dialing sequence would read:

9W10"ATT"0(205)-555-3161$314-555-222-4321

That would be a definite candidate for saving in Phone Dialer!

Using the Phone Dialer Log

The Phone Dialer comes with a log in which it keeps a record of your outgoing and incoming calls (see Figure 13.17). Each time you connect a phone call, an entry is placed in this text file. You can cut, copy, and delete from this log using the Edit menu commands, and you can redial an entry in your Log by double-clicking it or by selecting Log, Dial.

FIG. 13.17
You can use log entries to redial or copy and paste into other documents.

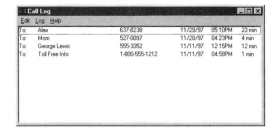

Playing Games

Windows 98 includes four games for your diversionary pleasure: FreeCell, Hearts, Minesweeper, and the classic Solitaire. To start a game, open the Start Menu and choose Programs, Accessories, Games. Then select the game you want to play from the Games submenu.

If you don't see any games, they weren't installed when you installed Windows. See "Adding Windows Accessories" (earlier in this chapter) to find out how to add the games using your Windows 98 installation CD-ROM or disks.

After you open a game, use the Help topics to learn about the objective and rules of the games and to get some tips on strategy. If you are connected to a network, check out Hearts, which you can play with other players who are connected to your network. ●

CHAPTER 14

Using Notepad and Wordpad

by Bob Voss

In this chapter

Using Notepad

Notepad is a miniature text editor. Just as you use a notepad on your desk, you can use Notepad to take notes onscreen while working in other Windows applications. Notepad uses little memory and is useful for editing text you want to copy into a Windows or DOS application that lacks editing capability.

Notepad retrieves and saves files in text format. This makes Notepad a convenient editor for creating and altering text-based files. Because Notepad stores files in text format, almost all word processing applications can retrieve Notepad's files. However, if you want the capability of formatting your documents, you'll need a true word processor. See "Creating Documents in WordPad," later in this chapter, to learn how to use the word processor that comes with Windows 98.

Starting Notepad

To start Notepad, open the Start menu and choose Programs, Accessories, Notepad. Notepad starts up and displays a blank document in the Notepad window (see Figure 14.1). You can begin typing.

FIG. 14.1

The initial blank Notepad file is ready for text.

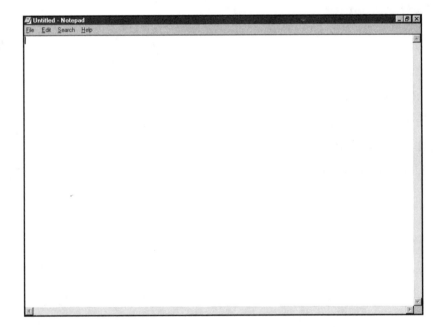

Working with Documents in Notepad

You can move the insertion point by using either the mouse or the keyboard. You select and edit text in Notepad the same way you select and edit text in WordPad. See "Selecting and Editing Text" later in the chapter for details.

Limited formatting is available from the File, Page Setup command. You can change margins and add a header or footer, but you cannot format characters or paragraphs in any way. You also can use the Tab, Spacebar, and Backspace keys to align text. Tab stops are preset at every eight characters.

With the commands on Notepad's Edit menu, you can cut, copy, and move text from one place in a file to another. Text that you cut or copy is stored in the Clipboard. When you paste text, the contents of the Clipboard is copied from the Clipboard to the document at the location of the insertion point.

▶ **See** "Using Simple Editing Techniques," **p. 43**

▶ **See** "Copying and Moving," **p. 43**

Creating a Time-Log File with Notepad

By typing a simple entry (**.LOG**) at the top of a Notepad document, you can have Notepad enter the current time and date at the end of a document each time you open the file. This feature might be convenient if you have to take phone messages or calculate the time spent on a project. Note that you must enter the text `.LOG` on the first line of the document, and it must be uppercase. As an alternative, you can choose Edit, Time/Date or press F5 to insert the current time and date at the location of the insertion point.

 Notepad can open binary files, but WordPad cannot. Although most of what you see when you open a binary file is unreadable, you can sometimes find helpful information in the header of the binary file. This is a good reason to keep Notepad on your computer, even if WordPad is more suitable for most tasks.

Creating Documents in WordPad

WordPad is the word processor that comes with Windows 98 that can perform most basic word processing tasks. Although it is not nearly as powerful and versatile as a full-featured word processing application (such as Microsoft Word 97), it is much more powerful than Notepad, the text editor that comes with Windows 98. Notepad is great for editing simple text files, such as AUTOEXEC.BAT, CONFIG.SYS, or any of the INI files, but it is limited to working with files under 50K in size, and it cannot be used to format text. With WordPad, you can perform all the basic editing tasks, such as cutting and pasting text and finding and replacing words and phrases. You can also format characters, paragraphs, and documents. In addition, WordPad is OLE-compliant, which means you can share data with other OLE-compliant applications. However, WordPad does not have many of the features found in advanced word processors, such as a spell checker, tables, headers and footers, and mail merge.

Part
III

Ch
14

Creating a New Document in WordPad

WordPad is located in the Accessories submenu of the Start menu. To start WordPad, open the Start menu and choose Programs, Accessories, WordPad. The WordPad window appears, as shown in Figure 14.2. When you first open WordPad, you are presented with a blank document. You might see different screen elements than those shown in Figure 14.2, depending on which elements have been added or removed using the View menu.

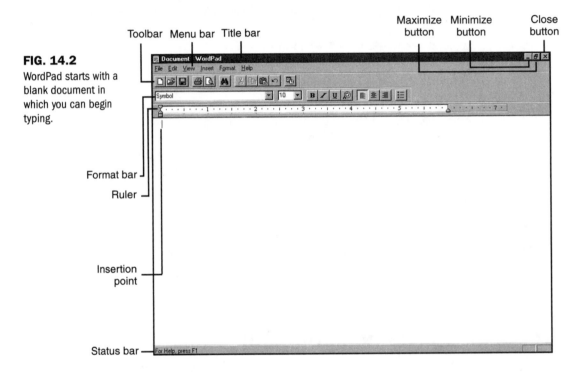

FIG. 14.2
WordPad starts with a blank document in which you can begin typing.

To create a new document in WordPad, follow these steps:

1. Choose File, New or click the New button on the toolbar to display the New dialog box (see Figure 14.3).

2. Select the type of document you want to create:

   Word 6 Document. This document type can be opened in Word 6, Microsoft Word 95, and Microsoft Word 97.

   Rich Text Document. This format (RTF) is compatible with several word processing programs and includes fonts, tabs, and character formatting.

   Text Document. This format includes only simple text characters with no formatting and is useful for creating batch files.

   Unicode Text Document. A universal character standard that uses a double-byte character set containing more than 38,000 characters, including characters for most of the major languages.

3. Click OK.

FIG. 14.3

Select one of the four document types when you create a new document.

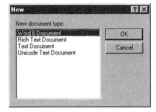

If you already have a document open, WordPad prompts you to save changes to that document if there are unsaved changes, and then WordPad closes that document. You can work on only one document at a time in WordPad because it does not support the Multiple Document Interface (MDI) standard.

You can enter and edit text in a WordPad document just as you would in any word processor, using the standard keys for moving around the document and deleting text. See "Selecting and Editing Text" later in the chapter for details.

Because WordPad is an OLE 2–compliant application, you can insert objects from other OLE applications into a WordPad document, or you can insert all or part of a WordPad document into another OLE application. You can, for example, insert a graphic created in Windows Paint as an object into a WordPad document and then double-click the Paint object and edit the graphic in place. When you do so, the WordPad menus and toolbars are replaced with the Paint menus and toolbars while you edit the object. You also can use the Insert, Object command or the drag-and-drop method for exchanging information with other OLE applications.

Opening WordPad Documents

To open an existing WordPad document, follow these steps:

1. Choose File, Open, or click the Open button in the toolbar. The Open dialog box appears (see Figure 14.4).

FIG. 14.4

Use the Open dialog box to locate and open WordPad documents.

2. Navigate to the disk and folder where the file you want to open is located.

3. Select the type of files you want to list from the Files of Type box.

4. Select the file you want to open and choose Open, or double-click the filename.

TROUBLESHOOTING

When I try to save a file in WordPad with a non-default extension, WordPad appends the filename with the .DOC extension. Why? When you save a file with an extension that is not associated with an application in the Registry, WordPad appends the default .DOC extension to the filename. In Notepad, the default extension .TXT is appended to the filename. To avoid this, enclose the filename in quotation marks.

Saving WordPad Documents

To save a document in WordPad, follow these steps:

1. Choose File, Save As, or click the Save button in the toolbar to display the Save As dialog box (see Figure 14.5).

FIG. 14.5

The Save As dialog box enables you to save a file in any drive, folder, or format you want.

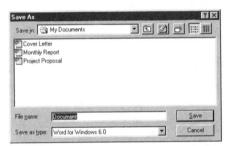

2. Select the drive and folder where you want to save the file.

3. Type the name for the file in the File Name text box.

4. Select a format from the Save as Type list if you want to save the file in a format other than WordPad.

5. Click Save or press Enter.

After you have saved a file for the first time, you can resave that file by choosing File, Save or by clicking the Save button in the toolbar.

Using WordPad to Create and Edit System, Batch, and Text Files

WordPad is very useful for creating and editing .TXT and system files (that is, files with the extensions .BAT, .SYS, .INI, and so on), especially when the file in question is too large for Notepad. When you open a .SYS, .INI, .BAT, or .TXT file in WordPad, edit or view it, and then resave it, it is saved with its original file extension. This feature eliminates the possibility of inadvertently saving a system file with the wrong extension, as can happen in a regular word processing program. In addition, WordPad provides more features (such as the Replace command) for editing your files than does Notepad.

To create a new text file in WordPad, choose File, New and select Text Document in the New dialog box. When you save the document, it is given the .TXT extension automatically. If necessary, change the extension (for example, to .BAT for a DOS batch file).

 T I P Create a shortcut for WordPad in the SendTo folder so you can quickly open any file with WordPad from Explorer or a folder window.

▶ **See** "Customizing the Send To Menu," **p. 112**

You can change the association for .TXT files so that they open in WordPad instead of Notepad when you open them from Explorer or My Computer. To change the association, follow these steps:

1. Choose View, Folder Options in Explorer or My Computer and select the File Types tab.
2. Select Text Document from the Registered File Types list, and then click Edit.
3. In the Actions list of the Edit File Type dialog box, select Open. Then click Edit.
4. Choose the Browse button. Then locate and select WORDPAD.EXE, which is located in the Program Files\Accessories folder.
5. Click OK and make sure that .TXT is selected in the Default Extension for Content list.
6. Click Close twice.

Creating Post-It Notes on Your Desktop

Because WordPad is an OLE 2–compliant application, you can drag and drop selected portions of a WordPad document into other OLE applications or onto the desktop. When you drag a selection onto the desktop, you create a scrap; double-click the icon for the scrap, and WordPad opens to display the information in the scrap. You can use these scraps as electronic Post-It notes—bits of information you might otherwise lose track of, secured to your desktop.

If you create desktop notes frequently, such as while you're on the phone, you can add WordPad to your StartUp folder so that it is immediately available, or you can simply create a shortcut on the desktop to WordPad. To create a note on your desktop, follow these steps:

1. Open WordPad and create the note.
2. Select the note and drag and drop it on the desktop. The scrap appears as a desktop icon, labeled with the first few words of the note. The data is saved as a file in the desktop folder.

You can rename the scrap if you want. Note also that you don't have to save the note in WordPad. Whenever you double-click the scrap icon, the note is opens in WordPad. If you open the scrap and make changes, the changes are automatically saved to the scrap when you close WordPad.

Part

III

Ch

14

Selecting and Editing Text

WordPad uses standard editing techniques, as found in most word processors. You can place the insertion point wherever you want to add text and begin typing. To delete characters, press Backspace (to delete characters to the left) or Del (to delete characters to the right).

When you need to work with larger blocks of text, such as words, sentences, or paragraphs, you can use your mouse to select the text using one of the techniques listed in Table 14.1.

Table 14.1   Mouse Techniques for Selecting Text

Selection	Action
One word	Double-click the word.
Several words	Double-click the first word and drag to the end of the last word.
Any amount of text	Hold down the mouse button and drag from the beginning to the end of the text.
Between two points	Move the insertion point to the beginning, click, move to the second point, press and hold down Shift, and click at the second point.
One line	Click the selection bar (white space) to the left of the line.
Several lines	Hold down the mouse button and drag up or down in the selection bar.
Paragraph	Double-click in the selection bar (blank area) to the left of the paragraph.
Entire document	Press Ctrl and click in the selection bar.

To select text with the keyboard, position the insertion point at the beginning of the text you want to select, hold down the Shift key, and move the insertion point to the end of the text using the arrow keys. To move the selection a word at a time, hold down the Shift and Ctrl keys as you press the arrow keys. You can select all the way to the end of a line by pressing the Shift and End keys.

After you have selected a block of text, you can delete it using the Del or Backspace keys. To move or copy the selected text, use the Edit, Cut or Edit, Copy keys, as described in the next section. If you start typing when text is selected, the selected text is replaced with whatever you type.

Moving and Copying Text

You can move or copy text using either the menu commands or the mouse. To move or copy text with the menu commands, follow these steps:

1. Select the text you want to move or copy using one of the techniques described in the previous section.

2. Choose Edit, Cut, or press Ctrl+X, or click the Cut button on the toolbar.

   or

   Choose Edit, Copy, or press Ctrl+C, or click the Copy button on the toolbar.

3. Position the insertion point where you want to move or copy the text.

4. Choose Edit, Paste, press Ctrl+V, or click the Paste button on the toolbar.

To move or copy text using the mouse, follow these steps:

1. Select the text you want to move or copy.

2. Point to the text with the mouse, hold down the mouse button, and drag the insertion point to the location where you want to move or copy the text.

   If you are copying the text, hold down the Ctrl key as you drag the text. A plus sign appears next to the mouse pointer, indicating that the text will be copied.

3. Release the mouse button.

WordPad is an OLE-compliant application, which means you can also drag text from a WordPad document into documents in other OLE-compliant applications. To simplify this operation, place the two application windows side by side before you move or copy the text.

Finding and Replacing Text

WordPad has find and replace commands that enable you to find a string of text, and if you want, to replace the found text with new text.

To find a string of text, follow these steps:

1. Choose Edit, Find or press Ctrl+F. The Find dialog box appears (see Figure 14.6).

FIG. 14.6
Use the Find dialog box
to search a document
for a string of text.

2. In the Find What text box, type the text string you want to find.

   (Optional) Select the Match Whole Word Only option to find text that exactly matches the text you typed in the Find What text box.

   (Optional) Select the Match Case option to find text that has the same case structure as the text you typed in the Find What text box.

3. Choose Find Next to find and select the first occurrence of the text.

4. Choose Find Next again to select the next occurrence of the text.

5. When you find the text you're looking for, click Cancel or press Esc.

Part
III

Ch
14

Even after you close the Find dialog box, you can repeat the last find operation by choosing Edit, Find Next or by pressing F3.

To find and replace a text string, follow these steps:

1. Choose Edit, Replace to display the Replace dialog box (see Figure 14.7).

FIG. 14.7
You can search for a text string and replace it with new text using the Replace dialog box.

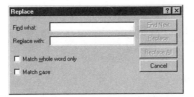

2. Type the text you want to replace in the Find What text box.
3. Type the text you want to insert in the Replace With text box.
4. Choose Find Next to locate the first occurrence of the text you typed in the Find What text box.
5. If you want to replace this text with the text in the Replace With text box, click Replace.

   or

   If you don't want to replace this text with the new text, click Find Next again to locate the next occurrence of the text.
6. To automatically replace all occurrences of the text in the Find What text box with the text in the Replace With text box, choose Replace All.
7. When you finish replacing text, click Cancel or press Esc.

Formatting in WordPad

WordPad enables you to format characters, paragraphs, and documents. At the character level, you can select a font, point size, and character attribute (such as bold and italic). At the paragraph level, you can align text to the left, right, or center. You can also specify the left, right, and first-line indents for a paragraph. At the document level, you can set the margins, change the orientation of the document (either portrait or landscape), and specify the paper size and which tray of your printer is used.

Formatting Characters

You can format characters using either the menu or the Format bar. To format text you have already typed, select the text first and then choose the formatting. To format text you are about to enter, position the insertion point where you will enter the text, and then choose the formatting.

To format characters using the menu commands, follow these steps:

1. Choose Format, Font to open the Font dialog box (see Figure 14.8).

FIG. 14.8
Select character
formatting in the Font
dialog box.

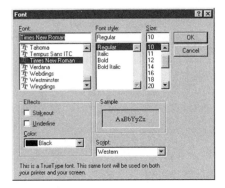

2. Select a font from the Font list box, a font style from the Font Style list box, and a point size from the Size list box. To preview your selections, look in the Sample box.

   (Optional) You can also select the Strikeout and Underline effects in the Effects box, and you can select a font color from the Color list.

3. When you finish making your selections, click OK.

You can make the same formatting selections from the Format bar. If the Format bar is not visible, choose View, Format Bar to display it. You can also toggle the font effects (bold, italic, and underline) on and off from the keyboard. Press Ctrl+B for bold, press Ctrl+I for italic, and press Ctrl+U for underline.

Formatting Paragraphs

In WordPad, you can adjust the text alignment and indentation of paragraphs. To format a paragraph, place the insert point in the paragraph you want to format and then make your formatting selections. If you want to format more than one paragraph, select all of the paragraphs you want to format. You can make your paragraph formatting selections using either the menu commands or the Format bar and ruler.

To format paragraphs using the menu, follow these steps.

1. Select the paragraphs you want to format.

2. Choose Format, Paragraph to display the Paragraph dialog box (see Figure 14.9).

3. Specify the indentation settings in the Left, Right, and First Line text boxes.

   WordPad uses inches to measure indentations and margins, not number of characters. This is because WordPad uses both proportionally spaced fonts and fonts of different sizes. Make sure you enter your settings in inches.

4. Select a paragraph alignment from the Alignment list.

5. When you finish making your selections, click OK.

Part
III

Ch
14

FIG. 14.9
Adjust the alignment and indentation for paragraphs in the Paragraph dialog box.

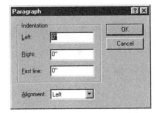

To set indentations using the ruler, follow these steps:

1. Choose View, Ruler if the ruler is not displayed.

2. Select the paragraph or paragraphs you want to change.

3. Drag the indent markers on the ruler to the desired settings.

You can change paragraph alignment using the Format bar. Select the paragraph or paragraphs you want to change, and then click the Align Left, Center, or Align Right button on the toolbar.

Creating a Bulleted List

WordPad enables you to add bullets to a list of items. To create a bulleted list, first type the items in the list. Each item should be a separate paragraph. Then select all the paragraphs and choose Format, Bullet Style to add the bullets. You can remove bullets by selecting the bulleted items and choosing Format, Bulleted Style again. If you press Enter at the end of a bulleted item to start a new paragraph, the new paragraph will also be bulleted.

Formatting a Document

Document formatting affects the appearance of an entire document. When you set the margins for a document, for example, those settings affect every page of the document.

To change the document formatting, follow these steps:

1. Choose File, Page Setup to display the Page Setup dialog box (see Figure 14.10).

FIG. 14.10
Use the Page Setup dialog box to change the margins, orientation, and paper size for a document.

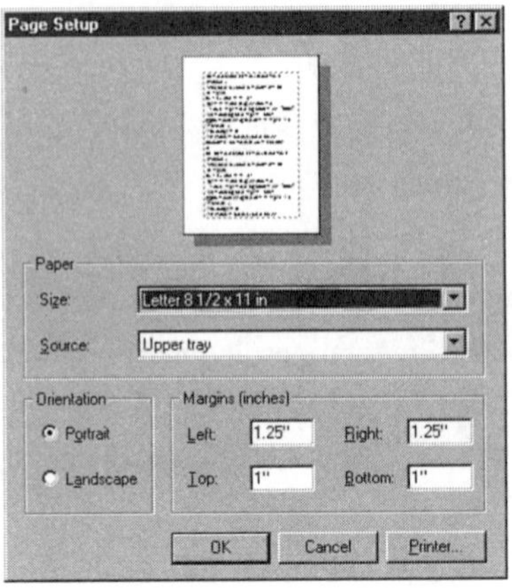

2. Enter the settings for the margins (in inches) in the Left, Right, Top, and Bottom text boxes.

3. Select either Portrait or Landscape orientation.

4. Select a paper size from the Size list.

5. If necessary, make a different selection from the Source list.

6. Click OK to put your changes into effect.

Setting Tabs

By default, WordPad has tab settings every one-half inch. You can also set custom tabs by using either the menu or the ruler. WordPad only uses left-aligned tabs.

To set a custom tab with the menu, follow these steps:

1. Select the paragraph in which you want to set the custom tabs.

2. Choose Format, Tabs to display the Tabs dialog box (see Figure 14.11).

FIG. 14.11

Set custom tabs in the Tabs dialog box.

3. Enter the setting for the custom tab in the text box (in inches).

4. Choose Set.

5. Repeat steps 3 and 4 to set up additional custom tabs.

6. To clear a tab, select it in the list of tabs and choose Clear.

7. When you finish settings tabs, click OK.

To set a custom tab using the ruler, select the paragraph in which you want to set custom tabs, and then click on the ruler wherever you want to set a tab. You can move an existing tab by dragging it along the ruler with the mouse. To remove a tab, drag it off the ruler.

Printing a WordPad Document

Printing a document with WordPad is very easy. You can preview a document to see exactly how it will appear on the printed page before you actually print the document, which will save you time and paper. Choose File, Print Preview to preview a document. Figure 14.12 shows the Print Preview window.

Part

III

Ch

14

FIG. 14.12

Save time and paper by previewing your document before you print it.

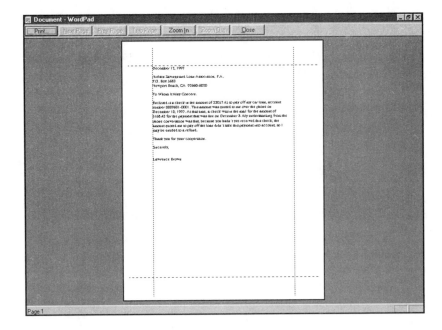

To zoom in for a close-up view of the document, click the magnifying glass on the area of the document you want to see up close or choose the Zoom In button. To zoom back out, click again or choose Zoom Out. Choose Close to close the Print Preview window.

To print a document, follow these steps:

1. Choose File, Print or click the Print button in the toolbar to display the Print dialog box (see Figure 14.13).

FIG. 14.13

Make your selections for printing a document in the Print dialog box.

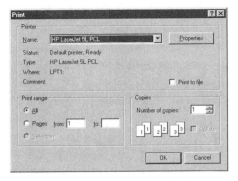

2. Select a printer from the Name list.

   After you make this selection, you will not have to do it again for printing other documents unless you want to change printers.

3. In the Print Range box, indicate what you want to print:

   Select All to print the entire document, or select Pages and specify a range of pages in the From and To text boxes. WordPad does not enable you to print a block of selected text.

4. To print the document to a file instead of to a printer, select the Print to File box. When you start the print job, you will be prompted for a filename and location.

5. Specify the number of copies you want to print in the Number of Copies box.

6. Click OK.

FIG. 14.14
You can customize some of WordPad's default settings in the Options dialog box.

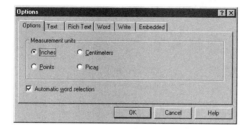

Changing WordPad Settings

You can change several of WordPad's default settings in the Options dialog box (shown in Figure 14.14). Your choices, available on each of the six tabs, include setting the measurement units, determining how word wrap operates, and presetting the toolbars that are displayed. To change any of these settings, choose View, Options, select the tab you want, make your selections, and click OK. ●

Part
III

Ch
14

CHAPTER 15

Using Paint and Imaging

by Ron Person

In this chapter

Editing Graphics in Windows

Windows 98 gives you two capable graphic file editors, Windows Paint and Imaging for Windows. Windows Paint is simple and easy to use, but it also might be as powerful a graphics application as you will ever need for creating and modifying bitmap (BMP) as well as GIF and JPEG graphics used on web pages.

Imaging for Windows enables you to open, modify, and annotate a wide range of graphic file formats, including TIFF, BMP, PCX, JPEG, GIF, fax documents, and more. With Imaging for Windows, you can add annotations to documents, highlight areas or text, rotate or magnify, and combine individual documents into a single multipage document. Imaging includes the ability to control scanners.

Using Windows Paint

When you need to make simple modifications to a BMP, GIF, or JPEG image, you might want to choose Windows Paint. It's quick to learn, yet has a full set of basic bitmap drawing tools.

Starting Windows Paint

To start Paint, click Start, Programs, Accessories, Paint. Paint starts up and opens a new, empty Paint file (see Figure 15.1).

FIG. 15.1
When you start Paint, a new file opens.

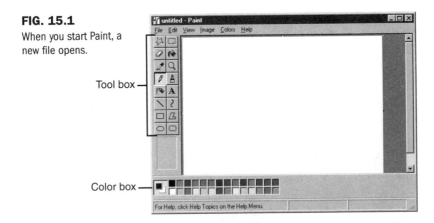

Tool box ⎯

Color box ⎯

To open a previously saved Paint file, click File, Open. Double-click the file in the Open dialog box.

Viewing Images in Paint

Use different levels of magnification to examine your drawing more closely or to paint and modify an image at the smallest, pixel, level. Use the View, Zoom or View, View Bitmap commands or the Magnifier tool to magnify an image so you can work on fine details. Figure 15.2 shows a small GIF image that has been magnified. When an image is magnified, you can edit the individual pixels in letters or the drawing.

FIG. 15.2
Magnify image details for more precise editing control.

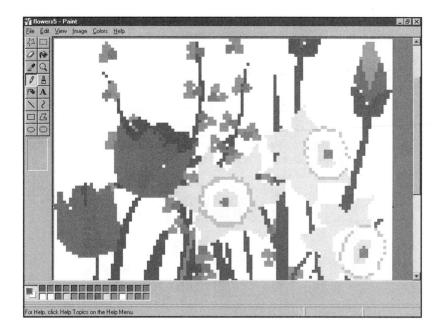

The larger magnifications of the picture display the *pixels*, or tiny squares of color, which make up your painting. Paint with any of the tools you use in normal magnification.

To change the view, follow these steps:

1. Click View, Zoom.
2. Click Normal Size (Ctrl+Page Up), Large Size (Ctrl+Page Down), or Custom. If you select Custom, the Custom Zoom dialog box is displayed. Select 100%, 200%, 400%, 600%, or 800%; then click OK.
3. Use the scroll bars to display the part of the painting you want to see.

To zoom back out to regular editing view, choose View, Zoom; then click Normal Size or click the Magnifier tool and then click in the picture.

Editing a Graphics File

Because Paint is a bitmap graphics application, the shapes you create are painted on screen in one layer. Although you can't layer objects, you can select portions and move, rotate, stretch, and change colors. As an aid for web graphics, you also can make graphics backgrounds transparent so a web page background shows through.

As you edit, be aware that completed objects cannot be edited, only erased or painted over and replaced. You can edit any object while creating it, but not after you complete the object. To remove an object you have just drawn, click Edit, Undo.

Whenever you reach a stage in your drawing where you are satisfied to that point, save the drawing with a unique name. This will enable you to return to previous stages. When the drawing is finished, erase the unneeded files.

Using the Paint Toolbox

The Paint toolbox includes tools for selecting areas, airbrushing, typing text, erasing, filling, brushing, drawing curves or straight lines, and drawing filled or unfilled shapes. Most of the tools operate using a similar process, as described in the following steps.

To create or modify an image you first must select the appropriate tool. If the tool uses a color you must also select a color. Figure 15.3 shows the individual tools in the tool box located on the left side of the screen.

FIG. 15.3

Paint's tool box provides the tools you need to create and modify a picture.

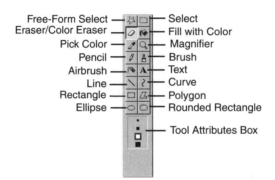

The color box offers foreground and background color choices. At the left end of the color box (see Figure 15.4) is a box overlaying a box. The top box is the foreground color; the bottom box is the background color. When you draw with the left mouse button the line is in the foreground color and the background color fills the object. Drawing with the right mouse button reverses the use of foreground and background colors.

FIG. 15.4

Choose foreground and background colors from the color box.

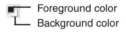

To select a tool or foreground color, click the left mouse button on the tool or color. Select a background color by right-clicking on a color.

To draw with the tools from the tool box, follow these steps:

1. Click the tool you want to use.
2. Position the pointer where you want to begin drawing; then press and hold down the mouse button as you draw with the mouse.
3. Release the mouse button to stop drawing.

The exceptions to this process are as follows:

- The Text tool, which you click to position the insertion point; then you type the text
- The Paint Fill tool, which works by pointing and clicking
- The Curve tool, which works by dragging a line and then clicking to the side of the line to create an arc
- The Polygon tool, which requires a click at each vertex of the polygon

Using Simple Tools The toolbox tools listed in Table 15.1 use simple procedures for operation. Tools not in this table are described in their own sections following this. Drawing with the left mouse button down uses the foreground color. Drawing with the right mouse button down uses the background color.

Table 15.1 Simple Tools

Function	Tool Name	Description
Select a rectangle	Select	Click the tool; then select an area by dragging a rectangular box.
Erase under tool	Erase	Click the tool; then select the eraser size at the bottom of the tool box. Drag with the left mouse button to erase. Background color is used to erase.
Fills interior of connected borders with color	Fill with Color	Click the tool. Left-click inside shape to fill with foreground color. Right-click for background color.
Pick color from picture for use with a drawing tool	Pick Color	Click tool; then click color in picture for use with drawing tool.
Magnify the picture to work at pixel levels	Magnifier	Click tool; then click magnification value at bottom of tool box. Use any tools while magnified.
Draw free-form lines	Pencil	Click tool; then drag to draw a one-pixel-wide free-form line.
Draw with variable width brush	Brush	Click tool; then select from the brush shapes at the bottom of the tool box. Drag to paint.
Paint with patterns of dots of varying density	Airbrush	Click the tool; then select a sprayer size at the bottom of the tool box. Select a color. Click or drag to spray. Hold the tool in one position longer to spray more densely.

continues

Table 15.1   Continued

Function	Tool Name	Description
Draw a straight line	Line	Click the tool; then select a line width at the bottom of the tool box. Drag the mouse to draw a straight line. Cancel the line that you're drawing by clicking the right mouse button before you release the left mouse button. Draw vertical, horizontal, or 45-degree angles by holding the Shift key.
Draw rectangle or square borders or filled shapes	Rectangle	Click the tool; then click the border only, border and fill, or fill only icon at the bottom of the tool box. Drag to draw a rectangle. Border size is the last line size selected. Hold the Shift to draw squares.
Draw an oval or circle	Ellipse	Click the tool; then click the border only, border and fill, or fill only icon at the bottom of the tool box. Drag to draw an oval. Border size is the last line size selected. Hold the Shift to draw a circle.
Draw a rectangle with rounded corners	Rounded Rectangle	Click the tool; then click the border only, border and fill, or fill only icon at the bottom of the tool box. Drag to draw a rectangle with rounded corners. Border size is the last line size selected. Hold the Shift key to draw a square with rounded corners.

Selecting a Free-Form Area   The Free-Form Select tool enables you to select an area of any shape by drawing a free-form boundary around the area. Click the Free-Form Select tool and two additional icons will be displayed in the toolbox. From these two, select either the Opaque (includes the background) tool or the Transparent (omits the background) tool at the bottom of the toolbox. Draw any shape to enclose the area to be selected. If you make a mistake while using the Free-Form Select tool, click the left mouse button outside the cutout area to cancel the selection.

Adding Text to a Picture   Use the Text tool to add text to your painting. Click the Text tool and, in the tool attributes box below the tool box, select Opaque (the background color fills the text box behind the text) or Transparent (the picture appears behind the text). Next, in the picture area, drag to determine the size of the text box. The text toolbar will be displayed, as shown in Figure 15.5. If it does not, click View, Text Toolbar to display it. Select a font, a point size, and bold, italic, or underline. There also is a button to orient text vertically or horizontally. Click in the text box and type.

FIG. 15.5

Type text in the text box and format with the Text toolbar.

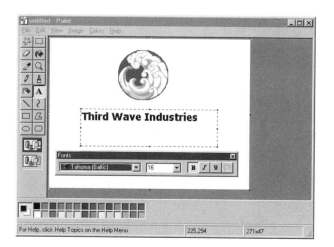

TIP If your painting includes a lot of text, you might find editing easier if you type the text in a word processor, select and copy it, and then paste it into Paint.

Drawing Curves   The Curve tool draws a curve. To draw a curve, follow these steps:

1. Click the Curve tool.

2. Select a line width from the tool attributes box.

3. Drag to draw a straight line. Release the mouse button at the end of the line.

4. Move the pointer to the side of the line; then drag the pointer to pull a curve in the line.

5. When you've achieved the arc you want, release the mouse button.

6. Click in the same spot to freeze the curve; to create an S-shaped curve, click on the other side of the line and repeat the process.

Drawing Objects with Many Sides (Polygons)   The Polygon tool draws a multi-sided shape. Each side on the shape is a straight line. To draw a polygon, follow these steps:

1. Click the Polygon tool; then click the border only, border and fill, or fill only icon in the tool attribute box.

2. Click and drag to draw the first side of the polygon. As with the Line tool, you can use the Shift key to draw a straight line segment oriented in 45 degree increments.

3. Release the mouse button and click at the next corner of the polygon. Continue to click at each of the remaining corners until the next-to-last corner.

4. Double-click at the next-to-last corner and Paint will automatically draw the last connecting line that finishes the polygon.

Choosing a File Format

To save a Paint file, click File, Save As. Type the name in the File Name text box; then click the Save As Type box to select one of the following file formats:

Format	File Extension Assigned
Monochrome Bitmap	BMP
16 Color Bitmap	BMP
256 Color Bitmap	BMP
24-bit Bitmap	BMP
JPEG	JPG, JPEG
GIF	GIF

Finally, click Save.

Using Imaging

Windows 98 includes free imaging software provided by Kodak called Imaging for Windows. Imaging for Windows can be used to view, annotate, print, manage, store, and share images that have been created from faxes, scanned documents, or computerized images. If you have a scanner, you can scan documents into Imaging for Windows.

You can annotate stored documents with graphics, highlights, and text. It even includes pre-defined or custom "rubber stamps" that can be stamped on an image. Documents can be passed on to others as a file. The imaging software is OLE-compatible, so you can select and then drag documents from the imaging software and drop them into applications such as Microsoft Word, Exchange, or Lotus Notes. Double-clicking on an embedded image of a document activates the image and switches the applications menus and toolbars to those of the Imaging for Windows software.

File formats read include AWD (Fax), BMP, PCX/DCX, JPG, XIF, GIF, WIFF, and TIF. The software stores documents in an industry standard multipage TIF 6.0, AWD (Microsoft FAX), or BMP (bitmap) format.

Starting Imaging

Open Imaging for Windows by clicking Start, Programs, Accessories and selecting Imaging. Imaging will open with a blank new document. By default, AWD and TIF files will open when the files are opened from an Explorer window.

Imaging for Windows runs either in a Read Only mode to preview images or in an editing mode. If you want editable files to open in the Imaging Preview mode so they cannot be edited, choose Tools, General Options and click the Preview button in the General Options dialog box.

TIP If the title bar for a document shows (Read Only), the document is in a format that Image cannot edit. Save the document to TIF, AWD (Fax), or BMP formats if you want to edit it.

Modifying Images

Imaging for Windows includes several tools to help you modify images, although you should not consider it a graphics editing application. If you will be modifying images, you might want to display the Imaging and Annotation toolbars by choosing View, Toolbars and selecting these two toolbars. From the Page menu or the Imaging toolbar, you can rotate an image in 90-degree increments clockwise or counterclockwise.

The Annotation menu or toolbar enables you to draw freehand lines and rectangles, highlight areas, create text boxes, and stamp with rubber stamps. The annotations you make are objects. Objects remain distinct and editable from the picture background. You can select an object with the Annotation Selection arrow and move, copy, or delete it. Saving the file in TIF format will enable you to make further changes to the objects when you reopen the file. Saving to BMP or AWD format freezes the annotations.

Inserting and Appending Images into a Multipage Document

Build a multiple page document by opening a new document or opening one of the documents that will be contained (see Figure 15.6). To insert a document before the current document, choose Page, Insert. If you want to insert a scanned image, choose Scan Page from the submenu and following scanning procedures. To insert an image from an existing file, choose Existing Page and select the file from the Open dialog box.

FIG. 15.6

Construct and view multipage documents in Imaging for Windows.

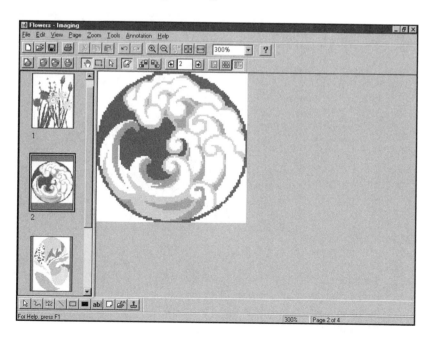

If you want to insert an image at the end of a multi-page document, choose Page, Append and then choose either Scan Page or Existing Page from the submenu depending on the source of the file you want to append.

Working with Scanned Images or Digital Photos

Use Imaging for Windows to scan documents and images directly. Before you can scan a document, you must install your scanner; then click File, Select Scanner. Select the scanner you want and choose OK. After you have selected a scanner you can scan a new document by clicking File, Scan New. The control window for your scanner or digital camera will be displayed. Follow the procedure described for your scanner or digital camera.

Imaging for Windows works with TWAIN-compliant scanners and digital cameras. If your scanner or camera does not work with Imaging for Windows, check to make sure the scanner is TWAIN-compliant and is correctly installed.

Viewing and Annotating Fax Files

Use Imaging for Windows to collect and annotate fax documents like the one shown in Figure 15.7. You also can create a multipage fax document from separate fax documents or image files, as described in the preceding section.

FIG. 15.7

View, annotate, and aggregate fax documents.

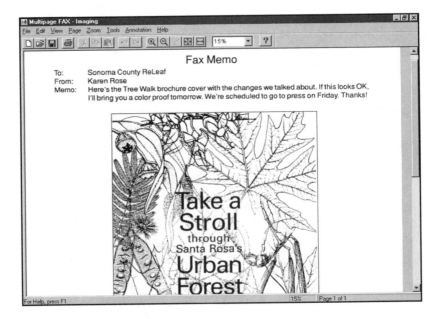

Add comments to a fax image by annotating the image with a text overlay or by drawing on it. To annotate an image with a drawing, highlight, text, note, or rubber stamp, choose the type of annotation you want from the Annotation menu. The highlighter will draw with a color over the fax image. When the file is saved to an AWD format, the highlight color changes to black-and-white shading.

Make multipage documents easier to browse by choosing <u>V</u>iew, <u>P</u>age and Thumbnails. This displays the thumbnails in a scrollable left pane and the full image of the selected thumbnail in the right pane, as shown in Figure 15.6.

Choosing a File Format

The file format in which you save your work affects changes you have made to the document or image. The default format for new files is TIFF although you can select AWD (Fax) or BMP format from the New Blank Document dialog box. When you create the new document, you can also specify the color depth, compression, resolution, and size.

If you create a TIFF file, you have a variety of color palettes available and you can use compression to reduce the file size. AWD files are limited to black and white, and compression is automatic. If you annotate an AWD file, the annotation will become a permanent part of the file when saved. BMP files can have different color palettes, but they are limited to a single page and cannot be compressed.

Change a file type by opening the file and then resaving it with the new file type. The new file will be limited by the color palette, size, and compression options available to the new file type.

PART IV

Managing Your System

CHAPTER 16

Maintaining and Troubleshooting Your System

by Ty Belknap and Larry Passo

In this chapter

Keeping Windows 98 Up-to-Date

No software is perfect, whether it's an operating system, a program, or the drivers for a piece of hardware. Companies are constantly working on their products to improve performance and reliability, and the main concern today is figuring out ways to get those improvements installed on user's systems.

Realizing this concern, Microsoft combined the use of the Internet with Windows 98 to get updates out quickly and easily, using the Windows Update Wizard.

Using the Windows Update Wizard

The Windows Update Wizard is a database maintained by Microsoft that contains drivers, system utilities, and other software. This gives you one convenient place on the Internet to check to see if there are Windows 98 updates available for your system. This is a Microsoft site, though, and Microsoft must approve all updated drivers on the site, so it might not have everything that you are looking for.

To search for updates using the Microsoft Update Wizard, follow these steps

1. Click Start and click the Windows Update icon. Internet Explorer comes up automatically and attempts to connect to Microsoft's Windows Update web site shown in Figure 16.1.

FIG. 16.1
The Update Wizard and Technical Support web sites are now combined.

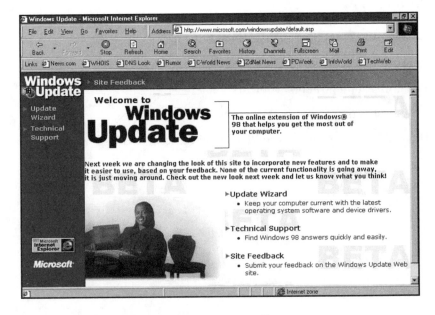

2. Click on Update Wizard. A registration wizard pops up if this is the first time you've used the Update Wizard (see Figure 16.2). You must fill out the registration to continue. Part of the registration is to upload your configuration files to Microsoft. You can deselect a check box so this doesn't happen if you want to.

FIG. 16.2

The Update Wizard will not start if you click No.

3. The Update Wizard web page contains two options: Update and Restore. Click Update to scan the Internet for updated system files. A new Internet Explorer window pops up, as shown in Figure 16.3. The Update Wizard loads necessary components into your system and then scans the database for updated drivers.

FIG. 16.3

When you click Update, a list of available files appears on the left side of the main window.

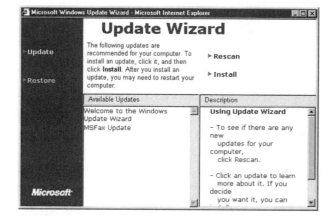

Part

IV

Ch

16

4. As updates are found, the wizard refreshes the screen and the list of files available for update. Select a file in the list on the left to see its description as well as its, size, and approximate download time on the right side of the main window.

5. Click on Install to install the file. Only one file can be installed at a time, and your computer may need to be restarted after a file is installed. Let the computer restart if necessary before downloading a second update in order to verify that it is still working properly.

The Update Wizard keeps track of where the new and old files are in case there's a problem. If your system crashes after you install a new file, or if some functions no longer work properly, you can go back and reinstall the old files. To do so, follow these steps:

1. Open the Update Wizard and click Restore. A new Internet Explorer window pops up, and the wizard scans your system and gives you a list of the files you have updated, as shown in Figure 16.4.

2. Select a file in the list on the left to show the description of the update.

3. To remove the update, click Uninstall. Restart your system if prompted.

FIG. 16.4
The Restore option allows you to uninstall files if they cause problems.

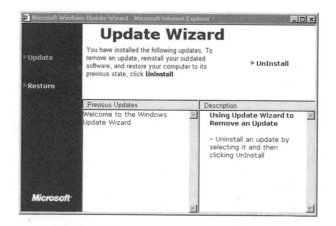

Reading Your Registration and Version Number

Your registration and version number might not seem important at first glance. But because Microsoft updates Windows 98 with patches and service packs, knowing where this information is will be helpful.

To view your current version of Windows 98 and Internet Explorer, as well as your product ID number, right-click on My Computer and select Properties. This opens the properties sheet shown in Figure 16.5.

FIG. 16.5
You will find the Windows and Internet Explorer version numbers in the System Properties dialog box. Your product ID number is the first number in the Registered To area.

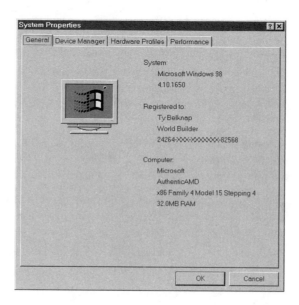

Improving Windows Performance

The performance of Windows 98 can degrade over time as you add and remove programs and make updates to the system files. This section describes how to use the Disk Defragmenter and ScanDisk features to help keep your system working at top speed. In the following subsections, you'll find steps on how to check your performance settings, adjust virtual memory, and track system resources, as well as a detailed explanation of what the Windows 98 Tune-Up Wizard is and how to use it to automate tasks.

Part
IV

Ch

16

Checking Performance Settings

Your computer's performance settings are vital tools in the war against problems. The main Performance page can warn you about old drivers or possible viruses and gives you an easy way to check your system resources.

Follow these steps to check your computer's performance settings:

1. Right-click My Computer.

2. Left-click Properties to access your system settings.

3. Choose the Performance tab at the top to view your performance settings (see Figure 16.6).

FIG. 16.6
Check the main Performance page often. Problems with your computer might show up here.

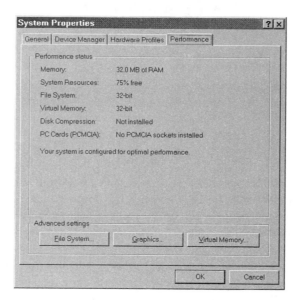

Look carefully through the main page of the Performance tab. Make sure that it lists the correct amount of memory and that the File System and Virtual Memory both say 32-bit. Incorrect amounts of RAM could show that there are bad RAM chips on your computer. Or it might mean that you are loading an old DOS program (like Smart Drive) in your AUTOEXEC.BAT or CONFIG.SYS files or the load= or run= lines at the beginning of your WIN.INI file.

> **CAUTION**
>
> If your File System area shows some or all of your hard drives using MS-DOS Compatibility Mode Paging, you might be using an old hard disk driver or the Disable All 32 Bit Protected-Mode Disk Drivers option on the Troubleshooting tab might be checked. Use the Update Manager or contact the disk manufacturer to see if updated drivers are available.
>
> A virus is another potential cause of Compatibility Mode Paging. Viruses and antivirus programs are covered toward the end of this chapter.

The Performance tab gives you access to three types of advanced settings: File System, Graphics, and Virtual Memory. Each of those types is outlined here.

File System   As you can see in Figure 16.7, the File System Properties dialog box has five tabs of options: Hard Disk, Floppy Disk, CD-ROM, Removable Disk, and Troubleshooting.

FIG. 16.7

The Hard Disk tab.

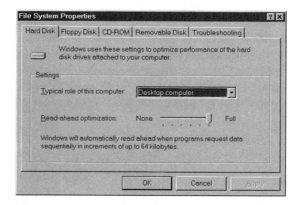

The Hard Disk tab configures the settings on how the hard disk reads files and how the VCACHE file system works. In the Settings area, you can configure the following options:

- *Typical Role of This Machine.* The three options are: Desktop Computer, Mobile or Docking System, and Network Computer. Laptop users should use the Mobile or Docking System option. The Network computer option could make the system run a bit faster than the Desktop Computer option, but it also can cause the system to hang during shutdown or restart if the file system cache is not able to completely clear itself.

- *Read-Ahead Optimization.* This should be set to Full by default, and unless your system does not shut down or restart properly, that is the best setting. If you have trouble using the normal shut down procedures, lower this option one step at a time to try to alleviate the problem.

N O T E   VCACHE is the Windows 98 Dynamic Swap File. This file grows and shrinks as programs are opened and closed. The Swap File, named Win386.swp, is a hidden file located on the root of your first hard drive.

The Floppy Disk tab contains only one option, which enables you to have the computer search for new floppy drives every time the system is restarted. This is a good option for laptop users who have removable floppy drives, but desktop users can save time by disabling it. The default option for this setting is off.

The CD-ROM tab configures the read-ahead and buffering for your CD-ROM system. Figure 16.8 shows the two options to be configured.

Part

IV

Ch

16

- ■ *Supplemental Cache Size.* Set this option to Large. This is another setting to lower if you are having problems shutting down or restarting your computer. If your computer hangs during shutdown, it could be because the CD-ROM cache is not flushing itself properly.

- ■ *Optimize Access Pattern For.* Choose the CD-ROM type you have. Raising the amount of the cache on smaller CD-ROM drives does not improve performance and may cause problems. Anything over a Quad (4) speed CD-ROM should use the Quad-Speed or Higher setting.

FIG. 16.8

The CD-ROM tab.

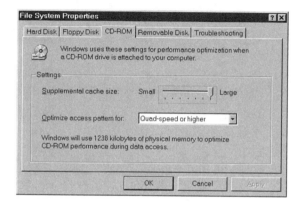

The Removable Disk tab also contains only one option: Enable Write-Behind Caching on All Removable Disk Drives. Removable disks include such drives as Zip, Jaz, and Syquest, and this is a good option to check if you have one of them. Write-behind caching allows your applications to execute faster by saving their disk writes to a buffer area in memory, which is must faster than actually writing the data directly to the disk. The contents of the buffer area will be written to the actual removable disk when the disk is ready to accept it. Because write-behind caching is enabled by default for your hard disks, the only reason to use this option is if you have removable media. The default option for this setting is off.

CAUTION

If you choose to use write-behind caching on removable disks, make sure the computer is done writing to the disk before you remove the disk, or some information might be lost. You should also consider using an Uninterruptible Power Supply (UPS) because you risk the loss of data if your computer loses power before it empties the buffer and finishes writing information to your removable disk.

The Troubleshooting tab is useful when you're working with older MS-DOS programs, especially file utility programs like Norton Utilities that weren't made for Windows 98. Figure 16.9 shows the six items on the Troubleshooting tab.

N O T E Windows 98 handles file systems much like Windows 95 did, and you can use most Windows 95 file utility programs in Windows 98. If you are using FAT32, make sure the utility is FAT32-compatible. ▇

▶ **See** "Choosing a File System," **p. 148**

FIG. 16.9
Click on a check box to disable or enable an item.

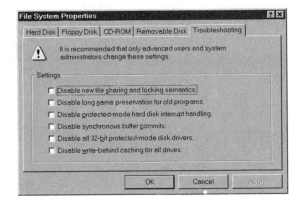

N O T E Every time you check (or clear) a box in the Troubleshooting tab, you must restart your computer. ▇

The six options on the Troubleshooting tab are:

- ▇ *Disable New File Sharing and Locking Semantics.* Some older MS-DOS programs cannot handle the new file sharing capabilities of Windows. Check this box to disable Windows file sharing so older programs can work properly.

- ▇ *Disable Long Name Preservation for Older Programs.* This option turns off the tunneling feature, which preserves long filenames when files are opened and saved by applications that do not recognize long filenames. You should use this option only if you need to ensure compatibility with important legacy applications.

    You can use this setting in conjunction with the utility LFNBK (located in the \tools\ reskit\file\lfnback subfolder of the Windows 98 CD). LFNBK allows you to back up long filenames while using older utilities; checking this option allows the long filenames to be unlocked so LFNBK can convert long filenames to 8.3 filenames.

N O T E To preserve long filenames with disk utilities that do not recognize them:

1. Turn off tunneling.

2. Close all other applications. (LFNBK cannot rename open files.)

3. At the command prompt, type **LFNBK /b *drive*** to back up and remove long filenames.

4. Restart the computer, and then run the disk utility. If it is an MS-DOS-based utility, run it in MS-DOS mode. If it is a Windows-based utility, run it in the usual way.

5. Turn tunneling on again, and then restart the computer.

6. At the command prompt, type **LFNBK /r *drive*** to restore long filenames.

The LFNBK utility actually renames each file with a long filename to its associated alias. The filename changes are stored in the LFNBK.DAT file in the root of the drive where you are running LFNBK. This file is used to restore long filenames (when you run LFNBK with the /r switch). ▪

Part

IV

Ch

16

CAUTION

The LFNBK utility is intended for use only by experienced Windows 95 users who have special needs for compatibility with older disk utilities. It is not intended for everyday use by average users.

▪ *Disable Protected-Mode Hard Disk Interrupt Handling.* This option prevents Windows 98 from terminating interrupts from the hard disk controller and bypassing the ROM routine that handles such interrupts. Some hard disk drives might require that this option be checked in order for interrupts to be processed correctly. If this option is checked, the ROM routine handles the interrupts, which slows system performance. This setting is off by default for all computers in Windows 95, and is on by default for all computers running Windows 3.x.

▪ *Disable Synchronous Buffer Commits.* This option causes a write initiation of the API buffers to the hard disk but allows users to continue working before the write is completed. This will not gain you better performance, but it might cause errors and data loss if the write is not completed. Use this option only when you're troubleshooting performance problems with specific programs that may require it.

▪ *Disable All 32-Bit Protected-Mode Disk Drivers.* Check this option if you think you are having problems writing information to the hard disk, or if your computer does not start due to disk writes. Note, however, that this will cause Compatibility Mode Paging to show up in the General properties tab for all hard drives. You should use this option only for troubleshooting because it will also slow your system significantly.

▪ *Disable Write-Behind Caching for All Drives.* Here is another thing to check if your system does not shut down or restart correctly. It will shut off all cache options for all disk drives, including the floppy disk, and it will slow your system down. So it's not really a fix, it just helps you determine where the problem lies.

Graphics The Graphics button off the main Properties tab takes you to the Advanced Graphics Settings dialog box, shown in Figure 16.10.

FIG. 16.10
Hardware acceleration can be a double-edged sword; it is not as stable as it should be.

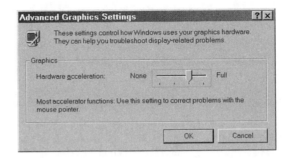

The only option here is Hardware Acceleration. If you're upgrading from Windows 95, the upgrade should keep the same settings you had before. Hardware acceleration is usually a performance boost to computers, but using hardware acceleration can cause Fatal Exception errors. The text of a Fatal Exception error usually looks something like this:

```
(filename) caused a Fatal Exception error in module (filename) at: 0128:bfff…
(more numbers)
```

The bfff series is what's important here. If the series of numbers starts with A, B, or C, the error could be a video problem. The first step toward correcting it is to look over the Internet or a Bulletin Board System to see if new drivers are available for your video card. If your video card has the latest drivers but you are still having problems, start lowering the Hardware Acceleration level one step at a time. After each restart, use your computer normally to see if the error reoccurs.

 Anytime you think your computer is experiencing problems related to hardware, check the Microsoft Windows Update Wizard for updated drivers. An updated driver might solve the problem.

Lowering the Hardware Acceleration option might also solve mouse pointer problems. If your pointer disappears or if your mouse pointer seems jerky (and the mouse itself is not dirty), lower the Hardware Acceleration option one or two notches and see if that helps.

Virtual Memory Virtual Memory is the last option on the Performance tab (see Figure 16.11). Virtual memory allows Windows to load and run faster and more efficiently. If you restarted your computer and ran System Monitor (discussed later in this chapter), you would find that Windows has about a 6MB disk cache. This is because Windows loads virtual drivers, video drivers, the drivers to run hard disks, and more in virtual memory. In addition, every program that you load adds drivers and files to that virtual memory area.

FIG. 16.11
Virtual memory is the
Windows 98 swap file.

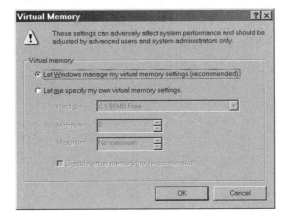

The best option is to let Windows manage your virtual memory settings. Windows 98 has a dynamic swap file that grows and shrinks in size depending on what you need.

Specifying your own settings can improve performance on your computer, but it imposes limitations on what Windows can swap to the file from RAM. Set the minimum and maximum sizes of the swap file to the same size if you decide to specify your own settings. That will make a permanent swap file on your hard disk that does not change size, so Windows doesn't have to manage the file. The more RAM you have, the smaller a swap file you need. A manually created swap file should be around 20MB if you have 32MB RAM (more if you have less RAM). The recommended minimum amount for a swap file is 12MB RAM, which can be eaten up quickly.

Defragmenting Disks for Faster Access to Data

Windows 98 writes information to the hard disk drive using whatever free space is available. As programs are removed, gaps form between the files that are left on the hard disk; those gaps are then filled by new programs that are installed. This process causes *fragmentation* of the hard drive, which cannot be prevented.

As the hard disk becomes fragmented, the computer has to search many different areas to execute programs or bring up data files. This causes a loss of performance because moving the read/write head of the hard disk to widely separated areas on the disk drive is a relatively slow operation. Fragmentation can also cause the computer to have problems during the normal execution of programs.

Disk Defragmenter was created to alleviate these problems. The Windows 98 Disk Defragmenter searches your hard disk for files and programs that belong together and then puts them in the right spots (like organizing a filing cabinet). The new Disk Defragmenter also watches how you use your computer and puts the programs you use the most at the front of the hard disk for faster access. This is done automatically if you check the option on the Settings submenu (detailed below), so you don't have to worry about picking and choosing which programs you might use the most.

 TIP   Setting your screen saver to None before you start to defragment your hard disk allows the process to end faster.

To begin using Disk Defragmenter, follow these steps:

1. Click Start, Programs, Accessories, System Tools, Disk Defragmenter.

2. From the screen shown in Figure 16.12, select the drive you want to defragment.

FIG. 16.12
Select the drive you
want to defragment.

3. Click the Settings button to open the dialog box shown in Figure 16.13.

4. Use the following options to specify your preferences:

   Rearrange Program Files So My Programs Start Faster. This tells the utility to choose the programs you use the most and put them at the front of the hard disk drive. This will cause Disk Defragmenter to run slower, but your computer could show improved performance once it's done.

Check the Drive for Errors. This tells the utility to test the sectors of the physical disk for problems. The utility might come back with a message to run ScanDisk if the error is something Disk Defragmenter can't handle. This will cause Disk Defragmenter to run slower, but it is a good option to use if you've been having system problems.

FIG. 16.13
Deselect both options if you just want a quick defrag of your hard drive.

Part

IV

Ch

16

5. If you want to save your settings, click Every Time I Defragment My Hard Drive. If you only want to use the settings for this time, click This Time Only.

6. Click OK to start the utility.

You also have the option of running Disk Defragmenter from the hard drive icon. To do so, open My Computer, right-click on a hard drive icon, and choose Properties. Then click the Tools tab to see the screen shown in Figure 16.14. The Defragmentation Status box at the bottom tells you how long it's been since your hard drive was defragmented. Select Defragment Now to start the Disk Defragmenter utility.

FIG. 16.14
You do not have the option of changing settings when you access Disk Defragmenter in this way, but it is a quick way to defrag a specific hard drive.

Using ScanDisk to Prevent and Repair Damage

ScanDisk can search all the files on your computer, as well as the physical disk(s), for errors. When it finishes the search, ScanDisk offers you options on how to fix any errors it has found.

> **N O T E**   ScanDisk checks and fixes problems in the following areas on hard disk drives, floppy disk drives, RAM drives, and memory cards:
>
> - File allocation table (FAT)
> - Long filenames
> - File system structure (lost clusters, cross-linked files)
> - Directory tree structure
> - Physical surface of the drive (bad sectors)
> - DriveSpace or DoubleSpace volume header, volume file structure, compression structure, and volume signatures
>
> ScanDisk cannot find or fix errors on CD-ROM drives, network drives, or drives created by using the MS-DOS commands Assign, Subst, Join, or InterInk. ▨

To start ScanDisk, click Start, Programs, Settings, System Tools, ScanDisk. The screen shown in Figure 16.15 appears. The Windows 98 version of ScanDisk can handle both FAT16 and FAT32 formatted hard disks.

▷ For more information on FAT16 and FAT32, **see** "Choosing a File System," **p. 148**

FIG. 16.15
The main ScanDisk window.

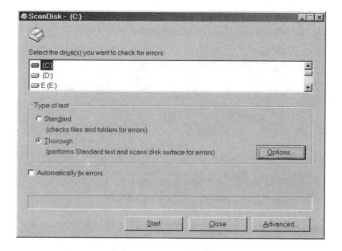

> **N O T E**   You can also start ScanDisk by selecting My Computer, right-clicking on the drive you want to scan, and choosing Properties. Select the Tools tab and click the Check Now button. ▨

The main ScanDisk window contains two options and a check box. Choose one of the following options:

■ *Standard.* This tells ScanDisk to check all files on your hard disk(s) for errors and to report any errors it finds. With this option, ScanDisk will not check the physical sectors on the hard disk(s). However, the Standard check is significantly faster than the Thorough check.

■ *Thorough.* This tells ScanDisk to check all files on your hard disk(s) and to do a surface scan to check the physical disk(s) for errors. If it finds errors on your physical disk(s), ScanDisk marks the affected sectors as bad and attempts to move any information in those sectors to good sectors.

Part
IV
Ch
16

If you choose the Thorough option, you can also specify what you want ScanDisk to do by clicking on the Options button and using the options shown in Figure 16.16.

FIG. 16.16
It's a good idea to do a surface scan if you're having trouble installing a new program.

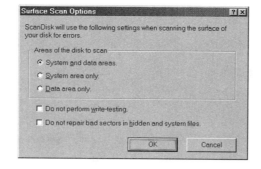

CAUTION

The files needed to run Windows reside in the System area. If your computer has a bad sector in the System area, you might not be able to restart Windows and might have to reinstall Windows from a DOS prompt.

Toward the bottom left corner of the main ScanDisk window is the Automatically Fix Errors check box. By default, this option is not checked, and ScanDisk simply shows you each error it finds. If you check this option, ScanDisk shows you the error and gives you the following options for choosing how to deal with the error:

■ *Ignore the Error and Continue.* You can ignore the error if it's not serious and continue scanning the rest of the disk. ScanDisk will tell you if the error is so serious that it cannot continue without fixing the error.

■ *Repair the Error by….* You can have ScanDisk repair the error and continue. ScanDisk will ask if you want to create an undo file. Always create one if you don't know what ScanDisk is trying to fix. You can always delete the undo file later.

■ *Delete the Affected… [file, folder, and so on].* ScanDisk will ask if you want to create an undo file. It's a good idea to create an undo file just in case.

N O T E ScanDisk will automatically fix the error and create an undo file if you choose to automatically fix errors.

At the bottom of the main ScanDisk screen, you'll see an Advanced button. Click the Advanced button to access these sets of options:

- *Display Summary.* You can tell ScanDisk to Always Display a Summary, Never Display the Summary, or Only Give a Summary When Errors Are Found.

- *Log File.* ScanDisk creates a log file called SCANDISK.LOG every time it is run. This file should be placed in the root of C:. You can choose to Replace Log, which will delete the previous log file; Append to Log, which will keep adding to the file; or No Log, which will never keep a log.

  You should generate a log file to keep track of errors. Use Append to Log only if you want to track errors over a period of time, though.

- *Cross-Linked Files.* Cross-linked files are two separate files that occupy the same space on a hard disk. This does not normally happen, and you may find other problems when this error comes up. The options for cross-linked files are: Delete to Remove Both Files from the Hard Disk, Make Copies to Re-Copy Each File to a Different Area of the Hard Disk, and Ignore If You Want ScanDisk to Keep Searching for Other Errors Without Fixing This One. It's recommended that you make copies.

N O T E The most frequent cause of cross-linked files is computers that are not shut down properly before they are turned off. That is why Windows 98 automatically runs ScanDisk when you turn your computer back on after it has been turned off improperly.

- *Lost File Fragments.* Generally, file fragments are created when Windows is not shut down properly. The two options are: Free to Delete the File Fragments Without Viewing Them and Convert to Files to Save Them and Look at Them Later. If you choose the Convert to Files... option, ScanDisk saves the fragments with an extension of .CHK in the root directory of your C: drive. You can view them with Notepad or WordPad. Most often they contain ASCII characters and can be deleted, but it's a good idea to save them if you were working on a file when Windows crashed.

- *Check Files For.* You have three options to choose from. Choose Invalid File Names to have ScanDisk search your hard disk for filenames that include invalid characters. Choose Invalid Dates and Times to have ScanDisk search for files that have improper dates or times associated with them. Choose Duplicate File Names to have ScanDisk search for duplicate files in the same directory.

  The latter option can slow ScanDisk down if it's searching directories with many files. In addition, if it finds duplicate files, you have the option of having ScanDisk repair the error (it will rename the files so they have different names), delete the affected files/ folders, or ignore the error and continue.

- *Check Host Drive First.* This option is useful if you have a DriveSpace compressed drive. It tells ScanDisk to automatically check both drives for errors.

■ *Report MS-DOS Mode Name Length Errors.* You can have ScanDisk check for filenames that are too long for MS-DOS mode to handle.

Click OK to apply the Advanced option settings you've selected and return to the main ScanDisk screen.

Then click Start to run ScanDisk. ScanDisk could take a long time to run (more than half an hour if you selected the Thorough option or if the hard disk is very fragmented).

Using the All-in-One Windows Maintenance Wizard

The Windows Maintenance Wizard is a program that automates ScanDisk and Disk Defragmenter, as well as clearing your system of temporary files and unwanted networking components. With this wizard, you can have Windows run ScanDisk and Disk Defragmenter automatically on specific days and during specific times when you are not using your system.

To run the Windows Maintenance Wizard, click Start, Programs, Accessories, System Tools, Maintenance Wizard. If you have never run the Maintenance Wizard before, the first screen you see asks whether you want to do an Express or Custom tune-up (see Figure 16.17).

N O T E If you have run the Maintenance Wizard before, performing the preceding steps takes you to a dialog box that asks whether you want to Perform Maintenance Now or Change My Maintenance Settings or Schedule. If you choose Change My Maintenance Settings or Schedule, the wizard responds with the screen shown in Figure 16.17. ■

FIG. 16.17
Express setup is quick and easy.

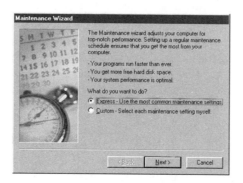

The Express method uses the most common tune-up settings and is a quick way to get the Maintenance Wizard up and running. Choose the Express setting and click Next. The next screen that appears asks what time of day you want the wizard to run (Nights, Days, or Evenings). Choose your preference and click Next. Windows shows you which tasks will be performed. Click Finish, and you're done.

The Custom method enables you to select each tune-up setting yourself. The Custom selection allows for more flexibility but is more difficult to set up. To use the Custom setting, follow these steps:

1. Choose the Custom button and click Next. The wizard asks what time of day you want the programs to run (Nights, Days, Evenings, or Custom). Choose the setting you want and click Next.

2. The Speed Up Programs window shown in Figure 16.18 appears. This window shows you what programs you have opening at startup. You can make Windows 98 start faster by not having any programs start automatically at startup. Click Next.

FIG. 16.18

Pick your startup files carefully. They can slow down the Windows startup process.

3. In the Speed Up Programs screen, you can specify when the Windows Disk Defragmenter should run. You can click on Reschedule or Settings to make any necessary changes to the schedule or settings. Click Next.

4. In the Scan Hard Disk for Errors screen, choose the options you want. Then click Next.

5. Delete Unnecessary Files is a tricky option. Every time your computer shuts off or restarts abnormally, a temporary file is created. Many newer Windows programs make a temporary file in the case of an accidental shut down as well. Most of the time, these temporary files are junk and can be deleted. However, there may be a time when you're writing an important document and your computer freezes. In that situation, a temporary file may have been created that can help you get your information back.

   If you do choose to have unnecessary files deleted, you can use the Settings button to indicate what types of files you want deleted (see Figure 16.19). Click Next.

FIG. 16.19

Disk Cleanup allows you to view the files that are marked for deletion.

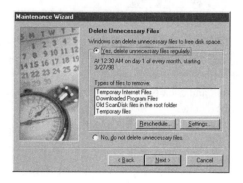

6. The last screen confirms your choices. Your computer must be on when the scheduled choices run. Verify the information, and then click Finish. This adds Task Scheduler to the System Tray on the right end of the taskbar.

 TIP You can perform the same functions on your system manually that the Maintenance Wizard performs automatically by using the Disk Defragmenter, ScanDisk, and Disk Cleanup utilities, all of which are located in the System Tools folder.

Keeping Track of System Resources

During a normal day at the computer, you might find yourself opening and closing a few programs, accessing the Internet for web pages or to read email, and perhaps playing a game that you end up having to hide in the background. Everything you do on your computer, whether it's moving the mouse around or loading the newest game, takes *system resources*, or memory. You should be able to reclaim resources by closing programs, but poorly written programs don't always give all the resources back. Unfortunately, the only way to get back all of your "missing" resources is to restart your computer.

There are several easy ways to keep track of your system's resources:

- Right-click My Computer, select Properties, and choose the Performance tab. The System Resources line shows a percentage of your free resources. My personal experience shows that my computer becomes very slow and I'm more likely to get errors when my system goes below 75 percent free resources with no programs running (using 32MB of RAM). Individual systems may vary, depending on the system and the amount of RAM it has.

- Resource Meter is a good way to keep constant track of your system's memory. To use it, click Start, Programs, Accessories, System Tools, and choose Resource Meter. Resource Meter runs in the System Tray of your taskbar. Hold your mouse pointer over the icon to see the free resources you have. You can also double-click the icon to bring up a bar chart that shows your free resources.

- System Monitor is another utility that tracks system resources. Because of its size and the number of options the utility offers, we've dedicated an entire section to System Monitor. See "Using System Monitor to Detect Bottlenecks," later in this chapter.

NOTE Keep in mind that Resource Meter uses system resources like all other programs do.

Repairing Configuration Problems

Windows 98 comes with a fantastic new utility called *System Information*. The System Information utility keeps track of all your computer's file versions, the resources your hardware is using, and the hardware and software components of your computer.

The Tools tab at the top of the utility also provides a means of quick access to Dr. Watson, System File Checker, Registry Checker, and more.

To access the System Information utility, click Start, Programs, Accessories, System Tools, System Information.

Gathering Details with the System Information Utility

The Microsoft System Information utility is a great tool for use in the battle against errors. It's a one-stop utility that enables you to view the resources, system components, and software environment on your computer. You can also run the following utilities from the Tools menu of the System Information utility:

- *Windows Report Tool.* Helps generate trouble reports.
- *Update Wizard Uninstall.* Enables you to select which of the packages that were automatically installed by the Update Wizard that you would like to uninstall and revert to their original version.
- *System File Checker.* Checks your system files to make sure that they are correct.
- *Signature Verification Tool.* Verifies that files have been distributed by an approved source.
- *Registry Checker.* Scans your Registry for errors and offers to back it up for you.
- *Automatic Skip Driver Agent.* Identifies hardware failures that occur when Windows 98 boots.
- *Dr. Watson.* Collects detailed information about the state of your computer when a General Protection Fault (GPF) occurs.
- *System Configuration Utility.* Offers a graphical interface that can be used to control the Windows 98 environment.
- *ScanDisk.* Scans your hard disk for errors.
- *Version Conflict Manager.* Checks for all system files that are present in more than one version number.

The main window of the System Information utility is used to gather details about your computer (see Figure 16.20). This window is divided into three sections: Resources, Components, and Software Environment.

NOTE This utility only allows you to view your hardware settings; you cannot change the settings from here. Chapters 19 and 27 contain details on changing settings.

▶ **See** "Using the Registry Editor," **p. 360** or "Inspecting Hardware Properties with Device Manager," **p. 548**

For troubleshooting purposes, Resources is the best section to keep track of. Although the Components section and the Software Environment section have good information on Registry settings and system file versions, the Resources section contains the majority of conflicts and settings needed to determine problems.

FIG. 16.20

The Microsoft System Information utility enables you to make sure Windows sees all the components in your computer.

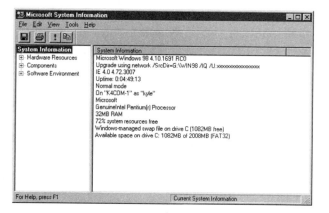

The Resources area in the left pane shows how the different hardware components on your computer are working together. The six specific types of resources you can view here include the following:

- *Conflicts/Sharing.* The utility scans your computer for hardware conflicts and software sharing violations. The right pane show any problems it finds.

- *DMA.* DMA (Direct Memory Access) allows hardware devices to bypass the CPU and work directly with memory. The right pane of this window gives you a list of which hardware device is using which DMA setting. This is a great area to check when you're adding new hardware to your computer.

CAUTION

No two hardware devices can use the same DMA channel.

- *Forced Hardware.* Plug and Play devices do not always play fairly. When PnP devices conflict, you can force the hardware to use specific settings. The right window pane shows you which devices are using forced settings.

- *I/O.* I/O (Input/Output) ports are memory locations (not associated with the main memory of the computer) in which information travels between the CPU and hardware devices. Each hardware device can use several I/O ports, but no two devices can use the same I/O port.

- *IRQs.* When two hardware devices try to use the same IRQ, a conflict arises, and in most cases, neither device will work properly. This is the most common type of hardware conflict.

- *Memory.* Details what memory address each piece of hardware uses. Again, no two devices can use the same memory address, but a single device can use several memory addresses.

From the File menu, you can choose to Export or Print any section of or the entire contents of the System Information utility. It's a good idea to print out the Resources area for reference. The information provided might come in handy if you're adding hardware, for example.

Repairing Damaged System Files

The System File Checker will automatically scan your computer's system files and repair any files that are damaged or corrupt. You can access System File Checker from the Microsoft System Information utility by choosing Tools, System File Checker. Figure 16.21 shows the main screen of the System File Checker.

As an added bonus, the System File Checker includes a file extraction utility. Anyone who has ever had to manually extract files out of CAB files will love this file extraction feature. Click the Settings button to change the default extraction settings.

FIG. 16.21

Now there's an easy way to extract files from a CD.

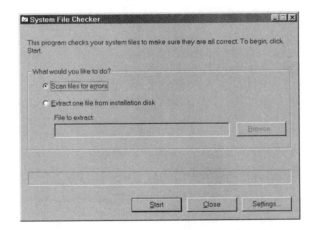

Follow these steps to use the file extraction feature:

1. Click the radio button to Extract One File from Installation Disk.

2. In the File to Extract box, type the filename (or you can browse your hard disk to find the file). Then click Start, and the screen shown in Figure 16.22 appears.

FIG. 16.22

You can type the location of the source file, or click Browse to search your hard disk or the CD for the CAB files.

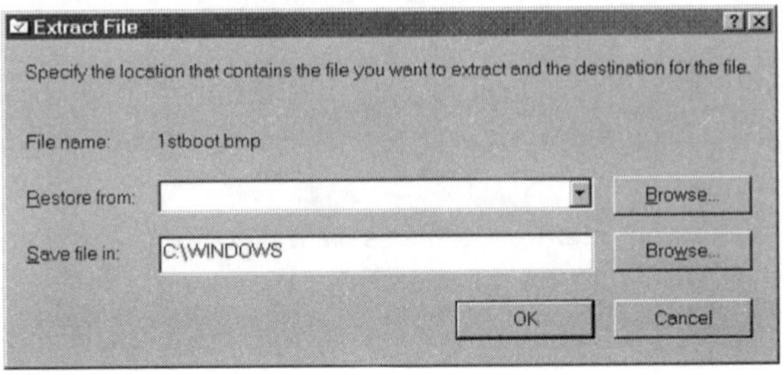

3. Verify the file's location (in the Restore From box) and the destination location (in the Save File In box). Use the appropriate Browse button if you need to change either one. Then click OK.

4. Windows asks if you want to back up the current file. This is a good idea if you are updating an older file, because the new file might not work properly. Choose a folder to place the backup in.

   If the folder you choose does not exist, Windows asks if you want to create it. Choose the option you want, and then click OK to continue and back up the file, or click Skip to continue without backing up the file.

5. Windows should display a successful replacement message. If an error occurs, run ScanDisk to make sure there are no file problems.

Scanning the Registry for Errors

Registry Checker is a simple yet powerful utility that's part of the Microsoft System Information utility. This program scans and then backs up the following system configuration files: the Registry (SYSTEM.DAT and USER.DAT), WIN.INI, and SYSTEM.INI. The backed up files are stored in a CAB file in the hidden folder \Windows\Sysbckup. To start Registry Checker, first start the Microsoft System Information utility. Then follow these steps:

1. Click Tools, Registry Checker. Registry Checker automatically begins to scan the Registry for errors.

2. If errors are found, Microsoft System Registry and Repair provides a list of known good *.CAB files (stored in the \Windows\Sysbckup folder) and allows you to choose which version of the Registry you want to restore.

3. Registry Checker will then ask if you want to back up the Registry. You should do so; having a current backup of the Registry is always good in case of future problems.

Changing Startup Options to Diagnose Problems

Microsoft's System Configuration utility is the next generation of the Safe mode feature that's used to troubleshoot problems. In the System Configuration utility, you can choose which parts of the startup process to use when restarting your computer.

To run the System Configuration utility, click Start, Run, and type **msconfig.exe** in the Run dialog box. Or, if you're in the Microsoft System Information utility, you can click Tools, System Configuration Utility. Either way, you will see the screen shown in Figure 16.23.

 TIP The System Configuration utility works in Safe mode. Use this to easily change startup troubleshooting options.

FIG. 16.23

You can now choose startup options from within Windows.

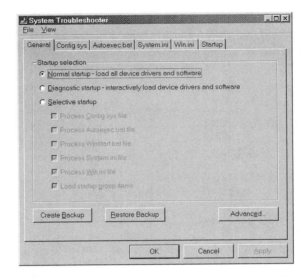

The Startup Selection area of the General tab offers these three startup options:

- *Normal Startup - Load All Device Drivers and Software.* This option is selected by default. It allows your computer to start as fast as possible, without loading any troubleshooting utilities.

- *Diagnostic Startup - Interactively Load Device Drivers and Software.* Select this option if you want Windows to display the Start menu each time you restart your computer. When the Start menu appears, you have 30 seconds to make your choice from among six options, which include MS-DOS mode, Safe mode, or your previous operating system. (You do not need this menu to run a step-by-step startup; that's part of the Selective Startup option.)

- *Selective Startup.* Selective Startup allows you to choose which files to load at startup. The details of using this option are outlined in the next section.

Using Selective Startup   Selective Startup actually offers two distinct options: using real-mode drivers and using protected-mode drivers. The real-mode drivers are CONFIG.SYS, AUTOEXEC.BAT, and WINSTART.BAT. The protected-mode drivers are WIN.INI, SYSTEM.INI, and the startup group items.

You may notice that one or more of the files listed under Selective Startup are grayed out so you can't select them. This indicates that the file is empty or missing. Most commonly grayed out is WINSTART.BAT, which is a real-mode networking file. Because Windows handles all networking components in protected mode, this file is usually not present. It is also possible that the AUTOEXEC.BAT or CONFIG.SYS might be blank or missing (and, therefore, grayed out) considering Windows handles most of the startup options those files used to control.

If the AUTOEXEC.BAT, CONFIG.SYS, and WINSTART.BAT files are all grayed out, ignore the following instructions for troubleshooting using real-mode drivers. Instead, skip down to the section on troubleshooting using protected-mode drivers.

> **CAUTION**
>
> You should make a backup of all your files before you start the troubleshooting process. To do so, click the Create Backup button at the bottom of the dialog box.

Part

IV

Ch

16

To troubleshoot your computer by using Selective Startup and real-mode drivers, follow these steps:

1. Open the System Configuration utility (as described in the previous section) and click the Selective Startup radio button.
2. Click the boxes to place check marks next to Process Config.sys File, Process Autoexec.bat File, and Process Winstart.bat File (or any of the three that are not grayed out).
3. Click the boxes to remove check marks next to Process System.ini File, Process Win.ini File, and Load Startup Group items.
4. Click OK to restart your computer.

Your system should go into a hybrid version of Safe mode. If your system freezes or encounters problems, you know that the problem resides in AUTOEXEC.BAT, CONFIG.SYS, or WINSTART.BAT. Go back through these steps and choose one file at a time until your system has the problem again. If necessary, you can choose view a specific file by selecting one of the tabs at the top of the System Configuration Utility dialog box. Then you can mark out individual lines in that file until you can narrow down the problem.

If you have no problems booting using real-mode drivers (or if you have no real-mode drivers to worry about), the next step is to troubleshoot the protected-mode drivers. Follow these steps:

1. Open the System Configuration utility (as described in the previous section) and click the Selective Startup radio button.
2. Click the boxes to place check marks next to Process System.ini File, Process Win.ini File, and Load Startup Group Items. (Load Startup Group Items may be grayed out; this is not a problem.)
3. Click the boxes to remove check marks next to Process Config.sys File, Process Autoexec.bat File, and Process Winstart.bat File.
4. Click OK to restart your computer.

Your computer should boot into normal mode Windows. If your system freezes or has problems, you know that the problem resides in SYSTEM.INI, WIN.INI, or the startup groups. Go back through these steps and choose one file at a time until your system has the problem again. If necessary, you can view a specific file by selecting one of the tabs at the top of the System Configuration Utility dialog box. Then you can mark out individual lines in that file until you can narrow down the problem.

Tracking System Crashes with Dr. Watson

Windows 98 comes with a new version of Dr. Watson to help track system crashes. Dr. Watson is loaded with Windows 98 but has no associated icons. Dr. Watson is not automatically activated when Windows 98 restarts. To get it up and running, follow these steps:

1. Click Start, Run.

2. Type **c:\windows\drwatson.exe** (assuming Windows 98 is loaded in the WINDOWS folder of your C drive). A new icon appears in the System Tray at the right end of the taskbar.

3. Double-click the Dr. Watson icon in the System Tray. Dr. Watson opens and takes a "snapshot" of your system.

With Dr. Watson running, you can easily keep track of any errors that occur. Dr. Watson intercepts each error and takes a "snapshot" of what your system is doing at the time the error occurs. Figure 16.24 shows one of Dr. Watson's snapshots.

FIG. 16.24
The Diagnosis window of Dr. Watson shows you what program or file caused the error.

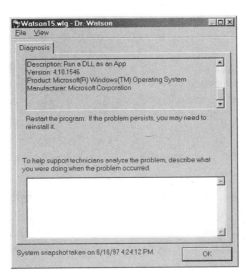

To keep track of the errors, click in the white section on the bottom of the screen and type a description of what you were doing at the time the error occurred. Click File, Save when you're done to save your report. This information will be a big help if you end up calling technical support.

T I P You can also configure how much information you want Dr. Watson to capture and retain by right-clicking the Dr. Watson icon in the System Tray and clicking on <u>O</u>ptions.

Troubleshooting Common Problems

Part

IV

Ch

16

Windows 98 comes with 13 troubleshooters to help with common problems. By using these troubleshooters in combination with the tools described earlier in this chapter, you should have a good basis for troubleshooting Windows 98.

The 13 troubleshooters cover the following topics:

Networking (which includes the Dial-Up Networking and Direct Cable Connection troubleshooters)

Modem	Display
Startup and Shutdown	DirectX
Print	Sound
DriveSpace	The Microsoft Network
Memory	Hardware Conflict
MS-DOS Programs	PC Card

To access any of them, click Start, Help. On the Contents tab, select Troubleshooting and then Windows 98 Troubleshooters (see Figure 16.25).

Each troubleshooter has options to choose from and gives advice on whether you should contact technical support depending on the problem you are having. Each step is written in plain English so it's easy to understand.

FIG. 16.25

Each troubleshooter provides a series of steps to guide you through testing different components of your computer.

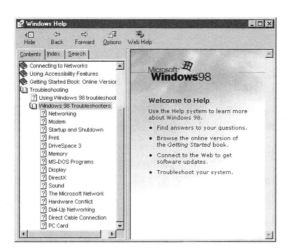

The following list outlines each of the troubleshooters.

- *Network Troubleshooter.* Whether you are hooking up a network adapter, logging on to a Microsoft or Novell network, or trying to use Network Neighborhood, this troubleshooter has a vast array of steps that will help you figure out your problem. The LAN Troubleshooter seems to be the most detailed of all the network troubleshooting wizards. It is well done and contains a lot of good information.

- *Modem Troubleshooter.* The Modem Troubleshooter goes far beyond just getting your modem to work. It also helps with problems such as setting up the dialing properties, working with communications programs, figuring out a missing dial tone, connecting to the Internet, and dealing with problems related to web pages. This is a great tool for the Net surfer.

- *Startup and Shutdown Troubleshooter.* Startup and shutdown problems are the worst to work with. The computer is doing so many things during these times that it's almost impossible to figure out what failed. This troubleshooter details many important areas to look at when dealing with startup and shutdown problems. Use this troubleshooter in combination with the System Configuration utility to fix the problem.

- *Print Troubleshooter.* This is an expanded wizard from the Windows 95 version. It goes into greater detail on specific problems and offers a larger assortment of possible fixes.

- *DriveSpace Troubleshooter:* This detailed wizard covers editing the SCANDISK.INI file to allow for compressed drives and unattended scanning. It deals mostly with mounting drives that are having problems, but it also addresses some specific errors.

- *Memory Troubleshooter.* A very basic wizard, the Memory Troubleshooter mostly deals with simple problems, such as having too many applications open at one time or not having enough available hard disk space. It is a good tool for addressing basic memory problems, but provides no in-depth information on the pesky errors that pop up from time to time.

- *MS-DOS Programs Troubleshooter.* This troubleshooter helps you configure MS-DOS based programs to work in the Windows 98 environment (so you don't have to restart in MS-DOS mode).

- *Display Troubleshooter.* A detailed area for display problems, this troubleshooter deals with many errors that might occur and what you can do to alleviate them.

- *DirectX Troubleshooter.* DirectX is a relatively new component to the Windows environment. It is constantly being updated and revised, and this troubleshooter takes that into account.

- *Sound Troubleshooter.* This troubleshooter goes in-depth on configuring sound cards and figuring out sound options, and it offers suggestions for fixing warbling sound. You'll find good coverage of CD audio drivers as well.

- *The Microsoft Network Troubleshooter.* This is a lightweight troubleshooter for MSN. It covers the basics for getting up and running on the Internet, where you can get more help from the online community.

> ■ *Hardware Conflict Troubleshooter.* This troubleshooter leads you through the basics of working with the Windows 98 Device Manager, providing explanations of the different types of conflicts and ways to resolve them.

> ■ *PC Card Troubleshooter.* Laptop users with PC Card services will appreciate the detail this troubleshooter goes into for fixing a service or card that has stopped working. This troubleshooter probably won't be used by people with desktop computers.

Protecting Your System from Viruses with McAfee VirusScan

A computer virus is a program designed to create abnormal behavior on a computer. Because the number of malicious viruses increases daily, some sort of antivirus program should be on every computer.

It's a common belief that viruses come from the Internet—through shareware or freeware programs or email. The fact is, however, that the first viruses created came out before the government allowed public access to the Internet. At that time, viruses sometimes came bundled with software that was bought in stores. Even today, you could go to a store and pick out a program that's wrapped in plastic, and there could be a virus on the disk (though it's less common).

N O T E　CD-ROM's are far less susceptible to viruses, but there is still a chance of infection if the manufacturer isn't watching closely. ■

Email viruses (or email "bombs," as they're sometimes called) are becoming a legend in today's world. It is impossible, however, for email to be infected with a virus. But this does *not* mean that you cannot get a virus from reading email. You might receive an email message with a file attached, and that file could contain a virus. For that reason, you should never have your email program automatically open attached files. Instead, use your email program to save the file to a special directory. Then, before you open the file, scan it using antivirus software.

Many brands of antivirus software are available these days, and they all seem to do a decent job. One of the best and most common of these is the McAfee VirusScan program.

You can download a shareware version of McAfee VirusScan from the Internet. Then click the SETUP.EXE file to start the installation process.

After it's installed, McAfee VirusScan pretty much runs itself. But be aware of the installation options you can choose from if you do a custom installation. Figure 16.26 shows all the options available with McAfee VirusScan.

FIG. 16.26

Choose Custom Install
to be able to pick which
components you want in
McAfee VirusScan.

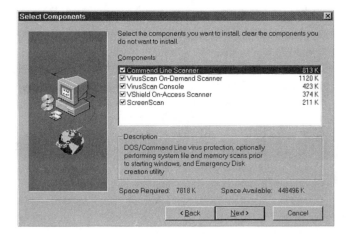

Each component slows your computer down a bit because McAfee searches every applicable file for possible viruses. So pick and choose which components you feel are most relevant in your situation. Here's what each component does:

- *Command Line Scanner* loads through the AUTOEXEC.BAT file when your computer boots. It checks all applicable files for infection. You may want to use this component only when virus security is an extremely important issue because the software loads in real mode and can take up valuable resources. This component might slow down the time it takes to boot your computer.

- *VirusScan On-Demand Scanner* should always be loaded. This component allows the user to scan the computer anytime he wants. This component also includes some added features. Because it's an on-demand utility, it doesn't slow the system down except when it's actually running.

- *VirusScan Console* contains administrations tools. You can set up automatic scanning, and you can lock it so other users can't shut off the scanning software.

- *VShield On-Access Scanner* runs in the background of Windows 98. An icon in the System Tray shows you that the program is running, but no other evidence is found. VShield scans all incoming files for viruses. This component uses few resources and usually causes no noticeable difference in performance. You can also prevent the icon from appearing in the System Tray if you want.

■ *ScreenScan* constantly scans your hard disk while your screen saver is running. The idea behind ScreenScan is sound, but the component is slow in responding when you want to access your system. Because it runs every time the screen saver is activated and it is slow to stop, it can be burdensome.

Other antivirus programs also have custom controls. Regardless of which program you use, choose the controls carefully so you don't lose too much performance.

Using System Monitor to Detect Bottlenecks

System Monitor is a Windows 98 tool you can use to help determine the cause of problems on a local or remote computer by measuring the performance of hardware, software services, and applications. When you make changes to the system configuration, System Monitor shows the effect of your changes on overall system performance. You can also use System Monitor to justify hardware upgrades.

Before you make major configuration changes, use System Monitor to evaluate your current configuration; this can help you determine whether a particular system or network component is causing a performance bottleneck.

The most common bottlenecks occur in memory (RAM) and the CPU. Follow these steps to track these two components using System Monitor:

1. Click Start, Programs, Accessories, System Tools, System Monitor. The utility comes up with nothing on the screen. For each item you want to add, you'll use the Edit, Add Item command.

2. To check the performance of your CPU, click Edit, Add Item. Then click Kernel in the left pane, select Processor Usage (%) in the right pane, and click OK.

3. To check the performance of your RAM, click Edit, Add Item. Then choose Memory Manager from the left pane, select Disk Cache Size from the right pane, and click OK.

4. Click Edit, Add Item again. Then choose Memory Manager from the left pane, select Other Memory from the right pane, and click OK.

5. In the main System Monitor window, click View, Line Charts. You should see a screen something like the one shown in Figure 16.27.

Here's an overview of the CPU and RAM performance statistics that System Monitor would display as a result of the previous procedure:

■ *Kernel: Processor Usage (%)*. Shows approximately how much time your CPU is active. The more active time, the more likely that this is causing a bottleneck. You will notice, however, that the Usage meter hits 100% every time you open a new program.

FIG. 16.27

You can switch among a chart, a graph, and a numbered list in System Monitor by clicking any of the right three icons.

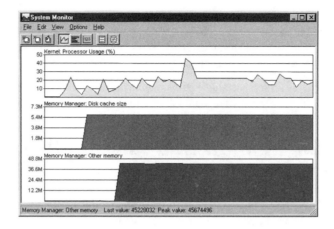

 TIP If your processor usage is too high, it might also be a symptom that you need more RAM. If your total RAM isn't large enough for your applications, and if your system is using large amounts of virtual memory, it will cause your processor usage to increase.

To see if you are using excessive amounts of virtual memory, check the counters for Memory Manager: Page-ins and Memory Manager: Page-outs.

■ *Memory Manager: Swapfile in Use.* Shows how much swap file is being used. Not enough memory (RAM) could cause a large swap file, which will make the hard disk work more. Hard disks are much slower than RAM, though, so adding RAM could be a good idea if you have a large swap file.

CHAPTER 17

System Information Utility

by Christopher Gagnon

In this chapter

System Information Overview

The System Information utility is an included application that allows you to view the configuration of every component, piece of hardware, and software environment setting in the system. It is divided into functional groups that enable you to locate information for any given subsystem easily and quickly.

The System Information utility is installed by default in the System Tools section of the Start menu. As you can see in Figure 17.1, the interface is similar to the Windows Explorer interface, with categorized systems on the left side that expand into detailed lists on the right side. The System Information utility displays three main categories: Hardware Resources, Components, and Software Environment.

FIG. 17.1

The System Information utility allows you to view resources and configuration settings on your system.

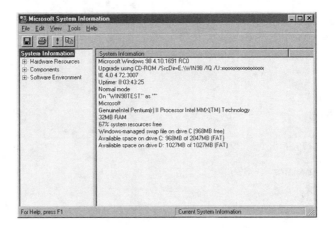

NOTE You can use different views to change the way certain components look in the System Information utility. The Basic view shows general information about the peripheral you are viewing. The Advanced view shows all details about the peripheral. The History view shows all settings made to the peripheral since Windows 98 was installed. ▪

Hardware Resources

The Hardware Resources section, shown in Figure 17.2, contains information regarding the resource settings used by hardware devices in the system.

This section is organized by resource type and displays information for the following resources:

■ *Conflicts/Sharing.* This section shows resource conflicts and resource sharing that exists on your system.

NOTE It is possible for two or more peripherals to share certain settings, such as interrupt requests. You might see more than one item listed on a particular IRQ. This is normal. As long as both items don't try to use the resource at the same time, there won't be a problem. ▪

FIG. 17.2

The Hardware Resources section allows you to view resource settings specific to your hardware.

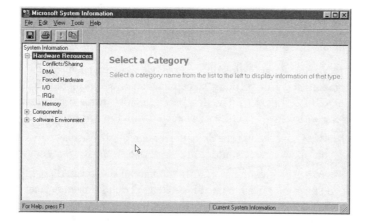

- *DMA.* This section shows you the hardware devices that use specific Direct Memory Addresses.

- *Forced Hardware.* This section lists all installed hardware that is forced to use specific settings. For instance, some older network cards can use only Interrupt 5. Such cards would be listed here.

- *I/O.* Here you'll find a list of I/O ranges, along with the components that use them.

- *IRQs.* This section shows which interrupt requests are claimed by hardware components. If there is a conflicting or shared IRQ, that IRQ is listed for each occurrence.

- *Memory.* This is a list of memory ranges assigned to specific components.

Components

The Components section, shown in Figure 17.3, contains information about specific subsystems of Windows 98. Information in this section comes in handy when you are experiencing problems with a specific area of Windows 98, such as printing.

FIG. 17.3

The Components section displays information specific to the Windows 98 subsystems.

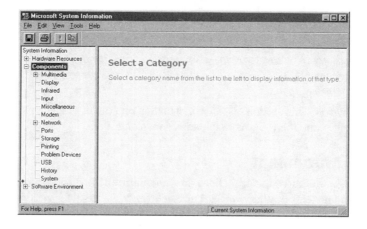

Because the subsystems can contain many components, some of the categories within the Components section are further subdivided. The following list outlines the main areas under the Components section:

- *Multimedia.* This section provides information on each of the installed multimedia components. This section also contains subsections for Audio Codecs, Video Codecs, and CD-ROM devices. These subsections give detailed information on the installed files, along with Registry settings associated with the component.

- *Display.* This section provides information on the display subsystem. It contains information on video cards, monitors, and drivers, and the Registry settings associated with them.

- *Infrared.* This section lists information about the infrared port (if you have one installed). If you have ever tried to troubleshoot an errant infrared device, you will appreciate this section.

- *Input.* This section covers the input subsystem, which includes your keyboard and mouse.

- *Miscellaneous.* Unclassified components are displayed here.

- *Modem.* This section displays valuable information regarding your modem and other telephony devices.

- *Network.* This section is one of the most valuable sections in the System Information tool. It gives you driver information, Registry settings, and resource settings for all your adapters, protocols, and network services.

- *Ports.* Here you can find resource settings and drivers for your LPT and COM ports.

- *Storage.* This section provides information about each disk drive on the system.

- *Printing.* This section contains information regarding each printer installed on the system.

- *Problem Devices.* This section lists all the components that are reporting problems to the system. You should always check this section if you are experiencing problems with your machine. It can serve as a detailed check list of tasks you need to complete to fix the system.

- *USB.* If your system contains a Universal Serial Bus, use this section to check USB settings and confirm driver versions.

- *History.* Whenever you make changes to the system, Windows 98 adds an entry to this section of the System Information utility. This helps you to track changes you have made to the computer.

- *System.* This section displays information on system-level components, such as the PnP BIOS and the Programmable Interrupt Controller.

Software Environment

The Software Environment section, shown in Figure 17.4, displays information specific to software components of Windows 98. This section is also useful for verifying such information as DLL versions and the use of 32-bit as opposed to 16-bit components.

FIG. 17.4

The Software Environment section contains information specific to software settings.

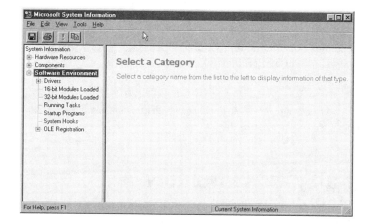

The following sections comprise the Software Environment section:

- *Drivers.* The Drivers section is broken into subsections labeled Kernel, MS-DOS, and User-Level. The Kernel and User-Level sections display driver information including filename, version, manufacturer, and the subsystem in which the driver resides. The MS-DOS section displays only the driver name and type. Any drivers listed in the MS-DOS section are installed for real-mode backwards compatibility.

- *16-bit Modules Loaded.* This section shows which software components on the system are 16-bit components. The display is similar to the Drivers section display; it contains areas for filename, version, manufacturer, description, path, type, and subsystem membership.

- *32-bit Modules Loaded.* This section is identical to the 16-bit Modules Loaded section, except that it displays 32-bit components.

- *Running Tasks.* This section gives you a glimpse of all the currently running tasks. If your computer begins to act up, you might want to jump to this section to determine which processes are running on the machine.

- *Startup Programs.* This section gives you an enhanced look at the programs that are started when you boot your machine. Previous versions of Windows did not give you an easy way of tracking down programs started from anywhere other than the Startup group. This section displays the program, where it is loaded from, and the command used to load it. This section comes in extra handy when you want to check startup parameters for programs starting during system boot.

- *System Hooks.* This section lists all hooks made to specific system resources from certain programs. These hooks can be to specific interrupts or to memory locations. For example, some older networking programs required the use of a certain memory range; such programs would be listed here.

N O T E In most cases, the System Hooks section will be empty. Most of today's software is not programmed to require a specific system resource. ▨

■ *OLE Registration.* This section displays information pertinent to Object Linking and Embedding. It is split into INI File and Registry subsections. The Registry section contains information that's stored in the Registry; the INI File section displays information stored in the INI files.

N O T E   Don't panic if you see identical entries in the INI File and Registry sections of OLE Registration. Entries often end up in both lists for backward compatibility with older software that doesn't support the Registry.   ■

Creating a System Inventory

One of the benefits of using the System Information utility is that it allows you to inventory each component of your computer. Unlike Device Manager, which allows you to view only basic settings and change device settings, the System Information utility allows you to save detailed information to a text file that can be used to create a report. This information can be invaluable when you're troubleshooting a system or speaking to technical support personnel. It can also be hard to keep up with the changes applied by service packs and updates. If you ever have to reload your system from scratch, a system inventory will ensure that you update each component, restoring your system to its exact state.

Saving System Information to a File

The System Information utility writes information to its own file type, which has an .NFO extension. This is a binary file that can be viewed only through the System Information utility. To save the information to the .NFO format, follow these steps:

1. Choose File, Save.
2. Specify a filename and location.

System Information also offers an export option with which you can save the file as ASCII text. It is a good idea to save a copy of your system inventory in this format. If your system becomes nonfunctional, you might not have access to the System Information utility, in which case the .NFO file wouldn't do you much good.

To save the information to a text file, follow these steps:

1. Choose File, Export.
2. Specify a filename and location.

The System Information utility converts the file and saves it to the disk. Figure 17.5 shows a system information text file as it appears in WordPad.

Printing System Information

The System Information utility provides an option for printing the system information. Printing the entire report can easily take more than 100 pages. The Print option in System Information uses the same conversion process to create the print job that it uses to create a .TXT file, so the print output will be identical.

FIG. 17.5

Exporting your system information to a text file allows you to access it from any text editor.

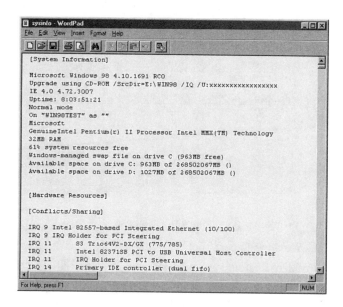

```
[System Information]

Microsoft Windows 98 4.10.1691 RC0
Upgrade using CD-ROM /SrcDir=E:\WIN98 /IQ /U:xxxxxxxxxxxxxxxx
IE 4.0 4.72.3007
Uptime: 8:03:51:21
Normal mode
On "WIN98TEST" as ""
Microsoft
GenuineIntel Pentium(r) II Processor Intel MMX(TM) Technology
32MB RAM
61% system resources free
Windows-managed swap file on drive C (963MB free)
Available space on drive C: 963MB of 268502067MB ()
Available space on drive D: 1027MB of 268502067MB ()


[Hardware Resources]

[Conflicts/Sharing]

IRQ 9  Intel 82557-based Integrated Ethernet (10/100)
IRQ 9  IRQ Holder for PCI Steering
IRQ 11     S3 Trio64V2-DX/GX (775/785)
IRQ 11     Intel 82371SB PCI to USB Universal Host Controller
IRQ 11     IRQ Holder for PCI Steering
IRQ 14     Primary IDE controller (dual fifo)
```

Probably a better way of printing is to convert the file to a .TXT document instead of printing from the System Information utility. Then you can open the file using WordPad, delete any unwanted information, and submit the print job.

System Information Tools

Although the System Information utility is a great tool for viewing settings, you cannot use it to make changes to the system. The Tools menu in the System Information utility contains links to several diagnostic programs that you can use to diagnose and fix problems in the system. This section covers the tools available in the System Information utility.

The Windows Report Tool

The Windows Report Tool, shown in Figure 17.6, gives you an easy method of reporting your problems to technical support personnel. You enter details about the problems you are experiencing, and the Windows Report Tool packages them with a snapshot of the current system configuration. This package gives the support technician all the information he or she needs to help you solve the problem.

Creating a Report Package   When you create a problem report, it is important that you provide as much detail as possible in the problem description. The more information you provide, the better the technician will understand the problem. Also, be sure to provide the steps needed to re-create the problem.

FIG. 17.6

The Windows Report Tool packages your system files along with a description of your problem.

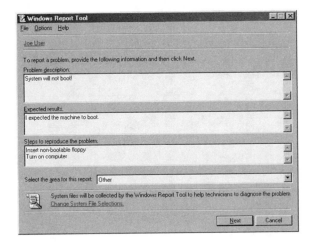

To create a new problem report, follow these steps:

1. Start the Windows Report Tool.

2. In the Problem Description box, enter a detailed description of the problem you are experiencing.

3. In the Expected Results box, detail the behavior you expected from the system when you experienced the problem.

4. In the next box, provide the exact steps needed to recreate the problem.

5. Select the category that best describes the problem.

6. Save the file to your hard drive.

You can then send the report package to your technical support personnel. This might be a technician from Microsoft, an OEM technician, or a member of your corporate help desk staff. Because the report is compiled into a file, you can easily attach it to an email message or copy it to a disk for delivery.

Modifying the Files Included in the Report   When the report is compiled into a file, Windows 98 takes the information you provided and packages it into a cabinet (.CAB) file along with your system files. In certain situations, you might not want to provide all your system settings to a third party (if, for example, you work in an environment where security is a top priority). You can pick and choose which components you want to include in the package by using the Collected Information dialog box, accessible through the Options menu (see Figure 17.7).

To remove an item from the package, simply locate the item in the list and remove the check mark from the box next to it. You also can add files if necessary. To add an item to the package, just click the Add button and use the browse dialog box to locate the file.

FIG. 17.7
You can specify which
files to include with the
problem report.

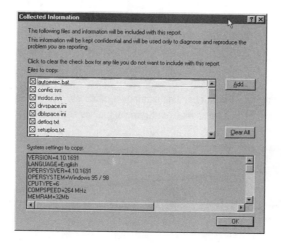

Update Wizard Uninstall

This tool allows you to uninstall any update made by the Update Wizard. This utility produces
the same results as using the Restore option from the Microsoft System Update web site.

When you start this application, Windows 98 searches the system for any applied updates and
displays them in a list, as shown in Figure 17.8. To remove an update, simply choose the one
you want to remove, and click the Uninstall button. All files affected by the update will be restored to the state they were in before the update was applied.

FIG. 17.8
With the Update Wizard
Uninstall utility, you can
selectively remove
updates that have been
applied to your system.

Signature Verification Tool

The Signature Verification Tool allows you to verify digital signatures on any signed files. A
digital signature ensures that a file is safe to use by giving you a way of verifying who created
the file. As you can see in Figure 17.9, the Signature Verification Tool looks nearly identical to
the Find tool. To use it, you choose Signed Files from the Look for box, select the location to
scan, and click the Find Now button. You can use this tool when you receive files from the
Internet or from a location you think might not be secure. For example, you might request an

updated DLL from somebody's web site. Although the file appears to have been created by Microsoft, it might have been altered to contain malicious code. You can use the signature verification tool to look for Microsoft's "signature" on the file. If that signature does not exist, you should discard the file and find one with the "signature" intact.

N O T E Signing files digitally has not become a standard practice in the software industry. This tool will become more valuable as more software companies start signing their files. ▢

FIG. 17.9
The Signature Verification Tool tells you who created the file (or lets you determine who didn't).

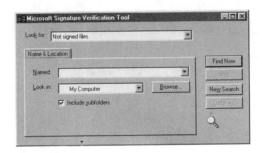

System File Checker

The System File Checker, shown in Figure 17.10, offers a quick, easy way for you to check for corruption in your system files. It scans your hard drive for a variety of file types and compares them with the originals from the installation media. If it finds a corrupt file, it gives you the option of copying the original from the CD.

N O T E The default file types scanned by the System File Checker are .386, .COM, .DLL, .DRV, .EXE, .MPD, .OCX, .SCR, .SYS, and .VXD. You can add and remove file types from this list by clicking the Settings button. ▢

To scan your system files for problems, simply open the System File Checker, check the Scan Files for Errors box, and click the Start button. Windows 98 scans the files and reports any errors it encounters. You can also choose to extract a file from the CD if you already know which file is giving you trouble.

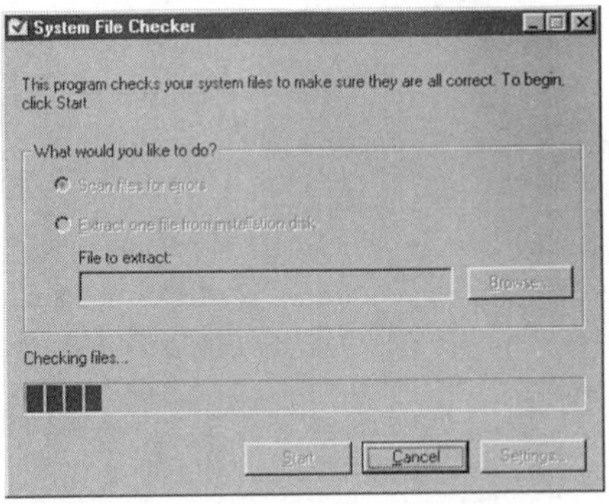

FIG. 17.10
The System File Checker identifies system critical files that might be corrupt.

Registry Checker

The Windows Registry Checker is a simple utility that checks for problems with the Registry. To use it, you simply run the application, and Windows 98 scans the Registry for corrupt keys. It also prompts you to back up the Registry, as shown in Figure 17.11. It's a good idea to back up the Registry after you install any new software or hardware.

FIG. 17.11
The Registry Checker scans the Registry for errors and gives you an easy way to perform a Registry backup.

Automatic Skip Driver Agent

Part
IV

Ch
17

One of the most beneficial features of Windows 98 is the new Automatic Skip Driver Agent. This component runs in the background during system startup to identify any piece of hardware that fails to start properly. The item is added to a list of troublesome devices. During subsequent boots of Windows 98, the Automatic Skip Driver Agent prevents the drivers for troublesome devices from loading, so that the system will boot without errors. Note, however, that the ASD does not fix the device; it just prevents the device from causing other system problems.

When you run the Automatic Skip Driver Agent from the System Information utility, you will see one of two things. If ASD does not find any problematic devices, you will receive a message that there are no critical operation failures on the machine. If ASD does determine that some piece of hardware is problematic, it will add that device to a list of troublesome devices. You can then re-enable the device and test any configuration changes you might have made. If the device fails again at startup, the ASD will disable it again and place it back in the list.

Dr. Watson

The Dr. Watson utility runs in the system tray of the taskbar. It is ideal for catching your system when it crashes. Dr Watson is aware of all processes and resources and can take a snapshot of the machine when problems occur.

The most convenient aspect of this application is that you can force it to take a snapshot at any time. If you receive a system error, you can use Dr. Watson to create a log entry that indicates the state of the machine. To do this, just double-click on the Dr. Watson icon in the taskbar. It takes a snapshot, which you can save and send to your technical support personnel. This snapshot is similar to the kind of file you can save with the System Information utility. Dr. Watson just enables you to create it immediately when you need it. Figure 17.12 shows the Dr. Watson diagnosis screen.

FIG. 17.12

Dr. Watson monitors the system for problems and can create a snapshot during system failure.

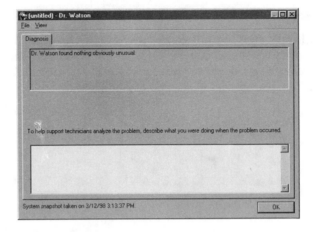

System Configuration Utility

The System Configuration Utility, shown in Figure 17.3, allows you to make changes to your system files through a visual interface instead of a text editor. The interface used to edit these files, however, is rather odd and forces you to press a new entry button for each entry you add. Therefore, you might find it easier to continue editing files with your favorite text editor. This utility also enables you to change your general boot options, as well as programs that start automatically during boot-up.

FIG. 17.13

The System Configuration Utility enables you to modify your system startup files from one location.

The System Configuration Utility contains the following tabs:

- General (This section allows you to specify whether to start the machine normally or in a diagnostic mode, and it provides a quick way for you to back up the boot files.)
- Config.sys
- Autoexec.bat

- System.ini
- Win.ini
- Startup (This section allows you to modify which programs to load at system startup.)

ScanDisk

The ScanDisk program, shown in Figure 17.14, is basically the same as the one that was included with Windows 95. With it, you can scan and fix problems on your hard drive. One of the benefits of ScanDisk is that it can perform a surface scan that can identify problems on the disk media itself. To run ScanDisk, simply start the program, select the drive, select the type of test, and click Start. If you check the Automatically fix errors box, ScanDisk will repair the disk without user input.

FIG. 17.14

ScanDisk performs several checks on the disk, including a surface scan.

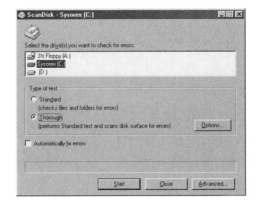

Version Conflict Manager

The Version Conflict Manager, shown in Figrue 17.5, keeps track of all installed files that replace newer existing files. Due to the manufacturing process, some software ships with drivers that are not the most current ones available. If you install some software that replaces a newer driver, Windows 98 will back up the newer driver so that you can restore it later. The Version Conflict Manager is the tool you use to restore the file.

Sometimes the newer driver that was overwritten will not work with the software that replaced it. To prevent problems from occurring after you restore the original driver, Version Conflict Manager will back up the driver currently in use before performing the restoration. This way, you can revert to the driver supplied with the software if necessary.

Part
IV

Ch
17

FIG. 17.15

The Version Conflict Manager allows you to revert to previous versions of files that have been replaced.

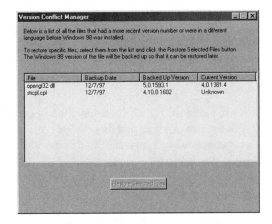

CHAPTER 18

Backing Up Your Data

by Phil Callihan and Larry Passo

In this chapter

Getting Started with Backup

As experienced users are well aware, regular system backups can save you hours of frustration. Windows 98 includes a fully featured backup utility, Microsoft Backup, at no extra cost. If you create and follow a regular backup schedule, you will be able to recover from the inadvertent corruption of the Windows 98 system Registry.

NOTE If you use Help in the backup utility, you might see references to "Seagate Backup Exec." This is because Microsoft licensed Microsoft Backup from Seagate Software, the company that makes the Backup Exec product line. ■

Windows 95 included a backup utility as an optional component that was available during setup. Windows 98 includes Microsoft Backup, which boasts the following improvements over the previous version:

- It is installed as a base component during Windows 98 setup.
- Improved wizard technology makes it easier to perform common tasks.
- It offers the capability to back up and restore the Windows 98 Registry.
- It works with the Windows 98 Task Scheduler so you can remind yourself to run your backups.

Microsoft Backup borrows interface elements from previous Backup Exec versions and the Windows 95 version. It includes the following useful features:

- Wizards to automate the process of backing up and restoring
- A graphical user interface that enables you to easily choose your backup selections if you don't want to use the wizards
- Support for many types of tape drives and fixed-media devices
- The ability to create backup "jobs" that target different files, allowing you to create a wide variety of backup strategies
- The option to create recovery disks that can revive your personal computer after a major loss of system data
- Password protection of your backups for extra security

The backup process is fairly straightforward. Wizards (as shown in Figure 18.1) lead you through common tasks such as backing up and restoring data. Backup also makes use of different-colored graphical "check marks" to indicate whether you have selected an entire folder or just specific files within a folder (see Figure 18.1).

You select the files you want to back up by clicking on folders or specific files. After you make your selections, you can save them for future use by creating a *backup job*. A backup job is a collection of files that you select within the Backup utility and save under a particular filename.

Having created a backup job, you can quickly back up that set of folders and files again by simply executing the previously saved backup job. This allows you to quickly back up or re-store your data or programs without having to manually re-select the same folders and files every time.

FIG. 18.1

Microsoft Backup allows you to select what to back up: entire folders or specific files.

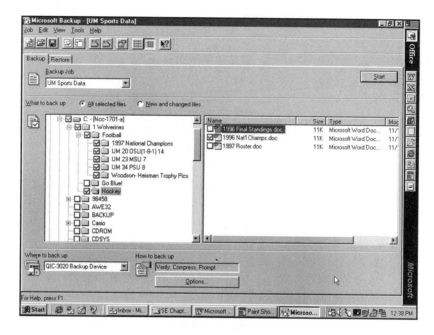

N O T E Backup jobs also save any settings that are selected when the job is saved. ■

Note the different colors of the selection marks. A bright blue mark signifies that a file or en-tire folder has been selected (the Football folder and the 1996 Nat'l Champs Microsoft Word document, in the case of Figure 18.1).

Also note that all higher-level folders that contain the 1996 Nat'l Champs document have a gray selection mark. This signifies that only a portion of the folder's contents have been selected to be a part of the backup job.

Another useful feature of Microsoft Backup is its capability to verify your files as you're back-ing them up. You should always verify your files after backing them up. You configure Microsoft Backup to verify files by selecting the check box on the option screen shown in Figure 18.2. The verification process double-checks to make sure that the original files match the files actually saved to your backup media by reading it back after it is written. Unfortu-nately, this adds to the time it takes to run your backup job, but the peace of mind it provides is well worth the extra time. Consider the extra time cheap insurance for your data.

Part

IV

Ch

18

CAUTION

If Microsoft Backup cannot verify your files, it might be time to replace the media or clean the read/write heads in your backup device.

FIG. 18.2

You can configure Microsoft Backup to verify files.

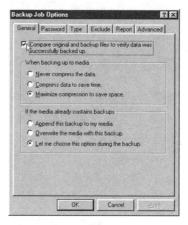

As a further safeguard for your data, you should store your backup media in a safe place—preferably offsite. One option for storing really important information is to hire a data archival service. For a monthly fee, such a company maintains your backup media in an environmentally controlled area, and sometimes it even picks up your backups at your location. For most home users, a closet or bookcase is a suitable storage location. Just don't store your backups right next to your computer system, where the same theft or fire could destroy both your system and your backup data.

 When deciding where to store backups, consider these potential dangers: electrical interference, temperature variations (including humidity), and theft. Balance these factors with convenience. Also, make a schedule for rotating your tapes between your computer and your storage area, and then follow it.

CAUTION

If you decide to store your backups in a safe, make sure the safe you use is certified for storing magnetic media. Most home "fireproof safes" are designed to protect only paper records, which can survive temperatures that will damage magnetic media.

The point of making backups is so that you can reverse the process and restore files to your system if you ever need to. The restoration process is very similar to the backup process. Microsoft Backup reads the catalog of files that have been saved on the backup media, and it allows you to choose which files and/or folders you want to restore. You can restore files or folders either to their original locations or to other locations.

Preparing a Backup Strategy

Many users don't create an overall backup strategy until it's too late. A realistic strategy should take into account available backup hardware, how much time you're willing to devote to backups, and ultimately how much data you're willing to lose given a worst-case scenario.

Choosing a Backup Format

You can perform three kinds of backups. Table 18.1 outlines them.

Table 18.1   Types of File Backups

Type	Description
Full Backup	Backs up every file selected. Marks files as having been backed up.
Incremental	Backs up every file created or changed since the last full or differential backup. Does not mark files as having been backed up.
Differential	Backs up every file created or changed since the last full or differential backup. Marks files as having been backed up.

To configure the backup type, select the Options button from Microsoft Backup's main screen, and then click the Type tab to see the options shown in Figure 18.3.

Part

IV

Ch

18

FIG. 18.3
Choose the type of backup you want to perform with Microsoft Backup.

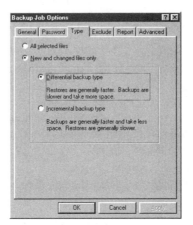

If you select the All Selected Files option and then select the root of each hard disk partition, Backup will perform a full backup of every file on your system. Backup and restore procedures will be slower if you use this option because of the volume of data that has to be processed. If you select New and Changed Files Only, you also need to choose between the Differential and Incremental backup options.

A differential backup saves new or changed files to your backup device but doesn't mark them as having been backed up. This means that if you create a file on Monday and perform a differential backup that night, and then you perform another differential backup on Tuesday, the file will be backed up on both days even if it was not changed on Tuesday.

Using the same example, if you create a file on Monday and perform an incremental backup that night, the file will be backed up and marked as having been backed up. If you perform another incremental backup on Tuesday, the file will not be backed up unless it has changed (been edited) since the Monday night backup. This means that subsequent incremental backups will take less time to run, because only new or changed files will be backed up.

> **CAUTION**
>
> Although it takes less time to create incremental backups, it takes more time to restore from them. You might need to restore from several different tapes of incremental backups if you have to restore files that were modified on different days.

Creating a Schedule

It's important to be realistic when creating your backup schedule. In a perfect world, we would all have lightning-fast multiple-gigabyte backup units attached to our personal computers that would allow us to do full system backups every day in a matter of seconds. But the reality is that system backups take time. On newer computer systems that have gigabytes of disk space, a full backup can take many hours. In addition, your hard disk capacity might be much larger than the capacity of your backup device, which can cause problems.

The following might be a good backup schedule for a moderately used home computer:

Full System Backup (everything)   Once every other month, alternating sets

Data Backup (user files)   Once a month, alternating sets

The idea of *alternating sets* stems from that annoying tendency of Murphy's Law to intervene when you need to restore important data. By alternating sets (Set A and Set B, Set 1 and Set 2, or whatever you choose), you ensure that you don't overwrite a good backup with a bad one. Multiple sets also help prevent the loss of data due to tape failure or other mishap.

If you create many files or create very large and detailed documents, the following backup schedule might be necessary:

Full System Backup (everything)   Once a month, alternating sets

Data Backup (user files)   Once a week, alternating sets

Deciding Which Files to Back Up

A backup strategy depends largely on how you use your computer and ultimately depends on how much data you are willing to lose in the event of a disaster.

For many users, system data changes infrequently—only during an operating system or application upgrade, for example. As a safeguard, you should back up your entire system before performing any major upgrade. For most users, personal data is much more important than application data. It's much easier to reinstall an application than to re-create personal data.

Organize your user files into subfolders in a common folder. This will ease backup and restoration procedures. It's much easier to back up one folder and its contents if you don't have to search through all your subfolders trying to find where you saved a particular file.

Assuming all your personal files are in one directory, you need to decide how often to back up that data folder. The advantage of backing up only data files is that these files are usually small compared to system data and program files. If you change data only once or twice a week, you might want to back up data only weekly or monthly. If you frequently change documents, on the other hand, you might want to back up your data files more often.

When deciding which files to back up, you should consider the priority of the following kinds of data:

- Files important to your system (operating system, Registry, and application files)
- Files that are important to you (personal documents and data)

Always maintain a reliable system backup. Fortunately, this data doesn't usually change very often, so you usually need to perform a full system backup only monthly or every other month. Although you should back up your user data more often, those backups are usually smaller than system backups and take less time.

Part

IV

Ch

18

Choosing the Right Backup Device

During the last few years, backup devices have become an economical option for many computer users. Many types of devices are now available, with varying degrees of capacity and speed. When choosing a backup device, make sure that it will fulfill the needs of your overall backup strategy.

Choosing the Right Backup Medium

Many hardware options are available for backing up the data on your personal computer. Here are a few guidelines you can use when purchasing a unit:

- *How much data do I need to back up?* Backup units vary greatly in capacity and speed.
- *Will my backup tapes be read by machines other than mine?* If so, you will want to get a tape device that uses tapes of the same type the other computers use.
- *How expensive is the backup medium?* You'll need more than one cartridge to implement a reliable system of backups.

You have many choices of backup media. Tape drives are the most common, but other options are available, depending on your specific needs and budget:

- *Tape drive.* This is the most common type of backup device, and it comes in a wide variety of shapes, sizes, and prices. Many tape drives offer high capacity and good speed and are the best way for most users to back up gigabytes of data. Some leading brands of tape drives are HP/Colorado, Exabyte, Seagate, and Conner.

- *Removable storage.* These devices are being used more and more in certain applications. They are fast, reliable, and easy to use and install. Unfortunately, most do not have the capacity of tape drives, and they are more expensive on a cost-per-megabyte basis. Some leading brands of removable storage media are SyQuest and Iomega's Jaz and Zip.

- *Compact disc (CD) writers.* These devices have been dropping in price and have begun to be used as archival devices. This medium is cheap (around $2 for a CD) but has limited storage (around 650MB). One advantage of this medium is that many more machines have CD drives than have tape devices, which gives you more options when you want to restore data. Unfortunately, the small capacity of the medium and the Write Once Read Many (WORM) nature of compact discs make this option impractical for most users. CD-R technology, which allows you to record and erase compact discs, might make this more feasible in the future, but capacity will always be a shortcoming.

- *Network drives.* This is a great solution—as long as your network resources have the capacity to handle the size of your backup file. Most network resources are backed up at the server level as well, offering even more safety for your data. The downside of saving your backups to the network is that you might not have enough storage space to perform a full backup. Check with your system administrator to ensure that you have the resources available on the network to handle your backup (.QIC) files and to schedule a time for running your backup that won't saturate the network during peak usage time.

- *Floppy disk.* Use this only as a last resort. Floppy disks are a very unreliable medium for backups. In addition, they are time-consuming, have limited capacity, and are unreliable and slow. Friends don't let friends do critical backups on floppy disks.

Installing and Configuring a Tape Drive

Microsoft Backup supports parallel, IDE/ATAPI, and SCSI backup devices. These devices range from external units that you can easily connect to your parallel port to internal devices that require varying degrees of knowledge for installation. Before you buy a tape drive, make sure you have the interface required to connect it to your computer system. Windows 98 supports tape drives manufactured by the following vendors: Conner, Exabyte, HP/Colorado, Iomega, Micro Solutions, Seagate, Tandberg, WangDAT, and Wangtek.

To install a tape drive, follow these steps:

1. Read any setup directions that came with your tape drive for specific instructions on installing your device.

2. Turn off your computer and install your tape drive according to the directions that came with it.

3. Turn on your computer and boot Windows 98.

4. If your device is Plug and Play-compatible, the system will detect it and install the proper drivers (best-case scenario).

If Windows 98 does not detect your tape device during bootup, open the Start menu and select Settings, Control Panel, Add New Hardware. The Add New Hardware wizard takes you through the steps for detecting and installing the sofware that runs your tape drive.

 TIP Microsoft Backup saves files in QIC format. QIC stands for Quarter-Inch Cartridge, which is a popular type of standardized tape cartridge used for tape backups. Microsoft Backup can be used with tape units that adhere to the following standards: QIC-40 low density, QIC-80 high density, and QIC-117. Even if you back up your files directly to disc instead of to tape, the file is saved in QIC format. Before you purchase a backup unit, always check to make sure that it is on the Windows 98 Hardware Compatibility List (HCL).

Formatting and Erasing Tapes

You usually must format a new tape before you can use it to perform a backup. (If you don't want to take the time to format tapes yourself, you can purchase preformatted tapes.) To format or erase a tape, follow these steps:

1. Insert the tape into your tape drive.
2. Start Microsoft Backup.
3. Select Tools, Media, Format. The program warns you that formatting will erase any data on the tape and that the process might take up to 30 minutes to complete.

 TIP Not all media need to be formatted. Some non-QIC formats are formatted automatically during the backup process.

 TIP You can save yourself time and effort by purchasing your QIC tapes preformatted. The time savings alone is usually worth the small additional cost of preformatted tapes.

Backing Up Files

If you perform consistent backups, you will have the tools you need to recover from both minor mistakes and computer disasters alike. The first place to begin is to perform a backup of your entire system.

Performing a Full System Backup Using the Backup Wizard

To perform a full system backup, follow these steps:

1. Start Microsoft Backup by opening the Start menu and choosing Programs, Accessories, System Tools, Backup. After the splash screen appears, the Backup Wizard begins to help you configure your backup procedure (see Figure 18.4).
2. Select Create a New Backup Job and click OK.

Part
IV

Ch
18

FIG. 18.4

The Backup Wizard opens immediately when you execute the Backup program.

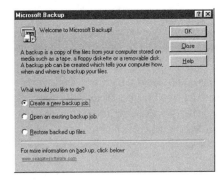

3. In the next dialog box, select Back Up <u>M</u>y Computer and click Next.

4. Select <u>A</u>ll Selected Files. Then click <u>N</u>ext to continue.

5. In the dialog box that appears, indicate where you want to save your backup. Click <u>N</u>ext.

 You can use a second hard disk as your backup device. Backing up your data to another hard disk is significantly faster than using a tape drive.

6. Next you specify how you want to perform your backup. The choices are Compare Original and Backup Files to <u>V</u>erify Data Was Successfully Backed Up (highly recommended) and Com<u>p</u>ress the Backup Data to Save Space (also recommended). Choose one and click <u>N</u>ext.

7. In the final screen of the Backup Wizard (see Figure 18.5), enter a name for your backup job.

FIG. 18.5

The final screen of the Backup Wizard lets you view your choices before executing your backup job.

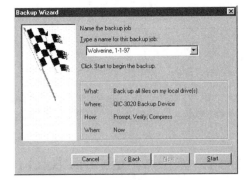

 Be sure to give the backup job a name that sufficiently describes what the backup does. All of your backup jobs will appear in a drop-down box in the Backup program from now on, so a good descriptive name will prevent confusion later.

8. Click Start to begin the backup. As the Backup job runs, you can monitor its progress onscreen. The Backup Progress screen, shown in Figure 18.6, keeps you updated, providing such useful information as the number of files being backed up and the estimated time the procedure will take.

FIG. 18.6
As the backup job runs, a status screen provides you with up-to-date information.

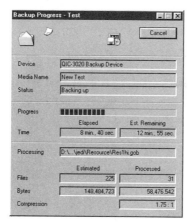

Ensuring That the Registry Is Backed Up Correctly

The Windows 98 System Registry files are crucial to restoring your system in the event of a major hardware failure. There are two ways to back up these critical files. The first is with regedit.exe, which is covered in Chapter 19, "Working with the Windows Registry." The second is to use Microsoft Backup.

When you use the Microsoft Backup method, you have to take a few steps to ensure that the System Registry is backed up properly. To do so, use the following steps (see Figure 18.7):

1. Select Tools, Preferences. The Preferences dialog box appears.

FIG. 18.7
Make sure that you back up the Registry.

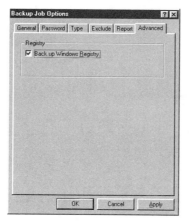

Part
IV

Ch
18

2. Check the box labeled <u>B</u>ackup or Restore the Registry When Backing Up or Restoring the Windows Directory. Then click OK.

3. Near the bottom of the Microsoft Backup screen, click the <u>O</u>ptions button.

4. In the Backup Job Options dialog box, select the Advanced tab. Then check the Back Up Windows Registry box and click OK.

After you complete the steps, the Registry will be backed up whenever you back up the Windows directory.

Selecting Folders and File Types for Partial Backups

As you learned earlier in this chapter, you can select specific folders that you want to back up. You select them in the What to Back Up section of the opening Microsoft Backup screen. A bright blue check mark appears next to files or entire directories that will be backed up. A gray check mark signifies that only a portion of a folder is selected for backup.

You also have the option of excluding certain file types from being backed up. This might come in handy, for example, if you do not want to back up temporary files or browser cache files.

To prevent a certain file type from being backed up, follow these steps:

1. At the bottom of the opening Backup window, click the <u>O</u>ptions button. The Backup Job Options dialog box appears.

2. Select the Exclude tab, and then click the A<u>d</u>d button. The Add Exclude dialog box appears (see Figure 18.8).

3. Select the file type you want to exclude.

FIG. 18.8

Microsoft Backup gives you the option of excluding certain file types from being backed up.

 If the file type(s) that you want to exclude are not already registered, click the <u>C</u>ustom Type button and enter the file extension that you want to exclude in the text box.

4. File types listed in the Do Not Back Up These File Types box will be ignored from now on during all backup procedures. When you've added all the file types you want to exclude, click OK.

Running a Saved Backup Job

To execute a saved backup job, follow these steps:

1. In the Backup Job drop-down list, select the saved backup job you want to execute.
2. Insert the tape on which you want to save your data.
3. Click the Start button to execute the job.

Scheduling Backups Using the Task Scheduler

An important feature of Windows 98 is its capability to automatically perform mundane tasks on a regular schedule. You can take advantage of this feature by letting Windows 98 remind you when it's time to run your scheduled backup.

To set up the Task Scheduler to remind you to perform a backup job, follow these steps:

1. Open My Computer.
2. Open the Scheduled Tasks folder.
3. Click the Add Scheduled Task icon to start the Add Scheduled Task Wizard. Click Next to continue.
4. The wizard prompts you to select a program to be scheduled. Select Backup and click Next.
5. Enter a name for the task and specify the frequency at which you want it to be executed. Then click Next.
6. Specify the desired Start Time and Start Date, and then click Next.
7. Click Finish.

At the specified time and date, Microsoft Backup executes automatically. You can then select the backup job you want to run.

Part
IV

Ch
18

> **CAUTION**
>
> Even though the Task Scheduler starts Microsoft Backup automatically, you must still run the proper backup job. The Task Scheduler only starts Microsoft Backup; it doesn't perform the actual backup.

Changing Backup Settings and Options

It's simple to change your backup settings and options. Follow these steps:

1. From the Backup Job drop-down box, select the name of the backup job you would like to change.
2. Make any changes you want to the file selections, options, and so on.
3. When you finish making changes, open the Job menu and select Save.

Restoring Backed-Up Files

Microsoft Backup gives you the ability to recover anything from a single file to your entire system.

Restoring Files to Their Original Locations

To restore files to their original locations, follow these steps:

1. Insert the tape that contains the backup you want to restore.
2. Start Microsoft Backup and select the Restore tab. Click the Refresh button.
3. Check the box next to the backup set you want to restore, and click OK.
4. In the What to Restore section, select the specific files you want to restore by checking the appropriate boxes.
5. From the Where to Restore drop-down list, select Original Location.
6. Click Start.
7. When the restoration process is finished, a dialog box displays the message `Operation Completed`. Click OK to finish.

Restoring Files to a New Location

To restore files to a new location, follow these steps:

1. Insert the tape that contains the backup you want to restore.
2. Start Microsoft Backup and select the Restore tab. Click the Refresh button.
3. Select the backup set you want to restore by checking the box next to it. Click OK.
4. In the What to Restore section, select the specific files you want to restore by checking the appropriate boxes.
5. From the Where to Restore drop-down list, select Alternate Location.
6. A selection box appears below the Where to Restore drop-down list. In that box, select the location to which you want to restore your files.
7. Click Start.
8. A window appears, updating you on the status of the restoration. When the process is finished, a dialog box displays the message `Operation Completed`. Click OK to finish.

Changing Restoration Settings and Options

To change the restoration options, select the Restore tab from Microsoft Backup's main program window and select the Options button. In the Restore Options dialog box, the General tab displays the rules that Microsoft Backup will use when restoring files (such as what to do if the files being restored have the same names as files that already exist at the restoration location).

TIP If you plan to restore the Registry from your backups, make sure that you have the Restore Windows Registry box selected on the Advanced tab of the Restore Options dialog box.

Part

IV

Ch

18

CHAPTER 19

Working with the Windows Registry

by Jerry Honeycutt

In this chapter

Words of Warning: Make a Plan

Changing the Registry is risky. The worst-case scenario is that Windows 98 will no longer start. The best case scenario is that you won't notice anything different, but on the whole, you'll probably cause certain applications or devices to behave improperly. No damage is irreparable, however, if you back up the Registry using the methods described in this chapter and if you stick to the plan you learn about in this section.

But just to be sure you know the risks, take a look at why editing the Registry using the Registry Editor is dangerous:

- The Registry Editor doesn't validate your changes.
- When you make a change to one value, you can easily miss related values in other parts of the Registry.
- The Registry Editor doesn't have an undo feature. Once you make a change, it's a done deal.

You can *learn* to make changes in the Registry without risking anything, and you can safely experiment with the Registry. After writing three books on the Registry (and through endless tinkering), this author has made only one change that he couldn't safely recover from. You can make sure that your experience with the Registry is just as good by making a plan before you strike out to make changes.

To that end, here's a sample plan that you can change to suit your own needs:

- Back up the Registry before you make any change. You learn many techniques for backing up the Registry in this chapter. Most of them are quick and painless.
- Make only one change at a time. If you make too many changes in one sitting, you're not as likely to figure out what went wrong if Windows fails.
- Don't delete data from the Registry until you're absolutely sure of the impact. Instead, rename data so as to hide it from Windows (which has the same effect as deleting it). When you're sure that everything is okay, delete the key.
- Don't make changes to a Registry setting until you're sure about the impact it will have. Make a copy of the setting in a new temporary entry; then make your change. If everything works out okay, remove the temporary value. At the very least, write down the original value so that you can easily go back to it if things don't work out.

 TIP You wouldn't think the Registry would be in peril when you install a new program because you don't change any Registry settings yourself. Regardless, my experience suggests that you should back up the Registry before you install programs with which you're unfamiliar so that you can easily recover from a wayward Setup program's *faux pas*.

Understanding the Windows Registry

Windows 98 stores the entire contents of the Registry in two files: SYSTEM.DAT and USER.DAT. These are binary files that you can't view using a text editor (as you can INI files). Windows 98 also turns on the Read-only, System, and Hidden attributes of SYSTEM.DAT and USER.DAT so that you can't accidentally replace, change, or delete these files. SYSTEM.DAT contains configuration data specific to the computer on which you installed Windows 98. USER.DAT contains configuration data specific to the current user.

Take a look. SYSTEM.DAT and USER.DAT are located in C:\Windows. The location of USER.DAT will be different if you've configured the computer to use profiles, though. In that case, Windows would have created a new system folder called C:\WINDOWS\PROFILES, under which you'll find a folder for each user that logs onto the machine. For example, C:\WINDOWS\PROFILES\JERRY contains my configuration data, and C:\WINDOWS\PROFILES\POMPY contains my dog's configuration data. Each user's profile folder contains an individual copy of USER.DAT. You'll still find a default USER.DAT in C:\WINDOWS, mind you, which Windows uses as a template for new users.

N O T E Profiles allow multiple users to log onto a single computer with their own familiar settings (Start menu options, desktop configuration, and so on). You enable profiles using the Enable Multi-Users Settings Wizard. To start the wizard, select the Users icon in the Control Panel, or open the Passwords Properties dialog box by selecting the Passwords icon in the Control Panel.

Understanding Registry Entries

Take a look at Figure 19.1. This Figure shows you how the Windows 98 Registry looks when viewed in the Registry Editor. In the left-hand pane, you see all the Registry's keys. In the right-hand pane, you see all the configuration data for the key that's selected in the left pane. Each group of configuration data in the Registry is called a *key*. Keys are very much like sections in INI files. They have names and can contain one or more bits of configuration data. Key names can be made up of any combination of alphabetical, numeric, and symbol characters, as well as spaces.

FIG. 19.1

The Registry Editor is a simple program that packs a lot of power.

Part

IV

Ch

19

Registry keys

Value entry data

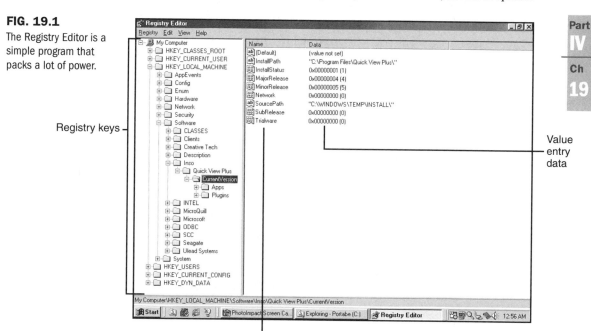

Value entry name

The most important difference between the Registry's keys and an INI file's sections is that a Registry key can contain other keys. That's the origin of the Registry's hierarchy. You can think of it as stuffing a bunch of file folders inside another file folder. At the top of Figure 19.1, you see My Computer. This just represents the computer whose Registry you're viewing (you can view remote computers, too). Below My Computer, you see a handful of *root keys*. Each root key contains a number of *subkeys*.

 TIP This chapter uses the terms *key* and *subkey* interchangeably. In reality, when referring to a child key (a key underneath the key being discussed), you should call it a *subkey*.

Below subkeys are *value entries*, where Windows stores the actual configuration data. Each key can contain one or more value entries, and each value entry has three parts:

- *Name.* The name can be any combination of alphabetical, numerical, and symbol characters, including spaces. The name uniquely identifies the value entry within a particular key. However, you might find the same name used in different Registry keys.
- *Data type.* Whereas INI files store only string configuration data, the Registry stores a variety of data types in a value entry. Table 19.1 describes the types of data you might find in the Windows 98 Registry.
- *Data.* Value data can be up to 64KB in size in Windows 98. An important concept you need to understand is that of an empty value entry. No such animal. If Windows or some other program has never assigned a value to a value entry, the value entry contains the *null* value. This is very different from assigning an empty string to a value entry; an empty string is a string of characters that just happens to be of zero length.

Table 19.1 Windows 98 Data Types

Type	Description
String	Text, words, or phrases. The Registry always displays strings within quotes.
Binary	Binary values of unlimited size, represented as hexadecimal. (These are similar to DWORDs except they're not limited to four bytes.)
DWORD	32-bit binary values in hexadecimal format (double words). The Registry displays a DWORD as an 8-digit (four bytes) hexadecimal number.

N O T E Every key contains at least one value entry, called (Default). This chapter just calls it the default value entry for a key. The default value entry is always a string value. Windows provides it for compatibility with the Windows 3.1 Registry and older 16-bit applications. In many cases, the default value entry doesn't contain anything at all. In other cases, a program needs to store only one value, so the default value entry is the only data stored in that key. ■

HKEY_LOCAL_MACHINE

You'll find six root keys in the Windows 98 Registry (take another look at Figure 19.1). HKEY_LOCAL_MACHINE and HKEY_USERS are real Registry keys; the others are *aliases*. Aliases are just shortcuts to branches within HKEY_LOCAL_MACHINE or HKEY_USERS that make accessing a particular set of configuration data easier for programmers and users. Take a look at the real keys first (we'll cover the aliases in a bit).

HKEY_LOCAL_MACHINE contains configuration data that describes the hardware and software installed on the computer, such as device drivers, security data, and computer-specific software settings (uninstall information, for example). This information is specific to the computer itself instead of to any one user who logs on to it. The following list describes the contents of each subkey immediately under HKEY_LOCAL_MACHINE:

- *Config.* Config contains information about multiple hardware configurations for the computer (in other words, hardware profiles). It contains groups of individual hardware settings from which Windows 98 can choose automatically or you can choose when you start the computer. Each subkey under HKEY_LOCAL_MACHINE\Config (numbered 0001, 0002, and so on) represents an individual hardware profile. HKEY_LOCAL_MACHINE\System\ CurrentControlSet\ControlNDConfigDB contains the name and identifier of the hardware profile that Windows 98 is currently using.

- *Enum.* This subkey contains information about each device installed on the computer. Each subkey under HKEY_LOCAL_MACHINE\Enum represents a particular type of bus (BIOS, ESDI, PCI, PCMCIA, or SCSI, for example.). Under each hardware class, you'll find one or more subkeys, which will in turn contain additional subkeys that identify a single piece of hardware. The organization of this branch and its contents depends largely on the devices you install on the computer and how the manufacturer organizes its settings.

- *Hardware.* Windows 98 doesn't do much with this subkey, as it provides hardware for compatibility with Windows NT.

- *Network.* This subkey contains information about the user who is currently logged on to the computer. Each time a user logs on to the computer, Windows stores details about the current network session (such as the user's logon name) in HKEY_LOCAL_MACHINE\ Network\Logon.

- *Security.* This subkey contains information about the computer's network security provider, administrative shares (for remote administration), and public shares. Windows 98 keeps track of all the open network connections other users have on your computer in HKEY_LOCAL_MACHINE\Security\Access. You'll find a single subkey for each connection.

- *Software.* This and the next subkey are the heart and soul of HKEY_LOCAL_MACHINE. Programs store settings that are specific to the computer in this subkey. These programs store their settings in branches that look like HKEY_LOCAL_MACHINE\Software\ *CompanyName\ProductName\Version*, where *CompanyName* is the name of the company, *ProductName* is the name of the product, and *Version* is the current version number of the product. You'll find many Windows-specific settings in this subkey, too, in HKEY_LOCAL_MACHINE\Software\Microsoft\Windows\CurrentVersion.

Part

IV

Ch

19

N O T E The single largest branch in the Registry is HKEY_LOCAL_MACHINE\Software\Classes. This subkey describes all the associations between documents and programs, as well as information about COM objects; thus, it is very large. You can also get to this branch through the root key HKEY_CLASSES_ROOT, which is an alias for HKEY_LOCAL_MACHINE\Software\Classes. ▪

■ *System.* Windows maintains *control sets*, each of which determines exactly which device drivers and services Windows loads and how it configures them when Windows starts. For example, a control set provides the various parameters Windows needs when it starts, such as the computer's name on the network and the current hardware profile. A control set also controls which device drivers and file systems Windows loads and provides the parameters Windows needs in order to configure each driver.

The Windows 98 Configuration Manager

The Configuration Manager is the heart of Plug and Play. It is responsible for managing the configuration process on the computer. It identifies each bus on your computer (PCI, SCSI, ISA) and all the devices on each bus. It also notes the configuration of each device, making sure that each device is using unique resources (IRQ and I/O address).

The Configuration Manager works with three key components to make all of this happen: bus enumerators, arbitrators, and device drivers. Here's a summary of the purpose of each component:

Bus enumerators	Bus enumerators are responsible for building the *hardware tree*. They query each device or each device driver for configuration information.
Arbitrators	Arbitrators assign resources to each device in the hardware tree. That is, they dole out IRQs, I/O addresses, and such to each device.
Device drivers	The Configuration Manager loads a device driver for each device in the hardware tree and communicates the device's configuration to the driver.

HKEY_USERS

HKEY_USERS contains all of the user-specific configuration data for the computer. That is, Windows stores configuration data for each user that logs on to the computer in a subkey under HKEY_USERS. If you haven't configured the computer to use profiles, all you'll find is a single subkey called .DEFAULT. The following list describes what you'll find in HKEY_USERS\.DEFAULT or within each user's subkey:

■ *AppEvents.* AppEvents contains associations between the sounds Windows produces and events generated by Windows and other programs. Under AppEvents, you'll find two subkeys: EventLabels, which describes each sound event, and Schemes\Apps, which assigns sound files to each event.

- *Control Panel.* Control Panel contains settings that the user can change using the Control Panel (such as Display and Accessibility Options). Many of the settings in Control Panel are migrated from the Windows 3.1 WIN.INI and CONTROL.INI files.

- *InstallLocationsMRU.* This itty-bitty subkey contains the last several paths from which you've installed Windows extensions. That is, every time you double-click the Add/Remove Programs icon in the Control Panel and click the <u>H</u>ave Disk button on the Windows Setup tab to install an extension, Windows 98 records the path of the INF file in InstallLocationsMRU.

- *Keyboard Layout.* Keyboard Layout defines the language used for the current keyboard layout. You change these values by clicking the Keyboard icon in the Control Panel.

- *Network.* Windows 98 stores persistent network connections in HKEY_CURRENT_USER\Network\Persistent. Each subkey represents a mapped drive letter (D, E, F, and so on). Under each drive letter's subkey, you'll find a handful of value entries—such as Provider Name, RemotePath, and UserName—that describe the connection.

- *Software.* Software is by far the most interesting subkey in this branch. It contains software settings that are specific to each user. Windows stores each user's desktop preferences under this subkey. In addition, each program installed on the computer installs user-specific preferences in this subkey. This subkey is organized just like the similarly named subkey in HKEY_LOCAL_MACHINE.

N O T E The Registry has an order of precedence. Often, Windows or other programs will store duplicate data in both HKEY_USERS and HKEY_LOCAL_MACHINE. In such cases, the configuration data stored in HKEY_USERS has precedence over the data stored in HKEY_LOCAL_MACHINE. Windows does this so that individual user preferences will override computer-specific settings. ▨

Aliases

Even though the Registry Editor does show six root keys, there are really only two: HKEY_LOCAL_MACHINE and HKEY_USERS. The remaining root keys are really just aliases that refer to *branches* (entire portions of the Registry beginning with a particular key) within the other two root keys. In other words, aliases are a bit like shortcuts in Explorer: If you change a value in one of the aliases, that value is actually changed in either HKEY_LOCAL_MACHINE or HKEY_USERS.

Here's more information about each alias:

- *HKEY_CLASSES_ROOT.* This is an alias for HKEY_LOCAL_MACHINE\Software\ CLASSES, which contains the associations between file types and programs.

- *HKEY_CURRENT_USER.* This is an alias for a branch in HKEY_USERS that contains the configuration data for the user who is currently logged on. Normally, it points to HKEY_CURRENT_USER\DEFAULT.

- *HKEY_CURRENT_CONFIG.* This is an alias for HKEY_LOCAL_MACHINE\Config\ *Profile*, where *Profile* is one of 0001, 0002, and so on. It contains the current hardware configuration for the computer.

- *HKEY_DYN_DATA.* This contains dynamic information about the current status of the computer. This isn't really an alias, but it is totally dynamic and is not permanently stored on disk.

N O T E When you export the Registry to a REG file, the file contains entries found only in HKEY_LOCAL_MACHINE and HKEY_USERS. That's because it is redundant to export the aliases. ▨

Abbreviations for Root Keys

You'll frequently see abbreviations for the root keys used in publications (but not this one). The following table gives the abbreviation used for each root key:

Root Key	Abbreviation
HKEY_CLASSES_ROOT	HKCR
HKEY_CURRENT_USER	HKCU
HKEY_LOCAL_MACHINE	HKLM
HKEY_USERS	HKU
HKEY_CURRENT_CONFIG	HKCC
HKEY_DYN_DATA	HKDD

Using the Registry Editor

REGEDIT might not be on your Start menu, but it is probably in your Windows folder (C:\WINDOWS). The file name is REGEDIT.EXE. To open it, choose Start, Programs, Run. Then type **regedit** and click OK. The REGEDIT window pops up. If you want, you can drag REGEDIT.EXE from your Windows folder to the Start button to create a shortcut to it.

TROUBLESHOOTING

I see REGEDIT.EXE in my Windows folder, but either I can't run it or it won't let me change anything in the Registry. If you're using a computer in a networked environment, your system administrator might have disabled it. You'll have to plead your case to the system administrator for access to REGEDIT.EXE. Note that the system administrator can also prevent REGEDIT.EXE from being installed on your computer if you're installing Windows from the network or doing a custom installation.

> **CAUTION**
>
> Preventing user access to the Registry Editor requires the cooperation of the program that the user is using to edit the Registry. REGEDIT cooperates. Other programs probably won't. Thus, in Windows 98, you can't be sure that a user doesn't have access to the Registry.

Searching for Keys and Value Entries

When you search the Registry, REGEDIT looks for keys, value names, and value data that match the text you specify. In other words, it searches using the name of each key, the name of each value entry, and the actual data from each value entry. You can use the search feature to find entries relating to a specific product, to find all the entries that contain a reference to a file on your computer, or to locate entries related to a particular hardware device.

Here's how to search the Registry:

1. Choose Edit, Find from the main menu, and REGEDIT displays the dialog box shown in Figure 19.2.

FIG. 19.2
Use these options to search for an item in the Registry.

TIP If you select any item in REGEDIT's left-hand pane and start typing the name of a Registry key, REGEDIT moves to the key that best matches what you've typed thus far. For example, expand HKEY_CLASSES_ROOT. Then press ., and REGEDIT selects .386; press **b**, and REGEDIT selects .bat; press **m**, and REGEDIT selects .bmp. Note that if you pause between keystrokes, REGEDIT starts your *incremental search* over with the next key you type.

2. Type the text for which you want to search. If you're searching for a number, try both the decimal and hexadecimal notations because both formats are common in the Registry.

3. In the Look At section, deselect the parts of the Registry in which you don't want REGEDIT to search: Keys, Values, and/or Data.

4. Click Find Next, and REGEDIT searches for a match. This can sometimes take quite a while (up to a few minutes on slower machines). If REGEDIT finds a matching key, it selects that key in the left-hand pane. If REGEDIT finds a matching value entry, it opens the key that contains the value entry in the left-hand pane and selects the value entry in the right-hand pane.

5. If the result isn't exactly what you had in mind, press F3 to repeat the search. When REGEDIT reaches the bottom of the Registry, it displays a dialog box telling you that it has finished searching.

TIP If the left-hand pane isn't big enough to easily tell which key REGEDIT found, look at REGEDIT's status bar to see the full name of the key. Alternatively, you can drag the window divider to the right to make more space in the left-hand pane.

Renaming a Key or Value Entry

Sometimes you have a really good reason to rename a key or value entry: to hide an entry from Windows while you test out a change. Well that's easy enough. Renaming a key or value entry in REGEDIT is similar to renaming a file in Windows Explorer except that you can't rename it by clicking on the name. Instead, you select the key or value entry that you want to rename, choose Edit, Rename, type over the name or change it, and then press Enter.

TIP You can also rename a key or value entry by selecting it and pressing F2.

Changing an Entry's Value

As a user, changing a value entry's setting is probably the number one activity you'll do with REGEDIT. You might want to personalize your desktop, for example, or you might need to adjust a TCP/IP setting to work better with your network.

Here's how to change a value entry:

1. Double-click a value entry in the right-hand pane to open the Edit dialog box. Remember that each value entry can be a string, DWORD, or binary data. This dialog box will be different depending on the type of data stored in the value. Figures 19.3, 19.4, and 19.5 show you what each dialog box looks like.

2. Change the value, and then click OK to save your changes.

FIG. 19.3

The Edit String dialog box shows you the original data before you start editing.

FIG. 19.4

Choose Decimal if your hexadecimal math is a bit rusty.

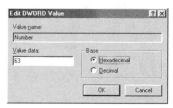

FIG. 19.5

You can use the
Windows calculator (in
Scientific mode) to
convert decimal values
to hexadecimal values
for use in this dialog box.

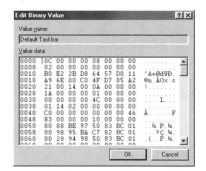

 Protect yourself when changing value data. Note the name of the value entry that you want to change and then rename it using some obscure name that Windows won't recognize such as MyValue. Then create a new Registry key with the name you assigned (as described in the next section) and set its value to what you want. This way, you can always restore the original setting by deleting the value entry you created and renaming the value entry you saved with its original name.

Changes that you make to the Registry might not be reflected immediately in Windows or the programs that are currently running. The only way to make sure is to close REGEDIT and restart Windows or the affected program.

To restart Windows 98 quickly, choose Shut Down from the Start menu. In the Shut Down Windows dialog box, select Restart the Computer and then hold down the Shift key and click OK. Windows 98 restarts without rebooting your computer.

Creating a New Key or Value Entry

Creating a new key or value entry is generally harmless—and equally useless unless, of course, you know for sure that either Windows or another program will use your new key. For example, the Microsoft Knowledge Base might instruct you to create a new Registry key to fix a problem. That's useful. Creating a new key out of thin air is pretty useless, however.

To create a new key or value entry, do one of the following:

- *New key.* Select the existing key under which you want your new subkey to appear. Choose Edit, New, Key from the main menu; type the name of your key; and press Enter.
- *New Value Entry.* Select the existing key under which you want your new value entry to appear. Choose Edit, New from the main menu and choose String Value, Binary Value, or DWORD Value from the resulting submenu. Then type the name of your new value entry and press Enter. You can edit your key as described in the preceding section.

Deleting a Key or Value Entry

Be very careful about deleting keys and value entries from your Registry. You'll likely prevent Windows from working properly if you carelessly delete keys or value entries from the Registry.

Part IV
Ch
19

If you don't know for sure what will happen or if you haven't been instructed to do so, *don't delete anything*. However, if you do need to delete a key or value entry, use these steps:

1. Highlight the key or value entry you want to delete.
2. Press Delete, and REGEDIT asks you to confirm that you want to delete it.
3. Click Yes to delete the key or value entry.

TIP   Before deleting a key, rename it with some obscure name such as MyNukedKey. This hides it from Windows and your applications. Then restart your computer and try it out. If everything works okay, go ahead and delete the key.

Importing and Exporting Registry Entries

There are two ways you can work with the Registry. You can work with it in its current form (SYSTEM.DAT and USER.DAT in Windows 98) using REGEDIT. Or you can export it to a text file (REG file) and edit it with your favorite text editor, such as WordPad (the file is too big for Notepad). If you export your Registry to a text file, you can use your editor's search-and-replace features to make massive changes to it. Be careful doing this, however, because you can inadvertently change a value you don't mean to change.

Aside from editing the Registry with a text editor, exporting the Registry to a text file has a more practical purpose. You're not limited to exporting your entire Registry. You can export a specific key and all its subkeys and value entries (the branch). Thus, you can export a tiny part of the Registry for the following purposes:

- *Backing up.* You can export a branch of the Registry in which you're making many changes. If you get confused or if things get out of hand, you can import that file back into the Registry to restore your settings.

- *Sharing.* You can export a key or a branch that contains a cool Registry hack. Then share that REG file with your friends so they can implement the same hack by importing the text file you provided (all they have to do is double-click the file).

To export your entire Registry or just a specific branch, perform the following steps:

1. In the left pane of the window, select the key that represents the branch you want to export. (If you're exporting the entire Registry, you can skip this step.)
2. Choose Registry, Export Registry File from the main menu. REGEDIT displays the dialog box shown in Figure 19.6.
3. If you're exporting the entire Registry, select All in the Export Range section. Otherwise, select Selected Branch, and REGEDIT automatically fills in the key you selected in step 1.
4. In the File Name text box, type the name of the file into which you want to export the Registry. If you don't add a file extension, REGEDIT uses the default file extension (.REG).
5. Click Save.

FIG. 19.6

You can export a branch of the Registry or the whole thing.

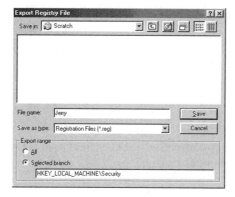

The resulting file looks very much like a classic INI file. To see it, open it in Notepad: Right-click the REG file and choose Edit. (Notepad will offer to open the file in WordPad if it's larger than 64KB.) The first line always contains REGEDIT4, which identifies the file as a REGEDIT file. The remainder of the file contains the keys and value entries REGEDIT exported. Figure 19.7 shows what exported Registry entries look like in a text file.

FIG. 19.7

A Registry export file looks a lot like an INI file.

Part
IV

Ch
19

The file is split into multiple sections, with each Registry key in its own section. The name of the key is shown in brackets. It is the fully qualified name of that key in the Registry file (in other words, you see the entire name of the branch including the name of the root key). Each value entry for a key is listed in that key's section. The value entry's name appears in quotation marks, except for default value entries, which REGEDIT indicates with the at sign (@). The value entry's data looks different depending on its type, as shown in Table 19.2.

Table 19.2   Formats for String, DWORD, and HEX Data

Type	Example
String	"This is a string value"
DWORD	DWORD:00000001
HEX	HEX:FF 00 FF 00 FF 00 FF 00 FF 00 FF 00

After you've made changes to your exported file, you might want to import it back into the Registry. In Windows Explorer, right-click an exported Registry file and choose Merge. Windows updates your Registry.

> **CAUTION**
>
> Be careful not to accidentally double-click a REG file. If you do, Windows automatically merges it with the Registry because merge is the default action for the REG file type.

Backing Up the Windows Registry

You'll find comfort in knowing that Windows 98 automatically backs up the Registry for you. Once each day, it uses the Windows Registry Checker (SCANREGW.EXE in C:\Windows) to back up the Registry to CAB files you find in C:\WINDOWS\SYSBCKUP. The first backup is named RB000.CAB, the second is RB001.CAB, and so on. The file with the highest number is the most recent backup file; thus, RB004.CAB is a more recent backup than RB002.CAB.

Right-click one of the CAB files, presumably the most recent, and choose View to examine its contents. You'll find four files in it: SYSTEM.DAT, SYSTEM.INI, USER.DAT, and WIN.INI. By default, Windows Registry Checker keeps only five backup copies of the Registry, but you can increase that by changing the MaxBackupCopies entry in SCANREG.INI to a higher number, perhaps 10.

You can also force Windows Registry Checker to make additional backup copies of the Registry after it has made its daily backup. Here's how:

1. Run SCANREGW.EXE (located in C:\Windows). After scanning the Registry for errors, the Windows Registry Checker asks you if you want to make another backup copy of the Registry.
2. Click Yes, and Windows Registry Checker backs up the Registry to another CAB file in C:\WINDOWS\SYSBCKUP. It displays a dialog box telling you when it's finished.
3. Click OK to close the Windows Registry Checker.

Windows Registry Checker is the preferred method for backing up the Registry. However, alternative methods might suit your needs better; you'll learn about those methods in the following sections.

Create a Startup Disk

If you're in a pinch and can't start Windows 98, you'll be very glad that you created a *startup disk*. This disk gets your computer going when it won't start from the hard drive. You'll also find a handful of utilities on the disk that you might be able to use to fix your computer. Here's how to create the startup disk:

1. Double-click the Add/Remove Programs icon in the Control Panel.

2. In the Add/Remove Programs Properties dialog box, click the Startup Disk tab.

3. Click the Create Disk button and follow the onscreen instructions. Windows 98 will likely ask you for your Windows 98 CD-ROM (or disks).

4. When Windows 98 finishes creating your startup disk, click OK to close the Add/Remove Programs Properties dialog box.

5. Label your Emergency Startup Disk and keep it in a safe place just in case you encounter problems starting Windows 98.

Windows 98 doesn't put CD-ROM or network drivers on your startup disk. If you think you might need access to either of these when you start from your startup disk, you'll have to copy the 16-bit DOS drivers to the disk. Then create a CONFIG.SYS and AUTOEXEC.BAT that loads them properly.

Copy the Registry Files to a Safe Place

The absolute easiest way to back up the contents of the Registry is to copy the files that contain the Registry to a safe place. You can even do this from Windows 98 Explorer, as explained here:

1. Create a folder on your computer to hold the backup copy of the Registry (C:\WINDOWS\REGISTRY, for example).

2. Make sure that you can view hidden files in Windows 98 Explorer (remember that SYSTEM.DAT and USER.DAT are hidden files). To make hidden files visible, choose View, Options from the main menu, select Show All Files, and click OK.

3. Copy SYSTEM.DAT from C:\WINDOWS to the backup folder.

4. Copy USER.DAT or your own personal profile folder from C:\WINDOWS to the backup folder.

5. Restore the Windows 98 Explorer window so that it hides those system files: Choose View, Options from the main menu, select Hide Files of These Types, and click OK.

If you'd rather do this more or less automatically, you can create a batch file that does the same thing. Then all you have to do is execute the batch file to copy SYSTEM.DAT and USER.DAT to a safe place.

The following batch file copies both files (SYSTEM.DAT and USER.DAT). It uses the Xcopy command with the /H and /R switches. The /H switch copies files with the Hidden and System attributes. You use this switch in lieu of changing the files' attributes with the attrib command. The /R switch replaces read-only files. That way, Xcopy will be able to write over previous backup copies of the Registry. %WinDir% expands to the location of your Windows folder when the batch file runs.

```
xcopy %WinDir%\system.dat %WinDir%\Registry\ /H /R
xcopy %WinDir%\user.dat %WinDir%\Registry\ /H /R
```

Part
IV

Ch
19

N O T E If you configured Windows 98 to use user profiles, you'll need to tweak this batch file to make it correctly back up your USER.DAT and USER.DAO files. In particular, you need to change the second line so that it copies these files from your profile folder instead of from the Windows folder. You can also enhance this batch file so that it copies USER.DAT and USER.DAO files for all users on the computer by copying the second line for each user. ▦

Back Up Your System Using a Tape Drive

Windows 98 comes with a tape backup utility that you can use as part of your regular backup strategy. Although Windows 98 Setup doesn't install it by default, you can use the Add/Remove Programs icon in the Control Panel to install the backup utility. After you install it, choose Start, Programs, Accessories, System Tools, Backup to run it.

By default, Microsoft Backup doesn't back up the Registry. Thus, to back up the Windows 98 Registry, you must perform the following steps before starting the backup:

1. Choose Job, Options from the main menu to display the Backup Job Options dialog box.
2. Click the Advanced tab, and you see the dialog box shown in Figure 19.8.

FIG. 19.8
By default, Microsoft
Backup doesn't back up
the Registry.

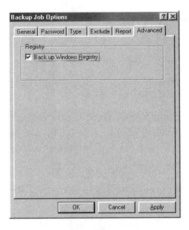

3. Select Back Up Windows Registry.
4. Click OK to save your changes.
5. Perform your backup as usual.

Export the Registry Using the Registry Editor

As you learned earlier in this chapter, you can export the entire contents of the Registry into a REG file (see "Importing and Exporting Registry Entries," earlier in this chapter).

CAUTION

Don't rely on an exported copy of the Registry as your only backup. Microsoft has recorded problems that have occurred when users attempted to restore a backup using this method. For example, Windows 98 might not correctly update all Registry data.

The best use for this method is to back up only the portion of the Registry in which you're making changes. That way, if something goes wrong while you're editing the Registry, you can easily restore that branch by double-clicking the REG file.

Use the Emergency Repair Utility

The Emergency Repair Utility (ERU) is a tool that you can use to back up your important configuration files. You can back up those files to a floppy disk or to another folder on your computer. Microsoft preconfigured it to back up your most important configuration files, including:

AUTOEXEC.BAT	PROTOCOL.INI
COMMAND.COM	SYSTEM.DAT
CONFIG.SYS	SYSTEM.INI
IO.SYS	USER.DAT
MSDOS.SYS	WIN.INI

You'll find ERU on your Windows 98 CD-ROM in \TOOLS\MISC\ERU. Copy all four files to a folder on your computer. Then add a shortcut to your Start menu by dragging ERU.EXE and dropping it on the Start button. After you've copied it to your computer, use these steps to back up your configuration files, including the Registry:

1. Start ERU by choosing it from the Start menu or by double-clicking ERU.EXE in Windows 98 Explorer.

2. Click Next after ERU pops up. In the dialog box that appears next, choose between backing up to a floppy or backing up to another folder.

3. Choose Drive A: if you want to back up your configuration files to disk, or choose Other Directory to back up your configuration files to another folder on your hard drive. Click Next to continue.

4. If you're backing up your configuration files to another folder on your computer, type the path of the folder in the space provided. Then click Next to continue. Otherwise, insert a formatted disk in drive A and click OK to continue. You see a list of files that ERU is backing up, as shown in Figure 19.9.

5. Click Custom to change the files that ERU includes in the backup.

6. Click Next, and ERU backs up your configuration files into the destination you chose.

7. ERU displays a dialog box that explains how to restore your configuration settings in the event that something bad happens to them. Click OK to close it.

Part

IV

Ch

19

FIG. 19.9

You can specify which files ERU includes in the backup.

Restoring the Windows Registry

As you learned earlier, Windows 98 uses a utility called Windows Registry Checker to back up copies of the Registry to CAB files stored in C:\WINDOWS\SYSBCKUP. You can restore any one of those backups using the real-mode version of this utility named SCANREG.EXE, which you find in C:\WINDOWS\COMMAND. To do so, follow these steps:

1. Start Windows in MS-DOS mode. To do so, select Command Prompt Only from Windows 98's boot menu. Or choose Shut Down from the Start menu, select Restart in MS-DOS Mode, and press Enter.

2. Type **scanreg /restore** to start the Microsoft Registry Checker.

3. Select a backup from the list provided. Microsoft Registry Checker displays the date, status, and filename of each backup. Ideally, you should pick the most recent backup; however, if you know the most recent one doesn't work, pick the next most recent backup.

4. Press Enter, and Microsoft Registry Checker restores the backup to your computer.

5. Press Enter to restart your computer.

Although using Microsoft Registry Checker is the preferred method for restoring the Registry, you can use other methods. The sections that follow describe methods for restoring the alternative backups you learned about in the previous sections.

Restore Your Copy of the Registry Files

Did you make a backup copy of SYSTEM.DAT and USER.DAT? If so, you can easily restore those files and continue with business. Here's how:

1. Make sure that you can view hidden files in Windows 98 Explorer. To make hidden files visible, choose View, Options from the main menu, select Show All Files, and click OK.

2. Copy your backup copy of SYSTEM.DAT to C:\Windows.

3. Copy USER.DAT or your own personal profile folder to C:\Windows.

4. Restore Windows 98 Explorer window so that it hides those system files: Choose View, Options from the main menu, select Hide Files of These Types, and click OK.

5. Restart your computer.

If you prefer, you can create a batch file that automatically restores your backup copies of SYSTEM.DAT and USER.DAT. Then all you have to do is double-click the batch file to restore them.

The following batch file restores your backup files. It uses the Xcopy command with the /H and /R switches. The /H switch copies hidden and system files. The /R switch replaces read-only files. That way, Xcopy will be able to overwrite the current copy of SYSTEM.DAT and USER.DAT. %WinDir% expands to the location of your Windows folder when the batch file runs.

```
Xcopy %WinDir%\Registry\System.dat %WinDir%\System.dat /R /H
Xcopy %WinDir%\Registry\User.dat %WinDir%\User.dat /R /H
```

N O T E If you've configured Windows 98 to for multiple user profiles, you'll need to tweak this batch file to make it correctly restore USER.DAT. In particular, you need to change the second line so that it restores the backup copy into your profile folder.

Restore Your System from a Tape Drive

If you used the Windows 98 tape backup utility (Microsoft Backup) to back up the Registry, you can easily (if not quickly) restore the Registry to the state it was in when you last backed up your computer. You must use the following steps to instruct Windows 98 to restore the Registry:

1. Choose Job, Options from the main menu and click the Advance tab.
2. Select Restore the Registry.
3. Click OK to save your changes.
4. Continue restoring the backup as usual.

N O T E Using Microsoft Backup to back up and restore the Registry is a method better suited for a full backup. That is, if you restore the Registry from a backup tape, you should also restore the entire system from the same tape. Doing so ensures that the files on your computer match the settings found in the Registry. If you restore just the Registry from an older tape, chances are good that your computer won't work correctly because the configuration data in the Registry doesn't match the remaining files on your computer.

Part
IV

Ch
19

Import an Exported Copy of the Registry

Earlier in this chapter, you learned how to export the Registry into a REG file. You can't import this file while Windows 98 is running, however, because the Registry Editor can't replace keys that are open. You need to start your computer to the DOS prompt, and then use the Registry Editor in real mode to import the Registry. Follow these steps:

1. Start Windows in MS-DOS mode. To do so, select Command Prompt Only from Windows 98's boot menu. Or choose Shut Down from the Start menu, select Restart in MS-DOS Mode, and press Enter.

2. Type **regedit /L:*system* /R:*user regfile*** at the DOS prompt. *system* is the path and filename of SYSTEM.DAT. *user* is the path and filename of USER.DAT. (Normally, *user* points to C:\WINDOWS\USER.DAT, but if you're using profiles, it might point to a USER.DAT file within a profile folder in C:\WINDOWS\PROFILES.) *regfile* is the path and filename of the REG file containing the backup.

3. Restart your computer.

N O T E   This method is better suited to restoring backups containing small portions of the Registry. For instance, you can back up a single branch in which you're making changes. If you make a mistake, you can restore that single branch, without affecting other parts of the Registry. ▪

Use the Emergency Repair Utility

The Emergency Repair Utility (ERU) is a tool that backs up all of your important configuration files, including the Registry. You learned how to backup the Registry with the ERU earlier in this chapter. Here's how to restore your configuration files from the backup:

1. Start your computer to the DOS prompt.

2. Change to the folder to which you backed up your configuration files. If you backed up your configuration files to a disk, put that disk in the drive and change to it.

3. Run ERD.EXE. It's mixed in with all the backup copies of your configuration files.

4. Select the files that you want to recover. Highlight a configuration file using the arrow keys, and then press the Enter key to select it.

5. Once you've selected the configuration files you want to recover, select Start Recovery and press the Enter key.

Restore SYSTEM.1ST

If all else fails, you'll find one more backup copy of the Registry on your computer. SYSTEM.1ST is a read-only, hidden, system file in the root folder of your boot drive. This is a backup copy of SYSTEM.DAT that Windows 98 made after you successfully installed and started Windows 98. It doesn't contain any custom settings, nor does it include any information added by the programs you've installed. The only thing this file does for you is get your machine running again if nothing else works.

Here's how to restore SYSTEM.1ST:

1. Start your computer to the DOS prompt.

2. Copy your C:\SYSTEM.DAT file to C:\Windows\SYSTEM.DAT. At the DOS prompt, type **Xcopy C:\system.1st C:\windows\system.dat /H /R**. Then press Enter.

3. Restart your computer.

CAUTION

Use this method as a last resort only. Once you've restored SYSTEM.1ST, all the configuration changes you've made to your computer since you first installed Windows 98 will be gone.

The Windows 98 Registry vs. Windows 95 and NT

You will see little or no difference between the Windows 98 and Windows 95 Registries. The organization is the same, and the Registry Editor is the same. Inside the Registry is a different story, however. Microsoft has optimized the code and data structures that implement the Registry so that it performs much faster. The only thing you might notice is how much faster the Registry works.

The Windows 98 and Windows NT 4.0 Registries, in many ways, are very similar. However, there are some pretty huge differences between HKEY_CLASSES_ROOT and HKEY_USERS that you should be aware of:

- Windows NT 4.0 stores the Registry in hives, whereas Windows 95 stores the Registry in two binary files.

- Windows NT 4.0 implements full security for the Registry hives and for each individual key in the Registry. Windows 95 provides little security.

- The structure of HKEY_LOCAL_MACHINE\System is very different in Windows 95 and Windows NT 4.0.

- Windows NT 4.0 provides an additional Registry Editor that takes advantage of security and the different types of data you can store in a value.

To learn more about the differences between the Windows 98 and Windows NT 4.0 Registries, take a look at Macmillan's own *Windows 95 and Windows NT 4.0 Registry & Customization Handbook*.

Part

IV

Ch

19

CHAPTER 20

Advanced Registry Hacks

by Jerry Honeycutt

In this chapter

Editing a Remote Computer's Registry

Remote administration enables you to inspect and change settings on one computer from another computer on the network. Typically, you change settings on the *target* (remote) computer from an *administrative* computer.

The cornerstone of Windows 98's remote administration capabilities is, of course, remote Registry administration. In fact, many of the other remote administration tools you learn about in this book, such as System Monitor, rely on the remote Registry to provide the information the tool uses. Closer to home, you can browse a remote computer's Registry or define policies that specify what users can and can't do on the remote computer.

Both the target and administrative computers must meet the following requirements to support remote Registry administration:

- *Common protocol.* The two computers (target and administrative) must have at least one common protocol: TCP/IP or NetBEUI, for example.

- *User-level security.* The two computers must use the same security type: share-level or user-level. For practical purposes, both should use user-level security.

- *Remote administration.* The target computer must have remote administration enabled. Note that, by default, when you enable user-level security, Windows 98 enables remote administration for the Domain Admins group on a Windows NT network, the Supervisor account on a NetWare 3.x network, or the Admin account on a NetWare 4.0 network.

- *File and Printer Sharing.* Both computers must have the appropriate File and Printer Sharing Service installed. Although Microsoft documentation states that this service isn't necessary for remote administration, my experience suggests otherwise.

- *Remote Registry Service.* Both computers must have the Remote Registry Service installed. This service uses the RPC (Remote Procedure Call) mechanism to provide access to the Registry API on the remote computer. The next section explains how to enable this service.

Creating a Custom Setup Script

Did you deploy Windows 98 without enabling remote administration? If so, you'll have to manually enable remote administration on each workstation in order to take advantage of the tools this chapter describes. Alternatively, you can enable remote administration using the System Policy Editor, as described in Chapter 38, "Configuring Windows Network Components."

If you haven't yet deployed Windows 98, however, you can use a custom setup script to enable remote administration as Setup installs Windows 98. Here's how. Copy the Windows 98 source files to an installation on the server and share that folder. Create a setup script in the MSBATCH.INF format that enables remote administration. Provide a means by which the user can launch Setup with the setup script, using either push or pull installation methods. (The section "Advanced Installation Techniques" in Appendix A, "Installing Windows 98," describes how to use login scripts to push the Windows 98 installation and how to email a batch file to the user so that he can pull the installation when he's ready.)

Enabling the Remote Registry Service

As you learned in the preceding section, before you can use remote Registry administration, you have to enable the Remote Registry Service on the target and administrative computers. Follow these steps:

1. Open the Network dialog box by double-clicking the Network icon in the Control Panel.

2. Click <u>A</u>dd to display the list of network components.

3. Select Service from the components list and click Add. Windows 98 might pause for a moment while it builds a driver information database. The Select Network Service dialog box appears, as shown in Figure 20.1.

4. Click <u>H</u>ave Disk to locate the Remote Registry Service on your Windows 98 CD-ROM. Then, in the dialog box that appears, type the path to the Remote Registry Service's installation files. (These files are located in \Tools\Reskit\Netadmin\Remotreg on the Windows 98 CD-ROM.) Click OK to continue, and you again see the Select Network Service dialog box.

FIG. 20.1

The services you see in this dialog box are described in the Remote Registry Service's INF file (REGSRV.INF).

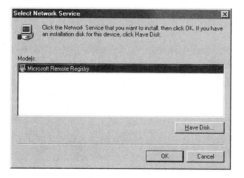

5. Select Microsoft Remote Registry from the list and click OK.

6. In the Network properties sheet, click OK. Windows 98 copies the appropriate files to your computer.

7. Restart your computer when prompted.

Opening a Remote Computer's Registry

Connecting to a remote computer's Registry gives you full access to it. You must be as careful editing a remote computer's Registry as you would be editing your own, because the implications of making careless changes are just as bad. Note that even though the changes you make are immediately reflected in the remote computer's Registry, the user might have to reboot his computer in order to reflect those changes in the rest of the operating system or in the applications that depend on those settings. As a general rule of thumb, if the user would have to re-start his computer after making a change in the Control Panel, he'll have to restart it after you make a similar change in the Registry.

Use the following steps to open a remote computer's Registry in the Registry Editor:

Part
IV

Ch
20

1. Open the Registry Editor by typing **regedit** in the Run dialog box and pressing Enter.

2. From the main menu, choose Registry, Connect Network Registry. You see the Connect Network Registry dialog box.

3. Type the name of the remote computer, or click Browse and select the computer in the dialog box that appears. Click OK, and you see the remote computer's Registry in the Registry Editor (see Figure 20.2).

FIG. 20.2

At any given time, the Registry Editor shows all the Registries to which you are connected.

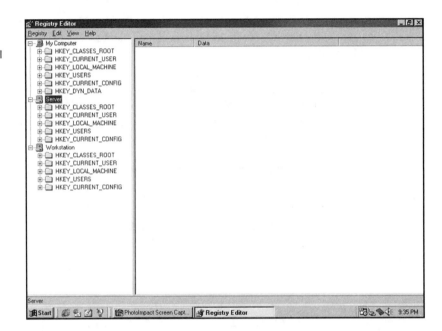

After you connect to the remote computer's Registry, everything works the same as usual. For example, you can add and remove Registry keys, and you can add, remove, and change value entries. Just make sure that you're selecting keys and value entries in the computer that you intend. Otherwise, you might change a Registry key on your own computer when you really intended to change a key on the remote computer.

Using the System Policy Editor

The System Policy Editor enables you to define restrictions that control the user's configuration. You can enforce a certain network configuration, for instance, or remove certain icons from the user's desktop. Figure 20.3 shows the System Policy Editor.

You learn how to use the System Policy Editor in Chapter 38. This chapter shows you how to install the System Policy Editor, set up machine and user policies, and apply policies to individual users, groups, and machines.

▶ **See** "Using the System Policy Editor," **p. 378**

The System Policy Editor provides access to a subset of the remote computer's Registry, whereas the Registry Editor gives you complete access to the Registry.

FIG. 20.3

Many of the forms in the System Policy Editor use drop-down list boxes to minimize the chance of error.

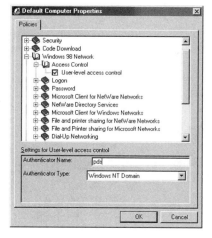

CAUTION

In many cases, the System Policy Editor is a better alternative than the Registry Editor because the risks are not as great when you use the System Policy Editor.

You have two options for using the System Policy Editor. The first is to create policy files that Windows 98 downloads from the network server and merges with the Registry. The second is to use the System Policy Editor in *Registry mode*, which allows you to change the remote Registry directly. Regardless of which method you use, you specify the values you want to change and their data by using forms and data-entry fields that make sense in their context. (In the Registry Editor, on the other hand, it's an editing free-for-all.)

To connect to a remote computer's Registry in the System Policy Editor, use the following steps:

1. Open the System Policy Editor.
2. From the main menu, choose File, Connect.
3. Type the name of the computer to which you want to connect, and then click OK.

TROUBLESHOOTING

I can't connect to a remote computer, even though I've enabled remote administration on the remote computer. You must enable remote administration and the Remote Registry Service on both computers. Make sure the Remote Registry Service is enabled on the computer from which you're administering as well as on the computer you're administering.

I can't administer a remote computer now, even though I've been able to administer the same computer before. Remote administration works only if someone is logged on to the remote computer. Thus, make sure someone is logged on before you attempt to administer the computer.

Part
IV

Ch
20

T I P To learn more about working with and administering the Windows 98 Registry, take a look at *Using the Windows 98 Registry* (Que, 1998). This book covers the Registry's organization in detail, discusses each of the tools that are available for managing the Registry, and shows you how to leverage the Registry in your organization.

Troubleshooting the Registry

The following sections contain information about specific tools and techniques you can use to diagnose and fix problems with the Registry. The following list contains answers to some of the most common questions and problems related to the Registry:

- *To prevent users from accessing the Registry:* Don't install the Registry Editor when you roll out Windows 98. Instead, set the Disable Registry Editing Tools system policy, as described in Chapter 38.

- *To fix Registry errors at startup:* If you see an error message that says `Windows 98 encountered an error accessing the system Registry, Windows will restart and repair the system Registry for you now`, allow Windows 98 to restart and repair the Registry in MS-DOS mode. If you see a message that says `Windows was unable to process the Registry. This may be fixed by rebooting to Command Prompt Only and running SCANREG /FIX. Otherwise, there may not be enough conventional memory to properly load the Registry`, follow the instructions in the next section to repair the Registry.

- *To remove references to missing device drivers:* If you see a message that says `Windows 98 can't find a device driver or other system file`, think back through the recent changes you've made to the computer. If you recently removed a program, reinstall the program and then use the uninstaller to remove it. If the missing file has a .VXD extension, remove all references to it in the Registry. If the file has a .386 extension, remove references to it in SYSTEM.INI file by commenting it out.

Fixing the Registry with the Registry Checker

As you learned in Chapter 19, "Working with the Windows Registry," Windows 98 runs the Windows Registry Checker each time you start your computer. The first time it runs each day, the Windows Registry Checker makes a backup of the Registry and stores the backup in a .CAB file that it stores in \Windows\Sysbckup.

You use the Registry Checker to scan the Registry for errors and fix them. Windows 98 includes two versions of the Registry Checker: one for MS-DOS and one for Windows. The MS-DOS version is a program called SCANREG.EXE, and the Windows version is a file called SCANREGW.EXE. Both versions can scan the Registry for errors, but only the MS-DOS version can restore backup copies of the Registry or actually repair a damaged Registry. Table 20.1 describes the command-line parameters you can use with both versions of the Registry Checker. Note that /restore and /fix work only with the MS-DOS version.

Table 20.1   Command-Line Parameters for Registry Checker

Parameter	Description
/backup	Backs up the Windows Registry
/restore	Restores a backup copy of the Registry
"/comment"	Associates a comment with a Registry backup
/fix	Fixes any errors found in the Registry
/autoscan	Scans for errors and backs up the Registry
/scanonly	Scans for errors without backing up the Registry

N O T E   Chapter 19 contains more information about using and configuring the Registry Checker. You learn how to increase the number of backup copies the Registry Checker keeps, for instance. ▓

Manually Removing Program Settings from the Registry

The way most programs use the Registry is rather predictable. They all store the same types of information in the same types of places. You can use this fact to help you successfully remove a program from the Registry.

T I P   Before you begin, back up the Registry. You'll be making significant changes to the Registry, and it's comforting to know you have a way out if things get out of hand.

First, delete all the program's installation folders. Most Windows 98 programs are installed in the folder C:\Program Files.

After you've removed the program's files, open the Registry Editor. Search the Registry for any entry that belongs to that program, and then remove it. The following list suggests some types of things you should search for:

- Search the Registry for each of the program's installation paths. If the program has two paths called C:\Program Files*Program* and C:\Program Files*Company**Program*, search for both of those paths in the Registry and delete any keys or value entries that contain them. Use common sense before removing any key that obviously contains configuration data used by other programs.

- Search the Registry for the program's name. If you're removing a program called "Elvis Lives for Windows 98," search the Registry for any key or value entry containing "Elvis" or "Elvis Lives." Delete any keys or value entries that contain the name of the program. Use common sense before removing any key that obviously contains configuration data used by other programs.

Part
IV

Ch
20

TIP If you find a key whose default value entry contains the name or path of the program you're removing, it's probably safe to remove the entire key, even if it has subkeys.

- Some programs name their DLLs and .EXE files with the same few starting characters. HiJaak 95 DLL files always begin with HJ, for example. Search the Registry for those characters. After verifying that the DLL files belong to the program you're removing (by finding that file in the program's installation folder or by looking at the file with Quick View), you can delete the key or value entry containing those letters. Use common sense before removing any key that obviously contains configuration data used by other programs.

 TROUBLESHOOTING

I can't start Windows 98 after I install a particular program. The program is loading shell extensions, drivers, or other files when Windows 98 starts, and those files are causing it to crash. Restart your computer and press F8 when Windows 98 displays the message Starting Windows 98. When the Startup menu appears, choose Command Prompt Only. Then completely delete the program's installation folder and subfolders (normally found under C:\Program Files). When you finish, restart Windows 98. You'll see a few messages about missing files, but Windows 98 will start successfully. Finally, remove the program's Registry entries using the steps in this section. After you remove the program's Registry entries, you won't see the messages about missing files.

Using Windows 98 to Repair the Registry

In most cases, you don't have to use the Registry Editor to repair the Registry. You can let Windows 98 do it for you. In fact, Windows will fix some errors before you even know they exist. The following list describes three techniques you can use to fix the most common problems associated with configuration data in the Registry:

- *To fix problems with the computer's hardware:* If your hardware configuration mysteriously breaks down, you won't be able to fix it using the Registry Editor. The hardware entries in the Registry are just too complicated. Use the Add New Hardware Wizard in the Control Panel to redetect your hardware.

NOTE If the Add New Hardware Wizard doesn't fix the problem, you'll need to remove the device from the Device Manager and then try the wizard again. To remove the device, double-click the Control Panel's System icon and click the Device Manager tab. Delete the device from the list and click OK to save your changes. ■

- *To fix problems with a particular application:* If a program's settings are bad, it's often easier to reinstall the program than to attempt a fix. You don't have to remove the program first; you just install right over it. You'll replace the program's files on the hard drive and the program's settings in the Registry. Be sure that you install into the same folder so you don't waste drive space. Some of the smarter programs know enough to leave your preferences alone while they correctly fix other Registry settings. If you reinstall Netscape Navigator, for example, it preserves all your server settings while it resets all the program's settings in HKEY_CLASSES_ROOT.

 TIP Many programs use .REG files to create their settings in the Registry. You might be able to use the .REG file again to restore the damaged settings without reinstalling the program. Look in the program's installation folders for a .REG file, and then inspect it by right-clicking the file and choosing Open. If it looks like it will fix your problem, double-click the file to merge its settings with the Registry.

■ *To fix problems with a particular file type:* The order in which you install programs on your computer affects a file extension's association with a file type. It's established on a last-come-first-served basis: If you install Microsoft Word first and the Microsoft Word Viewer second, the .DOC file extension is associated with the Microsoft Word Viewer program. Some programs, such as Internet Explorer and WinZip, automatically detect when they are no longer associated with a particular file type. In these cases, you can let the program fix the problem automatically. In other cases, you can use the File Types tab of the Folder Options dialog box in Windows Explorer to reassociate a file extension with a file type (see Figure 20.4).

FIG. 20.4
The bottom part of the File Types tab describes the extensions associated with the selected file type and the application that opens the file.

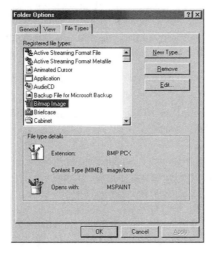

Configuring Windows 98 via the Registry

The following sections describe a variety of settings you can configure using the Windows 98 Registry. You won't find step-by-step instructions in these sections, however, because the instructions are very repetitive:

1. Open the Registry Editor.

2. Locate the given Registry key.

3. Add, change, or remove the given value entry.

4. Close the Registry Editor and restart the computer if necessary.

▶ **See** "Working with the Windows Registry," **p. 353**

ON THE WEB

The Windows 98 Annoyances web page contains a variety of customizations for Windows 98. You'll also find tips there that don't involve editing the Registry.

`http://www.creativelement.com/win98ann`

Adding Actions to the Context Menus

If you have more than one program that can access the same type of file, you'll want to add an action to the file extension's context menu that allows you to choose between the two programs. This gives you two options for opening a file: You can open with program A or open with program B, for example.

To better understand this, take a look at .DOC files. When you install Windows, it associates WordPad with .DOC files. WordPad is a fast editor that is file-compatible with Microsoft Word. The trouble begins when you install Microsoft Word. It associates .DOC files with itself—leaving you without a convenient way to open a .DOC file in WordPad if you so choose. To make it easy to open the file in WordPad, you can add a new action to the .DOC file's context menu that allows you to open .DOC files with WordPad, too. Here's how:

1. Add a subkey called \Open with Wordpad to the key HKEY_CLASSES_ROOT\ Word.Document.6\shell.

2. Under the new subkey, add another subkey called \command and set its default value entry to c:\Program Files\Accessories\WordPad.exe "%1".

N O T E The quotation marks around the %1 in the command line tell Windows 98 to put the file name inside quotation marks. The %1 is called a *placeholder*. If you don't put "%1" in the command line and you select a long filename with spaces in it, WordPad won't be able to open the file. ■

Now you can open .DOC files with either Microsoft Word or WordPad. Double-click a .DOC file to open it in Word. Right-click a .DOC file and choose Open with WordPad to open it in WordPad.

Changing the Desktop Icons

You're not stuck with the icons or icon names that Windows 98 and NT use for the special desktop icons (My Computer, Recycle Bin, and so on). You can change them all by following these guidelines:

■ *To change the name associated with an icon:* Open the key called HKEY_CLASSES_ROOT\CLSID. Table 20.2 describes some of the most common subkeys for desktop icons. Find the subkey that corresponds to the icon you want to change, and then change the default value entry to the name you want to display on the desktop.

■ *To change an icon's graphics:* Open the DefaultIcon subkey under the same key just mentioned, and then change the default value entry to the path of the icon file and index of the icon. If you want to use the fourth icon in Shell32.dll, for example, type C:\Windows\System\Shell32.dll,3. You can get icons from .DLL, .EXE, .ICO, and a variety of other files.

Table 20.2   Subkeys for Changing Desktop Icons

Name	Subkey
Briefcase	{85BBD920-42A0-1069-A2E4-08002B30309D}
Control Panel	{21EC2020-3AEA-1069-A2DD-08002B30309D}
Dial-Up Networking	{992CFFA0-F557-101A-88EC-00DD010CCC48}
Inbox	{00020D75-0000-0000-C000-000000000046}
My Computer	{20D04FE0-3AEA-1069-A2D8-08002B30309D}
Network	{208D2C60-3AEA-1069-A2D7-08002B30309D}
Printers	{2227A280-3AEA-1069-A2DE-08002B30309D}
Recycle Bin	{645FF040-5081-101B-9F08-00AA002F954E}
The Internet	{FBF23B42-E3F0-101B-8488-00AA003E56F8}
Microsoft Network	{00028B00-0000-0000-C000-000000000046}

N O T E   Most .EXE and .DLL files have icons in them. You'll find that some DLLs—such as MORICONS.DLL, COOL.DLL, PIFMGR.DLL, PROGMAN.DLL, and SHELL32.DLL in your \Windows or \Windows\System folder—have a large number of useful icons. ■

Changing the Location of System Folders

Part IV Ch 20

Have you ever tried to move the \ShellNew folder to a new location? How about the \My Documents folder? You can't unless you do so through the Registry. Delete any of these folders, if you can, and Windows creates the folder when you restart your computer. Windows keeps a list of shell folders in the Registry. This is how it knows where to find things such as your Start menu, desktop shortcuts, and recent documents.

You find these shell folders at HKEY_CURRENT_USER\SOFTWARE\Microsoft\Windows\CurrentVersion\Explorer\Shell Folders. Table 20.3 shows you the value entries you'll find in Windows 98.

Table 20.3 Default Shell Folders in Windows 98

Value Entry	Default
Desktop	C:\WINDOWS\Desktop
Favorites	C:\WINDOWS\Favorites
Fonts	C:\WINDOWS\Fonts
NetHood	C:\WINDOWS\NetHood
Personal	C:\My Documents
Programs	C:\WINDOWS\Start Menu\Programs
Recent	C:\WINDOWS\Recent
SendTo	C:\WINDOWS\SendTo
Start Menu	C:\WINDOWS\Start Menu
Startup	C:\WINDOWS\Start Menu\Programs\Startup\
Templates	C:\WINDOWS\ShellNew

Launching Explorer from My Computer

There are many different ways to get to Explorer. You can launch it from the Start menu. You can right-click My Computer and choose Explore. You can even double-click My Computer while you hold down the Shift key. So why can't you launch Explorer just by double-clicking My Computer? Well, you can. To do so, change the default value entry for HKEY_CLASSES_ROOT\CLSID\{20D04FE0-3AEA-1069-A2D8-08002B30309D}\Shell to **explore**.

Viewing Unknown File Types

Have you ever right-clicked CONFIG.SYS, hoping to open it in Notepad, only to find the Open With menu option? .SYS files are registered as system files and have no commands associated with them. There are plenty of other files that would be useful to open in Notepad that have no commands associated with them. You can remedy this situation, however, by associating Notepad with all unknown file types. Then, the next time you right-click on Config.sys or any other unregistered file type, you'll see Notepad on the context menu. Here's how:

1. Add a subkey called \Notepad to the HKEY_CLASSES_ROOT\Unknown\Shell Registry key.

2. Under the new key, add a subkey called command and set its default value entry to **C:\Windows\Notepad.exe "%1"**.

Comparing Snapshots of the Registry

Before you begin, make sure you understand how the Registry is organized. That means take a closer look at Chapter 19. A full understanding of this information can lead you to some of the best customizations.

The easiest way to find changes in the Registry is to compare a version of it before and after Windows 98 (or another program) makes a change. To do that, however, you need a program to compare two text files and point out the changes. I haven't found such a program on the Internet, but you'll find one included with Norton Utilities for Windows 98, Norton Navigator, Microsoft Win32 SDK, and Premia's Codewright for Windows 95. Many other utilities also include a program that compares two text files. The following example uses WinDiff from the Win32 SDK. Microsoft Word also allows you to compare two text files.

With the comparison tool in hand, use the following process to pin down a change made to the Registry:

1. Export the Registry to a .REG file, as you learned how to do in Chapter 19. Name this file BEFORE.REG.

2. Close the Registry Editor and run the program you believe will change the Registry. For instance, start Windows Explorer and change your settings in the Folder Options dialog box. Then close the program.

3. Open the Registry Editor and export the Registry to another .REG file called AFTER.REG.

4. Use the comparison utility to identify each change between the before and after versions of the .REG files.

You won't always be able to figure out which program on your computer will change a particular value entry. For that matter, you might not be able to figure out what actions on your part will cause a value entry to be changed. In these cases, you might have to resort to tinkering with the value entry until you see a noticeable change. Modifying the value entry is generally safe as long as you can re-create the previous value when things go awry. It's easy to give yourself some insurance. Create a temporary value entry and copy into it the contents of the entry that you're changing. If anything goes wrong, you can copy the contents that you saved back into the original entry.

Part
IV

Ch
20

Distributing Registry Hacks via .REG Files

.REG files are text files that you can easily import into the Registry. In fact, when you double-click a .REG file, Windows automatically imports it into the Registry by default. This fact makes it easy for you to distribute the .REG file. When the user opens it, Windows 95 automatically makes the changes that the .REG file contains.

CAUTION

Don't double-click a .REG file unless you know for sure what it contains. Double-clicking a .REG file merges its contents into the Registry without any confirmation.

.REG files resemble .INI files. Take a look at the following listing. The first line always contains REGEDIT4. This indicates that the file was created by REGEDIT. The remainder of the listing contains keys and value entries you'd normally find under HKEY_LOCAL_MACHINE\ SOFTWARE\Microsoft\Windows\CurrentVersion\FS Templates:

```
REGEDIT4

[HKEY_LOCAL_MACHINE\SOFTWARE\Microsoft\Windows\CurrentVersion\FS Templates]
@="Server"

[HKEY_LOCAL_MACHINE\SOFTWARE\Microsoft\Windows\CurrentVersion\
➥FS Templates\Desktop]
@="Desktop computer"

[HKEY_LOCAL_MACHINE\SOFTWARE\Microsoft\Windows\CurrentVersion\
➥FS Templates\Mobile]
@="Mobile or docking system"
"PathCache"=hex:10,00,00,00
"NameCache"=hex:51,01,00,00

[HKEY_LOCAL_MACHINE\SOFTWARE\Microsoft\Windows\CurrentVersion\
➥FS Templates\Server]
@="Network server"
"PathCache"=hex:40,00,00,00
"NameCache"=hex:a9,0a,00,00
```

The file is split into multiple sections, with each Registry key in its own section. The fully qualified name of the Registry file key is given—that is, you see the entire name of the path to that key, beginning with the name of the root key—between two brackets. Each value entry for a key is listed under that key's section. The value entry's name is quoted, except for default value entries, which REGEDIT represents with the at sign (@). The value entry's data looks different depending on its type, as shown in Table 20.4.

Table 20.4 Formats for String, DWORD, and HEX Data

Type	Example
String	"This is a string value"
DWORD	DWORD:00000001
HEX	HEX:FF,00,FF,00,FF,00,FF,00,FF,00,FF,00

Creating .REG Files by Hand

Creating a .REG file by hand is easy enough. Create a new file with the .REG extension. Then follow these steps:

1. Put REGEDIT4 at the very top of the file. This must be the very first line in the file. Also, make sure that you insert one blank line between REGEDIT4 and the first section of the .REG file, as just shown in the listing.

2. Add a section for each key that you want to add to or change in the Registry. Put each key name in square brackets, like this: [*Keyname*]. Make sure that you use the fully qualified path to the key, beginning with the root key.

3. Put an entry under each key for each value entry that you want to add or change. Each entry has the form "*Name*"=*Value*, where *Name* is the name of the value entry that you're adding or changing. If you're changing the default value entry, use the at sign (@) for *Name*, without the quotation marks. *Value* is the value to which you want to set the value entry. Make sure it follows one of the forms shown in Table 20.4.

4. Save your changes to the .REG file.

N O T E   You can't use a .REG file to remove a key from the Registry. If you need to create a script to do this, consider building an .INF file. The Windows 95 Resource Kit contains complete information about building .INF files. ▓

Creating .REG Files Using REGEDIT

Creating .REG files by hand seems easy enough, but it's not recommended. There are entirely too many opportunities for error—especially if you're a bad typist. Thus, you should use REGEDIT if at all possible. Chapter 19 shows you how to export a branch of the Registry to a .REG file.

You should be aware of a couple issues when you use this technique:

- When you export a key using REGEDIT, you're exporting all of that key's subkeys and value entries. Thus, you'll need to open the file (right-click it and choose Edit) and remove any keys and value entries that you don't want to distribute in the .REG file.

- You can change any of the values in the REG file. That is, if you're not satisfied with the settings you exported from the Registry, you can alter those settings in the .REG file before you distribute it.

Distributing .REG Files to Users

A good way to impress the users that you support is to distribute fixes to them without their asking. If you have an intranet in your organization, you can make .REG files available on a web page. Lacking an intranet, you can also distribute .REG files in mail messages or in the user's login script:

Part

IV

Ch

20

■ *To distribute .REG files on a Web page:* The default Windows 98 action for a .REG file is to import it. You can put a link to a .REG file on a Web page. Then, when a user clicks that link, the browser will download the file to the user's computer and automatically apply the change that it contains. This works fine for Internet Explorer users, but Netscape users will have to register a helper application for .REG files.

■ *To distribute .REG files in an email message:* If you don't have an intranet in your organization, the next best thing to do is distribute a .REG or .INF file in an email message. Attach the file to the message and instruct the user on how to apply the file. In most email programs, the user will just have to double-click the attachment to apply the .REG file or right-click on an .INF file and choose Install.

■ *To distribute .REG files in a login script:* You can put a command in each user's login script that automatically applies the .REG when the user logs onto the network. If you've set up a login script for multiple users, you can slip the command in that script instead. All you have to do is put the command `start` `filename.reg` in the script (`filename` is the name of the .REG file). The one problem with this method is that every time the user logs on to the network, the login script applies the .REG file. You can avoid this problem by putting this command in a batch file. Then the login script can check for the existence of this batch file on the user's computer. If it doesn't exist, the login script copies the batch file to the user's computer and executes it. Otherwise, the login script just ignores it.

CHAPTER 21

Scripting with the Windows Scripting Host

by Robert Ward

In this chapter

This chapter shows you how to use VBScript and the Windows Scripting Host (WSH) to automate administrative and production tasks. *Administrative tasks* are the little, frequently repeated, but critical configuration or maintenance tasks that are necessary to keep your system healthy. These include tasks such as the following:

- "Patching" the Windows Registry
- Mounting or unmounting network resources
- Performing frequent backups of selected files and directories
- Monitoring boot logs and other tracking information for unexpected changes
- Configuring more efficient desktops for inexperienced users

Production tasks are those operations that are always a part of completing one's work product. These are often trivial, but are repeated so often that they become frustrating time sinks. Alternatively, they can be error-prone, complex sequences of operations. Production tasks include tasks such as the following:

- "Closing the books" and printing financial reports
- Exporting names and addresses from an order-entry system to a word-processing program and performing a mail-merge to prepare pieces for a direct mail promotion
- Zipping a directory, FTPing the contents to a server, and sending email to notify the recipient
- Rearranging your desktop when you switch from one kind of project to another

This chapter shows how you can use WSH and VBScript to automate both administrative and production tasks. I'll introduce WSH scripting through a series of example scripts. Each of these scripts is chosen to illustrate an important scripting technique or an important WSH object. Before attacking the examples, though, I'll give you some background information about VBScript and COM and describe the WSH object model. The background information will help you understand the context in which WSH fits. The WSH object model is the technical foundation you'll need to understand the examples. To help you develop your own scripts, I'll also introduce you to the VBScript Debugger and other tools that make WSH scripting easier. Throughout, though, I'll assume you have some familiarity with VBA or some other dialect of VB. To teach programming (or even Visual Basic) from scratch is far beyond the scope of this chapter.

Background

In part because of the emphasis on user-driven interfaces, prior editions of Windows have not been well suited for production work. Until now, Windows has supplied only one user-oriented tool for automating tasks—the DOS command language. Unfortunately, few applications provide a command-line interface rich enough to allow them to be well controlled from a DOS batch script. While some applications supply a macro language that can support external automation using only the command interface, that solution imposes a heavy learning curve for the average administrator or power user. Stooping to a macro-based implementation for every automation task forces the administrator or user to become expert in every application's user interface and macro syntax. In any but the simplest production environments, that's just not realistic.

Recently, Microsoft has pushed two technologies that, combined, address this need. First is the *Common Object Model* (*COM*, formerly known as OLE and sometimes as OLE Automation or just Automation). The COM standard specifies how programs can expose their internal objects to other programs. The second technology is Visual Basic; both standard Visual Basic and Visual Basic for Applications (VBA). VB is a simple-to-learn language that can manipulate COM objects as if they were an intrinsic part of the language. During the last few years, Microsoft has revised their core applications to expose virtually all their functionality through some COM object and to use VBA as the application's internal macro language. Thus, a programmer can now incorporate an Excel spreadsheet, a Word document, or an Access database and all its functionality directly into a new application, just by referencing the appropriate COM object. Obviously, this is very attractive technology—so attractive that there are now hundreds of thousands of programmers conversant in Visual Basic and the use of various COM objects.

While VB and COM are powerful enough to "script" production and administrative tasks, for several reasons, VB isn't quite the right tool for the job. First, VB programs can't be modified outside the VB development environment. That makes VB impractical for scripting because administrative scripts often need to be modified ad hoc" on the station on which they are being used. It's just not cost effective to put a complete VB development environment on every work-station just so the administrator can make a quick adjustment to some script. For the same reasons, VB is not the right tool for production scripting. Production scripts are most effective when users can make changes. Users should be able to adjust scripts for small changes (like different directory names) without calling on the administrator. Finally, VB isn't the right language because it's too big. VB is geared for producing visual user interfaces. That means the runtime library is laden with large, complex visual objects. It's a waste of overhead to load such a library just to connect a network printer or execute a Word mail merge.

Enter *VBScript*, a VB dialect originally developed for use in web pages. Programs in VBScript are simple text files, so they can be written and modified by anyone with a text editor. Unfortunately, until recently, VBScript could only be executed as part of a web document. Because nearly everyone has a web browser, that wouldn't be a great limitation, but the security needs of a browser and the system-manipulation needs of a scripting language are directly at odds. For a browser to be secure, it should prevent a web page from modifying the file system or launching arbitrary tasks. For a scripting language to be useful, it must allow the script to do just those things and more.

Microsoft has now addressed these VBScript limitations by creating *WSH*, a stand-alone host that can execute VBScript programs directly. Because WSH occupies a minimal footprint and is being distributed free, it is ideal for production and administrative automation. Sites can easily afford to place a copy of WSH on every machine. (WSH is included as part of Windows 98.) Scripting in VBScript is a natural for Windows administrators because most are already familiar with the language features in VBScript, either from writing application macros in VBA or through using VBScript to create web pages. (The later sidebar "The VBScript Language Model" explains how VBScript differs from VBA.)

The VBScript hosted by WSH is the same language as that used to control the server in Active Server Pages and to control the browser in active web pages. (In fact, WSH, Internet Explorer, and Internet Information Server all use the same language engine—implemented as a separate OLE component—to interpret VBScript programs.) Even so, because WSH supplies a completely different execution environment (a different object model), using VBScript with WSH is substantially different than using it in web pages. Web scripts must manipulate the browser, various document components, and various server-side services. Automation scripts, on the other hand, must be able to manipulate file systems, execute programs, and configure system parameters. The following sidebar introduces the WSH Object Model.

The VBScript Language Model

VBScript is mostly a proper subset of VBA. (VBScript does include a suite of string manipulation and formatting functions that are not in VBA.) VBScript omits those VBA features that involve significant translation overhead (such as strong type checking facilities) or that comprise a security risk (such as file I/O). VBScript does not support the following:

- Types other than variant (in particular, there is no support for user-defined types)
- Many of the more advanced control statements
- Traditional Basic I/O features
- Conditional compilation features

While there are several other small differences (for example, you can't base arrays), these four categories encompass the most significant differences. As you can see from the following discussion, a lot is left out of VBScript; but then, it needs to be small and quick to fit its intended role.

Types and Type Checking   VBScript is almost type ignorant. While you can still declare variables by using Dim, you can specify only one type: variant. Everything—variables, object references, arguments—is represented as a variant. VBScript, however, is not a typeless language. Although everything is represented as a variant, VBS is aware of the underlying type and still warns you if a parameter doesn't match the type requirements of a COM interface. Unfortunately, that's about the only time you'll get warned about type mismatches. Oddly enough, even though everything is represented as a variant, type conversions are not automatic. You must still convert strings to integers before you can perform arithmetic on them.

Besides outlawing the intrinsic types, VBScript also outlaws user-defined types. This is not a language for creating complex data structures! In fact, you can't even use TypeOf to determine the type of existing objects. With only one all-purpose data type, it might seem reasonable to construct all data structures from an all-purpose aggregation, such as a collection. Don't count on it. VBScript also omits virtually all the collection manipulation features of VBA. Add, Count,

Item, Remove, and ! are all missing. The only operations supported on collections are For Each …. Next, ordinal selection, and selection using a key. (The keys themselves, though, are inaccessible.)

Although it's easy to say that all the type mechanism is gone, it's hard to get used to the implications. If you've been writing large, object-oriented programs, you'll be pretty uncomfortable when you realize that along with Type … End Type you've also lost New, ParamArray, Property Get, Property Let, and Property Set.

Control Statements   Several VBA control structures have been omitted, but most won't be missed. The most inconvenient changes are the omission of With…End With and the restriction of Select Case to single-valued cases. Other omissions include Do Events, GoSub…Return, GoTo, On Error GoTo, On Error…Resume, Resume, Resume Next, On…GoSub, On…GoTo, line numbers, and line labels.

Although this list includes many error-handling structures, the basic error handler, On Error Resume Next, is still present. The Error Method is gone, but the Err object and all of its properties are still available. Thus, you can still write capable error handlers, but you just have to work a little harder to craft the right expression.

Basic File I/O   What can I say? It's gone. All gone. So is the Debug object. Remember, VBScript was designed to use in web documents. Web documents aren't supposed to do file I/O.

A new runtime library for WSH does, however, include objects that allow you to do file I/O. I'll discuss these in more detail in the section on the WSH Object Model.

Conditional Compilation   Again, VBScript just doesn't have any—but then again, why would an interpreted language have support for conditional compilation? All the same, it would be nice to have a manifest constant and a file include capability.

Other Differences   The other differences are relatively few and innocuous (at least for most scripting users). For example, all financial functions have been omitted; as have the Lset and Rset string functions. You can get a complete language specification by downloading vbsdoc.exe from **www.microsoft.com/scripting/vbscript/download/vbsdown.htm**. Despite these omissions, VBScript is still a powerful, highly usable language. If you're wondering what's left, just scan the lists of keywords and functions in the language specification referenced previously. Even with all the omissions, VBScript is still a rich and versatile language.

The WSH Object Model

The *Windows Scripting Host* supplies objects to support parameterized execution, system configuration, network configuration, simple user interactions, and file system operations. The objects that supply these services, however, aren't all independent COM components. Many classes are only accessible through the methods or properties of some larger class. Table 21.1 lists the objects and details their access, methods, and properties.

Part
IV

Ch
21

Table 21.1 WSH/VBScript Objects

Class Name	Access	Methods	Properties
Supplied by Wscript.exe or Cscript.Exe			
Err	Err	Description HelpContext HelpFile Number Source	Clear Raise
Wscript	Wscript	CreateObject Disconnect Object Echo GetObject Quit	Application Arguments FullName Name Path ScriptFullName ScriptName Version
WshArguments	Wscript.Arguments	Item Count Length	
Supplied by WSHom.Ocx			
WshShell	Wscript. CreateObject ("WshShell")	Environment SpecialFolders	CreateShortcut ExpandEnvironmentStrings Popup RegDelete RegRead RegWrite Run
WshNetwork	Wscript. CreateObject ("Wscript. Network")	ComputerName UserDomain UserName	AddPrinterConnection EnumNetworkDrives EnumPrinterConnections MapNetworkDrive RemoveNetworkDrive RemovePrinterConnection SetDefaultPrinter
WshCollection	Returned from methods WshNetwork. EnumNetworkDrives or WshNetwork. EnumPrinter Connections	Item Count Length	

Class Name	Access	Methods	Properties
Supplied by WSHom.Ocx			
WshEnvironment	Returned as property WshShell.Environment	Item Count Length	Remove
WshShortcut	Returned from method WshShell.CreateShortcut	Arguments Description Hotkey IconLocation TargetPath WindowStyle WorkingDirectory	Save
WshSpecialFolders	Returned as property WshShell.SpecialFolders	Item Count Length	
WshURLShortcut	Returned from method WshShell.CreateShortcut	FullName TargetPath	Save
Supplied by SCRRUN.DLL			
Dictionary	Wscript.CreateObject ("Scripting.Dictionary")	CompareMode Count Item Key	Add Exists Items Keys Remove RemoveAll
Drive	Select from Drives collection or as return from method FileSystemObject. GetDrive(drivespec)	AvailableSpace DriveLetter DriveType FileSystem FreeSpace IsReady Path RootFolder SerialNumber ShareName TotalSize VolumeName	
Drives	Collection, available as property FillesystemObject.Drives	Count Item	
File	Select from Files collection or returned from method	Attributes DateCreated DateLastAccessed	Copy Delete Move

continues

Part

IV

Ch

21

Table 21.1   Continued

Class Name	Access	Methods	Properties
Supplied by SCRRUN.DLL			
	FileSystemObject.GetFile(filespec)	DateLastModified Drive Name ParentFolder Path ShortName ShortPath Size Type	OpenAsTextStream
Files	Collection, returned from method FileSystemObject.GetFolder(folderspec)	Count Item	
FileSystemObject	Wscript.CreateObject ("Scripting.FileSystem Object")	Drives	BuildPath CopyFile CopyFolder CreateFolder CreateTextFile DeleteFile DeleteFolder DriveExists FileExists FolderExists GetAbsolute-PathName GetBaseName GetDrive GetDriveName GetExtension-Name GetFile GetFileName GetFolder GetParentFolder-Name GetSpecialFolder

Class Name	Access	Methods	Properties
Supplied by SCRRUN.DLL			
			GetTemp-Name MoveFile MoveFolder OpenTextFile
Folder		Attributes DateCreated DateLastAccessed DateLastModified Drive IsRootFolder Name ParentFolder Path ShortName ShortPath Size SubFolders	Copy Delete Move CreateText-File
Folders		Count Item	AddFolders
TextStream		AtEndOfLine AtEndOfStream Column Line	Close Read ReadAll ReadLine Skip SkipLine Write WriteLine WriteBlank-Lines

The services provided by WSH objects are partitioned into six top-level objects: Wscript, WshShell, WshNetwork, Err, Scripting.Dictionary, and Scripting.FileSystemObject.

Wscript is the executive module. It supplies the methods to create and release other objects (including all COM components), to identify the running script and access its arguments, and to generate output messages (the Echo method).

WshShell provides primitive user interface capabilities and access to the local system. Through WshShell, you can manipulate environment variables, the desktop, and the Registry. You can get limited input from the user through the WshShell.Popup method.

Part
IV

Ch
21

WshNetwork supplies access to network resources and configuration. Through this object you can manage network drives and printers.

Err is the same object as available in VBA. By testing Err and querying its properties, you can collect information about program errors.

The *Dictionary* object implements an associative array. By using CreateObject, you can create as many dictionary instances as you might need. In most scripting applications, the flexibility and convenience of this object more than compensates for the loss of language support for user-defined types.

Similarly, the *FileSystemObject* compensates for the absence of intrinsic I/O functions. This object provides a rich set of methods and properties to support file and folder manipulation. One of its methods will create a TextStream object—a text file that acts much like traditional DOS or UNIX streams.

The Execution Environment

Microsoft actually supplies two implementations of the scripting host, Wscript and Cscript. *Wscript* is the native windows version of the host. All of the examples in this chapter were developed and tested under Wscript. To launch a script by using Wscript (assuming it has been selected as the default application for .vbs files) you merely double-click on some visual representation of the script file.

Cscript is a command-line-oriented implementation of the scripting host. You could think of Cscript as the native DOS version of the host. To launch a script with Cscript, you must either use Run on the Start menu or execute a command line in a DOS window.

When scripts execute under Cscript, all output generated by Wscript.Echo is redirected to the DOS standard output channel. Under Cscript, using the OpenTextFile method of the file system object, you can even open the console device (CON:) and read from standard input.

Thus, in addition to the WSH object model, a script executing under Cscript has limited access to standard input and standard output. Scripts executing under Wscript do not.

Another minor difference between the two hosts is the ease with which you can specify command-line arguments. Under Cscript, the arguments are simply part of the invoking command. If the script is to execute under Wscript, you have three alternatives:

- Launch the script by typing the command (with arguments) in the Start menu's Run dialog box
- Launch the script from a shortcut that includes the command-line arguments
- Create a .wsh file to specify the execution parameters

The .wsh file is a control file that specifies the execution parameters by using an .ini-like format. Using a .wsh file enables you to override (on a script-by-script basis) the default options for the scripting host. The .wsh file also allows you to specify the command line and arguments for the script.

These minor differences make Cscript a more natural fit for scripts that are to communicate with other DOS applications.

Writing Scripts

This section introduces you to some of the basics of scripting in the WSH environment. It isn't meant to be an introduction to Visual Basic. In fact, this section will be most meaningful to those who have already done some VB programming. This section isn't even meant to be a complete reference to the WSH environment, though in some instances I do give the syntax for specific WSH methods.

The goal in the following is to present a sampler—a collection of scripts and script fragments that will give you a feel for what can be accomplished in WSH/VBScript and what's involved in writing working scripts. To make the material accessible to as many as possible, I begin with some very basic topics, like generating output, and proceed to more complex topics. Except for the last program, I have attempted to keep the listings short, straightforward, and limited to a subset of the language—again, to help those who are not experts in Visual Basic get a feel for what's involved.

For full details about the language syntax and semantics and about the public interfaces to the WSH objects, you should see the reference materials listed in the "Scripting Resources" section near the end of this chapter.

Basic I/O

The simplest WSH script is probably the following one-liner:

```
MsgBox "Hello World"
```

This script generates the vbOK-style dialog box in Figure 21.1. As the Visual Basic title bar suggests, this program doesn't really use anything special from WSH. In particular, it doesn't use any WSH objects. But, it's important to remember that most of the VBA commands are still available in VBScript.

FIG. 21.1
This dialog box is generated by the MsgBox command. Note the contents of the title bar.

Although MsgBox is still available, administrative scripts should probably generate their output using the WSH Echo method. An Echo-based version of the Hello World program looks like this:

```
Wscript.Echo "Hello World"
```

This version uses the Echo method of the WScript object to generate the dialog box shown in Figure 21.2. Note that the Wscript object doesn't need to be instantiated—it's always available to a WSH script.

FIG. 21.2

The Echo-based Hello-World script produces this dialog box. Note that the title bar says Windows Scripting Host instead of Visual Basic.

The Echo method also generates a simple vbOK-style dialog box, but the box's title bar reads Windows Scripting Host instead of Visual Basic.

Wscript's Echo method takes any number of arguments, but doesn't really support any variations; you always get a vanilla vbOK-style dialog box that contains a concatenated list of the arguments. Even so, Echo does have advantages over MsgBox. The Echo method aims to be the Windows equivalent of the DOS ECHO command. Microsoft supplies the WSH executive in two different forms: Cscript, the command-line oriented version; and Wscript, the windows version. All output generated by the Echo method is directed to DOS's standard output channel when run under Cscript and to a vbOK dialog box when run under Wscript. Thus, using Wscript.Echo for simple output allows you to interactively test a script in the Windows environment, but then use the production version of the script in a traditional batch environment.

For greater control over the dialog box and for simple input you can use WshShell's Popup method. The Popup method understands most of the standard Visual Basic dialog box styles and returns a value indicating which button the user clicked to close the box. The calling syntax is as follows:

```
WshShell.Popup strText, [natSecondsToWait], [strTitle],[natType])
```

Popup returns an integer indicating which button the user clicked.

Because Popup is a member of the Shell object, programs must instantiate the Shell object by calling Wscript.CreateObject before calling Popup. The following program creates an instance of WshShell and then uses PopUp to collect some information about the user:

```
Option Explicit
Dim objWsh
Dim natIsOld
Set objWsh = Wscript.CreateObject("Wscript.Shell")
natIsMale = objWsh.Popup( "Are you Male?",, _
                          "User Information",vbYesNo)
```

Note the use of Set to save a reference to the object created by the call to CreateObject. If you omit the Set keyword, the following line will generate an Object Doesn't Support this Property or Method error.

The call to Popup creates a dialog box complete with a custom title bar (see Figure 21.3). The Popup function then returns either vbYES or vbNO, much like any similar call to VB's MsgBox function.

Enumerating the Environment

In addition to Basic I/O, the shell object supplies information about the script and its environment. The program in Listing 21.1 uses the Environment property of the Shell to generate a listing of all current environment strings. The report shown in Figure 21.4 illustrates one of the fundamental differences between Windows 98 and Windows NT. Windows NT partitions its variable space—Windows 98 does not. If this script were run on an NT machine, each section would include some output.

Listing 21.1   This WSH Script Reports the Contents of All Current Environment Variables

```
Option Explicit

Dim strMsg
Dim CRLF
Dim TAB
Dim wshShell
Dim strVar

CRLF = Chr(13) & Chr(10)
TAB = Chr(09)

'Uncomment the following line before debugging
'with the script debugger
'WScript.Echo "Envex waiting for Debugger"

Set wshShell = WScript.CreateObject("WScript.Shell")

StrMsg = "Current Environment Variables (Default):"
For Each strVar in wshShell.Environment
    strMsg = strMsg & CRLF & TAB & strVar
Next
```

continues

Listing 21.1   Continued

```
StrMsg = StrMsg & CRLF & CRLF & "Current Environment Variables (System):"
For Each strVar in wshShell.Environment("System")
      strMsg = strMsg & CRLF & TAB & strVar
Next

StrMsg = StrMsg & CRLF & CRLF & "Current Environment Variables (User):"
For Each strVar in wshShell.Environment("User")
      strMsg = strMsg & CRLF & TAB & strVar
Next

StrMsg = StrMsg & CRLF & CRLF & "Current Environment Variables (Volatile):"
For Each strVar in wshShell.Environment("Volatile")
      strMsg = strMsg & CRLF & TAB & strVar
Next

StrMsg = StrMsg & CRLF & CRLF & "Current Environment Variables (Process):"
For Each strVar in wshShell.Environment("Process")
      strMsg = strMsg & CRLF & TAB & strVar
Next

WScript.Echo strMsg

WScript.DisconnectObject(wshShell)
WScript.Quit
```

FIG. 21.4

The script in Listing 21.1 will always generate a report similar to this when run under Windows 98.

The following loop iterates over each of the strings in the Environment collection—available only as a property of the WSH Shell object:

```
For Each strVar in wshShell.Environment
      strMsg = strMsg & CRLF & TAB & strVar
Next
```

Listing 21.1 was written to report on the environment variables of an NT host, which are partitioned into four separate access spaces. Figure 21.4, however, was generated by running the script on Windows 98, in which the environment variables are all contained in a single name space.

You can use similar code and the Wscript.Arguments collection to generate a list of the command-line arguments passed to a script. Scripts can report singular environment characteristics just by echoing the property. For example, the following will report the filename of the script in which it appears:

```
Wscript.Echo Wscript.ScriptName
```

The following are the last two lines in Listing 21.1, which release the Script's instance of the WSH shell object, and then quit the WSH executive:

```
WScript.DisconnectObject(wshShell)
WScript.Quit
```

These lines aren't required. WSH automatically reduces the reference count to the Shell object and exits after it reaches the end of the script. Windows then frees the resources associated with the Shell object. I've included these lines because I believe it's good programming practice to clean up after yourself.

Using the Network Object

The network object, class WshNetwork, includes properties and methods that allow you to identify and manage network resources. Scripts can acquire their host's network name, the current user's name, and the current domain name by retrieving the appropriate properties from the network object.

Enumerating Resources   The network object also includes methods that return a collection of strings describing current network file and printer resources. These collections are of class WshCollection (an all-purpose container class) and are only accessible by walking the members of the collection.

The following two lines create a network object and use it to instantiate a collection of strings describing the network drives:

```
Set wshNet = WScript.CreateObject("WScript.Network")
set drives = wshNet.EnumNetworkDrives
```

The resulting drives collection is a set of paired strings. The first string in a pair describes the local mapping for the network resource. The second string in a pair is the network path to the same resource. When a network resource has no local mapping, the first string in the pair is a zero-length string. The same convention is used to represent printer resources.

To process these pairs properly, a script must walk the strings in order, keeping track of whether the current string is a drive designator or a path. Listing 21.2 shows how to access these collections to produce a report (see Figure 21.5) of currently connected network file and printer resources. Inside of the For Each loop, a Boolean (blnPath) is used to keep track of whether the current string represents a local mapping or a network path.

Part

IV

Ch

21

Listing 21.2   This WSH Script Reports All Currently Connected Network Resources

```
Option Explicit

Dim strMsg
Dim CRLF
Dim TAB
Dim wshNet

CRLF = Chr(13) & Chr(10)
TAB = Chr(09)

Set wshNet = WScript.CreateObject("WScript.Network")

strMsg = "Network Properties:"

strMsg = strMsg & CRLF & "Computer Name " & TAB & wshNet.ComputerName
strMsg = strMsg & CRLF & "User Domain "   & TAB & wshNet.UserDomain
strMsg = strMsg & CRLF & "User Name"      & TAB & wshNet.UserName

strMsg = strMsg & CRLF & "Network Drives"

Dim drives
Dim blnPath
set drives = wshNet.EnumNetworkDrives

blnPath = False
For each id in drives
   if blnPath then
       strMsg = strMsg & id
   else
       strMSG = strMsg & CRLF & TAB &  id & " = "
   end if
   blnPath = NOT blnPath
next

Dim printers, id
set printers = wshNet.EnumPrinterConnections
strMsg = strMsg & CRLF & "Network Printers"

blnPath = False
For each id in printers
   if blnPath then
       strMsg = strMsg & id
   else
       strMSG = strMsg & CRLF & TAB &  id & " = "
   end if
   blnPath = NOT blnPath
next


WScript.Echo strMsg

WScript.DisconnectObject wshNet
WScript.Quit
```

FIG. 21.5

The script in Listing 21.2 produces this report of network resources.

While it's useful to know what network resources are connected, it's even more useful to be able to modify those from a script. The next two examples show how to remove and connect network resources from a script.

Disconnecting Resources Listing 21.3 shows how to use the RemoveNetworkDrive and RemovePrinterConnection methods to drop all network connections. The script produces a dialog box that lists the disconnected resources (see Figure 21.6). The Remove methods have this syntax:

```
WshNetwork.RemoveNetworkDrive strName, [bForce], [bUpdateProfile]
WshNetwork.RemovePrinterConnection strName, [bForce],
                                        [bUpdateProfile]
```

Setting bForce to True will cause the resource to be disconnected even if it is currently in use by someone else. Setting bUpdateProfile to True will cause this mapping to be saved in the user's profile.

Listing 21.3 This WSH Script Disconnects All Network Resources

```
Option Explicit

Dim strMsg
Dim CRLF
Dim TAB
Dim wshNet

CRLF = Chr(13) & Chr(10)
TAB = Chr(09)

Set wshNet = WScript.CreateObject("WScript.Network")

Dim drives
Dim count, i
set drives = wshNet.EnumNetworkDrives
count = drives.count

strMsg = "Removing " & count/2 & " Drive Connections"

do while drives.count > 0
    if drives.item(i) <> "" then
        strMsg = strMsg & CRLF & TAB & drives.item(i) & " = " & drives.item(i+1)
        wshNet.RemoveNetworkDrive drives.item(i),1
```

continues

Part

IV

Ch

21

Listing 21.3 Continued

```
        else
        if drives.item(i+1) <> "" then
            strMsg = strMsg & CRLF & TAB & " = " & drives.item(i+1)
            wshNet.RemoveNetworkDrive drives.item(i+1),1
        end if
    end if
    set drives = wshNet.EnumNetworkDrives
loop

Dim printers
set printers = wshNet.EnumPrinterConnections
count = printers.count

StrMsg = StrMsg & CRLF & CRLF & "Removing " & count/2 & " Printer Connections"

do while printers.count > 0

    if printers.item(i) <> "" then
        strMsg = strMsg & CRLF & TAB & printers.item(i) & " = " &
        ➥printers.item(i+1)
        wshNet.RemovePrinterConnection printers.item(i),1
    else
        if printers.item(i+1) <> "" then
            strMsg = strMsg & CRLF & TAB & " = " & printers.item(i+1)
            wshNet.RemovePrinterConnection printers.item(i+1)
        end if
    end if
    set printers = wshNet.EnumPrinterConnections

loop


WScript.Echo strMsg
WScript.DisconnectObject wshNet
WScript.Quit
```

FIG. 21.6

The script in Listing 21.3 produces this report before disconnecting all network resources.

The Remove methods behave differently depending on whether they are called with a local resource designator or with a network path. When called with a local resource identifier, the Remove method will remove the entire resource. That is, the result of the call will be the removal of both local identifier and network path strings from the WshCollection. On the other hand, if called with a network path, both strings will be removed only if there is no local mapping for the resource.

Thus, the loop in Listing 21.3 invokes the Remove method on the local designator, if there is one, and invokes the Remove method on the network path otherwise. After removing a resource, the loop reinstantiates the network object. I found that if I didn't rebuild the network object, subsequent Removes wouldn't properly index the target string.

Connecting Resources   As promised, Listing 21.4 shows how to connect network resources from a script. This example assumes that the network resources are supplied by two different hosts that each require a different password from the user at the beginning of each session. Some users find such situations very confusing. This script simplifies the logon process by asking the user for each password and then using those passwords to connect to the appropriate resources.

Listing 21.4   This WSH Script Prompts the User for Two Passwords and Then Connects to Resources on Two Different UNIX Hosts

```
Option Explicit

Dim strMsg
Dim CRLF, TAB
Dim wshNet
Dim strPword, strPword2

CRLF = Chr(13) & Chr(10)
TAB = Chr(09)

Set wshNet = WScript.CreateObject("WScript.Network")

strPword = inputbox("Enter your Department password.", "Department Login")
strPword2 = inputbox("Enter your WebMaster password.",  "Web Master Login")
call wshNet.MapNetworkDrive ("M:", "\\DeptHost\Deptdir", ,,strPword)
call wshNet.MapNetworkDrive ("N:", "\\Gateway\WebRoot", ,,strPword2)
call wshNet.AddPrinterConnection ( "LPT2" ,"\\DeptHost\color 4200",,,strPword)

WScript.DisconnectObject wshNet
WScript.Quit
```

This example uses the InputBox function from Visual Basic to retrieve the two passwords (see Figure 21.7). Although InputBox is a convenient tool for getting textual input, it's not ideal for a password application because it echoes the password to the screen where others can see it. In a production environment, you would use a COM object for this task.

FIG. 21.7

The script in Listing 21.4 generates two password dialog boxes similar to this one.

After the password is available, the script calls AddPrinterConnection and MapNetworkDrive to connect the resources. The syntax for these methods is as follows:

```
WshNetwork.AddPrinterConnection strLocalName, ___ __
    strRemoteName, [bUpdateProfile], [strUser], [strPassword]
WshNetwork.MapNetworkDrive strLocalName, _
    strRemoteName, [bUpdateProfile], [strUser], [strPassword]
```

When the bUpdateProfile flag is True, the mapping will be stored in the user's profile.

Sequencing Jobs

Scripting for production tasks is primarily a matter of sequencing tasks or jobs. To handle this task well in the Windows environment, the scripting language must be able to manipulate not only traditional command-line-oriented applications, but also modern, complex COM objects. VBScript is well suited to this challenge.

Invoking Scripts or Programs   Listing 21.5 shows how to use the Shell's Run method to sequence three other scripts. This example uses the network scripts developed earlier to report on currently connected resources, disconnect all resources, and collect reconnect to specific resources. An administrator might use a script such as this to configure someone's workstation at logon. Alternatively, a power user might create a similar script to quickly reconfigure her network resources as she shifts from one task to another.

Listing 21.5   This WSH Script Invokes the Scripts in Listings 21.2, 21.3, and 21.4 to Reconfigure a User's Network Connections

```
Option Explicit

Dim strDTopPath
Dim wshShell

Set wshShell = WScript.CreateObject("WScript.Shell")

strDTopPath = wshShell.SpecialFolders("Desktop")

Call wshShell.Run(strDTopPath & "\netex2.vbs",,True)
Call wshShell.Run(strDTopPath & "\netex3b.vbs",,True)
Call wshShell.Run(strDTopPath & "\netex.vbs",,True)

WScript.DisconnectObject(wshShell)
WScript.Quit
```

This example assumes that the three network scripts reside directly on the desktop. The network scripts can be invoked directly (just as if someone had double-clicked their icons), because the WSH executive can exploit the file associations known to Windows.

The syntax for the Run method is as follows:

```
WshShell.Run strCommand, [intWindowStyle], [bWaitOnReturn]
```

By default, the Run method will spawn the task and return immediately to the script. In this example bWaitOnReturn is set to 1 to force the script to wait for each command to complete before launching the next command.

Manipulating COM Objects   The script in Listing 21.6 illustrates how easily VBScript can manipulate COM objects. This example uses Word to open a file, perform a mail merge, and print the result. You can do the same by using VB or VBA, but with WSH installed, any user can create or modify such a script without needing a full development environment.

Listing 21.6   This Script Opens an Instance of Word, Opens a File, Performs a Mail Merge, and Then Prints the Result

```
Option Explicit

Dim objWrd
Dim wrdDoc
Dim objMerge

Set objWrd = WScript.CreateObject("Word.Application")
'objWrd.Visible = True
Set wrdDoc = objWrd.Documents.Open ("d:\My Documents\labels.doc")
set objMerge = objWrd.ActiveDocument.MailMerge
objMerge.Execute
wrdDoc.PrintOut
objWrd.Quit 0
WScript.DisconnectObject objWrd
WScript.Quit
```

As you can see, VBScript makes the connection to the COM object nearly invisible. The challenging part becomes identifying the object, method, or property to perform the desired task. Microsoft's Office components help by recording their macros in VBA. If you need to automate some task involving an Office application, follow this procedure:

1. Open the Microsoft Office application.
2. Choose Macro from the Tools menu and start the macro recorder.
3. Using only keystrokes, perform the operation.
4. Stop the macro recorder.
5. Open the new macro for editing.

When you open the macro for editing, you'll be viewing the VBA code necessary to perform the task without the intervention of a user. This code seldom works directly—it depends too much on decisions made by the user as they position the cursor. The macro code does, however, show you what objects, methods, and properties you need to understand to write the script. Note also, that the method and property references in the macro are all relative to the unnamed Office application (for example, the Word.Application object if the macro was recorded in Word). In the WSH/VBScript environment, you must create an explicit reference to the application object and then invoke the appropriate methods as members of that reference.

Part

IV

Ch

21

Thus a Word macro might include only the following (or worse, only <u>MailMerge</u>, since the ActiveDocument is the default document):

```
ActiveDocument.MailMerge
```

The VBScript version, however, should look like this:

```
objWrd.ActiveDocument.MailMerge
```

After you have identified the key objects and methods by reviewing the macro, you can find the appropriate syntax in the online Visual Basic reference for that Office component. Word Help is not very friendly here—it doesn't index any of the VBA documentation.

If you have Visual Basic available (which sort of defeats the purpose of using VBScript), you can use VB's object browser to get similar information. Open a project (even an empty new project will do), select the References item from the Project menu, and check the Office component you plan to use. For example, checking the Microsoft Word entry makes the type library for Word.Application available. When the appropriate type library is available you can search quickly and conveniently for all the syntax information about any object, method, property, or intrinsic constant.

An Extended Example

As a final example, I've created a script that swaps different sets of shortcuts to and from the user's desktop. With this utility, when I switch from working on graphics projects to working on financial analyses, I can quickly remove all the graphics-related shortcuts from my desktop and replace them with shortcuts appropriate to financial work. When I'm ready to do some programming, I can remove all the financial clutter and replace it with programming shortcuts.

(Note that the Toolbars in Windows 98 implement virtually the same functionality—the shortcuts are just displayed as buttons or icons in the toolbars rather than as icons on the desktop.)

In addition to being a useful tool, this example demonstrates several WSH features. The script uses the Filesystem object to manipulate folders and files and various WshShell methods to create shortcuts. It reads arguments from its command line and manipulates Excel through the application's COM interface. Finally, unlike the other examples in this chapter, it is large enough to be structured as a collection of subroutines.

Overview   This utility uses an Excel Workbook as a database. Each distinct set of shortcuts (I call these sets "worksets") is stored on a separate sheet of the Excel Workbook. Each worksheet lists the information needed to create the related shortcuts with columns for the shortcut name, the program directory, the program name, and any command-line arguments (see Figure 21.8). The utility uses a special worksheet named XCLEANUPX to keep track of which shortcuts it last wrote to the desktop so that the script can reliably remove only its own postings each time it posts a new set.

The script expects to be called either with a single argument corresponding to the name of a worksheet in the Excel workbook, or with no arguments.

FIG. 21.8

This screen capture shows one of the worksheets in the Excel shortcut database. Notice that each sheet tab has been renamed to reflect the workset's name.

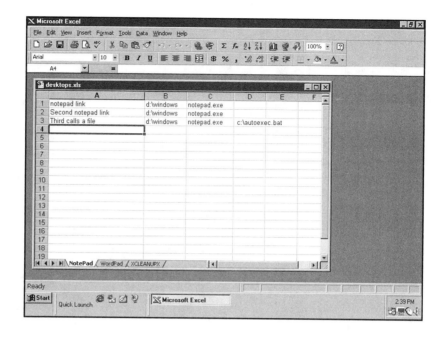

If called with no arguments, the script self-installs by creating a workset folder in the Start menu, creating submenu items for each of the labeled tabs in the Excel workbook, and adding desktop shortcuts for each of the shortcuts listed in the first worksheet (see Figure 21.9). Before creating the new folder, the script checks for an existing folder. It then creates one shortcut in that folder for each of the labeled worksheets in the Excel workbook. Finally, it finds the first worksheet and creates shortcuts (on the desktop) for each line in the worksheet.

Each of these shortcuts invokes the desktop script, passing an argument that specifies which workset is to be installed. (A special argument XCLEANUPX causes Desktop to delete all the shortcuts on the XCLEANUPX page without posting any new shortcuts.)

When invoked with an argument corresponding to the name of a regular worksheet, the Desktop script does the following:

- Deletes all shortcuts listed on the XCLEANUPX sheet
- Clears all entries from the XCLEANUPX sheet
- Adds the list of shortcuts from the worksheet named in the input argument to the desktop
- Copies the named worksheet to the XCLEANUPX sheet (for use during the next swap)

Figure 21.10 shows the results of calling Desktop with the argument wordpad. Note that the three notepad shortcuts present in Figure 21.9 have been removed and replaced by a single wordpad shortcut.

Part

IV

Ch

21

FIG. 21.9

The desktop utility installs itself in the Start menu. Note that the shortcuts corresponding to the Notebook worksheet have also been added to the desktop.

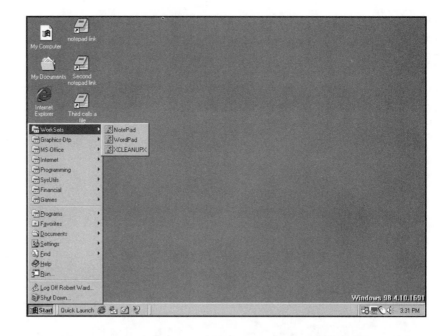

FIG. 21.10

This screen capture shows how the desktop looks after the wordpad workset is installed.

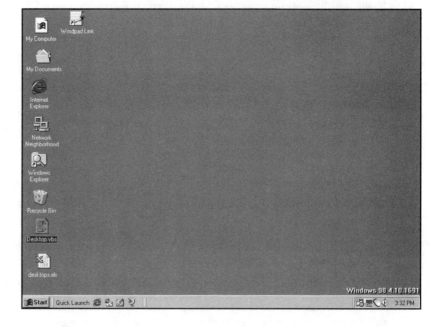

The Code   This example makes extensive use of the WshShortcut, the filesystem, and the Excell.Application objects. I'll limit my comments here to the two WSH specific objects.

Creating a Shortcut The MakeLink subroutine (at the end of Listing 21.7) shows all of the steps necessary to create a shortcut. First, the code creates a shortcut object using the WshShell.CreateShortcut method. Because this method returns an object reference, its return value must be assigned by using the Set keyword.

Listing 21.7 This Is the Code for the Desktop Utility

```
Option Explicit

Dim strScriptName
Dim strScriptDir
Dim strXlsName
Dim strRemoveName

strScriptName = "desktop.vbs"
strScriptDir = "d:\windows\desktop"
strXlsName = "desktops.xls"
strRemoveName = "OldLinks"
Dim wshShell


' Initialize shell and retreive path to desktop
Set wshShell = WScript.CreateObject("WScript.Shell")
'wshShell.Popup "Wait for debug"

Dim DesktopPath
DesktopPath=WshShell.SpecialFolders("Desktop")

' Start an invisible instance of EXCEL
' and open the shortcuts file
Dim objXL
Set objXl = WScript.CreateObject("EXCEL.application")
objXL.Workbooks.Open DesktopPath & "\Desktops"
'objXL.Visible = True

'Initialize an instance of the file system object
Dim fs
Set fs= WScript.CreateObject("Scripting.FileSystemObject")

'If called with no arguments, re-install the virtual desktop
'links in the start menu
'Otherwise, install the set requested by the input argument

Dim wshArgs
Set wshArgs=wscript.arguments

If wshArgs.Count = 0 Then
    Call InstallStartLinks(objXL)
    ' and install the first sheet links as the default
    Call InstallNewLinks(objXL, objXl.Worksheets(1).Name)
Else
    If wshArgs.item(0) = strRemoveName Then
      Call RemoveOldLinks(objXL)
```

continues

Part

IV

Ch

21

Listing 21.7   Continued

```
        Else
        If blnArgInSheet(wshArgs.item(0)) Then
          ' this is driven by the OldLinks sheet
          Call RemoveOldLinks(objXL)
          ' this writes a new OldLinks sheet
          Call InstallNewLinks(objXL, wshArgs.item(0))
        End If
    End If
End If

'Done, either because work is done, or because args are wrong
' either way, clean up and quit

objXL.activeWorkbook.Save
objXL.application.quit

' InstallStartLinks creates the Desktops folder, if necessary
' and inserts appropriate shortcuts to this script

Sub InstallStartLinks(objXL)

    'check for WorkSets folder in Startup Directory
    Dim strStartPath, strWorkPath
    strStartPath = wshShell.SpecialFolders("StartMenu")
    strWorkPath = strStartPath & "\WorkSets"
    if NOT(fs.FolderExists(strWorkPath)) Then
       fs.CreateFolder(strWorkPath)
    end if
    Dim objWs
    Dim strSheetName, strFilePath
    For each objWs in objXL.Worksheets
       objWs.activate
       strSheetName = objWs.Name
       strFilePath=strWorkPath & "\" & strSheetname & ".vbs"
       if NOT (fs.FileExists(strFilePath)) then
          ' build an appropriately named shortcut to this script
          Call MakeLink(strSheetName, strWorkPath, strScriptDir, strScriptName,
          ➥strSheetName)
       end if
    Next
End Sub

' blnArgInSheet makes certain that a sheet exits with
' a name that matches the requested argument ... just
' in case the script gets called with a bad argument

Function blnArgInSheet(strArgument)
    Dim objWs
    Dim strSheetName
    For each objWs in objXL.Worksheets
       objWs.activate
       strSheetName = objWs.Name
```

```
        if strSheetName = strArgument then
            blnArgInSheet = True
            exit function
        end if
    Next
    blnArgInSheet = False
End Function

Sub InstallNewLinks(objXL, strSheetName)

    ' Activate the sheet with the requested set of links
    objXL.Worksheets(strSheetName).Activate
    ' Select the first cell
    objXL.ActiveSheet.Range("A1").Activate

    ' Now loop through the rows until you find a blank
    Dim strShortCutName
    Dim strDirectory
    Dim strShortCutPgm
    Dim strShortCutArgs
    Dim NumRows
    NumRows = 0
    Do While objXL.ActiveCell.Value <> ""
        strShortCutName = objXL.ActiveCell.Value
        'reference the next column
        strDirectory =objXL.ActiveCell.Offset(0,1).Value
        'and the next
        strShortCutPgm =objXL.ActiveCell.Offset(0,2).Value
        'and now get arguments if any
        strShortCutArgs = objXL.ActiveCell.Offset(0,3).Value
        Call MakeLink(strShortCutName, DeskTopPath, strDirectory, strShortCutPgm,
        ➥strShortCutArgs)
        'now step to the next row
        objXL.ActiveCell.Offset(1,0).Activate
        NumRows = NumRows + 1
    Loop
    'Now copy the range to the OldLinks Sheet
    objXL.ActiveSheet.Range("A1:A10").Copy
    objXL.Worksheets(strRemoveName).Activate
    objXL.ActiveSheet.Range("A1").Select
    objXL.ActiveSheet.Paste

End Sub

' RemoveOldLinks deletes the shortcuts most recently
' installed by this script and clears the sheet
' named OldLinks as a side-effect

Sub RemoveOldLinks(objXL)

    ' Activate the sheet with the requested set of links
    objXL.Worksheets(strRemoveName).Activate

    ' Select the first cell
    objXL.ActiveSheet.Range("A1").Activate
```

Part

IV

Ch

21

continues

Listing 21.7 Continued

```
' Now loop through the rows until you find a blank
Dim strShortCutName
Dim strFullPath
Do While objXL.ActiveCell.Value <> ""
    strShortCutName = objXL.ActiveCell.Value
    objXL.ActiveCell.Value = ""
    strFullPath =  DesktopPath & "\" & strShortCutName & ".lnk"
    fs.DeleteFile(strFullPath)
    'now step to the next row
    objXL.ActiveCell.Offset(1,0).Activate
    Loop
End Sub

Sub MakeLink(strFriendlyName, strLinkPath, strDirectory, strProgram, strArgs)

    Dim Shortcut

    ' Create the link file on the desktop
    Set Shortcut = WSHShell.CreateShortcut(strLinkPath & "\" & strFriendlyName &
    ➥".lnk")

    ' Set shortcut object properties
    Shortcut.TargetPath = strDirectory & "\" & strProgram
    Shortcut.WorkingDirectory = strDirectory
    Shortcut.WindowStyle = 4
    Shortcut.IconLocation = strDirectory & "\" & strProgram
    If strArgs <> "" Then
        ShortCut.Arguments=strArgs
    End If
    ' Save it
    Shortcut.Save

End Sub
```

After it is instantiated, the shortcut object is initialized by a series of assignments to its various properties. In this instance, the code assumes that the target path and working directory are always the same. In other applications, those paths might be different.

Finally, after the object is initialized, it is saved. The .lnk file is not created until the object is saved.

Using the Filesystem Object   The filesystem object is used to remove shortcut (.lnk) files and to find and create folders. A new filesystem object is instantiated with the following:

```
Set fs=Wscript.CreateObject("Scripting.FileSystemObject")
```

The same filesystem object is used for all references to the file system, so it only needs to be instantiated one time.

The InstallStartLinks subroutine uses the FolderExists method of the file system to check whether a Worksets folder exists in the Start menu. If not, the subroutine immediately creates the Worksets folder using the filesystem object's CreateFolder method. Later in the same routine, the script uses the FileExists method to determine if new links should be installed in the Worksets directory.

The RemoveOldLinks subroutine uses the filesystem object's DeleteFile method to remove shortcut files.

The syntax for these four methods is as follows:

```
ObjFs.FolderExists( folderspec )
ObjFs.CreateFolder( foldername )
ObjFs.FileExists( filespec )
ObjFs.DeleteFile filespec [, force]
```

As you saw from inspecting Table 21.1, these four methods are only a fraction of the methods supported by the filesystem object. This object also supplies all the methods you need to read and write from text files (represented as TextStream objects). For more information about the filesystem object and specifically about using the TextStream object, see the *Microsoft Visual Basic Scripting Edition Language Reference*, available online at **http://www.microsoft.com/scripting/vbscript/download/vbsdown.htm.**

Using the Script Debugger

You can get Microsoft's Script Debugger v. 1.0 free from the Microsoft Scripting site, **http://www.microsoft.com/scripting**. This simple debugger was originally designed to support breakpoint tracing of web-hosted scripts—whether executing in the browser or on the server. It can also be used to trace execution of scripts executing in the WSH environment, although starting a session isn't quite as easy as in the web environment. (More on that later.)

The Script Debugger is very functional despite its simplicity. After it is attached to your running script, the debugger allows you to control execution using the familiar step, step over, and step into commands. An evaluation window (called the *command window*) allows you to probe variables and interactively experiment with troublesome expressions.

If you are accustomed to working with a type-smart debugger and browser such as the one in Visual Studio, you may be a little disappointed with Script Debugger. The Script Debugger is most useful when applied to the logic of your own script. It doesn't have enough type information or formatting flexibility to help in diagnosing interface problems between your script and a COM object, for example. Don't expect to examine pointer values or other low-level structures in the command window. This debugger doesn't understand much beyond VB strings and integers.

Starting a Session

Unlike the debuggers in an integrated development environment, the Script Debugger doesn't automatically have access to the executing source; you must manually attach the debugging process to the script process you want to examine. To attach the debugger you must perform these steps:

1. Modify the script so that it will pause and wait for user input as soon as it opens.
2. Launch the script.
3. Launch the debugger.
4. If the Running Documents window isn't visible, open it using the View menu.
5. Open the various branches of the Running Documents tree view until you find your script.
6. Double-click on your script. The debugger should load the script file into the source window at this point.
7. From the Debug menu select Break at Next Statement.
8. Click on the dialog (or do whatever else it takes) to make your script resume execution.

The debugger should now take control and halt execution on the first line following the line where your script was waiting.

I like to use the following line to pause the script while I attach the debugger:

```
WScript.Echo "Envex waiting for Debugger"
```

You can comment this line out (as in Listing 21.1) when you aren't debugging and then remove the comment apostrophe when you need to start a debugging session. Figures 21.11 and 21.12 show the debugger being attached to a debug version of Listing 21.1. Figure 21.13 shows the easiest way to examine a variable.

FIG. 21.11

In this screen capture, the script under test is waiting for user input, and the debugger is active and configured to break at the next statement.

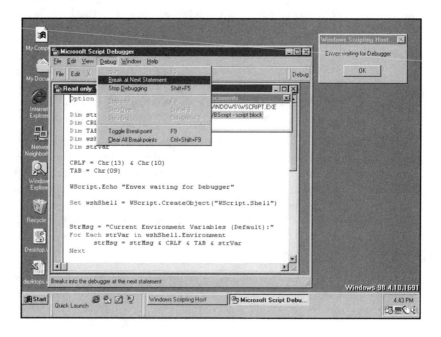

FIG. 21.12

At this point, the debugger has full control. The initial dialog box has been dismissed and the debugger has halted the script on the line following the initial call to Echo.

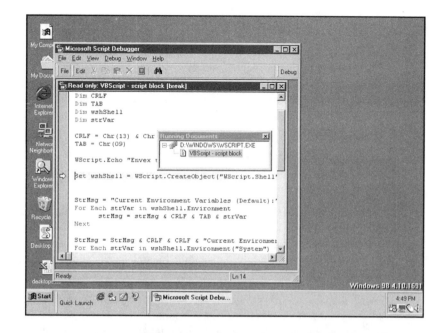

FIG. 21.13

Here I have used the debugger to step through the first iteration of the top loop and then printed the current contents of strMsg in the command window.

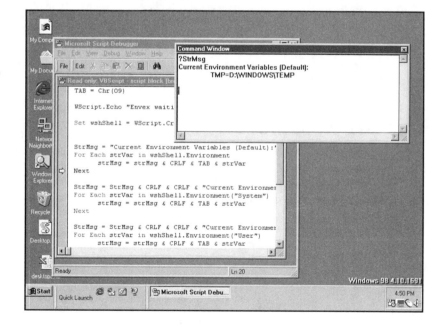

An Open Architecture

Earlier I mentioned that the VBScript engine was separate from the Windows Scripting Host. This reflects a design decision to separate knowledge about the scripting language from knowledge about how to manipulate the environment. When VBScript is used for client-side web scripting, the environment consists of the resources available in the browser, and the browser is connected directly to the scripting engine (the browser "hosts" the script). When VBScript is used in server-side web scripting, the http server functions as the scripting host.

It is this separation that allows the same language engine to be used in different environments. WSH is just another "container" that knows how to interface with the language engine and that provides certain general services.

One consequence of this design decision is that different language engines can be used with each of the scripting hosts. Microsoft supplies both a Jscript (Java) and VBScript engine with their browsers and with WSH. You can expect to see other language engines available in the future because Microsoft has made public the full specification of the language engine/ scripting host interface.

A second consequence is that developers are free to use the language engine and components of the scripting host in their own applications. Thus if you've written an editor, you could add VBScript as your editor's scripting (macro) language by simply embedding Microsoft's scripting control in the application. You must license this technology if you choose to use it, but as of this writing the license "fee" is simply an acknowledgment added to your application's About box.

For more information about this technology, see the ActiveX scripting links on the "Related Links" page at Microsoft's scripting site, described in the next section.

Scripting Resources

The main source for information about VBScript is Microsoft's scripting site at **http:// www.microsoft.com/scripting**. Although most of the information at this site assumes you are doing web scripting, it does have links to WSH resources. In particular, you can download the following executable components from this site:

- The Windows Scripting Host (Wscript and Cscript) and runtime library.
- The VBScript Scripting Engine.
- The Script Debugger.
- ACLIST, a handy utility for exploring the ActiveX controls available on your machine. This little utility also makes it much easier to reference ActiveX controls in web pages.

You can also view and download the latest version of these documents:

- A technical paper that describes the WSH object model
- The *Visual Basic Scripting Edition Language and Run-Time Reference*
- Script Debugger documentation

There are several discussion groups devoted to scripting:

- **microsoft.public.scripting.vbscript** covers web-based scripting.
- **microsoft.public.scripting.remote** covers remote scripting.
- **microsoft.public.scripting.debugger** covers use of the Script Debugger.
- **microsoft.public.scripting.hosting** covers issues related to writing your own scripting engine.
- **microsoft.public.scripting.wsh** covers WSH scripting.

Conclusion

The Windows Scripting Host opens a whole new realm of applications to Visual Basic programmers and plugs a significant hole in the Windows environment. Now administrators have a lightweight tool that is powerful enough to address the many configuration and monitoring issues present at any large site. Similarly, users and programmers have a convenient Windows-based tool for creating the little "productivity" scripts that make such a huge difference in the efficiency of any computing-intense work activity.

Because Microsoft has made it easy and inexpensive for other developers to add VBScript to their own applications, one can reasonably expect to see growing support for VBScript as a standard application scripting language.

While this chapter is certainly not the definitive reference for either VBScript or WSH, I hope it has convinced you that WSH/VBScript offers a well-chosen alternative for administrative and production scripting. With these examples and the resources named previously, you should have all you need to begin writing scripts for your own use. ●

Configuring and Customizing Windows

CHAPTER 22

Customizing the Look and Feel of Windows

by Curtis Knight

In this chapter

Establishing Custom Settings for Each User

Windows 98 allows you to create a profile for each user of the computer. Your user profile contains your individual customizations to Windows 98. This means that when you log on to the system, the settings you established for yourself are still there. When your coworkers log on, their settings are still there also.

 TIP As you read through this chapter, remember that where you are told to click on a file or folder and then click the OK or Open buttons, it is often possible to simply double-click the file or folder to finish the task.

If more than one person uses your computer, it is recommended that you set up user profiles before you begin implementing any of the customizations in this chapter. That way, when other people log on to the computer, they will be able to make their own customizations to Windows 98 without affecting one another's settings.

To establish user profiles, follow these steps:

1. Open Control Panel and activate Users. You'll see the dialog in Figure 22.1. Click the Next button to continue.

FIG. 22.1

Activate Users from Control Panel and Click Next to begin setting up a new user profile.

2. In the Add User dialog, type a username into the User name text box, and click Next to continue.

3. In the Enter New Password dialog, type a password into the Password text box, and press the tab key to move the insertion point to the Confirm password text box. Retype the identical password in the Confirm password text box and click Next to continue.

4. In the Personalized Items Settings dialog, check the items you want to customize. For example, if you want a separate My Documents folder for this user, check the My Documents Folder check box. If you want this user to have their own custom Start Menu, check the Start Menu check box.

   You also need to decide whether to tell Windows 98 to create a copy of each of these items or create new ones with default settings. Creating new items for each user will save disk space if the new user doesn't make very many changes to Windows 98 settings.

   When you've finished making your choices, click Next to continue.

5. When the Ready to Finish dialog displays, click Finish to continue. Windows will set up the new user profile and prompt you to reboot the computer.

To set up more profiles, run Users from Control Panel again, and you will be taken through the same setup routine for each new user.

Resizing the Taskbar

Occasionally, you might want to resize the Taskbar. For example, if your system has enough memory to allow several applications to be open simultaneously, the Taskbar can become so cluttered that the icons are too small to tell which is which. In this case, resizing the Taskbar will help you read the icon text.

Another reason you would resize the Taskbar is that with all the customization features implemented in Windows 98, the Taskbar can contain numerous toolbars and Quick Launch icons. Resizing the Taskbar makes it easier to find the elements you need to work with.

N O T E Be careful not to add too much to your Taskbar. If you do, you might find yourself spending more time searching your Taskbar than it would take to just browse to the file, application, or shortcut the old-fashioned way.

To gain maximum benefit from toolbars and Quick Launch, only implement them for those programs you use frequently. If you access a file or program once a week or less, think twice before establishing a toolbar or Quick Launch icon. ■

To resize the Taskbar, follow these steps:

1. Move the mouse pointer over the inside edge of the Taskbar until it becomes a double-headed arrow.
2. Drag the edge of the Taskbar until it is the size you want. (It is possible to size it as large as one-half the screen area.)
3. Now release the mouse button.

Moving the Taskbar

By default, Windows places the Taskbar at the bottom of the screen. If you prefer the Taskbar in a different position, you can move it to any of the four edges of the screen. For example, photographers often need to drag the Taskbar to one side of the screen to allow more vertical desktop real estate when working with a vertically formatted photograph.

To move the Taskbar, point to a blank area of it and use the left mouse button to drag it where you want it.

Using the New Taskbar Features

When you right-click on a blank area of the taskbar, a shortcut menu (often called a *context menu*) pops up. The main purpose of this menu is to give you access to Taskbar customization. There are also options included in the menu to help you rearrange the open windows on your desktop.

The first item on the taskbar's shortcut menu is toolbars. Toolbars contains a menu with three options: Desktop, Quick Launch, and New Toolbar.

Figure 22.2 shows the taskbar with two additional toolbars.

FIG. 22.2

As you can see, the taskbar can become cluttered quickly. This taskbar has two additional toolbars: Address and Desktop.

- Address: Use the Address toolbar to access files and Web pages right from the taskbar. You use this toolbar exactly like you use the one in your favorite Web browser.
- Links: Remember the Links toolbar right next to the Address toolbar in Internet Explorer? This is the same toolbar. you don't have to open Internet Explorer to access these links.
- Desktop: When you select Desktop, the Desktop toolbar is added to the taskbar. The Desktop toolbar contains all the folders, files, and shortcuts on your desktop. Use the small arrows on the left and right ends of the toolbar to scroll through the icons.

  This toolbar can be a major advantage if you normally maximize the window of the application you're currently working with and your taskbar is set to be visible at all times. The Always on top setting for the taskbar is covered later in this section.

■ Quick Launch: By default, the Quick Launch toolbar appears just to the right of the start button on the Taskbar. When you install Windows, Setup automatically places four useful icons in the Quick Launch toolbar: Internet Explorer, Mail, Show Desktop, and View Channels. The Quick Launch toolbar provides one-click access to your most commonly used applications.

To add your own shortcuts to the Quick Launch toolbar, drag the file or shortcut to the Quick Launch toolbar, and a shortcut is created for your application or file.

Table 22.1 describes the four buttons added to Quick Launch during the Windows install.

Table 22.1   Built-In Desktop Toolbars

Toolbar Name	Description
Internet Explorer	Yep, you guessed it, this is a shortcut to Internet Explorer.
Mail	This is a shortcut to Microsoft's contact manager Outlook Express. Outlook Express is included with Internet Explorer 4.x.
Show Desktop	This is probably the most useful of the four buttons Windows places on the Quick Launch toolbar. If your desktop becomes cluttered with open application windows, or if your current application window is maximized and you need to get to your desktop, click the show desktop icon, and all your windows are automatically minimized. Click the icon again, and all your windows are restored to the previous state and position.
View Channels	When you click this button, you get a full screen browser to view your channels. If you have not set up your Internet access, the Internet connection wizard will guide you through the setup.

▶ **See** "Using the Internet Connection Wizard," **p. 568**

Creating Toolbars with Frequently Used Folders and Web Pages

Windows 98 provides you with a quick and simple way to establish your own custom toolbars for your most often used files and folders. In a nutshell, it creates a toolbar that contains shortcuts to all the files and subfolders within the folder you select.

To create a custom toolbar, follow these steps:

1. Select new toolbar from the Taskbar shortcut menu.
2. The New Toolbar dialog pops up. This dialog provides a Windows Explorer style view of your system.

3. Navigate to the folder you want to convert to a toolbar, and click the OK button. The folder is now represented in a toolbar.

 TIP My Briefcase is an excellent candidate for a custom toolbar.

You can also create a toolbar for your favorite web pages. If you have a permanent Internet connection (generally this is done through your local area network at the office), you can create a toolbar that displays a web page. You can create this even if you use a dial-up connection to the Internet, but it's not quite as useful.

To create a web page toolbar, follow these steps:

1. Point Internet Explorer to the web page you want to display.

2. Right-click the taskbar, point to Toolbars, and select New Toolbar.

3. In the New Toolbar dialog, scroll down to Internet Explorer, and click the plus sign to expand it.

4. Select the web page you want, and click the OK button to create your new toolbar and close the New Toolbar dialog. A new toolbar will be displayed on your taskbar.

 TIP At the taskbar's default size you can only see one line of your web page at a time. To see more of your Web page toolbar, you can either use the spinner buttons at the right or resize the taskbar. See the section "Resizing the Taskbar" earlier in this chapter for details.

To remove a custom toolbar, right-click the taskbar or a toolbar, point to Toolbars, and click on the toolbar you want to remove.

Arranging Your Open Windows

Your taskbar context menu contains five options for rearranging the windows on your desktop. Can't make sense of what's open? Desktop too cluttered? Don't want to close any applications? No worries, this section will help you get a handle on the mess.

These options are accessed by right-clicking on the taskbar:

- Cascade Windows: When you select this option, all open windows are displayed in a cascading arrangement beginning in the upper-left corner of the screen and going toward the lower-right corner.

- Tile Windows Horizontally: When you select this option, your windows are tiled from left to right, top to bottom in alphabetical order.

- Tile Windows Vertically: To arrange your windows from top to bottom, left to right in alphabetical order, select this option.

- Minimize All Windows: If you need to minimize all open windows, select this option. This effect is similar but not identical to the Show Desktop button in the Quick Launch toolbar. The difference is that Show Desktop is a toggle that will restore your windows to their previous size. Minimize All Windows is not a toggle. You have to restore your windows one at a time.

- Changing Taskbar Options: You have several options available for giving your taskbar an attitude adjustment. These adjustments are made from the Taskbar Properties dialog.

Right-clicking the taskbar and selecting Properties is the quickest way to access the Taskbar Properties dialog. Figure 22.3 shows the Taskbar Properties dialog.

FIG. 22.3

With the Taskbar Properties dialog, you select the options you want and click the OK button.

Taskbar Properties can also be accessed through Start, Settings, Taskbar.

Table 22.2 describes the four options available for customizing the taskbar.

Table 22.2 Taskbar Options Tab

Check box	Description
Always on top	When you check this box, your taskbar is always visible, even when you maximize a window.
Auto hide	When you check this box, your taskbar changes to a very thin line. To make the taskbar visible again, simply point to the thin line.
Show small icons in Start menu	If you check this box, the icons and start menu are slightly smaller and the Windows logo down the left side of the menu is removed. To see the difference, watch the preview window as you check and uncheck this box.

continues

Table 22.2   Continued

Check box	Description
Show Clock	Check this box to make the clock visible in the system tray, which appears to the far right of the taskbar. To remove the clock from the system tray, uncheck the box.

TIP If you check both Always on top and Auto hide, you can maximize your application window and still have easy access to the taskbar any time by pointing to the edge of the screen where your taskbar is.

Setting the Date and Time

To change the date and time on your computer, follow these steps:

1. Double-click the clock in the taskbar. The date/time Properties dialog box is displayed as shown in Figure 22.4.

FIG. 22.4

Double-click the clock to bring up the Date/Time Properties dialog.

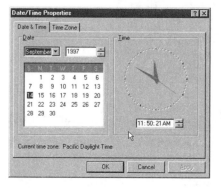

2. The dialog is divided into two sections: date and time. To change the month, click the down arrow to the right of the month list box. This brings a drop-down list from which you can select the month. Click the month you want.

3. To change the year, either highlight the text in the year text box and type the year directly, or use the spinner buttons to advance one year at a time up or down.

4. Select the day of the month by clicking in the calendar box below the month in year text boxes.

5. The time section shows an analog clock and a digital clock in a text box. The time is changed using the digital clock text box. This text box is divided into four fields: hour, min., seconds, and a.m./p.m. To change the time, place the insertion point in the field you need to change, and use the bar to the right of the text box to increment or detriment the field. You can also type directly into the fields. For instance, if the current time reads 11:00:00pm and you need to change it to 3:00:00pm, simply use your mouse to highlight the 11 and type the number 3.

Changing the Time Zone

After adjusting the date and time, double-check the current time zone display at the bottom of the Date and Time tab. If it displays the wrong time zone, select the Time zone tab in the Date/ Time Properties dialog.

This displays a world map and a drop-down list box from which you can select the proper time zone. To select the time zone click the down arrow to the right side of the time zone drop-down list box. Select the proper time zone from the list and click apply.

Also at the bottom of this tab is a check box titled Automatically adjust clock for daylight saving changes. If you check this box, Windows will automatically adjust for daylight savings time twice a year. If you live in an area where daylight savings time is not in effect, such as Indiana, make sure this box is not checked.

When you're finished, click the OK button to close the Date/Time Properties dialog. Your changes are applied when you click the OK button, or if you want that warm fuzzy, click Apply after making your changes; then close the dialog.

Managing Buttons on a Toolbar

Now that you've been experimenting with your taskbar, you might have too many toolbars, or one or more of them might be too big. Table 22.3 explains some taskbar management techniques.

Table 22.3   Taskbar Options Tab

Task	Description
Resizing Toolbars	When you get too many toolbars, you can't see everything. To get around this, you can resize your toolbars, shrinking those that you don't need to see and expanding the others.
	To resize a toolbar, point to the small vertical bar at the left edge of the toolbar, and drag left to expand it, right to make it smaller.
	When you resize a toolbar, the toolbar to the left of it expands or contracts automatically.
Removing Toolbars	If you got carried away with those custom toolbars and you want to get rid of some, right-click the taskbar or the title of one of the toolbars, point to Toolbars, and click the toolbar you want to remove.

continues

Table 22.3 Continued

Task	Description
Removing Buttons from the Quick Launch bar	The buttons on your Quick Launch bar are just fancy shortcuts.
	To remove a button from the Quick Launch bar, right-click it, and choose Delete from the context menu.
Hiding Text and Titles on the Custom and Desktop Toolbars	Another way to reduce the size of your toolbars is to tell Windows not to display the text for each icon.
	To hide the toolbar title, right-click the toolbar title, and click Show title to remove the check mark.

Removing Toolbars

Figure 22.5 shows the right-click menu for a Quick Launch button.

FIG. 22.5
This is the Context menu for a Quick Launch button; to remove the button, click Delete.

Adding and Removing Programs in the Start Menu

There are two ways to add items to the Start menu. If you prefer to add to the Start menu using a Wizard approach, follow these steps.

N O T E The Start menu is actually a folder on your hard disk, located in the Windows directory. Any files or shortcuts you place in \Windows\Start Menu\ will show up in your Start menu. ▪

1. Right-click a blank area of the taskbar, and select Properties.
2. Select the Start Menu Programs tab.
3. Click the Add button. This starts the Create Shortcut wizard (see Figure 22.6).
4. The first dialog in this wizard asks for the command line of the executable file for the program. If you know the path and filename of the executable for the application, type it into the command-line text box. If you don't know the path and filename, you can click the browse button to bring up the browse dialog. Find the executable name and click the open button.

    When the path and filename for the executable are displayed correctly in the command-line text box, click the next button.

FIG. 22.6

Click the Add button from the Start Menu Programs tab to start the Shortcut Wizard. Type the path to the document or program, or click Browse to search for it. Then click Next.

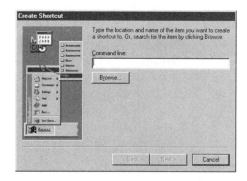

5. The Select program folder dialog is displayed. This is a tree-style view of your Start menu. You can select an existing folder, or you can click the new folder button to create a new folder. If you decide to create a new folder, you will see a new folder with the name program group (1), highlighted in rename mode. Type a new name for the folder and press Enter.

6. When you've selected a folder or created a new one, click the next button.

7. The Select a Title for the Program dialog is displayed. In the Select a name for the shortcut: text box, type an intuitive name for your new shortcut.

8. Click the Finish button.

9. Now check Start menu to make sure it works properly. If it does, close the Taskbar Properties dialog with the OK button.

To remove a program shortcut from the Start menu, follow these steps:

1. Right-click a blank area of the taskbar, and select Properties.

2. Select the Start Menu Programs tab.

3. Click the remove button. The remove shortcuts/folder's dialog is displayed.

4. Navigate to the shortcut you want to remove, and click the close button.

5. Now go to the Start menu to make sure the shortcut was removed properly. If it was, close the Taskbar Properties dialog with the OK button.

 You can remove an entire folder from the shortcut menu by selecting the folder. When you select a folder name, all shortcuts and folders under that folder are removed from the Start menu.

If you prefer to create and remove folders and shortcuts for the Start menu using Windows Explorer, click the Advanced button. The Advanced button launches Explorer and takes you directly to the Start menu folder. From here, simply create new folders and shortcuts the same way you would any other folder on your hard drive.

Clearing the Documents List in the Start Menu

Windows 98 maintains a history of the documents you've accessed. You can access these documents by clicking Start, Documents and selecting the document you need to access. Clearing the list is useful if you have accumulated several documents in your Documents history that you no longer access frequently or that don't exist anymore.

To empty your Documents menu, follow these steps:

1. Right-click a blank area of the taskbar, and select Properties.
2. Select the Start Menu Programs tab.
3. Click the clear button in the Documents menu section located at the bottom of the page.

Customizing the Windows Display

Today's video cards and monitors give you a wide choice of resolutions and color schemes. This section shows you how to adjust the display to your needs.

Using Desktop Themes

One of the coolest customization features of the Microsoft Windows 95 Plus Pack now comes with Windows 98. You can use Desktop Themes to customize wallpaper, screen savers, mouse pointers (animated cursors), and many other elements of your Windows display.

Microsoft includes all the themes from the original Plus Pack as well as a few new ones, or you can create and save your own themes by either mixing existing elements or using your own sounds, wallpaper, animated cursors, and so on.

You can access Desktop Themes from Control Panel. Select a theme from the Theme drop-down list and proceed to customize as you wish.

Changing the Screen Resolution

Screen resolution is a measure of the density of the pixels displayed. More pixels means finer detail. One side effect of high resolution is that everything appears smaller. The advantages are more content on the screen, and you get more detail.

To adjust the screen resolution, follow these steps:

1. From the Display Properties dialog box shown in Figure 22.7, select the Settings tab. The top portion of this page contains one or more icons that represent your monitor(s). Multiple monitors are covered later in the chapter.
2. If you have more than one monitor attached, single-click the monitor you want to adjust.
3. Click the down arrow at the right of the Screen Area drop-down list box, and select the resolution you want.
4. Click Apply.

FIG. 22.7

Right-click the desktop and select Properties to make changes to your display. To change screen resolution, select the Settings tab.

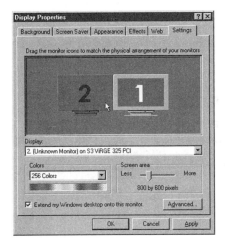

5. Click the OK button.

6. The resolution will change, and you'll see a confirmation dialog. If you're happy with the display, click the OK button within 15 seconds. If the display is unreadable, wait 15 seconds, and Windows will restore the settings to the previous resolution.

Changing the Number of Colors Available to Your Monitor

The Color palette box in the Display Properties dialog allows you to determine the number of colors your applications and Windows send to the monitor. The number of colors available depends on several factors: the quality of the video card, the quality of the video driver, and the amount of video RAM available. The combination of these factors determines the color palette and video resolution combinations you have available.

To change the number of colors available, follow this procedure:

1. From the Display Properties dialog box, select the Settings tab. The top portion of this page contains one or more icons that represent your monitor(s). Multiple monitors are covered in the section "Configuring Multiple Monitors."

2. If you have more than one monitor attached, single-click the monitor you want to adjust.

3. Click the down arrow to the right of the Color drop-down list, and select the number of colors you want your applications and Windows to display.

N O T E Remember that 3D graphics require more video RAM than 2D graphics. Therefore, depending on the selected resolution, your 3D graphics might not use the number of colors you choose here. If this happens, your 3D graphics will be a bit on the ugly side until you choose a lower resolution.

Changing your resolution is covered in the previous section, "Changing the Screen Resolution."

4. If you choose a color palette too high for the resolution selected in the Screen Area section, Windows will decrement the resolution to the highest resolution that can be used with the color palette you select. Experiment until you find an acceptable combination.

Changing Font Sizes

By default, Windows uses a font size of 96 dots per inch. This is referred to as Small Fonts, or Normal size. Large Fonts is 125 percent of Normal size, or 120 dots per inch. You can also specify a custom font size if neither of these is satisfactory.

To change your font size, follow these steps:

1. From the Display Properties dialog box, select the Settings tab. The top portion of this page contains one or more icons that represent your monitor(s). Multiple monitors are covered in the section "Configuring Multiple Monitors."

2. If you have more than one monitor attached, single-click the monitor you want to adjust.

3. Click the Advanced button. This brings up a property sheet for you video adapter.

4. On the General tab, click the down arrow to the right of the Font size drop-down list box, and select Small Fonts, Large Fonts, or Other.

5. If you selected either small or large, click the OK button to apply the changes, and close the dialog.

6. If you want to specify a custom font size, select Other.

7. In the Custom font size dialog, you can select from a drop-down list in the Scale fonts to be ___% of normal size drop-down list or type the scale you want directly into the box. The minimum scale is 20 percent. If you type something smaller into the box, Windows will change it for you to 20 percent.

8. The scale sample is displayed in the sample box and states the pixels (dots) per inch. You can also drag to the scale you want by clicking anywhere within the ruler and dragging left or right to decrease or increase the font scaling.

9. When you find the scale you want, click the OK button.

10. When you finish making your adjustments, click the OK button to apply the settings and close the Display Properties dialog.

Adjusting the Refresh Rate

To adjust the refresh rate for your video adapter, follow these steps:

1. From the Display Properties dialog box, select the Settings tab. The top portion of this page contains one or more icons that represent your monitor(s). Multiple monitors are covered in the section "Configuring Multiple Monitors."

2. If you have more than one monitor attached, single-click the monitor you want to adjust.

3. Click the Advanced button. This brings up a property sheet for your video adapter.

4. At the bottom of the adapter tab is a drop-down list called Refresh rate. Most adapters only have two settings available: Adapter default and Optimal. Some will list specific refresh rates measured in Hz.

   Generally, you want to set this to optimal, especially if you're having trouble with screen flicker.

Configuring Multiple Monitors

This section shows you how to use a dual monitor setup. This text assumes a setup of two monitors and does not give details on hardware installation.

▶ **See** "Adding a Second Display," **p. 540**

For details on changing resolution, refresh rate, and color settings for each monitor, refer to the appropriate sections in this chapter.

Windows 98 supports up to eight monitors. Each must have its own PCI VGA video adapter. Your monitors are numbered from 1 through 8.

Setting up Windows to work with your monitors is very simple when you have the hardware installed. Follow these steps:

1. From the Display Properties dialog box, select the Settings tab. The top portion of this page contains one or more icons that represent your monitors. The icons are squares containing large digits representing the number of the monitor.

2. Click once on monitor number 2. In the bottom-left corner of the Settings page, click the I want to use this monitor check box.

3. By default, monitor number 2 is assumed to be on the left side. You can move the icons around to better represent the physical setup of your monitors. If your main monitor is on the right side, simply move the icons around with the mouse until they represent the actual positioning of your two monitors. You can even arrange them in a vertical or diagonal arrangement.

4. The positioning of the icons is significant because it determines how you access each monitor.

5. When you have the icons arranged, click the OK button.

That takes care of getting your second display ready to use. Now let's see how to use it.

The secondary display(s) becomes an extension of your desktop. Therefore, it does not have its own Taskbar. In fact, there is nothing on the secondary display until you put something there.

Getting objects to the other monitor is very easy. All you do is drag the object to the other monitor. If your secondary monitor is to the left, just drag the object off the left side of your primary monitor. If you want to work with Netscape and Internet Explorer at the same time, drag one to the other monitor. You can even drag the taskbar over there to get it out of your way.

Customizing the Windows Desktop

You can customize your desktop so it has a look and feel that reflects your personality and how you work.

This section shows you how to create your own color schemes, put a nice nature photo on your desktop, and add texture to your desktop background.

Using Existing Color Schemes

To use an existing color scheme, follow these steps:

1. In the Display Properties dialog, select the Appearance tab.

2. The top half of the Appearance tab shows the different elements of the Desktop and your application windows that can be modified. This preview window shows the effect of the currently selected colors for each component or scheme.

3. To select an existing scheme, click down or to the right of the scheme list box, and select a scheme from the list. The effects of the scheme are displayed in the preview window.

4. If one of these schemes is suitable, select it and click Apply. The new color scheme will be applied immediately. If you like what you see, click the OK button to close the dialog.

Creating Custom Color and Text Schemes

If none of these schemes are appropriate and you only want to change a few elements, follow these steps to create your own color scheme:

1. Click the down arrow to the right of the Item: drop-down list box, and select the element you want to change.

2. Click the Color: button to display the color palette. If you see the color you want, select it. If the color you want is not there, select Other to display a larger color palette and the custom colors dialog. Select an existing color or create your own, and click the OK button.

3. When you've finished making color changes, click Apply to see what the changes will really look like. If you don't like them, switch back to the Windows standard color scheme and start over, or modify the colors you don't like. When you get the colors you want, click the OK button.

   Some elements are also sizable. If this is possible for a particular element, the Size: box will no longer be grayed.

 TIP If you find a scheme that is very close to what you want, you can select that scheme, change the colors of the few items you want to change, and then use the Save As button to give the new scheme the name.

4. To change the fonts, click the down arrow to the right of the Font: drop-down list box, and select the desired font from the drop-down list.

5. To change the font size, either select from the existing lists by clicking the Windows size text box, or highlight the contents of the size text box and type the font size directly into the box.

6. To change the color of the font, click the down arrow in the color box to display the palette, and click on the color you want to use. Click the Other button to create a custom color or select from a larger color palette.

7. To the right of the color palette button are the style buttons and italics. These are toggle buttons. If the button is depressed, that font style is turned on. To turn off, simply click the button again.

8. When you have selected all the colors fonts and sizes you'll need, click the Save as button. This brings up the Save scheme dialog box. In the Save color scheme as text box, type the name you want to give to your new color scheme and click the OK button.

Wallpapering Your Desktop with a Graphic

Would you prefer to display a graphic or even a photo on your desktop instead of that blasé background? No problem; here's how:

1. From the Display Properties dialog box, select the Background tab. The top half of this property page is a graphic representation of your monitor/desktop. When you select wallpaper from the wallpaper list, a preview of the wallpaper is displayed there. Figure 22.8 shows the Background tab with a photo of Mount St. Helens selected as the wallpaper.

FIG. 22.8
Right-click the desktop and select properties. Use the background tab to change the wallpaper and pattern for your desktop.

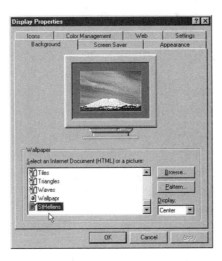

2. Scroll through the items in the Select an Internet Document (HTML) or a picture: and click the one you want to use.

   If the graphic you want to use for your wallpaper is not visible in the wallpaper list, click the browse button, and navigate to the location of your bitmap or HTML file. Select the file you want, and click the Open button.

T I P To get your own files to show up in the Wallpaper list, simply copy them to the Windows folder. The next time you go to the Display Properties dialog, your Custom wallpaper will show up in the wallpaper list.

3. Most wallpaper bitmaps are very small and can be tiled to create a wallpaper effect. In the lower-right corner of the Background property sheet, you'll see the drop-down list called Display. Click the down arrow to the right of this list box to display the list. Select either tiled or center. If you choose center, only one copy of the bitmap is displayed directly in the center of your desktop. This is the recommended method for displaying photographs and HTML files.

Changing the Background Pattern

To change the background pattern:

1. Select (None) in the wallpaper list.

2. Click the pattern button to display the pattern dialog.

3. Click on the pattern you want to display. See the effect in the preview window to the right of the pattern list.

4. To modify the pattern click the Edit pattern button. This brings up the pattern, which allows you to modify the pattern to your liking. When you're finished editing the pattern, click the Change button to view the sample. If the sample is satisfactory, click Done.

5. Click the OK button to return to the Display Properties dialog.

6. Click Apply to see the changes. If you like the changes, click the OK button.

Changing Desktop Icons

Want to change those system icons on the desktop? Follow these steps:

1. From the Display Properties dialog box, select the Effects tab. In the Desktop icons box you'll see the system icons that can be changed, including an option to use large icons.

2. In the Desktop icons box, single-click the icon that you want to change, and click the Change icon button. This brings up the Change icon dialog.

3. By default you'll see the icons inside explorer.EXE. Scroll to the right and left until you find the icon you want and click on it. Then click the OK button to close the dialog. You'll see the changes in the Desktop icons box.

4. If none of these icons suits your fancy, you can select another file to choose icons from. To do this, click the Browse button. This brings up a standard Windows browsing dialog. In the Files of type drop-down list select the file type you want to search for. Navigate the directory of the file you want to search.

Icons are small images embedded inside files. Generally the icon for a particular application is embedded inside the executable file. Some of these have a .DLL extension and some have .ICO extensions, but virtually any file can contain an icon. In fact, most Windows applications' executable files (.EXE or .COM) contain their own icon. This is the icon Windows uses by default.

Some .DLL files and most .ICO files are nothing more than a large collection of files. Shell32.dll is such a file. You can find Shell32.dll in the Windows directory.

The two check boxes in the Visual settings area are pretty self-explanatory. To turn the feature on, click it to place a check in the check box. To disable the feature, remove the check mark.

- Use large icons simply displays larger versions of all the icons.
- Show icons using all possible colors uses the maximum number of colors in the icon, depending on what color palette you have set for your display.

Using the Screen Saver

Many of the Windows NT screen savers have been included in Windows 98. This gives you a much broader and more interesting selection of screen savers than previous versions of Windows.

Experiment with the individual setting for each screen saver, and make changes often to keep your computer a little more interesting.

Protecting Your Computer with a Screen Saver Password

If you don't want someone walking up to your computer and snooping around while you're getting coffee, follow these steps to set up password protection:

1. From the Display Properties dialog box, select the Screen Saver tab.
2. Click the down arrow to the right of the screen saver list box, and select a screen saver if one isn't already selected.
3. Click the password protected check box.
4. Click the Change button. This brings up the Change Password dialog.
5. In the New password: text box, type the new password you want to use, and press the tab key to move to the Confirm new password: text box. Retype your new password and click the OK button.
6. A dialog box will be displayed in the middle of the screen telling you that your password has been successfully changed. Click the OK button. If the two passwords don't match, you'll receive a dialog box in the middle of the screen saying the passwords do not match and you must type them again.

Using Your Display's Energy-Saving Feature

The IBM XT (with the Intel 8086 processor) and its clones had a 100-watt power supply. This meant that at its peak usage it used about the same power as a 100-watt light bulb. And the monitor was a CGA that also used very little power, less than a television set.

With all the modern computing power and high-resolution video and other components now available, today's systems now use three to five times more power than they did in the 1980s.

Energy Star includes several Environmental Protection Agency (EPA) programs that set standards for energy efficiency. These standards are implemented in most modern computer hardware and office equipment.

ON THE WEB

The EPA has complete information on the Energy Star programs on their web site:
`http://www.epa.gov/appdstar/esoe/es_office.html`

To take full advantage of the power saving features of your Energy Star–compliant monitor, follow these steps:

1. From the Display Properties dialog box select the Settings tab.

2. You will see the property sheet for your video adapter. Select the Monitor tab. Table 22.4 describes the options on the Monitor page.

Table 22.4   Power-Saving Features

Option name	Description
Monitor is Energy Star compliant	If your monitor is Energy Star compliant, check this box. It is generally pretty obvious. Most ES-compliant monitors will have two power indicator lights on the front: yellow to indicate power has been reduced and green to indicate full power mode. Sometimes there is only one light that will change colors.
Automatically detect Plug and Play monitors	If your monitor is Plug and Play compatible, check this box. Windows will detect the power saver features of the monitor and use the appropriate software.
Reset display on suspend/resume	Most adapters don't need to reset the display after a suspend. If your display is working properly, ignore this setting. Some monitors will flicker during a reset. If this bothers you, try unchecking this box.

Remember that you can also use your computer's CMOS settings to make your hard drive spin down when it's not in use. Refer to your BIOS manufacturer's documentation for information on adjusting these settings.

Changing the Screen Saver and Screen Saver Settings

To select a new screen saver, follow these steps:

1. Click the down arrow next to the screen saver drop-down list, and select the screen saver you want. The screen saver you select will show in the preview area.

2. Click the Settings button to change the behavior and appearance. The types of settings vary with each screen saver. Experiment with the different settings; you can preview settings you have selected by clicking the Preview button.

TIP The best way to use the preview is to use the Alt+v keyboard shortcut. Often after you click on the Preview button and you let go of the mouse, you inadvertently move the mouse slightly. The slightest mouse movement will turn off this screen saver preview. If you use the keyboard shortcut, you won't accidentally move the mouse before you're finished previewing.

3. To display your customized text, select scrolling marquee or 3D text from the screen saver list, and click the Settings button. Type the text you want to display on screen, and experiment with the other adjustments.

Changing the Sounds Related to Windows Events

Windows 98 associates different sounds with each event. For example, if an error occurs, the default sound is a chime. You can change this so that a different sound bite is played for any particular event. In fact, you can record your own sounds if you have a microphone for your sound card. For instance, you can record a wave file that says, "An error has occurred." This kind of customization is great for sight-impaired users.

Only sound files in the WAV format can be associated with Windows events. WAV files have the extension `.WAV`. For your own wave files to show up in the Name drop-down list box, you need to store them in a media folder under your Windows folder, for example, `c:\windows\media\My sound.wav`.

 ON THE WEB

Sound America is an excellent source for WAV files on the Internet. The Sound America Web Site has literally thousands of sound files most of which are WAV format. They are free for the downloading, and most of them are less than 100k in size.

The web site address is **http://www.soundamerica.com**.

To change the sound associated with a Windows event, follow these steps:

1. From the Control Panel, select the sounds icon. The sounds Properties dialog box is displayed.

2. In the Events box, select the event you want to change the association for. If there is a Speaker icon to the left of the sound events, there is a sound already associated with that event. If there's no Speaker icon, no sound has been associated with that icon (see Figure 22.9).

3. In the Name drop-down list box, select the sound file you want to associate with this event. If you want to associate a WAV file that is not in the media folder, click the Browse button, and navigate to that location of the file, and select from the Browse dialog.

4. To preview the sound, click the right arrow to the right of the preview icon.

TIP Windows also supplies several preset schemes that you can select from the Schemes drop-down list box. Click the down arrow to the right of the Schemes drop-down list to select the scheme you wish to use.

FIG. 22.9
Sounds Properties
dialog.

5. When you finish making your custom sound associations, you can save this sound scheme with a unique name. Click the Save as button, type a name for the new sound scheme into the Save this sound scheme as text box, and click the OK button.

 One very practical use for this feature is to find or record an intuitive or unique sound to associate with New Mail Notification. This way when new mail comes in, you get something more than just a chime.

Now, when you receive a new email message you will know right away, and you can check to see if it's the important one you've been waiting all day for.

Customizing Mouse and Keyboard Settings

You can customize the behavior of the mouse and keyboard to make them work exactly the way you want them.

From Control Panel, select mouse. You'll see the Mouse Properties dialog.

Table 22.5 describes the options in the three tabs in the Mouse Properties dialog.

Table 22.5   Mouse Properties—Buttons Tab

Option Name	Description
Button configuration	To configure your mouse for left-handed use, click the Left-handed radio button. This reverses the functionality of the left and right mouse buttons.
Double-click speed	To adjust the double-click speed, move the slider bar in the double-click speed section of the buttons tab. Double-click the Jack-in-the-box in the Test area: to test your new speed setting.

Mouse Pointers and Animated Cursors

Depending on what task you're doing, your mouse pointer changes its appearance. The normal pointer is a white arrow pointing up and slightly left. If the computer is busy, such as when loading an application, your mouse pointer becomes an hourglass. This indicates that no other processing can occur until the current process is finished. If a process is working in the background, the mouse pointer becomes a combination of an arrow and an hourglass.

Windows provides several other mouse pointer schemes. To select a different scheme, click the down arrow to the right of the Scheme drop-down list. Select the pointer scheme you want to use.

The bottom half of this page shows what the mouse pointers look like. The square in the upper-right corner is a preview area for the highlighted pointer. This is really only useful if it is an animated cursor (mouse pointer). For example, if you select the animated hourglass scheme, click on the Busy cursor, and you can watch the animation in the Preview box.

If you want to create your own scheme of mouse pointers, select the pointer you want to change, and click the Browse button. This brings up a dialog box showing the contents of the cursors folder under Windows (`c:\windows\cursors`).

If you select a particular scheme but you want to use the Windows default for a few of the pointers, select the pointer you want to change and click the Use default button.

When you finish creating your disk pointer scheme, click the Save as button, type the new name in the Save this cursor scheme as: text box, and click the OK button.

Calibrating Mouse Movement

The Motion tab gives you the following options:

- Pointer speed sets the speed the pointer moves across the screen when you move the mouse. Move the slider to the left to slow down mouse movement and to the right to speed up mouse movement.

- Pointer trail displays pointer trails. Click the Show pointer trails check box. Adjust the length of the pointer trail with the slider bar below the check box. Kids love this feature. If you don't like the mouse trails, try not to let your kids find out about this one.

- Working with the new Intellipoint mouse: Microsoft has developed a great alternative to the three-button mouse. Its new mouse, called the Intellipoint mouse, has a left and right mouse button with a small wheel/button combination between the two buttons.

  To take full advantage of the wheel, your application must specifically support the mouse wheel.

  The wheel-button behaves differently in each application. Table 22.6 describes the functions of the wheel-button in Word 97.

Table 22.6   Functions of the Intellipoint Mouse Wheel-Button

Action	Effect
Single click	This activates a scrolling feature. The scroll box in the vertical scrollbar changes appearance, and the pointer changes to a dot with an arrow above and below it when the pointer is directly over the scroll box. If the pointer is above or below the scroll box, one of the arrows will disappear, and the page will begin to scroll in that direction. The farther the pointer is from the center of the document window, the faster the document will scroll.
Click and hold	The pointer changes to a dot with an arrow above and below. When you move the pointer up, the bottom arrow goes away and the document scrolls up. The reverse is true if you move the pointer down. A "ghost" pointer is visible at the position the pointer was in when you pressed the wheel. The farther the pointer is from the "ghost" pointer, the faster the document will scroll.
Spin without click	The document scrolls up or down three lines at a time.
Hold left button and spin	The text is highlighted as if you were doing a drag operation with the mouse.

Making Windows Accessible for the Hearing, Sight, and Movement Impaired

The Accessibility Options are indispensable for computer users with disabilities. Microsoft has done a fantastic job here. Many of these features are also useful for nonimpaired users as well. Even if you don't think you need any of these features, take a glance through them; you might be surprised at what you can do!

To open the Accessibility Options property sheet, double-click Accessibility Options in Control Panel. You'll see the dialog in Figure 22.10.

Keyboard Tab

The keyboard tab has three features:

- StickyKeys makes it easier to use multiple key combinations that include the Shift, Alt, and Ctrl keys. These keys are called Modifier keys. For example, Shift+F10 activates the right-click menu. When StickyKeys is enabled, you can press and release the Shift key and then press and release the F10 key to get the same effect (see Figure 22.11).

FIG. 22.10
Run Accessibility
Options from Control
Panel.

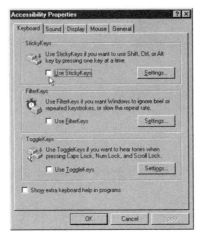

FIG. 22.11
StickyKeys Settings
dialog.

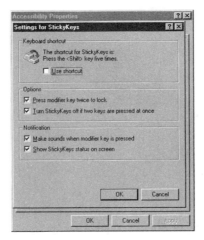

■ FilterKeys tells Windows to ignore repeated keystrokes (see Figure 22.12).

■ ToggleKeys gives audio feedback whenever Caps Lock, Num Lock, or Scroll Lock are pressed. To activate this feature, press the Num Lock key for five seconds, click the Settings button, and check the Use shortcut box.

Sound Tab

The Sound tab contains two visual feedback features: SoundSentry and ShowSounds.

Sound Sentry tells Windows to give visual feedback at times when normally only audio feedback would occur. The settings button allows you to select what type of visual feedback is given.

ShowSounds tells your applications to give visual feedback when they would normally only give audio feedback.

FIG. 22.12
FilterKeys Settings
dialog.

Display Tab

The Display tab feature forces your applications to use the color scheme specified in the Settings dialog (click the Settings button).

In the Settings dialog, you can check the Use shortcut box to enable the Left Alt+left Shift+Print Screen keyboard shortcut to enable the feature.

In the High contrast color scheme section, you can specify what scheme to use.

MouseKeys

MouseKeys allows you to use the arrow keys and the numeric keypad keys to control your mouse pointer. Click the Settings button to fine tune the feature's behavior.

General Tab

The general tab allows you to make a few global adjustments to the Accessibility Options.

Automatic reset tells Windows to turn off all Accessibility Options after a specified time of inactivity.

Notification provides two options for giving visual and audio feedback when features are turned on or off. This helps avoid accidentally toggling features on and off.

SerialKey devices is used when special input devices are attached to any of the serial ports. Use the Settings button to tell Windows what port the device is plugged into.

Using the Windows "Power Toys" Collection

The Windows Power Toys is a collection of small utility programs developed for Windows 95. Some of them have been built into the new operating system, and many of the others are still useful.

For instance, the AutoPlay Extender gives you AutoPlay capabilities for CD-ROMs that don't have AutoPlay support.

Cabview is a tool for viewing and extracting files from cabinet archives. An updated `Cabview.dll` is now included in the Windows 98 install. Installing the older version of Cabview from Power Toys is not recommended. CAB, short for cabinet, is a file archive format for distributing software and was implemented with the original release of Windows 95.

There are 13 different Power Toys and a `readme.txt` file is included that explains the functionality of each Power Toy.

> **CAUTION**
>
> Remember that Microsoft does not provide support for these utilities, and they were originally designed for Windows 95. Some of them might not work properly under Windows 98.
>
> Carefully read all documentation available before using any of the Power Toys.

ON THE WEB

You can download the Power Toys from Microsoft's web site at **http://www.microsoft.com/windows95/info/powertoys.htm**

CHAPTER 23

Working with Fonts

by Dan Logan

In this chapter

Understanding Fonts

Windows 98 provides several fonts that enable you to vary the look of your onscreen and printed text. A *font* is a set of characters in a single style defined by size, weight, and other features. Fonts are often members of type faces (type families) that are variations on that same style, for example Arial, Arial Black, Arial Bold, Arial Bold Italic, and Arial Italic. The Arial font is shown in Figure 23.1.

FIG. 23.1

The Windows 98 Arial font of the Arial type family.

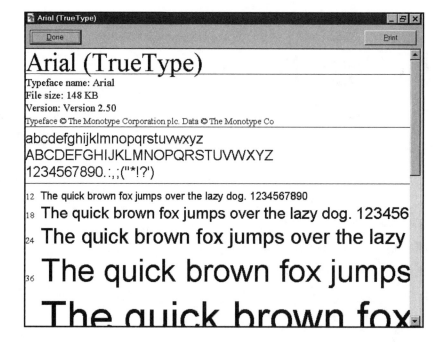

There are two general categories of fonts: bitmap fonts and scaleable fonts. Bitmapped (raster) fonts are tailored to the pixels on a monitor or the dots of ink put down by a printer. They are fixed in size; they can be enlarged or reduced, but their edges become jagged in the process.

Bitmapped fonts look best in the sizes in which they were created. At even multiples of their original size they might scale well, but in other sizes, or rotated, the likelihood is that the image quality will suffer. Generally speaking, bitmapped fonts should not be enlarged.

Scaleable fonts, originally developed for high-end computers and printers, allow you to change the size of the font while retaining the characters' proportions and without causing the edges of the letters to become jagged.

Windows 98 uses Microsoft TrueType fonts, which are scaleable. Every character in a TrueType font is stored as an outline that is used in the creation of every size of that character. The TrueType font file also contains all the other data it needs to produce an image, including the rules (hints) for fine-tuning the outline of the character at any given size. When the image has been sized, Windows rasterizes it to produce the image best suited to the capabilities of the monitor or printer, even if the monitor or printer is capable only of low resolutions. Hinting is needed on low-resolution monitors and printers, including VGA monitors and 300 dpi laser printers.

Installing and Removing Fonts

Windows 98 comes with a collection of TrueType and bitmap fonts (see Table 23.1). These are installed in the Fonts folder (c:\windows\fonts). TrueType fonts have the extension .TTF, whereas bitmap fonts have .FON extensions (see Figure 23.2). You can add more fonts to the system or remove many of them. You can install roughly 1,000 TrueType fonts in Windows 98. (The number is limited by the file size limits for the Registry key and the graphics device interface.)

FIG. 23.2
When you view font files as large icons, TrueType fonts display a TrueType icon.

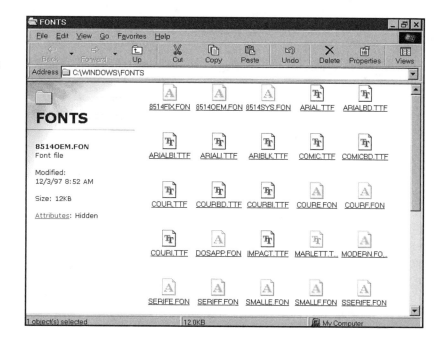

Windows ships with a number of fonts that serve special purposes. Windows uses a small number of system fonts to create its own screens (see Table 23.1). Deleting these fonts can cause glitches on your Windows screens or prevent you from booting Windows. OEM fonts support older equipment installed on the system. And the fixed-width fonts provide compatibility with older versions of Windows.

Windows 98 also supplies a few vector fonts. *Vector fonts* are a type of scaleable font typically used with plotters and high-resolution output devices. Modern.fon is a vector font.

Table 23.1 Specialized Fonts Supplied with Windows 98

Font Filename	Description
VGASYS.FON	VGA (640×480) resolution system font
VGAOEM.FON	VGA (640×480) resolution terminal font
VGAFIX.FON	VGA (640×480) resolution monospaced system font
8514SYS.FON	8514/a (1024×768) resolution system font
8514OEM.FON	8514/a (1024×768) resolution terminal font
8514FIX.FON	8514/a (1024×768) resolution monospaced system font
VGA850.FON	VGA (640×480) resolution terminal font (International)

Previewing Fonts

The Fonts folder in Control Panel works a bit differently from other folders. You can preview the system fonts and TrueType fonts in the Fonts folder using the Windows 98 font viewer. To see the fonts that come with Windows 98, follow these steps:

1. Click on Start, point to Settings, activate Control Panel, and activate Fonts.

2. Point to the font you want to preview and activate.

N O T E Keep in mind the term "activate" means click if the web desktop is enabled and double-click if it isn't.

You can use this procedure to preview a font file even if it is located in another folder. Font files need not be in the Fonts folder. New printer fonts can be installed when you install a new printer; these new fonts won't be placed in the Fonts folder, but they will show up with the fonts listed in Windows programs, such as Word for Windows.

Following is a list of the TrueType fonts that come with Windows 98. These additional fonts are available as both screen and printer fonts.

Arial	Small Fonts (VGA resolution)
Arial Black	Small Fonts (8514/a resolution)
Arial Bold	Symbol
Arial Bold Italic	Symbol 8,10,12,14,18,24
Arial Italic	Tahoma
Comic Sans MS	Tahoma Bold
Comic Sans MS Bold	Times New Roman
Courier New	Times New Roman Bold
Courier New Bold	Times New Roman Bold Italic

Courier New Bold Italic	Times New Roman Italic
Courier 10,12,15 (VGA resolution)	Verdana
Courier 10,12,15 (8514/a resolution)	Verdana Bold
Courier New Italic	Verdana Bold Italic
Non-Windows Application Font	Verdana Italic
Impact	Webdings
Marlett	WingDings
Modern	
MS Sans Serif 8,10,12,14,18,24	
MS Serif 8,10,12,14,18,24	

Adding New Fonts

There are hundreds of fonts available that you can purchase or find for free on the Internet. However, new fonts must be installed, not simply copied into the Fonts folder, in order for Windows and Windows applications to recognize them.

To add a font to the Fonts folder, follow these steps:

1. Click on Start, point to Settings, activate Control Panel, and activate Fonts.
2. Activate the File menu, and then activate Install New Font.
3. Activate the drive, and then activate the folder with the font you want.
4. Activate the font you want to add.

N O T E If you want to add more than one font, press and hold the Ctrl key while activating the font files you want to add. ▩

If you are on a network, you can add fonts from a network drive without using your computer's disk space. To do this, follow these steps:

1. Activate File, and then activate Install New Font.
2. In the Add Fonts dialog box, be sure the Copy fonts to Fonts folder check box is not checked. This option is available only when you install TrueType or raster fonts from the Install New Font command.
3. Choose OK.

ON THE WEB

Microsoft periodically makes more TrueType fonts available for no charge at **http://www.microsoft.com/typography/free.htm**.

Printing a Font Sample

To print a sample of a font, follow this procedure:

1. Click on Start, point to Settings, activate Control Panel, and activate Fonts.

2. Point to the font you want to print, and activate.

3. Choose Print on the font sample page.

N O T E   If you want to choose more than one font, press and hold the Ctrl key; then activate each font you want. ▨

Looking at Font File Properties

Using the Windows 98 font utility, you can look at useful information about the font file on the Properties sheet. Follow these steps:

1. Click on Start, point to Settings, activate Control Panel, and activate Fonts.

2. Point to the font and right-click.

3. Point to Properties and activate.

The Properties sheet for a TrueType font has a single tab called General (see Figure 23.3) that shows the font file name, type of file, location, size, attributes, and other information.

FIG. 23.3

Font Properties–
General tab.

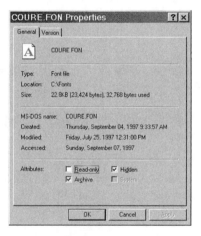

For other types of font files such as .FON files, the Properties sheet will also show a Version tab. See Figure 23.4, which shows additional information about the font file, including the file version, description, copyright, and other version information including company name, internal name, language, original filename, and product version.

FIG. 23.4

Font Properties–
Version tab.

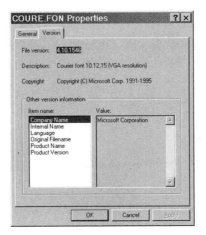

Deleting a Font

Many users will not need dozens or hundreds of fonts. If you don't use many fonts and would rather have more disk space, you can delete many of the fonts. To uninstall a font and delete it to the Recycle Bin, follow these steps:

1. Click on Start, point to Settings, activate Control Panel, and activate Fonts.
2. Activate the font icon or font file you want to delete.
3. Activate File and activate Delete.

N O T E   If you want to delete more than one font, press and hold the Ctrl key while activating each of the fonts. ▨

If you want to uninstall a TrueType font without deleting it from your hard drive, you must create a folder where you can keep a copy of the font file. To uninstall a TrueType font without deleting it (the font information will remain in the Registry), follow these steps:

1. Click on Start, activate Programs, and activate Windows Explorer.
2. Create a new folder for copies of the TrueType font files.
3. Copy the fonts you want to remove from the Fonts folder to the new folder.
4. Follow the procedure for deleting a font described in the previous section.

When you want to reinstall a font you removed, follow these steps:

1. Click on Start, point to Settings, activate Control Panel, and activate Fonts.
2. Activate the File menu, and then activate Install New Font.
3. Activate the drive, and then activate the folder with the font you want.
4. Select the Copy Fonts to Fonts folder option, so the font file is copied rather than moved. Activate the font you want to install. Choose OK.

Using Fonts in Applications

When a font is installed, Windows 98 applications can access it. Figures 23.5 and 23.6 show the font dialog boxes for WordPad and Word. To access the font dialog box from within the application, follow these steps:

1. Point to <u>F</u>ormat on the menu bar and activate.

2. Point to Font and activate.

3. Activate the font you want to use.

ON THE WEB

Microsoft maintains an informative Typography page at **http://www.microsoft.com/typography/**. Here you can find details on the development of TrueType, free TrueType fonts and utilities, developer information, descriptions of the features of TrueType and OpenType, and links to other typography-related sites.

Managing Fonts

If you do a lot of document design and use a variety of fonts, you spend a fair amount of time installing and previewing fonts, printing out font samples, and studying font file properties. The Windows 98 applet for managing fonts gives you the tools to perform these tasks—and also to sort the available fonts by their similarity to the font.

FIG. 23.5

Font Access in WordPad.

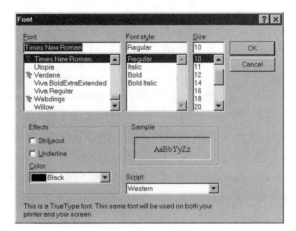

FIG. 23.6
Font Access in
Microsoft Word 97.

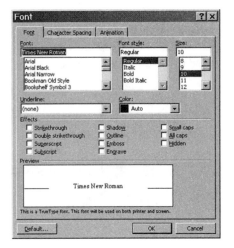

Sorting by Font Similarity

To sort the fonts in the Fonts folder according to their similarity to a specified font, follow these steps:

1. Click on Start, point to Settings, activate Control Panel, and activate Fonts.
2. Activate the View menu, and then activate List Fonts By Similarity.
3. Activate a font. The fonts will be listed in their order of similarity to the chosen font.

The fonts are sorted as very similar, fairly similar, or not similar.

Using Third-Party Font Management Software

Although the Windows 98 font manager will handle many tasks, third-party font management software is available that can provide more extensive capabilities if you must manage large numbers of fonts. For example, there are third-party font managers that will group fonts into sets that suit your work habits, activating or deactivating a font or sets of fonts as you need them.

Adobe Type Manager (ATM) Deluxe version 4.0 from Adobe Systems allows you to manage not only Windows TrueType fonts but Adobe PostScript Type 1 scaleable fonts. (Earlier versions of ATM didn't work with TrueType files; TrueType fonts, while in some instances appearing very much like their Adobe counterparts, are not the same and do not share the same file formats.) Heavy font users often have Type 1 fonts in their collections. Adobe sells more than 2,000 Type 1 typefaces.

ATM (see Figure 23.7) has other useful features. It can simulate fonts that a document calls for but aren't on your computer. It will automatically load an inactive font into Windows when a document calls for it. It can use anti-aliasing to smooth the edges of Type 1 fonts, and it has a multiple master feature that you can use to create your own typefaces.

ON THE WEB

You can find an overview of Adobe Type Manager Deluxe 4.0 at `http://www.adobe.com/prodindex/atm/overview.html`.

FIG. 23.7
Adobe Type Manager
Control Panel.

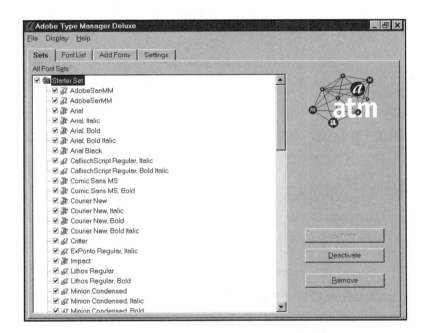

There are other popular font managers such as Bitstream Font Navigator, Agfa Font Manager, and FontMinder. FontMinder was created by Ares Software Corporation, but Adobe purchased the program from Ares in 1996, and some of its features, in particular the capability to automatically activate sets of fonts when a given application is launched, might be incorporated into Adobe Type Manager in the future.

Using Other Font Technologies

With Microsoft TrueType and Adobe's Type 1 fonts, you might have all the font power you need. However, there are other font technologies such as Bitstream TrueDoc, Monotype ESQ, and Adobe's Type 3 format that can extend the range of typefaces available to you.

Adobe Type 3 fonts are used by a narrow market of print professionals. Type 3 fonts come in both scaleable and bitmapped fonts, but they don't use hinting. The Type 3 format was designed to produce high-quality output on high-end PostScript-capable printers and service bureau imagesetters that have hardware for interpreting PostScript commands. Type 3 fonts make use of the full set of PostScript PDL capabilities.

Making Fonts Look Their Best on the Screen

Bitmapped fonts are best used at their design sizes. Enlarging bitmapped fonts produce jagged edges ("jaggies"). And how the font looks onscreen also depends on the resolution capabilities of the monitor and graphics card. At lower resolutions, instead of smooth lines or smooth curves, you might see jagged edges on the characters in your display or print output. Jaggies will appear when the monitor or printer doesn't have the resolution to display a smooth line.

Font smoothing or anti-aliasing is a method used to make the edges of characters appear smoother. To turn on font smoothing in Windows 98, follow this procedure:

1. Click on Start, point to Settings, activate Control Panel, and activate Fonts.
2. Activate View, Folder Options, View.
3. Check the box titled Smooth edges of screen fonts.
4. Choose OK.

If your text still doesn't appear smooth enough for your purposes, you might need to purchase a monitor and graphics card capable of higher resolutions.

Matching Screen Fonts with Printed Output

One of the computer user's most frustrating problems develops when the printed page coming out of the printer doesn't match what is seen onscreen. Fonts are one of the likely culprits for this problem. If the printer doesn't have access to the same font shown onscreen, the font that is substituted is likely to have minute differences that are enough to throw off spacing.

How do you make sure the screen and printer fonts are the same? Windows applications using TrueType download the fonts to the printer, so the printer uses the same fonts as on the screen.

Although in most cases you want the same screen and printer fonts, there are circumstances in which you want to use screen fonts in your document that your printer cannot print. This is useful if the document will be printed on another printer or used by a service bureau on an imagesetter. In this case, you can select fonts that you know are supported by the other printer or service bureau, and you can see onscreen how your document will look, even though you can't obtain an accurate printout from your own printer.

T I P Keep in mind that most Windows TrueType and Adobe PS fonts are licensed and copyrighted, and they can't legally be copied to a disk or across a network unless covered by license.

The appearance of the text and graphics on a page printed on a laser printer is controlled through a page description language (PDL). The two standard page description languages are Adobe's PostScript and Hewlett-Packard's Printer Control Language (PCL). PCL and PostScript printers will both run under Windows 98. Windows 98 uses a 32-bit universal printer driver that works with the printer-specific drivers supplied by printer manufacturers for their machines.

Hewlett-Packard was one of the pioneers in laser printer development for personal computers. The Hewlett-Packard LaserJet series is the standard for laser printers, and other manufacturers adopt a subset of the PCL commands in their printer drivers for some degree of HP compatibility.

PostScript became the standard for desktop publishing because service bureaus have used it for years with their imagesetters to produce camera-ready copy. Users' familiarity with PostScript has helped it retain its dominant position despite competition from Hewlett-Packard and TrueType.

Your printer can be configured using the Windows 98 Printer Properties screen. The Windows 98 Printer Properties screen gives you useful information about your printer's configuration and enables you to control its operation. Each printer has its own configuration options, and these vary widely among printers (see Figure 23.8).

To use the Printer Properties screen, follow these steps:

1. Click on Start, point to Settings, and activate Control Panel.
2. Select Printers.
3. Right-click on the PostScript printer you will be using.
4. Activate Properties.

FIG. 23.8

The Fonts tab on this Printer Properties screen shows the choices available on an HP LaserJet PostScript printer.

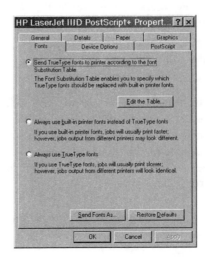

Printers come with resident fonts—some with more, some with less, depending on the model. A resident font is a font permanently stored in a printer's read-only memory. You can also add fonts by inserting font cartridges designed for the printer or by downloading soft fonts from the computer.

Some laser printers have slots that accept font cartridges, which are read-only memory boards loaded with a collection of fonts. Font cartridges have the advantage of using none of the computer or printer memory.

Printers can also take advantage of soft fonts. A *soft font* is one that is downloaded from the computer to the printer's random access memory (RAM) (it is also referred to as a *downloadable font*). The TrueType fonts that come with Windows 98 are soft fonts. Soft fonts use both disk space and printer memory. If you don't have enough memory in your printer to handle your printing needs (including a set of soft fonts), look into installing more RAM; on most laser printers you can increase the amount of RAM. Soft fonts must be downloaded to the printer and that takes time, but when they are downloaded, subsequent print jobs will print faster.

To force the use of TrueType fonts on a PostScript printer, follow these steps:

1. Click on Start, point to Settings, and activate Control Panel.
2. Select Printers.
3. Right-click on the PostScript printer you will be using.
4. Activate Properties.
5. Choose the Fonts tab.
6. Choose the Always Use TrueType Fonts button.
7. Choose OK.

Using the Character Map

The computer's keyboard offers only a worm's-eye view of the characters available to the user. To present what is actually available to users in a particular font, Windows 98 uses the Character Map (see Figure 23.9).

FIG. 23.9

In the lower-right corner of the window, the Character Map for MS Sans Serif shows the keystroke shortcut for the character.

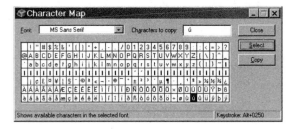

Part

V

Ch

23

To insert a character from the Character Map, follow this procedure:

1. Click on Start, Programs, Accessories, Character Map.
2. Double-click on the character you want. (Continue to hold the mouse button down if you want to see the character magnified.)
3. Activate Copy.
4. Return to your application.
5. Place the cursor where you want to insert the character, and Paste.

There are keyboard shortcuts that will allow you to insert extended ASCII characters in your documents. These shortcuts eliminate your having to keep returning to the Character Map. You can create a document with your most frequently used keyboard shortcuts or create macros for them in your Windows applications.

Figure 23.9 shows the keystroke combination for the character ú. To use the keystroke shortcut to a character, follow these steps:

1. Place the cursor at the point you want to insert the character.
2. Press Num Lock.
3. Press and hold the Alt key.
4. Using the numeric keypad on the keyboard, enter the four digits for the character you want to insert.
5. Release the Alt key. The character will be displayed at the insertion point.

Using WingDings, Symbols, and Other Unconventional Fonts

To give a taste of the plethora of distinctive fonts available to users beyond those that come with Windows 98, Windows includes three TrueType fonts of signs and symbols. `Wingdings.ttf` is an array of pointers and borders that can be used to dress up a document. `Symbol.ttf` is a collection of characters including the uppercase and lowercase Greek alphabets for mathematical and scientific notation and common business use. And the recently developed `Webdings.ttf` typeface reflects the growing interest in the Internet with a selection of characters for Web designers; these font images will move more quickly across the Internet than graphics files will.

Using Fonts on the Web

The Internet has expanded the concept of document publishing. In its early days the Net used only a limited number of fonts. But with the introduction of the graphically oriented World Wide Web and the spreading recognition of the Internet's possibilities, users demanded greater typeface options than the Net was capable of providing.

Typeface limitations revived the old problem of making onscreen and printed output look the same. There are widespread efforts being made to overcome the typeface limitations inherent in existing HTML specifications. The World Wide Web Consortium, an organization founded to develop common protocols for the evolution of the web, has identified the following typeface-related needs that must be addressed in order to give users greater flexibility in their use of fonts on the Internet or on intranets:

A font format that supports resolution independence, kerning, and ligatures

A mechanism for downloading fonts and converting them to the platform format

An inventory of fonts available over the Net, and copyright protection and payment schemes for those fonts

A means for addressing, naming, and matching fonts on the web

Part

V

Ch

23

ON THE WEB

For information and discussion of developments regarding fonts and the World Wide Web, visit the World Wide Web Consortium's Fonts and the web page at `http://www.w3.org/Fonts/`. There's also a mailing list for font/web issues at www-font; subscribe by sending the word *subscribe* to **www-font-request@w3.org**.

Embedding TrueType Fonts

To overcome the problem of disrupted document formatting due to changed fonts, font vendors are incorporating font embedding technology that allows you to embed the needed fonts in the document file.

Windows 98 supports TrueType font embedding. There are four levels of font embedding, and the TrueType font vendor builds the embedding level into the font. The embedding levels include the following:

1. Restricted license. No embedding allowed.
2. Print & preview. Document can be opened only as read-only. Fonts must only be installed temporarily on the remote system.
3. Editable. The selected font can be viewed on the monitor and printed, and the host document can be edited but must only be installed temporarily on the remote system.
4. Installable. The embedded fonts can be viewed, printed, edited, and permanently installed on another computer and used in other applications.

TIP

A useful tool that will help you with embedding is Microsoft's font properties extension for Windows. Download the free self-extracting file `ttftext.exe` from `http://www.microsoft.com/typography/property/property.htm`. When the software is installed, the font properties extension (see Figure 23.10) adds tabs to the Properties screen to give you additional information about a font. Activating the Embedding tab tells you the embedding level of the font.

FIG. 23.10
You can install the Font Properties extension applet for more information about your font files.

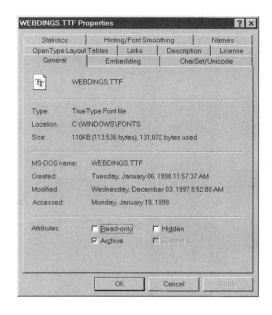

To save a file with embedded fonts in a Windows application such as Microsoft Word 97, follow these steps:

1. In the document window, choose File, Save As.
2. Select Options.
3. Select Embed TrueType fonts.
4. Choose OK.

Moving to OpenType Fonts

OpenType is a new format initiative by Microsoft and Adobe, aimed at making it easier for users to use and organize sets of TrueType and PostScript Type 1 fonts onscreen and in print. An OpenType font can have either TrueType outlines, Type 1 outlines, or both. Type 1 files can be rasterized by a Type 1 rasterizer or converted to TrueType data for rasterization.

The OpenType format will enable Web page designers to use high-quality fonts in their online documents. The new format should also reduce download times.

Dealing with International Character Sets

Windows 98 offers multilanguage support. Windows 98 supports Greek and Turkish, and the Baltic, Central European, and Cyrillic language groups. With this support enabled, you can view documents written in these scripts. With multilanguage support installed, a 652-character set is available in the Arial, Courier New, and Times Roman fonts.

To install the multilanguage support, follow this procedure:

1. Click on Start, point to Settings, activate Control Panel, and select Add/Remove Programs.
2. Choose the Windows Setup tab, check Multilanguage Support, and then activate Details.
3. Place check marks next to the languages you want to include.
4. Choose OK and then choose OK again to restart your computer and make the changes take effect.

If you want to write or edit documents in any of these languages, you must add keyboard support for the language. To do so, follow these steps:

1. Click on Start, point to Settings, activate Control Panel, and select Keyboard.
2. Select the Language tab, and then activate Add.
3. Select the languages you want.
4. Check the Enable Indicator On Taskbar box.

When you have installed multilanguage and keyboard support, the language indicator will be displayed on the taskbar. You can choose a toggle (Left Alt+Shift or Ctrl+Shift) to switch between two language scripts. The taskbar will show the language currently active (see Figure 23.11).

Windows 98 supports other languages such as Japanese, Chinese, Korean, and Arabic, but you must buy a language-specific version of the program to do so. These versions also support the pan-European language groups.

Part
V

Ch
23

FIG. 23.11

The active language (in this instance "EN" for English) is displayed on the Windows 98 taskbar.

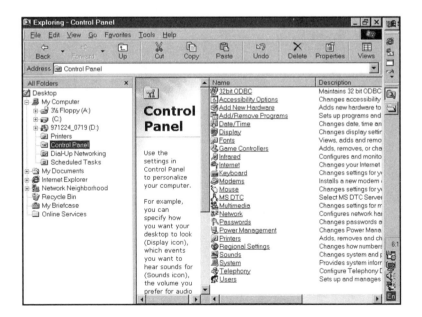

CHAPTER 24

Setting Up Windows 98 Multimedia

by Michael Desmond

In this chapter

Using Video Tools in Windows 98

Windows 98 extends and improves the video handling talents found in Windows 95. The old Media Player applet is still on-hand to play back video files, but the new video workhorse is ActiveMovie. This up-to-date facility enables you to do one-stop-shopping for popular video formats.

Understanding the Video Properties Box

You can instantly find information on any video file by right-clicking its icon and selecting Properties from the shortcut menu. The Properties dialog box includes three tabs: General, Details, and Preview. The General tab features information such as file size and dates.

You'll find useful information in the Details sheet, as shown in Figure 24.1. In addition to the run-time of the video clip, you will see information on the audio and video encoding schemes used to create the file—which can be very useful information if you are trying to get optimal performance. The Video Format section includes helpful data on the pixel resolution of the captured video, as well as the frame rate and data rate.

FIG. 24.1
Detailed information about frame rates, playback data rates, and capture resolutions can help you trouble-shoot video playback problems.

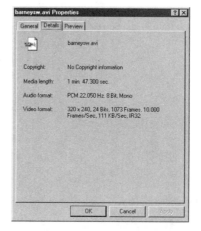

Click the Preview tab to view the selected video clip directly from the Properties dialog box. Then click the Play button. The slider bar control, which scrolls to the right as the video plays, lets you jump to any portion of the clip. To stop the clip, click the Stop button.

 T I P   If a video file fails to play or suffers from jerky playback, use the Properties dialog box to see how it was encoded. If the file was encoded at a resolution higher than 320×240 pixels or if the file uses 16-bit or 24-bit color, your system might need an upgrade in order to handle the playback. If the file will not play at all, also check to see which codec is identified in the Properties box. You might need to install the proper video playback driver in order for your system to recognize the video format.

Playing Video Files

Windows 98 provides two different applets for playing back digital video clips. They are:

- ActiveMovie control
- Media Player

New to Windows 98 is the ActiveMovie control. This applet takes over the video handling duties from the venerable Media Player and adds greater file support and better performance. However, you can still use Media Player to view files with the .AVI extension.

The easiest way to play a video clip in Windows 98 is to launch it directly from Windows 98 Explorer by selecting the icon. The ActiveMovie player launches, and after a brief pause, the video begins to play.

Playing Video Files from ActiveMovie

To play a video using the ActiveMovie control, do the following:

1. Open the ActiveMovie control from the Windows 98 Start menu by clicking Start, Programs, Accessories, Multimedia, ActiveMovie Control.
2. In the Open dialog box, select Movie Files from the Files of Type drop-down list.
3. Navigate to the directory that contains the file you want to play. All files with valid file extensions (AVI or MPG) appear in the dialog box.
4. Click the Open button, and the ActiveMovie control appears.
5. Click the Play button to play the video clip.
6. To stop playback, click the Stop button.

> **TIP** If the ActiveMovie player is already open, you can play back videos by dragging and dropping the desired file's icon onto the ActiveMovie window.

Playing Video Files from Media Player

To play your video clips from the Media Player, do the following:

1. Open the Media Player applet from the Windows 98 Start menu by clicking Start, Programs, Accessories, Entertainment, Media Player.
2. Select File, Open to go to the Open dialog box.
3. Click the Files of Type drop-down arrow and select Video (*.avi).
4. Navigate to the directory that contains the file you want to play. All files with the .AVI file extension appear in the dialog box.

> **TIP** You can launch files from the Device menu. To do so, click Device, and then select the media type from the numbered list. The Open dialog box then appears, displaying only files matching the selected type.

Part
V

Ch
24

5. Click the Open button. The filename appears in the window bar of the Media Player.

6. Click the Play button, and the AVI file begins playing. The slider control will advance as the file plays.

7. To stop the file, click the Stop button.

Working with ActiveMovie Video

In addition to providing support for many video file formats beyond AVI, ActiveMovie provides useful tools for customizing video playback.

Open an ActiveMovie File

You can load a video file into ActiveMovie by dragging and dropping any recognized video file type—including AVI and MPEG—onto the application window. It takes a few seconds to load the file, during which time the application bar will display something like this:

```
Demo.avi (Opening)
```

Once the file is loaded, ActiveMovie displays the following file information in the interface window:

- The total file runtime is shown at the left.
- The current position in the file is displayed in large characters in the center, as measured in either frames or seconds. (The word frame or time appears directly below the number to identify the unit of measure.)

Play an ActiveMovie File

To play a file, do any of the following:

- Double-click anywhere on the information display or the video window.
- Right-click anywhere on the information display or video window and select Run from the context menu.
- Click the Play control button at the bottom of the window.

Explore the Properties Sheet

You can optimize video playback by right-clicking the ActiveMovie display interface and selecting Properties from the context menu. The ActiveMovie Control properties sheet includes four tabs:

- *Playback* enables you to select a section of the clip to play back and to set the clip to rewind or keep playing upon reaching the end.
- *Movie Size* enables you to control the size of the video playback window.
- *Controls* enables you to customize ActiveMovie interface elements.
- *Advanced* provides information on ActiveMovie filters.

Using the Playback Sheet   The Playback properties sheet, shown in Figure 24.2, provides useful tools for controlling the way the open audio file plays.

FIG. 24.2

From the Playback sheet, you can select a section of the file to play or make a file repeat a specific number of times.

The slider bars in the Volume area are grayed out, but you can still tweak your video clips from the Timing area of the Playback sheet by doing the following:

Part

V

Ch

24

■ To constrain playback to a desired portion of the audio file, enter time valued into the Start and Stop text boxes.

N O T E   The format of the Start and Stop boxes changes depending on whether you have selected a time-based or frame-based display of the video clip duration. For precise work, it is generally more convenient to work with frame values than to work with time. ■

■ To play a file over a specific number of times, select the Play Count radio button and enter the desired value in the text box.

■ To play a file over continuously until interrupted, click the Auto Repeat radio button.

■ To automatically reset the file to the beginning after it plays, check the Auto Rewind check box.

Using the Movie Size Sheet   The Movie Size sheet lets you set the size of the playback window for the open file. Click the Select the Movie Size drop-down arrow and select from the following size options:

■ *Original Size.* Playback window will be the same size as that at which the original video was captured.

■ *Double Original Size.* Doubles the height and width of the original captured video size.

■ *1/16 of Screen Size.* Plays in a window that is 1/16 the size of the current display area.

■ *1/4 of Screen Size.* Plays in a window that is 1/4 the size of the current display area.

■ *1/2 of Screen Size.* Plays in a window that is half the size of the current display area.

■ *Maximized.* Plays in a standard playback window that occupies the entire display.

> **CAUTION**
>
> Playing video at expanded resolutions can reduce frame rates and result in jerky playback because the CPU and graphics card struggle to output the increased number of graphics pixels. A doubled video window, for example, contains four times the graphics information of a video played at native resolution (two times the height plus two times the width yields a 4X increase in pixels).

As does the Maximized option, the Run Full Screen check box causes the open video file to expand to the size of the display. However, this mode does not run in a standard playback window; instead, all the other elements on the display are disabled to allow the video playback to take over the screen. For systems with older graphics cards, this dedicated video playback mode can help boost the playback frame rate of full-screen video clips.

Using the Controls Sheet The Controls sheet gives you access to interface controls for playing files.

- Check the Display Panel check box to show the file information box.
- Check the Control Panel check box to display the VCR-like control buttons and the Trackbar slider bar.
- Inside the Control Panel area, check any one of the Position controls, Selection controls, and Trackbar check boxes to make the appropriate controls available on the ActiveMovie interface.
- In the Colors area, you can customize the ActiveMovie display panel by selecting colors from the Foreground and Background color buttons.

Working with Media Player Video

With its improved performance, wider file support, and enhanced features for developers, ActiveMovie is the video playback tool for Windows 98. Still, Microsoft has kept the Media Player applet around for those who want to use it. After a file is loaded into Media Player, you can access a number of controls from the menu bar.

Working with the Options Dialog Box

The Options dialog box lets you control how video clips play back. To get to it, click Edit, Options. You can then do the following from the Options box:

- Check the Auto Rewind check box to set the file back to the beginning after it stops playing.
- Check the Auto Repeat check box to have the video continuously play over and over until stopped by the user.

The OLE Object area, shown in Figure 24.3, contains tools for customizing playback of video files within external applications, such as word processors or spreadsheets.

FIG. 24.3
You can customize the playback of video files inside of other applications by using the Media Player's Options dialog box.

Follow these guidelines for using the objects in the OLE Object area:

- Check the Control Bar on Playback check box to have VCR-like control buttons appear beneath the embedded video window inside documents. Enter the name you want to appear with embedded clips in the Caption text box.

- Check the Border Around Object check box to have a thin border appear around the embedded video image.

- Check the Play in Client Document check box to have the video clip play in its window without invoking the Media Player interface.

- Check the Dither Picture to VGA Colors check box to use the basic 16-color palette in the playback window.

N O T E The dither control should only be used with systems with very limited graphics resources, such as graphics boards that cannot support 16-bit color output. Dithering to the limited VGA palette will result in very poor color reproduction, making many video clips all but unusable. ▪

Working with the Selection Dialog Box

Click Edit, Selection to go to the Selections dialog box. From here, you can demarcate a portion of the file to be played back or to be sent to another application.

- Click All to select the entire audio file so you can copy the entire file for pasting elsewhere.

- Click None to clear any existing selection.

- Click From to enter the start point (measured in minutes:seconds:tenths) of the selected area. Then enter the end point in the To box, or enter the length of the desired selection in the Size box.

N O T E The position information in the From, To, and Size boxes will be displayed either as number of frames or in amount of time (minutes:seconds:tenths), depending on which format (either frames or time) you select from the Scale menu. ▪

Working with the Device Menu

You'll also find useful tools in the Device menu.

■ To open files from the Device menu, choose the desired file type from the numbered list. The Open box then lists only files whose extension matches the type you selected.

■ To launch the Windows 98 Volume Control applet, click Device, Volume Control. For more on this resource, go to the section "Working with the Volume Control Tool," later in this chapter.

Using the Properties Dialog Box

Click Device, Properties to go to the Video Properties dialog box. Here you can set the size of the playback window for the open file, as shown in Figure 24.4. A representation of a monitor with a video window serves as a guide to let you preview the size of the video window. Open the Window drop-down list to see the size options.

FIG. 24.4
The display image in the Video Properties dialog box provides a graphic example of how large the adjusted video window will be.

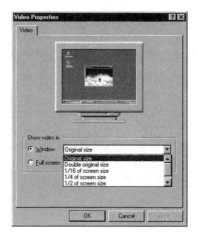

> **CAUTION**
>
> As it does in ActiveMovie, expanding the video window can impair performance.

The Full Screen radio button sets the video file to play back at the full size of the display. However, this mode does not run in a standard playback window; instead, all the other elements on the display are disabled to allow the video playback to take over the screen. For systems with older graphics cards, this dedicated video playback mode can help boost the playback frame rate of full-screen video clips.

Working with Video in the Windows 98 Device Manager

The Windows 98 Device Manager gives you access to all your hardware settings. Here, you can examine the graphics settings that might be affecting your video playback. To access graphics controls under the Device Manager, do the following:

1. Click Start, Settings, Control Panel, and click the System icon.
2. Click the Device Manager tab.
3. Click the plus sign (+) next to the Display Adapters item. The name of the currently loaded driver appears beneath the entry.
4. Select the device that appears and click Properties.

The Properties box features three tabs: General, Driver, and Resources. The General sheet provides basic information, such as the manufacturer of the device driver and the hardware it is tailored for. Click the Resources tab, and you will find the standard resource interface for Windows 98 hardware. This display lets you view and adjust memory address settings for the graphics adapter.

Part

V

Ch

24

N O T E You are not likely to make use of this facility to fix conflicts with the display hardware because any such conflict would render the display inoperable. However, you might be able to cross-reference the address information provided with that shown in another device's Resource sheet, which could help you determine which devices are in conflict. ▧

A welcome new feature of Windows 98 is the Driver tab of the device properties sheet. You will see two buttons at the bottom of this sheet. The Driver File Details button lets you view the actual driver files used to operate the graphics adapter. More interesting is the Upgrade Driver button, which launches Windows 98's automated hardware update scheme. To automatically upgrade your graphics adapter driver, do the following:

1. Click Start, Settings, Control Panel, and select the System icon.
2. Click the Device Manager tab.
3. Click the plus sign (+) next to Display Adapters. The name of the currently loaded driver appears beneath the entry.
4. Select the device that appears and click Properties.
5. Click the Driver tab and click the Upgrade Driver button.
6. Click the Next button.
7. Click the top radio button to search for a newer driver, and then click Next.
8. Activate the appropriate check boxes to find the newest driver software, as shown in Figure 24.5. In most cases, you will want to check the Microsoft Windows Update check box to check Microsoft's Internet-based index of driver updates.

9. The Internet Download Agent launches, connecting you to the Internet and taking you to the appropriate driver site. Follow the onscreen instructions to download the device driver software and install it on your system. When you finish, restart your PC.

 T I P   If you are experiencing graphics problems, you might be able to resolve them by turning off acceleration features within your graphics card. From the System Properties sheet, click the Performance tab and click the Graphics button. If the Hardware Acceleration slider bar is set all the way to the right, as shown in Figure 24.5, drag the control a step to the left and click OK. Click Yes when Windows 98 prompts you to restart. If the problems continue, you can repeat this process, further disabling acceleration features that might be causing the problem.

FIG. 24.5

The Advanced Graphics Settings dialog box lets you incrementally turn off hardware acceleration features in order to improve stability.

Working with the Multimedia Properties Controls

The Multimedia properties sheet, accessible through the Control Panel, gives you control of a variety of multimedia settings under Windows 98. To open the Multimedia properties sheet, click Start, Settings, Control Panel, and then click the Multimedia icon. The properties sheet appears.

There are five tabs arrayed across the top of the Multimedia properties sheet. Two of these directly impact video playback:

■ *Video*. Lets you size video playback windows.

■ *Advanced*. Provides access to driver and configuration settings for all audio, video, and other multimedia devices

Using the Video Sheet

The Video sheet of the Multimedia Properties dialog box provides the same video windows size controls found in both the ActiveMovie and Media Player applets. When you select a window size option, the image in the display shows a facsimile of what the clip will look like. Open the Window drop-down list, and you will see the following options:

■ *Original Size*. Makes the playback window the same size as that at which the original video was captured.

■ *Double Original Size*. Doubles the height and width of the original captured video.

- *1/16 of Screen Size.* Plays in a window that is 1/16 the size of the current display area.
- *1/4 of Screen Size.* Plays in a window that is 1/4 the size of the current display area.
- *1/2 of Screen Size.* Plays in a window that is half the size of the current display area.
- *Maximized.* Plays in a standard playback window that occupies the entire display.

The Full Screen radio button sets the video file to play back at the full size of the display. However, this mode does not run in a standard playback window; instead, all the other elements on the display are disabled to allow the video playback to take over the screen. For systems with older graphics cards, this dedicated video playback mode can help boost the playback frame rate of full-screen video clips.

Working with the Devices Sheet

The Devices sheet of the Multimedia Properties dialog box gives you access to drivers and hardware configurations for video devices and other multimedia components. The sheet provides a list of multimedia components under the Multimedia Drivers heading. To view the installed devices for a given component, click the plus sign (+) next to the item.

Part

V

Ch

24

When it comes to video controls, the most important stop is the entry called Video Compression Codecs. Here you will find a laundry list of video compression/decompression drivers, as shown in Figure 24.6, which allow the ActiveMovie and Media Player applets to recognize and play back digital video files.

FIG. 24.6

More codecs than you can shake a stick at: The Devices tab lets you see what types of video files your PC is equipped to handle.

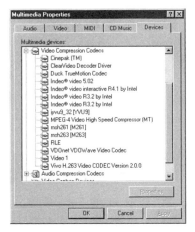

You can view the controls and properties associated with each codec by selecting an item and clicking the Properties button. The Properties dialog box also lets you remove the selected codec if you want. Some codec property boxes also include a Settings button, which might simply provide a splash screen showing the vendor and date (as the Cinepak codecs do, for example) or might provide controls for managing compression settings.

Also under the Devices tab is a heading for Video Capture devices. Here you will find driver entries for video capture cards, parallel port cameras (such as Connectix's QuickCam), and other video input devices. Individual configuration options for these devices (which are provided by the vendor) might be available from the Devices sheet using the Settings tab. If you do not have a capture device installed, the Video Capture Device item will not contain any underlying entries.

Understanding Video Compression

Behind the video formats are compression/decompression schemes called *codecs*. Codecs squeeze digital video down to a manageable size, but they require a matching driver on the playback to allow the video to be uncompressed and played. Windows 98 comes with a variety of codec drivers, which are listed in the Multimedia Properties dialog box found in the Control Panel.

While most codecs provide only video playback, some are designed to both compress and decompress video. The VDOWave codec from VDONet, for example, lets users conduct video conferences over the Internet. The Settings button in the VDOWave property box lets you set compression levels (see Figure 24.7).

FIG. 24.7
The web-centric VDOWave video codec lets you tailor the level of compression to suit the speed of your Internet connection.

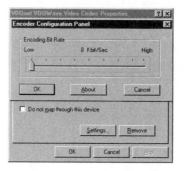

> **N O T E** Don't confuse video codecs with video file formats. A file format like AVI or MOV can often be compressed using a number of codecs. For example, AVI files can be compressed using Indeo, Cinepak, Video1, and TrueMotion codecs, just to name a few. ∎

Unlike file compression schemes such as PKZip, video compression is *lossy*. That means the codec throws out some visual data in an effort to achieve compression ratios as high as 100:1 or more. *Lossless* compression schemes, such as PKZip typically achieve compression ratios of about 1.7:1 or 2:1 in the best cases. By throwing out data, codecs allow video to play at data rates as low as 28.8Kbps for web-based video and 300Kbps for CD-ROM titles. However, the quality of these clips suffers, with poor resolutions, color degradation, and low frame rates that result in jerky playback.

These are some of the most common codecs:

- *Indeo.* Windows 98 provides version 5 of this venerable codec from Intel, which can provide improved quality over previous Indeo codecs. It also incorporates streaming capability, so that video clips can begin playing while the file loads—a critical feature for Internet-based video playback.

- *Cinepak.* Popular for both QuickTime and AVI file formats, Cinepak is widely used in multimedia titles because of its ability to handle high-action clips.

- *MPEG.* The most significant addition is support for MPEG in the ActiveMovie player. This high-quality, low-data rate codec provides near-VCR quality playback on fast Pentium PCs outfitted with video-accelerating graphics hardware.

- *Motion JPEG.* Used by video editing programs, this codec maintains every individual frame, so that users can later go in to the video file and make frame-by-frame changes and edits. Data rates do not go as low as MPEG, and video creators usually recompress to a more common format (such as Indeo or MPEG) after they finish editing. Motion JPEG is not provided in Windows 98.

Part
V
Ch
24

Looking at Windows 98 Video Handling

Underneath the interface, Microsoft speeds video performance using a technology called *DirectDraw*. This suite of developer tools, device drivers, and operating system components is part of the larger DirectX technology, which provides multimedia support for Windows 98.

DirectDraw is important because it allows inexpensive graphics hardware to boost video playback. The technology also provides a critical shortcut for video playback, so that graphics data can get to the screen faster. The most recent version of DirectDraw (part of DirectX 5.0), includes support for Intel's MMX-enhanced processors. Windows 98's ActiveMovie and Media Player applets both provide enhanced video playback on MMX-capable CPUs.

Graphics hardware can also help boost video performance. Virtually all of today's graphics boards use DirectDraw to provide video acceleration. These boards handle the following tasks:

- *Image scaling.* Often, video is played at twice its captured size in order to be large enough for the user to view comfortably. DirectDraw lets graphics cards create the additional pixels on the card (instead of inside the overburdened CPU) to keep things moving smoothly. It also lets cards average out the new pixels so that video doesn't become chunky or blocky when it is expanded.

- *Color space conversion.* DirectDraw also lets graphics cards convert video color data into a format your monitor can understand. This operation, which can account for up to 30 percent of the video playback workload, happens on the card so the CPU can be freed to improve frame rates.

Understanding the Video Underpinnings of Windows 98

Playing digital video is one of the most demanding things your PC can do. In order for digital video to play back under Windows 98, a variety of hardware and software underpinnings must be in place. These include:

- Windows 98 DirectDraw components and drivers
- Video-capable graphics hardware
- Appropriate video compression/decompression (codec) drivers
- Fast processor, disk media, and powerful CPU

Understanding File Formats

To make digital video comprehensible to PCs, a number of standard file formats are used. These formats all use a frame-based approach to displaying video, much the way cellulite film consists of a string of visual frames that are played quickly to deliver the illusion of motion. Sound is laid on top of the image stream, creating video.

In order to recognize a video file format, Windows 98 must have the proper drivers installed. By default, Windows 98 includes support for the following formats:

- *Audio Visual Interleave (AVI).* The most prevalent Windows-based video format, AVI was developed by Microsoft and is automatically recognized by the Media Player and ActiveMovie controls. It is designed to run on systems without dedicated video playback hardware, including older 486 machines.
- *QuickTime for Windows (MOV).* The first video file format remains popular both in multimedia titles and on the web. Unlike with AVI, Windows 98 won't automatically recognize video files with the .MOV file extension; however, ActiveMovie will.
- *Motion Pictures Expert Group (MPEG).* MPEG-1 video provides higher quality than AVI or QuickTime, but you'll need a fast Pentium (at least 90MHz) to get acceptable results with this complex codec. Windows 98's ActiveMovie control recognizes MPEG format-ted video files, but Media Player does not.

There are a variety of other less-common video formats on the market, including streaming video formats intended for web-based video playback. In fact, ActiveMovie provides streaming video support, in which it actually begins playing a video file before the entire file has loaded. This lets your video clips start with less delay.

Introducing DVD Video

One of the most significant advances in PC-based multimedia is the arrival of DVD, or Digital Versatile Disc. Based on 5.25-inch discs that look identical to CD-ROMs, DVD-ROM can store up to 4.7GB on a single side. Down the road, enhanced DVD-ROM discs will be able to nearly double the amount of data on each side. The standard also allows for two-sided discs, meaning that DVD-ROM discs will eventually hold as much as 17GB of data—perfect for broadcast-quality, high-resolution video.

In fact, DVD uses the same MPEG-2 video format seen in Direct Satellite Services (DSS) such as DirecTV, USSB, and PrimeStar. The problem is that MPEG-2 video is very complex, requiring hardware-based decompression to provide smooth playback of the broadcast-quality video. While fast MMX-enhanced PCs can play MPEG-2 video, hardware is needed to make it acceptable for viewing.

Windows 98 provides support for DVD-ROM drives and hardware, including components for handling MPEG-2 video and AC-3 surround sound audio. However, you will need to make sure you have the proper drivers to operate the DVD-ROM drive and the add-in board. Check with your vendor to make sure you have the proper drivers in place.

Part
V

Ch
24

Using Audio Tools in Windows 98

Windows 98 provides a variety of tools to let you play, edit, and create audio files. Those familiar with Windows 95 will find that many of the tools are largely unchanged in Windows 98, while new ones such as Windows 98's ActiveMovie control await.

PC-based audio comes in two forms: wave audio and MIDI. Wave audio, or WAV files, are digital representations of analog sound. When you record speech or music to the hard disk, for example, the resulting file is a wave audio file.

MIDI files (or musical instrument device interface) use a series of commands to tell your PC's sound hardware what notes and instruments to play. This makes for smaller files, but you are limited by the library of instruments available to your hardware and software.

Understanding the Audio Properties Box

You can find information on any audio file by right-clicking any WAV or MIDI file icon and selecting Properties from the shortcut menu. The properties sheet for WAV and MIDI files displays key information regarding the size, length, and format of the file. The General page displays file size and type information. Click the Details tab, and you'll get useful information such as the encoding scheme used to create a WAV file, as well as the duration of WAV and MIDI files (see Figure 24.8). You can sample both WAV and MIDI files from the Preview sheet of the Properties dialog box by clicking the Play button on the sheet. The clip will play directly from the sheet.

FIG. 24.8

From the Details sheet of the File Properties dialog box, you can check useful information such as the encoding format of wave files and the overall runtime of the audio clip.

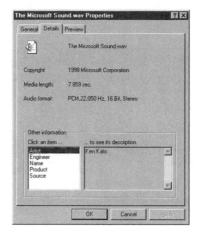

Playing Audio Files

Windows 98 provides a number of tools for playing back wave audio files, including:

- ActiveMovie control
- Sound Recorder
- Media Player

Both the Media Player and Sound Recorder are unchanged from Windows 95. The ActiveMovie control, however, is new and is an important resource for handling audio.

The easiest way to play a WAV or MIDI file in Windows 98 is to launch it directly from Windows 98 Explorer. For MIDI files, the ActiveMovie player launches and the file begins to play immediately. For WAV files, the Sound Recorder applet launches. In both cases, the applet closes immediately after the file finishes playing.

Playing Audio Files from ActiveMovie

To play an audio file using the ActiveMovie control, do the following:

1. Open the ActiveMovie control from the Windows 98 Start menu by clicking Start, Programs, Accessories, Multimedia, ActiveMovie Control.
2. In the Open dialog box, select Audio Files from the Files of Type drop-down list.
3. Navigate to the directory that contains the file you want to play. All files with valid audio file extensions (WAV or MID) appear in the dialog box.
4. Click the Open button, and the ActiveMovie control appears.

 If the ActiveMovie player is already open, you can play audio files by dragging and dropping the desired file's icon onto the ActiveMovie window.

5. Click the Play button. The WAV or MIDI file begins to play (see Figure 24.9).

FIG. 24.9

A position bar and time display prompt you during playback of files under ActiveMovie.

6. To stop the file, click the Stop button.

Playing Audio Files from Sound Recorder

You can also play wave audio file from the Windows 98 Sound Recorder. To do so, follow these steps:

1. Open the Sound Recorder applet from the Windows 98 Start menu by clicking Start, Programs, Accessories, Entertainment, Sound Recorder.

2. Select File, Open.

3. In the Open dialog box, navigate to the file you want to open. Select it and click the Open button.

4. The Sound Recorder interface reappears. Click the Play button to hear the sound file.

5. Click the Stop button to stop playing the file.

Playing Audio Files from Media Player

To play audio files from the Windows 98 Media Player, do the following:

1. Open the Media Player applet from the Windows 98 Start menu by clicking Start, Programs, Accessories, Entertainment, Media Player.

2. Select File, Open to go to the Open dialog box.

3. Open the Files of Type drop-down list and select either Sound (*.WAV) or MIDI Sequencer (*.MID;*.RMI).

4. Navigate to the directory that contains the file you want to play. All files with the selected audio file extension appear in the dialog box.

 You can also launch files from the Device menu. Click Device, and then select the media type from the numbered list. The Open dialog box then appears, displaying only files of the selected file type.

5. Click the Open button. The file name appears in the window bar of the Media Player.

6. Click the Play button, and the WAV or MIDI file begins to play. The slider control will advance as the file plays.

7. To stop the file, click the Stop button.

Playing Audio CDs

Like Windows 95, Windows 98 lets you play audio CDs in your CD-ROM drive using the CD Player applet shown in Figure 24.10.

Part
V

Ch
24

FIG. 24.10

The CD Player applet provides all the functions of a standard audio CD player.

To play CDs, do the following:

1. Open the CD Player applet from the Windows 98 Start menu by clicking Start, Programs, Accessories, Multimedia, CD Player.

2. Place an audio CD into the CD-ROM drive.

3. Click the Play button just to the right of the information display screen.

4. Jump to the previous or next track by clicking the Back or Forward button.

5. To reverse or fast forward within a track, click either the Reverse or Fast Forward button until you reach the desired point in the song.

6. To stop play, click the Stop button. (Or, click the Pause to keep your place in the current track.)

7. Eject the audio CD by clicking the Eject/Load button.

Working with the Windows 98 Sound Recorder

If you want to record or edit WAV files in Windows 98, you'll want to use the Sound Recorder applet. This section introduces you to Windows 98 audio editing and recording.

When you open a file in Sound Recorder, you see a visual representation of the audio file, including a status bar that indicates how far along in the file you are. The buttons beneath the slider bar control operations such as fast forward and rewind, similar to those on a tape recorder. The Position reading shows the current point in the audio file, and the Length reading tells you the complete duration of the file in seconds.

The File menu contains a number of familiar options, including commands for saving audio files. The Revert command lets you undo edits.

Recording WAV Files with Sound Recorder

If you want to record a WAV audio file, the only way to do so within Windows 98 is with the Sound Recorder applet. To record an audio file, do the following:

1. Open the Sound Recorder by clicking Start, Programs, Accessories, Entertainment, Sound Recorder.

2. To begin recording, click the red record button.

3. When you finish recording, click the Stop button.

4. Prepare to save the file by clicking File, Save As.

5. Click the Change button in the Save As dialog box.

6. In the Sound Selection dialog box, set the audio quality for the file. You can select Telephone, Radio, or CD quality settings from the Name drop-down box, or you can fine-tune the file encoding by using the options in the Format and Attributes drop-down lists.

7. When you're satisfied with the settings, click OK and then click Save to save the file to the desired location.

Editing WAV Files

Sound Recorder provides some useful editing tools that let you enhance existing WAV files. These capabilities can be accessed from the application menus. You can perform any of the following tasks:

- *Insert a wave file within another wave file.* Go to the point in the open file where you want to insert a file. Click Edit, Insert File. From the Insert File dialog box select the file you want to insert.

- *Mix two sound files together.* With the initial wave file open, click Edit, Mix with File. In the Mix with File dialog box, select the file you want to mix with the original wave file.

- *Delete part of a wave file.* To shave a portion off the front or back of an open wave file, go to the point in the file you desire, and click Edit. Select either Delete Before Current Position or Delete After Current Position. The file will then begin or end at the selected point.

- *Adjust volume and speed.* From the Effects menu, click Increase Volume (by 25%) or Decrease Volume to make the file play back more or less loudly. To speed or slow the rate of playback, click Effects, Increase Speed (by 100%) or Decrease Speed.

- *Reverse playback of the file.* To play the open wave file from back to front, click Effects, Reverse.

- *Add an echo.* Click Effects, Add Echo to make the file sound as if it is echoing.

Part
V

Ch
24

Saving Wave Files

When you save WAV files in Sound Recorder, you can set the compression and audio format to best suit your needs. While recordings of your favorite CDs might need high-fidelity digital playback, simple sound effects and speech clips can use less space-consuming formats. Click File, Save As. In the Save As dialog box, click the Change button. The Sound Selection dialog box lets you set the compression format, as well as the bit rate and depth of the wave file. From the Name drop-down list (shown in Figure 24.11), select one of the following three options:

Telephone Quality: 8-bit, 11.025-kHz, mono

Radio Quality: 8-bit, 22.05-kHz, mono

CD Quality: 16-bit, 44.1-kHz, stereo

CD quality is best for recorded music or any clip that requires very precise playback. Radio quality is a good compromise for music or speech clips because it conserves disk space while keeping much of the audio fidelity. Telephone quality minimizes file sizes but results in limited audio quality.

FIG. 24.11
From the Sound Selection dialog box, you can choose from preconfigured audio formats, or you can create customized schemes of your own.

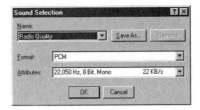

Working with ActiveMovie Audio

You can use ActiveMovie to play wave and MIDI files. In both cases, the new applet gives you a number of controls to let you customize playback.

Open an ActiveMovie File

You can load a file into ActiveMovie by dragging and dropping a Wave or MIDI file onto the application window. It will take a few seconds for the file to load, during which time the application bar will display something like this:

```
Canyon.mid (Opening)
```

After the file is loaded into ActiveMovie, you will see the following file information displayed in the black window:

- The total file runtime is shown at the left.
- The current position in the file is displayed in large characters in the center (the word time appears directly below it to indicate the unit of measure).

Play an ActiveMovie File

To play a file, do any of the following:

- Double-click anywhere on the black window
- Right-click anywhere on the black window and select Run from the context menu that appears.
- Click the Play control button at the bottom of the window.

Explore the Properties Sheet

You can optimize audio playback by right-clicking the ActiveMovie display interface and selecting Properties from the context menu. The ActiveMovie Control properties sheet includes four tabs:

- *Playback* enables you to control volume and playback selection.
- *Movie Size* enables you to set the size of the video playback window.
- *Controls* enables you to customize ActiveMovie interface elements.
- *Advanced* provides information on ActiveMovie filters.

Of these, Playback and Controls are important for audio playback.

Using Playback Properties   The Playback sheet of the Properties dialog box (see Figure 24.12) provides useful tools for controlling the way the open audio file plays.

Part

V

Ch

24

FIG. 24.12
Volume and Timing controls let you customize playback of audio files.

Slider bars located in the Volume area on the left side of the Playback sheet control volume and balance. Here's how to use them:

- Slide the vertical slider bar up or down to increase or decrease playback volume.
- Slide the horizontal slider bar to the left to increase output on the left speaker, or to the right to increase output on the right speaker.

In the Timing area, you can do the following:

■ To constrain playback to a desired portion of the audio file, enter a time value in the Start and Stop text boxes.

■ To play a file over a specific number of times, enter the desired value in the Play Count text box.

■ To play a file over continuously until you stop it, select the Auto Repeat radio button.

■ To automatically reset the file to the beginning after it plays, check the Auto Rewind check box.

Using Controls Properties   The Controls sheet of the Properties dialog box gives you access to interface controls for playing files, as shown in Figure 24.13.

FIG. 24.13

You can slim down the ActiveMovie interface by turning off many of the VCR-like control elements on the display. You can even tweak the colors.

Follow these guidelines for using the controls on this sheet:

■ Check the Display Panel check box to view the file information box.

■ Check the Control Panel check box to view the VCR-like control buttons and the Trackbar slider bar.

■ In the Control Panel area, check any one of the Position controls, Selection controls, and Trackbar check boxes to make the appropriate controls available on the ActiveMovie interface.

■ In the Colors area, you can customize the ActiveMovie display panel by selecting colors from the Foreground and Background color buttons.

Working with Media Player Audio

The Media Player applet has been replaced by ActiveMovie in Windows 98, but the Media Player program is still available if you want to use it. Once a file is loaded into Media Player, you can access a number of controls from the menu bar.

Working with the Options Dialog Box

The Options dialog box lets you control how audio files play back. To get to it, click Edit, Options. You can do the following in the Options box:

- Check the Auto Rewind check box to set the file back to the beginning after it stops playing.

- Check the Auto Repeat check box to have the file continuously play over and over until it's stopped by the user.

The OLE Object area contains tools for customizing playback of audio files within separate applications. Follow these guidelines for using the objects in the OLE Object area:

- Check the Control Bar on Playback check box to have VCR-like control buttons appear on audio clips embedded into documents. Enter the name you want to appear with embedded clips into the Caption text box.

- Check the Border Around Object check box to have a thin border appear around the embedded audio file icon.

- Check the Play in Client Document check box to have the audio clip play without invoking the Media Player interface.

You'll also find useful tools in the Device menu. These are some of the things you can do:

- To open files from the Device menu, choose the desired file type from the numbered list. The Open dialog box appears, showing only files whose extensions match the type you selected.

- To launch the Windows 98 Volume Control applet, click Device, Volume Control. For more on this resource, go to the section "Working with the Volume Control Tool," later in this chapter.

- Click Device, Properties to open the MCI Waveform Device Setup dialog box. Here you can adjust the size of the wave audio buffer by sliding the horizontal scroll bar element left or right, as shown in Figure 24.14.

Part
V

Ch
24

FIG. 24.14

Avoid choppy audio playback by increasing the memory buffer in the MCI Waveform Driver Setup dialog box.

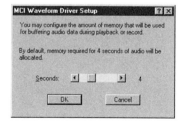

Working with the Selection Dialog Box

Click Edit, Selection to go to the Selections dialog box. From here, you can demarcate a portion of the file to be copied to the Windows 98 Clipboard. Use these methods to select the portion you want to copy:

- Click All to select the entire audio file so you can copy it to the Clipboard for pasting elsewhere.

- Click None to clear any existing selection.

- Click From to enter the start point (measured in minutes:seconds:tenths) of the selected area. Then enter the end point in the To box, or enter the length of the desired selection in the Size box.

Using the CD Player

The CD Player lets you create custom play lists by entering information about the currently loaded CD and then setting up the list of tracks you want to play. When the audio CD is loaded later, Windows 98 recognizes the unique bit pattern of the disc and calls up the information you entered. Other features for tweaking playback are outlined in the next two subsections.

Creating a Custom Play list

To create a custom play list for a loaded audio CD, you use the controls in the Disc Settings dialog box, shown in Figure 24.15.

FIG. 24.15
The play list feature is one of the most powerful options offered by the CD Player.

Follow these steps to build a play list:

1. Click Disc, Edit Play List to bring up the CD Player: Disc Settings dialog box.

2. Enter the artist's name and title of the album in the Artist and Title text boxes.

3. To name the album tracks, select a track in the Available Tracks scroll box and enter the song title in the Track text box. Click Set Name. Repeat for each track.

4. In the Play List scroll box, select any tracks you want to remove and click the Remove button.

 You can select multiple tracks at once by holding down the Ctrl key and clicking on the tracks. To select a range of continuous items, click the first track, hold down Shift, and then click the last track; the two you selected and all of those in between are selected.

5. To reorder tracks, click the desired track and wait until the note icon appears above the selected item. Then drag the item so that the position arrow to the left of the Play List scroll box points above the track you want to move it to. Then release the mouse button.

6. You can restore any deleted tracks to the Play List scroll box by selecting the track in the Available Tracks scroll box and clicking the Add button.

Touring the CD Player

The CD Player provides a lot of controls in its compact interface, matching the functionality of dedicated CD players. In the View menu, you will find the following commands:

- *Toolbar* hides and displays icons that let you set play lists, change the information display view, and adjust play rules.

- *Disc/Track Info* hides and displays the Artist, Title, and Track drop-down controls.

- *Status Bar* hides and displays text at the bottom of the applet showing total play time of the CD as well as the play time of the selected track. The status bar also provides information about icons on the toolbar.

- *Track Time Elapsed*, *Track Time Remaining*, and *Disc Time Remaining* determine what information appears in the main display window of the CD Player applet.

- *Volume Control* launches the Windows 98 Volume Control applet.

The Options menu offers several other useful commands. Random Order, Continuous Play, and Intro Play let you determine how the CD Player will move through the tracks on the installed audio CD. The Preferences command gives you access to the Preferences dialog box, where you can adjust appearance display, limit the intro play length, and set other options, as shown in Figure 24.16.

FIG. 24.16

Use the Preferences dialog box to tweak the CD Player interface and behavior.

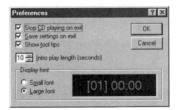

Part
V

Ch
24

Working with the Volume Control Tool

Windows 98 provides one-stop shopping for tweaking the level and balance settings for your sound card's various inputs and outputs. Not only can you adjust overall volume, you can adjust the volume and balance of individual inputs and outputs, including wave and MIDI audio output and CD audio playback.

You can access the Volume Control using any of the following methods:

■ Double-click the speaker icon on the Windows 98 taskbar.

■ Launch the applet from the Start button by clicking Start, Programs, Accessories, Entertainment, Volume Control.

■ Launch the applet from the Media Player by clicking Device, Volume Control.

N O T E   The easiest way to adjust volume is to click the taskbar speaker icon. A small slider bar control appears that lets you either adjust the volume level or mute the audio altogether. The small control disappears when you click on any other area of the screen. ▨

The Volume Control (shown in Figure 24.17) provides controls for playback and recording operation, as well as for specific audio applications such as voice recognition. Each audio component is represented by a horizontal slider bar with which you adjust the balance and a vertical slider with which you adjust volume. A Select check box allows you to turn a given component on or off.

FIG. 24.17

The Windows 98 Volume Control is the master control for setting balance and volume settings.

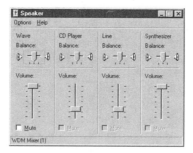

Available Controls

The default view for the Volume Control is for playback devices. Table 24.1 outlines the Volume Control components.

Table 24.1 Component Support in the Volume Control Tool

Control Name	Operation	What it does
Volume Control	Playback	All audio output
Line-In	Playback, Record	Audio originating from the sound board's line-in port
Microphone	Playback, Record	Audio captured by the microphone
CD	Playback, Record	Audio played from the CD-ROM drive's analog out port
MIDI	Playback	Playback of MIDI files
Wave	Playback	Playback of wave files
Record Control	Record	All audio input
Voice Commands	Other	Voice input from microphone

Part
V

Ch
24

Accessing Volume Control Settings

To access the volume control settings for playback, record, or other applications, click Options, Properties and then click the desired radio button in the Adjust Volume For area of the Properties dialog box.

In the Show the Following Volume Controls list, select the check boxes for the items you want to have displayed in the Volume Control. Any item that you deselect (remove the check mark from its box) will not be displayed when the Volume Control is launched.

If more than one audio device is installed in your PC, you can select which device to work with. To do so, select the desired device from the Mixer Device drop-down list.

Working with Audio in the Windows 98 Device Manager

If you want to tinker with hardware under Windows 98, you need to know your way around the Device Manager. To access audio controls under the Device Manager, do the following:

1. Click Start, Settings, Control Panel, and click the System icon.
2. Click the Device Manager tab.
3. Click the plus sign (+) next to Sound, Video, and Game Controllers. An entry for your audio hardware appears, as shown in Figure 24.18.

FIG. 24.18
Click the Sound, Video, and Game Controllers item, and your installed audio hardware will be displayed.

4. Select the audio device that appears, and click Properties.

The Properties dialog box that appears features three tabs: General, Driver, and Resources.

Inside the General Sheet

The General sheet identifies the manufacturer and model of the selected device, as well as information on any conflicts in the Device status area. It also lets you tailor the device for use by a specific system profile.

Inside the Driver Sheet

The Driver sheet lets you view information about the device drivers used to run the selected hardware. To see which driver files are loaded for the device, click the Driver File Details button and browse the Driver files list on the page that appears.

An intriguing new feature is the automated driver update facility in Windows 98. Here's how to use it:

1. On the Driver tab of the properties sheet, click the Update Driver button. The Upgrade Device Driver Wizard launches.
2. Click the Next button.
3. Select the top radio button to search for a more recent driver, and then click Next.
4. In the next dialog box, tell Windows 98 where to look for the new drivers. Click the appropriate check box to have Windows 98 search the floppy drive, the CD-ROM drive, a subdirectory on the hard disk, or the Internet.
5. Click Next to begin searching the selected areas and download the new driver.

Inside the Resources Sheet

Finally, the Resources sheet lets you change the hardware resources for the audio device, including IRQ, DMA, and base I/O address settings. The Conflicting Device list box at the bottom of the sheet prompts you if a hardware device conflict is present. If so, you can adjust the resource settings of a device by doing the following:

1. Deselect the Use Automatic Settings check box.

2. Select the desired resource item from the Resource Type list, and then click the Change Setting button.

3. On the next page, enter the desired resource settings. You can also use the spinner controls to advance or decrease the number.

4. Click OK twice to put the new settings into effect.

Working with the Multimedia Properties Controls

Part
V
Ch
24

The Multimedia Properties dialog box, accessible through the Control Panel, is ground zero for managing multimedia settings in Windows 98. Here you will find resources for handling audio drivers and hardware, as well as for using compression schemes when saving files. To open the Multimedia Properties dialog box, click Start, Settings, Control Panel. Select the Multimedia icon, and the Properties dialog box appears.

The Multimedia Properties dialog box contains nine tabs, five of which directly affect audio:

- *Audio.* Provides record and playback line level controls, as well as record-quality settings.

- *Video.* Lets you size video playback windows.

- *MIDI.* Provides controls for adding and configuring additional MIDI devices such as keyboards.

- *CD Music.* Controls volume of audio CD playback through the CD-ROM drive's analog out port.

- *Advanced.* Provides access to driver and configuration settings for all audio, video, and other multimedia devices.

Using the Audio Sheet

The Audio sheet of the Multimedia Properties dialog box is divided into two sections: Playback and Recording. Each lets you adjust overall volume level settings. What's more, Windows 98 adds intriguing controls for audio playback and recording.

Controlling Audio Playback Settings   You can select the audio playback device you want to control by picking it from the Preferred Device list. To change settings for the device, click the Advanced Properties button.

The Speakers sheet, shown in Figure 24.19, lets you configure Windows 98 for your particular speaker setup. The large image depicting a PC with speakers changes to reflect your selection. Click OK to put the new settings into effect.

FIG. 24.19

The Speakers sheet of the Advanced Audio Properties dialog box lets you tweak audio playback to suit your speakers.

To tweak audio playback and your system's performance, click the Performance tab. The Hardware Acceleration slider bar tells Windows 98 to employ more available hardware features to audio playback. If you experience problems with playback, try moving the slider to the left. Deactivating acceleration features can help eliminate conflicts.

The Sample Rate Conversion Quality slider bar determines how much processing power the PC applies to creating realistic audio playback. If your system is very fast, move this slider to the right. You should enjoy better audio without an unacceptable loss of performance. To return to the original settings, click the Restore Defaults button.

Customizing Wave Audio Recording Profiles   As with playback, you can adjust settings for audio recording. Select the recording device from the Preferred Device list, and then click the Advanced Properties button to go to the Advanced Audio Properties dialog box.

Here you will find only a Performance tab, which looks identical to that for audio playback described above. Moving the Hardware Acceleration and the Sample Rate Conversion Quality slider bars lets you trade audio quality for smoother performance and better stability. To return to the original settings, click the Restore Defaults button.

Using the MIDI Sheet

The MIDI sheet of the Multimedia Properties dialog box lets you configure and install MIDI devices such as keyboards and MIDI-capable sound cards. By default, the Single Instrument radio button is selected, denoting the primary MIDI device on the sound board.

Create a Custom MIDI Scheme   If you have external MIDI devices attached to your PC, you can create a custom configuration to employ these devices. To create a custom configuration, do the following:

1. Click the Custom configuration radio button.
2. Click the Configure button.
3. In the MIDI Configuration dialog box, select the desired channel and click the Change button.
4. In the Change MIDI Instrument dialog box, select the desired MIDI device in the Instrument drop-down control and click OK.
5. To assign the new configuration a name, click the Save As button (or simply click OK to make the changed settings your default configuration).
6. Enter a name for the new MIDI scheme and click OK. Click OK again to return to the MIDI sheet.

If you select your custom MIDI scheme, the assigned device plays when the corresponding channel is called up in a MIDI score.

Add a MIDI Device   You can also use this dialog box to install a new MIDI device, such as a keyboard. To add a new device, follow these steps:

1. From the MIDI sheet on the Multimedia Properties dialog box, click the Add New Instrument button.
2. In the MIDI Installation Wizard dialog box, select the MIDI port the device will be connected to and click Next.
3. Install the disk with the device's MIDI definition into the A:\ drive and click Browse.
4. In the Open dialog box, select the appropriate .IDF file and click Open.
5. Click the Next button.
6. In the Instrument Name text box, enter a name for the new device. Then click Finish.

Adjusting Audio CD Playback

This sheet lets you set the volume of playback for audio CDs played in CD-ROM drives. Here's how to use the controls:

- The CD-ROM Drive drop-down list lets you select the drive to configure (allowing you to work with more than one drive).
- If your CD-ROM sends audio CD music over the system bus, select the Digital CD Playback Enable check box to get enhanced audio CD playback.
- Adjust the volume of the selected CD-ROM drive by moving the Headphone slider bar left or right.

When you finish adjusting the settings, click OK to put your changes into effect.

Part

V

Ch

24

Working with the Devices Sheet

The Devices sheet of the Multimedia Properties dialog box provides access to drivers and hardware configurations for audio devices and other multimedia components. This sheet provides a list of multimedia components under the Multimedia Drivers heading. To view the installed devices for a given component, click the plus sign (+) next to the item, as shown in Figure 24.20.

FIG. 24.20

The Device sheet of the Multimedia Properties dialog box provides access to a host of audio devices and controls.

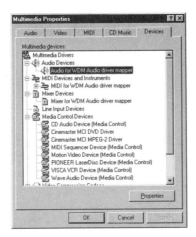

You can view the controls and properties associated with each device by selecting an item and clicking the Properties button. From the Properties dialog box for any component, you can deactivate or remove the device. Some device properties sheets also include a Settings button, which takes you to the corresponding controls for the hardware.

In addition to wave and MIDI devices, the Devices sheet includes a roster of items under the Audio Compression Codecs heading. These compression drivers let Windows 98 save sound files in compact format, and they are listed in order of priority. Higher priority codecs are more likely to be used by applications than are lower priority codecs. You can change the priority by selecting a codec, clicking the Properties button, and selecting a new priority number in the Change Priority From drop-down list (see Figure 24.21).

FIG. 24.21

Tell Windows 98 how to compress audio files from the Codec Properties dialog box.

Understanding the Audio Underpinnings of Windows 98

Much of what is new about audio in Windows 98 relates to the plumbing. Under the graphical interface, a technology called DirectSound works. DirectSound is a standard set of components, drivers, and development tools that provide audio handling for Windows 95 and 98. It also provides a standard interface for audio hardware and applications that work with Windows 98.

Understanding DirectSound

Does DirectSound make the Sound Blaster standard irrelevant? Not yet. DOS-based games continue to look for specific audio hardware, with Creative Labs' Sound Blaster boards remaining the most often supported hardware. And Windows 98 continues to provide driver support for Sound Blaster boards within the operating system because these boards make up a large percentage of the installed base.

Part

V

Ch

24

In addition to the basic audio handling of DirectSound, Windows 98 includes a technology called DirectSound3D. This component of Windows 98's multimedia toolbox lets the latest games and multimedia titles deliver 3D sound to provide enhanced realism. DirectSound3D allows games to produce so-called *positional audio*, which makes sounds seem like they are coming from specific directions. Programmers can tell Windows 98 where to put sounds based on what is going on inside a game at the time—a real benefit for immersive gameplay.

In order to take advantage of the new audio handling capabilities, you need a sound board that is DirectSound compliant. What does that mean? Basically, your sound card must have DirectSound drivers, which might be found on the Windows 98 web site or at the sound board vendor's web site.

For games and title to take full advantage of DirectSound and DirectSound3D, they must also support the technology. Those lacking the new audio tools will still work fine because Windows 98 continues to provide the familiar media control interface (MCI) commands that have been used by Windows programmers for years. However, you will get the best performance and audio features from new DirectSound-enabled programs.

Understanding Wave Audio Files

Digital audio comes in two forms: waveform audio (WAV files) and MIDI. WAV files are digital representations of analog sound, much as a graphics bitmap is a representation of a real-world image. In fact, Windows WAV files are similar to the digital audio stored on audio CDs.

When your system records a WAV file, the incoming signal is converted to a series of bits that represent the curve of the original analog signal. The quality of a digital audio file—and also its size—is related to its resolution and frequency. For example, CD-quality audio has a resolution of 16 bits and frequency of 44.1KHz, while the audio found in most AVI video clips is about 8 bits and 22KHz.

To understand what goes into a wave file, you need to know about its components:

- *Sampling rate.* The number of times each second that the system takes a snapshot of the analog audio signal. Sampling rate is measured in kilohertz (KHz), which represents thousands of samples each second. Audio CDs store sound at 44.1KHz.

- *Bit depth.* The number of bits that are dedicated to each sample. 16-bit audio, which is also used by audio CDs, puts two bytes of data to each sample.

- *Stereo/mono.* Stereo playback stores two channels of sound, which can vary to provide spatial quality to the audio playback. Mono playback uses a single channel.

The audio format determines the digital quality of the sound, but sound hardware is important, too. Interference inside the PC and the quality of audio components both affect sound output. Many sound boards have inferior frequency responses, which means they do not accurately reproduce sounds at the high and low range of human hearing. Most boards also produce poor signal-to-noise ratios (a measure of how much noise is in the output) with performance that falls far below that of CD players.

Some boards, such as Creative Labs' Sound Blaster AWE 64 Gold, provide good audio quality. However, even the best sound board won't match the quality of consumer audio components.

Hardware aside, why don't all clips use 16-bit 44.1KHz audio? Table 24.2 shows just how large a minute of uncompressed digital audio can get.

Table 24.2 Size of One Minute of Uncompressed Stereo Wave Audio

Frequency	8-bit	16-bit
11KHz	1.2MB	2.6M
22KHz	2.6MB	5.2M
44.1KHz	5.2MB	10.4M

To conserve disk space, you can reduce the number of bits dedicated to modeling the curve of analog audio. For example, by capturing to mono format instead of stereo, you cut the size of the file in half because only one channel of information is being stored. After that, you can reduce the number of times each second that you sample the incoming analog signal. By going from 44.1KHz (or 44,100 samples per second) to 22.05KHz (22,050 samples), you can cut the file size in half again. Dropping to 11.025KHz provides further economies. Finally, you can lower the number of bits dedicated to each audio sample. Dropping from 16-bit to 8-bit resolution again shaves the file size in half.

Unfortunately, the less sound you store, the less realistic the results. Losing the stereo data can render playback flat and leave it without spatial cues, such as when instruments or sounds come from one speaker or another. Dropping the bit depth can add audible hiss to sound files and can lessen the precision of reproduction. Lowering the frequency means that the audio is being sampled less often, so the card is unable to smoothly re-create the changes in sound.

Another way to conserve space is through compression. Like video files, audio compression techniques reduce file size by coding redundant information in a compact format and even by throwing out some aural information. Windows 98 includes several compression schemes:

- *DSP Group TrueSpeech.* (Speech-specific codec)
- *Fraunhofer IIS MPEG Layer-3 Codec.* (Streaming audio compression scheme)
- *Lernout & Hauspie Codecs.* (Speech-specific codec)
- *Microsoft ADPCM.* (General purpose codec)
- *Microsoft CCITT G.711 A-Law and u-Law.* (Video conferencing audio)
- *Microsoft GSM 6.10 Audio.* (General purpose codec)
- *Microsoft IMA ADPCM.* (Best general-purpose scheme)
- *Microsoft PCM Converter* (General purpose codec)
- *VivoActive Audio Decompressor.* (Audio handling for streaming video)
- *Voxware Audio Codecs.* (Speech-specific codec for audio conferencing)

Part
V

Ch
24

Understanding MIDI Files

The other half of the Windows audio scheme is MIDI. MIDI is actually a standard from the music industry, developed for synthesizers and other professional audio equipment. Unlike WAV files, which are digital representations of analog sound, MIDI files are composed of simple instructions that tell a MIDI device what to do. A MIDI file consists of instructions that tell your sound card which notes to play, with which instruments, and at what volume.

Of course, in order for these instructions to work, your sound board must be able to understand MIDI instructions. More importantly, all sound boards and MIDI audio equipment must work with the same set of instructions so that when a MIDI file calls for instrument number 98, the same instrument is played on all hardware. Instrument identifications are standardized under the General MIDI standard, which comprises 128 MIDI instruments.

 Make sure your sound card supports the General MIDI standard. General MIDI consists of 128 instruments and defines their identification for all audio equipment. Some boards can have more than 128 instrument sounds, but they must comply with General MIDI in order to work reliably with MIDI files.

There are two types of MIDI: wavetable synthesis and FM synthesis. Until about two or three years ago, most sound boards provided inexpensive FM synthesis MIDI. FM synthesis is an innovative scheme in which two or more signals are mixed to emulate the sound of actual instruments. While FM MIDI synthesis can play back any MIDI file, the scheme lacks the ability to produce realistic instrument sounds, particularly when many instruments are involved.

For top-quality MIDI playback, you need a board that supports wavetable MIDI. Wavetable MIDI cards use samples of actual instrument recordings to produce realistic music. When a

MIDI file calls for a trumpet to play a C note, the boards play an actual sample of that instrument. Because it would take too much room to store every note of every instrument, boards use algorithms to produce the proper sounds from the set of samples.

To get best results, your sound hardware should provide at least 16-voice polyphony. *Polyphony* refers to the capability to play more than one sound at once. For example, many MIDI scores play a veritable desktop orchestra, requiring 20 or even 32 MIDI voices to play at the same time.

N O T E   Creative Lab's Sound Blaster 64 AWE provides 64-voice polyphony, handling 32 voices in hardware on the card and another 32 voices through the PC's CPU. ▦

Many boards now provide software-based wavetable MIDI, which uses system memory and the PC's CPU to process MIDI sounds. While the scheme reduces cost on the sound board, the work of juggling MIDI sounds can bog down older Pentium PCs. In addition, software MIDI won't work with software that runs DOS mode, which includes some popular flight simulators.

Some sound boards also allow you to work with custom MIDI sounds, which is useful for adding effects and other noises to games and titles. Custom MIDI sounds are loaded from the system hard disk into the sound board or system memory so that the applications can play them back.

Looking at the New Sound Boards

Finally, Windows 98 is enabling a new market of audio products: PCI-based sound boards. Until recently, virtually all sound boards had to conform to Creative Labs' Sound Blaster scheme in order to ensure compatibility with the universe of software on the market. Under Windows 95 and 98, DirectSound now provides the new standard target for both software and hardware makers.

Unlike the Sound Blaster standard, which requires static IRQ, DMA, and base I/O assignments, DirectSound is tailored to work with the dynamic resource environment of Windows 98. The Plug and Play PCI bus can shift a sound board's resources to suit the current system needs, and software will still be able to find and use the hardware. With Sound Blaster cards, such a resource shift would disable the audio device until the resources were reconfigured.

What's more, PCI-based sound cards enjoy the high-speed data connection of the PCI bus, which runs at up to 132MB/s, versus 5MB/s for ISA. This allows software to send up to 20 independent channels of audio to the sound card, each of which can be managed and transformed individually. ISA cards, by contrast, can handle just one or two such channels.

Multi-channel audio is critical for true 3D sound and for home theater-like surround sound. DVD-ROM titles, for example, will use the Dolby AC-3 audio encoding scheme to push surround sound audio through five positioned speakers and a front-mounted subwoofer, while games will use multi-channel audio to independently juggle voices, music scores, and sound effects in real time.

Looking Ahead to USB Audio

Windows 98 is also opening up audio on the new Universal Serial Bus (USB). Using the Windows Driver Model (WDM) driver technology, which unifies Windows 95 and 98 and Windows NT drivers, future audio hardware will work over USB instead of the PCI or ISA bus. The benefit: greatly enhanced wave audio fidelity.

Some USB speakers from companies like Altec Lansing are actually digital. Normally, digital audio files are converted to analog electrical pulses on the sound board by a device called a *digital-to-analog converter* (DAC). Unfortunately, the electromagnetic frequencies (EMF) given off inside the PC's case distort the analog signal, producing poor audio fidelity. USB audio hardware will allow the digital audio to stay digital until it actually reaches the external speaker device, eliminating the disruptive EMF problem. Conversion will happen at the speaker itself.

Audio CD playback will also get a change. Gone will be the analog line-out connection running from the CD-ROM drive to the sound board. Instead, audio CD output will be moved digitally over the ISA or PCI bus to the sound card, where it will be converted to analog format—the same approach used to handle WAV files. ●

Part
V

Ch
24

Using Windows 98 to Play Games and Watch TV

by Michael Desmond

In this chapter

Windows and Arcade-Style Games

Windows 98 helps turn PCs into true entertainment centers. Windows 98 supports games, professional-quality video playback, and TV broadcasts. This chapter introduces you to some of Windows 98's most advanced and intriguing capabilities.

Gaming is big business, and Microsoft knows it. But until very recently, the majority of games were developed to play directly on DOS, inviting a raft of compatibility and resource problems for those who played them. Windows 98 includes a set of refined technologies and features designed to lure both game developers and game players to the new operating system.

What Is DirectX?

At the core of this effort is a set of technologies called *DirectX*. This set of device drivers, programming APIs, and Windows 98 components enables Windows 98 to handle a broad range of gaming applications, from rapid-fire screen updates to responsive and reliable input device operation. For users, the benefits are immediate. Games can be installed and played more reliably, and they can take advantage of accelerating hardware like 3D graphics cards and sound boards. What's more, they can even run side-by-side with mundane applications like spreadsheets and word processors.

DirectX includes the following components:

- *DirectDraw and DirectVideo:* Boost performance of 2D and 3D graphics for all applications.
- *Direct3D:* Enables standard 3D graphics handling and acceleration.
- *DirectSound and DirectSound 3D:* Provide a standard for managing audio, including positional 3D audio for producing the effect of surround sound on two speakers.
- *DirectInput:* Controls input devices such as joysticks and gamepads.
- *DirectPlay:* Provides standard tools for multiplayer gaming over phone lines, networks, and serial cables.

All of these provide a series of common interfaces to the hardware on your PC. Game makers write code to the appropriate DirectX components and then move on to making their games work well. Windows 98 and the DirectX components then handle the task of making things happen behind the scenes. The result: Vastly improved compatibility with all types of hardware.

N O T E Older DOS and Windows games not written for DirectX will still run fine on your DirectX-equipped PC, they'll just lack access to performance-enhancing shortcuts and acceleration. Games that use an older version of DirectX, such as DirectX 2.0 or 3.0, will enjoy some performance benefits but might not be capable of taking full advantage of all the available features. ■

Performance Issues

Just as important, DirectX enables much improved performance under Windows 98. One reason game makers wrote software for DOS was because the simple operating system—with its direct access to hardware devices—allowed developers to squeeze every ounce of performance out of systems. Windows 98, by contrast, uses thick layers of code to ensure compatibility, which produces the predictable result of slowed performance.

DirectX provides a shortcut for developers. While Microsoft still foists strict standards to maintain compatibility, DirectX lets developers send commands directly to graphics hardware, audio components, and other areas of the PC. The streamlined approach results in higher frame rates and more responsive play, as illustrated in Figure 25.1

In addition, the common set of gaming functions means that chip makers can design hardware to accelerate DirectX-based games. For example, games that use Direct3D to create 3D graphics can gain a performance benefit from a wide range of Direct3D-aware graphics cards. These cards take the performance burden off the CPU, allowing other areas of the game to become more responsive.

FIG. 25.1

Fast-action 3D games such as Quake 2 were impossible to create under Windows until DirectX APIs provided a standard way for developers to get top performance for demanding titles and games.

Part

V

Ch

25

When it comes to hard-core 3D game playing, nothing can replace a fast CPU. In fact, the best 3D boards, such as Diamond's Voodoo2 based on the 3Dfx Voodoo2 chip, are constrained mainly by the CPU. The reason: 3D graphics boards generally handle display operations, such as drawing textures and triangles, juggling lighting, and other effects. But before this happens, the CPU must do what is called geometry and setup. During that step, the system decides where all the triangles will go and how they will interact. If the CPU is slow in performing the setup operations, the graphics card must wait before it can draw the completed scene.

While the latest version of Direct3D can help move things along, you'll be much happier with a fast CPU. If you are buying a new system, make sure your CPU offers excellent floating point performance, which is critical to the complex mathematics involved in geometry processing. The Pentium II is the best x86 CPU in this regard, offering higher raw clock rates than any competing processor.

Finally, new versions of DirectX constantly extend and improve the features available to Windows-based games. DirectX 5 introduced AGP texturing, a feature that lets games use the large amount of system RAM for storing textures. AGP-enhanced games can deliver much greater visual realism when paired with compatible 3D graphics cards that plug into an AGP expansion slot. DirectX 5 ships as part of Windows 98.

Coming soon is DirectX 6, which continues to enhance 3D graphics quality and introduces DirectMusic. DirectMusic enables systems to play compelling music scores both for the web and for CD-ROM-based titles, and it eliminates delays and slowdowns that occur when playing MIDI scores while the system is busy.

Installing DirectX

How can you tell if DirectX is installed on your PC? Actually, Windows 98 comes with the full suite of DirectX software already installed. However, Microsoft is constantly updating the DirectX set, so you might need to install a new version down the road. You can get DirectX updates in either of two ways:

- Download from Microsoft's web site at www.microsoft.com.
- Load as part of the installation routine of a new CD-ROM-based game or multimedia title.

If an updated DirectX version comes with a game or some other software product you're installing, you will be prompted to install the new version during the process. If you download the files from Microsoft, however, you will need to launch the installation manually. The following steps outline the easiest way to do this:

1. Find the file DXSETUP.EXE in the directory where you originally downloaded the file.
2. Launch DXSETUP.EXE and follow the instructions that appear onscreen.
3. Restart your system after the installation routine is complete.

> **CAUTION**
>
> When DirectX installs, it examines your graphics card drivers to see if the drivers have been registered with Microsoft as approved DirectX drivers. In some cases, the installation might prompt you to overwrite the existing drivers with the generic DirectX drivers that are included with the update. In some cases, this can fix compatibility problems caused by incompatible drivers; in other instances, however, it can disable key features of your graphics card. If you recently downloaded graphics card drivers and are happy with their performance, click the No button when the prompt appears. You can always install the approved DirectX drivers later if you run into problems.

Configuring Joysticks and Other Game Controllers

Setting up joysticks was no picnic with DOS-based games. Most games supported only a few models, and calibration and setup usually had to happen outside the game itself. So if you noticed problems with response, you had to quit the game, enter a setup program, and restart the game—potentially a long process.

Windows 98 provides a standard applet interface for setting up joysticks and other devices. If you need to change controller settings, the game calls up the applet, which does all the real work. Best of all, you never have to close the game itself—it can stay active in the background (paused, of course) while you update your hardware settings.

Installing a Joystick or Game Controller

To setup a new game controller under Windows 98, do the following:

1. Click Start, Settings, Control Panel, and select the Game Controllers icon.

2. On the General tab of the Game Controllers dialog box, click the Add button.

3. Select the specific device type in the Game Controllers list box and click OK (see Figure 25.2).

FIG. 25.2

The Add Game Controller list includes support for popular joysticks, game pads, throttles, and steering wheels.

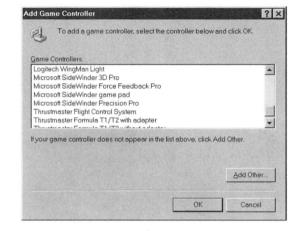

Part

V

Ch

25

4. If your device is not listed, click the Add Other button.

5. In the resulting dialog box, click the Have Disk button to install new device drivers. The new device should then be listed on the General tab, with an entry of OK in the Status column.

6. The new device is now installed. Click OK to finish the installation.

 If you have an older or unsupported joystick, don't despair. Windows 98 keeps a database of generic joystick types (defined by the number of buttons and other controls) from which you can select. In addition, most joysticks support emulation modes matching that of popular products from CH and Thrustmaster. Find out your joystick's preferred emulation, and then load the matching controller model. You should enjoy better performance.

Configuring a Joystick or Game Controller

To change the settings of an installed game controller, do the following:

1. Click Start, Settings, Control Panel, and select the Game Controllers icon.

2. On the General tab of the Game Controllers dialog box, select the device you want to adjust in the Game Controllers list. Then click Properties.

3. In the Test sheet, shown in Figure 25.3, a graphic depiction of the device provides a visual response when you push buttons or other controls. This lets you determine whether all the controls are working normally.

FIG. 25.3

The Test sheet lets you get familiar with your game input device's controls and make sure they are all working properly.

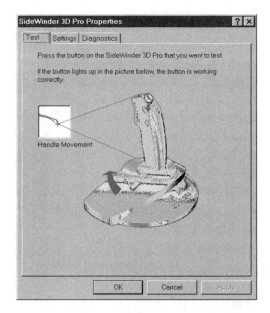

4. Click the Settings tab to see if all features are enabled. Click the appropriate check boxes next to identified features to enable or disable the specific controls.

5. Click the OK button to put your changes into effect.

N O T E Until about a year ago, almost all joysticks used analog signals to communicate position to the PC. The problem with these "dumb" joysticks is that the CPU must constantly check the game port to see what the joystick is reporting—even if nothing has changed. Game makers say this can sap 15 to 20 percent of your CPU's time, which is a major drag when fast frame rates spell the difference between success and defeat. New digital joysticks from Microsoft, Logitech, CH, and others are able to send updates directly to the CPU, freeing your system to perform other tasks and improving the precision and responsiveness of the device. If you are on the market for a new stick, consider a digital model. ■

The combination of DirectX and Windows 98's support for USB is ushering in a new class of joysticks, which use force feedback technology. These products actually include a small motor in the joystick base to create resistance, movement, and recoil based on events in your game. Microsoft's Flight Simulator 98, for example, sends DirectX data that tells force feedback joysticks to produce a rumbling vibration when your plane is accelerating down the runway. In addition, turbulence might cause the stick to move around, and high-G turns cause the stick to strain against your efforts to pull it back.

While some force feedback joysticks use the standard game port found on virtually all sound cards, the all-digital connection of USB provides better reliability and performance. It is also easier to plug and unplug joysticks by using the USB port, even during gameplay. The drawback to these products? The mechanics inside the stick add to the cost, causing force feedback products to sell for well over $100.

Using the WebTV

The WebTV software turns a properly equipped PC into a functioning television set. This feature allows you to view TV programming side-by-side with your applications, as well as to browse TV listings and capture video and images. You must have a TV tuner card installed in your PC to pick up broadcasts, and an Internet connection is useful for downloading the latest TV listings and schedules. You can find up-to-date listings at Starsight's web site, located at `http://www.starsight.com`.

To install the WebTV software, do the following:

1. Click Start, Settings, Control Panel, and select the Add/Remove Software icon.
2. Click the Windows Setup tab. Wait a moment while Setup searches for installed components.
3. In the Components box, scroll down to the WebTV item and click the box to the left to put a check mark in the box.
4. Click OK.
5. If the Windows 98 CD-ROM is not already in the drive, insert it when prompted. You will have to restart your system once or twice for all the changes to take effect.

When the software is installed, a small television icon appears on the taskbar in the group next to the Start button.

To watch a program, launch the WebTV application and go to the channel you want to watch. There are two ways to launch WebTV:

- Click the TV icon at the left end of the Windows 98 taskbar.
- Click Start, Programs, Accessories, Entertainment, WebTV.

Part

V

Ch

25

Using the Program Guide

When you launch WebTV, you first see the Program Guide, which displays the available channels in the main window. Use the scrollbar on the right side to browse through the channels, or use the scrollbar across the bottom to see what is on at different times during the day. A timeline across the top of the window shows the time of day for the programs being displayed.

T I P If your PC includes a separate TV tuner board, it's quite likely that the board vendor offers its own viewing application with the hardware. You should make a point to use both the WebTV applet and the bundled TV software with the board to see which you prefer.

Just above the display window, you can set the Program Guide to display programming for a specific date, time of day, or subset of channels, as shown in Figure 25.4. Clicking these reduces the amount of data displayed in the window and makes it easier for you to find the program you want.

FIG. 25.4
The Program Guide can overwhelm you with choices, but you can use one of the useful filters to pare things down to your viewing schedule.

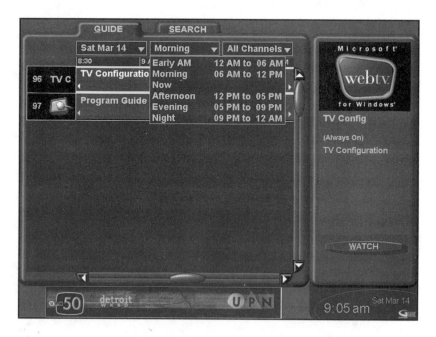

In addition, you can search for specific programming by clicking the Search tab at the top of the Program Guide window. A list of programming categories appears along the left side, and the window in the center displays the results of your searches. You can click one of the categories to see all the programs that fit that definition, or you can enter text into the Search box in the lower-left corner to look for a specific word or description. Just enter the text and click the Search button at the bottom to see the results in the main window.

You can further winnow your searches by using the pick list controls at the top of the screen (see Figure 25.5). The leftmost control lets you filter by days or by those programs that are broadcast at the moment. The rightmost control lets you sort the resulting search by time or by title.

FIG. 25.5

The useful Search screen lets you hunt for programs by category, text string, or time of day.

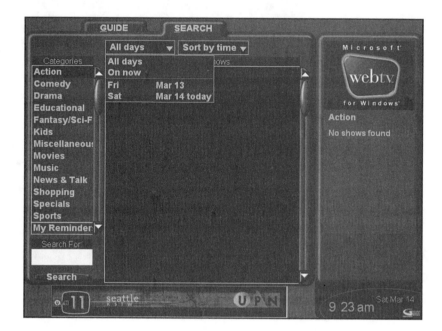

To view a program, select it from the results window. If the program is on, the WebTV application tunes to the appropriate channel and displays it.

Changing Channels

WebTV gives you several ways to select a channel to view. For most, you must access the TV Toolbar, which runs across the top of the WebTV screen. To invoke the TV Toolbar, shown in Figure 25.6, press F10 or the Alt key. To change the channel, do one of the following:

- Click the arrows on the spinner control in the left corner of the TV Toolbar, which appears across the top of the screen.

- Enter the number in the channel control on the TV Toolbar by dragging the cursor over the current entry and typing the new number over it. Press Enter to go to the channel.

- Click one of the pre-selected channel icons on the TV Toolbar.

- Use a remote control (if your system supports one) to enter channel changes.

Part

V

Ch

25

FIG. 25.6
The TV Toolbar makes it easy to change channels, adjust settings, and add or remove custom channels.

Full-Screen or Window?

By default, WebTV launches in full-screen mode, meaning you cannot see your other programs while watching TV. Of course, you can adjust WebTV so that it takes up only part of the screen by doing the following:

1. Press F10 or Alt to invoke the TV Toolbar.

2. Click the small double-box icon that appears in the upper-right corner of the TV Toolbar. (Be sure not to click the X icon; that closes WebTV!)

3. The WebTV screen shrinks so it takes up only a portion of the screen.

4. To resize the window, first position the pointer over a corner of the window so that it turns into a double arrow. Then click and drag the window border to the desired shape and size. Repeat on the other corner if necessary.

Other TV Options

WebTV mates some of the best features of the PC with its broadcast capabilities. For example, if a broadcaster provides data signals embedded in the broadcast, you can display running text, graphics, and other information alongside the program. A football broadcast, for example, might display the scoring statistics of the team that has just taken the field.

The additional data reaches your PC by way of the video blanking interval (VBI), essentially a segment of the broadcast frequency not used to produce the display. Because the rarely used VBI is part of the standard broadcast specification, it is the equivalent of an unused lane on a freeway. Your PC can be told to monitor the VBI and to interpret appropriate signals coming off it as data.

This technique can do more than just add text display or canned HTML pages to ongoing broadcasts. Broadcasters might team with software vendors and distributors to schedule bulk data broadcasts. Just as you can set your VCR to record that long-awaited episode of *ER*, you can tell your PC to receive a broadcast download of Internet Explorer 4.0. Because the transfer happens over the airwaves, you don't have to spend hours logged on to the web while a 30MB file creeps over the modem.

You can tell whether a particular broadcast is enhanced by looking at the TV Guide window: WebTV places a blue icon next to the entry. (A red circle icon indicates that the programming is unenhanced.) The icons also appear for programs shown on the TV Toolbar banner. Today, few broadcasters make use of this facility, but some NFL games, as well as NBC's drama *Homicide: Life on the Streets* have been providing additional content.

By default, WebTV enables the enhanced content. You must turn it off if you want to view only the broadcast. To turn off the enhancements on a broadcast, do the following:

1. Press F10 or Alt to invoke the TV Toolbar.
2. Click the blue icon that appears on the far-right side of the TV Toolbar banner.
3. In the context menu that drops down, the Enhancements item should have a check mark next to it. Click it to remove the check mark. The Enhancements is now disabled.
4. To re-enable this feature, click the blue icon again and click the Enhancements item.

WebTV also supports closed-captioning, in which it displays running text of dialog along the bottom of the screen. You can even have WebTV look for specific words in the text stream—say, "President Clinton"—and have the program perform a particular action, such as turning up the volume for you.

To turn on closed captioning, do the following;

1. Press F10 or Alt to bring up the TV Toolbar.
2. Click the Settings icon.
3. In the Settings dialog box, click the Show Closed Captioning check box. A check should now appear in the box.
4. Click OK.

Part V

Ch 25

Using DVD Players with Windows 98

DVD is a major improvement to the multimedia and data storage capabilities of desktop PCs. DVD-ROMs, which look identical to CD-ROM media, can hold up to 17GB of data—more than 30 times that stored on a CD-ROM. In addition, DVD-ROM enables vastly improved audio and visual quality from PC-based digital video (see Figure 25.7).

The numbers can get a bit confusing. DVD-ROM actually specifies a 4.7GB capacity per side, per layer. A two-sided single-layer DVD-ROM can, therefore, hold up to 9.4GB of data. Capacities can go up to 17GB for discs that use two layers of media on each side. In this scheme, the read laser fires at slightly different angles to read each of the two layers, making the untargeted layer transparent to the laser. However, the process of laying two layers forces slightly wider pit placement, which is why a dual-layered side of media holds only 8.5GB as opposed to the 9.4GB you might expect.

FIG. 25.7
High-quality MPEG-2 digital video delivers professional-quality video playback to the PC. In fact, it's the same format used by direct broadcast satellite providers like DirecTV.

Video-enabled DVD-ROM titles generally require two new hardware components to run:

- *DVD-ROM drive.* An optical disk drive, very similar in appearance to a CD-ROM drive, that can read both DVD-ROMs and CD-ROMs.
- *Decoder board.* A PCI add-in card that includes hardware for decoding compressed MPEG-2 video and audio for playback on the PC.

Installing the DVD Components of Windows 98

If your PC has this hardware, Windows 98 allows you to immediately take advantage of their features. In some cases, however, you must manually install the DVD components of the Windows 98 operating system. Follow these steps:

1. Click Start, Settings, Control Panel, and select the Add/Remove Software icon.
2. Click the Windows Setup tab. Wait a moment while Windows 98 reviews its configuration.
3. Scroll through the Components list and select the Multimedia entry.
4. Click the Details button to bring up the list of available Multimedia components.
5. Click the box next to DVD Player to place a check mark in the box.
6. Click OK, and then click OK again to have Windows 98 install the software. Insert the Windows 98 CD-ROM if prompted.
7. Restart the PC to put the changes into effect.

You've probably heard a lot also about the coming of recordable DVD formats. Unlike CD-R and CD-RW drives, which let you record full 650MB CD-ROMs, neither DVD-RAM nor DVD+RW can put 4.7GB of data on a single side. DVD-RAM allows for 2.6GB of data, while DVD+RW allows for 3GB. A greater issue with the recordable formats, however, is the lack of installed drives. While a recorded CD can be read by virtually any CD-ROM-equipped PC, systems with a DVD-ROM drive remain few and far between. So while DVD-ROM might be a good choice for playing multimedia titles, DVD recordable drives remain a marginal purchase.

Using the DVD Player Software

In general, most DVD-ROM drive kits come with their own player software, like that shown in Figure 25.8. Likewise, many DVD-ROM-based games and titles play video and audio within the confines of their own interface. In these cases, you don't need to access Windows 98's DVD Player software. In fact, you will generally find that the interface provided with your DVD-ROM drive and kit offer more features than the player included with Windows 98. However, the DVD Player is useful for browsing through DVD-ROMs and playing back selected MPEG video clips.

FIG. 25.8

Creative Labs uses a remote control-like interface to switch tracks, play video, and control playback settings. The capability to display either letter box or standard TV format video is just one of DVD's useful features.

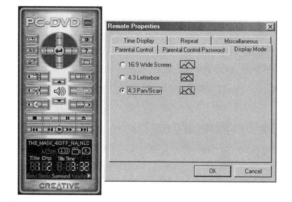

To open the DVD Player, click Start, Programs, Applications, Accessories, Entertainment. Click DVD Player. The player application loads.

The DVD Player applet offers a concise interface for browsing content on DVD-ROMs. A simple VCR metaphor lets you select among available video tracks, offering familiar push buttons you can use to play, advance, pause, and rewind video. A window displays the video track, elapsed time, time remaining, and other information for each track. Users can also access letter-box format, closed-captioning, and subtitling, provided those features are available on the disc. ●

CHAPTER 26

Adding New Hardware

by Michael Desmond

In this chapter

Using the Add New Hardware Wizard

Installing new hardware under Windows 98 is made easier by the use of Plug and Play technology and the Add New Hardware Wizard. Today, almost all new hardware provides Plug and Play capability; in addition, most systems sold over the last three years comply with PnP. The result: Easier hardware installations.

Not sure if your system is PnP-compatible? The following things must be in place for PnP to work with your installations:

- A Plug and Play BIOS (see Figure 26.1).
- A Plug and Play operating system, such as Windows 98 or Windows 95.
- Plug and Play–compliant hardware devices, including adapter cards.

FIG. 26.1

The Windows 98 Device Manager will indicate if your system's BIOS is Plug and Play–compliant.

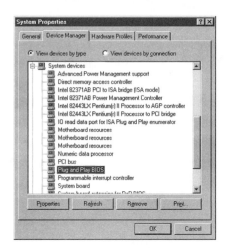

If you have a working PnP-compliant system, you'll notice that hardware installations go much more smoothly. Even when Windows 98 doesn't get it right—which does happen occasionally—the intuitive onscreen guides help prompt you as to what to do.

The Add New Hardware Wizard provides a common user-friendly interface for hardware installation procedures. Several things can happen to launch the wizard:

- Windows 98 detects a new hardware device during operation.
- Windows 98 detects a new hardware device during boot-up.
- The user selects the Add New Hardware icon from the Windows 98 Control Panel.

Installing Plug and Play Hardware

Regardless of how the wizard is invoked, it provides a consistent step-by-step approach. The following list represents a typical sequence of the events that occur when Windows 98's Add New Hardware Wizard detects a new device at startup.

1. Windows 98 displays a message saying that new hardware has been detected. After a period of time, the Message Building Driver database appears. A timeline in the dialog box shows the progress of the update.

2. The Add New Hardware Wizard dialog box prompts you to tell Windows 98 where to find drivers for the new device. Click the Next button to continue.

3. Windows 98 recommends that you search for new drivers; click the top radio button to do this. If you know exactly where the drivers are located, click the bottom radio button to display a list of all drivers located in a certain area. Click Next.

4. Tell Windows 98 where to search by checking the drives and locations to search. If you have checked either the CD-ROM or floppy disk, make sure the media with the drivers is in the appropriate drive.

5. When Windows finds the appropriate .INF file, you will be prompted to install it by clicking Next.

 TIP By default, the Add New Hardware Wizard often asks you to insert the Windows 98 CD-ROM. But depending on the age of your Windows 98 disc, you may find newer drivers included with the hardware itself. As a general rule, you should use the newest drivers you can when installing new products. In fact, I often check the manufacturer's or Microsoft's web site to download the newest driver before installing hardware.

NOTE If Windows 98 can't find the required device driver file in the expected location, you will be prompted to browse for the necessary files. ■

6. When the driver installation is complete, click the Finish button. You may be prompted to restart Windows 98.

Part
V

Ch
26

CAUTION

Installing new hardware involves making changes to the Windows 98 Registry, the central configuration database that is vital to your system's operation. Before you install a new device, you should make it a point to back up your Registry settings. Open the Registry by clicking Start, Run. Type **Regedit** in the text box and click OK. In the Registry Editor, select the My Computer icon at the top of the list on the left, click the Registry menu item, and then click Export Registry File. Save the file to a desired location (such as to a floppy disk) using the Export Registry File dialog box. Also give your exported Registry file a name. If your existing Registry becomes corrupt following an installation, you will be able to fix the problem by asserting your old, working Registry from your hard drive or floppy disk. Alternatively, an even better idea is to back up the entire Windows directory, which ensures that you can return your operating system to its native state should the installation overwrite or corrupt any key system files.

Using the Add New Hardware Wizard for Undetected Devices

What do you do if the wizard fails to properly detect your newly installed card? You need to intervene and manually tell Windows 98 what it is you are installing. But the wizard's consistent interface does help guide you. Follow these steps:

1. Follow steps 1 through 5 of the previous procedure. Windows 98 will prompt you by saying that it was unable to determine the new hardware device. Click Next.

2. The next dialog box offers a list of hardware device types, as shown in Figure 26.2. Select the appropriate device type and click Next.

FIG. 26.2

The Add New Hardware Wizard provides a comprehensive list of device types, from which you can pick out your specific hardware during installation.

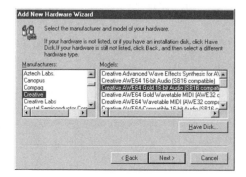

3. In the dialog box shown in Figure 26.2, click the device's vendor in the Manufacturers list box, and then click the device model in the Models list box.

4. If you are loading drivers from a floppy or CD-ROM, click Have Disk and navigate to the appropriate .INF file. The device drivers will then be loaded.

5. When the driver installation is complete, a message box advises you that system settings have changed and asks whether you want to restart Windows 98. Click Restart Now so that your driver change takes effect.

Adding Internal Adapters

Windows 98's Plug and Play, assisted by the Add New Hardware Wizard, makes it easy to install an internal adapter card. Sound boards, graphics cards, and internal modems are all common add-in card installations.

Installing an Internal Adapter

That said, you need to exercise caution when working inside your system. Rough handling or incorrect installations can damage delicate leads and electronics, rendering your PC inoperable. You should also be sure to always unplug your system before you open the case. This will ensure that a power spike does not damage components during installation.

CAUTION

Static electricity is a real concern when you're working inside a PC case. Before you touch or handle any cards, make sure you touch one of the PC's metal supports. This effectively grounds you and draws away any static charge you've accumulated.

To install an adapter card, do the following:

1. Shut down the PC and unplug the power cord from the back of the system box.
2. Remove the system case. Usually, this entails unscrewing a single thumbscrew or using a Phillips head screwdriver to remove two or more screws located along the back of the case.

N O T E If you own a Compaq system, you may have to find a Torx screwdriver for the unique screws that company uses to attach its cases. You can find a Torx driver at your local hardware store or at most computer stores.

3. If the system is a tower or minitower design, lay the system on its side so that the CPU and cards are pointing up. Be sure to place the PC on the ground or some other stable surface.
4. Use a Phillips head (or Torx) screwdriver to unscrew the backplate of the add-in slot you want to use. Remove the backplate protector or the card, if a card is already installed in the slot.
5. Insert the new card into the desired slot, applying gentle, even force along the top of the card. You may have to rock the card slightly from front to back to gain entrance to the slot.
6. Make sure the card is properly seated and is level inside the slot. The card's back ports should be accessible from the back of the system.
7. Attach any necessary wires or cables to the card. Leave the case off the PC until you are sure the device is working.

N O T E Some computers, including models from Compaq, will not boot with the cover off. If your PC fails to start, try reseating the cover and booting again.

8. Plug in the PC and start up the system. Windows 98 should detect the new card and launch the Add New Hardware Wizard. Follow the instructions as outlined above.
9. After the new drivers are installed, you will probably need to shut down the system and restart. Having verified that the new device is working properly, shut down the PC and reattach the case.

N O T E Be careful not to lose those backplates you remove when you're installing a new card. You'll want to keep them handy to cover up the open slot in the back of the chassis should you ever remove the device. Otherwise, your PC will be more susceptible to gathering dust on the motherboard and fans, which can lead to overheating. In addition, open backplane slots can reduce the efficiency of airflow in the PC chassis, again inviting heating problems with fast CPUs.

Part
V

Ch
26

Installing Older Adapter Cards

The easiest way to install a new older device in a Windows 98 system is to use the Add New Hardware Wizard's automatic detection feature to identify the new card or device. But the wizard can also determine if you have removed a card. Auto-detection is best suited for PCs that have few or no specialty adapter cards, such as sound and video-capture cards.

The following steps describe the automatic detection process for installing a Creative Labs Sound Blaster AWE 32 card:

1. Set non-conflicting resource values for your new adapter card by using jumpers or the card's setup program.
2. Shut down Windows 98 and turn off the power on your PC.
3. Install the new adapter card in an empty ISA slot, and then make any required external connections, such as audio inputs and speaker outputs for sound cards.
4. Turn the PC power back on and restart Windows 98.
5. Launch Control Panel and double-click the Add New Hardware icon to start the Add New Hardware Wizard.
6. Click Next. Then select the Yes (Recommended) radio button in the dialog box that appears.
7. Click Next to display the wizard's boilerplate.
8. Click Next to start the detection process. After a few minutes of disk activity, the wizard advises you that the detection is complete.
9. Click Details to display what the wizard detected.
10. If the wizard does not detect your newly installed card, you must install the card manually. Click Cancel to terminate the automatic detection process.
11. Click Finish to install the required drivers from the Windows 98 CD-ROM or floppy disks. The message box indicates the expected medium.
12. Insert the Windows 98 CD-ROM into the drive and click OK to install the drivers.
13. If Windows 98 can't find the required device driver file in the expected location, you will be prompted to browse for the necessary files.
14. When the driver installation is complete, a message box advises you that system settings have changed and asks whether you want to restart Windows 98. Click Restart Now so that your driver change takes effect.

N O T E   If the specific device model name does not appear in the list, don't panic. Click the Have Disk button below the Models list box, and then insert the driver disk or CD-ROM provided with the hardware. Navigate to the proper drive letter, and the appropriate .INF file will appear. Click OK, and the drivers and device information will be loaded into Windows 98 from the media. ■

Understanding Adapter Cards

While adapter installations are relatively similar, there are actually several types of adapters available for PCs. Depending on the age and model of your system, you will need to make sure you purchase cards that are supported in your PC's motherboard. Here are the four most common card types:

- *ISA.* A low-speed (8- or 16-bit) bus common on PCs since their inception; at least one or two slots available on most motherboards; generally used for sound cards, internal modems, and some network adapters. Data rate is limited to about 5Mbps.

- *PCI.* A fast, 32-bit bus common on Pentium and faster PCs; generally used for graphics, network cards, and—more recently—sound boards. The top data rate is 132Mbps.

- *VL.* A fast 32-bit bus common on 486 systems; generally used for graphics cards. The top data rate is about 132Mbps.

- *AGP.* A super-fast 32-bit bus that runs at 2 to 4 times the speed of PCI; used exclusively for advanced graphics on Pentium II–based systems. The top data rate is 528Mbps.

> **CAUTION**
>
> Graphics card companies and system makers tout AGP's advanced 3D features, which allow a lot of system memory to be used for rendering 3D textures. However, many AGP-compliant graphics cards lack this capability, and tests show that AGP fails to deliver a meaningful performance benefit in relation to standard 2D and 3D graphics.

Two other bus types, EISA and MicroChannel, provide faster-than-ISA performance and offer Plug and Play features. However, both are aging bus designs that have fallen out of favor and are generally being replaced by PCI cards and slots.

Before you make any upgrade, you need to make sure that you buy a card that matches the available slots in your PC. A VL bus graphics card, for example, will not fit into a Pentium MMX system that features slots for ISA and PCI cards. Likewise, a new ISA sound card won't be of any use if all the ISA slots are already occupied by other necessary peripherals.

Plug and Play is also a factor. While Windows 98 will recognize most ISA and VL bus cards, neither bus specifically requires that cards provide PnP capability. PCI and AGP, on the other hand, were designed with PnP in mind.

N O T E   Owners of 486 PCs may face a bigger issue: the disappearance of VL bus-based cards. Most graphics board makers have switched their efforts to PCI and, more recently, AGP. If you have an old 486 PC that you want to upgrade to handle 3D graphics and video playback, you may be out of luck. If you really want to use these applications, consider upgrading to a Pentium or faster system with PCI card slots. ■

AGP   The accelerated graphics port (AGP) bus dedicates a connection to your graphics card. Although the current top data rate of AGP is 528Mbps, there are actually several flavors of the specification. Before you install a new AGP graphics card, you should know which flavor your system and card adhere to. Table 26.1 outlines the various distinctions. You'll want to use faster versions of AGP hardware in order to maximize 3D performance.

Table 26.1 Types of AGP Buses

AGP Type	Bus Width	Clock Rate	Bandwidth
AGP 1X	32 bits	66MHz	264Mbps
AGP 2X	32 bits	133MHz	528Mbps
AGP 4X	32 bits	266MHz	1024Mbps

Today, AGP 2X is supported by the Intel 440LX and 440BX chipsets, which means virtually all Pentium-II motherboards support 528Mbps operation. However, many early AGP graphics cards support only AGP 1X, which limits your data rates to the lower 264Mbps specification.

Down the road, Intel will be releasing AGP 4X, an enhanced specification that doubles the clock rate yet again to deliver 1Gbps of bandwidth. Targeted for graphics workstations and 3D professional applications, AGP 4X will become critical as software really takes advantage of the fast bus.

Windows 98 provides AGP support directly within the operating system. However, most software still doesn't make use of its most compelling feature: the ability to share system RAM with the graphics card. AGP lets games and software store megabytes of texture data in system memory, where the AGP graphics card can access it directly for use in realistic 3D scenes. Opening more data storage for textures should result in a marked improvement in the visual quality of 3D software.

Windows 98 includes DirectX 5.0, the latest version of Microsoft's gaming APIs and components, which enables DirectX-based games to make use of AGP texture memory. However, only games written using DirectX 3.0 or later can recognize the additional memory.

Installing a Modem

Modem installations are among the most common of upgrades, if only because of the rapid-fire improvement of modem speeds to the current level of 56 kilobits per second (kbps). While I recommend that users always buy the fastest modem they can reasonably afford, the final decision always comes down to the question of internal versus external design.

The main advantage of internal modems is their lower cost: They often cost $20 to $30 less than their external counterparts. Part of the savings is due to the fact that internal models don't include the power supply, plastic case, and serial cable found on external modems. What's more, internal models are best for older 486 systems, which might not have a serial port fast enough to handle 28.8 kbps and higher transmission rates.

N O T E   You might see some low-cost modems referred to as "Windows modems" or "Winmodems."
These devices use the system CPU to handle controller functions usually conducted in the
modem. While this approach reduces parts costs in the modem, it requires that Windows be present to
handle the transactions. That means your DOS-only games might not be able to access the COM
hardware. If you use DOS to play online games, consider getting a full-function modem that uses a
hardware controller. ▤

For most people, however, external models provide valuable flexibility. For example, a locked-up signal can be fixed by toggling the external modem on and off, whereas an internal modem requires a system reboot. Likewise, informative status lights let you see if the modem is actually sending and receiving bits. (However, the Windows 98 modem status applet, shown in Figure 26.3, makes this less of a concern.)

FIG. 26.3
Double-click the
modem light icon on
the Windows 98
taskbar, and you'll see
a full-fledged dialog
box that shows you how
much data your modem
has moved.

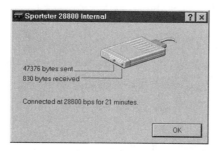

Physically installing an internal modem is the same as installing any internal adapter card. Physically installing an external unit simply means plugging the phone cords into the proper modem jacks, plugging in the power cable, and attaching the serial cable to the appropriate serial port on the back of your PC.

That done, you need to tell Windows 98 to work with the newly installed device. Do the following:

1. With the modem installed and powered on, click Start, Settings, Control Panel. Select the Modems icon.
2. In the Modems Properties dialog box, click the Add button.
3. Keep the check box unchecked and click Next to have Windows 98 detect the modem.
4. After a few moments, a final dialog box appears. Click Finish to complete the installation and return to the Modem Properties dialog box. The modem is now installed and available to your Windows applications.

Part
V

Ch
26

Installing a New Disk Drive

Windows 98 itself is large enough that it may motivate a hard disk upgrade, particularly given the low cost of disks with capacities as high as 6GB. Here are a few of those types of hard disks:

■ *Enhanced IDE (EIDE).* Common in PCs built within the past three years, these are the most common hard disks on the market.

■ *SCSI.* High-performance systems may use SCSI-based drives, which boast faster response and better multitasking features than do their EIDE cousins.

■ *IDE.* An aging standard that supports only disks up to 540MB.

The vast majority of users have EIDE hard disks, for the simple reason that they are less expensive than SCSI yet provide capacities of 9GB and beyond.

A new type of enhanced IDE interface, called ultra DMA or ATA-33, provides faster hard disk connections. Where enhanced IDE typically tops out at 15Mbps, ATA-33 drives can push up to 33Mbps of data—nearly as much as a fast and wide SCSI drive. Only the newest motherboards include ATA-33 interfaces, so you might have to purchase an add-in card to realize the benefit of an ATA-33 drive in an existing system.

Installing a Hard Disk

To install an EIDE hard disk, you must physically mount the drive in the system. First, however, you must decide whether the disk is to be the main bootable hard disk, or if it is to serve as a second disk for your system.

If the disk drive is to be a second disk, you should connect it to the same EIDE port as the first disk, using the available second connector provided on the cable running from the motherboard to the primary disk drive. Before installing the disk, make sure the pins near the back of the drive unit are set so that the disk is configured as a slave (the boot disk is already set as the master for its EIDE port).

N O T E   If you have an EIDE CD-ROM drive, you'll want to set it as the master device on the secondary IDE channel and set the two hard disks as master and slave on the primary channel. This will improve the performance of the CD-ROM drive and avoid possible time-out problems that can occur when the slow-response CD-ROM drive shares resources with quicker hard disks. ■

Having done that, you can proceed with the installation.

1. Power down the PC, unplug the power cord, and remove the case.

2. Locate an open internal drive bay (or an external bay if no internal ones are available). Make sure the bay matches the size of the drive, which in most cases is 3.5 inches.

3. Slide the new drive into the available bay, taking care to line up the screw holes in the drive with the slots in the drive mounting.

4. Using the supplied screws, secure the drive in the drive bay. Be careful not to over-tighten the screws; turning them too far into the drive can puncture the sealed casing.

5. Plug the available connector from the primary EIDE cable into the back of the drive. Align the red stripe on the cable with the side of the drive that contains pin 1. (Newer systems may use a connector that is keyed with a notch in the cable connector and a

corresponding tab that lines up on the port connector. Check the drive documentation carefully.)

6. Plug the power cable from the power supply into the back of the drive. The connector is shaped such that it can fit only one way. Make sure the connection is firm.

7. When you are sure everything is seated properly and secured, plug in the PC and boot it up. The new drive should automatically appear with an incremented drive letter that is one greater than the highest used by your original disk drive.

A Word About File Systems

Advancing hard disk capacities have outstripped the facilities inside the operating system. Windows 95 and Windows 3.x used the FAT16 file system, which can only recognize hard disk partitions of up to 2GB. In order to access all of a 6GB hard disk, you must partition the drive into three 2GB segments, each of which has its own drive letter. This fools the operating system into thinking there are three disks of 2GB installed.

In addition, larger hard drives have resulted in expanding amounts of lost disk space. This problem occurs because of the way FAT16 segments the hard disk into lots of same-sized clusters. Every file, no matter how small, consumes at least one cluster. On smaller drives with cluster sizes of 4KB or 8KB, the amount of space wasted in each cluster was not too severe. But at 1GB, cluster sizes are 32KB a piece. The result: Lots of lost disk space, also known as *slack*. FAT32, however, puts the squeeze on cluster size to optimize disk space, as outlined in Table 26.2.

Table 26.2   FAT16 versus FAT32 Cluster Sizes

Maximum Drive Partition	FAT16 Cluster	FAT32 Cluster
128MB	2KB	4KB
256MB	4KB	4KB
512MB	8KB	4KB
1,024MB	16KB	4KB
2,048MB	32KB	4KB
8,192MB	N/A	4KB

Part

V

Ch

26

As you can see from the table, a typical 2GB partition under FAT32 uses clusters one-eighth the size of those used by the same drive under FAT16. Multiplied over thousands of files, the more-efficient FAT32 scheme results in tens or even hundreds of megabytes of saved disk space.

To address this issue, Windows 98 uses the FAT32 file system by default. This update can recognize hard disks as large as TKGB, eliminating the need to create several drive letters. What's more, FAT32 is more efficient about disk space. A 2GB FAT16-formatted drive sets aside 32KB of space for every file, so even a 1KB file consumes 32KB. FAT32 cuts that number down to 4KB.

If you're installing a large IDE hard drive, you might want to format it using FAT32 (provided that is not the case already). Windows 98 includes a program called CVT1.EXE that automatically converts existing FAT16 drives to FAT32 format without requiring you to reformat the drive or back up its data. (However, it's generally a very good idea to back up your data before you switch file systems.)

You can also select your file system using the DOS-based FDISK.EXE application found in the WINDOWS\COMMAND subdirectory. This program lets you create and resize logical disk partitions, as well as select the file system to be used in each partition. In some cases, you might want to switch back to FAT16 from FAT32 (for example, to dual boot Windows NT or to regain compatibility with some antivirus and utility programs). Although you'll have to reformat your hard disk to do it, FDISK will let you switch your drives from FAT16 to FAT32.

N O T E   Windows NT works fine on FAT16 partitions. However, it will not run on or recognize FAT32 partitions. If you have a dual-boot Windows 98/Windows NT system, you must plan correctly for how to use FAT32 with Windows 98. Windows NT and all its associated applications and data files must be located on a non-FAT32 partition. If you decide to use FAT32 for the Windows 98 partition, be aware that you will not be able to share installed applications between the two operating systems. For example, you will have to have two copies of Word for Windows—one on the FAT16 partition and one on the FAT32 partition. ▧

Adding a SCSI Device

The Small Computer System Interface (SCSI) may be more common among Macintosh computers than most PCs, but the daisy-chained bus is still often found on scanners, high-performance hard disks, and other devices. While SCSI is more expensive than the popular enhanced IDE bus found on many PCs today, it enjoys several key advantages:

- Higher maximum throughputs
- More efficient multitasking
- Support for both external and internal devices
- Convenient daisy-chained setup

Explaining SCSI

SCSI comes in several varieties. Today, most devices use either Fast SCSI or Fast and Wide SCSI, though an even faster version—Ultra SCSI—is now available for high-performance peripherals. Table 26.3 shows how the various SCSI types compare.

Table 26.3 The Many Faces of SCSI

SCSI Type	Data Rate	What It's Good For
SCSI	10MBps	Scanners, tape backup drives
Fast SCSI	20MBps	CD-ROM drives, hard disks
Fast and Wide SCSI	40MBps	Hard disks
Ultra SCSI	80MBps	Fast hard disks

Unlike IDE, SCSI is a daisy-chained bus. That means that peripherals are connected in a row (much like a string of Christmas lights) from a point originating at the system motherboard. Daisy chaining allows users to connect as many as seven devices from a single SCSI card or port. Each SCSI device must be assigned a unique ID number, called a SCSI ID, that Windows 98 can use to identify devices on the chain. These numbers run from 0 to 7.

N O T E Although faster and slow SCSI products and cables can coexist neatly on a SCSI daisy chain, those of different bit widths (wide and narrow) generally cannot. If you are building a selection of SCSI peripherals, you should make a point to work with Wide SCSI variations (16 bits wide) in order to avoid problems.

While all devices should work regardless of their assigned ID—assuming that no ID is re-peated on the chain—the truth is a little less clear. Some SCSI devices, such as bootable hard disks, may require an ID number of 0 or 1, while others may have a preferred ID assignment. The result: You might have to tweak the ID assignments of the devices in order for all of them to work properly. Check your documentation closely for such requirements when assigning ID numbers.

Installing a SCSI Adapter

Most PCs sold today do not include a built-in SCSI card or connector—they rely on the less-expensive enhanced IDE bus to drive device-like hard disks and CD-ROM drives. So if you want to add a high performance CD-ROM drive, hard disk, scanner, or other peripheral, you may have to install a SCSI adapter card.

The process is identical to that of adding a new adapter card, which is detailed in the section "Installing an Internal Adapter," earlier in this chapter. When the Add New Hardware Wizard comes up, Windows 98 should detect both the card make and model (if it doesn't, you may have to select it manually from the list of SCSI adapters provided in the wizard itself). Once the appropriate driver software is loaded and the system restarts, the card will be ready to host SCSI devices.

N O T E Many SCSI adapters include a built-in floppy controller. You should check to make sure this feature is disabled to avoid a conflict with the working controller on your motherboard.

Part
V

Ch
26

Installing a SCSI Device

SCSI device installations under Windows 98 resemble those of other hardware: The operating system detects the new hardware and guides you through the driver installation process. There are a few tweaks, however:

1. Shut down the PC and unplug the power cord.

2. Remove the terminator plug SCSI Out port of the last device in the SCSI daisy chain, and plug the new device's cable into the port.

3. Plug the other end of the cable into the SCSI In port on the new device. Make sure the total length of your daisy chain doesn't exceed 15 feet, because devices won't behave reliably beyond that point.

4. Fit the terminator plug on the new device's SCSI Out port.

5. Select a unique SCSI ID for the new device, using the provided wheel control or other facility. This can usually be found on the back of the device.

6. Power up the system. The Add New Hardware Wizard should detect the new device and prompt you to install drivers for the device.

7. Once drivers are installed, restart the system. The new SCSI device should be ready to go.

N O T E SCSI termination can be tricky. If this is the first external device you are installing, you need to change the termination setting on the card itself because it will be terminated if no external devices are present. ▓

Installing a USB Peripheral

New to the PC landscape is the Universal Serial Bus (USB), a low-to-medium-speed bus designed to replace the serial, parallel, keyboard, and mouse ports on your computer. Windows 98 is the first operating system to provide full USB support, which makes it easier than ever to add external peripherals to your PC. Table 26.4 shows some of the devices served by USB.

Table 26.4 USB Changes Everything

Device Type	Devices
Input	Mice, keyboards, joysticks
Imaging	Scanners of all types
Multimedia	Videoconferencing cameras, speakers, wave audio
Output	Printers, monitor controls

Like SCSI, USB lets you connect hardware to each other, eliminating the need to plug everything into the back of your PC. So a scanner can be hooked to your monitor, which in turn is hooked to your PC. That spells welcome cable relief. What's more, devices such as scanners and speakers, which now require their own power plugs, can draw their power over the USB cable, reducing the number of necessary electrical plugs. USB lets you hook up a maximum of 127 devices to your PC—though few users are likely to test that limit.

It's no surprise that USB is a Plug and Play bus—more so than SCSI—so devices are automatically detected by Windows 98 (see Figure 26.4). If you attach a USB scanner to your running PC, Windows 98 automatically initializes the device, allowing you to conduct scans without having to reboot or go through other steps. Likewise, the operating system will unload drivers for USB devices that are unplugged.

USB can't match SCSI's performance, however, because data rates top out at 12Mbps, so don't expect USB hard disks and CD-ROM drives. Down the road, look for a faster Plug and Play external bus, called IEEE 1394, or FireWire. This bus supports up to 400Mbps data rates, making it suitable for video capture and networking. Windows 98 does not feature FireWire capability now, but Microsoft has said it will support the technology in the future.

FIG. 26.4

Like any other device, USB hardware is tracked by the Windows 98 Device Manager, as shown by the Logitech PageScan USB scanner that is logged under the Imaging Device entry.

Part

V

Ch

26

USB device installations can vary, but in most cases they're very simple. Just plug the hardware into the USB port on the back of the PC. Windows 98 will detect the hardware and might prompt you to insert a driver disk or the Windows 98 CD-ROM. After Windows loads the driver and initializes the new device, you will be able to use the device normally.

N O T E Most PCs feature two USB ports, but because of the way Windows 98 sets up USB devices, only one port—the one you installed in—will register the new device. If, at a later date, you plug into the other port expecting to get right to work, you will find that you must reinitialize the device. In some cases, this can confuse Windows and cause a system crash. Your best bet when installing a new USB device is to take the time to plug the peripheral into both ports so that both are initialized; that way Windows will recognize the device on-the-fly no matter what.

USB and IEEE 1394 are also slated to become an important platform for your PC's storage drives. The Device Bay specification defines a standard modular drive bay that includes USB and IEEE 1394 connectors. Users will be able to slip Device Bay–compatible drives in and out of future PCs without having to mess with screws and clumsy drive bays. The two ports will replace the IDE and SCSI buses often used to connect these devices to the system.

Because both buses are Plug and Play–compatible, Device Bay drives can be readily swapped in and out of systems. Windows 98 will detect the presence or absence of the hardware and react accordingly. Faster magnetic media will use the IEEE 1394 bus, while tape drives and slow removable discs will work over USB.

Adding a Second Display

Windows 98 adds the capability to send graphics to two displays at the same time, allowing you to expand the size of your Windows 98 desktop. For example, you can view a full-screen graphics layout on one display (at high-resolution true color) while the other shows your email or web browser at a different graphic setting. To run multiple displays, you'll need at least two VGA-compatible monitors, as well as a graphics card for each display. One important note: Because the graphics cards must run on the AGP or PCI buses, the number of free slots will probably limit display support.

To run a second display, you need to install a second graphics card. This process is identical to that outlined in the section "Installing an Internal Adapter," earlier in this chapter. After the new card is installed and running, you must shut down the PC, plug in the second monitor, and restart. The original card and display will boot up to the Windows 98 desktop, and the second display subsystem can be used to display desired programs.

Conclusion

Windows 98 does not dramatically change the installation procedure for hardware devices. Still, the Plug and Play routines have been tweaked for better performance, and useful additions such as the Upgrade Wizard should help keep your hardware up-to-date. Windows 98 also expands the recognized universe of devices to include DVD-ROM drives and peripherals operating on the USB bus. ●

CHAPTER 27

Configuring Hardware

by Michael Desmond

In this chapter

How Windows 98 Works with Hardware

Windows 98 doesn't radically change the way things were handled under Windows 95, but it does include some useful new tools and tweaks. At the center of all hardware, however, is Windows 98's Plug and Play (PnP), the combination of software and hardware that allows the operating system to automatically manage devices.

For PnP to work, your peripherals, system BIOS, and operating system must all incorporate PnP technology. When Windows 98 starts, the operating system and the PC go through a series of steps to establish configurations, arbitrate conflicts, and record changes.

- *System BIOS (basic input/output system).* The system BIOS is the low-level code that boots your system, detects the hard disk, and manages basic operations. Plug and Play systems employ a specifically tuned BIOS that adds 13 system function calls specific to Plug and Play. These calls provide the intelligence to detect hardware and manage configuration changes.

N O T E   To see if your BIOS is PnP-compliant, look for the BIOS information on your monitor at the beginning of the boot process. A text message identifying the BIOS version should include mention of PnP. You can also check the Windows 98 Device Manager for a PnP BIOS listing.

- *Operating system.* Windows 98 interacts with the system BIOS and the installed hardware and keeps track of hardware resources.
- *Hardware peripherals.* Adapter cards and other peripherals must incorporate PnP circuitry in order to provide automated configuration. PCI add-in cards, by definition, are PnP-compliant, whereas ISA cards must be specifically designed for the feature. External peripherals such as modems and printers can be PnP as well.
- *Device drivers.* The final piece of the PnP puzzle is the device driver. Peripherals must use dynamic drivers (called VxDs) that allow configurations to be changed on-the-fly. You can usually get the latest driver versions from the peripheral manufacturer.

N O T E   The best place to find the latest 32-bit device drivers for your peripherals is from the vendor. Often, the driver available from a vendor's Web site will be more up-to-date than those found on the Windows 98 CD-ROM.

These components all come together to eliminate the need for the user to tell each peripheral exactly which resources it can access. IRQ, DMA, and I/O address settings are all assigned by Windows 98 based on the overall picture that PnP provides.

While Windows 98 makes things easier, you need to be knowledgeable about the resources your devices need. This enables you to diagnose and fix simple conflicts without having to resort to time-consuming or costly repair services. IRQs, or *interrupt requests*, are the most critical of the system resources, if only because nearly all devices need them. IRQ numbers enable hardware devices to get the CPU's attention.

A PC has 14 IRQs, but not all of those are actually available to your peripherals. In fact, as PCs incorporate more and more devices, IRQs have become increasingly scarce, which sometimes results in failed installations and conflicts.

Table 27.1 lists the IRQs and their most common uses. As you can see, only about a third of these may be available, and often even those are occupied.

Table 27.1 Counting IRQs

IRQ Number	Application
2	Cascade from IRQ9
3	Available (or second COM port)
4	COM1, COM3
5	Available (or second printer port, LPT2)
6	Floppy disk controller
7	Printer port (LPT1)
8	System clock
9	Graphics adapter
10	Available
11	Available
12	Mouse (PS/2 systems)
13	Math coprocessor (if applicable)
14	Hard drive controller
15	Available

Walking Through Plug and Play

Each time you boot the system, a series of steps occur that launch the PnP process. All the hardware on the system is checked at boot time. If new hardware has been installed, it will be detected, and the appropriate steps will be taken by the PnP system.

The hard work of Plug and Play begins at the BIOS, the lowest level of system logic that controls the movement of information throughout the system.

The following list details the steps that Windows 98 goes through during system startup:

1. The system BIOS disables configurable motherboard devices and add-in cards.
2. PnP ISA and PCI devices are detected.
3. An allocation table is created for basic system resources, including ports, memory, and IRQ and DMA settings.

Part

V

Ch

27

4. I/O devices are enabled.

5. The read-only memory of ISA devices is scanned.

6. Initial program load (IPL) devices are configured in order to boot the system.

7. Specific resources are assigned to all configurable devices.

8. The booststrap loader starts. At this point, the operating system takes over.

9. Windows 98 allocates the remaining resources, after allowing for older resource assignments to each PnP device. If many older and PnP devices are in use, Windows 98 might have to perform many iterations of the allocation process, changing the resource assignments of the PnP devices each time, in order to eliminate all resource conflicts.

10. Windows 98 creates a final system configuration and stores the resource allocation data for this configuration in the registration database (the Registry).

11. Windows 98 searches the Windows\System folder to find the required driver for the device. If the device driver is missing, a dialog box appears, asking you to insert into drive A the manufacturer's floppy disk containing the driver software. Windows 98 loads the driver into memory and then completes its startup operations.

Notice that Windows 98 makes educated guesses about the identity and resource requirements of older devices. The operating system features a large database of resource settings for older devices, which enables it to detect and configure itself to a variety of existing hardware. However, this detection process is not perfect, and it forces dynamic PnP peripherals to be configured around the static settings of older hardware.

Installing Device Drivers

Device drivers are a critical part of hardware configuration. This software acts as a bridge between your hardware and the Windows 98 operating system, enabling the two to talk to one another. Drivers not only enable features, they can also enhance performance and fix bugs and conflicts. For this reason, users should always keep an eye out for improved versions of driver software for their hardware. Devices most affected by device driver updates include graphics cards, sound cards, scanners, printers, and video capture devices.

Windows 98 makes it easy to install new driver software, via the Update Device Driver Wizard. Simply follow these steps:

1. Click Start, Settings, Control Panel and select the System icon.

2. Click the Device Manager tab to display the list of device types available to your PC (see Figure 27.1).

3. In the scrolling list box, click the plus sign next to the hardware category you want to work with.

4. Double-click the specific device item that appears, and Windows displays the properties dialog box for that item.

5. Click the Driver tab, and then click the Update Driver button shown, in Figure 27.2.

FIG. 27.1

The Device Manager lets you browse among device types to access properties for specific hardware.

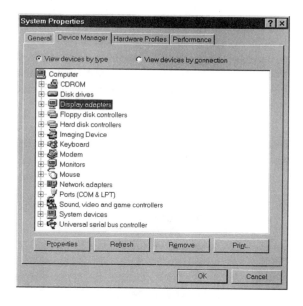

FIG. 27.2

The Update Driver button, found in the properties dialog box of many devices, makes it easy to search out the latest driver versions available on the web.

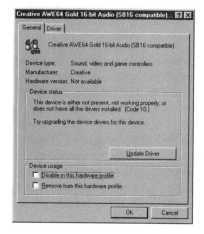

6. The Update Device Driver Wizard launches. Click Next.

7. At the next screen, click the top radio button to tell Windows 98 to search for a new driver. Click Next.

8. Tell Windows 98 where to look for a new driver. If you want to try to find the latest version on the web, make sure the Microsoft Windows Update check box is checked.

   Windows 98 searches the selected locations for a new driver. Again, the most recent versions will often be found via a search of Microsoft's web-based index of device drivers.

Windows 98 might carry you off to Microsoft's approved driver index, but you might find more recent—if unapproved—drivers at the manufacturer's web site. This won't happen automatically, however. You'll have to use your web browser to go to the vendor's site, find the appropriate driver files, and download them to an empty folder on your hard disk. If the file is compressed (using PKZip or some other utility), you'll need to expand it as well. Then use the Update feature to browse over to the folder containing the files, and install from there.

9. Windows 98 tells you if it finds a more recent driver. If you wish to install the software, continue through the dialog box prompts.

10. After the driver is installed, you will have to reboot your system.

Managing Older (Non-PnP) Hardware

Things get more complicated when non-PnP hardware is involved. These so-called older devices lack the capability to be dynamically configured by Windows 98, and they might be difficult to detect during setup. In addition, PnP device installations must be able to work around existing older devices already in the system.

Because of the large number of older non-PnP devices on the market, Windows 98's Plug and Play capability is designed to work with them. Windows 98 includes a large database of hardware devices that provides information on the preferred settings for hundreds of such devices.

Older adapter cards use one of the following two methods for setting device resources:

Mechanical jumpers. These create a short circuit between two pins of a multipin header. Jumpers are commonly used to designate resource values for sound cards, and they must be set to match the resource settings of Windows 98. If jumper settings do not match those set in Windows 98, the device will not operate.

Non-volatile memory (NVM). Nonvolatile memory—such as electrically erasable, programmable read-only memory (EEPROM)—retains data when you turn off your PC's power. Network adapter cards and sound cards commonly use NVM. Usually you must run a setup program for the card to match the board settings to those of the operating system.

TROUBLESHOOTING

Windows 98 doesn't recognize my external modem. What is wrong? If you are using a 9-pin to 25-pin serial adapter, it may lack the wiring needed to pass Plug and Play data to and from your PC. You need to purchase a newer adapter that allows Plug and Play to work with your external serial device.

Older Device Detection During Windows 98 Setup

When you run Windows 98's Setup program, the OS attempts to detect all the hardware devices in your PC, including older devices such as ISA sound cards and network adapters. It then installs 32-bit protected-mode drivers for peripherals for which updated drivers are available. However, Windows 98 often keeps references to real-mode (16-bit) device drivers in the CONFIG.SYS and AUTOEXEC.BAT files, which are used when the system runs DOS software in DOS-only mode.

> **CAUTION**
>
> The CONFIG.SYS and AUTOEXEC.BAT files—and their references to real-mode drivers—are intended as a compatibility tool. These drivers enable mice, CD-ROM drives, sound cards, and other devices to run in a DOS-only session, which is not uncommon for game play. Unfortunately, the 16-bit reference in these legacy configuration files can confuse Windows, causing it to preempt changes you make in the drivers. If you find your hardware mysteriously using real-mode drivers, check for references to the hardware in the following locations: CONFIG.SYS, AUTOEXEC.BAT, INI, SYSTEM.INI. If you find such references, try to remove them and reload the 32-bit drivers, and then reboot the system. Then your hardware might run under the enhanced 32-bit drivers. Just keep in mind that you'll need to reapply those references in order to use the devices in a DOS-only session.

If Windows can't identify an older device, you need to install the device manually.

Changing Settings After a Device Is Installed

If the resource values for a newly installed device are incorrect, or if you receive a Resource Conflict message, you need to stop the detection process and do the following:

1. Open the Control Panel's System Properties sheet (click Start, Settings, Control Panel, and double-click the System icon).

2. Click the Device Manager tab. If you see an exclamation point superimposed on the new device's icon, that device is experiencing a resource conflict with other hardware.

3. Double-click the entry for the new card to display the properties sheet for the device.

4. In the Resource Settings list box, select the resource whose value you need to change and click the Change Settings button (see Figure 27.3).

> **N O T E** In some instances, such as with serial port settings, you will not be able to change the resource setting from the Resources sheet. The reason: These resources are managed down at the BIOS level, so the operating system is unable to change them. In such cases, your only option might be to change the settings from the system BIOS, which you can access at startup by pressing Delete, F1, or some other key. Check your system documentation for details. ▪

5. Use the spinner controls to adjust the number in the Value box to match the number that's preset on the device hardware.

   If a conflict with an existing card occurs, the card with the conflicting resource is identified in the Conflict Information text box. When you find a value setting that displays the No Devices Are Conflicting message in the Conflict Information text box, stick with that setting.

Part
V

Ch
27

FIG. 27.3

The Resources tab enables you to override Windows 98's automatic settings to work around IRQ, address, and DMA conflicts.

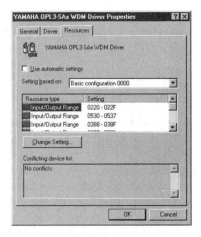

6. Make the corresponding change in the card either by using the jumpers or via software.

7. After making all the changes necessary to eliminate resource conflicts, click OK to close the resource's edit dialog box. Then click OK to close the properties sheet for the specific device.

8. Click OK to close the System Properties sheet.

9. You will be prompted to restart the system. Shut down and then restart Windows 98 to put your new settings into effect.

 TIP Plug and Play is not perfect. When you make multiple configuration changes, it can take Windows two or more restarts to sort out the situation. If you run across problems with the installed device after finishing the process, don't give up too easily. Try rebooting the system—from a cold boot, just to be sure—one or two times. Doing so might enable the hardware detection algorithms to catch all the variables in your system.

Inspecting Hardware Properties with Device Manager

The Windows 98 Device Manager is ground zero for managing resources and controlling devices. You can access this useful facility from the Windows 98 Control Panel by clicking Start, Settings, Control Panel, and then selecting the Systems icon. From the System Properties dialog box, choose the Device Manager tab. (Or, you can simply right-click the My Computer icon on the desktop, choose Properties from the context menu that appears, and click the Device Manager tab to access its interface.)

When you get to the Device Manager, you will see a scrolling list box. To see the resources for any hardware device, follow these steps:

1. Click the plus symbol next to the category of hardware you want to examine (see Figure 27.4).

FIG. 27.4
Clicking the plus (+) sign next to a device category reveals the installed hardware.

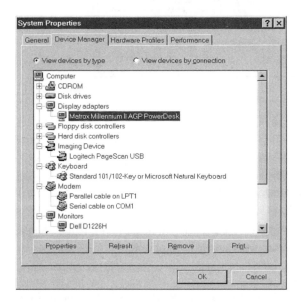

2. Select the specific device from the expanded tree-and-branch listing and click Properties. The properties dialog box for the device appears.

3. Depending on the device, you will be able to change system resources, update driver software, and alter settings from this dialog box. Make any necessary changes.

4. To put your changes into effect, click the OK button in the properties dialog box.

N O T E   The Device Manager is really nothing more than a window into the Windows 98 Registry. All the hardware configuration data provided in the Device Manager is stored in the HKEY_LOCAL_MACHINE Registry key. In some instances, you can even tweak Registry settings to achieve customizations not possible through the device's interface. ■

Part
V

Ch

27

You'll also find a very useful tool in the Device Manager. Click the Properties button at the bottom of the dialog box, and the Computer Properties dialog box appears, as shown in Figure 27.5. Click the four radio buttons to see up-to-the-minute information on IRQ, DMA, I/O, and memory settings. If you are installing a new device, it's a good idea to browse through the DMA and IRQ listings first to look for free resources before you perform the installation.

FIG. 27.5

The Computer Properties sheet features a roster of assigned IRQ, DMA, I/O, and memory resources.

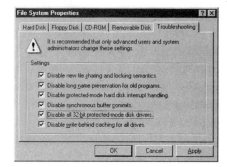

Configuring a Modem

Modems are among the most frequently updated peripherals, in part because of the rapid advance in communication data rates. In addition, many users have several dial-in routines set up for calling into various services or locations, which can require additional tweaking of the hardware. Fortunately, Windows 98 provides a sensible standard interface for adjusting modem settings.

To access modem controls, click Start, Settings, Control Panel, and then select the Modems icon. The Modem Properties dialog box appears.

 Want to see how well your modem is connecting? Launch the System Monitor by clicking Start, Programs, Accessories, System Tools, System Monitor. In the System Monitor dialog box, click Edit, Add Item. From the Category list, choose the Dial Up Adapter entry. Then click the Connection Speed item and click OK. A System Monitor chart will report the bit rate of the modem.

General Properties

When you open the Modem Properties dialog box, the General page appears first. You can have one or more modems set up under Windows 98, and they will appear in the main window of this dialog box. To change settings on a particular modem, select the desired device in the main window and click the Properties button.

In the General sheet of the dialog box that appears, you can assign the modem a new COM port address. Simply click the Port drop-down button and select the desired address. This control is often useful when your modem is conflicting with a mouse or another modem; switching to a free COM port enables the modem to work properly.

The Speaker Volume slider bar appears just below the Port control. This control lets you adjust volume so that the sound of dialing and connecting is not too loud to live with, yet remains loud enough to hear in case there is a problem.

Finally, the Maximum Speed drop-down list enables you to set the serial port to accept a desired data rate. In general, it is best to give yourself a little head room because modem compression can boost data rates above that of the reported connection rate. A setting of 57,600 or 115,200 is recommended.

Connection Properties

The Connection page of the Modem Properties dialog box lets you adjust settings that allow your modem to speak the language of other modems. If your modem is working (if you can hear it dial numbers) but fails to connect, changing some of the settings on this page might resolve the problem.

Connection Preferences   The first stop is the Connection Preferences area, where you can adjust your modem's data bit, stop bit, and parity values. In general, you should assume the following default values will work for the named controls:

> Data bit: 8
>
> Parity: None
>
> Stop bits: 1

If you continue to have problems, check with the ISP or provider on the other end to see if they use these values.

Call Preferences   The Call Preferences area enables you to customize calling behavior. It provides the following controls:

- *Wait for Dial Tone Before Dialing.* Avoids dialing if someone else is on the line. Uncheck this if you have a call messaging service that notifies you by using a stuttered dial tone.

- *Cancel the Call If Not Connected Within xxx.* Keeps your modem from indefinitely hogging the phone line if a connection is not made. The default value is 60 seconds; just be sure to allow enough time for the connection to be made.

- *Disconnect a Call If Idle for More Than xxx.* When this option is activated, Windows 98 hangs up if no modem activity is detected in the number of minutes specified in the text box.

Advanced Settings   You'll also find some less-important controls by clicking the Advanced button. From the dialog box that appears, you can turn hardware compression on and off and take control of default error-checking modes.

The Port button takes you to the Advanced Port Settings dialog box. A pair of slider bars let you commit more or less memory to storing bits coming into or going out of the modem. Moving the slider controls all the way to the right can help speed performance and avoid buffer overruns that can result in lost data.

Part

V

Ch

27

Resolving Conflicts

When it comes to resolving conflicts, the Device Manager is again the best place to start. Problems often occur when hardware devices try to grab the same system resource; however, incompatible hardware may also be the culprit.

Using the Device Manager for Conflicts

If a device is conflicting, you will see an indication on the Device Manager page of the System Properties dialog box. An exclamation point next to a device, as shown in Figure 27.6, means that a conflict has been detected.

FIG. 27.6

Windows 98 eases troubleshooting by pointing out device conflicts in the Device Manager.

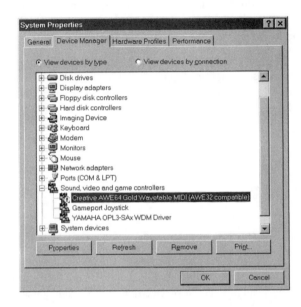

You can alter the settings for the offending device by double-clicking the highlighted item and clicking the Resource tab of the device's properties dialog box.

When a conflict exists, it is described in the Conflicting Device list box at the bottom of the sheet. To resolve the conflict, do the following:

1. Uncheck the Use Automatic Settings check box.
2. In the scrolling list box in the center of the dialog box, scroll to the desired item and double-click it.
3. Use the spinner control that appears to assign a new setting for the resource. Click OK.
4. Click OK again to put the changes into effect. You will usually have to restart the system.

Exploring File System Properties

If you experience chronic system crashes and data loss, you might try tweaking the way Windows 98 works with your disk I/O. The System Properties dialog box includes some potentially helpful tools. Follow these steps to see what you can do:

1. Click Start, Settings, Control Panel, and select the System icon.
2. Click the Performance tab, and then click the File System button.
3. In the File Systems Properties dialog box, click the Troubleshooting tab.

You will see a dialog box similar to the one shown in Figure 27.7. Use the options in this dialog box to disable key performance aspects of the Windows 98 file system, including advanced disk cache features, 32-bit file I/O, and long filename preservation. Your performance will take a hit, but turning off these features might allow you to stabilize your system long enough to replace the errant disk drives.

FIG. 27.7

Windows 98's advanced caching and file access features can upset some older hard disk and CD-ROM drives. Use the File Systems Properties dialog box to disable some features in an attempt to restore reliability.

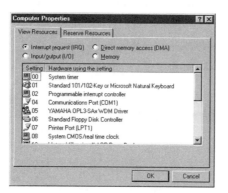

Tweaking Graphics Performance Levels

Problems can also occur when hardware such as graphics and audio accelerators don't properly support advanced features. Windows 98 lets you troubleshoot these problems by selectively turning off individual features until you find a profile that works properly.

To scale back graphics acceleration features, follow these steps:

1. Click Start, Settings, Control Panel, and select the System icon.

2. Click the Performance tab, and then click the Graphics button to display the Hardware acceleration slider bar, shown in Figure 27.8.

FIG. 27.8

Adjusting the Hardware acceleration control might help alleviate problems related to your graphics card.

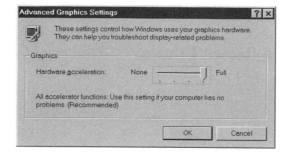

3. Drag the Hardware Acceleration slider bar to the left one notch and click OK.

4. Click Yes when Windows 98 tells you to restart the system. If the problem disappears, you know your graphics hardware can't effectively provide full capabilities.

Part

V

Ch

27

N O T E You can access this same control from the Windows 98 Control Panel by selecting the
Display icon, clicking the Settings tab, and then clicking the A<u>d</u>vanced button. In the dialog
box that appears, click the Performance tab, and the same control appears. ■

You can tweak audio capabilities in much the same way. If you are experiencing audio problems, try disabling some of the hardware acceleration in an effort to ferret out a problem.

1. From the Windows 98 Control Panel, select the Multimedia tab.

2. In the Audio sheet, click the Advanced <u>P</u>roperties button.

3. Click the Performance tab to display the audio performance controls, shown in
Figure 27.9.

FIG. 27.9

The Performance tab
lets you adjust the
sample rate of audio
data to achieve higher-
quality results or to
alleviate hardware-
related problems.

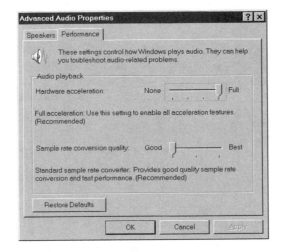

4. Drag the Hardware acceleration slider bar to the left one notch to disable part of the
audio acceleration capabilities.

5. Click OK, and then click Yes to restart the system when prompted.

Removing Unneeded Device Drivers

Sometimes problems can occur if the driver for a previously removed device has not been
uninstalled. You can remove the device driver from Windows 98's Device Manager list by following these steps:

1. Click Start, <u>S</u>ettings, <u>C</u>ontrol Panel, and double-click the System icon.

2. Click the Device Manager tab and double-click the icon for the hardware type of the
device that was removed to display the installed devices. An exclamation point superimposed on a device icon indicates a removed or inoperable device.

3. Click the list item to select the device you want to remove, and then click Re<u>m</u>ove.

4. Confirm that you want to remove the device by clicking OK in the Control Device Removal message box.

If you have more than one hardware configuration, a modified version of the Confirm Device Removal message box appears. Make sure the Remove from All Configurations option button is selected; then click OK to remove the device and close the message box.

N O T E Once again, if the driver you are removing has a reference in CONFIG.SYS, AUTOEXEC.BAT, WIN.INI, or SYSTEM.INI, you might have to remove the mention of the device from those files as well. Otherwise, Windows might load the old 16-bit version of the driver. How can you tell? After you've removed a device, restart the system and see if Device Manager shows an entry for it. If it doesn't, you're in the clear. If it does, you need to remove the offending lines from those files. ▦

Creating Hardware Profiles

Windows 98 lets you create multiple hardware profiles—a useful feature for notebook users who need different hardware settings when they are on the road or plugged into a docking station at the office. You can create hardware profiles from the Hardware Profiles page of the System Properties dialog box, shown in Figure 27.10.

Do the following:

1. Go to the System Properties dialog box by clicking Start, Settings, Control Panel, and clicking the Systems icon.
2. Click the Hardware Profiles tab.
3. Select the hardware profile present in the list box and click the Copy button.
4. In the To text box of the Copy Profile dialog box, enter the name you want to assign to the new profile.
5. Click OK. The new entry will now appear next to your default hardware profile, as shown in Figure 27.10.

N O T E The profile you create will be identical to the one you copied. To tailor the profile to meet your needs, you need to go to the properties dialog box of each peripheral, found in the Device Manager. At the bottom of the General page, you can set the device to be associated with one or all hardware profiles. ▦

Part
V

Ch
27

FIG. 27.10

Create new hardware profiles by simply copying from an existing profile.

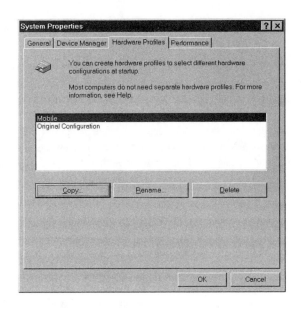

CHAPTER 28

Power Management

by Dean Andrews and Larry Passo

In this chapter

Understanding Power Management

New portable and desktop PCs feature power management capabilities that let you specify schemes for conserving power (and battery life) by shutting down devices (such as hard disks, CD-ROMs, parallel and serial ports, and so on) after a specified time of inactivity. The power management capabilities of Windows 98 allow you to control the power consumption of these various components by choosing a power scheme.

N O T E Power schemes are collections of settings for managing the power usage of your computer. ▣

CAUTION

Power management functionality might vary greatly from computer to computer because it depends on features that must be implemented in both the computer's hardware and its BIOS. Your computer might not support some or all of the power management features discussed in this chapter. See your computer's hardware documentation for details.

You can also adjust the power conservation settings for the various components of your computer in a power scheme. For example, depending on your hardware, you might be able to do any of the following:

- Turn off your monitor and hard disks automatically to save power.
- Put the computer on standby when it is idle. While on standby, your monitor and hard disks turn off, and your computer uses less power.
- Put your computer in hibernation, which turns off your monitor and hard disk, saves everything in memory on disk, and turns off your computer.

Typically, you turn off your monitor or hard disk for a short period of time to conserve power. If you plan to be away from your computer for a while, you should put your computer on standby, which puts your entire system in a low-power state.

Standby is particularly useful for conserving battery power in portable computers.

CAUTION

You might want to save your work before putting your computer on standby. While the computer is on standby, information in computer memory is not saved to your hard disk. If the power is interrupted for any reason, all information in memory will be lost.

You might put your computer in hibernation when you'll be away from the computer for an extended period of time or overnight. When you restart the computer, your desktop is restored to exactly what it was when you left it.

N O T E It takes longer to bring your computer out of hibernation than to bring it out of standby. ■

Advanced Power Management (APM)

Several specifications for PC power management have been adopted by the computer industry over the last few years. The original specification was called Advanced Power Management (APM) 1.0, and it defined interactions among a PC's hardware, BIOS, and software that let PCs operate at different levels of power consumption, such as full power, sleep, and standby. Subsequent revisions of APM added the capability to manage the power consumption of PC Card (also known as PCMCIA) devices and portables with multiple batteries, as well as other features.

However, APM has a major limitation in that it focuses on the system board and device access information when determining whether to power down devices. The BIOS might know that a PC Card device is present, but it has no way of determining if the card is actually being used. If the hard disk is being used, the BIOS has no way of determining if it is being used by a program or if the operating system is just using it as a page file for virtual memory.

Advanced Configuration and Power Interface (ACPI)

The very latest PC power management scheme, which is supported by newer computers, is called Advanced Configuration and Power Interface (ACPI) 1.0. ACPI supports the fine-tuned management of a wide variety of hardware devices.

Windows 98 supports both APM and ACPI on computers that have the appropriate BIOS and hardware for these power conservation schemes.

N O T E ACPI is an open industry specification co-developed by Intel, Microsoft, and Toshiba. ■

For notebook computers, the most important aspect of power conservation is extended battery life. By setting the appropriate power management options for your notebook's hardware under Windows 98, you can operate your notebook for several hours on batteries without being connected to an electrical outlet. Devices that can be set for power conservation under Windows 98 include hard disk drives; monitors and LCD panels; serial, parallel, and USB ports; CD-ROM drives; DVD-ROM drives; PC Card devices; and keyboards, mice, and joysticks.

N O T E Full power management capabilities are available only on systems that are compliant with the new ACPI specification. ■

Part
V

Ch
28

Legacy Hardware Support

But what if your existing hardware doesn't support ACPI? Table 28.1 outlines what will happen.

Table 28.1   What Happens if the Hardware Doesn't Support ACPI

Hardware Type	Legacy OS	Windows 98
Legacy hardware	A legacy OS on legacy hardware does what it always did.	Limited to power support that is supported by the hardware
Legacy and ACPI hardware support on the same machine	It works just like a legacy OS on legacy hardware.	During boot-up, Windows 98 tells the hardware to switch from legacy to ACPI mode, and full power management is enabled.
ACPI-only hardware management	No power	Full power management

Configuring Power Management Options

The Power Management icon in Control Panel lets you set a desired level of power management for your notebook or desktop system. Windows 98 automatically determines what type of power management capabilities your PC has. The Power Management properties sheet, shown in Figure 28.1, then displays a list of devices that can be set for different power conservation levels.

FIG. 28.1

Use the Power Management properties sheet to control the power management settings for your computer.

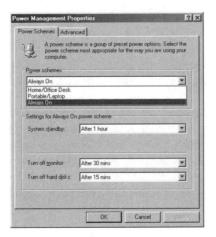

 Turn off your monitor and hard disks automatically to save power. While on standby, your monitor and hard disk use less power. When you want to use your computer again, it comes out of standby quickly, and your desktop is restored to the exact state in which you left it.

Selecting a Power Management Scheme

To modify the settings for your PC's power management, use the following procedure:

1. Click the Power Management icon in Control Panel and select the Power Schemes tab from the Power Management properties sheet, as shown in Figure 28.2.

2. In the Power Schemes box, choose the name of your power management scheme. The default schemes are Portable/Laptop, Home/Office Desk, and Always On.

3. The Settings box displays the complete list of devices in your PC that support power management.

    In the Settings for...scheme box, pick the power conservation settings for each individual device. After that device has been unused for the specified time interval, it will power down to conserve power.

FIG. 28.2

You can specify power conservation settings in the Power Management properties sheet.

 T I P If you never want a particular device to power down, choose Never in the Turn Off Hard Disks field.

4. Click OK to close the Power Management properties sheet.

 T I P If you'd like to enable the Power Meter icon in the system tray of the Windows 98 taskbar, put a check next to that option on the Advanced tab of the Power Management properties sheet. Then you can double-click the Power Meter icon in the system tray to open the Power Management properties sheet.

Part
V

Ch
28

Custom Power Management Schemes

In some cases, you might want to create a new power scheme. For example, when your notebook is docked or using AC power instead of batteries, you'll probably want to use different power management settings than when it's not docked or you're using battery power.

To create a new power scheme, use the following procedure:

1. Click the Power Management icon in Control Panel.

2. Choose the settings for the individual devices, as described in the preceding steps.

3. In the Power Schemes box, click the Save As button to display the Save Scheme dialog box, shown in Figure 28.3.

FIG. 28.3

You can save your own custom Power Management settings.

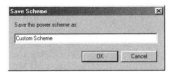

The OnNow Initiative

Windows 98 also supports a new feature called OnNow that makes your computer more responsive by reducing its startup time. Using power management techniques, OnNow can start your computer in just a few seconds and restore all your programs to the point where you left them. In addition, it allows your computer to continue working even though it appears to be turned off. This means you can leave all your programs running, download your favorite Web pages, send and receive email, back up your hard disk, or tune-up your operating system even when you're not at your computer.

Power management works on computers that support Advanced Power Management (APM), and it works even better on newer computers that support Advanced Configuration and Power Interface (ACPI). Power management also makes it possible for you to put your computer on standby or in hibernation mode to save power resources.

To humans, the PC appears to be either on or off. However, an OnNow PC is actually in one of three states:

- *Working.* The system is fully useable; power conservation occurs on a per-device basis.

- *Sleeping.* The system appears to be off. However, the system returns to the Working state in an amount of time inversely proportional to the power consumption.

- *Soft Off.* The system appears to be off. However, the system returns to the Working state after a full reboot.

N O T E Another name for OnNow might as well be NeverReallyOff. What appears to be an On/Off switch on the front panel of an OnNow computer really just signals Windows 98 to place all the hardware components of the system into a very low state of power consumption. Look for a hidden "real" power switch on the back of the system. ▪

Characteristics of an OnNow PC

New Windows 98 PCs that are compliant with the OnNow initiative have the following capabilities:

- The PC will be ready for immediate use when the power button is pressed.
- When the PC is not being used and it is considered "off," it is still capable of responding to wake-up events.

N O T E Typical wake-up events might include ringing phones or software requests (such as backup routines) that are scheduled to wake up the PC at a predetermined time.

- Software adjusts its behavior when the PC's power state changes.

CAUTION

If your applications inadvertently keep the PC busy unnecessarily, your PC will never be able to achieve the full power and noise savings that are possible with OnNow.

- All devices in the computer participate in the specified power management scheme, whether they were originally installed in the PC or added later by the user.

Part

V

Ch

28

Windows Internet Services

CHAPTER 29

Establishing a Dial-Up Internet Connection

by Ed Bott

In this chapter

Using the Internet Connection Wizard

If you can't access the Internet through an office network, look for one of the literally thousands of independent service providers and online services scattered throughout the world who will gladly give you a dial-up account—for the right price, of course. Windows 98 supplies all the software you need to make a fast, reliable Internet connection. All you need to add is a modem or other connecting device.

The first time you open the Internet icon on the desktop, you launch the Internet Connection Wizard (see Figure 29.1). After you run through this initial setup routine, when you click the Internet icon, the Internet Explorer program starts.

FIG. 29.1

These three options are just a small sampling of what you can do with the Internet Connection Wizard.

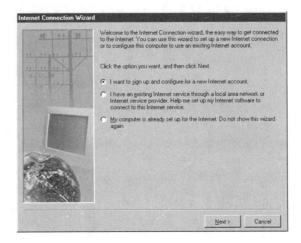

The Internet Connection Wizard is a remarkably versatile piece of software. After you get past the initial explanatory screen, you have three choices:

- You can sign up for a new Internet account. The Internet Connection Wizard offers a referral list of Internet service providers in your area.

- You can set up an existing Internet account for access through Windows 98, either over the phone or through a network.

- You can tell the Internet Connection Wizard to use your existing Internet connection. If you're comfortable with TCP/IP and networking, this is a reasonable choice.

The Internet Connection Wizard doesn't have to be just a one-time deal. You can make the wizard reappear at any time by following these steps:

1. Right-click on the Internet icon on the desktop.

2. Choose Properties, and then click the Connection tab. The dialog box shown in Figure 29.2 appears.

3. Click the Connect button.

FIG. 29.2

Want to use the Internet Connection Wizard again? Click the Conn<u>e</u>ct button on this dialog box.

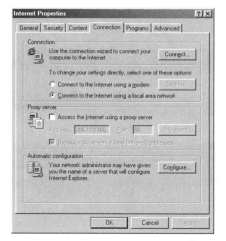

Don't underestimate the Internet Connection Wizard. Although it's easy to stereotype it as a tool for beginners, this wizard is useful for experts as well, and it handles nearly every imaginable task when it comes to setting up and managing Internet connections. Because of the sheer number of choices available when you run the Internet Connection Wizard, it's pointless (and probably impossible) to try to explain or illustrate every step in order. But this is a partial list of what you can use it for:

- Install and configure a modem (or set up a LAN connection for Internet access instead).
- Adjust the dialing settings you use, including the local area code and the prefixes you use to access outside lines.
- Create and edit Dial-Up Networking connection icons for one-button access to the Internet.
- Adjust advanced Internet settings.
- Enter and edit account information you use to connect with an Internet service provider.

N O T E   If you have not yet installed Dial-Up Networking, the Internet Connection Wizard installs these system services automatically. You will need your original Windows CD-ROM or disks, and you will need to restart the computer to complete the installation.

Installing and Configuring a Modem

There are two obvious prerequisites to any dial-up connection: You need a modem (or another type of connecting device, such as an ISDN adapter), and you need a phone line. If you haven't set up a modem previously, the Internet Connection Wizard includes a series of steps that automatically install the correct drivers and configure your modem. You can also use the Modems option in Control Panel to add a new modem or to configure an existing one.

Although most dial-up connections use only one modem at a time, you can install multiple communication devices. The system depicted in Figure 29.3, for example, includes an analog modem and an ISDN adapter. Note, however, that you can assign only one device to each Dial-Up Networking connection.

▶ **See** "Installing a Modem," **p. 532**

FIG. 29.3
This system includes two communication devices: a 3Com ISDN adapter and a Microcom analog modem. Both are available for dial-up connections.

Adding a New Analog Modem

Windows 98 does a super job of identifying and configuring the correct modem type from a list of hundreds of choices. If your modem is Plug and Play compatible, Windows should detect it automatically, install the correct drivers, and configure all relevant settings. For modems that don't take advantage of Plug and Play detection, you might have to do the installation and configuration duties manually.

N O T E PC Card modems for mobile computers require different installation procedures. Appendix E provides step-by-step instructions.

▶ **See** "Using PC Card Devices," **p. 1045** ■

To add a new modem, follow these steps:

1. Open the Modems icon in Control Panel.

2. If you have not previously set up a modem on this system, the Install New Modem Wizard appears. If you are adding a new modem, click the Add button.

3. In the Install New Modem dialog box, click the Next button to allow Windows to detect your modem, and then proceed to step 4. If you've downloaded a driver or if the manufacturer supplied a driver on disk and you're certain that this driver, is more up-to-date than the built-in Windows drivers, select the option to skip detection, click Next, and skip to step 5.

4. If Windows detected your modem properly, click Finish to install the driver. Skip over all additional steps.

   If Windows did not correctly detect your modem, click the Change button and proceed to step 5.

5. If you bypassed the detection process or if Windows did not correctly detect your modem, you'll see a list of available modem drivers. Choose the modem manufacturer from the list on the left and the model name from the list of modems on the right. If you have an updated Windows 95 or Windows 98 driver, click the Have Disk button and specify the location of the driver.

6. Select the port to which the modem is attached. Most desktop PCs have two serial ports (COM1 and COM2), and a mouse is often attached to one; Windows will not list a serial port if the mouse is attached to it. If you have multiple free serial ports, Windows should detect the correct one. You might need to check the system documentation or the label on the physical port to verify which port the modem is using.

7. Click Finish to install the driver and configure the modem.

TIP If you can't find a compatible Windows 95 or Windows 98 driver for your modem, select (Standard Modem Types) from the top of the Manufacturers list and choose the generic model that most closely matches your modem's speed. Although you will lose any advanced features included with your modem, you should be able to send and receive data at the modem's rated speed.

Configuring an Analog Modem

After you've installed drivers for an analog modem, it should be configured correctly. Still, it can't hurt to double-check settings to guarantee that the device is properly set up for maximum performance. A series of nested dialog boxes includes options for adjusting drivers, connection speeds, port assignments, and hardware-specific connection settings, including control over the volume of the modem's built-in speaker.

To set basic modem options, open the Modems icon in Control Panel, select the modem whose settings you want to adjust, and click Properties. A dialog box like the one shown in Figure 29.4 appears. Click the General tab.

FIG. 29.4

Use this properties sheet to adjust the volume of the modem's internal speaker. (Confusingly, the Maximum Speed setting does not control modem-to-modem speeds.)

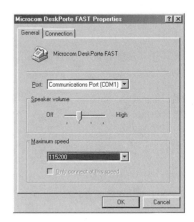

Three basic options are available here:

- *Port.* This dialog box displays the port the modem is configured to use. To switch the modem to another port, use the Port drop-down list.

- *Speaker Volume.* This is also the place to adjust the modem's speaker. The slider control uses four positions: Off, Low, Medium, and High (from left to right). For most circumstances, the Low setting is the best because it enables you to hear the dial tone and handshaking sounds so that you know to retry a connection when your modem and the one at the other end are not communicating correctly.

- *Maximum Speed.* Don't be confused by the Maximum Speed control at the bottom of this dialog box. This setting controls the internal speed at which your computer communicates with the modem, and on most Pentium-class computers, that speed is invariably faster than the transmission speed of the modem itself. Previous versions of Windows typically set this value too low. On most Pentium PCs, you can safely set the port speed to 115,200bps. Reduce this setting only if you experience persistent data errors when sending and receiving. Avoid the check box labeled Only Connect at This Speed.

To set general connection options, click the Connection tab. You'll see a dialog box like the one shown in Figure 29.5.

FIG. 29.5

Avoid the temptation to tinker with these connection settings. For most circumstances, the default settings work best.

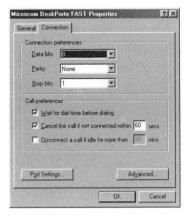

You can adjust four settings here:

- *Connection Preferences.* The Connection Preferences section at the top of the dialog box specifies settings for data bits, parity, and stop bits. These settings are typically used for direct modem-to-modem communications rather than TCP/IP connections that use the Internet-standard Point-to-Point Protocol (PPP) or Serial Line Interface Protocol (SLIP). You should not have to adjust these settings for Internet access.

- *Call Preferences.* Note the check mark in front of the box labeled Wait for Dial Tone Before Dialing. If your phone system uses a dial tone that differs from the standard U.S. dial tone, Windows mistakenly believes the line is dead and refuses to dial until you clear this box. Likewise, voice-mail systems that alter the normal dial tone to a "stutter" signal can confuse Windows unless you clear this box.

If you choose the option Cancel the Call If Not Connected Within *XX* Secs, you must enter a value for a number of seconds in the box. The 60-second timeout is sufficient for most domestic calls. If some of your dial-up connections routinely require lengthy connect times, you should increase this value to avoid timeout errors.

The Disconnect a Call If Idle for More Than *XX* Mins option lets you specify the amount of time the connection can be idle before Windows disconnects automatically. This setting is appropriate only for modem-to-modem connections; for Internet connections, use the timeout settings defined by the Internet Explorer Connection Manager.

Finally, you can set hardware-specific options that control the basic functioning of your modem. Click the Advanced button to see the dialog box shown in Figure 29.6.

FIG. 29.6

Adjust these advanced connection settings only if you understand the consequences of your actions. Unnecessary tinkering here can reduce data transmission speeds.

Four advanced options are available in this dialog box:

- *Use Error Control.* Error control options reduce the likelihood of noisy phone lines causing data corruption. Most modern modems support both data compression and error control. The modem information file should set these options for your specific modem. The Use Cellular Protocol box enables the MNP10 error-control protocol, which can be used with some (but not all) cellular modems.

- *Use Flow Control.* Flow control governs the integrity of the connection. By default, Windows 98 enables hardware flow control, and most modern modems support this mode for best performance. Software flow control should never be used for an Internet connection.

- *Modulation Type.* Do not change modulation types unless the manufacturer of your modem specifically recommends that you do so.

- *Extra Settings.* If necessary, click in the Extra Settings box and add AT commands that enable or disable a particular feature of your modem or adapter. For example, S0=5 tells your modem to answer automatically after five rings. Check your modem documentation for AT commands applicable to your hardware.

ON THE WEB

Zoom Telephonics offers a comprehensive source of information about modem technology and the AT command set. You can browse its listings at

`http://www.modems.com`

Configuring an ISDN Adapter

Most home and small-office dial-up connections use conventional analog lines. In some areas, you can use the Integrated Services Digital Network (ISDN) to establish high-speed digital connections. Compared with analog lines, ISDN circuits offer significant advantages:

- Connection times are practically instantaneous, for example, unlike on analog lines that require 20 seconds or more to establish a connection.

- Transmission speeds are typically 2–5 times faster than on most analog modems.

- The connection is digital from end to end, which means you won't lose data because of noise on the line—something that can't be said for the typical analog connection.

- A typical ISDN configuration includes two digital data channels and one analog data port, which enable you to plug in a conventional telephone or modem and then talk or send data over an analog connection while simultaneously sending and receiving data on a digital channel.

ISDN technology has its share of disadvantages as well. Generally, these lines cost more—sometimes many times more than an analog line. Not all ISPs support ISDN, and those that do often charge a premium as well. And finally, configuring an ISDN connection can be a nightmare, and the technology is difficult and filled with jargon.

ISDN hardware comes in all shapes and sizes, and every piece of hardware uses a different setup routine. Some devices install as network adapters, others as modems, and still others as routers on a network. When you choose an ISDN device using the Add Hardware option in Control Panel, Windows installs the ISDN Wizard. This tool allows you to configure the technical details of your ISDN line, as shown in Figure 29.7.

FIG. 29.7

Although some ISDN adapters emulate modems, this device from Eicon Systems looks like a network card to Windows 98.

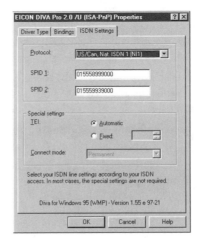

ON THE WEB

For more information about ISDN technology, check out Dan Kegel's detailed web page at

`http://www.alumni.caltech.edu/~dank/isdn/`

For details on how to order ISDN service, plus links to updates of the ISDN software for Windows 98, try Microsoft's Get ISDN page.

`http://www.microsoft.com/windows/getisdn/about.htm`

Although the ISDN Configuration Wizard makes setup somewhat easier than it used to be, the process is still complex. When connecting an ISDN line, you must get detailed instructions from the manufacturer of the adapter and from the phone company—and then follow those instructions to the letter. At a minimum, you'll need to know the service provider IDs (SPIDs), the telephone numbers for each channel, and the switch type used in the telephone company office. Some ISDN hardware includes a utility that enables you to upload this information to the adapter itself.

TIP After you successfully install your ISDN adapter, it appears as a choice in the Internet Connection Wizard and the Dial-Up Networking Wizard.

Other High-Speed Access Options

Telephone companies are no longer the only sources of access to the Internet. There is an increasing number of high-speed alternatives to traditional dial-up access that use different types of wires—and in some cases no wires at all.

Hughes Network Systems, for example, sells a small satellite dish called DirecDuo, which provides Internet access at speeds of up to 400Kbps as well as several hundred channels of TV programming. Not to be outdone, many phone companies are rolling out systems that use Digital Subscriber Line (DSL) technology to provide Internet access at speeds in excess of 1MB per second, while allowing you to use the same line for voice calls. And some cable TV companies now offer Internet access over the same cable you use to receive television signals.

Depending on the system configuration, these solutions can deliver data at speeds of up to 10MB per second, roughly on a par with local area network performance. Although Windows 98 does not offer built-in support for any of these cutting-edge technologies, third parties offer hardware and Windows drivers that work well. If you plan to use any of these services, be sure to ask the provider for detailed instructions on how to access the service from Windows 98.

Configuring a Connection to an Existing Internet Account

Windows 98 uses a service called Dial-Up Networking (DUN) to connect your system to the Internet over telephone lines. The Internet Connection Wizard automatically installs DUN if necessary. Individual connection icons within the Dial-Up Networking folder contain all the information you need to connect with the Internet. You'll find the Dial-Up Networking folder in the My Computer window. To open this system folder from the Start menu, click Start and choose Programs, Accessories, Dial-Up Networking.

If you already have an account with an Internet service provider, the wizard's step-by-step procedures can help you create a Dial-Up Networking connection with a minimum of clicking and typing. The default settings assume you're making a standard PPP connection, with IP address and DNS settings assigned dynamically. Follow these steps:

1. Start the Internet Connection Wizard and choose the option to set up a new connection to an existing account. Click Next to continue.

2. Choose the option to connect using your phone line and click Next.

3. Choose the modem you want to use with this connection and click Next. (If you haven't set up a modem, you'll be able to do so here.)

4. You can choose an existing connection icon if there are any in your Dial-Up Networking folder. In this case, or if you don't have any existing connections, select the option to create a new icon. Then click Next to continue.

5. Enter the dial-in phone number of your Internet service provider and click Next.

6. Enter your username and password and click Next.

7. The wizard asks whether you want to adjust advanced settings for the connection. For standard PPP connections for which you don't need to specify an IP address or DNS servers, select No and click Next. (See the next section, "Adjusting Advanced Settings," for more information on when and how to adjust the advanced settings.)

8. Give the connection a descriptive name, as in Figure 29.8, and click Next.

FIG. 29.8

The default connection icon uses a generic name. You can add location info to make the icon's purpose easier to identify.

9. If you need to set up mail and news accounts or a directory server, the wizard provides separate steps to help with each of these tasks. (See Chapter 32 for instructions on setting up these accounts.) When you reach the end of the wizard, click Finish to create the Dial-Up Networking connection icon.

Adjusting Advanced Settings

As you saw in step 7 of the previous procedure, the Internet Connection Wizard includes an option for adjusting advanced connection settings. If your Internet service provider uses a SLIP connection or requires scripting, or if you need to enter a fixed IP address and specify addresses for DNS servers, select Yes in the Advanced Settings dialog box (see Figure 29.9) and fill in the four boxes that follow.

FIG. 29.9

When you select Yes in the dialog box, the Internet Connection Wizard takes a brief detour into advanced configuration options.

Advanced settings include the following:

- *Connection Type.* Choose PPP or SLIP connection.
- *Logon Procedure.* Select the manual option to bring up a terminal window when connecting, or specify a logon script.
- *IP Address.* If your ISP provides a fixed IP address, enter it here.
- *DNS Server Address.* If your ISP requires you to specify primary and backup name servers, enter their IP addresses here.

 These advanced settings are useful if you have multiple dial-up accounts (a corporate dial-up server and a personal account with an ISP, for example). Create a separate Dial-Up Networking icon for each account, and then individually adjust the IP address and other settings for each connection icon.

Using Multilink Options for Faster Connections

Most dial-up Internet connections are simple one-modem, one-line propositions, and transmission speed is limited by the slower of the two modems at the ends of the connection. Under specialized circumstances, though, you can use two or more connecting devices to increase the speed of a dial-up connection. These so-called *multilink connections* require the following conditions:

- You must have multiple devices to bind together into a single virtual connection.
- Each device requires its own driver software.

■ Each device needs access to a separate analog phone line or a channel on an ISDN line.

■ The dial-up server at the other end of the connection must support multilink PPP connections.

The most common use of multilink connections is to join two 56KB or 64KB channels on an ISDN line to create a 112KB or 128KB connection.

To enable multilink options on an existing connection, follow these steps:

1. Open the Dial-Up Networking folder, right-click on the connection icon you want to modify, and choose Properties from the shortcut menu.

2. Click the Multilink tab. The dialog box shown in Figure 29.10 appears.

FIG. 29.10

If your Internet service provider supports multilink PPP, use these settings to combine two modems to create a faster virtual connection.

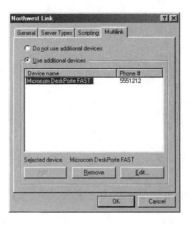

3. Select the Use Additional Devices option, and the grayed-out buttons at the bottom of the dialog box become available.

4. Click the Add button and choose a modem or ISDN adapter from the drop-down list. If no choices are available, click Cancel and set up your additional hardware. Then continue.

5. Enter a separate phone number for the additional device, if required. The hardware documentation and service provider can supply more details about your specific configuration.

6. Select any entry in the list and use the Remove or Edit button to modify the entry.

7. Click OK to save your changes.

Creating and Editing Logon Scripts

Today, most commercial Internet service providers use logon servers that communicate easily with Windows Dial-Up Networking connections. Some older providers or noncommercial dial-up sites, however, might require additional keyboard input that the Windows connection can't provide. In such cases, you must create a logon script for use with the Dial-Up Networking connection. When you open a connection icon whose configuration details include a script,

Windows opens a terminal window and sends the additional commands. The script might operate unattended in the background, or it might stop and require that you make an entry in the terminal window.

Script files are simple text files that end in the extension .SCP. You'll find these four general-purpose scripts in the Program Files\Accessories folder:

- CIS.SCP establishes a PPP connection with CompuServe.
- PPPMENU.SCP logs on to a server that uses text menus.
- SLIP.SCP establishes a SLIP connection with a remote host machine.
- SLIPMENU.SCP establishes a SLIP connection on a menu-based host.

TIP Some scripts require editing before use. If so, it's prudent to back up the script file you plan to modify before you make any changes.

To assign a script to a connection icon, follow these steps:

1. Open the Dial-Up Networking folder, right-click on the icon, and choose Properties from the shortcut menu.
2. Click the Scripting tab. The dialog box shown in Figure 29.11 appears.

FIG. 29.11

Choose a logon script from this dialog box. Then click the Edit button to open Notepad and edit the script.

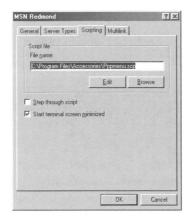

3. Click the Browse button and navigate to the Accessories folder. Select a script from the list and click Open.
4. If you need to modify the script, click the Edit button. The script opens in Notepad. Make any necessary changes and save your changes before closing the editing window.
5. To avoid being distracted by the script as it runs, check the Start Terminal Screen Minimized box.
6. To tell Windows that you want the script to pause after each step so you can see where modifications are needed, check the Step Through Script box.
7. Click OK to save your changes.

When you open a Dial-Up Networking connection with a script attached, the terminal window appears. If you selected the Step Through Script option, you'll also see the Automated Script Test window shown in Figure 29.12.

FIG. 29.12

Use the step option to walk through a logon script one step at a time for debugging purposes.

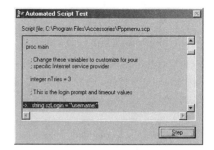

Normally, the terminal window doesn't accept keyboard input. If you need to respond to a prompt, check the Allow Keyboard Input box. When the script has finished processing, you might need to click Continue to complete the connection.

N O T E For detailed documentation of the dial-up scripting language, look in the Windows folder for a file named SCRIPT.DOC. ■

Setting Up a New Account with an Internet Service Provider

The top option on the Internet Connection Wizard lets you choose an Internet service provider and set up a new Internet account. Although you can research available ISPs and sign up for an account on your own, this wizard offers a quick, hassle-free way to change service providers or set up a new account.

Using the wizard is a straightforward process. You specify the country you live in, the area (or city) code, and any necessary dialing instructions. The wizard installs a handful of required software components, including support for TCP/IP and Dial-Up Networking. During the setup and configuration process, the wizard may restart your system one or more times. Although the wizard manages the details of shutting down and restarting, you'll have to respond to dialog boxes like the one in Figure 29.13 to move the installation process along.

Eventually, the wizard makes two phone calls. The first is to Microsoft's Internet Referral Service, which uses your area (or city) code and the first three digits of your phone number to identify Windows 98-compatible Internet service providers available in your area and language. Because Microsoft regularly updates the roster of eligible service providers, the exact choices you see will vary; the list should resemble the one shown in Figure 29.14.

FIG. 29.13

The Internet Connection Wizard's automatic signup option requires almost no intervention except for input in this dialog box.

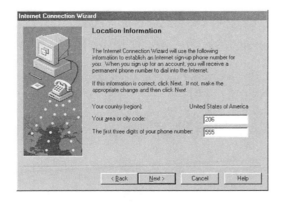

FIG. 29.14

The Microsoft Internet Referral Service generates a list of available Internet service providers just for you, based on your location and operating system.

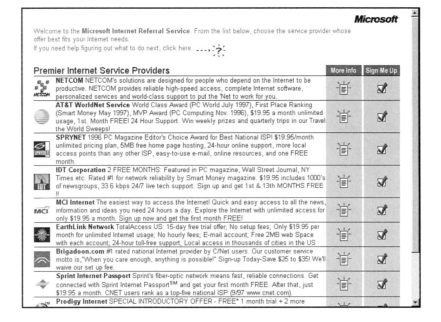

If the summary information isn't enough to help you decide, click the More Info icon to the right of a listing for extra details about that company's services. When you're ready to choose, click the Sign Me Up icon to the right of the entry you want. The Internet Connection Wizard makes a second phone call—this one to the provider you've chosen.

Each provider's signup procedure varies, but in general you'll have to supply your name, address, and credit card info. The wizard takes care of all remaining details, including setting up Dial-Up Networking connection icons and installing any necessary access software.

Managing Dial-Up Networking Connections

Windows stores every connection icon you create in the Dial-Up Networking folder. Although you can make copies and shortcuts for use elsewhere, the only way to create or manage these icons is to open the Dial-Up Networking folder (see Figure 29.15). You'll find it in the My Computer folder or inside the Accessories folder on the Start menu.

N O T E Believe it or not, some Microsoft documentation calls these icons *connectoids*. ■

FIG. 29.15
Open the Dial-Up Networking folder to create or manage your connection icons. Note the additional Create and Dial icons in the toolbar.

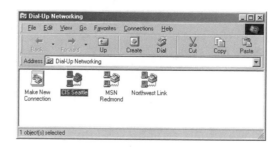

Like the Desktop, Control Panel, and Printers folders, the Dial-Up Networking folder is a special system folder and doesn't have a corresponding MS-DOS–style directory. To make this folder more accessible, open the My Computer window and drag the Dial-Up Networking icon onto the Quick Launch bar, or drag the icon onto the Start button to create a shortcut at the top of the Start menu.

Adding a New DUN Connection

As you've seen, the Internet Connection Wizard creates connection icons as part of the process of configuring your Internet connection. If you're comfortable working directly with connection icons, you can create them from scratch using a two-step wizard accessible from the Dial-Up Networking folder. Follow these steps:

1. Open the Dial-Up Networking folder and open the Make New Connection icon.

2. In the Make New Connection Wizard, give the connection a name and select a modem or other communication device. Then click <u>N</u>ext.

3. Enter the area (or city) code, country code, and phone number of the server you want to dial. Click <u>N</u>ext.

4. Click Finish to save the connection in the Dial-Up Networking folder, where you can edit it later.

CAUTION

Although this is a quick way to create a Dial-Up Networking icon, the default settings will almost always require editing. For example, by default these connections use three different protocols; for most Internet connections, only TCP/IP is needed.

Adjusting the Properties of an Existing Connection Icon

Regardless of how you create a Dial-Up Networking connection icon, you can change its properties at any time. Open the Dial-Up Networking folder, select an icon, right-click the icon, and choose Properties. You'll see a multi-tabbed dialog box like the one in Figure 29.16.

FIG. 29.16

Use this dialog box to change the phone number or modem associated with a connection.

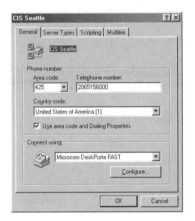

On the General tab, you can adjust the area code, country code, and phone number for any connection. You can also change the modem or other connecting device you use for the connection.

Click the Server Types tab to adjust properties specific to the server with which you plan to connect. Figure 29.17 shows the choices available.

FIG. 29.17

If your ISP uses any nonstandard settings, you need to adjust them here.

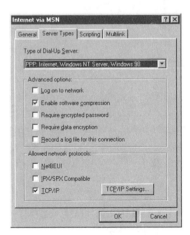

The Type of Dial-Up Server drop-down list contains five choices. You'll select PPP in most cases. If you're dialing in to a UNIX server with a shell account, however, you might need to choose SLIP or CSLIP.

N O T E *PPP* stands for Point-to-Point Protocol. *SLIP* is short for Serial Line Interface Protocol. PPP has largely replaced SLIP as the standard method of remotely accessing Internet service providers, thanks to its better error-checking features and its capability to handle automatic logons. ▪

Unless your ISP recommends that you change settings in the Advanced Options area, leave that section alone; the defaults are correct for standard PPP connections. For example, most ISPs support Password Authentication Protocol (PAP) or the Challenge-Handshake Authentication Protocol (CHAP). If you check the Require Encrypted Password box, you won't be able to log on.

For Internet access, you can improve performance by clearing the check marks in front of NetBEUI and IPX/SPX in the list of Allowed Network Protocols. TCP/IP is all you need unless you're dialing in to a Windows NT server.

▶ **See** "Connecting to a Remote Access Server," **p. 950**

Finally, click the TCP/IP Settings button to check the configuration details of your connection. You'll see a dialog box like the one in Figure 29.18.

FIG. 29.18

If your ISP has assigned you a static IP address, enter it here, along with the addresses of DNS servers.

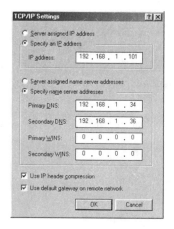

The default settings for a Dial-Up Networking connection assume you're dialing in to a network that assigns you an IP address automatically each time you connect, without requiring that you specify DNS servers. On networks that use static IP addresses, you manually fill in your IP address and the addresses of DNS servers. For access to an ISP, leave the WINS server entries blank and don't change the default gateway or IP header compression unless your ISP specifically recommends it.

Creating a Shortcut to a Dial-Up Connection Icon

Although connection icons can exist only in the Dial-Up Networking folder, you can create shortcuts to those icons and put them anywhere you want. To place a shortcut on the desktop, open the Dial-Up Networking folder, select an icon, right-click it, and choose Create Shortcut. You can also right-drag a connection icon to any folder or onto the Start menu and choose Create Shortcut(s) Here from the menu that appears when you release the icon.

Moving or Copying Connection Icons

Right-clicking a connection icon does not produce Cut, Copy, or Paste menus. But you can share these icons with other users or copy them to other machines if you know the undocumented technique. When you drag a connection icon out of the Dial-Up Networking folder and drop it in any legal location, including the desktop or a mail message, Windows creates a special Dial-Up Networking Exported File, which has the .DUN extension.

Although these exported files resemble shortcuts, they behave differently. There's no shortcut arrow, for example. In addition, when you right-click a Dial-Up Networking Exported File icon and choose Properties, you see an abbreviated properties sheet in place of the normal shortcut information. But if you drop one of these files in the Dial-Up Networking folder of another machine running Windows 95 (with Dial-Up Networking version 1.1 or later) or Windows 98, it works just as though you'd created the connection from scratch. This is an excellent technique for quickly giving other users access to Dial-Up Networking without forcing them to go through the process of creating a connection icon from scratch.

Renaming and Deleting Connection Icons

To rename a connection icon, open the Dial-Up Networking folder, select the icon, right-click, and choose Rename. To delete a connection icon, select the icon, right-click, and choose Delete.

Using Locations to Control Dial-Up Connections

Each time you use a Dial-Up Networking connection icon, you have the option of specifying which *location* you want to dial from. Settings for each location include the area (or city) code for that location, calling card information, prefixes required to reach an outside line or to dial long distance, and much more. Locations are especially useful for owners of portable PCs: By doing nothing more than selecting a location entry from a list, you can tell Windows to simply dial the access number for your ISP's server when you're at home, but to use a dialing prefix, area code, and calling card number when you're on a business trip in another location.

Even if you always dial in from your home or office, you can still take advantage of multiple locations. This is especially true if your Dial-Up Networking calls sometimes incur long distance or toll charges or if your telephone company requires special dialing procedures for nearby area codes.

To set up dialing locations for the first time, use the Telephony option in Control Panel. To adjust dialing options on-the-fly when you're making a dial-up connection, click the Dial Properties button to the right of the phone number in the Connect To dialog box. And if you've opened the Modems option in Control Panel, you can click the Dialing Properties button on the bottom of the General tab. Regardless of which technique you use, you'll see a dialog box like the one in Figure 29.19.

FIG. 29.19

Don't be fooled by the name; you can use dialing locations to define dialing prefixes and area code preferences or to bill your calls to a telephone credit card.

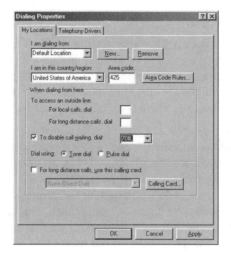

N O T E   Why are dialing settings grouped under the Telephony icon? All 32-bit Windows communications programs use a common feature set called the Telephony Application Programming
Interface, or TAPI for short. Programs that use TAPI can detect when another TAPI-aware program wants
to use a phone line, which makes it easier for the two programs to share a single line gracefully. A
simple TAPI function lets them use centrally defined dialing settings as well. ▪

If your ISP has multiple access numbers and you sometimes get a busy signal on your local
number, you might want to call a number outside your area code. To that end, you can set up a
location that lets you charge the daytime calls to a less-expensive long-distance provider using
a telephone credit card.

Follow these steps to set up a new location called "Credit Card Call from Home":

1. Use the Telephony option in Control Panel to open the Dialing Properties dialog box.
2. Click the New button, and then click OK in the message box that confirms you've
   created a new location.
3. Note that the text in the box labeled I Am Dialing From is selected. Start typing to replace
   the default location name with a descriptive entry, such as **Credit Card Call from Home**.
4. Check the box labeled For Long Distance Calls, Use This Calling Card.
5. Select your calling card number from the drop-down list. If you're using a prepaid card
   or if your telephone card isn't in the list, select None (Direct Dial).
6. Click the Calling Card button, and the dialog box shown in Figure 29.20 appears.
7. If you're creating a new card type, click the New button and give the entry a name. Enter
   your PIN (if required) and enter or verify access numbers for long distance and international calls.
8. Click the Long Distance Calls button. The dialog box shown in Figure 29.21 appears,
   with suggested default settings for your call. Make a note of the sequence of steps your
   long distance company requires for you to make a call with your calling card, and then
   use the drop-down lists to add or edit those steps here.

FIG. 29.20
Use the Calling Card dialog box to set up access options for a telephone calling card.

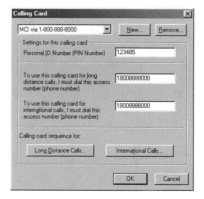

FIG. 29.21
Although this dialog box looks daunting, it's remarkably effective for scripting calls you make with a calling card.

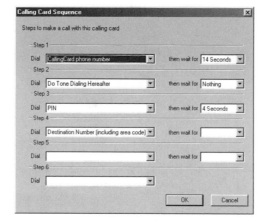

9. Click OK to save this sequence. Repeat the process for international calls if necessary.

10. Click OK to save your dialing settings.

Now, whenever you want to call a Dial-Up Networking connection using a telephone calling card, select the appropriate location in the Connect To box, and Windows will automatically dial the correct sequence of tones.

 T I P Because Telephony locations work with all TAPI applications, you can use these same calling card settings with the Windows 98 Phone Dialer (found in the Accessories group) and other communication programs as well.

Another good use of dialing options, at least for residents of the United States, is to help cope with the explosion of new area codes over the past few years. There was a time when you dialed all local calls direct and dialed 1 plus the area code and number for long distance. No more. Today, most large metropolitan areas have already been partitioned into smaller zones, each with its own area code. As a result, some local calls demand an area code, but others don't. And there's no firm set of rules that dictate when you dial 1.

The version of Dial-Up Networking that debuted in Windows 95 worked well enough, but it fell down completely on this job. Windows 98 vastly improves your ability to deal with nonstandard area codes and dialing configurations. To adjust these options, open the Dialing Properties dialog box and click the Area Code Rules button. You'll see the dialog box shown in Figure 29.22.

FIG. 29.22

Have local dialing rules changed for you? Use these advanced area code options to tell Windows exactly how to dial.

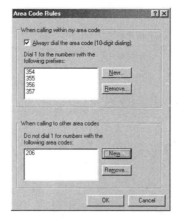

Use the options at the top of the dialog box to specify dialing rules for prefixes within your own area code. The bottom options specify how to handle nearby area codes.

> **T I P** Would you prefer to not use dialing properties at all? When you create a Dial-Up Networking connection icon, clear the check mark from the box labeled Use Area Code and Dialing Properties. Then enter the phone number exactly as you'd like Windows to dial it, complete with any prefixes, area codes, city or country codes, and calling card numbers.

Using The Microsoft Network for Internet Access

Although it started out with the launch of Windows 95 as on online service competing with America Online and CompuServe, today The Microsoft Network (MSN) is a curious hybrid. Though partly an entertainment medium with "channels" of content ranging from the Disney Blast to Microsoft Investor, it's also a low-cost Internet service provider with worldwide coverage and a variety of access plans.

Naturally, Microsoft makes it easy to install the MSN access software and sign up for a trial account. Look on the Windows desktop for an icon called Set Up the Microsoft Network. If you choose this option, it will load nearly 4MB of software and call a Microsoft server to establish your account. Although MSN uses many of the same components as Windows 98 (most notably Internet Explorer 4.0), it also adds its own distinctive touches, including a custom Connection Manager.

A typical MSN setup makes these changes to your system:

- MSN's Connection Manager replaces the Internet Explorer dialer.
- MSN automatically configures email and news accounts with the username you choose at startup.
- The icon in Outlook Express and Internet Explorer changes from the stylized Explorer logo to MSN's logo.
- An additional icon appears in the taskbar's notification area when you're connected to MSN. Right-click on that icon to access a cascading menu with access to all of MSN's services.

In addition, MSN makes other subtle changes throughout the operating system, including installing and configuring a handful of multimedia players.

 TIP If you use MSN to access the Internet but aren't fond of its interface, you can have the best of both worlds. When you install MSN, it adds a connection icon to the Dial-Up Networking folder. Use that icon to connect, and you'll bypass all of the MSN interface changes. Even if you uninstall the MSN software completely, you can still access your MSN account with this connection icon. If you do so, for your username, enter MSN/*username* (include the slash, but substitute your username) and dial your local MSN access number.

Using Other Online Services

Increasingly, online services resemble Internet service providers both in the services they offer and the rates they charge. When you open the Online Services folder on the Windows desktop, you have access to shortcuts with which you can connect to America Online (AOL), AT&T WorldNet, CompuServe (which is now owned by AOL), and Prodigy Internet.

The icons in the desktop folder are shortcuts to much larger setup files stored on the Windows 98 CD-ROM. You can use these icons to open a new account or to enable access to an existing account with one of these services.

For more details about each of the online services, including technical support numbers, see the text file in the Online Services folder.

Connecting to the Internet

After you've created a Dial-Up Networking icon that contains your connection settings, you can establish a connection using any of these three methods:

- Open the Dial-Up Networking folder and use that icon to manually connect to the Internet. This option gives you maximum control over when and how you connect to the Internet.

■ Set up Internet Explorer to automatically open a Dial-Up Networking connection whenever you attempt to access a web page. By default, this option requires you to respond to a confirmation dialog box before actually dialing. This is your best choice if you use a single line for voice and data calls.

■ Use advanced settings in the Dial-Up Networking folder to make a hands-free connection that doesn't require confirmation from you whenever you attempt to access any Internet resource. This option is best if you have a dedicated data line and don't want any interruptions from Windows.

Making a Manual Connection

To connect to the Internet manually, follow these steps:

1. Select the connection icon and open it. A dialog box like the one shown in Figure 29.23 appears.

FIG. 29.23
Regardless of the settings you defined for the connection icon, this dialog box lets you temporarily change the phone number, username, location, and other settings.

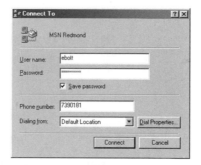

2. Check your username and enter a password if necessary. To store the password for reuse, check the Save Password box.

3. Check the entry in the Phone Number box. If the format is incorrect, choose a new location or edit the number to include the required prefixes.

4. Click the Connect button. Windows opens a modem connection and attempts to dial the number. You'll see a series of status messages, like the one in Figure 29.24, as the connection proceeds.

FIG. 29.24
Status messages like this can help you identify problems when making an Internet connection.

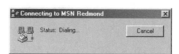

After you successfully complete the connection, you'll see an informational dialog box like the one in Figure 29.25. At the same time, a Dial-Up Networking icon appears in the notification area to the right of the taskbar.

FIG. 29.25

If you'd prefer not to see this dialog box after every completed connection, check the option just above the Close button.

Connecting (and Disconnecting) Automatically

Internet Explorer includes a component called Connection Manager, which can automatically establish an Internet connection whenever you attempt to access a web page. You can configure Connection Manager to pause for confirmation or to dial automatically.

N O T E   Connection Manager does not work with other Internet programs. If you want Outlook Express to dial automatically each time you check your mail, you'll have to set up separate dialing options using that program. See Chapter 32 for details on how to set up an automatic mail and news connection. ▓

To set up Connection Manager, open the Internet Options dialog box and click the Connection tab. Choose the option labeled Connect to the Internet Using a Modem, and then click the Settings button. The Dial-Up Settings dialog box shown in Figure 29.26 appears.

FIG. 29.26

Internet Explorer can handle the dialing duties, but you'll have to specify these options first.

Use the Add button to create a new connection.

Enter your username and password here; domain name is unnecessary for most ISP connections.

Set this interval to disconnect automatically if there's no activity.

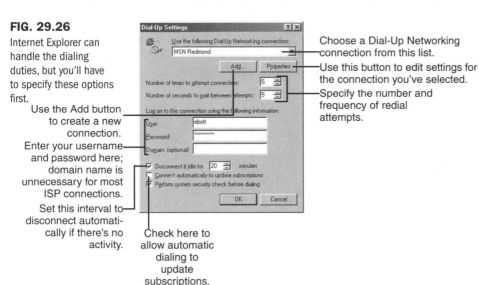

Choose a Dial-Up Networking connection from this list.

Use this button to edit settings for the connection you've selected.

Specify the number and frequency of redial attempts.

Check here to allow automatic dialing to update subscriptions.

After you've configured all Connection Manager options, click OK to close the Dial-Up Settings dialog box, and click OK again to close the Internet Options dialog box. Then open Internet Explorer and try to access a web page. If you don't have an open Internet connection, you'll see a dialog box like the one in Figure 29.27.

FIG. 29.27
By default, Connection Manager prompts you before trying to make a dial-up connection.

Here are some tips for getting maximum benefit out of Connection Manager:

- Check the Save Password box to store your password in the Windows cache. Remove the check from this box if you don't want other users to be able to access your Internet account.
- If you see the Connection Manager dialog box but you're not ready to connect, click the Work Offline button.
- Check the box labeled Connect Automatically, and you won't need to confirm your action each time you dial.

The Disconnect If Idle option automatically closes your dial-up connection if there's been no activity for the amount of time you specify. The default value is 20 minutes, but you can reset the idle time to any value between 3 and 59 minutes.

If you're working with a web page when the idle-time setting expires, Internet Explorer won't suddenly close the connection. Instead, you'll see an Auto Disconnect warning dialog box like the one shown in Figure 29.28. You have 30 seconds to respond before Connection Manager shuts down access to the Internet.

The Auto Disconnect dialog box gives you these options:

- Click the Disconnect Now button to close the connection immediately.
- Click the Stay Connected button to reset the timer and continue working with Internet Explorer.
- Check the Don't Use Auto Disconnect box to disable this feature until you reset it. (This has the same effect as clearing the check box in the Dial-Up Settings dialog box.)

FIG. 29.28
You'll receive fair warning before Connection Manager shuts down an open connection.

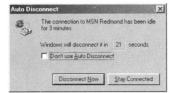

> **CAUTION**
>
> Some sites can keep an Internet connection open indefinitely. For example, stock tickers that automatically refresh every few minutes will keep your connection from hanging up, as will sites that deliver streaming data such as RealAudio. Don't expect Internet Explorer to disconnect automatically if you leave one of these pages open and then walk away from your computer.

Making a Hands-Free Manual Connection

If you prefer not to use the Connection Manager, open the Internet Options dialog box and configure Internet Explorer to connect using a local area network. You'll have to connect manually using a Dial-Up Networking connection icon before attempting to access a web page. To turn this into a single-click process, follow these steps:

1. Open the Dial-Up Networking folder.

2. Open the connection icon you want to automate, and then enter your username and password. Check the Save Password box.

3. Click Connect. When the status dialog box appears, click Cancel to abort the connection and return to the DUN folder.

4. Choose Connections, Settings.

5. Clear the check marks in front of the boxes labeled Prompt for Information Before Dialing and Show a Confirmation Dialog After Connected, as shown in Figure 29.29.

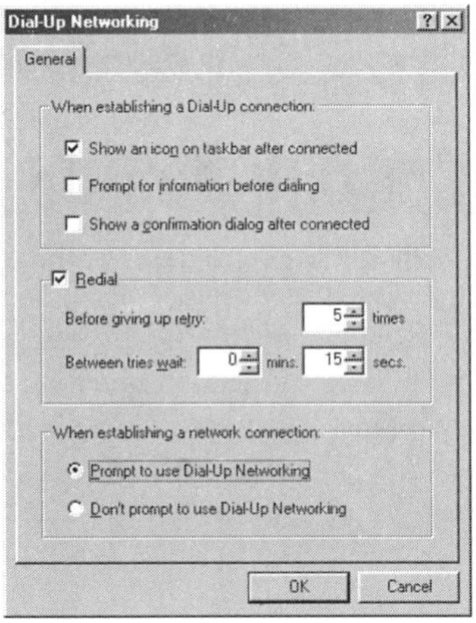

FIG. 29.29
Use these settings to bypass all dialog boxes when you click on a connection icon.

6. Check the Redial box and set automatic retry options if desired.

7. Click OK to save your changes.

Monitoring Connection Status

Whenever you have an open connection to the Internet, you can check its status in a variety of ways. For example, you can double-click the icon in the notification area, or you can right-click and choose Status to see a display showing the total length of time this connection has been open and the total number of bytes you've received and sent (see Figure 29.30).

FIG. 29.30

To eliminate the display of connection information in the bottom of this status window, click the No Details button.

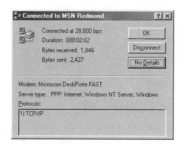

 T I P To see status information at a glance without opening a dialog box, simply point to the icon in the notification area. After a few seconds, a ScreenTip will appear.

Closing Your Internet Connection

When you've finished working with your Internet connection, you have three options for closing it:

- Right-click the icon in the notification area and choose Disconnect.

- Right-click the connection icon in the Dial-Up Networking folder and choose Disconnect. (Note that the same menu is available if you right-click on a shortcut to a connection icon.) This technique is useful if the taskbar icon is not available for some reason.

- If the connection status dialog box is open, click the Disconnect button.

Troubleshooting and Optimizing Dial-Up Connections

In a perfect world, your computer would be able to process data packets as fast as your modem could deliver them. Unfortunately, there's rarely anything perfect about online communications. Some users find it nearly impossible to connect to the Internet at their modem's rated speed under any circumstances; others find that connection speeds are maddeningly variable (dialing the same access number with the same hardware might result in a high-speed connection one time, while a few minutes later the system might connect at a fraction of its rated speed).

Diagnosing connection problems can be extremely frustrating. Connecting with an Internet server can involve dozens of computers and network links, and the slowest link in that chain dictates the speed of the connection. Sometimes the bottleneck is at the server itself; when Microsoft releases a new version of Internet Explorer, for example, its servers invariably slow to a crawl in the face of overwhelming demand. In addition, physical problems such as a sliced fiber-optic cable on the Internet's backbone can cause slowdowns for every server that depends on that segment.

The initial connection speed doesn't always tell the full performance story either. Using the V.34 and V.90 standards, modems can shift speeds on-the-fly, varying up or down to compensate for changes at either end of the connection. The only surefire way to measure the effectiveness of a connection is to measure net throughput; if you download a file from a web site, for example, Internet Explorer will display throughput statistics in a dialog box (see Figure 29.31). With experience, you'll learn to detect when a connection is abnormally slow and when you should begin the diagnostic process.

FIG. 29.31

How fast is that connection, really? Use data throughput statistics such as these to measure performance instead of relying on the reported connection speed.

When you encounter performance problems with dial-up connections, try using the following steps to isolate and repair the problem.

1. Check Hardware Settings and Driver Files

First, make sure you're using the correct driver for your modem. If you must use a generic driver for your 56KB modem, be sure to choose the correct one. (Windows 98 includes separate high-speed drivers for older modems that use the incompatible K56flex and X2 technologies, for example.)

T I P In early 1998, the International Telecommunications Union finally agreed on a standard for 56KB modems. The final standard goes by the designation V.90; if you own a high-speed modem that uses an earlier version of 56KB technology, contact the modem manufacturer for up-to-date information on upgrades, and check with your ISP to see which standards it supports.

Next, check with the modem manufacturer to see whether an upgrade is available for the modem's *firmware*, the internal microcode that dictates how the hardware works with communications software, including Windows Dial-Up Networking. Many newer modems store this code in programmable flash memory, which allows you to download bug fixes and install them just as you would upgrade a system BIOS.

Finally, make sure that you've configured your serial port to work at the proper speed. If you've throttled the port rate to 19,200bps, for example, that will be the maximum throughput you can expect—regardless of the modem's capabilities. For a 28.8 or 33.6 modem, you must set your port rate to at least 38,400bps, and 56KB modems require a minimum port speed of 57,600bps. (See the section "Configuring an Analog Modem," earlier in this chapter, for details on how to adjust the Maximum Speed setting for a modem.)

N O T E Don't be misled by advertisements for high-speed modems. Although it's theoretically possible for analog modems to communicate at 57,600bps, limitations on phone lines in the United States restrict maximum transmission speeds to roughly 53KB, and that speed is available downstream only (when the data is flowing to your modem). The upstream data speed (data flowing to your ISP or between two modems over a conventional analog line), cannot exceed 33.6KB. ■

2. Check for Phone Line and Wiring Problems

Faulty wiring and noisy phone lines are among the most common causes of connection problems. If you routinely connect at speeds well below your modem's rated capabilities and you've ruled out configuration problems, try the following suggestions:

- Connect to a variety of numbers in different geographic areas to verify that the problem is on your end of the connection and is not caused by a faulty modem on the other end of the line. If your connection speed remains the same for local and long distance calls to a variety of locations, the problem is probably on your end.

- Dial a number that you know connects to a clean line and listen carefully to the resulting connection. If you hear clicks, static, or a pronounced hissing or humming, chances are good that noise is affecting your data calls. (Water or frayed insulation on a phone wire might be the culprit.)

- If possible, try connecting to a different RJ-45 outlet in your home or office to isolate internal wiring problems. If you can plug your modem directly into the terminating block where the telephone line enters your home or office, you might be able to tell whether the problem originates on the incoming line rather than within your premises.

- Ask the phone company to test the quality of your incoming line. If you're fortunate, the phone company will agree to send a data specialist with test equipment designed to identify line problems. Some phone companies might be reluctant to guarantee any level of performance for data connections; in that case, it sometimes help to complain about the quality of voice or fax connections. You might also find an ally in the regulatory body that governs telephone service, such as your state public utilities commission.

3. Double-Check Your Logon Settings

When you use the Internet Connection Wizard to create a Dial-Up Networking icon, the resulting connection settings use only the TCP/IP protocol. That's not the case, however, when you create a DUN icon using the Make New Connection icon in the Dial-Up Networking folder. If you notice that it takes an inordinately long time to establish a connection, Windows might be attempting to negotiate a connection over multiple protocols unnecessarily.

To solve this problem, open the Dial-Up Networking folder, right-click the connection icon, and choose Properties. Click the Server Types tab and look at the settings in the dialog box that appears. If the NetBEUI and IPX/SPX Compatible boxes are checked (see Figure 29.32), remove the check marks from both boxes and try again.

FIG. 29.32

When you create a connection icon manually, Windows attempts to use this full array of protocols. To improve performance, clear the check boxes for all but the TCP/IP protocol.

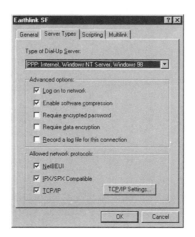

4. Use Diagnostic Utilities

One of the most effective ways to track down problems with a dial-up connection is with the help of *Tracert*, a command-line utility included with Windows 98. As the name implies, you can use this command to trace the route that packets take as they move between your computer and a distant server. With the information that Tracert reports, you can often identify problems with Internet servers.

To use Tracert, open an MS-DOS Prompt window and type **tracert *hostname*** (where *hostname* is the name of the server you're trying to reach, such as www.microsoft.com). When you press Enter, this command sends packets of data to the destination you specified.

The output shows how many *hops* each packet requires; each hop is an intermediate computer that hands off the data to the next link in the chain. The list also shows the time (in milliseconds) that each hop requires. A time of 10ms or less is typical of a high-speed connection; when times exceed 250ms, as they often will for servers running over slow links, you've found the source of sluggish throughput. ●

CHAPTER 30

Web Browsing with Internet Explorer 4.0

by Ed Bott

What Is Internet Explorer 4.0?

Internet Explorer 4.0 delivers all the basic functionality you've come to expect from a web browser. It lets you gather information from servers located on your company's intranet or on the World Wide Web. It displays text and graphics in richly formatted pages, runs scripts, accesses databases, and downloads files. With the help of Internet Explorer 4.0, you can establish secure, encrypted sessions with distant servers so that you can safely exchange confidential information (like your credit card number) without fear that it will be intercepted by a third party.

Internet Explorer 4.0 also makes it easier for you to protect your computer. It uses the concept of security zones, for example, to tightly restrict the ability of unknown web servers to interact with local computers and network resources. With one set of security settings for your local intranet, another for trusted sites, and another for the Internet at large, you can automatically download files from local servers but control downloads from external sites.

Using subscriptions, you can transfer web-based information automatically to a desktop or notebook PC and then view those pages even when you're not connected to the Internet.

Internet Explorer 4.0 looks different, too. You can use the versatile Explorer bar—a simple frame that locks in place along the left edge of the browser window—to organize your Favorites list, search for information on the web, or browse pages stored in your local cache. Because the browser shares code with the Windows Explorer, you can display the contents of a folder on your local PC or network and then jump to a web site in the same window. And there are dozens of configuration options to make the interface more comfortable.

To open Internet Explorer and display your home page, click the Internet icon on the desktop or the Quick Launch bar. Figure 30.1 shows the default browser window.

Decoding URLs

In order to open a web page, you have to specify its location, which you do either by clicking on a shortcut or link that points to the file, or by entering its full name and path in the Address bar. For an HTML document stored on your local PC or a network server, use the familiar *drive:\filename* or *\\servername\sharename\filename* syntax. For web pages stored on a web server on the Internet, you'll need to specify a Uniform Resource Locator, or URL.

N O T E   Some otherwise-credible sources insist that URL actually stands for Universal Resource Locator, but the organizations that set Internet standards agree that U is for Uniform. Opinion is evenly divided on whether to pronounce the term "earl" or say the letters "U-R-L." ■

As Figure 30.2 shows, each URL contains three essential pieces of information that help Internet Explorer find and retrieve information from the Internet. (Some optional types of information, including port numbers and query parameters, might also be part of a URL.)

The Standard toolbar gives you one-click access to frequently used tasks

Explorer bars help you find information and revisit favorite web pages

You can hide the Quick Links bar or move it to another location at the top of the browser window

FIG. 30.1

The Internet Explorer interface includes these basic navigational elements.

The Uniform Resource Locator for the current page appears in this Address bar

Check this status bar for useful information about the current page, especially as it loads

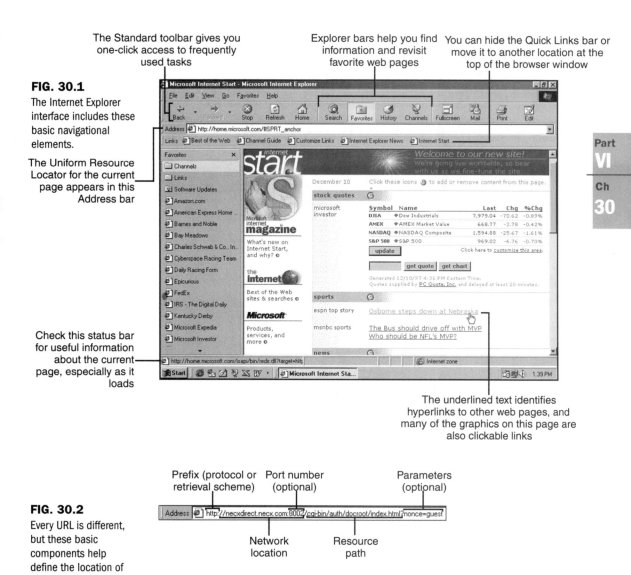

The underlined text identifies hyperlinks to other web pages, and many of the graphics on this page are also clickable links

Prefix (protocol or retrieval scheme)

Port number (optional)

Parameters (optional)

FIG. 30.2

Every URL is different, but these basic components help define the location of all sorts of web resources.

Network location

Resource path

Here's a breakdown of the parts of a URL:

■ The *prefix* tells Internet Explorer which protocol or retrieval scheme to use when transferring the document. The prefix is always followed by a colon. Standard web pages use the http: prefix, while secure web pages use https:. The URL for a file stored on an FTP server uses the prefix ftp:. Internet Explorer will automatically add the http: or ftp: prefix if you type an otherwise valid web or FTP address.

■ The *network location*, which appears immediately to the right of the prefix, identifies the Internet host or network server where the document is stored (www.microsoft.com, for example). Note that you must separate the prefix from the network location in URLs with two forward slashes. This part of an URL might also include a username and password for connecting with resources on servers that require you to log on. If the server requires connection over a nonstandard TCP port number, you can add a colon and the port information at the end of this entry.

■ The *resource path* defines the exact location of the web page or other resource on the specified server, including its path, filename, and extension. This entry begins with the first forward slash after the network location. If the URL doesn't include the name of a page in the resource path, most web servers will load a page called DEFAULT.HTM or INDEX.HTM. Two special characters define parameters that appear after the path: A ? indicates query information to be passed to a web server, and a # identifies a specific location on the page.

 T I P To display a blank page in your web browser, use the URL about:blank.

There are a surprising number of prefixes you can type in the Address bar. Each uses its own protocol or retrieval method to gather information. For a detailed listing of the most common URL prefixes, see Table 30.1.

Table 30.1   Legal URL Prefixes

Prefix	Description
about:	Displays internal information about the browser. IE4 uses this prefix to display some error messages, including about:NavigationCanceled.
file:	Opens a local or network file. Used in other browsers but not required with IE4 when the Windows Desktop Update is installed.
ftp:	Connects with a server running the File Transfer Protocol.
gopher:	Connects with a server running the Gopher or Gopher+ protocol.
http:	Retrieves information from web servers using Hypertext Transfer Protocol.
https:	Creates a connection with a secure web server and then encrypts all page requests and retrieved information over Secure Hypertext Transfer Protocol.
mailto:	Launches the default email client and begins composing a message to the address named in the URL.
news:	Connects with a Usenet news server using the default news reader.
nntp:	Connects with a Usenet news server using the NNTP access.
res:	Resource within a binary file; IE4 uses information with DLL files to display some help information.
telnet:	Launches the system's default Telnet client to create an interactive session with a remote host computer.
wais:	Connects with Wide Area Information Servers that contain large databases.

Working with Web Pages

The basic building blocks of the World Wide Web are simple text documents written in Hypertext Markup Language, or HTML. To communicate with the web server where a given page is stored, your browser uses Hypertext Transfer Protocol, or HTTP.

Every time you open an HTML document, Internet Explorer interprets the formatting tags and other coded instructions in that document and displays the fully formatted results in your browser window. A single web page might contain text, graphics, links to other pages or to downloadable files, and embedded objects such as ActiveX controls and Java applets. When you load that web page, it might in turn load dozens of additional linked files, especially graphic images.

▶ **See** "Restricting ActiveX Control," **p. 663** and "Limiting Java Applets," **p. 668**

HTML pages can incorporate scripts that cause specific actions to take place in response to a trigger event (such as the clicking of a button to submit data from a web-based form for processing by a web server). Dynamic HTML instructions let the contents of the browser window change as you work with the page.

To see the underlying HTML code for the current web page, choose View, Source. Internet Explorer uses its basic text editor, Notepad, to display HTML source code, as shown in Figure 30.3.

FIG. 30.3
Because HTML documents are strictly text, you can view the underlying source code in the bare-bones Notepad editor.

```
index - Notepad
File  Edit  Search  Help
<CENTER><IMG SRC="/graphics/index/gifs/headsup.gif" WIDTH=241 HEIGHT=66
ALT="Heads Up"></CENTER>

<!-- <IMG ALIGN=LEFT SRC="/graphics/index/gifs/spacer.gif" WIDTH=10
HEIGHT=280>
<IMG ALIGN=RIGHT SRC="/graphics/index/gifs/spacer.gif" WIDTH=10
HEIGHT=280> -->
<BLOCKQUOTE>
<FONT SIZE=2>
<P>
<FONT SIZE=5><B>B</B></FONT>ack by popular demand...
<BR>    
If you are looking for a reliable, high-capacity removable storage
solution for your Mac or PC, the <A
HREF="/cgi-bin/auth/docroot/iomega.html?nonce=guest">Iomega Jaz</A>
drive should top your list.  Fast, quiet and priced-to-move, these 1Gig
drives may well be the last storage device you will <I>ever</I> have to
buy.
<BR>    
And to sweeten the deal, we are giving away 3-packs of Jaz media
($269.95 value) to ten more lucky winners during December.  Just
think...three more gigs of space for all of your stuff...<B>for
FREE!</B>  <I>(No purchase necessary.  See contest rules for your <A
```

 TIP FrontPage Express adds an Edit button to the Internet Explorer toolbar. When you install Microsoft's full-strength web page editor, FrontPage, it takes over this function. Click this button to begin editing the current web page.

Working with Hyperlinks

Hyperlinks are HTML shortcuts you can activate with a single click. Clicking a link has the same effect as typing its URL into the browser's Address bar. The specific action that occurs depends on the prefix: Clicking a link with the http: prefix, for example, allows you to jump from page to page. Other prefixes typically found in links carry out specific actions. For example, a link can allow you to begin executing a script (javascript:), download a file (ftp:), begin composing a mail message (mailto:), or open Outlook Express to read a linked newsgroup message (news:).

On a web page, the clickable portion of a hyperlink can take several forms. Text links appear in color (blue, by default) and are underlined. A web page designer can change the look of a text link and can also attach a link to a picture or button on the screen. Internet Explorer changes the shape of the pointer when it passes over a link. To see additional information about a link, look in the status bar or inspect its properties. Some web pages, such as the one in Figure 30.4, include pop-up help text for the image under the pointer; the status bar shows where the link will take you.

FIG. 30.4

The pop-up ScreenTip and the status bar offer helpful information about this link; you can also right-click to inspect its properties.

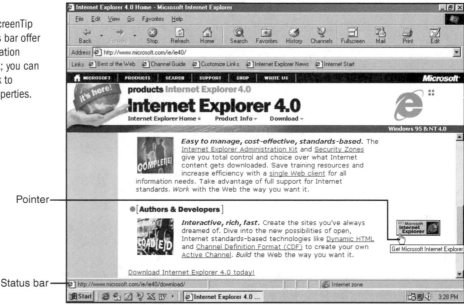

Pointer

Status bar

TROUBLESHOOTING

I click a link, but the linked page doesn't open properly. Most of the time when clicking a link fails it's because the specified page has been moved or no longer exists on that server. It's also possible that the author left out a crucial portion of the web address or simply mistyped it. You can sometimes open the link (or its parent) anyway, although it might take several extra steps: Right-click on the link and choose Copy Shortcut; select the entire contents of the Address bar, right-click, and choose Paste; then edit the URL as needed and press Enter.

To copy the underlying URL in text format from a link to the Windows Clipboard, right-click on the link and choose Copy Shortcut. For a link that's attached to a graphic, choose Copy only if you want to copy the image itself to the Clipboard.

Normally, clicking on a link replaces the page displayed in the current window. To open the linked page in its own window without affecting the current page, right-click on the link and choose Open in New Window.

Starting Internet Explorer

The browser window opens automatically when you click on a hyperlink or an Internet shortcut. To open Internet Explorer and go directly to your home page, use the Internet Explorer icon on the desktop or on the Quick Launch bar.

Part

VI

Ch

30

 You can have two or more browser windows open at one time—a technique that's handy when you're gathering and comparing information from multiple sources. To open a new browser window, use any of these three techniques:

- Choose File, New, Window. The new window displays the same contents as the current browser window.

- Press Ctrl+N. This keyboard shortcut has the same effect as using the File menu. In both cases, the new browser window "remembers" previously visited sites, so you can use the Back button just as you would in the original window.

- Click the Launch Internet Explorer Browser button in the Quick Launch toolbar. The new window opens to your home page.

Navigating Internet Explorer

There are at least six ways to display a web page in the current browser window:

- Type a URL in the Address bar or choose a previously entered URL from the drop-down list, and then press Enter.
- Select Start, Run and type a URL in the Run box.
- Click a link on an HTML page.
- Open an Internet shortcut on the desktop, in a folder, in the Favorites list, or in an email message.
- Click a shortcut on the Links bar.
- Use the Back and Forward buttons, the File menu, or the History list to return to previously viewed pages.

Using the Address Bar

You can click in the Address bar and painstakingly type a full URL to jump to a particular web page, but Internet Explorer 4.0 includes several shortcut features that reduce the amount of typing required for most web addresses.

There's no need to start with a prefix when you enter the address of a valid Internet host. For example, when you type

www.microsoft.com

the browser automatically adds the http:// prefix. If the address you enter begins with ftp, it adds the ftp:// prefix.

CAUTION

There's an important distinction between the forward slashes used in URLs and the backslashes used in local files and in UNC names that refer to network resources. If you enter *servername* in the Address bar, you'll see a list of all the shared resources available on a network server; if you enter //*servername*, you jump to the default HTML page on the web server with that name.

If you type a single word that doesn't match the name of a local web server, Internet Explorer automatically tries other addresses based on that name, using the common web prefix www and standard top-level domains—.com, .edu, and .org. To tell Internet Explorer to automatically add www to the beginning and com to the end of the name you typed, press Ctrl+Enter.

Using AutoComplete to Fill In the Blanks

As you move from page to page, Internet Explorer keeps track of the URL for every page you've visited. Each time you begin to type in the Address bar, Internet Explorer checks the History list and attempts to complete the entry for you, suggesting the first address that matches the characters you've typed. You can see the results of this AutoComplete feature in Figure 30.5. Note that the characters you type appear on a plain white background, while the suggested completion is highlighted.

FIG. 30.5
The AutoComplete feature suggests the first address that begins with the characters you've typed.

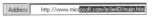

When it makes an AutoComplete suggestion, Internet Explorer scans the list of addresses you've entered previously, in alphabetical order, and then chooses the first matching address. If you type www.m, for example, `www.matrox.com` might be the first suggestion. To accept the completed address, just press Enter.

If the suggested address isn't the one you want, you have two alternatives: If you continue typing, Internet Explorer will revise its suggestion based on the new text you type. In the previous example, if you press i so that the contents of the Address bar read www.mi, Internet Explorer might suggest `www.microsoft.com`.

What do you do if there are dozens of pages in your History list that begin with the same domain name? After AutoComplete makes its first suggestion, use the down arrow to cycle through every entry in your history list that begins with that string of text. When you reach the right address, press Enter to load that page.

You can simply ignore AutoComplete suggestions and continue typing the address. If you find the feature more confusing than helpful, follow these steps to turn AutoComplete off:

1. Choose <u>V</u>iew, Internet <u>O</u>ptions.
2. Click the Advanced tab.
3. Clear the check mark from the box labeled Use AutoComplete.
4. Click OK to close the dialog box and save your changes.

Navigating with the Mouse

Click the Back button to jump to pages you previously visited, and then click the Forward button to return. When you right-click on either button (or use the arrow at right), a list of the nine most recent pages appears, as seen in Figure 30.6. (The same list of up to nine pages also appears at the bottom of the <u>F</u>ile menu.)

FIG. 30.6

Right-click or use this drop-down arrow for a faster alternative to repeatedly clicking the Back or Forward button.

If you own a Microsoft IntelliMouse, you can use the wheel (located between the buttons) to take advantage of three navigational shortcuts:

- Hold down the Shift key and roll the wheel downward to return to the previously viewed page; hold down Shift and move the wheel up to go forward again.

- Roll the wheel up or down to scroll three lines at a time through a web page (the Advanced tab of the Internet Options dialog box lets you adjust this setting).

- Hold down the wheel button and move the mouse in any direction to scroll. Release the wheel button to stop scrolling.

- Click the wheel to turn on continuous scrolling. When you see the indicator in Figure 30.7, move the pointer, and the page will scroll automatically in that direction like a TelePrompter. The farther you move the pointer, the faster the page will scroll. To resume normal scrolling, click the wheel again or press Esc.

 Virtually every object on a web page is accessible via shortcut menus. Right-click to inspect properties, copy or print an image, or add a page to your Favorites list, for example.

▶ **See** "Using the Favorites Folder to Organize Your Favorite Web Sites," **p. 634**

Working with Frame-Based Pages

Frames are an effective way for clever designers to make web pages more usable. Unlike ordinary pages, which fill the browser window from border to border, frame-based pages split the window into two or more zones, each with its own underlying HTML code and navigation controls. The most common use of frames is to add a table of links along one side of the browser window, with pages displayed in the frame on the other side; because the frame containing the list of links is always visible, it's easy to quickly move through the site without constantly hitting the Back button. Not surprisingly, Microsoft's developer pages (Figure 30.8) make good use of frames.

FIG. 30.7

Use your IntelliMouse to automatically scroll at a controlled speed; in this example, moving the pointer down makes the page scroll more quickly.

FIG. 30.8

Look carefully and you'll see four frames in this page. In addition to the obvious navigation area at left, there are two frames along the top. The main browser window is a frame with its own scrollbar.

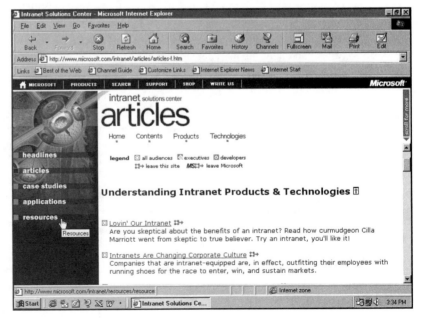

Working with frames takes practice. The Back and Forward buttons, for example, won't let you navigate within a frame. To move back and forth within a frame, you have to select the frame itself, right-click, and then click the Back or Forward shortcut menu choices. Likewise, to view the source code for a frame, you'll need to right-click in the area of interest and choose View Source from the shortcut menu. When you save or copy a frame-based page, make sure you've selected the portion of the document you want and not just the small master document that contains pointers to the frames!

▶ **See** "Arranging Frames on the Printed Page," **p. 645**

Part

VI

Ch

30

Navigating with the Keyboard

For most people most of the time, the mouse is the best way to navigate using Internet Explorer. But the web browser also offers superb keyboard support, which is important for users who have physical disabilities that make it difficult or impossible to use a mouse. Keyboard shortcuts are also a useful way to accelerate web access for skilled typists who prefer to keep their hands on the keyboard while they work.

Most of the movement keys in Internet Explorer 4.0 work as they do elsewhere in Windows. Home and End go to the top and bottom of the current page, for example. The Up and Down arrow keys move through the page, and the Page Up and Page Down keys move up and down in bigger jumps.

You can use shortcut keys to choose commands and view documents. Many of the pull-down menus include pointers to keyboard alternatives. Table 30.2 lists the most useful keyboard shortcuts in Internet Explorer.

Table 30.2   Internet Explorer's Keyboard Shortcuts

To Do This...	Press This
Go to the next page	Alt+Right Arrow
Go to the previous page	Alt+Left Arrow, Backspace
Display a shortcut menu for a link or object	Shift+F10
Move forward between frames	Ctrl+Tab
Move back between frames	Shift+Ctrl+Tab
Move to the next link on a page	Tab
Move to the previous link on a page	Shift+Tab
Activate the currently selected link	Enter
Refresh the current page	F5
Stop downloading a page	Esc
Open a new location	Ctrl+O

continues

Table 30.2   Continued

To Do This...	Press This
Open a new browser window	Ctrl+N
Save the current page	Ctrl+S
Print the current page or active frame	Ctrl+P

Using Image Maps

One popular navigational aid on some web pages is the image map. Instead of assigning links to a series of graphic objects or buttons, a web designer can create links to specific coordinates of a single large image. The image map in Figure 30.9, for example, lets you jump to linked pages using a map of Houston, Texas. How do you know when you're working with an image map? Watch the status bar at the bottom of the browser window as the mouse passes over the image; if you see coordinates, as in this figure, there's an image map under the pointer.

FIG. 30.9
The coordinates at the end of the URL in the status bar are your tip-off that this site is using an image map for navigation.

Image maps are clever and useful jumping-off points on web sites. Their only drawback is that they require the use of the mouse. There's no way to use an image map with the keyboard.

Gathering Information from the Status Bar

Each time your browser makes a connection with a web server, valuable information appears on the status bar along the bottom of the screen. Figure 30.10 shows the Internet Explorer status bar.

FIG. 30.10

You'll find important information about the status of the current page here.

Status bar

The status bar shows the following:

- *The status of the current download.* Look for an hourglass over a globe as a page loads, and a full-page icon when the download is complete.

- *The status of objects currently loading,* including linked graphics, ActiveX components, and Java applets. This area also counts down the number of items that have not yet been downloaded.

- *A link's destination URL.* Point to a link to see its associated URL in the status bar; use the Advanced tab of the Internet Options dialog box to switch between full URLs (`http://www.microsoft.com/default.asp`) and friendly names (`Shortcut to default.asp at www.microsoft.com`).

- *Loading progress.* A blue progress bar shows what percentage of the entire page has been loaded.

- *Security status.* Look for a padlock icon to indicate when you're viewing a page over a secure connection or using international language support; when you print a page, you'll see a printer icon here.

- *Security zone.* The security zone for the current page appears at the far right of the status bar.

▶ **See** "Establishing and Maintaining Internet Security Zones," **p. 658**

T I P Want to quickly adjust Internet Explorer options? Double-click on the status bar; that has the same effect as choosing View, Internet Options from the pull-down menus.

Stopping Downloads and Reloading Pages

There are many reasons why a web page doesn't load properly, but the most common is too much traffic on the server you're trying to reach or on one leg of the connection between your browser and the remote server. Click the Stop button (or press Esc) to immediately stop a download. Take this step if you're certain the page you requested has stalled or is unavailable and you don't want to wait for the browser to time out. It can also be a time-saving tactic if the page contains many bulky graphic elements and you can already see the link you want to follow or the section you want to read.

The Refresh button is especially valuable when you're viewing frequently updated pages—such as weather information, traffic maps, or stock quotes—because it guarantees that the version you see is the most recent and not a stale copy from the Internet Explorer cache. You should also click the Refresh button when a download fails in the middle of a page or when one or more objects on a page fail to load, as in the example in Figure 30.11.

FIG. 30.11
The icon in each empty box means that a graphic file failed to load. Click the Refresh button to reload the entire page, or right-click to download just one image.

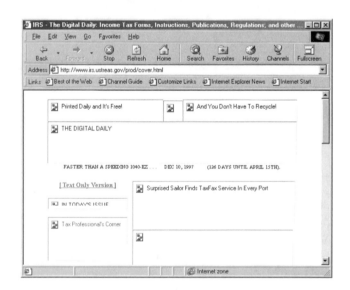

 T I P You don't have to refresh the entire page if a small portion of the page failed to load. Look for a red X or a broken image icon, which indicate that a linked file failed to load. To refresh just that portion of the page, right-click and choose Show Picture.

Setting Your Home Page

Every time you start Internet Explorer, it loads the page you designate as your home page. By default, Microsoft takes you to `home.microsoft.com`, where you can follow links to assemble a home page based on your own interests. You can designate any web page as your home page; if you're connected to a company intranet, you might prefer to set a local page to load automatically at startup.

To reset your home page, load the page you want to use and then choose View, Internet Options and click on the General tab (see Figure 30.12). Click Use Current to set the current page as your home page. Click Use Default to restore the default Microsoft home page. Click Use Blank to replace the home page with a blank page that loads instantly.

Part VI

Ch 30

FIG. 30.12
Choose your preferred home page, and then navigate to this dialog box to designate that page as the default that runs every time you start Internet Explorer.

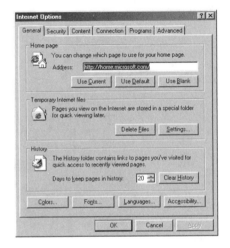

 TIP When you're choosing a home page, make sure it's readily accessible so it won't cause delays when you start your browser. Better yet, use FrontPage Express to construct your own home page, with links to favorite sites inside your intranet and on the World Wide Web. See Chapter 36 for more details on how to use FrontPage Express.

Increasing the Size of the Browser Window

Pieces of the Internet Explorer interface can get in the way of data, especially on displays running at low resolutions. There are several ways to make more space available for data in the browser window. Most involve hiding, rearranging, or reconfiguring these optional interface elements.

The simplest way to reclaim space for data is to hide the toolbars and status bar. To hide the status bar, choose View and click Status Bar; to eliminate one or more of the three built-in toolbars, right-click on the menu bar and remove the check marks from Standard Buttons, Address Bar, or Links.

You can also rearrange the three toolbars, placing them side-by-side or one on top of the other. You can even position any toolbar alongside the menu bar. To move a toolbar, click on the raised handle at the left and then drag the toolbar to its new position. Drag the same handle from right to left to adjust the width of the toolbar.

Want to cut the oversize buttons on the browser window down to size? Choose View, Internet Options, click on the Advanced tab, and check the option to use the smaller Microsoft Office-style buttons instead; then choose View, Toolbars and clear the check mark from Text Labels. The results should resemble what you see in Figure 30.13.

FIG. 30.13

These smaller buttons without labels fit comfortably alongside the Address bar to make room for more data in the browser window.

To configure Internet Explorer for the absolute maximum viewing area, load any page, and then click the Full Screen button. This view, shown in Figure 30.14, hides the title bar, menu bar, Address bar, and Links bar. The Standard buttons toolbar shrinks to its smallest setting, and even the size and position of the Minimize and Close buttons in the upper-right corner are adjusted.

 If you prefer the extra screen real estate you get with Full Screen view, you can configure IE4 to automatically open all web pages this way. You can also configure IE4's channels to appear by default in Full Screen view. To set up either option, choose View, Internet Options, click the Advanced tab, and check the boxes labeled Launch Browser in Full Screen Window or Launch Channels in Full Screen Window.

In Full Screen view, right-clicking on the toolbar lets you add the menu bar, Address bar, or Links bar to the same row. The Auto Hide choice on the same shortcut menu lets every last piece of the interface slide out of the way; to make the toolbar reappear, move the mouse pointer to the top edge of the screen.

To switch back to normal view, click the Full Screen button again.

FIG. 30.14
Click the Full Screen button to expand the Internet Explorer browser window to its maximum size.

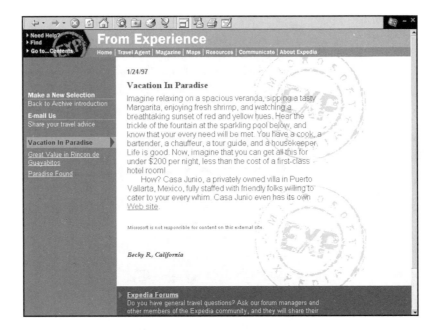

Adjusting Fonts and Colors to Make Web Pages More Readable

Can you change the look of a web page? That depends on decisions the designer of the page made when creating it. Some web pages use only generic settings to place text on the page. Sophisticated designers, on the other hand, use web templates called cascading style sheets to specify fonts, colors, spacing, and other design elements that control the look and feel of the page. You can specify fonts and colors you prefer when viewing basic web pages; advanced settings let you ignore style sheets as well.

The primary benefit is for people with physical disabilities that make it difficult or impossible for them to read the screen. To adjust any of these settings, choose View, Internet Options, and then click the General tab.

 T I P If you're curious about how a web designer created the specific look of a page, use the View Source option to inspect the HTML code. If you like a particular look, you might be able to copy and paste the code to adapt the design for use in your own web page.

To adjust the default fonts, click the Fonts button. Besides selecting from a limited assortment of options for proportional and fixed fonts, you can also change the size that Internet Explorer uses for basic web pages from its default Medium. Choose smaller settings to pack more information onto the screen; use larger values to make text easier to read.

Click the Colors button to change the default values for text and backgrounds on basic web pages. By default, Internet Explorer uses the window colors you defined using the Windows Display; with the Standard Windows settings, that means black text on a white page. To change the defaults, you must change that systemwide setting or click to clear the Use Windows Colors check box and then specify different Text and Background colors, as shown in Figure 30.15. Internet Explorer also allows you to reset the colors for links here.

FIG. 30.15

Setting alternate font choices affects only basic web pages—those that don't use style sheets.

Changes you make to default fonts and colors will not apply to pages that use style sheets unless you make one final adjustment. Click the Accessibility button and check the appropriate boxes to tell the browser to ignore colors, font styles, and font sizes specified in style sheets.

You can increase or decrease default font sizes exclusively for pages you open in the current session. Choose View, Fonts, and select one of the five relative sizes from that menu. This change will apply only when viewing pages that use standard fonts, and Internet Explorer will return to normal settings if you close and then reopen the browser window. When you adjust font sizes, be aware that pages can look odd and, in some cases, can even become unreadable. If you find yourself using this feature regularly, go to the Advanced tab on the Internet Options dialog box and check the option to add a Fonts button to the Standard toolbar.

Viewing Web Pages in Other Languages

Do you frequently find yourself browsing pages created by designers using an alphabet that's not the same one used in your Windows language settings? Before Internet Explorer can display foreign-language pages, you must use the IE4 setup program to install Multi-Language Support for the appropriate languages. You'll find a Pan-European add-on that enables Internet Explorer to display most Western European languages correctly. There are Japanese, Korean, and Chinese add-ins as well.

After you install the additional font support, you should be able to see pages in any of those alphabets, as shown in Figure 30.16.

FIG. 30.16
If you try to view foreign-language web pages, you might see only a garbled mess (left); you'll need to add fonts for the extra languages to see them correctly (right).

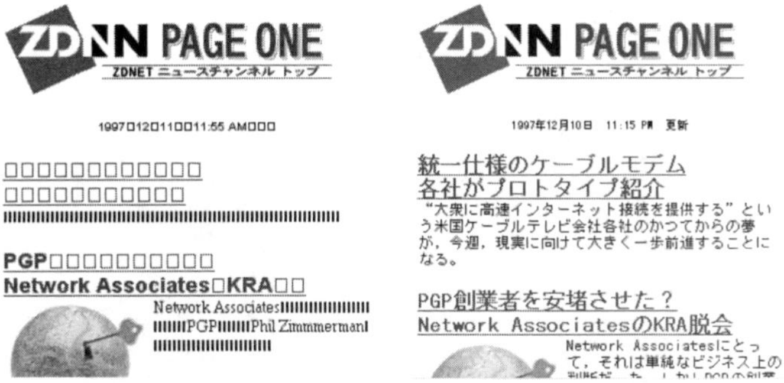

Part

VI

Ch

30

 If you regularly view web pages that are designed to be displayed in your choice of languages, tell IE4 which one you prefer. Choose View, Internet Options and click the Languages button on the General tab. Add support for the appropriate languages, and then place your preferred language at the top of the list.

Configuring IE to Work with Other Programs

When you first install Internet Explorer, it includes most of the capabilities you need for browsing basic web pages and handling other types of data, such as streaming audio and video. IE4 allows you to dramatically expand its capabilities using a variety of add-in programs. Some install themselves automatically with your permission, while others require that you run a separate setup program.

Installing and Using Add-Ins and Plug-Ins

Core components of Internet Explorer let you view text formatted with HTML as well as graphics created in supported formats, including JPEG and GIF images. To view other types of data, you must install add-in programs that extend the capabilities of the basic browser. Add-ins can take several forms:

■ ActiveX controls offer to install themselves automatically when needed. Depending on your security settings, Internet Explorer might refuse to install ActiveX add-ins, or you might have to click in a confirmation dialog box. ActiveX controls can perform a practically unlimited variety of functions; examples range from simple data-viewing panels to sophisticated analytical engines for tracking stock quotes. MSNBC's home page, shown in Figure 30.17, includes an ActiveX control that automatically turns current headlines into entries on a cascading menu, making it easier for you to navigate through the day's news.

▶ **See** "Internet Security," **p. 653** for a detailed discussion of ActiveX and Java security issues.

FIG. 30.17
This ActiveX control on MSNBC's home page allows you to browse news headlines and jump to linked pages using cascading menus.

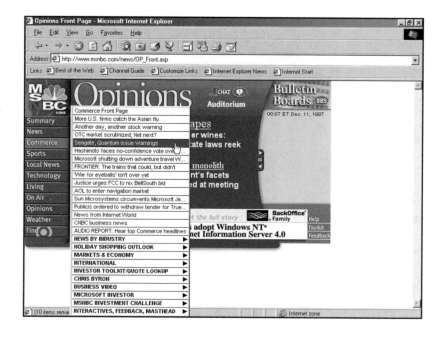

 T I P There's no need to seek out ActiveX controls. Pages that require add-ins will offer to install the control when you need it, and most controls download in a matter of minutes, even over relatively slow connections.

- Java applets download and run each time you access a page containing the helper program. The security settings for Java applets prohibit them from interacting with local or network resources except on the machine where they originated, and you can't install them permanently as you can ActiveX controls.

- Other add-in programs and plug-ins use standard installation routines and can often run on their own. Two must-have add-ins for Internet Explorer are RealNetworks' RealPlayer, which allows your browser to receive live audio and video broadcasts over the Internet, and Adobe's Acrobat Reader (shown in Figure 30.18), which lets you display and print richly formatted documents complete with graphics, columns, and other design elements that go far beyond HTML. Both are free (in fact, RealPlayer 4.0 is included with IE4); upgrades to more powerful versions are available for a price.

ON THE WEB

To download the most recent streaming audio and video player from RealNetworks, follow the links from this site:

http://www.real.com

ON THE WEB

To find the most recent version of Adobe's Acrobat Reader, follow the links from this site:

http://www.adobe.com

FIG. 30.18

When you view a formatted document using the Adobe Acrobat Reader, it takes over the browser window and adds its own toolbars.

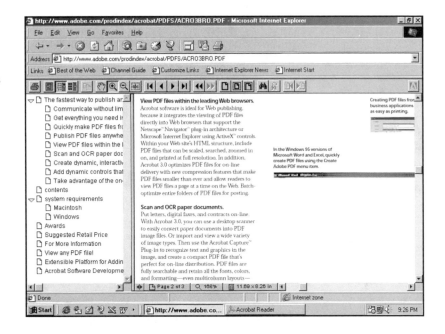

Tuning In to the Internet with NetShow 2.0

One of the most intriguing uses of Internet bandwidth is the delivery of so-called *streaming media*. Unlike conventional sound and video files, which require that you download the entire file before beginning to play it back, streaming media begins playing as soon as the first bits reach your browser. With streaming media, radio stations can "broadcast" their signals over the Internet, making it possible for sports fans, for example, to follow the exploits of their hometown heroes no matter how far they roam.

Streaming media can consist of audio, video, or both. On a normal dial-up connection at 28.8KB, audio will typically work well, but video signals are unbearably choppy because the pipe between server and client simply can't deliver data fast enough. Video broadcasts are more practical on company intranets, where network cables can deliver data fast enough to handle broadcast-quality signals.

Internet Explorer includes two useful streaming-media players—RealPlayer and NetShow. For video broadcasts, the NetShow player can function as an ActiveX control, with the viewing screen embedded in the HTML page, or it can run as a standalone application with its own menus and VCR-style controls. (See Figure 30.19 for an example of the NetShow player in action.)

NetShow includes several useful customization options. To access the NetShow properties sheet, right-click on the image window or on the player controls and choose Properties. You'll see a dialog box like the one in Figure 30.20.

FIG. 30.19

With its menu bar and VCR-style controls, the NetShow player looks like a standard Windows application. If only the video window is visible, right-click to set options.

FIG. 30.20

Use the settings on the Advanced tab to configure NetShow to work through a proxy server.

Click the Settings tab to shrink the video window to half-size or expand it to double the default size. Another drop-down list on this tab lets you choose full controls, simple controls, or none at all.

Use the options on the Advanced tab to configure NetShow on a network that uses a proxy server. You'll need to check the documentation from the server to see which TCP and/or UDP ports are required.

Basic title information appears on the General tab, while the Details and Statistics tabs display information about the current connection.

Setting Default Mail and News Clients

The Mail button on the Standard toolbar launches your default email program. Links that begin with the news: prefix fire up your default news reader. If you have more than one program that can work with Internet Explorer, you can control which one starts up when it's needed. To switch between Outlook 97 and Outlook Express as your default mail program, for example, choose View, Internet Options, click the Programs tab, and choose the preferred program from the drop-down lists shown in Figure 30.21.

FIG. 30.21

To switch from one helper program to another, use these drop-down lists. Only programs specifically written to work with Internet Explorer will appear here.

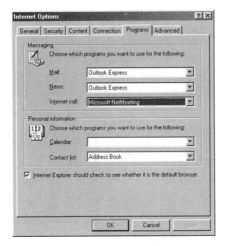

Speeding Up Web Connections

Tuning Internet Explorer for speed and responsiveness involves inevitable tradeoffs between rich content and quick results. Elaborate graphics, video clips, sound files, and other large elements add fun and extra dimensions to the web, but waiting for those elements to download over a slow connection can quickly become frustrating.

Selectively filtering out some types of downloadable content can reduce the amount of time it takes to load a page the first time. Intelligently managing the browser's cache makes it much faster to access pages a second or subsequent time. Of course, even the most careful configurations can't overcome traffic jams on the Internet.

Browsing Without Graphics

When slow downloads are a problem, the most common culprit is a page that's overstuffed with graphics, sound, and video files, which take time to download. To turn Internet Explorer into a lightning-fast text-only browser, follow these steps:

1. Choose View, Internet Options and click on the Advanced tab.
2. Scroll down to the Multimedia branch of the tree.
3. Remove the check marks from all boxes in this section, as shown in Figure 30.22.
4. Click OK to apply your changes.

With multimedia options turned off, Internet Explorer will show generic icons, empty boxes, and simple text labels where you would normally see images. It will also ignore any sound files, animations, or video clips embedded in the page. Some sites work perfectly well without images; Fortune magazine, for example, offers an all-text page (see Figure 30.23) that loads quickly and doesn't require any graphic images. (You can always use right-click shortcut menus to manually request any content you've turned off.)

FIG. 30.22
Clear all the check boxes in the Multimedia section to transform Internet Explorer into a speedy text-only browser.

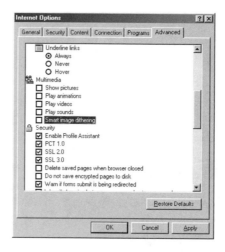

FIG. 30.23
Who needs graphics? Even without images for its buttons, this all-text page is eminently readable, thanks to excellent labels.

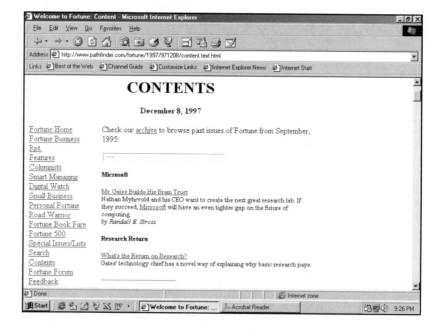

Although turning off the browser's ability to load image and multimedia files can dramatically improve performance, it can also block important information. On sites that use image maps as their only navigation tool, for example, there's literally no way to get around without displaying that image. To selectively show a picture after downloading the text-only page, right-click the icon that represents the image and choose Show Picture from the shortcut menu.

T I P One of the most useful Internet Explorer Power Toys adds a Toggle Images button to the Standard toolbar. If you want to speed up downloads by selectively turning off the display of images—without having to continually open and close dialog boxes—this add-in is essential. You'll find it at the following location:

`http://www.microsoft.com/ie/ie4/powertoys`

Managing the Browser's Cache

With or without graphics, the best way to improve performance is to make sure the browser's cache is correctly configured. Each time you retrieve a new web page, Internet Explorer downloads every element and stores a copy of each one in a cache directory on your hard disk. The next time you request that page, the browser first checks the cache; if it finds a copy of the page, it loads the entire document from fast local storage, which dramatically increases performance.

When the cache fills up, Internet Explorer throws out the oldest files in the cache to make room for new ones. To increase the likelihood that you'll be able to load a cached copy of a page instead of having to wait for it to reload from the Internet, adjust the size of the cache. Choose View, Internet Options, and click the General tab (see Figure 30.24) to find all the controls you need to fine-tune the web cache.

FIG. 30.24

Give the browser cache extra working room, and you'll increase Internet Explorer's performance.

Checking the cache less frequently improves performance but increases the risk you'll see an outdated page.

Move this slider to increase or decrease the space allotted to the web cache.

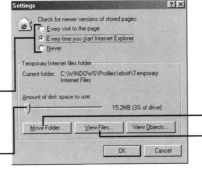

Moving the cache to a new location is not recommended; if you must, be sure to restart the computer afterward.

Click here to view all files in the cache.

CAUTION

If you tell Internet Explorer you never want to check for a more recent version of cached pages, your browser will seem remarkably faster. Beware, though: For pages that update frequently, such as news headlines or stock quotes, you'll have to work to see the most recent version. If you choose this setting, get in the habit of clicking the Refresh button to make sure the page is up-to-date.

When should you click the Delete Files button? This action completely empties the Temporary Internet Files folder and can have a noticeable negative impact on how fast your favorite pages load. Under ordinary circumstances, Internet Explorer manages the size of the cache by itself. You might need to clear the cache manually, though, if a corrupt cached file is causing Internet Explorer to crash, or if you run out of disk storage and you need to make room for crucial files, or if you plan to do a full system backup and you don't want to include all these cached web files.

Viewing Cached Files and Objects

Normally, you use the History Explorer bar to browse full pages stored in the browser cache. But you can also view the individual objects in the cache—HTML pages, graphics, ActiveX controls, and even cookie files. Click the <u>V</u>iew Files button in the Settings dialog box to see a full listing, like the one shown in Figure 30.25.

▶ **See** "How Safe Are Cookies?" **p. 672**

FIG. 30.25

The Temporary Internet Files folder holds a copy of every object you've viewed in the browser recently. Right-click to open, copy, or delete any file.

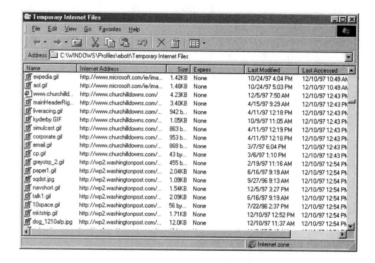

The Temporary Internet Files folder is unlike any other folder you'll see in Windows. Notice the column headings, for example, which track the time a file was last created. Double-click on column headings to re-sort the list—that's particularly useful for finding and deleting large files that are cluttering up the cache. Use right-click shortcut menus to inspect the properties of stored objects and to open, copy, or delete objects.

N O T E   Where are cached pages really stored? Windows organizes all cached files using a maze of hidden folders inside the Temporary Internet Files folder. These folders have randomly generated cryptic names like 25NMCE84; shell extensions in Windows pull the contents of all these folders together into a single display in the Temporary Internet Files folder. Although you can use the DOS Attrib or Windows Find commands to see these files in their actual locations, avoid the temptation to move or delete these hidden objects. Instead, use Internet Explorer's <u>V</u>iew Files button to manage them. ■

Controlling Advanced Internet Explorer Options

Literally hundreds of options control how Internet Explorer browses web pages. Many of these settings are bunched together on the Advanced tab of the dialog box that appears when you choose <u>V</u>iew, Internet <u>O</u>ptions. Although most of these options are the same as those found in previous releases of IE4, a handful are new to Windows 98, and a small number are irrelevant to Windows 98 users!

The following sections describe what effect each of the Advanced options has.

Accessibility

Internet Explorer's Accessibility options are designed to make web browsing easier for users with physical disabilities. The options in Table 30.3 were not available in the original release of IE 4.0, but were added in IE 4.01 and are available in Windows 98.

Table 30.3 Accessibility Options

Option	Description	Default Setting
Move System Caret with Focus/ Selection Changes	This option makes it easier for screen-reading programs, typically used to help translate screen contents for users with impaired vision.	Unchecked
Always Expand Alt Text for Images	If you've turned off the display of pictures, you will see alternate text only when the size of the image box is large enough to contain the text. This option expands the size of the image box to display the alternate text associated with any image, even small ones.	Unchecked

Browsing

The set of options outlined in Table 30.4 helps define the basic behavior of the browser window.

Table 30.4 Browsing Options

Option	Description	Default Setting
Notify When Downloads Complete	Normally, IE displays a confirmation dialog box and requires that you click OK after successfully downloading a file; clear this check box (new in Windows 98) to prevent the dialog box from appearing.	Checked

continues

Table 30.4 Continued

Option	Description	Default Setting
Disable Script Debugging	This option is meaningful only if you have installed a debugger for use with JavaScript and VBScript; check this box to hide the Script Debugger choice on the View menu.	Unchecked
Show Channel Bar at Startup (if Active Desktop is off)	Adds a channel bar to the desktop.	Unchecked
Launch Channels in Full Screen Window	By default, channels display in full screen mode; clear this check box to display in a normal browser window.	Checked
Launch Browser in Full Screen Window	Changes the default browser setting to full-screen display; this option hides the IE title bar, menu bar, status bar, and Address box, as well as the taskbar and Start button.	Unchecked
Use AutoComplete	Clear this box to prevent Internet Explorer from suggesting completions as you type a URL in the Address box.	Checked
Show Friendly URLs	Abbreviates the display of information in the status bar at the bottom of the browser window.	Unchecked
Use Smooth Scrolling	Removing this check mark might speed up the scrolling of web pages, but the effect is barely noticeable on most computers.	Checked
Enable Page Transitions	Page transitions are movie-like effects (dissolves and fades, for example) that occur when you switch from one page to another. Unchecking this box might improve performance, especially over slow connections.	Checked

Option	Description	Default Setting
Browse in a New Process	Forces web browser to use a separate copy of Internet Explorer instead of sharing code with the Windows shell; requires more system resources but decreases the chance that Windows will crash when a web page hangs.	Unchecked
Enable Page Hit Counting	If you use Active Channels, IE logs the time and date that channel pages were loaded into the browser in both offline and online modes. Clear this check box to prevent IE from sending this information to web publishers.	Checked
Enable Scheduled Subscription Updates	Clear this check box to prevent IE from automatically connecting with a web site to update a subscription; this option is most helpful for users with dial-up connections.	Checked
Show Welcome Message Each Time I Log On	Has no effect in Windows 98.	Checked
Show Internet Explorer on the Desktop (requires restart)	Clear this box to remove the Internet Explorer icon from the Windows desktop; has same effect as choosing Delete from that icon's shortcut menu.	Checked
Underline Links: Never Hover Always	Normally, all links on a web page appear with an underline; choose another option so that underlines never appear or appear only when the pointer hovers over a link.	Always

Multimedia

Normally, Internet Explorer downloads all types of content associated with a page. Turning off one or more of the options in Table 30.5 can dramatically improve performance over slow connections, but it can also make navigation difficult or impossible.

Table 30.5   Multimedia Options

Option	Description	Default Setting
Show Pictures	Enables or disables display of photos and graphics; to display a picture when this option is unchecked, right-click the red X icon and choose Show Picture from the shortcut menu.	Checked
Play Animations	Enables or disables display of animated graphics, such as those used in banner ads.	Checked
Play Videos	Enables or disables display of video clips.	Checked
Play sounds	Clear this check box to disable automatic playing of sounds; a handy option if you browse the web in an open office and want to avoid annoying neighbors.	Checked
Smart Image Dithering	Dithering allows IE to display a larger number of colors than your display type normally allows by using a combination of available colors. Clear this check box only if you regularly see images with distorted colors.	Checked

Security

Table 30.6   Security Options

Option	Description	Default Setting
Enable Profile Assistant	Allows IE to store personal information in encrypted form and then exchange it with web sites; although this feature has been available since the first release of IE4, as of mid-1998 no sites supported it.	Checked
PCT 1.0	Enables communication with web sites using the Private Communication Technology standard to encrypt data.	Checked

Option	Description	Default Setting
SSL 2.0	Allows exchange of encrypted data (such as credit card numbers) using version 2.0 of the Secure Sockets Layer protocol. Because this is an older standard, some security-conscious users might choose to disable this feature, which will prevent access to some web sites.	Checked
SSL 3.0	Allows IE users to exchange encrypted data using version 3.0 of the Secure Sockets Layer protocol.	Checked
Delete Saved Pages When Browser Closed	Deletes all cached pages in the Temporary Internet Files folder when you close the browser; prevents unauthorized users from viewing your cache to see which pages you've visited recently.	Unchecked
Do Not Save Encrypted Pages to Disk	Prevents IE from storing secure pages (such as those you might use for online banking) in the browser cache; prevents other users of your computer from viewing private or sensitive information.	Unchecked
Warn If Forms Submit Is Being Redirected	Displays a warning dialog box when you submit a web-based form whose contents will go to a web server other than the one that appears in your Address box.	Checked
Warn If Changing Between Secure and Not Secure Mode	Displays a dialog box when you switch in or out of secure mode; for some users, the https:// prefix and padlock icon are sufficient notice, and the warning dialog box is unnecessary.	Checked
Check for Certificate Revocation	Specifies that IE check the status of a web site's certificate before continuing with a secure transaction; this extra check can significantly increase the time required to begin a transaction.	Unchecked

Part

VI

Ch

30

continues

Table 30.6   Continued

Option	Description	Default Setting
Warn About Invalid Site Certificates	Displays a warning message if the URL associated with a site certificate is not valid.	Checked
Cookies: Always Accept Cookies Prompt Before Accepting Cookies Disable All Cookie Use	Lets you specify how IE handles cookie files, which store information about your interactions with the current page; see Chapter 32, "Internet Security," for a full discussion of cookies.	Always Accept Cookies

Java VM

Internet Explorer includes a Java Virtual Machine (VM), which provides the system support and security features needed to download and run Java applets. Table 30.7 lists the Java VM options.

Table 30.7   Java VM Options

Option	Description	Default Setting
Java Console Enabled (requires restart)	Developers can use the Java console to display messages about the status of a Java program; this option is not relevant for ordinary browser use.	Unchecked
Java JIT Compiler Enabled	Enables the Just-In-Time (JIT) compiler, which speeds up performance of some Java applets. If you encounter a Java applet that doesn't run correctly, try disabling this option and reloading the page.	Checked
Java Logging Enabled	Another developer-oriented option, which captures messages from Java programs to a text file in the Windows folder; this option is not relevant for ordinary browser use.	Unchecked

Printing

This category includes only one option (see Table 30.8).

Table 30.8   Printing Option

Option	Description	Default Setting
Print Background Colors and Images	On black-and-white printers, complex backgrounds can make text difficult or impossible to read; check this box if you have a color printer and you want to reproduce background images or colors on a printed page.	Unchecked

Part
VI

Ch
30

Searching

If you type an address that IE doesn't recognize, it will attempt to find the page for you either by trying to automatically complete the address or by taking you to Microsoft's search page. Table 30.9 lists the Search options.

Table 30.9   Searching Options

Option	Description	Default Setting
Autoscan Common Root Domains	If you enter a single word in the Address box, IE will first look for a local server by that name; if it can't find that server, it will add the prefix **www** and add the root domain suffixes **.com**, **.edu**, **.org**, and **.gov**. Clear the check box to disable this feature.	Checked
Search When URL Fails Never Search Always Ask Always Search	Controls how IE responds when you enter an invalid URL. By default, it offers to help you find the correct address using Microsoft's default search page.	Always Ask

Toolbar

Although the IE toolbar is not customizable, you can change the two settings listed in Table 30.10.

Table 30.10   Toolbar Options

Option	Description	Default setting
Show Font Button	Adds a button that lets you specify one of five font sizes for the current browsing session; use the Fonts button on the General tab to set a default font size that lasts from one session to the next.	Unchecked
Small Icons	Changes the size of the buttons on the main IE toolbar; if you run at 640×480 resolution , you must use this setting to see the Print and Edit buttons.	Unchecked

HTTP 1.1

Version 1.1 of the Hypertext Transfer Protocol significantly improves the performance of web pages. Windows 98 and IE4 fully support HTTP 1.1. Table 30.11 shows the HTTP 1.1 options.

Table 30.11   HTTP 1.1 Options

Option	Description	Default Setting
Use HTTP 1.1	Tells the Web browser to send page requests using HTTP 1.1; if you experience difficulty with some older web sites that require HTTP 1.0, try disabling this option.	Checked
Use HTTP 1.1 Through Proxy Connections	Check this option to send HTTP 1.1 requests through a proxy server; check with your network administrator before making this change.	Unchecked

CHAPTER 31

Finding, Organizing, and Saving Web-Based Information

by Ed Bott

In this chapter

Using Internet Shortcuts

Regardless of where you find a web page—on a corporate intranet or on a distant server—deep down inside it's nothing more than a document file. And just as you use conventional shortcuts to organize documents stored locally, Internet shortcuts are the most effective way to organize web-based information. When you inspect the properties of an Internet shortcut, you see a page of settings like the one in Figure 31.1.

FIG. 31.1
The target for an Internet shortcut is an URL rather than a local or UNC file specification.

Internet shortcuts behave just like other shortcuts. You can add Internet shortcuts to the desktop or Start menu, move them between folders, send them to other people in mail messages, or rename the shortcut without affecting the target it points to.

▶ **See** "Using Shortcuts," **p. 94**

If you start the Create Shortcut wizard and enter a valid URL in the Command line box, Windows creates an Internet shortcut. You can drag that shortcut into the browser window or the Address bar to open the target page, or drop it into the Favorites folder or Links bar to make the page more readily accessible.

 It's easy to create a shortcut that points to the web page you're currently viewing in the browser window. Just choose File, Send, Shortcut to Desktop. Once the shortcut is on your desktop, you can rename it, modify its properties, move it to another folder, or send it to a friend or co-worker in an email message.

Using the Favorites Folder to Organize Your Favorite Web Sites

If you've used a web browser before, you're already familiar with the concept of saving pointers to web sites you visit frequently. Netscape Navigator calls them bookmarks, while prior versions of

Internet Explorer saved shortcuts to web pages in a Favorites folder. Internet Explorer 4.0 also lets you collect Internet shortcuts in a Favorites folder, but the user interface for working with Favorites is dramatically different.

 TIP If you had a copy of Netscape Navigator installed when you upgraded to Windows 98, all your Netscape bookmarks would be available in the Favorites folder. This conversion is a one-time process, however; New Navigator bookmarks you create after installing Windows 98 are not saved in the Favorites folder.

Click the Favorites button to open the Favorites Explorer bar; this frame along the left border pushes the main browser window to the right. When you choose an entry from the Favorites list, the page you selected appears in the browser window, as in Figure 31.2.

FIG. 31.2
Click on a shortcut in the Explorer bar at left, and the target page appears in the browser window at the right. Arrows at the top and bottom of the Favorites list let you scroll to additional entries.

Part VI

Ch 31

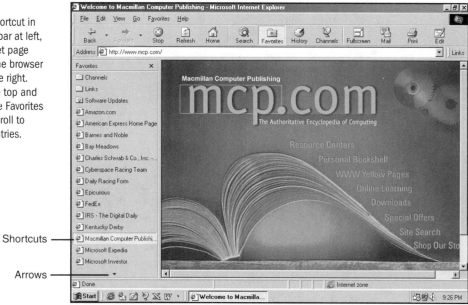

The Favorites folder is located within the Windows folder; if you've enabled multi-user settings, each user with a profile on the computer gets a personal Favorites folder. The contents of the Favorites list appear in alphabetical order on the pull-down Favorites menu and in the Explorer bar. To reorder the shortcuts in the Favorites menu, drag any entry to a new position by holding down the mouse button instead of clicking.

 TIP Although the Favorites folder is most useful with Internet shortcuts, you can move any object there, including files, folders, and shortcuts to documents or programs. Clicking on a document or program shortcut in the Explorer bar usually launches the associated application in its own window.

Adding a Web Page to the Favorites Folder

To add the current page to the Favorites list, use one of these two techniques:

- Drag the page icon from the left of the Address bar and drop it into the Favorites Explorer bar.
- If the Explorer bar is not visible, choose Favorites, Add to Favorites.

You can also use shortcut menus to create new entries in the Favorites folder. Follow this simple procedure:

1. Right-click on any blank space or text in the current page.
2. Choose Add to Favorites from the shortcut menu; you'll see a dialog box like the one in Figure 31.3.
3. Give the shortcut a descriptive name, if you wish, or use the default page title.
4. Click the Create In button and choose a subfolder in the Favorites list.
5. Click OK to create the new shortcut and close the dialog box.

FIG. 31.3

When you create a new entry in the Favorites folder, give it a new name if necessary to help you identify the page later.

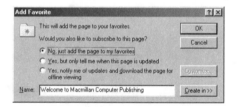

 TIP If the current page contains a link to a page you'd like to add to your Favorites folder, you can use the same technique without having to open the page. Point to the link and right-click, and then follow the steps outlined earlier.

When you add a web page to your Favorites list, you also have the option to download pages automatically at scheduled intervals.

▶ **See** "Using Subscriptions to Download Web Pages," **p. 683**

Deleting and Renaming Favorites

To delete an Internet shortcut in the Favorites folder, point to the shortcut, right-click, and choose Delete.

To rename an Internet shortcut, point to its entry in the list and choose Rename. Edit the name of the shortcut and press Enter to save your changes.

Using Subfolders to Organize Favorites

As you add items to the Favorites folder, the list can quickly become too long to work with comfortably. When you reach that point, use subfolders to help organize the Favorites list. You can create an unlimited number of subfolders in the Favorites folder, and you can even add new folders within those subfolders.

With the Favorites Explorer bar open, it's easy to move one item at a time from folder to folder. However, you can't use the Explorer bar to create new folders or to move more than one shortcut at a time. For these more serious organizing tasks, choose Favorites, Organize Favorites; that opens the dialog box shown in Figure 31.4, which includes the full set of tools you need.

FIG. 31.4
Use the buttons along the bottom of this dialog box to organize your Favorites folder. Right-click or use ScreenTips like this one to gather more information about a shortcut.

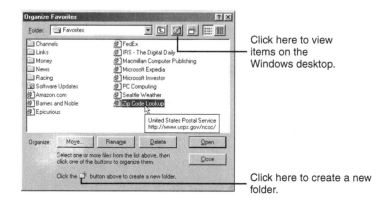

Click here to view items on the Windows desktop.

Click here to create a new folder.

Moving shortcuts to a new folder is a simple process, as long as you perform the steps in the right order. Open the Organize Favorites dialog box and do the following:

1. Click the New Folder button; the new folder appears at the end of the current folder list, with a generic name selected for editing.

2. Type a name for the new folder and press Enter.

3. Select one or more shortcuts from the Favorites list and click the Move button.

4. In the Browse for Folder dialog box, click the name of the folder you just created.

5. Click OK to make the move and click Close to return to Internet Explorer.

 You can also drag and drop Internet shortcuts within the Organize Favorites dialog box. If your collection of Favorites is relatively small, you'll probably find it easier to rearrange them this way than by using the cumbersome procedure outlined earlier.

Folders appear in alphabetical order at the top of the Favorites Explorer bar. To see the contents of a folder, click on its entry there; the list of shortcuts in the folder appear just below the folder icon, also in alphabetical order. Click the folder icon again to close it.

 For fastest access to the Favorites folder, click the Start menu. The cascading Favorites menu appears between the Programs and Documents choices.

Changing or Adding Quick Links

Although the Favorites folder is a convenient way to organize web pages, it still takes a couple of clicks and some scrolling to find a particular page. For the handful of sites you visit most frequently, use the Links toolbar instead. The shortcuts on this toolbar are never more than a click away, and you can easily arrange them for fast, convenient access.

To show or hide the Links bar, right-click on the menu bar and click Links. When you first start Internet Explorer, there are only five shortcuts on the Links bar, and they all point to pages at Microsoft. In less than five minutes, you can give the Links bar a complete makeover and give your productivity a dramatic boost in the process.

 T I P   Do you really need all those Microsoft pages on the default Links bar? Not likely. The Internet Start link, for example, is completely unnecessary; anytime you want to jump to `home.microsoft.com`, just click the spinning Explorer logo in the upper-right corner of the browser window. The Customize Links button leads to a simple Help screen that tells you how to change links; after you learn the technique, you can safely delete this link.

There's no limit to the number of shortcuts you can add to the Links bar. To keep navigation simple, though, you probably want to limit the number of links to no more than 10 or 12, depending on your screen resolution. On the Links bar in Figure 31.5, for example, there are nine shortcuts; adding even one more would push the last link off the screen. When that happens, arrows appear at either side of the Links bar to aid in scrolling.

FIG. 31.5

To squeeze the maximum number of shortcuts onto the Links bar, change long page titles to shorter labels.

To give your Links bar a makeover, follow these steps:

1. Right-click on any Links you don't plan to keep and choose <u>D</u>elete from the shortcut menu.
2. To add the current page to the Links bar, drag the icon from the left side of the Address bar and drop it alongside any existing link. The shortcut icon tells you when it's OK to drop.
3. Click the Favorites button and drag shortcuts from the Favorites folder to the Links bar.
4. To rearrange the order in which links appear, grab an icon and move it to its new location. Other links shift left or right to make room for it.
5. To rename a link, open the Favorites Explorer bar, click on Links, right-click on the entry you want to change, and choose Rena<u>m</u>e.

 T I P   The width of each shortcut on the Links bar is defined by its label. The shorter the name, the more links you can use. "FedEx," for example, takes up much less space than "Federal Express Home Page," without sacrificing any meaning.

Using the Search Bar to Find Information on the World Wide Web

How many pages are there on the World Wide Web? No one can say for sure, but the number is at least 50 million, probably more than 100 million, and growing every day. How do you find specific information in the billions of words and hyperlinks on all those pages? That's where search engines come in.

Internet Explorer offers easy access to several popular search engines through an Explorer bar that works much like the Favorites bar. When you click the Search button, an Explorer bar like the one in Figure 31.6 takes over the left side of the screen.

FIG. 31.6
Use the default search engine or pick another one from the drop-down list in the Explorer bar, and then enter the text you're looking for. Click links in the search results to view pages in the window at the right.

Part

VI

Ch

31

Finding information on the web is a two-step process. First, you have to choose a search engine that's appropriate for the type of information you're looking for. Then you have to construct your search so the pages you're looking for appear at the top of the list.

Choosing the Right Search Engine

In general, search engines can be divided into two types. Category-based sites like Yahoo! organize the Internet by classification. Indexed search engines, such as Excite and AltaVista, use web robots to gather text and create searchable databases of information. Most popular search sites now combine both techniques on their home pages.

Category searches are ideal for broad, open-ended questions, while indexed sites are better for finding specific facts. In either case, getting the right results takes practice and some basic understanding of how the search engine works. To avoid playing favorites, Internet Explorer picks one of its featured search engines at random every day and spotlights that choice when you click the Search button. You can accept the default, or you can study Table 31.1 and make your own selection using the drop-down list.

Table 31.1 Popular Internet Search Engines

Name	URL	Description
AOL NetFind	`www.aol.com/netfind`	America Online calls on a huge database of reviews to help you find people, companies, places, and information. Powered by Excite technology, it's open to non-AOL members as well.
Excite	`www.excite.com`	If you can't find it using Excite, it probably isn't on the Internet. Click on "Channels" to find information by topic or use its massive database to search the entire web.
Infoseek	`www.infoseek.com`	Enter text or click on topic links to find information. Jump to Infoseek's main page to try its impressive capability to process plain-English questions.
Lycos	`www.lycos.com`	One of the oldest search engines around, Lycos began as a research project at Carnegie-Mellon University. Today it offers Yahoo!-style category lists and superb international support.
Yahoo!	`www.yahoo.com`	The original category-based search engine now uses AltaVista's indexing software to do keyword searches as well. Make sure you choose the correct search method before sending your request.

 TIP Don't like any of the built-in search options? Then choose List of All Providers from the drop-down list in the Search bar. This option opens Microsoft's all-in-one search page, with links to dozens of general-purpose and specialized search sites.

Performing the Search

After you've selected a search engine, follow these steps to carry out your search:

1. If you see a category that's relevant to your search, click that link. Otherwise, enter the text you're looking for in the search box.

2. If the search engine provides any options, check them carefully. For example, do you want to search the web, Usenet newsgroups, or both?

3. Click the button that submits your request to the search engine.

4. A list of search results appears in the Search bar, as in the example in Figure 31.7. Scroll through the list and click on any links that look promising. The page appears in the browser window to the right of the Search bar.

5. Use the Next button at the bottom of the results list to see more entries in the results list.

6. If the search request doesn't produce the correct results, change your search or choose a different search engine and try again.

FIG. 31.7
This search produces a staggering 247,558 matches, but the most relevant pages appear in the top 10. Use the Next button to move through the list 10 links at a time.

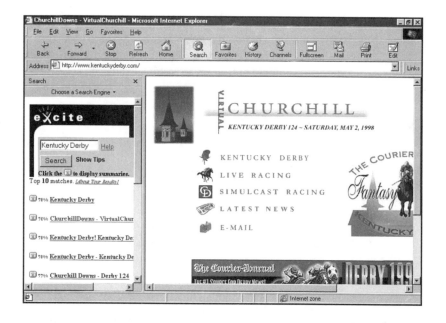

 There's no need to click the Search button if you simply want to look for a keyword or two. If you type **find**, **go**, or **?** in the Address bar, followed by one or more words, Internet Explorer's AutoSearch feature submits your request to Yahoo! for processing, returning results in the main browser window.

If you've found a favorite search engine, you can tell Internet Explorer to take you to that site instead of Yahoo! each time you use AutoSearch. To make the change, you first have to download Microsoft's Tweak UI utility, one of the unofficial Power Toys for Windows 95 and Windows 98. You can find all the Power Toys, with full instructions for their use, at

```
http://www.microsoft.com/windows95/info/powertoys.htm
```

After installing Tweak UI, open Control Panel and start the utility; click the General tab and use the drop-down list to change the default search engine.

Tips and Techniques for More Successful Searches

How can you guarantee better results when you search the web? Try these techniques:

■ Visit the major search sites often. They regularly add new features and upgrade search interfaces. If you use only the Internet Explorer Search bar, you won't see those improvements.

■ Learn how to combine search terms using the logical operators AND, OR, and NOT to narrow the results list. Every search engine uses a slightly different syntax for these so-called Boolean queries; check the help pages at the search engine's site. The default operator is usually OR, which means if you enter two or more words, you get back any page that contains any of the words; use an ampersand, AND, or quotation marks to be more specific.

Part
VI

Ch
31

■ Don't stop at simple searches. Some search engines let you specify a range of dates to search, for example, to avoid being bombarded with stale links. Others let you specify or exclude a particular web server. Still others let you progressively narrow down a list of results by searching only in those results. Read each search engine's online instructions to see what advanced features it offers.

Saving a Successful Search

When you find a search that you think you'll want to reuse, follow these steps to save it:

1. Right-click anywhere in the Search bar and choose Properties.

2. Select the entire URL that appears on the General tab, and then right-click and choose Copy from the shortcut menu. Click OK to close the Properties dialog box.

3. Select the entire contents of the Address bar, right-click, and choose Paste.

4. Press Enter to load the page whose URL you just copied.

5. Create a shortcut to the current page, either on the desktop or in the Favorites folder, and give it a descriptive name.

Searching for Information on the Current Page

A web page can consist of a single paragraph, or it can run on for tens of thousands of words. Internet Explorer's Find feature lets you search for words or phrases on the current page or within a selected frame. This feature can be extremely helpful when a search engine turns up a list of pages and you're trying to find the matching word or phrase in a specific page. To begin, press Ctrl+F and enter your text in the Find dialog box shown in Figure 31.8.

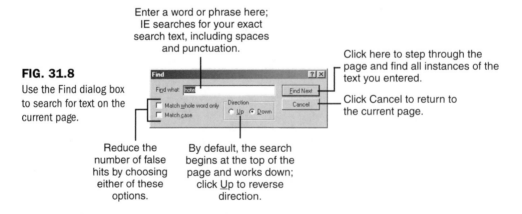

FIG. 31.8
Use the Find dialog box to search for text on the current page.

Enter a word or phrase here; IE searches for your exact search text, including spaces and punctuation.

Click here to step through the page and find all instances of the text you entered.

Click Cancel to return to the current page.

Reduce the number of false hits by choosing either of these options.

By default, the search begins at the top of the page and works down; click Up to reverse direction.

Note that the Find dialog box searches only text that actually appears on the page; it won't look at hidden text or HTML tags in the source for the page. To search for hidden text or tags, choose View, Source and use Notepad's Search menu.

TROUBLESHOOTING

Your search for text turned up no matches, but you're certain the word you're looking for is on the page. Looking for text on frame-based pages can produce unexpected results if you're not careful. On these pages, the Find feature searches only in the current frame, not in all frames visible in the browser window. Before you open the Find dialog box and enter your search text, make sure you click in the frame in which you want to search.

Using the History Bar to Revisit Web Sites

In addition to the cache in the Temporary Internet Files folder, Internet Explorer keeps a record of every URL you load. This History list is indispensable when you want to return to a page you visited recently, but you can't remember its address. If you've enabled multiple user settings on your Windows 98 PC, each user who logs in gets a private History folder.

▶ **See** "Managing the Browser's Cache," **p. 623**

Part
VI

Ch
31

Click the History button to open an Explorer bar similar to the one in Figure 31.9. The History bar looks and acts just like the Favorites bar, snapping into position along the left edge of the browser window and pushing the main viewing window to the right.

FIG. 31.9
Every time you visit a web page, it gets an entry in this History list. If you can remember when you saw the page, you can find it here.

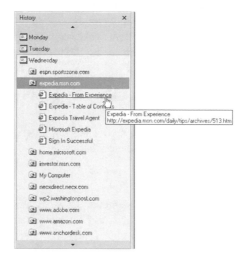

N O T E From the Windows Explorer, you can examine the History list by double-clicking the History icon. Individual shortcuts are not actually stored in the History folder, however; instead, Internet Explorer uses an internal database to manage the collection of shortcuts, with a single data file for each day. The entire collection is organized in one or more hidden folders. Although it's possible to view these hidden files from a DOS prompt, there's no way to see their contents without using Explorer's system extensions. ■

Navigating Through the History Folder

By default, the History folder keeps a pointer to every page you've accessed for the past 20 days. When you click the History button to open the Explorer bar, you see the list of shortcuts organized by day, with the most recent day's collection at the bottom of the list. Click on the entry for any day to see the list of shortcuts for that day, with a single entry for each resource location. Click again on any of these entries to see a shortcut for each page within that domain. When you click on an Internet shortcut in the History list, Internet Explorer loads the page in the browser window at the right.

 To increase or decrease the size of the History list, choose View, Internet Options and change the number of days to keep pages in history. Use the spinner control on the General tab to select a number between 0 and 999. Choosing 0 clears the History list every day, although you can still recall any page you visited earlier in the same day.

Although you cannot directly add an Internet shortcut to the History list, you can copy an entry from the History list to a variety of places: the desktop, the Start menu, the Favorites folder, or an email message, for example. Drag a shortcut from the History list to any legal destination or use the right-click menu to copy the shortcut to the Windows Clipboard.

Clearing Out the History

Internet Explorer allows you to empty the History folder completely or to delete entries one at a time. Clearing out the History folder can reclaim a modest amount of disk space, and it can also make the list easier to navigate. But a more practical reason to remove items from this list is for privacy reasons—to keep another user from seeing the list of sites you've visited recently.

- To clear a single shortcut from the list, point to the shortcut, right-click, and choose Delete.
- To remove a group of shortcuts, point to the entry for a given web location or day, right-click, and choose Delete.
- To empty all entries from the History folder, choose View, Internet Options, click the General tab, and click the button labeled Clear History.

Browsing the Web Offline

Internet Explorer's cache and History folders work together exceptionally well when you choose to work offline. With the History folder visible in the Explorer bar, you can choose File, Work Offline and view any files stored in the cache, even if you have no current connection to the Internet.

When you work with Internet Explorer offline, a network icon with a red X appears in the status bar along the bottom of the browser window. Except for that indicator, you can browse pages in the History cache just as if you were working with a live Internet connection. When you point to a link that isn't cached locally, the pointer changes shape, and you see the dialog box shown in Figure 31.10. Before you can view the selected page, you must open an Internet connection.

▶ **See** "Using Subscriptions to Download Web Pages," **p. 683**

FIG. 31.10

The X in the status bar means you're working offline. You'll see this pointer when you attempt to access a page that isn't stored in the web cache.

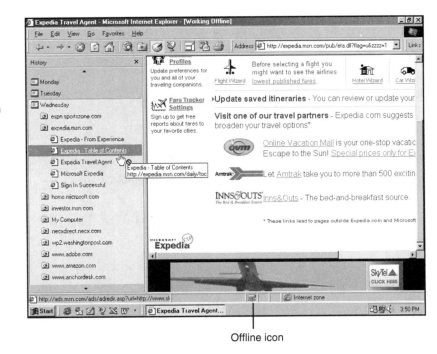

Offline icon

Printing Web Pages

Successfully transferring a web page to paper can be as simple as clicking a button, although complex page designs require some preparation for best results.

To print a full web page that doesn't include frames, click the Print button on the Standard toolbar. This action sends the current page to the printer without displaying any additional dialog boxes. Internet Explorer scales the page to fit on the standard paper size for the default printer. The entire web document prints, complete with graphics, even if only a portion of the page is visible in the browser window.

TIP By default, Internet Explorer ignores any background images or colors when printing. That behavior is by design, because most of these decorations simply make printed text harder to read. To add background images or colors to printed pages, choose View, Internet Options, click the Advanced tab, and check the appropriate box in the Printing section. Be sure to reverse the process after printing.

Arranging Frames on the Printed Page

For more complex pages, especially those that include frames, choose File, Print (or press Ctrl+P). That opens the Print dialog box, shown in Figure 31.11, and lets you specify how you want to arrange the page on paper.

FIG. 31.11
Watch the display at the left of the Print Frames box to see how a frame-based page appears when printed.

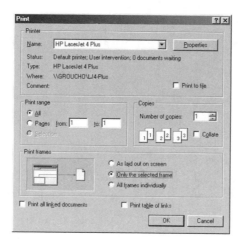

Follow these steps for maximum control over any printed page:

▶ **See** Chapter 12, "Printing," for more details on configuring and using a printer.

1. Choose the area to be printed. The Selection option is grayed out unless you've selected a portion of the page.

2. Choose the number of copies to print. The default is 1.

3. Tell Internet Explorer how to deal with frames—print a single frame, print the page as it appears onscreen, or print each frame on a separate page.

4. Choose either of the two options at the bottom of the dialog box to specify whether and how linked pages will print.

5. Click OK to send the page to the printer. An icon on the status bar confirms that the page has gone to the printer.

CAUTION

An option at the bottom of the Print dialog box lets you print all linked documents along with the current page. Exercise this option with extreme care, because printing indiscriminately in this fashion can consume a ream of paper with a single click.

Adding Headers and Footers to a Printed Web Page

To control most options that Internet Explorer applies before printing a web page, choose File, Page Setup. By using this dialog box (shown in Figure 31.12), you can change the orientation, margins, and paper specifications for the current page. More importantly, though, you can specify a header and footer to print on each page.

FIG. 31.12

Use these formatting codes to specify a header and footer to appear on each page you print. Internet Explorer saves the format you enter here as your default.

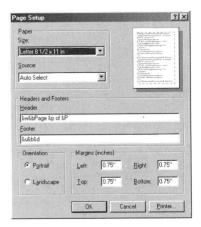

You can enter any text as part of the header or footer; in addition, Internet Explorer uses a set of arcane codes, each prefixed by an ampersand, to add information about the current page to the header or footer. Table 31.2 lists each of these codes.

Table 31.2 Custom Header/Footer Variables

To Print This	Enter This Code
Window title	&w
Page address (URL)	&u
Date (short format)	&d
Date (long format)	&D
Time (default format)	&t
Time (24-hour format)	&T
Single ampersand	&&
Current page number	&p
Total number of pages	&P
Right-align following text	&b*text*
Center *Text1*, right-align *Text2*	&b*text1*&b*text2*

N O T E If you can't remember the codes for headers and footers, click the question mark icon in the title bar of the Page Setup dialog box and point to the Header or Footer box. Watch out for a bug in the documentation, though: Any text you add after the characters &b will be right-aligned, not centered, in the header or footer. ■

Saving and Editing Web Pages

Only the simplest web pages consist of a single, simple document. More often, the page you see in your browser consists of one or more HTML documents and several linked images. There's no way to save all the elements on the entire page in one smooth operation. Instead, when you choose File, Save As, Internet Explorer saves the underlying HTML document and ignores any images or pages linked to that page. (You can also choose to save the current page as a plain-text document instead of an HTML-formatted page.)

To save graphics, frames, and other files linked to the current page, you must right-click on each one and choose Save Target As from the shortcut menu. Right-click on any link and use the same menu choice to save a linked page without opening it.

 With the help of a handy Internet Explorer keyboard shortcut, you can turn any web graphic into wallpaper for your desktop. When you find an image you'd like to install on the desktop, right-click and choose Set As Wallpaper.

▶ **See** "Customizing the Windows Display," **p. 438**

You can also edit any web page by loading it directly from your browser into FrontPage Express. By using the web browser, open the page you want to edit, and then click the Edit button on the Standard toolbar. You can also create a shortcut to the current page, and then right-click on that shortcut icon and choose Edit.

▶ **See** "Creating Web Pages with FrontPage Express," **p. 779**

Downloading Files from FTP Sites

One of the most common ways to distribute files of all types over the Internet is with FTP servers. Unlike web servers, which are designed primarily to assemble hypertext documents for viewing in a browser window, FTP servers use File Transfer Protocol (FTP) to move files between computers. Internet Explorer is capable of acting as a basic FTP client.

To connect directly to an FTP site using your web browser, enter the name of the site in the Address bar. Because FTP servers don't include graphics support, the display you see in the browser window is as austere as the one in Figure 31.13.

Click on any link in the FTP window to begin downloading that file. When you click on a link to a file stored on an FTP server, Internet Explorer handles the details of logging on to that server and negotiating the details of how to transfer the file. If Internet Explorer succeeds in connecting to the FTP server, you typically see the dialog box shown in Figure 31.14. Choose the option labeled Save This program to Disk, and then designate a name and destination for the downloaded file to begin the transfer.

FIG. 31.13
Don't expect fancy graphics or menus when you connect to an FTP site. Although this listing is plain, it's easy to find your way around.

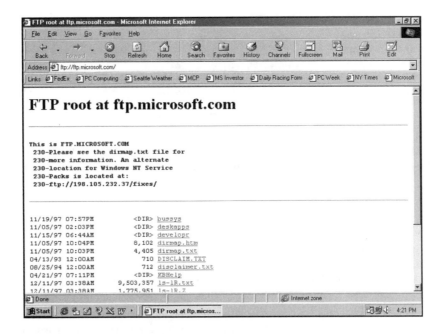

FIG. 31.14
Under most circumstances, you want to save a file rather than run it directly from an FTP server.

Based on the size of the file and the speed of your current connection, Internet Explorer attempts to estimate the time remaining on your download. This process isn't always successful; in particular, it fails when the FTP server at the other end of the connection fails to report crucial information about the file you've chosen to download. In those cases, the dialog box you see tells you how much of the file has been downloaded so far.

When downloading a file of any sort using IE4, you see a dialog box like the one in Figure 31.15, which may include an estimate of the amount of time remaining for the file to download.

FIG. 31.15
You see this progress dialog box whenever Internet Explorer downloads a file to your computer.

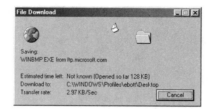

 T I P If you minimize the Download dialog box, you see the progress of your download in the label and ScreenTip of the Taskbar button. You can close the browser window or switch to another page without interrupting the download.

Logging on to Password-Protected FTP Servers

Many FTP servers allow anonymous access without a designated user name and password. Microsoft, for example, uses its FTP server to freely distribute patches and updates for Windows and other products. Internet Explorer handles anonymous logons easily. Other FTP servers, however, may refuse to allow logon unless you enter valid account information; this is especially true of corporate sites intended for use only by employees and other authorized users. Because Internet Explorer does not properly respond to password prompts from FTP servers, you have to construct a custom URL to connect to a password-protected FTP server. Click in the Address bar and enter the URL in the following format:

```
ftp://<username>:<password>@<ftp_server>/<url-path>
```

Substitute the proper username, password, and FTP server address in the preceding example.

Using Windows 98's FTP Client

Because Internet Explorer offers only the most basic FTP capabilities, it is incapable of connecting properly with some FTP servers. If you encounter such a server, use the Windows 98 command-line FTP client instead. Follow these steps to download a file from `ftp.microsoft.com`; the same techniques should work with any site:

1. Click Start and choose Run.

2. In the Open box, type **ftp** and press Enter.

3. At the ftp> prompt, type **open ftp.microsoft.com.**

4. Enter **anonymous** as the username; although any password will suffice on an anonymous FTP server, the widely accepted custom is for you to enter your email address as the password.

5. Use the **cd** command to navigate to the proper directory and use **ls** or **dir** to list the contents of the current directory.

6. If the file you want to download is a binary (nontext) file, enter **bin** and press Enter.

7. Type **get** *filename* to begin the download (substitute the name of the file for *filename*). To retrieve multiple files, type **mget** *filespec* (*filespec* can include wildcards, such as *.zip).

8. When your FTP session is finished, type **close** to disconnect from the server and **quit** to close the FTP window.

For rudimentary help with FTP commands, type **help** at the FTP> prompt.

ON THE WEB

If you use FTP regularly, invest in a full-featured FTP client like FTP Explorer. You can find this shareware product at

http://www.ftpx.com

Part

VI

Ch

31

CHAPTER 32

Internet Security

by Ed Bott

In this chapter

Setting a Security Policy

By its very nature, the Internet is an insecure place. Packets of data move from machine to machine across connections that anyone with a little technical knowledge can tap into. On the Internet, clicking a link can download and run a program written by someone you've never met, whose motives you can't even begin to guess. When you transmit sensitive data over the Internet, it can be intercepted by complete strangers. If you run a server program, a stranger can connect directly to your computer, with consequences you might not be aware of. There's no need for paranoia, but everyone who accesses the Internet should have a healthy respect for its risks.

Windows 98 and Internet Explorer 4.0 include a broad set of security tools. Before you can properly configure these options, however, you need to establish a security policy. This policy should balance the need to protect sensitive data against the undeniable value of open access to information and the wealth of information available on the world's largest network. Different environments have different security requirements as well. With a dial-up Internet connection at home, you might not worry about the risk of break-ins, but on a corporate network, firewalls and other sophisticated security precautions are a must.

These elements should be central to any security policy:

- Authentication. When you connect to a web site, how do you know who's really running that server? When you download and run a program, how do you know that it hasn't been tampered with or infected with a virus? When extremely sensitive information is involved, you may want to insist on secure connections guaranteed by digital certificates.

- Encryption. Certain types of data—usernames and passwords, credit card numbers, and confidential banking information, for example—are too sensitive to be sent "in the clear," where they can be read by anyone who can intercept the packets. For these transactions, only secure, encrypted connections are acceptable.

- Control over executable content. The Internet is filled with programs and add-ins that can expand the capabilities of your browser. Unfortunately, poorly written or malicious add-ins can carry viruses, corrupt valuable data, and even expose your network to unauthorized break-ins. On most networks, administrators try to limit the potential for damage by restricting the types of files that users can download and run.

Protecting Your PC from Attack

The idea that your computer might fall victim to a random attack from a stranger sounds like the stuff of science fiction or sensationalist headlines. Unfortunately, this scenario is depressingly common on the Internet, especially where users use direct connections to Internet service providers.

Mainstream news stories stress incidents in which hackers break into a system and steal data, such as credit card numbers. A far more common form of mischief on the Internet, however, is the so-called denial of service attack. The specific techniques vary, but in general these attacks exploit bugs in the way Windows handles TCP/IP packets. When an attacker targets an unprotected Windows machine, the result might be a fatal crash, or the flood of data might cause the system to slow to nearly a halt, forcing the user to reboot.

How Denial of Service Attacks Work

There's nothing new about denial of service attacks; users of UNIX-based computers have been fighting off attacks of this nature for years. Because Windows 95, Windows 98, and Windows NT are so widely used, they're logical targets for new attacks, and would-be attackers spread the details of successful new techniques with shocking speed.

Since the original release of Windows 95, Microsoft has issued several patches to Windows' TCP/IP networking components. Each of these updates was a direct response to a popular denial of service attack. For example, an underground program called Winnuke sends packets that contain out-of-bounds data; without the corrective patch, a Windows system crashes with a blue-screen error when it encounters this type of data. Other attacks include Teardrop, which works by sending fragmented packets of data that cause unpatched Windows systems to crash when they try to reassemble them; Land, which uses phony IP addresses to slow Windows to a crawl as it tries to handle a flood of unidentified data; and Ssping, also known as the "Ping of death," which uses a bug in the popular Ping utility to crash Windows.

The good news is that Windows 98 is invulnerable to these and all other known attacks as of the date it was first released. The bad news? History demonstrates conclusively that there are more networking bugs in Windows, just waiting to be discovered; when they emerge, Microsoft will need to develop and distribute patches to keep Windows users safe from the newly discovered exploits, and users will need to install those patches to avoid data loss and downtime.

 T I P Whenever a new Windows security hole is discovered, Microsoft publishes security alerts with links to downloadable patches. To keep abreast of the latest developments, visit the Microsoft Security Advisor web site, at

http://www.microsoft.com/security

Are You Vulnerable?

Before a would-be attacker can target your PC, he (most are young males) has to identify your IP address and discover an unprotected TCP port. The surest way of protecting yourself from denial-of-service attacks, therefore, is to make sure you have neither a public IP address nor any accessible TCP ports. In other words, never open a direct, modem-based Internet connection. Of course, that's a drastic step that most users of dial-up Internet connections would hardly be willing to take.

For most users, the risks of Internet attacks are low. If you use a modem to access the Internet for brief online sessions, during which you simply browse web pages, your risk of attack is relatively low. The odds that an attacker will stumble across your IP address during a short online session are small.

Users who are most vulnerable to Internet attacks are those with direct, full-time connections, those who run web and FTP servers, and those who use interactive services like Internet Relay Chat (IRC). In all these cases, your IP address is easily available, and an attacker has ample opportunity to probe your system in search of weak spots.

Protecting Yourself from Attack

To keep mischief-makers out of your physical offices, you install and use secure locks. To keep cyber-vandals from breaking into your network, you install, configure, and use a *firewall*, a secure gateway computer that sits between your network and the router at your Internet service provider. This combination of hardware and software is designed to intercept and filter packets of information, letting through only those that meet your strict standards of security.

There are practically an infinite number of firewall designs, ranging in price from absolutely free to well into six-figure territory. In general, though, firewalls fall into one of two broad categories:

- Network-level firewalls intercept each packet that attempts to go in or out of your network, scanning its address header to determine its point of origin. Screening rules determine whether the packet passes through to its destination or is rejected.

- Application-level firewalls are more complicated, using a carefully isolated machine outside the network that runs proxy services for news, HTTP access, FTP, Telnet, and other services. When a host machine inside the firewall requests a service from the Internet, the proxy server intercepts the request and handles the transaction. To the machine on the other end of the connection, the request looks as though it came from the proxy server; there's no possibility of a direct (and possibly compromised) connection between it and the host machine inside the firewall.

Firewalls can do much more than simply keep out intruders. Because they serve as a central point of access for all traffic in and out of the network, they can enforce business-level restrictions on Internet use—denying access to X-rated sites, for example, or restricting FTP access to trusted sites only. Full-featured firewall packages typically include detailed usage logs and audit reports as well, making it possible to detect attacks as they happen. If you can spot a successful break-in early enough, you can take steps to boot out the bad guys and shore up security as needed.

ON THE WEB

Want more information about firewalls? You'll find links to the definitive Firewalls FAQ and mailing list at **http://www.greatcircle.com**.

Configuring Internet Explorer to Use a Proxy Server

With ordinary dial-up Internet connections, client machines connect directly to web or FTP servers, making it possible for a would-be hacker to break into the network. To minimize that risk, most corporate networks include a firewall and one or more proxy servers.

Before Internet Explorer 4.0 can use a proxy server, you must specify its name or IP address. Some proxies (Microsoft Proxy Server 2.0 or later, for example) can automatically configure client machines; in that case, you need to enter the name of the machine that contains the configuration files.

TROUBLESHOOTING

You're connected to a corporate network and some or all of the options described in this chapter are unavailable. That's usually a sign that the network administrator has used Microsoft's Internet Explorer Administration Kit to enforce security policies from a central server. In that case, most security settings (and many other options, for that matter) will be grayed out and inaccessible. See your network administrator if you need to change one of these settings.

Follow these steps to set up Internet Explorer for use with a proxy server:

1. Choose View, Internet Options, and click the Connection tab. A dialog box like the one in Figure 32.1 appears.

FIG. 32.1

Check this box and enter the name or IP address of your proxy server; port 80 is the standard setting for virtually all web proxies.

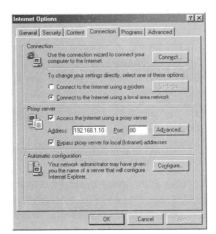

2. Check the box labeled Access the Internet Using a Proxy Server.

3. If your network includes a server that can automatically configure Internet Explorer, click the Configure button, enter the full URL of the server, and click OK. No additional configuration is necessary.

4. If your network does not include an autoconfiguring proxy server, click in the A<u>d</u>dress text box and enter the name or IP address of the proxy machine.

N O T E When configuring a proxy server, you may use either the server's name or its IP address. The effect is identical no matter which technique you use. The administrator in charge of the proxy server can supply information about your network's configuration. ■

5. Click in the <u>P</u>ort text box and enter the name of the TCP port that the proxy server uses. In the overwhelming majority of cases this will be port 80, the standard for web traffic.

6. If your network uses separate proxy servers to handle other protocols, click the Ad-<u>v</u>anced button to open the dialog box shown in Figure 32.2. Enter those settings here.

FIG. 32.2

Click the Exceptions text box and specify URLs that you want to access directly, without using the proxy server.

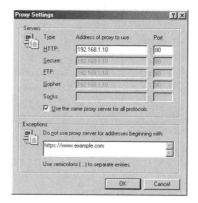

7. Your network administrator might provide direct access to some sites and block access through the proxy server. If instructed to do so, click the Exceptions text box and enter the names of any domains that do not require access through the proxy server. Be sure to enter a protocol prefix (typically http:// or https://) for each address. Use semicolons to separate entries in this list.

8. Click OK to close the Advanced dialog box.

9. Click OK to close the Internet Options dialog box and begin using the proxy server.

 T I P On most corporate networks, you should check the box labeled <u>B</u>ypass Proxy Server for Local (intranet) Addresses. The proxy's safety features shouldn't be necessary inside the firewall, and routing intranet requests through the proxy will hurt performance without improving security.

Establishing and Maintaining Internet Security Zones

Internet Explorer 4.0 includes dozens of security settings. Applying each of those options to individual web sites would be impractical; instead, the system lets you group sites into four security zones, each with its own high, medium, or low security settings. Initially, as Table 32.1 shows, all sites are divided into two groups: those inside your company's intranet and those on the Internet. As part of a comprehensive security policy, you can designate specific web sites as trusted or restricted, giving them greater or less access to machines inside your network.

Table 32.1 Security Zones at a Glance

Security Zone	Default Locations Included in Zone	Default Security Settings
Local intranet zone	Local intranet servers not included in other zones; all network paths; all sites that bypass proxy server	Medium
Trusted sites zone	None	Low
Internet zone	All web sites not included in other zones	Medium
Restricted sites zone	None	High

As you move from one address to another by using Internet Explorer, the system checks to see what zone the address has been assigned to and then applies the security settings that belong to that zone. If you open a web page on a server inside your corporate intranet, for example, you can freely download files and work with ActiveX controls or Java applets. When you switch to a page on the Internet, however, your security settings might prevent you from using any kind of active content or downloading any files.

There are three built-in security levels, plus a Custom option that lets you pick and choose security settings for a zone. Table 32.2 summarizes the security options available when you first start Internet Explorer 4.0.

Table 32.2 Default Security Levels

Security Level	Default Settings
High	ActiveX controls and JavaScript disabled; Java set to highest safety level; file downloads prohibited through browser; prompt before downloading fonts or logging on to secure site.
Medium	ActiveX enabled for signed controls only, with prompt before downloading; file and font downloads permitted; Java set to medium safety level; all scripting permitted; automatic logon to secure sites.
Low	Enable all ActiveX controls, but prompt before using unsigned code; Java set to low safety; desktop items install automatically; file and font downloads permitted; all scripting permitted; automatic logon to secure sites.
Custom	Enables user or administrator to select security settings individually.

Part
VI

Ch
32

Adding an Internet Domain to a Security Zone

Initially, Internet Explorer includes every external web site in the Internet zone. Over time, you'll identify some sites that are extremely trustworthy, such as a secure server maintained by your bank or stockbroker. On these sites, you might want to relax security settings to allow maximum access to information and resources available from that domain. Other sites, however, might earn a reputation for transferring unsafe content, including untested software or virus-infected documents. On a network, in particular, you might want to tightly restrict access to these unsafe sites.

To add the addresses for specific web sites to a given security zone, open the Internet Options dialog box, and click the Security tab; the dialog box shown in Figure 32.3 appears.

FIG. 32.3

Adding a web site to the Restricted Sites zone lets you tightly control the site's ability to interact with your PC and network.

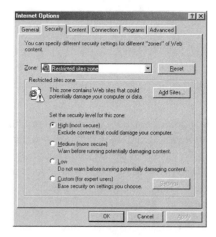

By definition, the Internet zone includes all sites not assigned to other zones. As a result, you can't add sites to that zone. Follow these steps to assign specific sites to the Trusted Sites or Restricted Sites zones:

1. Open the Internet Options dialog box and click the Security tab.
2. Choose a zone from the drop-down list at the top of the dialog box.
3. Click the Add Sites button.
4. Enter the full network address of the server you want to restrict in the text box and click the Add button.
   - Be sure to include the prefix (http://, for example), but don't add any address information after the host name—Internet Explorer applies security settings to all pages on that server.
5. Repeat steps 3 and 4 to add more server names to the selected zone.
6. Click OK to close the dialog box.

To remove a web server from either the Trusted Sites or Restricted Sites zone, click the A<u>d</u>d Sites button, select the address from the list, and click the <u>R</u>emove button. Any addresses you remove from a zone again belong to the default Internet zone.

Some special considerations apply when adding sites to the Trusted sites or Local Intranet zone:

- By default, only secure sites (those with the https:// prefix) can be added to the Trusted sites group. To add other sites, clear the check box that reads Require <u>S</u>erver Verification (https:) for all sites in this zone.

- To add sites to the Local Intranet zone, you'll have to go through one extra dialog box (see Figure 32.4). Clear the middle check box if you want resources that you access without using the proxy server to fall into this group by default. Click the <u>A</u>dvanced button to add sites to the Local Intranet zone.

FIG. 32.4

Clear one or more of these check boxes to move sites from the Local Intranet zone to the default Internet zone.

 The status bar always displays the security zone for the current page. After you add a site to a security zone, load the page to confirm that the change was effective.

Changing Security Settings by Zone

When you first run Internet Explorer 4.0, all web pages use the same Medium security settings, but it doesn't have to stay that way. If your intranet is protected by a reliable firewall and you use ActiveX components developed within your company, you might want to reset security in the Local Intranet zone to Low. Likewise, if you're concerned about the potential for damage from files and programs on the Internet, you can reset security for the Internet zone to High.

To assign a different security level to any of the four built-in zones, follow these steps:

1. Open the Internet Options dialog box and click the Security tab.
2. Choose the appropriate zone from the drop-down list.
3. Click the <u>H</u>igh, <u>M</u>edium, or <u>L</u>ow option button.
4. Click OK to save your new security settings.

When you choose the <u>H</u>igh option for the Internet zone (or use custom options to choose similar security settings), don't be surprised if many pages don't work properly. Because ActiveX controls are disabled by default, for example, you're likely to see dialog boxes like the

Part

VI

Ch

32

ones in Figure 32.5 when you load an ActiveX-enabled page or attempt to download and play a streaming audio file.

FIG. 32.5

With the security level set to High, many forms of rich content simply won't work. Instead of hearing multimedia files, for example, you'll see a dialog box like this one.

Setting Custom Security Options

If none of the built-in security levels is quite right for the policy you've established, you can create your own collection of security settings and apply it to any of the four security zones. Instead of choosing High, Medium, or Low, use Internet Explorer's Custom option to step through all the security options and choose the ones that best suit your needs. Follow these steps:

1. Open the Internet Options dialog box and click the Security tab.

2. Choose the appropriate zone from the drop-down list.

3. Click the Custom option button.

4. The Settings button, which is normally grayed out, should now be available. Click it, and the Security Settings dialog box appears (see Figure 32.6).

FIG. 32.6

Internet Explorer includes a long list of security settings for each zone. Use context-sensitive help for a concise explanation of what each one does.

5. Scroll through the list and choose the options that best apply to your security needs. If you're not sure what an option means, right-click its entry and choose What's This for context-sensitive help.

6. After you've finished adjusting all security settings, click OK to apply the changes to the selected zone.

 TIP Have you experimented with security settings to the point where you're afraid you've done more harm than good? Just start over. Open the Security Settings dialog box, choose a security level in the Reset To box, and click the Reset button. That restores the custom settings to the default security settings for that level and lets you begin fresh.

Restricting ActiveX Controls

The single most controversial feature of Internet Explorer 4.0 is its support for ActiveX controls. ActiveX technology, an extension of what was known in previous versions of Windows as Object Linking and Embedding (OLE), commonly refers to component software used across networks, including the Internet. Internet Explorer 4.0 uses ActiveX components in the browser window to display content that ordinary HTML can't handle, such as stock tickers, cascading menus, or Adobe Acrobat documents. An ActiveX chart control, for example, can take a few bits of data from a distant server and draw a chart at the speed of the local PC, instead of forcing you to wait while downloading a huge image file. The Microsoft Investor page (see Figure 32.7) offers a particularly rich example of this capability to quickly gather and manipulate data.

Part
VI

Ch
32

FIG. 32.7
An ActiveX control on this page makes it possible to quickly analyze and display complex data such as stock prices.

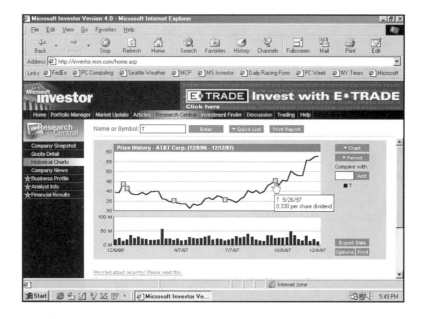

When you view a page that includes an ActiveX control, you don't need to run a setup program and restart your browser; the program simply begins downloading, and then offers to install itself on your computer. That's convenient, but automatic installation also allows poorly written or malicious applets free access to your computer and network. Internet Explorer security options let you take control of ActiveX components and apply security settings by zone. You can completely disable all such downloads, or you can rely on digital certificates to decide which components are safe to install.

Customizing ActiveX Security Settings

Whenever Internet Explorer encounters an ActiveX control on a web page, it checks the current security zone and applies the security settings for that zone:

- The default Medium security settings disable any unsigned ActiveX controls and prompt you before downloading and installing those that have a valid certificate.

- The most drastic ActiveX security option completely disables any components you encounter in a given security zone, signed or not. To enable this setting in the Internet zone, set the security level to High.

- When security is set to Low, the browser runs any ActiveX control. Signed controls download and install automatically; Internet Explorer prompts you before using an unsigned control.

> **CAUTION**
>
> Low security settings put your computer and network at risk. The only circumstance in which we recommend this setting is in the Local Intranet zone, to allow access to trusted but unsigned ActiveX controls developed by other members of your organization.

In zones where some or all ActiveX controls are disabled, Internet Explorer downloads the prohibited control but refuses to install it. Instead, you'll see an error message like the one in Figure 32.8.

FIG. 32.8
Unless you set security options to Low, you'll see this dialog box anytime you encounter an unsigned ActiveX control. With High security, all ActiveX components are disabled.

Table 32.3 shows default ActiveX settings for each security zone. If you don't see a mix of options appropriate for your security policy, choose a zone and use Custom settings to redefine security levels.

Table 32.3 ActiveX Security Settings by Zone

Security Setting	Option	High	Medium	Low
Download unsigned ActiveX controls	Prompt			X
	Disable	X	X	
	Enable			
Script ActiveXPrompt controls marked safe for scripting	Disable			
	Enable	X	X	X
	Prompt		X	X
Initialize and script ActiveX controls not marked as safe	Disable	X		
	Enable		X	
Download signed Prompt ActiveX controls	Disable	X		
	Enable			X
	Prompt			
Run ActiveX controls and plugins	Disable	X		
	Enable		X	X

Custom security settings offer a way to take advantage of only the ActiveX controls you specifically approve, while prohibiting all others. Choose the Custom security level for the Internet zone, click Settings, and enable two options: Run ActiveX Controls and Plugins, and Script ActiveX Controls Marked Safe For Scripting. Disable all other ActiveX security settings. With these security settings, currently installed ActiveX controls function normally. When you encounter a new page that uses an ActiveX control, it refuses to install; you can choose to install it by temporarily resetting the security options for that zone.

Using Certificates to Identify People, Sites, and Publishers

Internet Explorer uses digital certificates to verify the publisher of an ActiveX control before determining how to handle it. This feature, called Authenticode, checks the ActiveX control for the existence of an encrypted digital signature. IE4 then compares the signature against an original copy stored on a secure web site to verify that the code has not been tampered with. Software publishers register with certifying authorities such as VeriSign, Inc., who in turn act as escrow agents to verify that the signature you're viewing is valid.

ON THE WEB

For more information about how Authenticode uses digital signatures and certifying authorities, see

http://www.verisign.com/developers/authenticodefaq.html

If Internet Explorer cannot verify that the signature on the ActiveX control is valid, you see a Security Warning dialog box (see Figure 32.9). Depending on your security settings for the current zone, you might be able to choose to install the control anyway.

FIG. 32.9

You'll see this warning when Internet Explorer can't verify that a certificate is valid. Click Yes to install the software anyway or No to check again later.

If the Certifying Authority verifies that the signature attached to the control is valid, and the current security zone is set to use Medium settings, you will see a dialog box like the one in Figure 32.10.

FIG. 32.10

Use the links on this certificate to see additional information about the publisher of ActiveX controls you download.

The Security Warning dialog box confirms that the signature is valid. In addition, it offers links that you can follow for more information about the publisher and gives you the option to add that publisher to a list of trusted sites.

- Click Here for Detailed Information About the Publisher, Gathered from its Certificate. If the applet or control is requesting permission to access system resources, an additional link appears. Detailed Help is available.

- Click Here To See Additional Information About The Applet Or Control. This link typically points to a web site run by the software publisher.

- Choose Yes to install the software, and No to abort the installation.

- Check this box to add the certificate to your list of trusted publishers. Future downloads accompanied by certificates on your trusted publishers list install automatically, without requiring your approval.

N O T E To view and edit the full list of trusted publishers and certifying authorities, choose View, Internet Options, click the Content tab, and look in the Certificates box. ■

■ Click here for general information about certificates and ActiveX security.

> **CAUTION**
>
> A valid certificate provides no guarantee that a signed ActiveX control is either bug-free or safe. The certificate simply identifies the publisher with reasonable certainty. Based on that identification and the publisher's reputation, you can decide whether to install the software, and in the event something goes wrong you know who to call for support.

Managing ActiveX Components on Your Computer

Every time Internet Explorer adds an ActiveX control, it downloads files to the local computer and makes adjustments to the Windows Registry. Unlike conventional programs, you can't use the Control Panel's Add/Remove Programs applet to remove or update components; but there is a way to manage this collection. Follow these steps:

1. Choose View, Internet Options and click the General tab.
2. In the box labeled Temporary Internet files, click the Settings button. The Settings dialog box appears.
3. Click the View Objects button to open the Downloaded Program Files folder. You'll see a list of all installed ActiveX controls and Java class libraries (see Figure 32.11). If you're not sure what a control does, right-click and choose Properties to see additional information.

FIG. 32.11

All installed ActiveX controls appear in this folder. Use the right-click shortcut menus to inspect the file's properties, update it, or remove it.

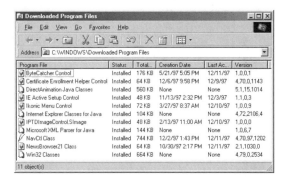

4. To delete one or more components, right-click the entry or entries and choose Remove from the shortcut menu. This step deletes each component's executable file and clears out any registry settings as well.
5. To update one or more components with the most recent versions, right-click the entry or entries and choose Update from the shortcut menu. This step checks the original

source for each file (usually an Internet address), replaces the component with new versions, and updates applicable registry settings as needed.

6. Close the Downloaded Program Files window and click OK to close the Settings dialog box.

Limiting Java Applets

Like ActiveX controls, Java applets extend the capabilities of Internet Explorer by displaying and manipulating data and images in ways that HTML can't. There's a significant difference between ActiveX and Java, though. Java applets run in a virtual machine with strict security rules. The Java Security Manager (sometimes referred to as the sandbox) prevents applets from interacting with resources on your machine, whereas ActiveX controls are specifically designed to work with files and other applications.

Unlike ActiveX controls, Java applets are not stored on your machine. Instead, every time you access a Java-enabled page, your browser downloads the applet and runs the program in the Java virtual machine. When you are finished with the applet, it disappears from memory, and the next time you access the page you have to repeat the download. Over slow links, large Java applets can take excruciatingly long times to load, although the results can be impressive, as the example in Figure 32.12 shows.

FIG. 32.12
This stock-charting page is an excellent illustration of the rich capabilities of Java applets.

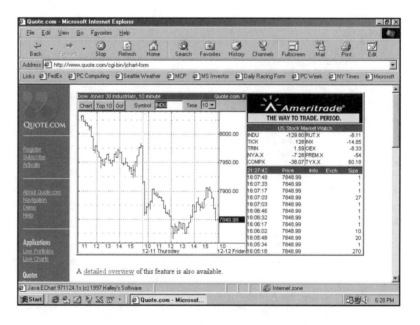

Internet Explorer's Security Settings dialog box lets you control specific aspects of the Java interface. Like the security settings for ActiveX controls, you can assign ready-made Low, Medium, or High options to Java applets, or disable Java completely. There's even a Custom option, although most of its settings are meaningful only to Java developers. To adjust Java security, follow these steps:

1. Choose <u>V</u>iew, Internet <u>O</u>ptions, and click the Security tab.
2. Choose a zone from the drop-down list and click the <u>C</u>ustom option button.
3. Click the <u>S</u>ettings button.
4. Scroll through the Security Settings dialog box until you reach the Java section.
5. Choose one of the five safety options.
6. If you select the Custom option, a new <u>J</u>ava Custom Settings button appears at the bottom of the dialog box. Click this button and the Custom Permissions dialog box appears (see Figure 32.13).

FIG. 32.13

Internet Explorer lets you tightly control the Java virtual machine, but only an experienced Java developer will be able to work comfortably with these options.

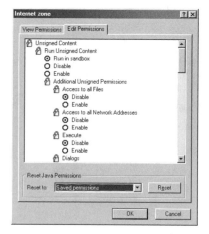

7. To change permissions in the Permissions dialog box, click the Edit Permissions tab. Select individual security options from the top of the dialog box, or use the drop-down list at the bottom of the box to select High, Medium, or Low security settings.
8. Close all three dialog boxes to apply the changes you've made.

ON THE WEB

Earthweb's Gamelan site is the best place on the Internet to look for Java applets and detailed information about the Java language. You'll find a link to these pages at

http://www.developer.com/directories/directories.html

Part

VI

Ch

32

Blocking Dangerous Scripts and Unsafe File Downloads

In addition to its ability to host embedded controls and applets, Internet Explorer supports simple scripting, using JavaScript and VBScript. With the help of scripts, web designers can create pages that calculate expressions, ask and answer questions, check data that users enter in forms, and link to other programs, including ActiveX controls and Java applets.

Although the security risks posed by most scripts are slight, Internet Explorer gives you the option to disable Active scripting as well as scripting of Java applets. You'll find both options in the Security settings dialog box when you choose Custom settings.

A far more serious security risk is the browser's ability to download and run files. Although the risk of executing untrusted executable files is obvious, even document files can be dangerous. Any Microsoft Office document, for example, can include Visual Basic macros that are as powerful as any standalone program. To completely disable all file downloads, select the built-in High security level. With this setting turned on, you'll see a dialog box like the one in Figure 32.14 whenever you attempt to download a file from a web page.

FIG. 32.14

With the security level set to High, no file downloads are allowed. When you attempt to download any file, including programs and documents, you'll see this dialog box instead.

Working with Secure Web Sites

When is it safe to send confidential information over the Internet? The only time you should transmit private information, such as credit card numbers and banking information, is when you can establish a secure connection by using a standard security protocol called Secure Sockets Layer (SSL) over HTTP.

To make an SSL connection with Internet Explorer 4.0, the web server must include credentials from a designated Certification Authority. The URL for a secure connection uses a different prefix (https://), and Internet Explorer includes two important indications that you're about to connect securely. You'll see a warning dialog box each time you begin or end a secure connection, as well as a padlock icon in the status bar (see Figure 32.15).

FIG. 32.15

Internet Explorer warns you when you switch between secure and insecure connections.

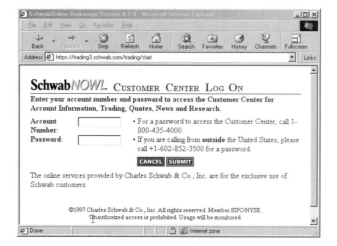

After you negotiate a secure connection, every bit of data is encrypted before sending and decrypted at the receiving end; only your machine and the secure server have the keys required to decode the encrypted packets. Because of the extra processing time on either end, loading HTML pages over an SSL connection takes longer.

ON THE WEB

For more information on certificates for commercial web servers, visit

http://www.verisign.com/microsoft

Although the built-in encryption capabilities of Internet Explorer 4.0 are powerful, one option can help you ensure even greater security. Because of United States Government export restrictions, the default encryption software uses 40-bit keys to scramble data before transmission. That makes it difficult to decode, but a determined hacker can break 40-bit encryption in relatively short order. A much more powerful version of the encryption engine uses 128-bit keys, which are nearly impossible to crack; some banks and brokerage firms require the stronger encryption capabilities before you can access personal financial information online.

At this writing, the 128-bit security software is available only in the United States and Canada, although Microsoft has won permission to make this code available to banks and financial institutions overseas as well. To check which version you have, find a file called Schannel.dll, normally stored in the \Windows\System folder. Right-click the file icon and choose Properties; then inspect the Version tab (see Figure 32.16).

Part
VI

Ch
32

FIG. 32.16
If your copy of Internet Explorer includes the Export version of this security code, your commercial transactions are not as safe as they could be.

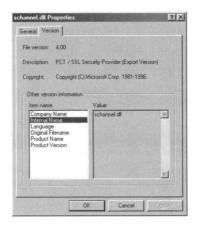

The weaker, 40-bit encryption code includes the words Export Version on the Properties tab. The stronger 128-bit security engine includes the label U.S. and Canada Use Only. You can download the 128-bit upgrade, as long as you do so from a machine that is physically located within the United States or Canada. You'll find complete download instructions for the 128-bit upgrade at

http://www.microsoft.com/ie/ie40.

How Safe Are Cookies?

When you view a page in your web browser, some servers give you more than you asked for; quietly, without your knowledge, they record information about you and your actions in a hidden file called a cookie. In more formal terms, these data stores are called client-side persistent data, and they offer a simple way for a web server to keep track of your actions. There are dozens of legitimate uses for cookies. Commercial web sites use them to keep track of items as you add them to your online shopping basket; the *New York Times* web site stores your username and password so you can log in automatically; still other sites deliver pages tailored to your interests, based on information you've entered in a web-based form.

The first time you access a cookie-enabled server, the server creates a new cookie file in the Temporary Internet Files folder. That record contains the server's domain name, an expiration date, some security information, and any information the webmaster chooses to store about the current page request. When you revisit that page (or access another page on the same site), the server can read and update information in the cookie record. Although information stored in each cookie is in plain text format, most sites use codes, making it nearly impossible to decipher exactly what's stored there.

If you're troubled at the thought of inadvertently sharing personal information with a web site, you can disable cookies completely, or you can direct Internet Explorer to ask your permission before setting a cookie. To control your cookie collection, follow these steps:

1. Choose <u>V</u>iew, Internet <u>O</u>ptions, and click the Advanced tab.

2. Scroll to the Security heading and find the section labeled Cookies (see Figure 32.17).

FIG. 32.17

If you'd prefer not to share personal information with Web sites using hidden cookie files, change this default option.

3. Choose the option you prefer: Disable All Cookie Use or Prompt Before Accepting Cookies.

4. Click OK to record the new security settings.

Should you be overly concerned about cookies? The privacy risks are minimal, thanks to strict security controls built into your web browser that limit what the server can and cannot do with cookies. They can't be used to retrieve information from your hard disk or your network; in fact, a server can only retrieve information from a cookie that it or another server in its domain created. A cookie can only track your movements within a given site; it can't tell a server where you came from or where you're going next.

Many web designers set cookies simply because that's the default for the server software they use; the information they collect gathers dust, digitally speaking. So when you ask Internet Explorer to prompt you before accepting a cookie, be prepared for a barrage of dialog boxes like the one in Figure 32.18. Try saying no; the majority of web sites work properly without cookies.

FIG. 32.18

You can ask Internet Explorer to warn you before it accepts a cookie; click the More Info button to see the contents of the proposed cookie file, as shown here.

Simplifying Online Purchases with Microsoft Wallet

A new feature in Internet Explorer 4.0 makes it possible to conduct safe transactions over the Internet without having to continually reenter your credit card and address information. The Microsoft Wallet lets you store address and credit card information in encrypted form on your hard disk. When you encounter a web site that allows payments from the Microsoft Wallet, you select a credit card and address from the lists you created earlier, and then complete the transaction.

You can add multiple addresses and credit card entries to the Address Selector and Payment Selector lists. By entering separate home and work addresses, you're free to order products and services for shipment to either address (see Figure 32.19).

FIG. 32.19

With multiple entries in the Microsoft Wallet Address Selector, you can easily tell a merchant where you want to receive goods you order over the Internet.

To add credit card information to the Payment Selector, follow these steps:

1. Choose View, Internet Options. Click the Content tab.

2. Click the Payments button to open the Payment Options dialog box.

3. Click the <u>A</u>dd button and choose a payment method—Visa, MasterCard, American Express, or Discover—from the drop-down list.

4. Use the wizard (see Figure 32.20) to enter credit card information, select a billing address (or create a new address entry), and protect the information with a password.

FIG. 32.20
The display name you enter here identifies this card when you use the Microsoft Wallet. The following screen lets you protect this information with a password.

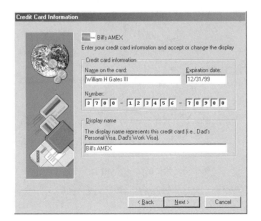

5. To add another credit card, repeat steps 3 and 4.

6. Click <u>C</u>lose to exit the Payment Options dialog box.

Note that address information is not encrypted; anyone with access to your computer can view, edit, or delete this information. Credit card details, on the other hand, are password-protected; if you forget your password, you'll have to delete the entry from the Payment Selector and re-enter it.

Part VI
Ch 32

Controlling Access to Undesirable Content

Not every site on the Internet is worth visiting. Some, in fact, are downright offensive. That can represent a problem at home, where children run the risk of accidentally stumbling across depictions of sex, violence, and other inappropriate content. It's also potentially a problem at the office, where offensive or inappropriate content can drain productivity and expose a corporation to legal liability in the form of sexual harassment suits.

Internet Explorer includes a feature called the Content Advisor, which uses an industry-wide rating system to restrict the types of content that can be displayed within the borders of your browser. Before you can use the Content Advisor, you have to enable it: Choose <u>V</u>iew, Internet <u>O</u>ptions, click the Content tab, and click the <u>E</u>nable button. You'll have to enter a supervisor's password before continuing. After you've handled those housekeeping chores, you'll see the main Content Advisor window(see Figure 32.21).

FIG. 32.21

Use the Content Advisor's ratings system to restrict access to web sites that contain unacceptable content.

The Content Advisor interface is self-explanatory: You use slider controls to define acceptable levels of sex, violence, language, and nudity. After you click OK, only sites whose ratings match your settings are allowed in the browser window.

Surprisingly, many adult sites adhere to the rating system, and an increasing number of mainstream business sites have added the necessary HTML tags to their sites as well. Unfortunately, many mainstream business sites don't use these ratings; as a result, you'll want to avoid setting the option to restrict unrated sites. ●

Web Subscriptions and the Active Desktop

by Ed Bott

In this chapter

Adding Web Content to the Active Desktop

The Active Desktop represents a key change in the Windows interface. The classic Windows 95 interface uses the desktop simply as a holding area for icons; however, the Active Desktop treats the entire Windows desktop as if it were a web page. You can still store icons there, but you can also add live web pages, components written in HTML, ActiveX controls, and Java applets. To see the Active Desktop in operation, look at Figure 33.1.

FIG. 33.1

Add live web content, including the headline and stock tickers shown here, to the Active Desktop.

N O T E   Don't confuse the Active Desktop with the Windows Desktop Update. The Windows Desktop Update, standard in Windows 98, makes sweeping changes to the Start menu, taskbar, Explorer, and other parts of the Windows interface. The Windows Desktop Update offers a number of options, including the choice of web-style single-click navigation or the traditional double-click style. The Active Desktop is one choice in the Windows Desktop Update, but even if you choose to disable web-based content on the desktop, the other changes in the Windows Desktop Update remain in place. ■

When you choose web style as your preferred interface, the Active Desktop is automatically enabled. If you choose Classic style, on the other hand, the Active Desktop is automatically disabled, and your desktop looks and acts like Windows 95.

▶ **See** "Classic or Web? Choosing a Navigation Style," **p. 62**

▶ **See** "Classic or Web? Choosing a Navigation Style," **p. 62**

You can enable or disable the Active Desktop at any time, regardless of which navigation style you've chosen. Follow these steps:

1. Right-click on any empty space on the desktop and choose <u>A</u>ctive Desktop from the shortcut menu.
2. To enable or disable the Active Desktop, select the View As <u>W</u>eb Page option. A check mark appears in front of this menu choice when the Active Desktop is enabled.
3. To hide or show individual web items, select <u>A</u>ctive Desktop, <u>C</u>ustomize my Desktop. Uncheck items on the web tab of the Display Properties dialog box to prevent them from displaying on the Active Desktop. Restore an item's check mark to show it on the Active Desktop again.

 TIP What good is information on the Active Desktop if your application windows cover it up? To quickly clear away all windows, use the Show Desktop button on the Quick Launch toolbar.

Using an HTML Page as Your Desktop

If you're a skilled web page designer, it's a trivial task to create a custom page that organizes essential information and links. In corporate settings, using a standard HTML-based background page can be an excellent way to ensure that every user has access to the same crucial information on the intranet. Windows 98 enables you to specify an HTML page as the desktop background, just as previous versions of Windows enabled you to use a graphic image as wallpaper.

You can use any HTML editor, including FrontPage Express, to create your background page. Think of this page as the base layer of the Active Desktop. Standard desktop icons sit on top of this layer, and you can add other web elements as well. The HTML page you use as your Windows background can include hyperlinks, graphics (including a company logo), tables, HTML components, scripted objects, and ActiveX controls.

▶ **See** "Creating Web Pages with FrontPage Express," **p. 779**

After you've created the background page, save it to local or network storage. To begin using the page as your desktop background, follow these steps:

1. Right-click any empty space on the desktop and choose P<u>r</u>operties.
2. In the Display Properties dialog box, click the Background tab (see Figure 33.2).
3. Click the <u>B</u>rowse button to display the Browse dialog box. Select the HTML file you want to use as the desktop, and then click <u>O</u>pen.
4. Click <u>A</u>pply to see your new background immediately.
5. Click OK to close the Display Properties dialog box.

Part

VI

Ch

33

 TIP If you prefer to see only your custom background when you view the Active Desktop, open the Display Properties dialog box, click the Effects tab, and choose <u>H</u>ide icons when the desktop is viewed as a web page. To switch between the Active Desktop and the desktop icons, right-click any empty space on the desktop, choose <u>A</u>ctive Desktop from the shortcut menu, and enable or disable the View As <u>W</u>eb Page choice.

FIG. 33.2
Create a custom web page and use it in place of wallpaper to make a truly custom interface.

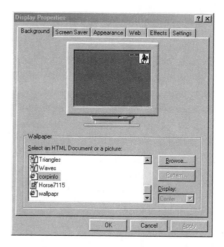

Displaying Objects on the Active Desktop

Enabling the Active Desktop lets you use the Windows desktop to display a variety of content. You can add the following:

- An HTML page as the Windows background; unlike wallpaper, this background can contain text, hyperlinks, images, and HTML code.
- One or more web pages, each in its own self-contained region.
- Web components, including ActiveX controls and Java applets.
- Active Channels, which let you download prepackaged collections of web content for offline browsing.
- Pictures, stored locally or from a web server.

Adding a New Web Page to the Active Desktop

Before adding a new web page to the Active Desktop, create an Internet shortcut to the page. Then follow these steps:

1. Right-click any empty space on the desktop and choose Properties from the shortcut menu. The Display Properties dialog box appears. Select the web tab to display the dialog box shown in Figure 33.3.

2. Click the New button. (Choose No if you're prompted to connect to Microsoft's gallery of Active Desktop components.)

3. If you know the exact filename or URL of the item you want to add, enter it. Otherwise, click the Browse button.

4. The Browse dialog box displays only files you can add to the Active Desktop—typically, images and Internet shortcuts. Select the item you want to add and click Open.

FIG. 33.3

Enter a filename or web address to add pictures or entire web pages to your Active Desktop.

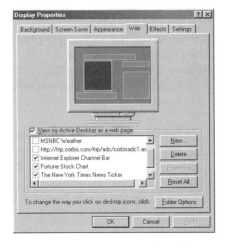

5. Click OK. If you entered an Internet shortcut, you'll see the dialog box shown in Figure 33.4. Click the Customize Subscription option if you need to enter a password or reschedule updates. Click OK to continue.

FIG. 33.4

Click OK to customize login and update options for web pages on the Active Desktop.

6. The new object appears in the list at the bottom of the web tab. Note that the screen display at the top of the dialog box shows the approximate position of each desktop item. Click Apply to display the new item and add another. Click OK to save your changes and close the dialog box.

There's a far easier way to add a new element to the Active Desktop. First, view the web page or open the graphic file in the browser window; size the window so you can see a portion of the desktop. To add a web page, hold down the right mouse button and drag the icon from the left of the address bar onto the desktop. To add a picture to the Active Desktop, right-drag the image onto the desktop. Choose Create Active Desktop Item (or Image) Here.

To move or resize objects on the Active Desktop, let the mouse pointer hover over the object until a gray border appears around the object. Click the thick bar at the top of the object and drag it to a new location. Use the borders to resize the windows. Scrollbars appear if the object is larger than the window you've created.

Part
VI

Ch
33

Placing a Picture on the Active Desktop

The Classic Windows 95 interface lets you add one graphic, centered or tiled, as wallpaper on the Windows desktop. Using the Active Desktop, you can add multiple pictures to the desktop and rearrange them as you see fit. You can use saved image files, such as a family picture or a postcard of your favorite tropical resort. Alternatively, you can select a web-based image that is regularly updated, such as a weather or traffic map.

N O T E   The Active Desktop supports three standard graphic file formats: Windows Bitmap (BMP), GIF, and JPEG File Interchange Format (JPEG). GIF and JPEG are the most common graphic formats on the Internet. ■

For photographs and other images that remain static, your best strategy is to create the Active Desktop item from a file stored on your local drive. Linking to a graphic file on a web site forces the browser to try to update the file for no good reason. To save an image you find on a web page, right-click the image and choose Save Picture As from the shortcut menu. Give the picture a meaningful name, and store it where you can find it later.

▶ **See** "Saving and Editing Web Pages," **p. 648**

> **CAUTION**
>
> Images and other original elements on most web sites are protected by copyright. Displaying an image file on your personal desktop is generally considered acceptable, but reusing a copyrighted graphic on a commercial web site without permission could land you in court.

Adding a Component to the Active Desktop

Unlike web pages, which sometimes have to be forced into service as an Active Desktop object, components are made for this very purpose. A component can be a simple scrap of HTML, or it can include an ActiveX control or a Java applet. Some components are actually miniprograms that you can customize to match your own preferences.

▶ **See** "Restricting ActiveX Controls," **p. 663** and "Limiting Java Applets," **p. 668**

ON THE WEB

Microsoft's Active Desktop Gallery includes an assortment of interesting desktop components, including a useful search box, stock tickers, and several clocks. Browse the entire collection at the following address:

http://www.microsoft.com/ie/ie40/gallery

Adding a new component to your Active Desktop is simple. In most cases, the web page designer includes an Add to Active Desktop button (see Figure 33.5). Click this button to download and install the component.

FIG. 33.5

Choose a component like this weather map from Microsoft's gallery; then click the Add to Active Desktop button to add it to your desktop.

Hiding, Removing, and Editing Objects

You don't have to display every installed component, picture, and web site on your Active Desktop. Hide objects you use infrequently so that they remain available when you need them. To display, hide, remove, or edit objects on the Active Desktop, right-click the desktop, and then choose Properties. Select the web tab in the Display Properties dialog box.

- To hide an object, clear the check box next to its entry. The object remains in your list of installed objects.
- To remove an object from the list, select the object and click Delete. The object will be removed from your system.
- To adjust the subscription settings for the object, click the Properties button.

  Click OK to accept your changes.

Using Subscriptions to Download Web Pages

When you subscribe to a web site, you instruct IE4 to regularly visit the site in search of new content. Don't let the term *subscription* mislead you; there's no fee associated with the process. Subscriptions are simply a way for you to automatically search for and download content from your favorite sites.

If you can load a web page into the browser window, you can subscribe to it. You can specify the amount of information to download from the site, although this capability is limited and might not produce the results you're expecting.

Part
VI

Ch
33

You can also subscribe to Active Channels—prepackaged collections of web content that include a site map and a recommended schedule for updates. With the help of Channel Definition Format (CDF) files, a webmaster can assemble just the information you need and not a page more.

> **CAUTION**
>
> With an IE4 subscription, you can instruct the browser to retrieve a given page and all pages linked to it, to a depth of as many as three pages. On web sites that contain large collections of files, this "web crawling" can cause an unacceptable performance hit. For this reason, some sites ban web crawlers, and you'll find that your subscriptions to these sites won't update correctly.

Subscribing to Web Sites

To subscribe to a web site, you start by adding it to your Favorites list. Follow these steps:

1. Open the web page in the browser window.

2. Choose Favorites, Add to Favorites. Rename the shortcut, if you want to, and choose a folder. Note that the Add Favorite dialog box includes two subscription options (see Figure 33.6).

FIG. 33.6
Choose one of these options to add a web page to your Subscriptions list.

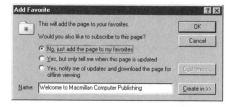

 When you subscribe to a web site, IE4 adds a shortcut in your Favorites folder and in the Subscriptions folder. Deleting the shortcut in the Favorites folder does not delete your subscription, nor does deleting a subscription remove the entry from your Favorites list. The property sheet for an Internet shortcut includes extra tabs when you've subscribed to that site.

3. If you simply want IE4 to notify you when new content is available on this page, choose Yes, But Only Tell Me When This Page Is Updated. Click OK to accept these settings and skip all remaining steps.

4. To set up a subscription that automatically downloads content from the specified web site, choose Yes, Notify Me of Updates and Download the Page for Offline Viewing.

5. Default subscription settings download only the specified page; the update is scheduled daily at 1:00 a.m. To accept these settings, click OK and skip all remaining steps.

6. If the web site to which you're subscribing requires a password for access, or if you want to adjust any other subscription properties, click the Customize button. That launches the Subscription Wizard (see Figure 33.7).

FIG. 33.7
To customize subscription options, follow the wizard's prompts.

The wizard includes four options (for further details on each of these options, see the following section):

- Download pages linked to the specified page. Choose a number between 1 and 3.
- Ask IE4 to send you an email message when the page is updated.
- Adjust the schedule IE4 uses to update this subscription. Choose Daily, Weekly, Monthly, or Custom options.
- Enter a username and password if the site requires it.

7. When you're finished with the Subscription Wizard, click OK to add the entry to your Subscriptions list.

Managing Subscriptions

Internet Explorer maintains your list of subscribed sites in the \Windows\Subscriptions folder. Special extensions to the Windows Explorer let you view subscription details, edit update schedules, and delete sites when you no longer want to subscribe.

To open the Subscriptions folder, choose Favorites, Manage Subscriptions. You'll see a window like the one in Figure 33.8.

Select one or more sites from the list and use the right-click shortcut menus to open, copy, delete, or update the selection. Select a single site and choose Properties to adjust the subscription's settings.

Customizing Subscriptions

By default, each subscription downloads one page, once a day, around 1:00 a.m. For most subscriptions, you'll probably want to change those defaults. Most often, you'll want to increase the amount of content that IE4 downloads as well as the update schedule.

Part
VI

Ch
33

FIG. 33.8
Switch to Details view to
see information about
each entry in the list,
including error
messages from the last
update attempt.

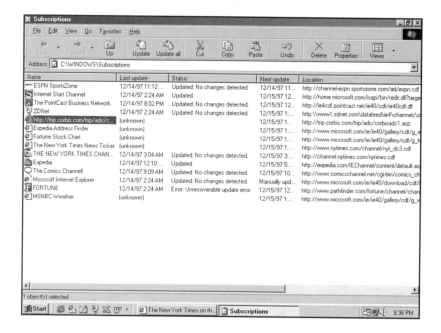

You can adjust all the following options when you first create a subscription, using the Subscription Wizard. To change a subscription's properties after that, open the Subscriptions
folder, right-click the entry for the site, and choose Properties from the shortcut menu. Select
the Subscription, Receiving, or Schedule tabs and make any of the following changes.

Controlling the Size and Depth of Subscriptions   Chances are you'll want to see more than
one page for your favorite web sites. On the front page of a newspaper like the *Los Angeles
Times*, for example, you'll usually find links to the day's top stories. When you go to those
pages, you'll find links to still more stories.

As part of the settings for each subscription, you can tell IE4 to follow all the links on the subscribed page. For subscriptions you plan to read offline, it's crucial that you enter a number
large enough to gather the information you need. However, it's also important to monitor the
amount of material that IE4 must download. The number of pages that need updating might
increase dramatically with each additional layer. If you don't set the correct limits when setting
up a subscription, the downloaded content might consume all the space in your Temporary
Internet Files folder.

 If you typically read only one portion of a web site, don't start at the site's home page; instead, pick
the site that contains the links you plan to follow. On highly structured sites, this page might be deep
within the site. However, you might not be able to be selective with an active server page or a page that
was created in response to your query.

To define exactly which pages IE4 will download with each update, follow these steps:

1. Right-click the site's entry in the Subscriptions folder, and then choose Properties.

2. Select the Receiving tab. You'll see a dialog box like the one in Figure 33.9, with the lower option selected in the Subscription type box.

FIG. 33.9
If you've opted to download a subscription for offline viewing, click the Advanced button to adjust the amount of content to retrieve.

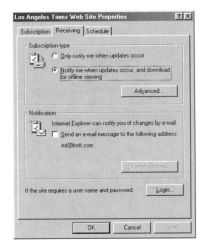

3. Click the Advanced button. The Advanced Download Options dialog box appears (see Figure 33.10).

FIG. 33.10
Balance these options to download the right amount of content without consuming too much disk space.

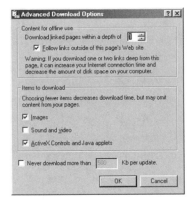

Part
VI

Ch
33

4. To download pages linked to the main page in your subscription, adjust the Download Linked Pages option. Enter a number between 1 and 3. To restrict the download to pages on the main site, clear the check box labeled Follow Links Outside of This Page's Web Site.

5. To restrict the total amount of content downloaded with each update, check the box labeled Never Download More Than X Kb Per Update. Enter a limit in kilobytes (the default is 500 K).

6. To further limit downloads, review the list of options in the center of the dialog box. By default, IE4 gathers image files, such as ActiveX controls and Java applets, but does not retrieve sound and video files.

CAUTION

Many web pages use images to help with navigation and to supply information. Don't restrict image downloads unless you're certain a site is useful in text-only mode.

---

7. Click OK or select another tab to further customize the subscription.

Specifying a Format for Update Notifications   How do you know when there's been a change in a web site to which you subscribe? Look at any Internet shortcut, on the desktop, in the Favorites bar, in the Channel bar, or in the Subscriptions window; a red gleam in the upper-left corner of an icon means there's new content.

If you prefer a more emphatic notice, ask IE4 to send you an email message every time it notices a change in a web site to which you subscribe. The email message can be a simple notice with a hyperlink, or it can contain a copy of the updated HTML page.

To set up email updates, follow these steps:

1. Select an entry in the Subscriptions folder, right-click, and choose Properties.

2. Click the Receiving tab.

3. Choose one of the two Subscription types at the top of the dialog box. If you select the option to download content for offline viewing, IE4 sends you the page via email.

4. Check the box labeled Send an Email Message to the Following Address. If necessary, click the Change Address button and enter or change the address and server information.

5. Click OK to close the dialog box and save your changes.

Scheduling Automatic Updates   By default, IE4 updates your subscriptions once a day, at 1:00 a.m. You can adjust the update interval or set the subscription for manual updates only. You can also specify whether IE4 will dial your Internet connection automatically.

To adjust a subscription's update schedule, open the Subscriptions folder and select the Schedule tab. You'll see a dialog box like the one in Figure 33.11.

To use a regularly scheduled interval, choose the Scheduled option and select Daily, Weekly, or Monthly from the drop-down list. Click the Edit button to adjust the details of this schedule. For example, if you subscribe to an online magazine that appears every Friday at midnight, you can tell IE4 to update your subscription each Friday morning at 5:00 a.m., before you arrive at work.

FIG. 33.11

Use these options to control how and when IE4 updates your subscriptions.

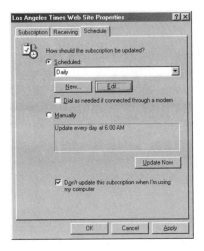

Network administrators might be horrified at the thought of thousands of users requesting web updates on the hour. IE4 attempts to minimize that problem by randomly varying the exact time for each update by a few minutes in either direction. To take maximum control over how users work with Internet Explorer 4.0, make sure you check the Internet Explorer Administrator's Kit, available from Microsoft. For more information about the most current release of IEAK, see **http://ieak.microsoft.com/**.

You can also create a custom schedule, using a dizzying variety of options. For example, if you have a favorite business-oriented site, you can set a subscription to update once an hour, from 8:00 a.m. through 5:00 p.m., every weekday. You can update a subscription every Monday, Wednesday, and Friday. You can even specify that a site update at 9:00 a.m. on the second Tuesday of every other month. When you save a custom schedule, you can reuse the schedule with other subscriptions as well.

To create a custom schedule for updates, follow these steps:

1. Select an entry in the Subscriptions folder, right-click, and choose Properties.

2. Click the Schedule tab and click the New button. The Custom Schedule dialog box opens (see Figure 33.12).

3. Choose the day or days to update. Select Daily, Weekly, or Monthly and adjust the available options that appear to the right.

4. Choose the time or times to perform the update. Options let you repeat the update throughout the day; if the exact time of each update is not important, check the option to vary the exact time of each update to avoid causing network congestion.

5. Give the schedule a descriptive name and click OK.

Part
VI

Ch
33

FIG. 33.12

Be sure to give each custom schedule a descriptive name, so you can reuse the schedule with other subscriptions.

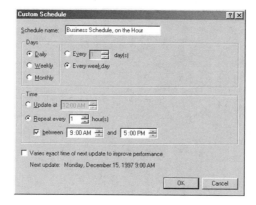

6. Set two final options to tell Internet Explorer whether it should automatically dial up your Internet connection or update a subscription when you're working with your computer.

7. Click OK to save your changes.

Updating Subscriptions Manually   IE4 lets you manually update all of your subscriptions with the click of one button. This capability is especially useful if you are about to leave on a trip and you want to make sure your notebook computer contains the most current versions of all your web subscriptions. You can also update an individual site if you know there's new content and you don't want to wait for the next scheduled update.

To manually update all subscriptions, follow these steps:

1. Verify that you have a working Internet connection. If necessary, open a Dial-Up Networking connection.

2. If the Subscriptions folder is open, click the Update All button.

3. If the Subscriptions folder is not open or the toolbar is not visible, choose Favorites, Update All Subscriptions.

4. If you have a lengthy list of subscriptions to update, the process might take a long time. The Downloading Subscriptions dialog box displays the status of the operation, including any error messages that might appear (see Figure 33.13). To cancel all further updates, click Stop. To skip over one site's update and proceed with the next site, click Skip. Click the Hide button to move the Downloading Subscriptions dialog box out of the way and continue working. You can close the browser window or view other sites while the update process continues.

To update an individual subscription, follow these steps:

1. If the Subscriptions folder is open, click the Update button.

2. If the Subscriptions folder is not open or the toolbar is not visible, choose Favorites, Manage Subscriptions.

3. Right-click the name of the site you want to update and choose Update Now.

FIG. 33.13

If you don't see this full status window, click the <u>D</u>etails button.

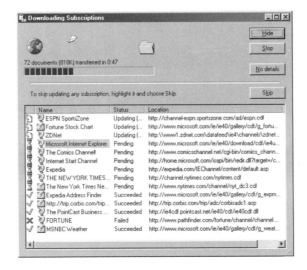

If you subscribe to a site that rarely changes or one you rarely visit, you can tell IE4 to update that subscription only when you manually choose to do so. Right-click the subscription icon and choose P<u>r</u>operties. Click the Schedule tab and choose the option labeled <u>M</u>anually. The Update Now button at the bottom of this dialog box also lets you refresh the subscription with the most current content.

Subscribing to Password-Protected Sites   Sites like the *Wall Street Journal* (**http:// www.wsj.com**) require that you enter a username and password before browsing their site. If you're using IE4 interactively, you can type the information directly into a login text box. When you subscribe to a password-protected site, IE4 lets you include the login information so that you can get the information you're looking for automatically.

You do not have to subscribe to the specific page that includes the login screen. You can subscribe to a page above the login screen and specify a depth of delivery that reaches below the login screen. When IE4 reaches the page that requests your user ID and password, it supplies them and continues updating the subscription.

To enter a username and password for use with a web subscription, follow these steps:

1. If you are initially creating the subscription, click the <u>L</u>ogin button. If you are editing an existing subscription, right-click its entry in the Subscriptions folder, and then click P<u>r</u>operties. Click the Schedule tab and click the <u>L</u>ogin button to display the Login Options dialog box (see Figure 33.14).

2. Enter the username and password you use to gain access to the site. Make sure both entries are spelled correctly and that the case (the mix of capital and lowercase letters) is correct.

3. Click OK to return to the Schedule tab. Click OK again to close the dialog box and save your changes.

Part

VI

Ch

33

FIG. 33.14

Enter login information here for IE4 to gain access to password-protected sites when updating a subscription.

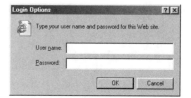

After setting up a subscription to a password-protected site, it's a good idea to verify that it works. Update the subscription manually; if the update fails because of an incorrect username or password, try logging in manually to make sure the site is working and the information you enter is correct. Then edit the subscription's username and password to match those you've tested.

Speeding Up Subscription Updates

If you're about to hit the road and you're running short on time, two shortcuts can dramatically reduce the time it takes to update all the subscriptions on your notebook. First, cut the update list to the bare minimum. Choose Favorites, Manage Subscriptions, and hold down the Ctrl key as you select the sites you want to update. When you're finished, right-click and choose Update Now from the shortcut menu.

To speed the update process even more (and save precious disk space), tell IE4 to concentrate on text and ignore large graphics and media files. Note that some sites use images for navigation, and at other sites images might contain important information; as a result, the pages you end up with when you use this technique might be of limited use. Still, when time is short, you can follow these steps:

1. Open the Subscriptions dialog box.
2. Right-click each site you plan to update, choose Properties, and click the Delivery tab.
3. Click the Advanced button to open the Advanced Download Options dialog box.
4. In the Items to download box, clear the check mark next to the options labeled Images, Sound and video, and ActiveX Controls and Java applets.
5. Repeat steps 2 through 4 for each subscription you plan to update.
6. Select the group of icons to update, right-click, and choose Update.

Subscribing to Active Channels

Channels are prepackaged subscriptions. Instead of indiscriminately delivering web pages to your hard disk, a webmaster can put together a collection of pages, just as a newspaper publisher assembles a daily paper. When you subscribe to an Active Channel, you download a single file that was created using the Channel Definition Format (CDF). Channel files typically include multiple HTML files, graphics, a map of the web site (including links to pages not included in the CDF file), and a publisher's recommended schedule for updates.

By default, Windows 98 adds a Channel bar that contains shortcuts to dozens of brand-name channels to your desktop. Note that you don't have to subscribe in order to view the content in a channel.

The Channel bar contains an Internet shortcut that takes you to Microsoft's Active Channel Guide. Browse through this lengthy list by category, or search for keywords using the built-in search button. The Active Channel Guide is updated frequently (see Figure 33.15).

FIG. 33.15
Microsoft maintains this exhaustive list of channels to which you can subscribe.

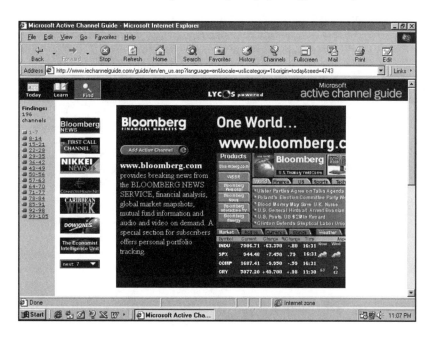

ON THE WEB

If you inadvertently delete the Channel Guide shortcut from the Channel bar, don't worry. You'll find the latest list of Active Channels at

http://www.iechannelguide.com

Adding a Channel to the Channel Bar

Most channels include an Add Active Channel button that allows you to add its shortcut to the Channel bar. When you add a channel to the Channel bar, you typically have the option of subscribing to the channel. You can use the publisher's recommended schedule or a custom schedule of your choosing; if there's no Add This Channel button on the preview pane in the Channel Guide, right-click and choose Subscribe from the site icon at the left.

Part
VI

Ch
33

Viewing Channels

When you click a shortcut in the Channel bar on the Windows desktop, Internet Explorer opens in full-screen mode, with the Channel bar visible along the left side of the browser window.

Although the Channel bar in the browser window includes the same sites as its desktop counterpart, the two bars behave differently. In the browser's Channel bar, for example, the icon for each channel is black and white until the mouse pointer passes over it. When you click a shortcut, the channel's home page opens in the pane to the right. If the CDF file for that channel includes a site map, clicking the channel button opens the list of available pages.

 TIP   You can view channels as ordinary web pages, as desktop components, or in full-screen mode. To specify whether IE4 should use full-screen mode for all channels, choose View, Internet Options, click the Advanced tab, and check the option labeled Launch Channels in Full Screen window.

Some channels include a Screen-Saver view. You might see this option during the initial Channel setup. To enable, disable, or adjust the Channel screen saver at any time, right-click the desktop, choose Properties, click the Screen Saver tab, and choose the Channel Screen Saver option.

When you view a channel in full-screen mode, the Channels bar slides off the screen when you read the page; it reappears when you move the pointer to the left edge of the screen. If you're running at a high screen resolution, use the pushpin icon to lock the Channels bar in place (see Figure 33.16).

Browsing Channels Offline

To view Channels and other subscriptions without making an active Internet connection, choose File, Work Offline. Like all subscriptions, Active Channels share the Temporary Internet Files with pages you browse interactively. When the cache fills up, IE4 pitches the oldest pages to make way for the newest ones.

▶ **See** "Browsing the Web Offline," **p. 644**

If you encounter frequent error messages when you attempt to update or view subscriptions, you might have used all the available space in your Temporary Internet Files folder. To make room for more content, increase the size of the web cache.

▶ **See** "Managing the Browser's Cache," **p. 623**

N O T E   Don't be surprised when you discover that some channels provide only a table of contents and links. Although these sites can give you a good idea of what's available when you go back online, you won't find enough information to justify keeping a subscription to this sort of channel. ■

Pushpin icon

FIG. 33.16
Watch the colorful logo appear when the mouse pointer passes over each entry in the Channel bar.

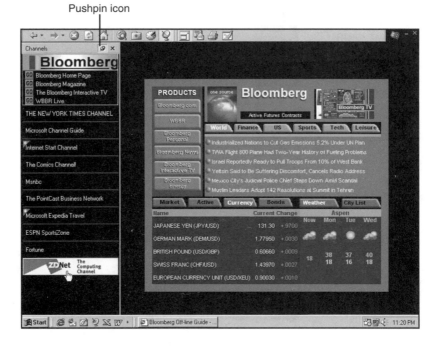

Managing the Channel Bar

The Channel bar appears on the Desktop when you install Windows 98. It also appears as an Explorer bar within the browser window when you click the Channels button.

By default, the Channel bar includes built-in shortcuts to channels delivered by some well-known companies, including Disney, America Online, and MSNBC (see Figure 33.17). There are also shortcuts to categories—news, entertainment, and business, for example—which include shortcuts to additional channels.

Although the Channel bar initially gets a place of honor on the Windows desktop, it's just another HTML component on the Active Desktop. That means you can customize its look and feel to suit your computing style. After you've sampled the selection of built-in channels and subscribed to a handful, give your Channel bar a makeover (see Figure 33.18).

- To move the Channel bar to a different location on the desktop, click any empty desktop space; then let the mouse pointer hover over the top of the bar until the gray sizing handle pops up (see Figure 33.18). Click and drag to a new location.

- To resize the Channel bar, aim the mouse pointer at the bar and wait for a thin, gray border to appear. Click any border and drag to change the size and orientation. Note that as the size of the bar changes, shortcuts on the bar reorder themselves automatically.

- To add or delete channels from the bar, right-click any channel icon and choose Add or Delete from the shortcut menu.

Part
VI

Ch
33

FIG. 33.17
Out of the box, the
Channel bar includes
these preset selections.
You can change the
collection of shortcuts
and rearrange the
Channel bar itself.

FIG. 33.18
After deleting unneces-
sary channels and
changing its size and
orientation, this Channel
bar looks vastly different
from its default settings.

CAUTION

Be careful when deleting any of the category icons on the Channel bar. If you've subscribed to a channel
within that category, you'll lose easy access to the channel.

- To rearrange channels on the bar, simply drag them to the location you prefer. Other
  shortcuts on the bar will rearrange themselves automatically.

- To remove the Channel bar from the desktop, let the mouse pointer hover over the top of
  the bar until the gray sizing handle pops up. Click the X in the upper-right corner.

 The Channel bar on the desktop is identical to the one that appears in the browser window. When you
add or remove channels from one, the other changes accordingly. If you'd rather use the Windows
desktop for other items, close the Channel bar there and use the Channels button on the Internet
Explorer toolbar when you want to work with channels.

Disabling the Active Desktop and Channels

Of all the features in Internet Explorer, the Active Desktop is by far the most controversial. Some organizations, in fact, prefer to disable all active Internet features, including the ability to display live content on the desktop, to use Active Channels, or to create subscriptions that update automatically. It's easy to turn off the display of live Internet content on the Active Desktop, but clearing out other active features takes a determined effort. To eliminate most active features, follow this seven-step program:

 TIP A knowledgeable user can easily circumvent most of the steps outlined in this section and restore virtually all of IE4's active features. For sites where security is a high priority, use the Internet Explorer Administration Kit to enforce strict Internet access policies. Full details about this program are available at **http://ieak.microsoft.com**.

1. Turn off the Active Desktop. Right-click any empty area on the desktop and choose <u>A</u>ctive Desktop from the shortcut menu; then make sure there's no check mark next to the View As <u>W</u>eb Page menu choice.

 TIP The TweakUI utility includes an IE4 tab that lets you adjust some of the options listed here. For example, clearing the check box labeled Active Desktop enabled removes the Active Desktop option from the desktop's shortcut menu, and it also hides the web tab on the Display properties sheet. For more details about TweakUI, see Appendix C, "Using Power Toys."

2. Remove the Channel bar from the desktop. Open Control Panel and choose the Display option. Click the web tab, and select Internet Explorer Channel bar from the list at the bottom of the dialog box. Click the <u>D</u>elete button. If any other items are listed, repeat this step for each one.

3. Disable IE's ability to display Active Channels. IE4 uses a file called Cdfview.dll (stored in the Windows\System folder) to display the contents of Channel files, which include the CDF extension. If you delete or rename this file, IE will lose its ability to display Active Channels, and you'll see an error message like the one in Figure 33.19 when you attempt to open a channel. To break the association between Cdfview.dll and the Channel File type, open any Explorer window, choose <u>V</u>iew, Folder <u>O</u>ptions, and click the File Types tab. Select Channel File from the list of Registered file types, and then click the <u>R</u>emove button. Click OK to save your changes.

Part
VI

Ch
33

 TIP Unfortunately, there's no way to remove the Channels button from the Internet Explorer toolbar. Likewise, you'll waste your time trying to delete the Channels folder from the Favorites menu, because IE re-creates this file the next time you restart your computer.

FIG. 33.19

To completely disable IE4's ability to view Active Channels, rename the Cdfview.dll file. When you attempt to open a channel, you'll see this error message instead.

4. Remove Channel bar content. The default Windows 98 installation adds more than 250K of icons and miscellaneous HTML files that make up the default settings for the Channel bar (Disney, AOL, MSNBC, and so on). To remove these files, open the \Windows\Web folder and remove the following four types of files:

- Channel files—it's safe to remove any file with the extension CDF.

- GIF images—look for files whose names end with _wl or _sl; these are the wide and narrow versions of the images IE uses to identify content on the Channel bar.

- Icons—you can safely delete all 40 or so icon files, with the extension ICO.

- Any file with Microsoft HTML Document file type and a name that begins with **cc** can be deleted; these are the category templates that IE displays when you browse the list of available channels.

5. Remove the Channels shortcut from the Quick Launch bar. Although it's impossible to remove all traces of the Channels icon, this one is easy to get rid of. Right-click the icon and choose <u>D</u>elete from the shortcut menu.

 The Windows 98 Start menu includes a cascading Favorites menu that includes the Channels folder. If you'd prefer not to see this cascading menu, you can remove it by editing the Registry. Open RegEdit and navigate to the following Registry key:

HKEY_CURRENT_USER\Software\Microsoft\Windows\CurrentVersion\Policies\Explorer

Add the DWORD value **NoFavoritesMenu** and set its data value to 1.

The TweakUI utility (described in Appendix C) includes a check box that will make this modification for you.

6. Empty the Subscriptions and Channels folders. If you've previously set up any web subscriptions, this step removes them completely.

7. Disable automatic subscription updates. IE4 gives you many options for controlling when and how you connect to the Internet to update subscriptions. If you prefer to update subscriptions only when you specifically choose to do so, open the browser window, choose View, Internet Options, and click the Advanced tab. Clear the check mark next to the check box labeled Enable Scheduled Subscription Updates, and then click OK.

Part
VI

Ch
33

CHAPTER 34

Using Outlook Express

by Ed Bott

In this chapter

Should You Switch to Outlook Express?

Outlook Express, the default email client software in Windows 98, includes the basic tools you need to compose, send, and receive mail over the Internet. It uses this basic email interface for a second purpose as well—to let you read and participate in threaded discussions on Internet newsgroups. If you originally set up an email account using the email software included with Windows 95, you have an important decision to make when you upgrade. Should you stick with your old mail software or switch to Outlook Express?

Starting with the first release of Windows 95, every version of Windows has included a desktop icon labeled Inbox. In the original version of Windows 95, this icon launched a program called the Exchange Inbox. Microsoft promised that this universal inbox would be capable of storing email from just about anywhere, as well as faxes, voice mail, and other types of data. If you've used Exchange Inbox, though, you know it's hard to configure, slow, and notoriously buggy; the fax components in particular are a usability nightmare.

In the years since the original release of Windows 95, Microsoft has updated the Exchange Inbox program slightly. The new version, which is included with every copy of OSR2, was renamed Windows Messaging. The update fixed several bugs (and added a few new glitches), and the new name was supposed to help dispel confusion with Microsoft Exchange Server, Microsoft's mail server package for businesses.

Although the Windows Messaging application is included with Windows 98, the Inbox icon no longer appears automatically on the desktop, and Microsoft no longer recommends that you install it. The program is now officially an orphan, replaced by the new Windows default mail program, Outlook Express. Microsoft also sells a full-featured mail package called Outlook 97 (an Outlook 98 upgrade is due in mid-1998).

If you currently use Exchange Inbox or Windows Messaging, should you switch to Outlook Express? The correct answer depends on how the rest of your mail system works.

- If you have been using Exchange Inbox or Windows Messaging to gather email exclusively through industry-standard Internet mail servers, you should switch to Outlook Express. It's simple to set up and much easier to use, and it does a superb job of handling Internet mail.

- If you send and receive email using a Microsoft Exchange server on a corporate network, you must use an Exchange-compatible client program. Acceptable options include the Exchange Inbox, Windows Messaging, Outlook 97 (included with Microsoft Office 97), or Outlook 98. In this situation, Outlook Express is an option only if your Exchange Server uses the IMAP format.

- If you use Microsoft Fax or another MAPI-compatible application, it will not work with Outlook Express. (MAPI stands for *messaging application program interface*, a Microsoft standard for communication between email applications. Outlook Express supports only Simple MAPI, which allows programs like Word and Excel to use Outlook Express for sending messages.) For full MAPI compatibility, you must use an Exchange-compatible mail client.

▶ **See** "Using Windows Messaging and Microsoft Fax," **p. 981**

Starting Outlook Express

When you install Windows 98, you also install Outlook Express. There's no way to avoid adding Outlook Express on initial setup. However, you can uninstall the program if you decide you prefer other mail and news clients. (To uninstall Outlook Express, open the Add/Remove Programs option in Control Panel, click the Install/Uninstall tab, choose Microsoft Outlook Express, and click the Add/Remove button.)

To find the shortcut for Outlook Express, click the Start button, choose Programs, and look in the Internet Explorer group. You'll also find shortcuts to Outlook Express on the desktop and in the Quick Launch bar.

The first time you run Outlook Express, it prompts you to select a location for storing data files (see Figure 34.1). By default, the program creates Outlook Express and Address Book folders in \Windows\Application Data\Microsoft, with separate Mail and News folders within the Outlook Express folder. If your computer is configured to enable multiple users to log in with their own settings, the default folders appear under \Windows\Profiles*profilename*.

▶ **See** "Establishing Custom Settings for Each User," **p. 428**

FIG. 34.1

To avoid problems later, accept this default data location when you first set up Outlook Express.

Your best choice is to accept the default location that Outlook Express offers. What if you want to move these data files after setting up Outlook Express for the first time? There's no simple way to accomplish this chore. You'll have to first use the Windows Explorer to move all the data folders, and then open the Registry Editor, find HKEY_CURRENT_USER\Software\Microsoft\Outlook Express, double-click on the Store Root value, and change that value to reflect the new location.

Part

VI

Ch

34

> **CAUTION**
>
> Think twice before using the Registry Editor, and always make a backup. Incorrectly editing the Windows Registry can result in data loss and cause programs to fail to start and run properly.

After you've configured Outlook Express, running the program will take you to the Start Page (see Figure 34.2), which lets you move quickly between your Inbox, newsgroups, and your address book.

FIG. 34.2
From this Start Page, you can jump to your email inbox, follow threaded discussions on an Internet newsgroup, or search for address information.

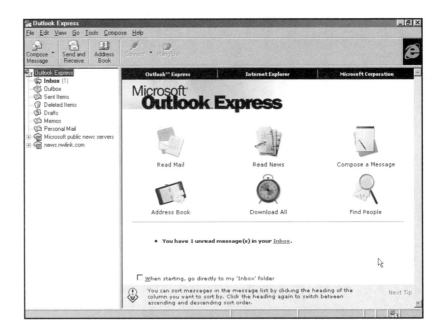

 T I P You can bypass the Outlook Express Start Page and jump straight to your mail. Choose Tools, Options, click the General tab, and check the box labeled When Starting, Go Directly to My Inbox Folder.

Configuring Outlook Express

Before you can use Outlook Express to send and receive email, you must supply some basic configuration information. At a minimum, you'll have to enter the name and type of the mail server that stores and forwards your messages, along with the username and email address associated with your mail account. Before you can access newsgroups with Outlook Express, you'll need to enter similar configuration information, including your username and email address as well as the name of the news server you plan to use.

The Internet Connection Wizard handles all Outlook Express setup details, although you can also configure accounts manually. If you did not use the wizard when you first set up IE4, or if you skipped the mail and news steps, the Internet Connection Wizard runs automatically the first time you use Outlook Express.

If you receive Internet mail from multiple sources—from a corporate server and a personal account with an Internet service provider, for example—you'll need to establish separate

Outlook Express mail accounts for each one. Each news server requires its own news account as well. There are no limits to the number of mail and news accounts you can set up in Outlook Express.

▶ **See** "Migrating from Exchange or Outlook 97," **p. 712**

Setting Up a Default Mail Account

When you first launch Outlook Express, the program prompts you to set up a default mail account using the Internet Connection Wizard.

Follow the wizard's prompts to enter the following information:

- Your name. This is the display name that will appear in the From field when you send a message. Most people enter their real name; you might want to add a company affiliation or other information to help mail recipients identify you more readily.

- Your email address. When recipients reply to messages you send, this is the address their mail software uses.

- Mail server information. As Figure 34.3 shows, you must fill in addresses for incoming and outgoing mail servers, even if a single server does both jobs. Be sure to specify the mail protocol your incoming server uses: POP3 (the default setting) or IMAP.

FIG. 34.3

You must enter names for the servers that handle incoming and outgoing mail. In most cases, the same server handles both chores.

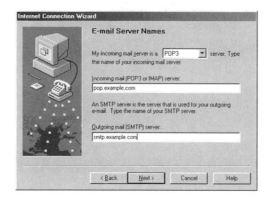

N O T E   Outlook Express supports three widely used mail standards. The overwhelming majority of Internet service providers transfer email using servers that run *Simple Mail Transfer Protocol (SMTP)*. To download messages from an SMTP server, most mail clients use version 3 of *Post Office Protocol (POP3)*. A newer standard, *Internet Message Access Protocol (IMAP)*, is less widely used. ■

- Logon information. Enter the account name you use to log on to the mail server. If you enter a password in this dialog box, Outlook Express stores the password and uses it each time you check mail. For extra security, leave the password text box (see Figure 34.4) blank and you'll be asked to enter it each time you check for mail. The Secure Password Authentication option is rarely used by Internet service providers; if you receive mail over The Microsoft Network, however, you should check this box.

Part VI

Ch

34

FIG. 34.4

Leave this password box blank if you want to keep other users from accessing your mail. Outlook Express will ask for your password each time you connect to the server.

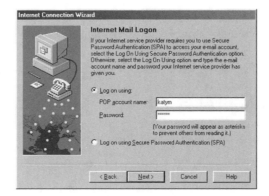

- A friendly name for the account. This is the label that appears in the Accounts list.
- Connection type. Tell Outlook Express whether you access the Internet through a LAN or over a dial-up connection.

To configure additional mail accounts, choose Tools, Accounts. Click the Add button, choose Mail, and the relevant portions of the Internet Connection wizard will run again.

Setting Up One or More News Servers

Outlook Express does more than email; it's also a full-featured news-reading client that enables you to download and read messages from newsgroup servers, post replies, and manage locally stored messages. With a few minor exceptions, the user interface is the same one you see when you send and receive mail, and the program uses the same system services to help you compose and send messages to public or private newsgroups.

▶ **See** "How Newsgroups Work," **p. 745**

Before you can read newsgroup messages, you must provide Outlook Express with the name of a news server to which you have access. Most Internet service providers offer a news feed to their customers. If your ISP's name is acme.com, for example, you'll probably find a news server at news.acme.com. The Microsoft Network provides newsgroup access on servers at **msnnews.msn.com** and **netnews.msn.com**. Microsoft's public newsgroups are available from **msnews.microsoft.com**. If you have access to a private news server, it might require that you log on with an account name and password.

ON THE WEB

If your ISP or corporate site does not maintain a news feed, try connecting to a public-access news server. You get what you pay for, of course; most such sites are slow and unreliable for serious news access. There's a well-maintained list of public news servers at

http://wkweb1.cableinet.co.uk/tony.dane/access/public.htm.

As with mail accounts, setting up a news account with the Internet Connection Wizard is a simple fill-in-the-blanks process. The wizard appears the first time you click the Read News icon on the Outlook Express Start Page, or when you choose Tools, Accounts, click the Add button, and choose Mail.

You'll have to enter a name and email address for each news account. Enter the name of your news server when prompted (see Figure 34.5), and check the option at the bottom of this dialog box if the server requires you to log on with a username and password.

FIG. 34.5
You must supply the name of a news server before accessing newsgroups with Outlook Express.

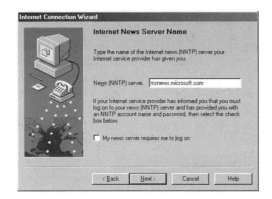

Give the account a friendly name to help identify it in the account list. The default entry is the server name, but a descriptive name like "Microsoft public newsgroups" is easier to understand than **msnews.microsoft.com**.

 You don't have to be truthful when entering your name and email address. In fact, some experienced newsgroup participants never use their real address when posting, because it's too easy for unscrupulous marketers to skim addresses from newsgroup participants and target them for unsolicited email, or spam.

Managing Mail for More Than One User

On many Windows 98 computers, one user gathers mail from one or two Internet mail accounts. However, Outlook Express lets you manage mail in more complex environments, with multiple users of the same computer accessing separate mail accounts.

Before multiple users can store messages in separate mailboxes, you must open the Users option in Control Panel and enable multi-user settings. Each user who logs on to Windows with a separate username and password creates separate data files for addresses and messages when they use Outlook Express.

Adjusting Properties for an Existing Mail or News Account

To change the settings for a mail or news account after you've set it up using the Internet Connection Wizard, click Tools, Accounts, select the entry you want to change, and click the Properties button. With minor exceptions, the options for mail and news accounts are identical.

The first account you create in the mail and news group becomes the default account for that category. That's an important distinction, because it determines which information appears on-screen when you click the Read Mail or Read News icon on the Start Page, and it defines which SMTP server Outlook Express uses when sending messages. To change default mail or news accounts, select the account and click the Set as Default button.

For both types of accounts, use the General tab (see Figure 34.6) to change the friendly name for the account or to edit personal information. This dialog box lets you add the name of your organization and specify a different reply-to address. For example, if you send a message using your corporate mail account but prefer to receive replies via your personal Internet mail account, enter the personal address in the Reply address box. When recipients reply to your message, their mail software should automatically insert the preferred reply-to address.

FIG. 34.6
Edit the reply-to address for a mail or news account if you want to receive replies at an address other than the one from which you send messages.

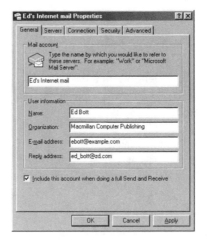

The Server tab lets you change the name or logon settings for mail and news servers. The Advanced tab lets you adjust timeout settings (sometimes necessary over very slow connections) and break apart lengthy messages (required by some mail servers running older software). Do not adjust these settings unless specifically instructed to do so by the server's administrator.

Selecting Connection Options

For each Outlook Express mail and news account, you can specify how you prefer to connect to the Internet—over a LAN, manually, or by using a modem. If your computer is permanently connected to a network with Internet access, you can set all your accounts for LAN access and be done with it. However, on machines with dial-up Internet access, particularly notebook computers, you should pay close attention to these settings.

Each time you create a new account, you'll have a chance to specify connection properties. To adjust these settings after you've created an account, choose Tools, Accounts, select the account name, click Properties, and click the Connection tab. You'll see a dialog box like the one in Figure 34.7.

FIG. 34.7

The choice shown in this dialog box allows Outlook Express to dial your Internet service provider automatically every time you access a mail server.

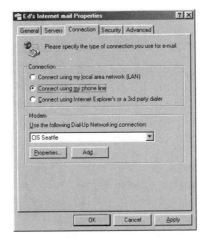

What's the difference between the three connection options?

- Connect Using My Local Area Network (LAN). The LAN option assumes you have a full-time connection to the Internet through a local area network. Unless you choose to work offline, Outlook Express checks for mail every 30 minutes. To change the interval for checking mail, choose Tools, Options, click the General tab, and use the spinner control.

- Connect Using My Phone Line. Choose a Dial-Up Networking connection from the list at the bottom of this dialog box, or click the Add button to create a new one; Outlook Express dials this connection whenever you attempt to access a mail or news server. Use this option if you do not use the IE4 dialer (for example, if you access the web through a proxy server) but you must use a dial-up connection for email.

- Connect Using Internet Explorer's or a 3rd Party Dialer. Outlook Express uses the connection settings you specify for your web browser. This is your best choice if you use the same phone line for voice calls and Internet access, because Internet Explorer and Outlook Express can share the same connection.

Notebook users might wish to create multiple copies of mail and news accounts, each with a different connection type, to handle different working environments. For example, you would specify a LAN connection when you're connected to the office network, but use the IE4 dialer to make a manual connection when you're working in a hotel room.

Part

VI

Ch

34

Choosing HTML or Plain Text as Your Message Format

Each time you compose a message using Outlook Express, you choose whether to use plain text only or to add graphics, colors, and rich text formatting using HTML. If most of your messages go to users of Outlook Express or other HTML-compatible mail programs, rich text formatting can make your messages livelier and more readable. With HTML formatting, your messages look and behave like web pages; you can specify fonts and their sizes, change text colors, use paragraph styles, and control text alignment. You can add background colors and graphics, bulleted and numbered lists, and hypertext links to other web pages.

All that fancy formatting is lost, though, if your correspondents use email software that can't interpret HTML. They'll see a plain text version of your message, along with a file attachment that they can open in a web browser. In fact, there's a good chance they'll be annoyed when they receive your HTML messages because even a simple one-sentence message typically occupies 1K or more of disk space when translated into HTML.

N O T E   Users of Netscape mail products can send and receive HTML-formatted mail as well, although you may notice minor differences in the look of messages sent between Netscape and Microsoft clients. ■

Outlook Express lets you set separate default formats for mail and news messages, and it enables you to override those settings on individual messages. Unless you're certain that the overwhelming majority of your email recipients can handle HTML attachments, your best bet is to choose plain text for mail messages. Likewise, on newsgroups where people use a variety of news reader clients, it's good manners to specify plain text as your default format.

To adjust the default settings, follow this procedure:

1. Choose Tools, Options, and click the Send tab. You'll see the dialog box shown in Figure 34.8.

FIG. 34.8

Using these default settings, all your mail messages go out in HTML format, with plain text the preferred format for news messages.

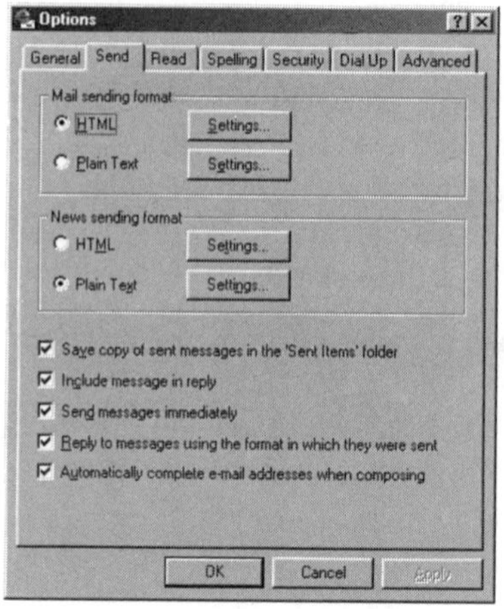

2. In the box labeled Mail Sending Format, select HTML or Plain Text as the default format for mail messages.

3. In the box labeled News Sending Format, select HTML or Plain Text as the default format for messages you post to newsgroups.

4. After you've specified a format, the Settings buttons let you specify additional formatting options. These additional choices are shown in Figure 34.9.

FIG. 34.9

If recipients complain about stray characters (especially equal signs) in text messages, try changing text encoding from Quoted Printable to None.

TROUBLESHOOTING

Some recipients complain that all your paragraphs appear as a single long line, or that your messages are filled with equal signs. Mail Format options control how Outlook Express encodes your messages using Multipurpose Internet Mail Extensions (MIME). Quoted-Printable MIME replaces line endings and special characters (such as accented vowels) with an equal sign and an optional numeric code. This technique enables you to send some formatting information using ASCII characters. Your recipients are seeing this encoding through a mail reader that isn't fully compliant with the MIME standard. If they're unable or unwilling to switch to another mail client, choose Tools, Options, click the Send tab, and click the Settings button to the right of the mail format you've chosen. Change the text encoding option to None and the problem should disappear; unfortunately, you will also lose the ability to use extended ASCII characters.

▶ **See** "Composing a New Message," **p. 723**

Exchanging Data with Other Mail Programs

If you currently use another email package and plan to switch to Outlook Express, the process is simple and straightforward. Outlook Express can import address books and archived messages from the following popular mail clients:

- Eudora Pro or Eudora Light (version 3.0 or earlier)
- Netscape Mail (versions 2 or 3)
- Netscape Communicator
- Microsoft Internet Mail

- Microsoft Exchange Inbox
- Windows Messaging

In addition, you can import messages from Microsoft Outlook 97 or Outlook 98. (See the following section for detailed instructions on how to transfer address information from Outlook 97 to Outlook Express.)

Migrating from Exchange or Outlook 97

Do you currently use the Exchange Inbox email program that Microsoft introduced with Windows 95? In versions of Windows 95 sold after late 1996, this program may go by the name Windows Messaging. Outlook 97 and Outlook 98 both use the Windows Messaging system services and the same format for messages and Personal Address Books. If you use any of these programs, Outlook Express offers to convert your messages and addresses the first time you run the program, as shown in Figure 34.10.

FIG. 34.10

Switching from the older Exchange Inbox to Outlook Express can be as easy as clicking Next in this dialog box.

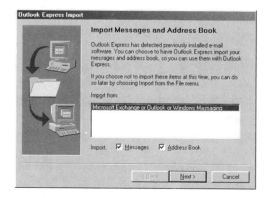

Converting data from most mail programs is a simple process, but there's one notable exception. To transfer your Contacts folder from Outlook 97 to the Windows Address Book in Outlook Express, you'll need to go through a cumbersome two-step conversion process. The first step is to export the Contacts information into an Exchange-compatible Personal Address Book (PAB); then you can import the PAB into Outlook Express. Follow these steps:

1. Open Outlook 97, choose File, Import and Export, and select Export to a File. Click the Next button.

2. Following the wizard's prompts, select the Contacts folder, click Next, and choose Personal Address Book from the list of export formats. Click Next again.

3. When you click Finish, Outlook 97 copies the information to the Personal Address Book in your current profile.

4. Next, open Outlook Express, choose File, Import, Address Book, and select Microsoft Exchange Personal Address Book from the list of available formats. (This choice is

available only if you have Windows Messaging or Outlook 97 installed and you have created a Personal Address Book.)

5. Click the Import button to finish the process. Your collection of email addresses and other contact information appears in the Windows Address Book.

Restoring Outlook Express as the Default Mail Client

Note that you can set up more than one mail program on a system running Windows 98. When you install another mail program, however, it might take over as the default email program that starts when you click the Mail icon on IE4's Standard toolbar or click a mailto: hyperlink on a web page. To restore Outlook Express as the default mail client, follow this procedure:

1. Start Outlook Express, choose Tools, Options, and click the General tab.

2. Check the option labeled Make Outlook Express My Default Email Program.

3. When you check that box, the grayed-out option below it becomes available. Check Make Outlook Express My Default Simple MAPI Client if you want Outlook Express to start up when you choose File, Send from an application's menu. This option prevents Windows Messaging or Outlook 97 from performing this function.

Importing Data from Another Mail Program

When you choose File, Import, Outlook Express offers a cascading menu with three additional choices. The Address Book and Messages options are self-explanatory; the third choice, Mail Account Settings, lets you reuse the information (server and logon names, for example) that you've entered for one mail account when setting up another. When importing messages or addresses, Outlook Express first asks you to specify the mail program and then checks data-file locations specified for that program in the Registry. If Outlook Express can't find the program on your system, you'll see a dialog box that lets you specify the location.

Each import option steps you through a series of dialog boxes, with slightly different choices that depend on the mail program or data type you start with. If you choose to import data from a text file with comma-separated values, for example, you'll have to specify which Outlook Express fields should receive each column of data in your text file. As Figure 34.11 shows, Outlook Express makes a reasonable guess at mapping fields in your text file to those in your Address Book. You can manually adjust the relationship between fields; check the box to the left of each field to include or remove it from the import operation. Click the Change Mapping button and you'll see a drop-down list of available Outlook Express fields.

You can use the Import choices to bring in messages or addresses even if there's already data in your Address Book or message store. When the program detects that a record you're trying to import already exists in your Address Book, you'll see a dialog box like the one in Figure 34.12. At this point, you can choose whether to keep the existing entry or replace it with the new data.

Part
VI

Ch
34

FIG. 34.11
Outlook Express won't recognize the Organization label in this text file; click the Change Mappings button to tell the program that its data belongs in the Company field.

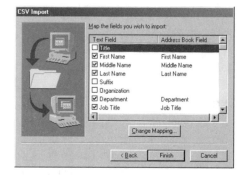

FIG. 34.12
Click Yes to All and you'll completely replace matching records in your Address Book with new data from an import file.

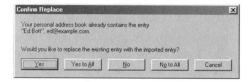

Exporting Data to Another Program

Unfortunately, Outlook Express isn't nearly as cooperative when it comes to moving messages and address information back to competing mail programs. When you choose File, Export from the Outlook Express menu, you can easily move information into Outlook 97 or Microsoft Exchange. To transfer addresses into other programs, you'll first have to convert the information into a text file with comma-separated values and then find the corresponding import feature in the destination program. There's no easy way to move messages from Outlook Express into another mail client.

Reading Messages in Outlook Express

When you first click the Read Mail or Read News icon on the Outlook Express main screen, you'll see a display much like the one in Figure 34.13.

The folder list at the left of the screen includes the default mail folders, any additional folders you've created, all news servers you've set up, and any newsgroups to which you've subscribed. The right side of the screen includes the column-oriented message list, which shows the contents of the currently selected folder or server. Below is a preview pane that shows the contents of the currently selected message. There's a customizable toolbar at the top and a status bar at the bottom of the window.

Two optional parts of the Outlook Express screen—the Outlook Bar and the Folder bar—are hidden by default. The message list is always visible; there's no way to make it disappear. Using a few menu choices and check boxes, though, you can show, hide, and rearrange virtually every other aspect of the Outlook Express interface.

Toolbar   Folder list

FIG. 34.13
The default Outlook Express layout includes the folder list at left, message list at top right, and a preview pane below.

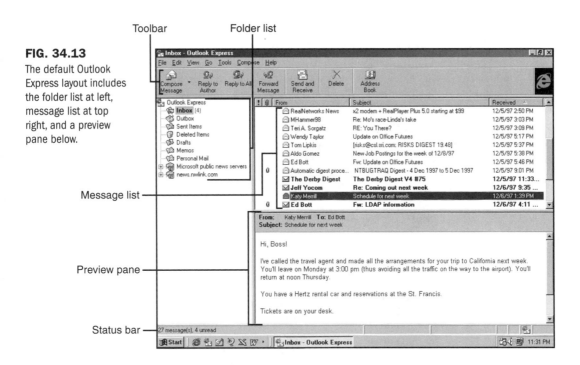

Message list

Preview pane

Status bar

Changing the Layout

To alter the basic look of Outlook Express, choose View, Layout. You'll see a dialog box like the one in Figure 34.14.

FIG. 34.14
These options produce a layout that closely resembles the Outlook 97 interface.

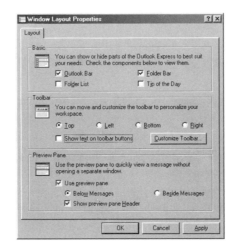

These settings rearrange the Outlook Express interface so that it closely resembles the Outlook 97 interface, as shown in Figure 34.15. The Outlook bar at left shows all the default folders plus any top-level folders you've created; it doesn't include icons for subfolders you create. The Outlook bar also includes icons for news servers and subscribed newsgroups. Just above the message list is the drop-down folder bar, which shows all folders in an Explorer-style hierarchy.

FIG. 34.15

The Outlook bar at left resembles the one in Outlook 97, with one difference—you can't change the order of icons.

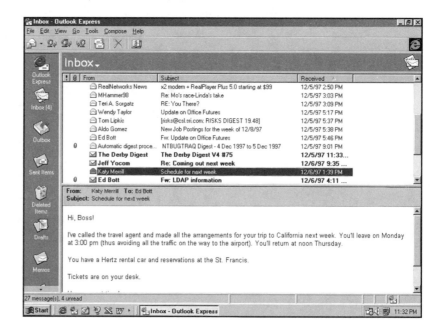

Using the Preview Pane

As you move between messages in the message list, the contents of the currently selected message appear in the preview pane. Use the layout options to change the appearance and behavior of this pane.

- To toggle the preview pane on and off, choose View, Layout and click the Use preview pane check box.

- To move the preview pane, choose the Below Messages or Beside Messages option.

- To show or hide the address and subject line in the preview pane, check the box labeled Show Preview Pane Header.

- To change the size of the preview pane, point to the bar between the message list and the preview pane until it turns to a double-headed arrow, and then click and drag.

TIP Each entry in the message list first appears in bold to indicate you haven't yet read it. The unread status changes when you open the message or allow it to appear in the preview pane for more than a few seconds. To filter the message list so it shows only those messages you haven't yet read, choose View, Current View, Unread Messages.

Navigating Through Folders

After you move past the Start Page, the Outlook Express message list always shows the contents of the currently selected folder, newsgroup, or news server. To move from folder to folder, use one of these three navigational tools:

- Click any icon in the folder list to switch to the contents of the message list.

- If the Folder bar is visible, the name of the currently selected folder, server, or newsgroup appears just above the message list. Click that folder name to unfurl a drop-down folder list. The down arrow to the right of the name provides a visual clue; after you make your selection the list snaps out of the way again.

- Click any icon in the Outlook bar to show the contents of that location.

To view or adjust the properties of any icon, right-click the icon and choose from the shortcut menu.

TIP Use one of three Internet links at the top of the Outlook Express Start Page to launch Internet Explorer, jump to Microsoft's home page, or navigate to the Outlook Express Start Page on the web. The icon for the Outlook Express Start Page is always available at the top of the folder list, Folder bar, or Outlook bar.

Sorting the Message List

To sort the contents of the message list, click any column heading. Choose View, Columns to add or remove columns and change the order of those that are displayed. (Note that different types of objects provide different choices of columns.) Click the border between two column headings and drag to adjust column widths.

To group mail or newsgroup messages using threads, choose View, Sort By, and toggle the Group Messages by Thread setting.

Opening Individual Messages

Double-click any item in the message list to open it in its own window, as shown in Figure 34.16.

Part
VI

Ch
34

FIG. 34.16

This full message window offers more space than the preview pane. Maximize the window and use the up or down arrows to navigate without the message list.

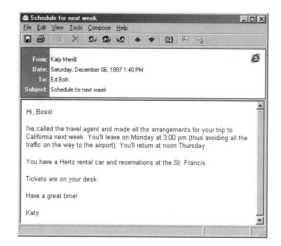

Icons on the message window toolbar let you save, print, or delete the current message.

It's possible to navigate through your entire message list without switching back and forth between the message list and the message window. Here's how:

1. Open any message in its own window. Maximize the window if you want to see as much of the message as possible without having to use the scrollbars.

2. To move to the next message in the list, click the up arrow on the toolbar. Click the down arrow to move back to the previous message

3. To move to the next unread message in the list, press Ctrl+U.

4. In threaded message lists, such as those found in newsgroups, press Ctrl+Shift+U to move to the next unread thread.

5. To move or copy a message to a folder, choose File, Move To Folder or File, Copy to Folder. To delete a message, click the Delete button on the toolbar.

Changing the Way Plain Text Messages Look

When you receive an HTML-formatted message, the formatting codes in the message itself control how it looks in the preview pane and in individual message windows. If the message doesn't specify font information, Outlook Express uses default fonts and sizes to control the display of proportional fonts (used for general text) and fixed fonts (used for tabular material that must line up precisely).

When you receive a plain-text message, Outlook Express displays it using the default proportional font and the default font size. On most systems, that means plain-text messages appear in Arial, using the Medium Size setting (12 point). Follow these steps to change the font and font size to improve readability or to see more text in a message window.

1. Open any plain-text message and choose View, Fonts. Select the size you prefer from the five available choices. Note the size and close the message window.

2. From the main Outlook Express window, choose Tools, Options.

3. Click the Read tab, and then click the Fonts button in the box labeled Font Settings

4. To change fonts, use the drop-down list labeled To Proportional Font. (Adjusting the Fixed-Width Font setting affects only HTML-formatted messages.)

5. To change to the default font size you noted earlier, use the drop-down list labeled Font Size.

6. Click OK to save your changes. You might need to close and restart Outlook Express to see the font changes in both the preview pane and individual message windows.

Customizing the Outlook Express Toolbar

To change the look of the Outlook Express toolbar, choose View, Layout; use the check boxes to move the toolbar to either side or to the bottom of the window. Hide the text labels to dramatically reduce the amount of space the toolbar takes up. To add, remove, and rearrange buttons, click the Customize Toolbar button; you can also open this dialog box, shown in Figure 34.17, by right-clicking the toolbar and choosing Buttons from the shortcut menu.

FIG. 34.17
Use the Add and Remove buttons to rearrange the toolbars for mail and news windows.

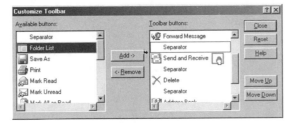

Note that there are separate toolbars for mail and news windows, so you'll have to customize them individually. You can't customize toolbars used in Outlook Express message windows or those in the Windows Address Book.

 TIP If you use the folder list regularly but don't want to sacrifice the screen real estate it demands, add the Folder List button to your toolbar. It acts as a toggle, revealing or hiding the folder list so you can have more room for the message list and preview pane and still navigate between folders without having to wade through pull-down menus.

Part
VI

Ch
34

Using the Windows Address Book

Outlook Express organizes email addresses using a module called the Windows Address Book. Each contact record includes fields that enable you to track additional details about a person, including home and business addresses, and phone numbers. The Windows Address Book also lets you create group records so you can send email to several individuals by entering an alias instead of a lengthy list of addresses.

Address Book information is stored in a single file with the .WAB extension. Each user profile on a machine can contain its own Address Book file, but there is no way to maintain multiple address books within a single profile.

N O T E   Although the Windows Address Book appears to be an integrated part of Outlook Express, it's actually a separate application called WAB.EXE. If you use the Address Book frequently, you might want to create a shortcut to this program and place it on the Start Menu or the Windows desktop. ■

To open the Windows Address Book, click the Address Book icon on the Outlook Express toolbar. As in an Explorer window, you can choose one of four different views for the contents of the Address Book. In the default Details view (see Figure 34.18), click a column heading to sort the records by the values in that field; click again to sort in reverse order.

FIG. 34.18

As the mouse passes over each Address Book entry, a ScreenTip displays the contents of that record.

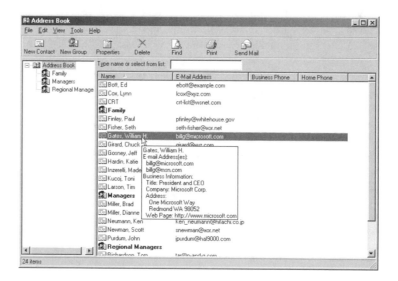

- ■ To open an individual record, double-click the item, or select it and click the Properties button.
- ■ To delete a record, select it and click the Delete button.
- ■ To copy the text from a contact record to the Windows Clipboard, right-click the item and choose Copy from the shortcut menu.
- ■ To begin composing a message to a recipient whose email address is in your Windows Address Book, select the person's record and click the Send Mail button.

Creating and Editing Address Book Entries

To create a new record from scratch, click the New Contact button and begin filling in fields on the Personal tab. As Figure 34.19 shows, you can enter more than one email address for a contact. Choose one address and click the Set as Default button to tell Outlook Express to use that email address when you click the Send Mail button.

FIG. 34.19
You can enter multiple email addresses in a contact record—personal and business addresses, for example.

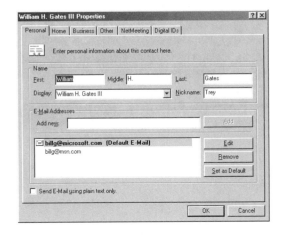

 TIP Note as you enter information in the First, Middle, and Last fields that the value in the Display field automatically fills in as well. This field is what you'll see under the Name heading when you look at the Address list. The drop-down Display list lets you choose from several defaults, but you can enter anything you like here, including a descriptive name like "Caterer," "Travel agent," or "Boss."

Creating Mailing Groups

A mailing group (also known as an alias or distribution list) lets you send messages to multiple people without having to enter each name in the message. When you enter the name of a mailing group in the address box of a message, Outlook Express substitutes the names that make up that group before sending the message. To create a mailing group, follow these steps:

1. Click the New Group button.
2. Enter a name for the mailing group in the Group Name text box. The name can be up to 255 characters long and can contain spaces and special characters.
3. Click the Select Members button. A dialog box containing names from your Address Book appears.
4. Click a name in the list and then click the Select button to add that person's entry to the list. Continue adding names individually, or hold down the Ctrl key to select more than one name at a time. Use the New Contact button to add an entry to the list.
5. When you've finished adding names to the group, click OK.
6. Add notes about this group in the field at the bottom of the Group Properties dialog box, if you like, and then click OK.

Part
VI

Ch
34

TIP A mailing group can contain group entries as well as individual names. You can use this feature to avoid having to update multiple groups. For example, you might create separate mailing groups for each department in your company: Accounting, Sales, Marketing, and so on. Then create an All Employees list consisting of each of the department lists. When a new employee joins the company, update the department list, and the master list automatically updates as well.

To see all the groups in your Address Book, choose View, Groups List.

Adding Address Book Entries Automatically

The easiest way to create contact records in your Windows Address Book is to copy email addresses from messages you receive. Outlook Express lets you add contact records one at a time or automatically.

For one-at-a-time addressing, open a message and right-click any name in the From, To, or CC fields; then choose Add to Address Book from the shortcut menu, as shown in Figure 34.20.

FIG. 34.20

Right-click any address and use the shortcut menu to add the name and address to your Windows Address Book.

TIP You can automatically create a new entry in your Windows Address Book whenever you reply to a message. Choose Tools, Options, click the General tab, and check the box labeled Automatically Put People I Reply To in My Address Book.

Finding People Using Public Directories

What's the best way to find someone's email address? Copying it from an email or a business card is still the surest way to be certain your message will reach its destination. However, the next best technique is to use a public directory server. When you click the Find button on the Windows Address Book toolbar, you'll see a dialog box like the one in Figure 34.21.

FIG. 34.21
Use a public directory server to track down email addresses and add them to your address book.

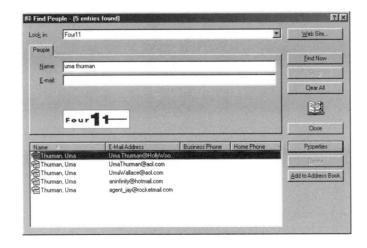

Outlook Express gives you a choice of several public servers that use the Lightweight Directory Access Protocol (LDAP), an Internet standard for exchanging directory information. Select a server in the Look In list box, and then click in the Name text box and enter all or part of the name you're searching for. Click Find Now to begin the search.

ON THE WEB

For more information about how LDAP works, check this web site, managed by the university where the protocol was invented:

http://www.umich.edu/~dirsvcs/ldap/index.html

Matching records appear in a list at the bottom of the Find People dialog box. Select a name and click the Properties button to view more information about that directory entry. Right-click and choose Send Mail to begin composing a message to that person. Click Add to Address Book to save the contact's name and address in your Windows Address Book.

Composing a New Message

To begin a new mail or news message from scratch, click the New Message button or press Ctrl+N. You'll see a blank New Message window (see Figure 34.22).

Addressing a Mail Message

Although you can simply begin typing your message within the New Message window, it's easier to start by filling out the address box. Enter the main recipient(s) for the message on the To: line, and then use the Tab key to move to the Cc:, Bcc:, and Subject lines before tabbing into the body of the message.

FIG. 34.22

Follow these prompts to begin addressing and composing a message.

Click the small Address Card icon at the beginning of any line in the address box to open a special window on your Windows Address Book. This Select Recipients dialog box, shown in Figure 34.23, lets you pick names from a list and add them to the address box.

FIG. 34.23

Click the small index-card icon at the beginning of any address line to open this view of the Windows Address Book.

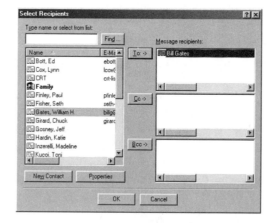

Use other buttons in this dialog box to create a new contact and add it to the list, to see more details about an address-book entry, or to find an address on a public directory server. To clear a name from any of the three message recipient boxes, select the name, right-click, and choose Remove from the shortcut menu.

When you've finished adding recipients, click OK to return to the New Message window.

Checking a Recipient's Address

You don't need to use the Windows Address Book to add recipients. Simply type one or more valid email addresses and continue; be sure to separate address entries with a semicolon or comma.

If you know a name is in your address book, enter a few characters from the first or last name. Outlook Express fills in matching names as you type; this AutoComplete feature works almost exactly like its equivalent in Internet Explorer. When the correct name appears in the address box, press Enter to add the address and a semicolon, with the insertion point positioned for you to add another address. Press Tab to move to the next address field.

> **CAUTION**
>
> Check the contents of the address box carefully before sending a message. If you type even a single incorrect character here, the AutoComplete feature might insert the wrong address, and you might wind up sending a sensitive or personal message to someone other than the recipient you intended.

If you don't like this AutoComplete feature, turn it off. Choose Tools, Options, click the Send tab, and deselect the check box labeled Automatically Complete Email Addresses When Composing. Even with this feature disabled, you can still enlist the help of the Address Book in completing addresses; just type a few characters from the first or last name, and then click the Check Names button (see Figure 34.24). If only one address-book entry matches the characters you typed, that entry appears in your address box; if there's more than one match, you'll have to pick the correct address from a dialog box. After Outlook Express has verified that the address is valid, it adds a link to that address entry; you know the process was successful when you see the underline beneath each address entry.

FIG. 34.24
The Check Names button returns address records that contain the characters you typed in any position.

Composing the Message

If you've chosen HTML format for your message, the Formatting toolbar appears just above the box in which you enter the message text. Use the toolbar buttons to change font and paragraph formatting, colors, and alignment. The three rightmost buttons, shown in Figure 34.25, insert a rule, a hyperlink, or a graphic image.

The New Message window includes most of the features you expect from a formatting editor, including the ability to specify fonts, colors, and alignment. There's even a multilevel Undo. Press Ctrl+Z to roll back changes you made or text you typed.

FIG. 34.25

Use these formatting buttons to control the look of an HTML message. Buttons at the far right let you insert this rule and hyperlink.

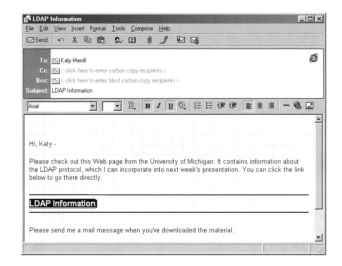

TROUBLESHOOTING

You tried to check the spelling of your message, but the Tools, Spelling command was grayed out and unavailable. Outlook Express does not include its own spell-checking module; instead, it borrows the spelling checker from other Microsoft applications, such as Word and Works. You must install one of these applications before you can check the spelling of an Outlook Express message.

To create a hyperlink in a message, follow these steps:

1. Select any piece of text or a graphic image.
2. Click the Insert Hyperlink button. A dialog box lets you choose from an assortment of formats, including the default http:// for web pages, ftp:// for file locations, and mailto:// for mail links.
3. Type the URL and click OK to assign the link to the object you selected. Notice that the hyperlink appears underlined in your message.

Changing Message Formats

To change the format of a message from HTML to plain text and vice versa, choose the appropriate entry from the Format menu. You can use the General tab of a contact record to specify that an addressee always receives messages in plain text. By default, when you respond to a message, Outlook Express uses the same format as the original. When you reply to an HTML-formatted mail message, your reply uses that same format unless you specifically tell Outlook Express not to do so.

Giving Messages a Consistent Look

When you create a message from scratch, you start with a blank slate. Your electronic messages lack basic information that you take for granted when you print correspondence on letterhead, such as your name, company name and logo, your job title, and your phone number. Outlook Express offers two features that help you apply a consistent look to your messages and supply some of this missing information.

With HTML-formatted messages, use templates called *stationery* to add background graphics, fonts, paragraph formatting, and other standard elements to mail and news messages. Use *signatures* with all kinds of messages, including text messages, to add standard information at the end of every message you create.

Using Signatures   For daily use, especially in a business setting, create a standard signature to make sure important information goes out with every message you send. A signature might include your name, return email address, company affiliation, and telephone number, for example. At some companies, employees routinely add a disclaimer stating that the views expressed in email messages are personal opinions and do not represent the company.

To set up a personal signature, choose Tools, Stationery, click the Mail or News tab, and click the Signature button. You can compose a simple text signature, like the one in Figure 34.26. You can store your signature in a text file if you prefer, or use FrontPage Express to add graphics and formatting codes and then store the result in an HTML file. To use a file as your signature, choose the File option and specify its location.

FIG. 34.26

Netiquette dictates that signatures should be short and to the point. At five lines, this signature is long enough.

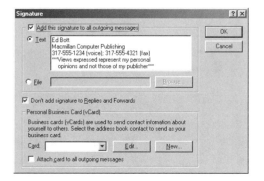

▶ **See** "Creating Web Pages with FrontPage Express," **p. 779**

Check boxes on the Signature dialog box let you specify whether you want Outlook Express to automatically add the signature to every message you create. There's also an option to skip signatures on replies and forwarded messages. Leave both check boxes blank if you prefer to add a signature only to selected messages.

Part
VI

Ch
34

To add a signature to a message while composing it, choose Insert, Signature.

Applying a Look with Stationery   Outlook Express includes a collection of HTML templates called stationery. These starter documents typically incorporate background graphics, standard fonts, and a few styles. To see and use the sample stationery, choose Compose, New Message Using, and then select an entry from the cascading menu.

Most of the sample stationery, built around personal themes including party invitations and greeting cards, is inappropriate for business use. However, it might supply some ideas for stationery you can create for your own use. For example, you might use a company logo as a background graphic, and add your signature in a formatted block of text set off from the main text by HTML rules.

To modify one of the sample stationery formats, follow these steps:

1. Choose Tools, Stationery. Choose the option labeled This Stationery, and then click the Select button to open a list of stationery installed on your computer.

2. Pick a format that includes the basic elements you want in your custom stationery. Use the Preview window to see what each stationery type looks like.

3. Click the Edit button to launch FrontPage Express with the selected stationery type.

4. Add text and graphics, and make any other formatting changes.

5. Save the document with a descriptive name in the same folder with the other stationery samples. (By default, these are in \Program Files\Common Files\Microsoft Shared\Stationery.) Close FrontPage Express.

6. Select the stationery you just created and click OK.

To use a stationery file for all mail or news messages you compose, make sure its name is selected in the Stationery box. To compose an HTML message without using the default stationery, choose Compose, New Message Using, No Stationery.

Exchanging Address Information with vCards

When you meet a new business contact in person, you exchange business cards. To send the digital equivalent of a business card in an email message, Outlook Express uses the vCard format. When you attach a vCard to your mail or news messages, recipients with a vCard-compatible address book (the Windows Address Book or Netscape Communicator, for example) can merge the attachment into their personal address book, which creates a new record that includes all of your address information.

Before you can send a vCard, you have to create a personal record in the Windows Address Book and then tell Outlook Express to use that card as your business card. Choose Tools, Stationery, and click the Signature button to choose your card.

CAUTION

You can set an option in the Signature dialog box that automatically adds your electronic business card to every mail message. Think twice before you check that box, though. Your regular correspondents probably won't appreciate the extra disk space consumed by every one of those redundant business card attachments, and correspondents without a vCard-compatible address book will probably also resent the useless attachments. It's far better to selectively attach business cards, by choosing Insert, Business Card.

Composing a News Article

Composing a message to a newsgroup uses tools that are virtually identical to those you use to create mail messages, with one major exception. Instead of picking addresses from your Windows Address Book, choose Tools, Select Newsgroups (or click the News Server icon to the right of the To: in the address box). You'll see a dialog box like the one in Figure 34.27, which you can use to fill in one or more newsgroup names in the address box.

FIG. 34.27

Posting the identical message to multiple newsgroups, as in this example, is generally considered bad Netiquette.

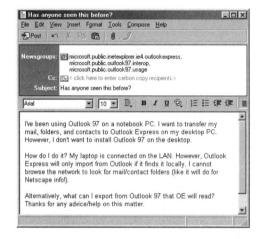

▶ **See** "Working with Newsgroups," **p. 744**

See "Working with Newsgroups," **p. 744**

TIP Before posting a question to a newsgroup, see if it's already been answered in a FAQ—a list of frequently asked questions. It's the fastest way to get answers, and you'll also avoid being flamed for not reading the FAQ. The mother of all FAQs, with upwards of 900 files, is news.answers. There, you'll find information ranging from the laughably trivial (every cult TV program ever made is there, along with more information on body piercing than any human should need) to the deadly serious. (You can read about a half-dozen religions or find detailed information on organ transplantation, depression support groups, and other sober topics.)

Part
VI

Ch
34

Sending Your Message

After you've finished addressing and composing your message, you have a variety of options for actually launching it on its way.

- To send a mail message immediately using the default mail account, click the Send button.

- To post a newsgroup message immediately, click the Post button.

- To choose which mail account to use when sending a message, choose File, Send Message Using, and pick the account from the cascading menu.

- To tell Outlook Express you want to choose when to send a message, choose File, Send Later.

- To save a mail message in the Drafts folder so you can work on it later, choose File, Save.

Working with File Attachments

In addition to formatted text and graphics, you can attach a file to any message you compose using Outlook Express. Binary files, such as images and programs, can safely travel across the Internet, but only if you encode them into ASCII text before sending. When an incoming message includes an attachment, Outlook Express and other MIME-compatible mail clients are capable of converting the encoded text back into binary files.

To add a file attachment to a message you're composing, click the Paper Clip icon on the tool bar. You can also attach one or more files by dragging them from an Explorer or folder window into the message window.

> **CAUTION**
>
> Not all mail client software is capable of decoding all attachment formats. If you're certain the recipient uses Outlook Express or another modern, MIME-compatible program, you should have no problem exchanging attachments. If you're not certain what mail software the recipient uses, try sending a small test attachment to verify that the process works before you send important files via email.

To view or save a file attachment in a message you've received, look for its icon.

- In the preview pane, click the Paper Clip icon at the right of the preview header to see a list of attached files. Choose an item from the list to open it; you can't save an attachment from the preview pane.

- In a message window, look for file icons in a separate pane just below the message text (see Figure 34.28). Double-click to launch the file, or use right-click shortcut menus to save the file to your local hard disk or a network location.

FIG. 34.28
Right-click its icon to open, save, or print a file attachment. When composing a message, you can also right-click to add or remove files.

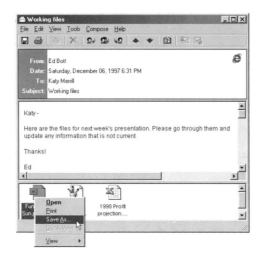

TROUBLESHOOTING

Your recipients report that file attachments appear as gibberish in messages they receive from you. Your recipient is probably using a mail client that is not fully MIME-compatible, or their Internet service provider's mail server can't process the attachments correctly. If you can't convince them to change mail clients, try resending the attachment using the Uuencode format instead of MIME encoding. You must send the message as plain text; choose Tools, Options, click the Send tab, and click the Settings button opposite the Plain Text option to adjust the format for outgoing attachments. Many older mail clients that don't handle MIME formatting can process Uuencoded attachments just fine. If that still doesn't work, your recipient will need to find a third-party program that can decode attachments. There are free and shareware programs that can help convert MIME-formatted and Uuencoded text to its original binary format.

Sending and Receiving Mail

Exchanging messages with a mail server is an interactive process. A mail server does not automatically send messages to your computer; to begin the transfer process, your mail client has to send a request to the server. Outlook Express can poll for mail at regular intervals, or you can send and receive messages on demand by clicking a button.

Collecting Mail Automatically

If you have a LAN connection, Outlook Express automatically checks for new messages and sends outgoing mail every 30 minutes. To check for mail more or less frequently, follow these steps:

1. Choose Tools, Options, and click the General tab. You'll see the dialog box shown in Figure 34.29.

FIG. 34.29

On a LAN connection, Outlook Express checks for new mail every half-hour. To pick up messages more frequently, adjust this setting to 5 or 10 minutes instead.

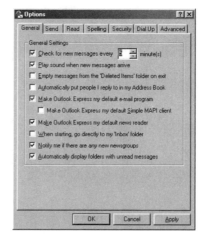

2. Make sure there's a check mark in the box labeled Check For New Messages Every X Minute(s).

3. Use the spinner control to adjust how often Outlook Express sends and receives mail. This number must be in the range of 1 (every minute) to 480 (every 8 hours).

4. Click OK to make the change effective.

How do you know when new mail has arrived? Outlook Express gives you two cues when you've received mail. A letter icon appears in the notification area at the right of the taskbar, and the program also plays a sound. If you find the sound disturbing, it's easy to kill the noise. Choose Tools, Options, click the General tab, and remove the check mark for that option.

You can also choose a different sound file to play when new mail arrives. Open the Control Panel and use the Sounds applet to assign a different .WAV file to the New Mail Notification event.

▶ **See** "Changing the Sounds Related to Windows Events," **p. 447**

TIP As Outlook Express checks for mail, look in the status bar for messages that display the results of the connection attempt. Double-click the icon at the far right to display a dialog box with more details, including any error messages you might have received.

Delivering the Mail Manually

Of course, you can check for new messages anytime by using the Send and Receive button. This technique works even if Outlook Express is set to check messages at regular intervals.

The Send and Receive command automatically connects with every mail account and your default news account. To add or remove a server from this group, follow these steps:

1. Choose Tools, Accounts and select the account from the list.

2. Click the Properties button to display the account's property sheet.

3. Click the General tab and check or uncheck the setting labeled Include this account. (The exact wording is different for mail and news accounts.) A check mark means Outlook Express will automatically check for messages when you click the Send and Receive button.

4. Click OK to make the change effective, and then close the Accounts dialog box.

If you have multiple mail providers and you want to connect with only one of them, regardless of the default settings, choose Tools, Send and Receive from the menus. Outlook Express presents a cascading menu that lets you choose which mail providers you want to connect with.

Checking the Mail When You're Out of the Office

Outlook Express lets you file and save all the messages you send and receive. But what happens when you need to read your email from a machine other than the one you normally use? This might be the case if you normally use an office PC but occasionally check your email from home or the road. If you use the default settings, you'll end up with a collection of messages on different PCs.

The cure is to adjust the account settings on your away PC so that it downloads messages but does not delete them from the mail server. Later, when you return to the office, you can connect to the server and download all the messages, saving and filing the important ones.

You must specifically set this option for each account you intend to check. Choose Tools, Accounts, select the account, and click the Properties button. Click the Advanced tab, then check the Delivery options (see Figure 34.30).

FIG. 34.30
If you check your mail when you're away from the office, tell Outlook Express to leave messages on the server so you can retrieve them when you return to work.

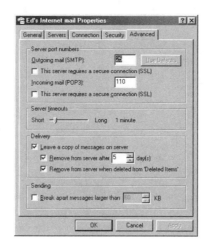

Part
VI

Ch
34

The other two Delivery options help you avoid cluttering up the mail server by automatically deleting messages after a set number of days or when you delete them from your away machine.

Replying to Messages You've Received

The simplest way to compose a message is to reply to one you've received. The format for replies varies slightly between mail and news messages.

Replying to a Mail Message

When you select a message and click the Reply button, Outlook Express opens a New Message window, selects the same format as the message to which you're responding, fills in the To: line with the sender's address from the original message, adds Re: to the beginning of the original Subject line, and positions the insertion point at the top of the message. When you click the Reply to All button, Outlook Express picks up every addressee from the To: and Cc: lines in the original message and adds them to your new message.

By default, all replies include the full text of the original message, with a separator line between your reply and the original text. How that message appears depends on the format of your reply.

- With HTML-formatted messages, all graphics are included and the original text is indented
- With plain-text messages, each line of the original text begins with the > character.

Choose Tools, Options, and click the Send tab to adjust these defaults (see Figure 34.31).

FIG. 34.31
If you routinely reply to replies, lower the default text wrap to 72 characters. That will lessen the chance that your prefix character will cause lines to wrap inappropriately.

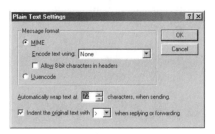

To change the default setting so all replies start with a blank message, uncheck the Include Message in Reply option.

Replying to a Newsgroup Message

When reading newsgroup messages, you have a choice of two reply buttons. Click Reply to Group to begin composing a message to the current newsgroup; just as with a mail message, your reply includes the original posting, although the format of the separator text is different.

To reply in a private email to the person that posted the original newsgroup message, click the Reply to Author button. Although there's no Reply to All button, that option is available: Choose Compose, Reply to Newsgroup and Author to post your reply to the newsgroup *and* send a copy to the author via email.

> **CAUTION**
>
> Check the email address carefully when responding to newsgroup postings. Many newsgroup contributors deliberately corrupt the Reply-To address in their messages to frustrate junk emailers. You might need to edit stray characters or words to see the real address.

Forwarding Messages

You have two choices when you forward a message you've received to another person. Select the message and click the Forward button to open a New Message window containing the original message; the message uses the same indent settings as if you had chosen to reply to the sender. Enter one or more addresses, add any comments of your own, and click the Send button.

You can also forward an email message as an attached file; choose Compose, Forward as Attachment. That's the correct choice when you want another person to see the message exactly as you saw it, without prefix characters or other reply formatting.

Organizing Messages with Folders

By default, Outlook Express includes five top-level mail folders. There's no way to delete these basic mail folders, which perform the following crucial functions:

- All incoming messages hit the Inbox first; use the Inbox Assistant to file or process messages automatically as they arrive.

- Mail that you've sent goes to the Outbox until the next time you exchange messages with your mail server.

- By default, a copy of every message you send goes to the Sent Items folder. To change this setting, choose Tools, Options, click the Send tab, and uncheck this option.

- When you delete a message, Outlook Express moves it to the Deleted Items folder. An option on the General tab lets you empty this folder each time you exit. By default, this folder stays full until you right-click its icon and choose Empty Folder.

- The Drafts folder stores messages you've composed and saved but haven't yet sent.

Part

VI

Ch

34

N O T E You can't organize newsgroup messages using mail folders, although you can drag a newsgroup message from the message list and copy it into a mail folder.

Creating a New Folder

You can add an unlimited number of top-level mail folders and subfolders to Outlook Express. The easiest way to create a new folder is to follow these steps:

1. If the folder list is not visible, choose View, Layout; check the box labeled Folder List and click OK.

2. Select the folder in which you want to create the new subfolder. To create a new top-level folder, choose the Outlook Express icon at the top of the folder list.

3. Right-click the icon you selected and choose New Folder from the shortcut menu.

4. Enter a name for the new folder. (This dialog box also lets you use the tree at the bottom of the dialog box to change the location in which the new folder will be created.)

5. Click OK to create the new folder.

Moving or Copying Messages Among Folders

To move messages, drag them from the message list and drop them on the folder icon in your folder list. To copy messages to a folder while leaving the original file intact, hold down the Ctrl key as you drag the messages.

If you use folders extensively, use right-click shortcut menus in the folder list to move and copy messages. As Figure 34.32 shows, these commands let you create a new folder on-the-fly. Better yet, add the Move To button to the toolbar for instant access to this dialog box.

FIG. 34.32

Use the New Folder button to create a folder and move or copy messages from the same dialog box.

▶ **See** "Customizing the Outlook Express Toolbar," **p. 719**

> Adding a new top-level folder creates a matching shortcut on the Outlook bar. If you create a folder within an existing folder—under the Inbox, for example—it appears in the folder list but not on the Outlook bar.

Moving, Renaming, and Deleting Folders

Open the folder list and simply drag folder icons to move them from one location to another. Right-click and use the shortcut menus to delete or rename a folder. You can freely move, delete, or rename any folders you've created, but you can't change any of the five default mail folders.

Compacting Folders to Reduce the Size of Your Mail File

As you receive new messages and organize them into folders, the size of your mail file grows. When you move and delete messages, Outlook Express removes the messages but leaves the empty space in the mail file. Over time, this can cause your mail folders to waste a significant amount of space. To eliminate wasted space in a single folder, select its icon and choose File, Folder, Compact. To remove slack space from every mail folder, choose File, Folder, Compact All Folders.

> After you compact your mail folders, it's a good idea to back up all your mail files. Click the Start Menu, choose Find, Files or Folders, and search for the data files for each folder; these files use the extension .MBX, while a matching index for each file has the same name but the .IDX extension. Folders you create go by the name FOLDER1.MBX, FOLDER2.MBX, and so on.

Using the Inbox Assistant to Process Mail Automatically

In some busy organizations that live and die by email, it's not uncommon for workers to receive dozens or even hundreds of messages per day. Managing that torrent of messages can be a full-time job, but Outlook Express can do at least part of the work. The secret is a tool called the Inbox Assistant, which lets you define rules for Outlook Express to follow when you receive new mail.

Defining Rules for Processing Mail

To define rules that automate mail processing, choose Tools, Inbox Assistant. Click the Add button and you'll see a dialog box like the one in Figure 34.33.

FIG. 34.33

To create a mail-processing rule, define one or more criteria in the top of this dialog box, and then select an action to be performed when a message meets that condition.

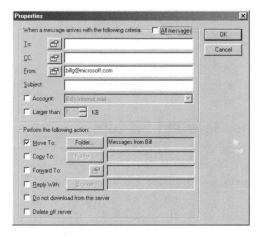

Each rule consists of two parts: a set of criteria and a matching action. Each time a message arrives in your Inbox, Outlook Express compares it with the conditions defined in your Inbox Assistant rules; when it finds a match, it performs the action defined for that rule.

You can define a variety of conditions to trigger mail actions:

- search for text in the address box or in the subject line
- look for messages that come through a specific mail account
- check the size of each incoming message
- apply the rule to all messages

N O T E   If you're familiar with filtering options in other mail programs, such as Eudora Pro, you might be disappointed in the limitations of the Inbox Assistant. For example, you cannot define complex "or" conditions; when you specify multiple criteria, Outlook Express acts only on messages that meet all those criteria. Nor can you check the text of the message itself or see whether a message has a file attachment. ■

When a message meets the conditions you define, you can order Outlook Express to move or copy it to a folder, forward it to another recipient, reply automatically with a saved message, leave the message on the server, or delete the message from the server.

Figure 34.34 shows some rules you might find useful for weeding out junk mail and helping to identify important messages:

- Automatically move mail sent by a VIP or from your company's domain (mcp.com, for example) to a special Read Me Now folder.
- Look for messages where your name is in the CC field and move them to a Read Me Later folder.

FIG. 34.34
Use Inbox Assistant rules to help identify important messages and eliminate junk mail.

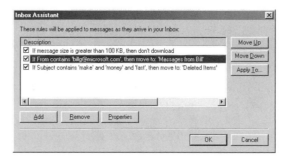

- Move messages to the Deleted Items folder if the subject contains key junk-mail phrases (make money fast, for example) or if the message was sent by someone from who you do not wish to receive mail. (This feature is often called a bozo filter.)

- When you're out of the office on business or on vacation, use an Inbox Assistant rule to forward all your mail to an assistant and send an advisory message to the sender.

- If space on your notebook computer is tight, tell Outlook Express not to download messages that are larger than a specified size—say, 100KB.

Changing Inbox Assistant Rules

Note that rules are applied in the order in which they appear in your list. If two or more conditions apply to the same message, the Inbox Assistant can apply only the first rule. This type of conflict between rules can produce effects you didn't anticipate.

- To adjust the order in which the Inbox Assistant applies rules, select a rule from the list and use the Move Up and Move Down buttons.

- To completely eliminate a rule, select it and click the Remove button.

- To temporarily disable a rule without eliminating it, clear the check box to the left of its entry in the list.

- To change the conditions or actions associated with a rule, select it and click the Properties button.

 To clean up a cluttered mail folder, select a rule, click the Apply To button, and pick a folder from the dialog box that pops up. The Inbox Assistant will process all the messages in that folder and any subfolders.

Part
VI

Ch
34

Enhancing Email Security

By its very nature, an ordinary email message is as insecure as a postcard. It takes only the most rudimentary technical knowledge to spoof a message so that it appears to be coming from someone other than the actual sender. In fact, a favorite hacker trick is to send bogus mail messages that appear to have come from famous individuals such as Bill Gates. Additionally, because email travels in packets across the Internet, it's theoretically possible for anyone to intercept a transmission, read a message sent to someone else, and possibly change the contents of that message.

Outlook Express includes two features that enhance email security, although neither offers foolproof protection from a skilled and determined data thief. *Encryption* lets you encode the contents of a message so that only a recipient with a matching code key can decipher the text. A *digital signature* tacked onto the end of a message guarantees that the message originated from the sender and was not tampered with in transit.

Before you can use either security feature, you'll first have to acquire a digital certificate from a certifying authority and add it to Outlook Express. You'll also need to enable that certificate for every mail account with which you plan to use it, as in Figure 34.35.

ON THE WEB

Internet Explorer 4.0 includes a special offer for a free Class 1 digital ID from VeriSign, Inc. Read full details at **http://digitalid.verisign.com.**

FIG. 34.35
Before you can encrypt or digitally sign an email message, you'll need to enable a certificate like this one. Click the button at the bottom of the dialog box for more information.

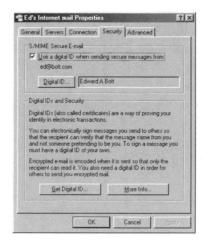

To install your digital ID, follow the instructions provided by the certificate provider. The certificate includes two parts: a *public key*, which you distribute freely to others, and a *private key* to which only you have access. Anyone can encrypt a message using your public key, and once they've done so, only you can unscramble it using the private key.

How Encryption Works

The basics of cryptography aren't difficult to understand. School children, for example, use simple ciphers to create secret messages by substituting letters: A in place of B, B in place of C, and so on. Of course, these encryption systems are ridiculously easy to crack, rendering them unsuitable for applications where privacy is essential.

Computer technology enables users to create far more complex encryption systems that are essentially impervious to all but the most determined attempts at cracking. The more complex the system, the more time and computer power it takes to break the code. With the 128-bit keys used to encrypt secure browser connections, for example, it would take several millennia for even the most powerful desktop computer to run through all possible combinations and decode the original text.

Today's computer-based cryptographic systems use a variety of standards. The official encryption technique of the United States government, for example, is the Data Encryption Standard (DES). This system, originally developed in the mid-1970s and standardized in 1981, requires that both parties exchange a secret key consisting of a randomly generated 56-digit number and then use this key to scramble the encrypted data. Without access to the key, you would have to try more than 200 trillion combinations to read the encrypted text. DES encryption is widely used by banks and other financial institutions.

For everyday use, DES encryption has an enormous drawback. It requires that you exchange digital keys with the party on the other end, either physically (on a floppy disk, for example) or over an electronic connection. Of course, if you had a secure electronic connection, why would you need to use encryption? The solution is to use the RSA Public Key Cryptosystem. With this technique, you generate a matched pair of keys, one public and one private. You freely distribute the public key, via email, on your company's intranet, or on public servers, for example. The private key, on the other hand, stays on your system, where only you have access to it.

N O T E RSA isn't a technical acronym. Rather, the name identifies the three Massachusetts Institute of Technology professors who invented the process in 1977—Ronald Rivest, Adi Shamir, and Len Adleman. The patents for the RSA technology belong to a company they later founded, called RSA Data Security. ◼

The beauty of the RSA system is that it's *asymmetrical*; you can use either key to encrypt a message, and the only way to decrypt it is by using the matching key of the pair. When you exchange secure mail with another person or organization, the other party has a pair of public and private keys as well. By exchanging public keys with one another, you can work with two types of secure messages:

Part

VI

Ch

34

- ◼ When you use the recipient's public key to encrypt a message, only the owner of the private key can read the resulting message; even the sender will see only gibberish. The recipient must use the private key to unscramble the message contents. This technique guarantees that the message contents remain private.

- ◼ When you use your own secret key to encrypt a message, anyone with a copy of your public key can decrypt the message. This doesn't protect the contents of the message, but it does guarantee that only the holder of the secret key could have encrypted it. Anyone receiving such a message knows for certain that you sent it and that a third party has not been tampered with or forged the message.

Encryption Support in Outlook Express

Outlook Express supports a standard called Secure Multi-Purpose Internet Mail Extensions (S/MIME), which uses RSA encryption technology. At the core of any S/MIME client, you'll find support for the Public Key Cryptography Standards (PKCS). PKCS is ancient by Internet standards; it was first adopted in 1991 by a consortium of computer industry pioneers from private industry and the research community. S/MIME clients (including Outlook 98 and Netscape Communicator) use the PKCS #7 Cryptographic Message Syntax, which defines the basic structure of the digital signature and envelope. This technology is also at the core of Microsoft's Authenticode technology, which is used to verify the integrity of ActiveX controls, and other vendors, including Netscape and Sun, have incorporated it into code-signing mechanisms used with Java applets.

When you install a digital certificate in Outlook Express, Windows 98 asks you to select a cryptographic key (see Figure 34.36). The key you choose defines the encrypting algorithm that the program will use; the more bits, the more secure the encrypted results will be.

FIG. 34.36
Any of these crypto-graphic providers will be sufficient to encrypt ordinary mail messages with a high degree of security.

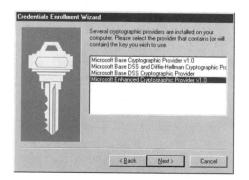

N O T E   If you have multiple mail accounts, you'll need a separate certificate for each one because each certificate is tied to a unique email address. Outlook Express selects the correct certificate based on the account you use to send messages. ■

Windows 98 includes the following four encryption algorithms:

- Microsoft Base Cryptographic Provider v1.0
- Microsoft Base DSS Cryptographic Provider
- Microsoft Base DSS and Diffie-Hellman Cryptographic Provider
- Microsoft Enhanced Cryptographic Provider v1.0

For all intents and purposes, these cryptographic providers are identical. They use slightly different mathematical formulas to generate keys, but the results are fully interoperable with other S/MIME-compatible clients.

Sending a Digitally Signed Message

To add a digital signature to a message, click the Digitally Sign Message button on the toolbar in the New Message window. A red icon in the lower-right corner of the address box tells you this is a signed message.

> **CAUTION**
>
> Outlook Express includes the option to digitally sign and/or encrypt all your messages. Don't activate this feature unless you're certain that most of your correspondents use mail software that can accept digital certificates. For the overwhelming majority of email users, it's best to choose secure email options one message at a time.

Encrypting a Message

To scramble a message so that only a trusted recipient can read it, click the Encrypt message button in the New Message window. A blue padlock icon in the address box lets you know the message is encrypted. You must have a copy of the recipient's public key before you can encrypt a message to that person. (You can ask a correspondent to send you their public key; you can also find public keys on some directory servers.)

ON THE WEB

Pretty Good Privacy, Inc. has one of the best online sources of information about encryption and secure email. You'll find it at

http://www.pgp.com/privacy/privacy.cgi.

Reading a Signed or Encrypted Message

Anyone can encrypt a message and send it to you, as long as they have a copy of your public key. When you receive the encrypted message, Outlook Express uses your private key to unscramble the text so you can read it. When you receive a digitally signed message, you'll see an introductory message like the one in Figure 34.37.

Using Secure Mail on Corporate Networks

Although the encryption tools in Outlook Express are extremely powerful, their feature set is basic at best. The underlying design assumes that the user has an SMTP account with an Internet service provider, and it also assumes that the user will acquire a digital certificate from an independent certifying authority, such as VeriSign, Inc.

Organizations that require secure email within the company should consider installing Microsoft Exchange, which supports the use of digital certificates that comply with the X.509 standard. These certificates might be issued by an Internet certificate authority such as VeriSign, but a more manageable corporate solution uses the Certificate Server in Internet

Information Server 4.0 and later. Most organizations that choose this configuration will also want to replace Outlook Express with a more robust, full-featured email client, such as Outlook 98.

FIG. 34.37
Outlook Express offers this help screen when you receive a digitally signed message. Note the additional information in the address header, too.

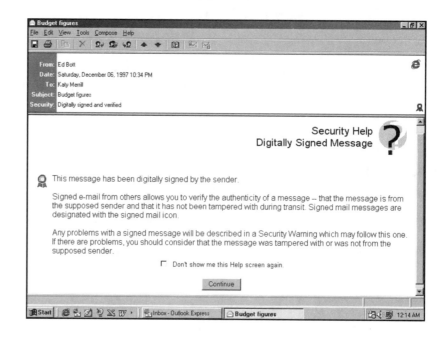

 Organizations that require exceptional levels of security should not rely on software and passwords to protect sensitive systems and data. An increasing number of hardware devices support the Microsoft Cryptography Application Programming Interfaces (CryptoAPI). These supplement software-based security with smart cards, fingerprint recognition, and other types of hardware that uniquely identify a particular user.

Working with Newsgroups

Although newsgroup messages appear in the same window as mail messages, the mechanics of downloading and managing newsgroup messages are dramatically different. Unlike mail messages, which are addressed directly to you, newsgroup messages are posted on public servers for all to see. You probably don't want to read every message in busy newsgroups, which can get hundreds of new messages per day.

Getting the maximum benefit from Internet newsgroups takes careful setup and management. Before you can get started, you have to identify potentially useful or interesting newsgroups.

How Newsgroups Work

Newsgroups are nearly as old as the Internet itself. They get only a fraction of the publicity that goes to the newer and flashier World Wide Web, but that doesn't mean they're less useful. On the contrary, public peer-support newsgroups can be an excellent source for quick answers to thorny software and hardware support questions. Newsgroups are also popular among hobbyists ranging from BMW enthusiasts to cat owners, and moderated newsgroups are important gathering places for computer and science professionals.

Don't be misled by the name; newsgroups have nothing to do with the *New York Times* or CNN. They function more like public bulletin boards, organized by topic, where individuals post messages (sometimes called *articles*) that anyone with access to that group can read and reply to. Just as web servers use Hyper Text Transfer Protocol, or HTTP, to communicate, news servers use Network News Transfer Protocol, or NNTP, to share information.

The oldest collection of newsgroups is called Usenet, a distributed network of servers that continually exchange messages with one another. When you post a newsgroup article to your local news server, it works its way across the network until every Usenet news server has a copy.

ON THE WEB

For the definitive description of what Usenet is and isn't, read this web page:

http://www.netannounce.org/news.announce.newusers/archive/usenet/what-is/part1

Not all Usenet news servers carry all newsgroups, and it's up to the manager of a news server to decide when older messages "expire" and drop off the server. The past few years have seen a steady increase in the number of private newsgroups as corporations have seen how easy it is for employees to communicate using these forums.

> **CAUTION**
>
> Don't expect to find useful information in a newsgroup just because the name sounds appealing. As the Internet has grown, newsgroups have become increasingly vulnerable to spam—posts (usually commercial in nature) that are unrelated to the stated purpose of a newsgroup and simply serve to clutter the listings of articles. On some once-popular newsgroups, the only traffic these days consists of variations on chain letters and enticements to visit X-rated web sites.

Part
VI

Ch
34

Viewing the Full List of Newsgroups

The first time you connect to a news server, Outlook Express offers to download a list of all the newsgroups available there. On a well-stocked server, that can represent thousands of newsgroups. Click the Newsgroups button to view the complete list of groups available on a news server. If you've defined multiple accounts, make sure you select the correct server from the list at the left of the window (see Figure 34.38).

FIG. 34.38

To see a complete list of available newsgroups, first select a news server icon from the list at left.

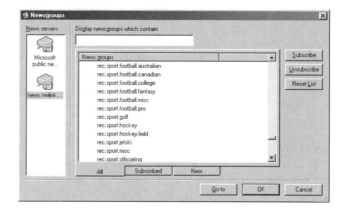

Deciphering a Newsgroup Name

Newsgroups use a dotted naming convention like those found elsewhere on the Internet, with strict hierarchies that identify what subscribers can expect to find in each one. To read a newsgroup name, follow the hierarchy from left to right as it goes from general to specific. In Usenet newsgroups, for example, the first entry is the top-level domain. Table 34.1 lists many (but not all) of the most common top-level domains.

Table 34.1   Common Top-Level Domains

Top-Level Domain	Description	Sample newsgroup
comp	general computer subjects	comp.os.ms-windows.networking.tcp-ip
rec	hobbies, the arts, pop culture	rec.music.beatles
soc	social issues and world culture	soc.culture.irish
sci	science-related, many highly specialized	sci.space.policy
gov	government newsgroups	gov.us.fed.congress.documents
news	newsgroup administrative issues	news.newusers.questions
misc	miscellaneous, often commercial groups	misc.taxes.moderated

There are a variety of unofficial newsgroup hierarchies as well, including the infamous alt category. When people complain about pornography on the Internet, they're talking about newsgroups whose names begin with alt.sex and alt.binaries.pictures.erotica.

There are also local newsgroups, whose top-level domain identifies a geographic region. (Try ba.food for San Francisco Bay Area restaurant recommendations, or nyc.jobs for employment in the Big Apple.) Additionally, there are private groups intended for subscribers of Internet service providers like Netcom.

Microsoft now provides its first level of technical support through newsgroups in the microsoft.* hierarchy. You'll find them on **msnews.microsoft.com**, and an increasing number of Internet service providers are replicating the Microsoft news feed to their own news servers.

Finding a Specific Newsgroup

On Microsoft's public news servers, there are nearly 600 separate groups. Some well-stocked Usenet news servers include more than 15,000 distinct newsgroups. Instead of scrolling through the full Newsgroups list to find relevant ones, use the text box at the top of the dialog box to show only groups whose names contain certain letters or words. If you're looking for information about Outlook Express, for example, type the word Outlook to see a filtered list like the one in Figure 34.39.

FIG. 34.39
After you've found the newsgroup you're looking for, double-click its name to add it to your list of subscribed groups.

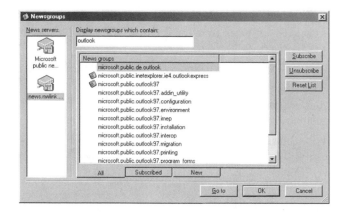

ON THE WEB

You can't use Outlook Express to search the contents of a newsgroup for specific information, but web-based news archives like Deja News can search newsgroups for messages and threads that match your interests. If you find a wealth of information in a particular newsgroup, use Outlook Express to go there directly. You'll find Deja News at

http://www.dejanews.com

Part
VI

Ch
34

Refreshing the List of Newsgroups

On Usenet servers in particular, it's common for new groups to appear and old ones to disappear regularly. If you suspect that there are new groups available on a server,

1. Select the News Server icon in the folder list.

2. Click the Newsgroups button to show the list of all newsgroups.

3. Click the Reset List button to update the master list. This operation might take some time, especially over a slow Internet connection.

4. After you've refreshed the list, click the New tab along the bottom of the Newsgroups list to see only new groups.

Managing Newsgroup Subscriptions

Don't be confused by the buttons to the right of the Newsgroups list. Subscribing to a newsgroup doesn't cost anything, and it doesn't require that you send any information about yourself to a news server. (There's also no connection with web subscriptions.) In Outlook Express, subscriptions are simply a way of managing the Newsgroup list to show only your favorite groups.

Follow these steps to manage your newsgroup subscriptions:

1. Select the News Server icon in the folder list, and then click the Newsgroups button.

2. Click the All tab at the bottom of the dialog box to see the full list of newsgroups.

3. Select at least one name from the list; to select more than one name at a time, hold down the Ctrl key as you click.

4. Use the Subscribe button to add a newsgroup to your personal list. An icon appears to the left of the newsgroup name.

5. Use the Unsubscribe button to remove a newsgroup from your personal list. (You can also double-click an entry in the Newsgroups list to toggle the subscribed icon.)

6. Click the Subscribed tab at the bottom of the Newsgroups list to see only the list of newsgroups you've selected. Icons for all subscribed newsgroups appear under the News Server icon in your folders list (see Figure 34.40).

 T I P   You needn't subscribe to a newsgroup to see its contents. Select a name from the Newsgroups list, and then click the Go To button to open the newsgroup. Use the choices on the Tools menu to manage subscriptions for the newsgroup you're currently viewing.

FIG. 34.40
When you select a news server in the folder list at left, the list at right shows only newsgroups to which you've subscribed.

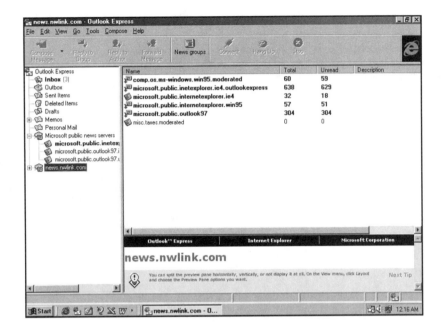

Downloading and Reading Newsgroup Messages

Before you can read the messages in a newsgroup, you have to download them from the server to your computer. That process is not as straightforward as it sounds. For starters, you can't tell from the Newsgroup list how many messages are currently available for each newsgroup. Some obscure groups generate only a handful of messages, but popular groups might contain thousands of messages at one time, with some containing binary attachments or graphic files that occupy significant amounts of disk space. Downloading every message without first checking the newsgroup's contents is clearly a bad idea.

To make newsgroup traffic more manageable, Outlook Express distinguishes between message headers and bodies. Regardless of the size of the message itself, the header contains only the subject line, the author's name, and the message size. By default, when you open a newsgroup for the first time, Outlook Express connects with the server and asks it to transfer the 300 most recent subject headers.

Look at the status bar (see Figure 34.41) to see how many headers were left on the server. To download more headers, choose Tools, Get Next 300 Headers. Outlook Express always chooses the most recent headers that have not yet been downloaded.

Part
VI

Ch
34

FIG. 34.41

The status bar tells you how many message headers you've downloaded from the total available on the server.

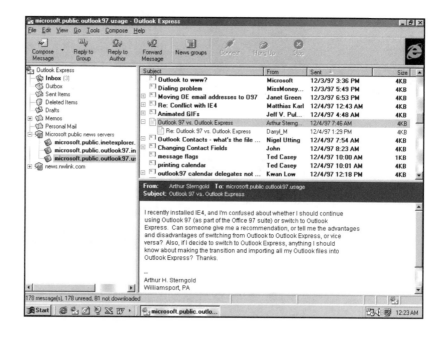

 TIP   To adjust the number of headers Outlook Express retrieves on each pass, choose Tools, Options and increase or decrease the number shown on the Read tab.

Navigating Through Newsgroups

The window in which you read news messages works much the same as the mail window, with a single notable exception. Outlook Express organizes news messages so you can follow a discussion that takes place over days or even weeks.

Newsgroups facilitate *threaded conversations*, in which one user posts a message and others reply to that message. News servers keep track of the links between original posts, replies, and replies to replies. By default, Outlook Express maintains these threads regardless of the sort order you've chosen for messages in a given newsgroup. These messages remain grouped together even when the reply title begins with the Re: prefix.

Replies to a message are indented below the original message, and replies to replies are indented another level. To see all the messages in a thread, click the plus sign to the left of the message header that begins the thread. To collapse the thread so you see only the first header, click the minus sign to the left of the thread.

Navigating through threads with the keyboard is fast and easy. Use the up and down arrows to move through the list of messages. In the default view, where all message threads are collapsed, the up and down arrow moves from thread to thread. To work with threads from the keyboard, use the right arrow to expand and the left arrow to collapse each thread.

If messages are not grouped together properly, choose View, Sort By, Group Messages by Thread.

Reading Messages Online

As long as the connection between Outlook Express and the news server is active, you can read messages by opening a message window or by using the preview pane. When you select a header, Outlook Express automatically retrieves that message from the server and adds it to your file. When you double-click to open a message window, or if you keep the preview pane open for more than 5 seconds, the header text changes from boldface to normal type, indicating that you've read the message.

If you'd prefer to keep your connection open while you scroll through the headers and retrieve only those messages that look most interesting, choose Tools, Options, click the Read tab, and clear the check mark from the box labeled Automatically Show News Messages in the Preview Pane. As Figure 34.42 shows, with this option set you must select a header and tap the spacebar to retrieve a message.

FIG. 34.42
Note the different icons in this list: Downloaded messages show a full page, and the corner is turned down after reading.

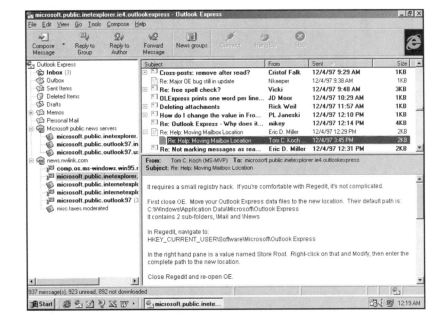

Working Offline for Maximum Efficiency

The most efficient way to work with large newsgroups is offline. Outlook Express lets you download a batch of headers, then scroll through the list and mark the ones you want to download. The next time you connect to the server, Outlook Express retrieves the marked messages, which you can read anytime.

Follow these steps to work offline:

1. To begin working offline, choose File, Work Offline.

2. When you see a message header you'd like to read, mark it for retrieval. You can use the right-click shortcut menu, but it's easier to select one or more message headers and press Ctrl+M.

3. To select an entire thread for retrieval, make sure the thread is collapsed, with a plus sign visible to the left. Select the first message in the thread and press Ctrl+M. The icon to the left of a message header that has been marked for retrieval changes (see Figure 34.43).

FIG. 34.43

The tiny arrow to the left of some headers means they've been marked for retrieval the next time you connect with the news server.

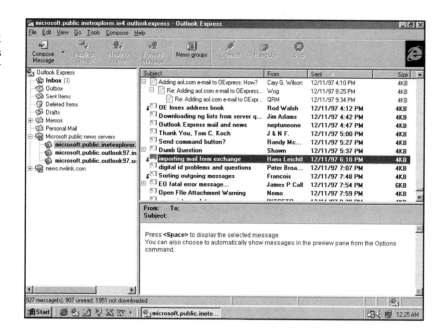

4. To remove marks, select one or more marked messages and choose Tools, Mark for Retrieval, Unmark.

5. To go online again, choose File and clear the check mark from the Work Offline choice.

6. To retrieve all marked messages, choose Tools, Download This Newsgroup. In the dialog box that appears, check the option labeled Get Marked Messages (see Figure 34.44).

FIG. 34.44

Check the option at the bottom of this dialog box to retrieve messages whose headers you've marked.

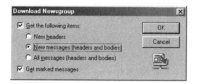

Reestablishing Connections with a News Server

Unless you've set up your news account to hang up immediately after downloading messages or headers, the connection remains active while you work with messages and headers. By default, Outlook Express disconnects from the server after a minute; when that happens, the text in the status bar changes and you'll see a dialog box like the one in Figure 34.45.

FIG. 34.45

After a period of inactivity, you might lose your connection to the news server. To reconnect, choose File, Connect, or press F5.

If you're using a dial-up connection, you might need to redial at this point. Click the Connect button or choose File, Connect to redial the server. If you're connected through a LAN, you can re-establish the connection by pressing the Refresh key, F5.

Using Filters to Make the News More Readable

After a while, the sheer bulk of downloaded headers and messages from some newsgroups is overwhelming, and navigation can become nearly impossible. To cut the display down to manageable proportions, use filters to show only messages that meet specific criteria. Outlook Express includes three built-in filters, or you can create your own.

News filters are analogous to mail-processing rules created by the Inbox Assistant. Unlike those rules, however, newsgroup filters can't move or forward messages or reply automatically on your behalf to messages.

To use a built-in filter, choose View, Current View and pick one of these three choices:

- Unread Messages. Use this filter to quickly pick up new messages, especially when they're part of older threads.
- Downloaded Messages. This choice works especially well after you've marked a widely scattered group of messages for offline reading.
- Replies to My Posts. For active participants in a busy newsgroup, this filter is essential.

You can also create your own filter based on one or more rules, which can be used in conjunction with the built-in filters. To create the rules for your filter, choose Tools, Newsgroup Filters, and then click the Add button. You'll see a dialog box like the one in Figure 34.46.

You can apply filters to a single newsgroup or server or to every server. Filters let you suppress messages from specific individuals or domains, or messages with a key word or phrase in the subject line. You can also hide messages that are too old or too big.

FIG. 34.46

Use filters to reduce the amount of clutter in crowded newsgroups. This filter, for example, hides all "make money fast" postings.

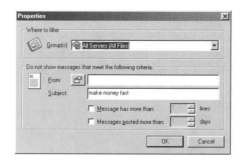

To apply all active filters to the current display, choose View, Current View, and make sure Filtered Messages is checked.

To temporarily disable a single rule, clear the check box next to its entry in the Filters list. To change the order in which rules are applied, use the Move Up and Move Down buttons. To edit a rule, select its entry and click the Properties button. To eliminate a rule permanently, click the Remove button.

Controlling Message Downloads for Each Newsgroup

Eventually, as you develop experience, you'll build up a list of favorite newsgroups, each with its own characteristics. Outlook Express lets you create different settings for each one, so that you can download messages and/or headers according to your preferences.

To set up each newsgroup, open the folder list, right-click a newsgroup entry, and choose Properties. The General tab provides information about the number of messages and headers; click the Download tab (see Figure 34.47) to tell Outlook Express whether you want only headers or full messages each time you download a newsgroup.

FIG. 34.47

Be careful with this option; downloading extremely active newsgroups can consume more disk space than you think.

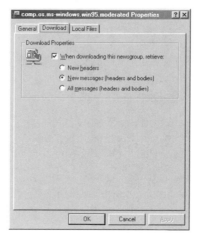

After you've set your preferences for each newsgroup to which you're subscribed, use one of the Download choices from the Tools menu to gather mail and news. Figure 34.48 shows the status screen you'll see if you choose Download All Messages.

FIG. 34.48

Watch this status screen for details as Outlook Express gathers mail and news from all your accounts.

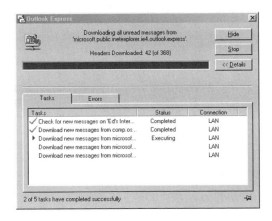

CHAPTER 35

Collaborating and Communicating with NetMeeting

by Paul Sanna

In this chapter

Introducing NetMeeting Works

NetMeeting is an application that allows users to both work and play over the Internet in a collaborative fashion. By using NetMeeting, users can converse (if each has audio equipment), exchange ideas, exchange files, see what each other is working on, and even see what each other is doing (if each person has video equipment installed on his or her computer). The opportunity to collaborate and communicate over the Internet has a number of potential applications. In this first section of the chapter, we look at these potential applications, as well as explain how the various components of NetMeeting work with these applications. Here's what we cover:

- How NetMeeting works
- Audio conferencing
- Video conferencing
- Application sharing and collaboration
- Share clipboard
- Whiteboard
- Chatting

How NetMeeting Works

Understanding how NetMeeting works can help you make sense of the large number of components associated with the application. In this short section, we review a few points that will help you make sense of NetMeeting:

- **Internet/intranet connection:** You need to connect to the Internet or to your organization intranet to use NetMeeting. If you are in a corporate organization, it is likely you have a connection to the Internet as part of your network. Otherwise, you must connect to the Internet using an Internet Service Provider.

- **NetMeeting:** This is the software that allows you to collaborate and communicate as described in the chapter so far. This software is available from Microsoft's web site for free. It is also available with Internet Explorer version 4.0 when you purchase the CD, as well as with Windows 98.

- **ILS server:** For the purposes of NetMeeting users, an ILS server is nothing more than a list of NetMeeting users you can call or who can call you. There are a number of ILS servers, so you need to be looking at the correct server to find a specific person (though SpeedDial can address this problem, which is addressed later).

- **Meeting:** The meeting is the basic element in NetMeeting. If you are speaking with one person or many, you are involved in a meeting. If you are involved in a business discussion with co-workers or you are chatting about popular music and the weather, you are involved in a meeting.

Audio Conferencing

NetMeeting allows users to converse over the Internet. Provided a computer has a sound card with a working microphone that is capable of either full-duplex or half-duplex, the computer can be used to help you converse with someone over the NetMeeting. You can also have audio conferences with groups of persons using NetMeeting. When you are in NetMeeting conversations with more than one person, you can direct your audio to one person or to all persons in the NetMeeting.

In addition, NetMeeting supports Intel MMX technology, which means you will see improved audio performance over systems without MMX.

You can find more information on audio conferencing later in the chapter in the section, "Placing and Receiving a NetMeeting Call."

Video Conferencing

Video conferencing with NetMeeting makes it possible for users to hold face-to-face meetings if they are not in the same location. The only requirement for video conferencing is that users have installed on their computers any video equipment compatible with Windows 98. This video equipment amounts to the following:

- A video capture card
- A camera

NetMeeting provides users with a number of different capabilities and features for video conferencing. These features are covered in more detail, where appropriate, in later sections in this chapter:

- **Switchable audio and video:** When you're in a meeting with more than one person, NetMeeting allows you to easily switch to different, specific persons involved in the meeting. This way, you can direct your conversation, both the audio and video portions, to one person in the meeting rather than to all persons.

- **Receive images even with no video hardware:** NetMeeting allows you to receive video images from other users if you do not have video capture.

- **Dock and move video windows:** NetMeeting makes it easy to manage the numerous windows that are displayed when you are using the application for video conferencing. You can dock both the My Video and Remote Video within the Current Call pane, or allow them to float over the NetMeeting window.

- **Support for H.323:** NetMeeting supports the H.323 standard in audio and video conferencing, though you must first install the H.263 codec.

You can find more information later in this chapter in the section, "Placing and Receiving a NetMeeting Call."

Application Sharing and Collaborating

NetMeeting allows persons to share applications over the Internet. This feature makes it easy for someone to use other applications as part of their NetMeeting conversation or meeting. Examples of the use of application sharing are

- Show updated sales of financial statistics in a spreadsheet during a NetMeeting meeting
- Preview a presentation to a group
- Demonstrate a software application in a sales situation

Application sharing can be configured for one-person use, where only the person sharing the application can modify it; or application sharing can be collaborative, where any users in the meeting also can work with the application. More information on collaborative application work can be found later in the "Sharing Applications" section.

Shared Clipboard

The clipboard is always available to all users in a meeting. This makes for an easy method for sharing data. Any data on a NetMeeting user's clipboard is available and is visible to other persons in the meeting. Naturally, NetMeeting users must be careful that sensitive information is not on the clipboard during a NetMeeting meeting.

Whiteboard Work

NetMeeting's whiteboard application allows users to draw ideas using painting and drawing tools. This application is useful for drawing processes or business flow, rough-sketching graphics ideas, or for any collaborative work that requires illustrations or rudimentary drawings. You can find more information on the NetMeeting later in this chapter in the "Using the Whiteboard to Sketch Your Thoughts" section.

Chatting

NetMeeting provides a simple application for those times when users do not want to or cannot communicate either by audio or video. Chat provides a vehicle for NetMeeting users to simply write each other messages. These messages can be sent to all the people in a meeting or to just one person. You can find more information on the Chat application later in the chapter in the "Exchanging Ideas in the Chat Window" section.

File Transferring

You can send a file to any person involved in a meeting with you. You can select the file to send at the point you want to send, you can continue your meeting with the recipient of the file as it is being sent, and the recipient of the file can specify a default location for all files sent via NetMeeting. You can find more information on transferring files in the "Transferring Files" section later in this chapter.

Running NetMeeting

Once installed, Microsoft NetMeeting is available from the Start menu in Windows 98. To start NetMeeting, select it from the menu. Depending on how you installed it, NetMeeting can appear in one of two places:

- **Installed with Windows 98:** If you installed NetMeeting as part of an Internet Explorer installation with Windows 98, you start NetMeeting by opening the Start menu and choosing Programs, Internet Explorer, Microsoft NetMeeting.

- **Installed from a download:** If you chose not to install NetMeeting with Windows 98 and instead downloaded NetMeeting from the Internet and then installed it, you start NetMeeting by opening the Start menu and choosing Programs, Microsoft NetMeeting.

Running NetMeeting for the First Time

The first time you run NetMeeting, a number of configuration options are set. You can change any of these options at any time from NetMeeting. These options include:

- Default directory server
- Personal information
- Connection speed
- Audio equipment configuration

Each of these options is covered in the next five sections. Follow along in these sections as you respond to the prompts in the dialog boXEs that NetMeeting presents to you.

Figure 35.1 shows the first dialog box that appears the first time you start NetMeeting. Choose Next to continue.

FIG. 35.1
The first dialog box in NetMeeting describes some of the application's capabilities.

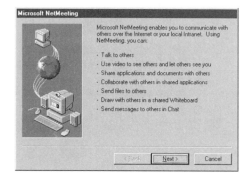

Sharing Applications

To take advantage of NetMeeting's capabilities to share applications and data with other NetMeeting users, you must enable sharing on your computer. The next dialog box to appear in NetMeeting (see Figure 35.2) reminds you to do so. Press Next to continue.

FIG. 35.2
You are reminded to enable sharing when NetMeeting starts.

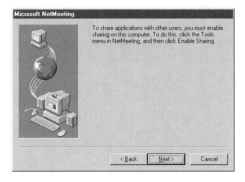

Specifying a Default Directory Server

The dialog box shown in Figure 35.3 is the next one displayed the first time you launch NetMeeting. This dialog box helps you specify that you are automatically logged on to an ILS directory server when NetMeeting starts. You learn more about directory servers later, but just remember that a directory server lists the names of the persons you can communicate with using NetMeeting. To automatically log on, click on the Log on to the Directory Server When NetMeeting Starts option. If you want to manually log on to a directory server when NetMeeting starts, leave the check box clear and choose Next.

FIG. 35.3
You can specify that you are automatically logged on to a specific ILS server as soon as NetMeeting starts.

If you specify that you be logged automatically, you must also choose a directory server. Unless you know of a specific directory server, just accept the default option of Microsoft's ils.Microsoft.com. Choose Next.

Specifying Personal Information

The next dialog box that appears the first time you run NetMeeting prompts you for personal information (see Figure 35.4). At the minimum, you must specify your first and last name and your email address; you will not be able to choose Next until you do so. You can also specify your location and country, as well as a general comment. Enter the information, and then press Next.

Keep in mind that this information is visible to everyone who is logged on to the same directory server as you. With this in mind, the Comment field can be used to let everyone on the server know what kind of meetings you might be interested in. For example, your comment might be `Business use only` or `Call me to test please`.

T I P While you are required to enter this information, Net Meeting has no way of knowing whether the information you have entered is correct. Therefore, if you do not want to reveal your real name or email address, enter fictitious information.

FIG. 35.4

The personal information you provide is visible to all NetMeeting users logged on to the same server as you.

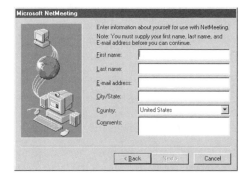

Categorize Yourself

You are next prompted to categorize the conversations you will have and the projects you will collaborate on with NetMeeting (see Figure 35.5). You must choose whether your use of the product will be mainly for personal/family use, business-use, or adult-only in nature. You must choose one of these options before continuing, but you can always change this option at any time from the NetMeeting menu. Choose one of the options, and then choose the Next button.

FIG. 35.5

You must categorize the content of your collaborations and content in NetMeeting.

Defining Connection Speed

You also must specify the speed of your connection the first time you run NetMeeting. If you are using a modem to connect to the Internet, choose the speed, 14000 bps or 28000 bps, that is closest to the speed of your modem. If your modem is faster than 28000 bps, select that option. If you use either a local or wide area network, or an ISDN connection, to work on the Internet, then select either of those two options from the dialog box. When you have made your selection, choose the Next button.

Configuring Audio with the Audio Tuning Wizard

As you know, NetMeeting can exchange audio information between users. Because of this, the initial configuration process must also check for the availability and status of any audio equipment installed on your computer. The set of audio configuration checks and tests are collectively known as the Audio Tuning Wizard. Choose Next to continue.

The first test the Audio Tuning Wizard performs is to see if the audio equipment installed on your computer works, and then to set the volume. In the next dialog box that appears, click on the Test button. If you hear a sound, click and drag the needle on the Volume bar to a comfortable setting, and then choose Next. This establishes the default volume level for NetMeeting.

The next test of your computer's audio equipment is to check the microphone. The dialog box shown in Figure 35.6 asks you to read a sentence. Read the sentence in your normal speaking voice, or at least the voice you will use when you are speaking over NetMeeting. As you read the sentence, the level of your voice is monitored, and the recording level for your computer is set. This recording level matches the loudness of your voice with the capabilities of the audio equipment installed on your computer, so your voice is always transmitted with strong, clear quality. Choose the Next button to continue, and then choose the Finish button.

FIG. 35.6

You read a sentence in order to test your computer's microphone.

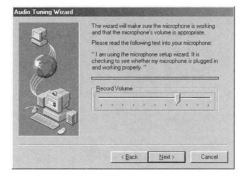

After the settings for your microphone are established, the Wizard's final dialog box appears. Choose Next, and the Audio Tuning Wizard closes.

> **N O T E**   You can always restart the Audio Tuning Wizard at any time from NetMeeting. To do so, choose Tools, Options from the menu, and then choose the Audio tab. Next, click on the Audio Tuning Wizard button. ▪

This marks the end of the configuration process. With NetMeeting now up and running, the next section of the chapter introduces you to the NetMeeting window and its components.

Navigating and Displaying Information in NetMeeting

NetMeeting provides you with a large amount of information at one time. Understanding what information is presented to you and knowing how to see other information is important to taking full advantage of NetMeeting. For example, you can switch between views of the people logged on to different ILS servers, and you can switch to a list showing people interested in chatting about the same content as you. In this section, you learn how to manipulate NetMeeting's user interface in order to navigate to the places you get to and see the things you need to see.

Understanding What You See in NetMeeting

The first step in helping you understand how to navigate and display information in NetMeeting is to identify what you see in NetMeeting. Figure 35.7 points out the major components of NetMeeting. Keep in mind that the Current Call, SpeedDial, and History views are not shown in the figure; pictures of the views are included later in the chapter.

FIG. 35.7
The NetMeeting window includes a number of components.

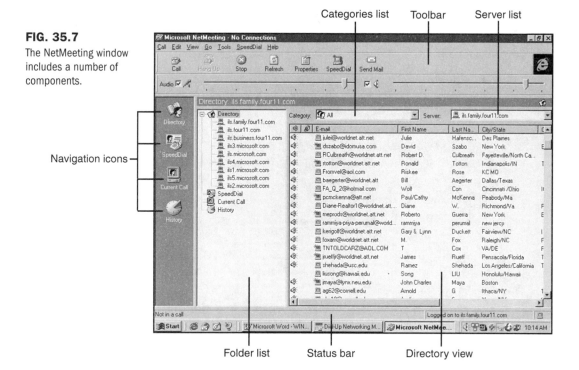

The following list explains the use of the major NetMeeting components.

- **Toolbar:** Like any other toolbar, the NetMeeting toolbar gives you quick access to the most useful functions. Unlike most other toolbars, however, the NetMeeting toolbar cannot be customized.

- **Folder list:** The Folder list provides a tree view of the NetMeeting components. Most users will choose either the Folder List or the Navigation icons as the primary tool for navigating in NetMeeting

- **Navigation icons:** The Navigation icons are nothing but a graphical presentation of the NetMeeting components.

- **Status bar:** Provides you with status information. Normally, the position to the left of the screen provides you status about your current call if you are in one. The Status area to the right usually provides you information about your connection to the current ILS server.

- **Server list:** The Server list shows all of the ILS servers visible to your Internet connection.

- **Categories list:** The Categories list provides groupings of the users logged onto the server. You can use the list to quickly select a set of users, such as business users, or only those with a camera.

Completing Common Tasks

Now that you have an understanding of the objects you see in NetMeeting, we will look at how to display, hide, and navigate in NetMeeting. The following list shows you how to complete common tasks:

- **To hide or display the toolbar, Folder list, Navigation icons, or status bar**, right-click anywhere on the screen and make the appropriate choice from the menu that appears.

- **To change the arrangement of columns in either the SpeedDial, Directory, or Current Call view**, click on the name of the column you want to move, drag it to the location where you want the column to appear, and drop.

- **To sort the list by any of the columns**, click on the column name. Click a second type on the column to reverse the sort order.

- **To see information about any person in any list**, right-click on the entry in the list and then choose Properties from the menu that appears.

- **To allow the video windows to float over the NetMeeting window**, drag the Remote Video and My Video window (only available if you have video equipment) to the left side of the screen.

- **To anchor the video windows to the right side of the NetMeeting window**, drag the Remote Video and My Video window (only available if you have video equipment) to the right side of the screen.

Placing and Receiving a NetMeeting Call

In this section, we examine the most basic of NetMeeting functionality: the capability to receive and send calls, and to converse by using audio or by writing messages to and from other NetMeeting communicators. Keep in mind as you review the information in this section that the operation of the application is much the same regardless of your computer's capabilities. You needn't do anything special if you do not have video equipment or if your audio equipment is not working properly. NetMeeting automatically manages the application and interface to match the capabilities of your computer and those who you are communicating with.

Logging On to a Server

You must be logged on to a server in order for persons to see your name in a directory list and to call you. By default, when NetMeeting starts, you are connected to the server specified in the Options dialog box on the Calling tab. This is the same server you specified when you ran NetMeeting for the first time, provided you specified that you be connected automatically to a server when NetMeeting begins. You can tell if you are logged on to a server by looking at the right pane of the status bar. A message appears there indicating to what server you are logged on.

If you are not logged onto a server, or if you want to log on to a server different from the one you are currently logged on to, follow these steps:

1. If you are logged on to a server already, choose Call, Log Off from *your server* from the menu.
2. Choose Tools, Options from the menu, and then choose the Calling tab.
3. Select the server you want to log on to from the list, and then choose OK.
4. A message appears informing you that you are not logged on to a server. Choose OK to be logged on.

Finding Someone to Call

Finding someone to call might not be as easy in NetMeeting as it is using the telephone or emailing someone. Unless the person you want to call is in your SpeedDial list, you must locate the person on one of the ILS servers you have access to with your Internet connection. Here are some methods for locating a particular person:

- **To see all of the users logged on to a particular server**, choose the server from the Server list. This list is available only in the Directory view.
- **To see only a set of users logged on to a server**, choose the server from the server list, and then choose the category of users you want to see from the Categories drop-down list.
- **To see the most up-to-date directory list**, choose Refresh from the toolbar.
- **To sort the list of persons logged onto a server**, click on the column of the information you want to sort by.

Part
VI

Ch

35

■ **To see the type of equipment other users have**, from the directory view, study the columns with the speaker and camera as headers. A speaker in the speaker column for any user indicates they have audio capability. A camera in the camera column indicates the user has video capability.

Placing a Call

Placing a call to a user is one of the most simple tasks in NetMeeting. As you learned in the preceding section, the tougher task in NetMeeting is locating a person to call. When you have located a person to call, calling them is simply a matter of clicking on their entry in the list where you found them (SpeedDial or directory) and then choosing Call from the toolbar. You also can right-click on the person's entry in the list and then choose Call from the menu that appears.

TIP If you know the IP of the computer you want to call, you can avoid having to locate that person's name on a list. To call a person by manually specifying their name, choose Call, New Call from the menu, enter the IP address, and then choose OK.

When you call a person, the left pane of the status bar indicates that the ILS is trying to locate the computer you are trying to call (see Figure 35.8). Once the ILS server has connected to the computer, the message changes to indicate that the server is waiting for a response from the user.

FIG. 35.8
The status bar tells you that the server is trying to locate the computer your are calling.

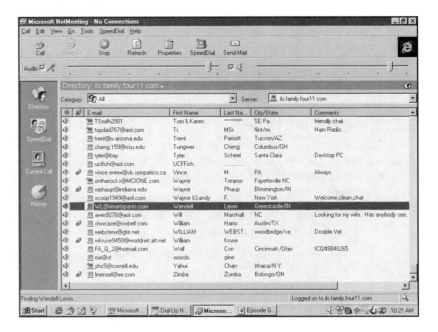

At this point, the person you are calling sees a message indicating that you are calling. The person can either accept your call or ignore it. If the person accepts your call, your display switches to the Current Call view. If the person ignores your call, a message appears indicating they have ignored your call.

Answering a Call

You are notified in two ways when a person is trying to contact you:

- You hear the sound of a phone ringing.
- A message appears on the status bar informing you of an incoming call (see Figure 35.9).

FIG. 35.9
You are notified with sound and a message when you have an incoming call.

Naturally, however, there are a number of requirements for you to receive a call with NetMeeting:

1. NetMeeting must be running.
2. You must be connected to the Internet.
3. To hear the phone sound, your audio equipment, if you have it, must be working properly, and the volume must be set at a level at which you can hear the sound.

To answer a call, choose the Accept button for the person calling. At that point, the person who called you is joined to your meeting (see Figure 35.10). If you do not want the person to join your meeting, choose the Ignore button. A message appears on that person's computer indicating that you have rejected their call.

One last note about answering a call. Your name automatically appears in the directory list of the directory you are logged on to. This means that anyone can call you. There are a few options to keep people from bothering you:

- Use the comment field of your personal information to say Friends only, or something similar.
- Choose Call, Do Not Disturb from the menu. This restricts all persons from calling you.
- Choose Tools, Options from the menu, and then select the Calling tab. Next, select the option to keep your name from appearing on the directory list.

Ending a Call

When you no longer want to participate in a NetMeeting meeting, simply choose Call, Hang Up from the menu, or choose Hang Up from to the toolbar.

Part
VI

Ch
35

FIG. 35.10

The name of the person whose call you accept is added to the list in the Current Call pane.

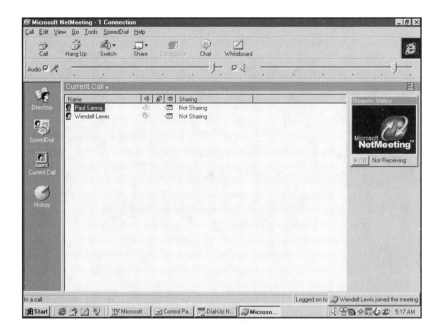

Hosting a Meeting

There might be occasions when you want to meet at a predetermined time with one or more NetMeeting users. This might be to have a casual conversation, or to collaborate on work projects. In this case, you will want to host a NetMeeting meeting. As the host of a NetMeeting meeting, you can define which people can participate in the meeting by accepting or ignoring calls into the meeting.

To host a meeting with NetMeeting, from the menu, choose Call, Host a Meeting. A message appears informing you that you are starting a meeting, and after you choose OK at the message, the Current Call pane appears. After you have started a meeting, an icon appears beside your name in the directory list indicating to anyone viewing the list that you are in a meeting (see Figure 35.11).

Using SpeedDial

SpeedDial is a feature in NetMeeting that helps you keep track of people who you communicate and collaborate with often. The SpeedDial list shows the people of your choosing and whether each is logged on or not. Seeing the list of the usual people who collaborate and communicate in one place makes it easy to check on them or to connect them without having to browse through each of the ILS servers to find them.

To display the SpeedDial list, choose View, Speed Dial from the menu, or choose SpeedDial from either the Folder list, Navigation bar, or the toolbar (see Figure 35.12).

FIG. 35.11
An icon appears beside the name of any person involved in a meeting.

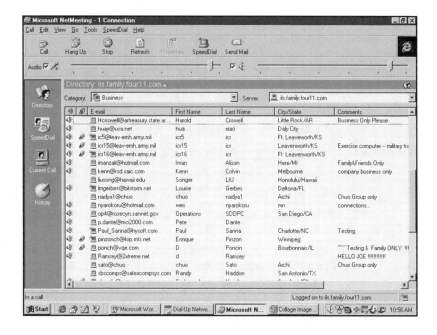

FIG. 35.12
The SpeedDial list shows people you can call without identifying their server first.

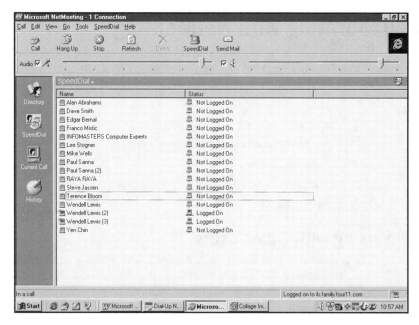

After the SpeedDial list is displayed, you can call anyone on the list by either double-clicking on their name or by right-clicking on their name and choosing Call from the menu that appears.

NetMeeting provides you with a few options to manage the SpeedDial list. Many of the SpeedDial options can be configured from the Calling tab on the Options dialog box. To display the dialog box, choose Tools, Options from the menu, and then choose the Calling tab. The following list shows some of the common SpeedDial list management tasks:

- Specify if and when a person who has called you or people you have called are added to the SpeedDial list.
- Automatically refresh the SpeedDial list as soon as NetMeeting starts.
- Specify the maximum number of entries that can appear on the SpeedDial list.

In addition to the options presented in the dialog box, you can manage the list with some choices made directly from the SpeedDial pane:

- **To delete a SpeedDial entry,** right-click on the name of the person to be deleted and then choose Delete from the menu that appears.
- **To refresh the SpeedDial list manually,** right-click anywhere in the SpeedDial list and then choose Refresh SpeedDial from the menu that appears.
- **To add a directory entry to SpeedDial,** from any Directory list, right-click on the entry for the person you want to add to the SpeedDial list and then choose Add SpeedDial to the menu.

Collaborating with NetMeeting

When you have connected with one or more users with NetMeeting, either by answering a call or by someone answering your call, it is time to begin collaborating and communicating. In this section, you learn how to extend NetMeeting through collaboration. Specifically, this section covers:

- Conversing with one or more users
- Using chat to exchange written information
- Sharing applications
- Using the whiteboard
- Transferring files

Conversing with Other Users

The most basic way to use the advantages of NetMeeting is to hold a conversation with one or more of the people in the same meeting as you. If you and the person you want to communicate with both have working audio equipment and/or video equipment, you can exchange audio and video signals.

Audio Conversations   If both computers have working audio equipment, you should be able to hear the other person you are communicating with speak. The volume and audio indicators flash when they pick up a signal. You can adjust any of the levels by clicking on and then dragging either the audio or volume needles. You can also specify that these settings are handled automatically from the Audio tab of the Options dialog box. You display the dialog box by choosing Tools, Options from the menu.

If you are in a meeting with more than one person, you can direct your conversation to one specific person in the meeting. To do so, choose Switch from the toolbar and then choose the person you want to converse with (see Figure 35.13).

FIG. 35.13

You can direct the audio of your meeting to one person.

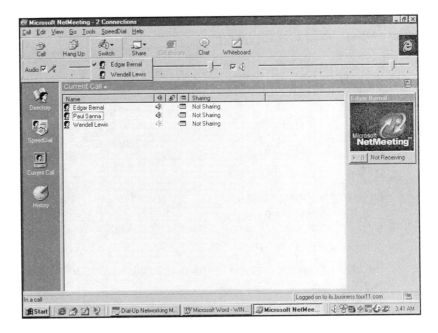

Video Conversations   Video conversations are dependent on the video capabilities of at least one of the persons in a meeting. If at least one person has a video capture card and a camera attached to his or her computer, that person can send a video signal from their computer, and that signal can be received by other members of the meeting. A user doesn't need to have the video capture card and camera to receive the video signal. Having this equipment, however, is a requirement for sending a video signal. As such, you should automatically receive a video signal when you hold a meeting with a person with capable equipment.

To start the video feed if you are not receiving it, press the Play button at the bottom of the Remote Video button. This starts the video feed from any person who has directed the feed to you. To stop receiving video, click again on the button at the bottom of Remote Video.

If your computer has capable video equipment, you will have an additional window on the screen, the My Video window. Click the button at the bottom of the My Video window to see a preview of how your video will appear to others.

To start sending video, choose Tools, Video, Send from the menu.

Part
VI

Ch
35

As with the audio portion of a meeting, you can direct the video portion of the meeting to one person in the meeting. To do so, choose Tools, Switch Audio and Video from the menu, and then choose the person you want to receive the signal. To stop sending video to a particular person, repeat this step.

Configuring Video   A number of options are available to help you configure the video capabilities of your system with NetMeeting. For example, you can specify the size of the video image you send. You can also choose to receive video faster and sacrifice quality, or specify the opposite. These choices, and others, are available from the Video tab of the Options dialog box, which you display by choosing Tools, Options from the menu.

Exchanging Ideas in the Chat Window

If you do want to communicate with audio, video, or by sharing applications or the whiteboard, or if your computer does not have the capabilities to do so, you can always communicate with Chat. The Chat application allows you to communicate with other NetMeeting users simply by typing messages. You have available standard editing capabilities from the Edit menu, and you can even save the text of your message by using standard File Save and File Save As commands.

You can direct messages to a specific person in Chat, or to all persons in Chat. The caption of the Chat windows always shows you how many people are involved in a Chat conversation. If you are in a conversation and you open the Chat window, the Chat application on the person's computer you are conversing with also opens.

To open Chat, choose Tools, Chat from the menu, or click on the Chat button on the toolbar. Figure 35.18 shows the Chat window.

To enter a Chat message, type your message in the Message box and then press the large Send button to the right of the Message box. You have the option in Chat to send your message to everyone in the meeting. To send a private message to one person, choose the person from the Send To: drop-down list before sending the message.

Figure 35.14 shows how the Chat window might appear during a conversation.

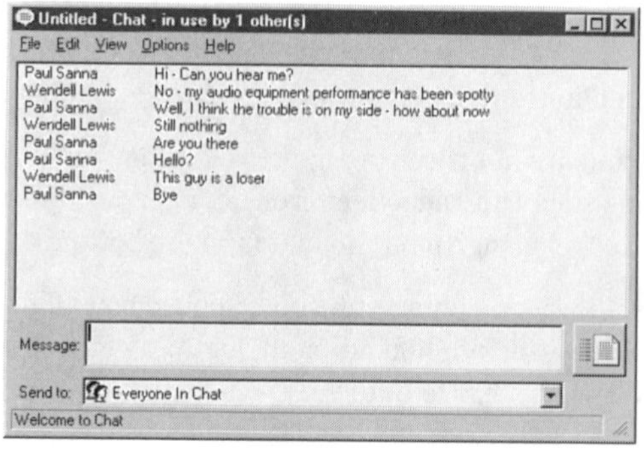

FIG. 35.14

Chat conversations many times are used to help debug audio and video problems.

Configuring Chat   You can configure Chat to behave how you like. These choices are found on the various Chat menus. Here are some ways you might customize chat:

- To change the font used in the Chat window, choose Options, Font from the window, make selections from the dialog box, and then choose OK.
- To change how messages are formatted in the Chat window, choose Options, Chat Format from the menu. You can choose what type of information is displayed, as well as how long messages are formatted. Make selections and then choose OK.
- To hide or display the status bar, choose View, Status Bar from the menu.

Sharing Applications

As discussed in the "How NetMeeting Works" section of this chapter, you can integrate applications into your NetMeeting collaborative efforts. This means you can use external applications as part of your collaborative efforts with NetMeeting. By default, only the person sharing the application can use it, but you can enable users you are conversing with to also work with the application.

Showing Your Work to Other Users   The most basic use of application sharing is showing users in your meeting an application on your computer. The only requirement for doing so, naturally, is that you have the application installed on your computer.

To show your work or application to others, follow these steps:

1. Start the application you want to share and load any document you want to share with others.
2. Next, from the NetMeeting window and the Current Call view, choose Share from the toolbar or choose Tools, Share Application from the menu. Notice that the list of all running applications on your computer is displayed (see Figure 35.15).

N O T E   If the Sharing button is dimmed on the toolbar, you probably have not enabled sharing on your computer. To do so, choose Tools, Enable Sharing. NetMeeting then installs files onto your system, and you probably will be asked to reboot your computer.

3. Select the application you want to share. At this point, an additional item appears on the taskbar of the other persons in your meeting. The item appears with a hand beneath a window icon. When people click on that item, their screen is hidden by a pattern. You must now select from the task bar the application you want to share with the other users on your computer in order for them to see it (see Figure 35.16). The other users will not be able to use the application, and their cursor will be inoperable.

   Keep in mind that they have the capability to switch to any other running application on their computer. When they switch to your shared application, however, they see it only if you are viewing it, too.

Part
VI

Ch
35

FIG. 35.15

You can share any application running on your computer.

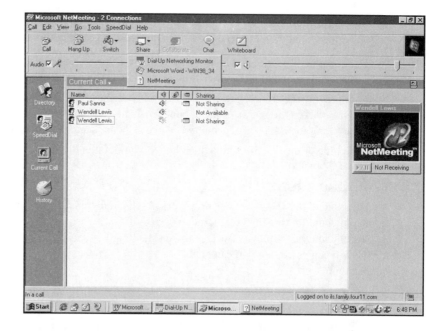

FIG. 35.16

When you display the application on your computer, people in your meeting see it, too.

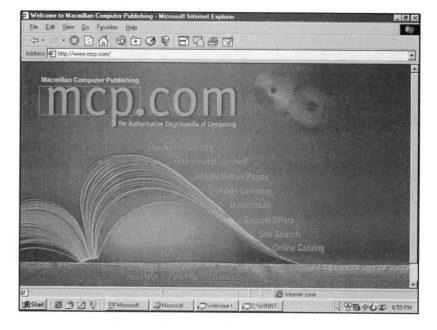

Here are two more important points related to sharing applications:

- To stop sharing an application, you can either shut down the application on your computer, or choose Share from the toolbar in NetMeeting and then reselect the application you are sharing. The check mark beside the application you were sharing will clear, indicating the application is no longer shared.

- You can share more than one application at one time. To share another application, choose Share from the NetMeeting toolbar, and then select the next application you want to share. Remember, people in your meting see only the application you select on your computer. So you have to control how the users switch between applications.

Giving Users Access to the Application   You can also give users control access to an application you have shared. This allows one person at one time to control an application on your computer. Provide this access carefully, as you, in effect, are giving a remote user control over one aspect of your computer.

To allow users control over a shared application, follow these steps:

1. Start by following the steps in the previous section, "Showing Your Work to Other Users."

2. Click on the person you want to give access to the application, and then choose Tools, Start Collaborating from the NetMeeting menu, or choose Collaborate from the toolbar.

3. Next, via audio or chat, let the person who you have given access to the application know you have done so. This user must now choose Collaborate from the toolbar.

4. At this point, the user to whom you have given access to the application controls the application. They have full cursor control, and the cursor on your computer changes to a hand with the initials of the person controlling the application.

5. To take control back from the user, press the Esc key from either the application being controlled or NetMeeting.

   For the user of the application to return control, the user chooses Collaborate again from the toolbar, or Tools, Stop Collaborating from the menu.

Using the Whiteboard to Sketch Your Thoughts

NetMeeting includes a whiteboard application. The whiteboard application is used to share information with persons you are collaborating with. By simulating the whiteboard or flipchart you would find in most corporate conference rooms, you can use NetMeeting's whiteboard to sketch out rough ideas, draw illustrations, or create outlines, lists, or plans. You can integrate clipboard data, as well as create multi-page whiteboard presentations.

Here is how whiteboard works:

- When one person in the meeting starts whiteboard, the application is launched on the computers of all other persons in the meeting.

- Any changes made to the whiteboard project are immediately displayed on the whiteboards of all other people in the meeting.

Part

VI

Ch

35

■ Whiteboard works much like any paint or drawing program. You click on different shapes, and then drag and drop on the screen to draw them.

■ A whiteboard project can be saved as a whiteboard file. To do so, choose File, Save As from the menu, give the project a name, and then choose OK.

■ Any user can lock the project so no other people in the meeting can change the drawing. To do so, the user must either click on the Lock button on the toolbar to the left of the whiteboard work area or choose Tools, Lock Contents from the menu.

Transferring Files

NetMeeting makes it easy to transfer files to people you are communicating and collaborating with. This makes it easy to exchange information as you hold a meeting with someone. Otherwise, you need to leave NetMeeting in order to start your email program.

To send a file, follow these steps:

1. From the Current Call pane, click on the name of the person to whom you want to send a file.

2. From the menu, choose Tool, File Transfer, Send File, or right-click on the recipient's name and choose Send File from the menu that appears. The Select a File to Send dialog box appears.

3. Select the file to send and then choose OK. The status bar at the bottom of the NetMeeting window is updated to show you the progress of the transfer.

   While the file is being received at the recipient's computer, the dialog box shown in Figure 35.17 appears.

   When the transfer is complete, a message appears on the sender's machine.

FIG. 35.17
A message appears on the recipient's computer as a file is being transferred.

Specifying Where Transferred Files Are Stored   You can define a default location where files you received via NetMeeting are stored. To do so, choose Tools, Options from the menu. From the General tab, choose the Change Folder button, and then select a folder and choose OK. From the Options dialog box, you can also view the contents of the directory you selected by choosing the View Files button. ●

CHAPTER 36

Creating Web Pages with FrontPage Express

by Paul Sanna

In this chapter

Introducing FrontPage Express

FrontPage Express is a near-WYSIWYG HTML page editor that enables you to build pages to be viewed in a web browser over either the Internet or local corporate intranets. First, take a quick look at what "HTML" and "near-WYSIWYG" mean.

WYSIWYG is an acronym for "What You See is What You Get." In the case of web pages, the workspace of a true WYSIWYG web page editor shows you exactly what you will see in a browser. FrontPage Express is actually a "near-WYSIWYG" web page editor because its display of a page is not always *exactly* the same as a browser's. That said, its display is very, very close to what will show up in a browser window. (In fact, there are no truly and completely WYSIWYG web page editors, partly because different browsers have slightly different ways of displaying certain page elements. This is because HTML is simply a markup language and does not specify the actual appearance of tags within a browser.)

HTML stands for Hypertext Markup Language. In HTML, special character codes are inserted into a text file to generate particular effects, such as bold or the appearance of a graphic, a hyperlink, or a table. When a browser opens a page, the browser reads and then translates the HTML into the text and images you see onscreen. You will see a few examples of HTML in this chapter, but you will not have to write any HTML. This is because FrontPage Express develops the HTML for you. As you lay out your pages in FrontPage Express, the HTML code is automatically written behind the scenes. When you save your work, FrontPage Express saves the HTML codes required to present the page you have developed.

Understanding Web Page Design

Web authoring is a young art, but already there is some agreement about its basic principles. The following guidelines list the fundamentals of text layout and hyperlink design.

- Use lots of white space on a text-heavy page.
- Avoid excessively long pages that require endless scrolling.
- Write clearly and pay close attention to spelling and grammar. Nothing undermines a page's authority as much as confusing language and bad spelling. Typos suggest that the author couldn't be bothered with checking the work—and what does that say about the other information that's offered?
- Because people usually like to take a look at the home page (it helps them get oriented), it's a good idea to include a go-to-home-page control on all your pages. This is especially true if you have a large or complex site or one whose organization isn't obvious when a person enters it from some point other than the home page.
- Make sure the links on the page accurately suggest what the viewer will find at their destinations, and verify that the links behave as advertised when the viewer does use them.
- Keep your navigation controls uniform in appearance; for example, a go-to-home-page button should look the same everywhere on your site.

■ Before making pages available to the viewing public, test them for behavior and appearance using the default settings of Netscape 3.0, Netscape 4.0 (also known as Communicator), Microsoft Internet Explorer 3.0, and Microsoft Internet Explorer 4.0. These are now the dominant browsers.

Launching FrontPage Express

You can launch FrontPage Express either from the Start menu or from the Internet Explorer browser. When you launch Front Page Express from the browser, the page you were viewing is loaded directly into FrontPage Express. With this technique, FrontPage Express enables you to edit any pages you see on the World Wide Web, right there on your desktop. Naturally, you won't be able to change the web pages you're viewing (unless you are working on a web to which you have rights), but this gives you a great way to see first-hand how real-life web pages are built. Furthermore, you can keep your own copy of the web page you're viewing by saving it as an HTML file on your own PC, and then you can examine it later at leisure. You can, of course, edit that copy you have of the page on your own machine.

In addition, if you are working on an existing web, say for your company or organization, this method makes it easy to select the page you want to work on without having to access the server where the pages are stored.

Here are the two methods you can use to launch FrontPage Express:

■ To launch FrontPage Express from the Start menu, open the Start menu, choose Programs, Internet Explorer, and then FrontPage Express. A new blank web page is displayed (see Figure 36.1).

■ To launch FrontPage Express from Internet Explorer, choose Edit, Page from the menu, or click the Edit button on the Standard toolbar. FrontPage Express opens, displaying the page you were viewing in the browser (see Figure 36.1).

Opening Existing Pages

You can open existing pages that are stored locally or on an existing web. Follow these steps to open a page.

1. Choose File, Open from the menu.

2. If you are opening a page that has not yet been published to a web or if it is stored locally, choose the From File option. Enter the name of the file in the text box. Use the Browse button if you need help locating the file and/or entering its name and location. Click OK.

   or

   If you are opening a page that already has been published to a web, choose the From Location option. Then enter the URL and the name of the page in the edit box and click OK.

FIG. 36.1
Launching FrontPage Express creates a new blank page in the workspace.

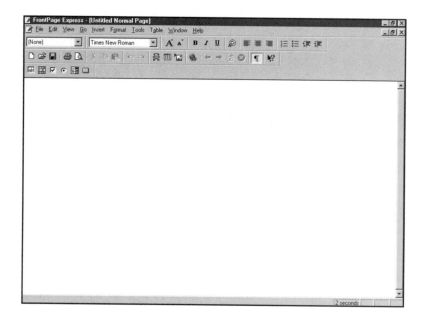

Hiding and Displaying Toolbars

FrontPage Express includes three toolbars. Like toolbars in other applications, the toolbars in FrontPage Express show buttons for common tasks, such as changing text size, indenting, inserting an image, and more. Unlike in other applications, however, you cannot modify the buttons on any of the toolbars.

Here is a description of each of the toolbars:

- *Standard.* The Standard toolbar provides buttons like those you see on toolbars in other applications, such as New, Open, and Save. In addition, it offers the Insert WebBot, Insert Table, and Image buttons.

- *Format.* The Format toolbar gives you access to most of the choices that appear on the Format menu, such as the style, font, and color selections. You will use the Format toolbar when you are formatting text you have entered onto your page.

- *Forms.* You will use the Forms toolbar when you are creating a web page that contains standard Windows controls, such as a push button or drop-down list. The Forms toolbar provides buttons with which you can add these controls to the page.

You can hide or display any of the toolbars. To display or hide a toolbar, just choose <u>V</u>iew from the menu bar and select the appropriate toolbar from the menu (see Figure 36.2). If a check appears beside the toolbar name, the toolbar is already displayed. If a check already appears beside a toolbar name and you click the name, the toolbar becomes hidden.

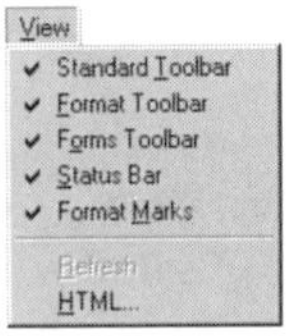

FIG. 36.2

Use the View menu to specify the toolbars you want displayed.

You can also drag the toolbars to different locations in the toolbar region. For example, drag the Forms toolbar up to the same line as the Format toolbar. Furthermore, you can drag the toolbars down into the workspace, where they will become floating toolbars.

 T I P Using the View menu, you can control whether or not the status bar is displayed along the bottom of the workspace; you can also turn on or off format marks, which show you symbols for page elements (such as line breaks) and inserted HTML code.

Saving Your Work

At some point, you will want to save the work you have completed on your web page. You have two choices for saving web pages. You can save your work to a file or to an existing web. How you originally opened the page and whether you have started a web will determine which choice you make. Here are your options:

■ *If your web has not yet been started,* save your page to a file (instructions follow). You will publish your pages to a web later.

■ *If your web has been started and you are adding a new page,* save your page to the web and be sure you provide the hyperlinks to the page. To do so, choose File, Save As, choose Location, and then supply the URL and the name of the file.

N O T E Adding a new page to an existing web only works if the server supporting the web has the Microsoft FrontPage extensions installed on it. ■

■ *If you are editing a page on your web,* just choose File, Save, and FrontPage Express updates the web with your changes.

■ *If you are editing a page from a web you don't control,* you probably will not be able to save to someone else's web. Instead, save the page to a file or save it to your own web.

To save a page you are working on to a file, follow these steps:

1. Choose File, Save As.

2. From the Save As dialog box, choose As File.

3. Select a folder from the Save As File dialog box, enter a name for the file, and then click Save.

Creating Web Pages Instantly

Almost all the information presented in this chapter helps you build web pages using FrontPage Express' long list of features. Luckily, FrontPage Express provides templates and wizards that remove much of the work that is normally involved with developing a page, such as positioning and formatting text. The list of templates and wizards appears when you choose the File, New command (see Figure 36.3).

FIG. 36.3

You see the list of available templates and page wizards when you choose File, New.

The following sections explain how to use the templates and wizards.

Using the Normal Page Template

If you select this option and click OK, FrontPage Express creates a new blank page in the editor workspace. It is exactly the same as if you had clicked the New Page icon on the Standard toolbar.

Using the Personal Home Page Wizard

Many Internet service providers (ISPs) and online services host web pages and even web sites for their subscribers—sometimes at no additional cost. Many universities and colleges also provide this service to their students. This means that even persons without access to the hardware required to run a web server can establish a presence on the web. Many times, this presence is nothing more than a personal home page with a number of links that provides an update on the life and activities of the person who posted the page.

The only requirement for this type of presence is for you to supply the content. FrontPage Express makes it easy to develop these types of pages with the Personal Home Page Wizard. This wizard walks you through the steps required to create a personal page. When you have answered all the wizard's questions, it creates an attractive page that you can then submit to the service that is hosting your web page. Your only work is to supply the details into the preformatted sections, which are created based on your responses to the wizard.

Here is the type of information you might supply for the Personal Home Page Wizard:

- Your employment
- Projects you're working on
- Your favorite web sites
- Biographical information
- Your interests
- Information on how to contact you
- A form to send information or comments to you

To use the Personal Home Page Wizard, follow these steps:

1. Choose the File, New command. The New Page dialog box appears.
2. Select Personal Home Page Wizard from the Template or Wizard list box, and then click OK. The Personal Home Page Wizard dialog box appears (see Figure 36.4).

FIG. 36.4

The Personal Home Page Wizard helps you set up a personal home page, using pre-established categories of information.

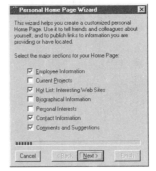

3. From the Personal Home Page Wizard dialog box, select the type of content you would like to include on your home page. Keep in mind that the wizard will create just one page, not a web of linked pages. This means that the more items you select from the Personal Home Page Wizard, the longer your home page will be. After making your selections, choose Next.
4. In the next dialog box, click in the Page URL text box and specify the filename of the page, as it will be stored on the web. In the Page Title text box, enter the title of the page as it will appear in the browser (see Figure 36.5). FrontPage Express provides a default filename and page title, but you should replace them with meaningful ones of your own.

FIG. 36.5

In this dialog box, you get the chance to specify a filename and page title for your home page.

5. Next, the wizard presents a series of dialog boxes in which you supply personal information that the wizard will use to build your page. What type of information it asks for depends on the choices you made in step 3. For example, if you chose to include biographical information, you would be prompted to select a format for the biographical section of the home page; in this case, you could choose from an Academic, Professional, or Personal format (see Figure 36.6). When you finish with one dialog box, choose Next to move to the next one or choose Back to change information you've already provided.

FIG. 36.6

The wizard gives you a choice of formats for your home page's biographical section.

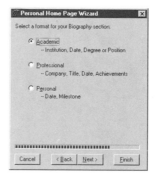

6. When the wizard has collected all the information it needs to build your page, it displays a dialog box similar to the one shown in Figure 36.7. This dialog box includes a list box that shows each of the major sections you're creating with the Personal Home Page Wizard. This is your opportunity to choose the order in which the sections appear on the page. Choose a section, and then click either the Up or Down button to specify the order of the sections. When you're done, choose Next.

7. Choose Finish from the final dialog box, and the almost-completed page appears in a window in FrontPage Express. Review the page, and replace any "instructions" that appear with the information required, as shown in Figure 36.8.

FIG. 36.7

You can choose the order of the sections that appear on your personal home page.

FIG. 36.8

When the wizard finishes building your page, you supply some of the detailed information yourself.

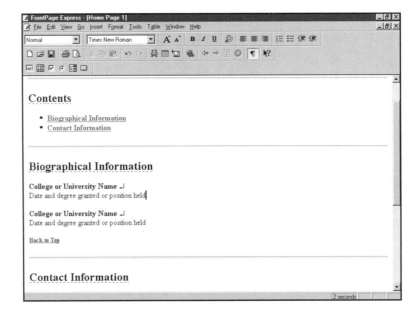

Using the Form Page Wizard

The Form Page Wizard creates a web page that collects different types of information from the person viewing the page in a browser. Examples of form pages you might create include an order form (if you were selling something over the Internet) or a list of questions (if you were conducting a survey).

Form pages can contain many of the controls used today in Windows applications (see Figure 36.9). Controls are the onscreen elements—list boxes, buttons, check boxes, and more—used in Windows and in Windows application to operate the system. The Form Page Wizard automatically places on the page whichever controls are necessary to collect the information you require from the user.

FIG. 36.9
Web pages can use many of the controls used in non-web applications.

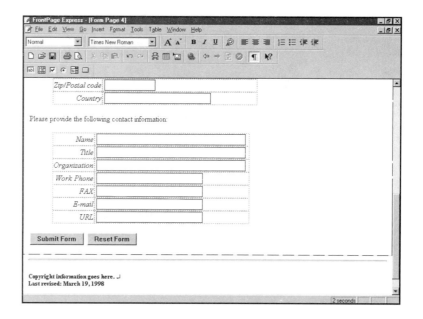

You should understand one important point about the Form Page Wizard: Your work is not close to being done when the wizard finishes creating your page. The wizard builds many of the controls your page requires based on your responses. However, most of the logic required to put your page to work (such as validating that a zip code supplied does not contain non-numeric values or calculating the total amount of an order) must be completed without the help of the wizard. This warning is not meant to discourage you from using the wizard, though, only to inform you that the wizard alone will not build a fully functioning form.

The following steps get you started with the Form Page Wizard.

1. Choose the File, New command. The New Page dialog box appears.

2. Select Form Page Wizard from the Template or Wizard list box, and then choose OK. The Form Page Wizard dialog box appears. Choose Next to continue.

3. In the Page URL text box, specify the filename of the page as it will be stored on the web. In the Page Title text box, enter the name of the page as it will appear in the browser. Choose Next to go to the Add/Modify/Remove dialog box (see Figure 36.10).

4. To add a question to the form, choose Add. A list of possible types of information your form can collect appears (see Figure 36.11).

N O T E   If the page you specified in step 3 already exists, the wizard will scan that page for any content it believes to be form-related. If it finds questions on the form, it displays them in the list shown in the dialog box in Figure 36.11. This enables you to open an existing form page and modify it, or to continue working on a page you've already started. ■

FIG. 36.10
Use the Form Page Wizard dialog box to set up the questions for your form. This one shows contact and ordering information.

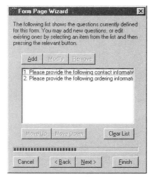

FIG. 36.11
The Form Page Wizard can collect many types of information.

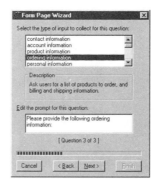

5. Scroll through the list presented and select the first of the types of information you want to collect on your form. Notice that when you select a particular type from the list, a note about the type appears in the Description frame beneath the list. Also notice that the prompt for the information, which will appear to the person viewing your page, appears in the edit box at the bottom of the dialog box. If you like, you can customize the prompt by editing the text in the box. When you have selected the information type you want to collect and perhaps edited the prompt, choose the Next button.

6. Depending on the type of information you selected, you might be presented with another dialog box requesting more detailed information about your prompt (see Figure 36.12). For example, if you specified "contact information" in step 5, the wizard will ask you if your form should request such information from the user as name, title, organization, address, and phone. Answer the prompts in the dialog box and choose Next.

7. The dialog box described in step 5 appears again. Choose the next type of information your form will request, and then follow the instructions in step 6. Repeat steps 5 and 6 until all the information your form will request is represented in the list box. When the list of prompts is complete, choose Next.

8. In the next dialog box, you set the presentation style for the form (see Figure 36.13). Specify the styles you want, and then click Next.

FIG. 36.12

You can choose several data items related to contacts in this section of the Form Page Wizard.

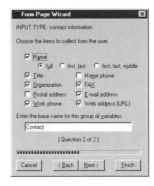

FIG. 36.13

You can customize the form's presentation with the option buttons in this dialog box.

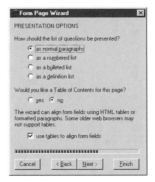

9. In the next dialog box, you specify how FrontPage Express should deal with the information the user provides. Choose from these options:

   Save Results to a Web Page creates an HTML file.

   Save Results to a Text File creates an ASCII text file.

   Use Custom CGI Script specifies that a CGI script (which you have to write) handles the user's input. You specify the name of the output file in the text box labeled Enter the Base Name of the Results File. "Base name" simply means that this is the filename to which the appropriate extension—HTM, TXT, or CGI—will be added (see Figure 36.14).

   Choose Next.

10. In the final dialog box, click Finish. FrontPage Express creates the page according to your input.

11. Review the page and replace any "instructions" with the information required. You can also customize many of the fields, specifying the default value, for example. You can display the options available to any of the fields by double-clicking on the field.

FIG. 36.14
In this dialog box, you specify the results file format.

Using the Survey and Confirmation Templates

FrontPage Express templates can also be used to quickly create content for the web. The templates provided with FrontPage Express work differently than the wizards. As you learned in the previous section, the wizards collect information and then build the page for you based on your answers. Templates do not prompt you for information. Instead, you choose the type of page you want to build from a list of templates, and then FrontPage displays a preformatted page with a series of placeholders you can replace with your own information.

For example, if you were to create a page based on the Survey Form template, you would need to replace the sample questions provided by the template (such as "What is your favorite color?") with the questions you want to include in your survey.

Follow these steps to create a page using a template:

1. Choose the File, New command. The New Page dialog box appears.
2. Select either the Survey or Confirmation template from the list, and then choose OK.
3. The page appears on the screen. Edit the page to replace its generic content with the information required. Figure 36.15 shows what the Survey form looks like before it's edited.

The usefulness of the Survey template is pretty obvious, but that of the Confirmation template is a little less so. Basically, it's the basis of a custom confirmation page that you can use to tell a user you have recorded the information he sent you. When he clicks the Submit button of a form you provided, assuming you have set that form up to use this custom confirmation page, the confirmation page appears in his browser.

FIG. 36.15
The Survey template can be customized to meet your particular information-gathering needs.

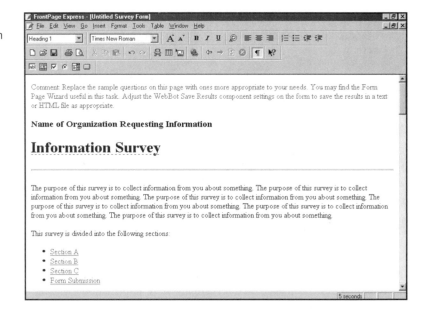

Formatting and Positioning Text

Entering text in FrontPage Express is very similar to entering text in any word processor. You click anywhere on the page and start typing. You can also copy text from another application and then paste it into the page that is currently open in FrontPage Express. FrontPage Express provides a wide range of text formatting options.

You can also specify the position and alignment of text on a line-by-line basis, or you can use built-in styles, which make it easy to apply groups of formatting commands with just one click. The next few sections cover the following formatting topics:

- Typeface, color, size, and text effects
- Paragraph alignment and formatting
- Use of line breaks
- Bulleted and numbered lists
- Horizontal line effects

Formatting Text

You format text in FrontPage Express much as you do in other Windows applications. You select the text to be formatted, and then make selections either from the toolbar or from choices on the Format menu.

To format text in FrontPage Express, follow these steps:

1. Select the text to be formatted.

2. Choose the Format, Font command to open the Font dialog (see Figure 36.16).

FIG. 36.16

From the Font dialog box, you cannot only change fonts and their sizes, but you can also apply special effects such as strikethrough.

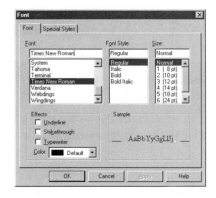

N O T E The font you choose will be used by the viewer's browser only if that font is also installed on the viewer's machine. If that font isn't installed, his browser will use its default font. In connection with this, be aware that FrontPage Express might add Microsoft-specific extensions to a page, and the effects of these extensions might not appear in other manufacturers' browsers. ▪

3. To specify the typeface for the text, choose the font name from the Font list.

4. To specify the style for the text, make a selection from the Font Style list. Keep in mind that the choices in the Style list will vary based on the font selected.

5. To specify the size of the text, make a selection from the Size list box. The choices in the Size list also vary based on the font selected.

6. Apply effects such as underlining, strikethrough, or a typewriter font by selecting the appropriate check box(es) in the Effects group.

7. To select a color for the text, click the Color drop-down arrow and select a color from the list that appears. To create a custom color, choose Custom from the list.

8. To create a subscript or superscript effect, choose the Special Styles tab. Select the appropriate effect from the Vertical Position drop-down list, and then set the amount of vertical offset using the By list.

9. Choose OK.

T I P If you experiment with character formatting on a large section of text and you mess it up and want to start all over again, you can easily do so. Select the offending text and choose Format, Remove Formatting. Character size, font, color, and attributes (such as bold) all revert to the default of Times New Roman, size 3 (12 point), regular typeface, color black.

Using Styles to Position and Format Paragraphs

To position text in FrontPage Express, you have two options:

- Use a combination of built-in styles and indent/outdent and alignment commands.
- Use a table to lay out your page, and then position text within the table's cells.

The difference between the two is that the table option allows you more precision in placing text on the page, but it also adds an extra layer of work and complexity. The basic rule of thumb is to use a table to lay out a page or a section of a page where graphics and text appear on the same line, such as in columns. Otherwise, the built-in styles and menu commands should suit your needs. Creating tables is covered in detail later in the chapter in the section "Creating and Editing Tables."

To use one of FrontPage Express's built-in paragraph styles and/or menu commands to position text, follow these steps:

1. Click anywhere in the paragraph to be formatted. If you want to format multiple paragraphs, select all of the paragraphs that will be positioned the same way.

2. To *indent* the selected paragraphs, click the Indent button on the Format toolbar.

   To *outdent* the selected paragraph(s), click the Outdent button on the Format toolbar.

   To choose a built-in style, choose one from the drop-down list on the Format toolbar. Table 36.1 provides a short description of each FrontPage Express built-in style.

Table 36.1 FrontPage Express Built-In Styles

Style Name	Formatting Description
Address	Italics, no indent, double spaced
Bulleted List	Bullet, indented, single spaced
Defined Term	Single spaced, first line left aligned, subsequent lines indented
Definition	Single spaced, first line indented, subsequent lines further indented from first
Directory List	Same as bulleted list
Formatted	Bullet, single spaced
Heading 1	Bold, left aligned
Heading 2	Bold, left aligned
Heading 3	Bold, left aligned
Heading 4	Bold, left aligned
Heading 5	Bold, left aligned

Style Name	Formatting Description
Heading 6	Bold, left aligned
Menu List	Bullet, indented, double-spaced
Numbered List	Same as standard numbered list

TROUBLESHOOTING

I wanted to change from Normal to Formatted style when I was part way through a paragraph. When I used the Paragraph Properties dialog box to do this, the whole paragraph changed to Formatted style. The same thing happened when I tried to do it using the Change Styles box. What's going on? Changing a paragraph style isn't the same as changing character style (such as applying bold or selecting a font). Character style changes (those you apply with the Font dialog box) affect only selected text or whatever characters you type after the change. However, when you select a paragraph style (the selection method makes no difference), the style is always applied to the entire paragraph. You cannot break the paragraph into chunks and apply a different style to each chunk.

Using Line Breaks to Control Text Formatting

Sometimes you need to keep short lines of text together and not allow a blank line of text between them. The trouble is, if you try pressing Enter where you want the text to break, you always get a blank line. The solution is to insert line breaks. A line break orders a browser to jump to the very next line of its window.

The procedure is simple: To keep short lines of text together, press Shift+Enter when you reach the end of the line. This inserts an HTML line break tag into the text stream, which orders a browser not to leave a blank line before the start of the next line of text. If you've turned on Format Marks (with either the View menu option or the Show/Hide Format Marks button on the toolbar), you'll see a line break symbol in the FrontPage Express workspace. These symbols, of course, don't show up in a browser.

Line breaks don't define the end of a paragraph. Therefore, the paragraph style affects all the text between the end of the previous paragraph and the start of the next, completely ignoring the presence of the line breaks.

Creating Bulleted and Numbered Lists

You can easily add a bulleted or numbered list to your web pages. FrontPage Express even provides a few styles of each so you can customize your lists to a certain extent. You can quickly format a list as a bulleted or numbered list from the Format toolbar, or you can make more specific choices from the Bullets and Numbering dialog box. Follow these steps:

1. Enter the list of items to be bulleted on the page. Be sure to press Enter at the end of each line.

2. Select all the paragraphs in the list.

3. To create a bulleted list, click on the bulleted list button the Format toolbar. To create a numbered list, click on the numbered list button on the Format toolbar.

4. If you want to exert a bit more control over the appearance of the bullets or numbers, choose Format, Bullets and Numbering from the menu. Select either the Bulleted or Numbered tab, select the format, and click OK.

TIP A fast way to start a list (of any kind) is to use the Change Style drop-down list box. It contains all the types of lists that FrontPage Express supports. Alternatively, click the Bulleted List button or the Numbered List button on the toolbar to start a list of that type.

Adding Horizontal Lines

You can add horizontal lines anywhere on your web page. These lines are useful for breaking your page into sections. You can specify the color, weight, alignment, and size of the line.

To add a horizontal line, follow these steps:

1. Click on the page in the location where you want the horizontal line to appear.

2. Choose Insert, Horizontal Line from the menu. A line appears on the page.

    If you are content with the appearance of the line on the page, your work is done. If you would like to customize the line, continue to step 3.

3. Double-click anywhere on the line, and the Horizontal Line Properties dialog box appears (see Figure 36.17).

FIG. 36.17

You can customize the appearance of a horizontal line on your page.

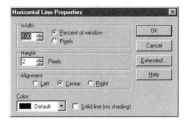

4. You can specify whether your line is a fixed length (in pixels) or whether it occupies a specific percentage of the width of your page. To specify your preference, select either Percent of Window or Pixels from the Width frame, and then enter the appropriate value in the scrolling list box.

5. Specify the height of the line (in pixels) in the height scrolling list box.

6. In the Alignment area, specify whether the line should be left-, center-, or right-aligned by selecting the appropriate option.

7. Select a color from the Color drop-down list.

8. To create a solid line with no shadow effect, select the Solid Line (No Shading) check box.

9. Choose OK to put your changes into effect.

> **CAUTION**
>
> Often when sizing various page elements, you get a choice between sizing in pixels and sizing by percentages. Generally, you should choose percentages. If you choose pixels and the user has his display set to a resolution different from yours, the element might not fit his screen properly.

Inserting and Managing Hyperlinks

The capabilities of HTML allow page developers to provide links to other web sites, and links on those web sites to other sites, and so on. Hyperlinks help the user navigate through the web (or just through your site) by means of following relevant, related information. You will most likely want to provide hyperlinks on your pages to other locations on the web.

To add a hyperlink, follow these steps:

1. Enter the text that will be used as a link. The text might be a word, or phrase, or a name that brings the user to a specific place on the web, or it might be the actual URL for the location that will be linked. Keep in mind that the text you want to use as a hyperlink might already have been entered. For example, you might provide a link from a word in a paragraph you entered when you first began developing the page.

N O T E You might prefer to add hyperlinks when you have completed almost all of the other work on your page instead of worrying about the links as you develop your page. You can add hyperlinks at any time, so you might want to focus on the content of your page first and then add hyperlinks at the end. ■

2. Select the text you entered in step 1 (or whatever text you want to use as the link).

3. Choose Insert, Hyperlink from the menu. The Create Hyperlink dialog box appears (see Figure 36.18).

4. You can create a hyperlink to a page that exists on the web, to a page you already have open in FrontPage Express, to a bookmark on an open page, or to a page that has not yet been created.

To create a link to an existing page on the World Wide Web, choose the World Wide Web tab (refer to Figure 36.18). Select the appropriate protocol from the Hyperlink Type drop-down list (more than likely, http: will be the type), and then specify the URL in the URL text box. Click OK.

FIG. 36.18
Use the Create
Hyperlink dialog box to
set up links to pages
open in FrontPage
Express, to locations on
the World Wide Web, or
to a new page.

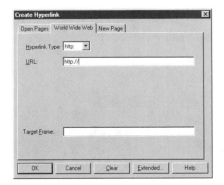

To create a link to a page you have open, including the current page, choose the Open Pages tab (see Figure 36.19). Each of the pages currently open in FrontPage Express is named in the Open Pages list. Click the name of the page, and then click OK to create the link. Keep in mind that this procedure will create a link to a specific file in a specific location in a directory. If the target file is moved to another directory, the link will become invalid.

FIG. 36.19
You can create a link to
any page currently open
in FrontPage Express.

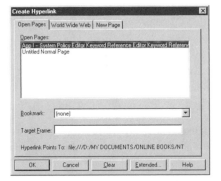

To create a link to a bookmark on an open page, choose that page from the Open Pages list, and choose the appropriate bookmark from the Bookmark drop-down list. Then click OK. (To find out how to place a bookmark on a page, see the section, "Creating Bookmarks.")

To create a link to a new page, choose the New Page tab. Enter the title of the page you want to create in the Page Title text box, and enter the filename of the page in the Page URL text box. Click OK, and the New Page dialog box appears (it was described earlier in the section "Creating Web Pages Instantly"). Select the type of page you want to create and click OK. Keep in mind that if you choose a page type based on a wizard, the appropriate wizard will be launched. If so, follow the onscreen directions. If not, click OK to create the link.

An easy way to specify a hyperlink to a World Wide Web target is to open that page in your browser when you define the link. The URL of the page currently open in your browser automatically appears in the URL text box of the Create Hyperlink dialog box. This eliminates any chance of typing the address wrong when you create the link.

If you need to modify the properties of a link, click on its text and choose Edit, Hyperlink. The Edit Hyperlink dialog opens. Except for its title, this dialog box is identical to the Create Hyperlink dialog box discussed in the previous steps.

To remove a hyperlink, select the hyperlink text and choose Edit, Unlink.

 If you put the cursor over a hyperlink but don't click it, the URL of the destination appears in the FrontPage Express status bar. This is handy for identifying the link's destination without actually having to go there.

Creating Bookmarks

A *bookmark* is a label that points to a specific location on your page. Users don't see bookmarks. A bookmark is used with hyperlinks when you want to provide a link on one page to another location on the same page. As an example, if you want to provide a link from the table of contents that appears on the top of the page to the relevant section later in the page, you would need to create a bookmark.

Here is how you create a bookmark on your page:

1. Select the text that is to serve as the bookmark.
2. Choose the Edit, Bookmark command. The Bookmark dialog box appears (see Figure 36.20).

FIG. 36.20

Creating a bookmark makes it easy to create a hyperlink to a specific position on a page.

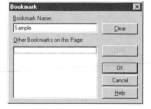

3. By default, the text you selected to bookmark appears as the name of the bookmark. If this is acceptable, choose OK. If you would like to specify some other text as the bookmark, enter the text in the Bookmark Name text box, and then choose OK.
4. The dialog box closes. Click anywhere outside the bookmark text, and you'll see that it now has a dashed underline. This tells you that there is a bookmark at that position. The dashed underline does not appear in a browser.

TIP To clear a bookmark, click anywhere in the marked text and choose Edit, Bookmark, Clear. The bookmark vanishes.

Adding Graphics

It's rare to find a web page without at least one graphic element. You can certainly add an aesthetically pleasing element to your page by adding some sort of graphic, even if you're not an artist. Many applications today come with dozens of clip art images you can borrow and use on your page. For example, Microsoft Word provides a wide selection of clip art, and you can borrow any of those images for use with FrontPage Express. In addition, your local software store probably stocks a selection of graphics libraries available on CD, each of which stores thousands of different images.

Your challenge as a web page developer, then, is not to create the graphics, but rather to decide how to integrate one or more graphic elements into your page. In this section, you'll look at how to add images to a web page. The first order of business, however, is to introduce two primary types of graphics used on the World Wide Web.

Understanding Graphics Types

Many software applications available today let you produce anything from the most basic to the most complicated drawing. Some of these applications save the drawings in a specific format, which means that only applications capable of reading the format can use the graphics. While many applications can read and write different formats, graphics for the web usually are found in two formats: GIF and JPEG.

GIF (pronounced *jiff*) is a graphics format developed by the online service CompuServe. While a number of versions of the GIF file exist, the most common one supports 256 colors. GIF is probably the most widely used format on the web, and almost every browser and image editor supports this format.

The GIF format also supports a process known as *interlacing*. An interlaced image is displayed in the browser in stages, which enables the user to begin viewing the image much sooner than he could if the graphic were not interlaced. You can specify for any GIF image you include on a FrontPage Express page to be interlaced by simply checking the Interlaced option when you select the image to be loaded.

Another option that FrontPage Express supports for GIF files is *transparent images*. When an image is created, a transparent color index is selected. This color blends with the background color of the browser when the image is displayed (only if the browser supports the display of transparent images). This effect blends the focal part of the graphic—such as a picture of the author of this chapter—with the background of the browser to give the appearance of a borderless image.

The other major web graphical format is JPEG. JPEG (pronounced *jay-peg*) was developed by the Joint Photographic Experts Group. The standard JPEG may contain up to 16 million colors. The most interesting, colorful, and detailed images you see on the Internet are most likely JPEG graphics. Considering the great resolution JPEG images provide, you may be wondering why all graphics are not JPEG format. One of the problems with JPEG images is that because of the detail they support, the file usually must be compressed when it is downloaded. And the compression process sometimes results in a loss of detail. In addition, a loss of detail sometimes occurs when a JPEG image is reduced from its original size to the size needed by the individual who is building the page.

T I P The GIF format is best for images without continuous-tone shading, such as line art drawings. JPEG is the format of choice for graphics with continuous-tone shading, usually photographs.

Inserting a Graphic

You can insert a graphic from two different sources: from a file on your computer or network or from another site on the web. When you insert a graphic from the web, you are actually creating a pointer to the web site where the graphic is located; the graphic is not actually copied to your web site. With that in mind, you should be sure that any graphic you are referencing on another web site will not be moved later.

N O T E You should also be sure that the viewers of your page will, in fact, have access to the referenced site if that's the approach you use to display the graphic. Thanks to proxy servers and intranet restrictions, many sites are unavailable to users on a company LAN. ▪

T I P The best method for including a graphic from another web site into your page is to copy the image. To do so, right-click on the target graphic, and then select the menu choice that saves the graphic locally. That way, you have your own copy of the graphic file. Remember, however, that copyright law applies to the Internet and the web: Many images are for free use, but not all. Don't use copyrighted images without permission from the owner. If you put something like a Disney character on your site, for example, you're asking for legal trouble.

To insert a graphic onto your web page, follow these steps:

1. From the menu, choose Insert, Image. The Image dialog box appears (see Figure 36.21).

2. To insert an image stored on your computer or a network resource to which your computer is attached, choose the From File option and then enter the name of the file in the edit box. Use the Browse button if you need help locating the file and/or entering its name and location.

   To insert an image stored on a web site, choose the From Location option, and then enter the URL for the site and the name of the image in the text box.

3. Choose OK, and the image appears on the screen

FIG. 36.21
You add graphics to your page by using the Image dialog box.

Managing the Size of Your Graphic

When you insert an image into your web page, the image occupies an area on your page matching its size. In other words, if the image is 100 pixels wide by 100 pixels tall, it will occupy a 100×100-pixel area of your page at the location where you inserted it. You might want to increase or decrease the size of the graphic. You can use either of two techniques to do so:

■ Select the image, and then click and drag the handles that appear around the image. If you drag a handle at one of the corners of the image, you can maintain the proportional ratio of the image. If you drag a handle either horizontally or vertically, you change the horizontal or vertical aspect only.

■ Double-click on the image to display the Image Properties dialog box. Choose the Appearance tab, and then modify the image's size using the Width and Height scroll boxes. You can specify the image's size as a certain percentage of the page's size by choosing the In Percent option for the width, the height, or both.

Adding a Hyperlink to Your Graphic

You may want to provide a hyperlink with a graphic on your web page. This gives the user the capability to link to another site via a graphic instead of a word or phrase.

To add a hyperlink to a graphic, follow these steps:

1. Insert the image into the page using the method described previously.

2. Click the image to select it and choose Edit, Hyperlink to open the Create Hyperlink dialog box.

3. Set up the link using the techniques you learned earlier in this chapter.

Specifying Options for Your Graphics

As you learned earlier in the chapter, depending on the format of your graphic, you might be able to specify a number of options for it, such as whether a GIF graphic is interlaced.

To specify options for a graphic, right-click on the graphic, and then choose Image Properties. The dialog box that appears will contain options appropriate to the image type you selected.

Using Backgrounds

You can add character to your web pages by adding a background image or colors. When you add a background image to your page, any text or graphics you add to your page appear against that background. The size of the graphic determines how your background appears. FrontPage Express will tile the graphic across your page, which means it copies the graphic across the page and down to the bottom. Therefore, if you require a broad background, such as the sky and clouds, be sure your graphic is at least 640×480 pixels. If you prefer a tiled effect, such as a company logo, almost any size is suitable.

 TIP An attractive effect is to present a border down the left side of the page. To create this effect, the graphic you use should be 640 pixels wide, but the illustration or picture to use as the border should occupy the leftmost area of the graphic. If you use a graphic that is wide as the screen, FrontPage Express cannot wrap the image. Instead, it repeats the image down the page.

To specify a background image or color for your page, follow these steps:

1. Select File, Page Properties from the menu. The Page Properties dialog box appears. Choose the Background tab (see Figure 36.22).

FIG. 36.22
You can specify a background image and color for your page.

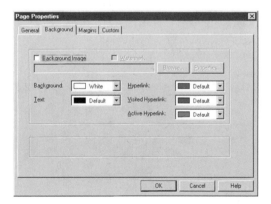

2. To add a background image, choose the Background Image check box, and then enter the filename and location of the image in the edit box. Use the Browse button if you need help locating the file and/or entering its name and location.

3. To specify a background color for the page, select the color from the Background drop-down list.

4. Choose OK.

Creating and Editing Tables

Tables are a critical component of all but the most basic of web page designs. However, the application of tables in web pages isn't strictly to handle columns and rows. Tables also make it easy to position graphics and text at any location required. By merging and splitting rows and columns, you can use tables to place graphics and text in locations that would be difficult to access using only indenting and alignment commands.

Adding a Table to Your Page

You can add a table to your web page from either the Standard toolbar or the menu. If you use the menu, you can specify a number of options for your table when it is created (such as cell padding and border size). When you use the toolbar to create the table, your choices are limited to the number of columns and rows. Of course, after you create a table with the toolbar, you can always select the entire table to customize it. To do so, choose Table, Table Properties from the menu.

The following list explains each method for creating a table:

■ *Toolbar.* To create a table from the toolbar, click on the Insert Table button on the Standard toolbar. Drag down to select the number of rows for your table and—*without releasing the mouse button*—drag across to select the number of columns. When you have selected the correct number of rows and columns, release the mouse button (see Figure 36.23).

■ *Menu.* To create a table from the menu, choose Table, Insert Table. The Insert Table dialog box appears (see Figure 36.24). In the Size area, enter the number of rows and columns in the respective text boxes. Use the up and down arrow buttons in each of the controls to increment or decrement the current value.

FIG. 36.23
You can add a table to your page quickly by using the toolbar.

Adding Rows or Columns

Even with the best planning, you might discover a class of information you didn't allow for and decide you need a new row or column in your table for it. To add either one, select the existing row or column that is to be adjacent to the new one. Choose Table, Insert Rows or Columns. The Insert Rows or Columns dialog box appears. Fill in the data for the number of rows or columns you want to insert and specify where they should go relative to the selection you made. Then choose OK.

FIG. 36.24

The Insert Table dialog box provides you with more options than you have when you create a table from the toolbar.

Selecting Table Components

After you create your table, it is likely you will need to customize it, possibly modifying its size or changing column layout, for example. In order to customize a table in FrontPage Express, you must first select either the entire table or the component of the table you want to work with. The following list explains how to select the various components of the table.

- *Entire table.* Click and drag over the table until all the rows and column are selected.

  or

  Click anywhere in the table, and then select Table, Select Table from the menu.

- *One cell.* Move the mouse pointer towards the leftmost edge of the cell until the pointer becomes an arrow pointing to the right. Then double-click.

  or

  Click anywhere in the cell, and then choose Table, Select Cell from the menu.

- *One column.* Move the mouse pointer above the top border of the first row in the column. When the mouse pointer changes shape to become a darkened downward-pointing arrow, click.

  or

  Click anywhere in the column, and then choose Table, Select Column from the menu.

- *Range of columns.* Move the mouse pointer above the top border of the first row in the first column. The mouse pointer will change shape to become a darkened downward-pointing arrow. Press and hold down the Shift key, and then click and drag to select additional columns.

- *One row.* Move the mouse pointer to the left edge of the table, adjacent to the row to be selected. When the mouse pointer changes shape to become a darkened arrow, click.

  or

  Click anywhere in the row, and then select Table, Select Row from the menu.

■ *Range of rows.* Move the mouse pointer to the left edge of the table, adjacent to the first row to be selected. The mouse pointer will change shape to become a darkened arrow. Press and hold down the Shift key, and then click and drag to select additional rows.

Deleting a Table or Parts of a Table

When you're experimenting, you need to know how to delete an experiment gone wrong. To get rid of a table entirely, click anywhere in it, choose Table, Select Table, and press the Delete key. Another way is to double-click in the left margin to select the entire table, and then press the Delete key or choose Edit, Clear.

You remove columns or rows using the same method: Select those to be cut, and then press Delete. If you delete a cell (as distinct from deleting its content), all the cells to its right slide over to fill the empty space, and a gap appears at the right side of the table.

Splitting and Merging Rows, Columns, and Cells

You can use other techniques to further define the layout of the rows and columns in your table. These techniques are useful when you want to vary either the row or height of cells with respect to other cells in the same columns or row. You can merge columns, rows, and cells together to achieve this type of effect. Figure 36.25 shows an example of a table in which a combination of splitting and merging is used to create a fairly elaborate layout.

FIG. 36.25

You can use merged and split cells to put information precisely where you want it.

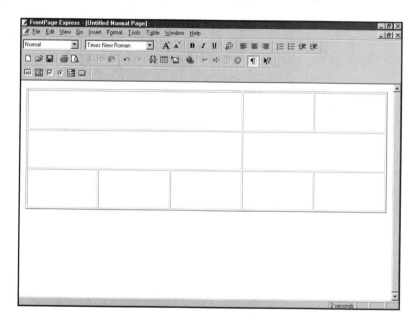

The following list outlines the techniques for splitting and merging columns, rows, and cells:

■ *Split a cell.* Select the cell to be split, and then choose Table, Split Cells from the menu. The Split Cells dialog box appears (see Figure 36.26). Choose either Split into Columns or Split into Rows. Then specify the number of columns or rows into which the cell should be split in the Number of Columns scroll box. Choose OK.

FIG. 36.26

You can split cells into columns or rows—as many of each as you need.

■ *Split all the cells in a column.* Select the column, and then choose Table, Split Cells from the menu. The Split Cells dialog box appears. Choose the Split into Rows option. In the Number of Rows scroll box, specify the number of rows each of the cells in the column should be split into. Then choose OK.

■ *Split all of the cells in a row.* Select the row, and then choose Table, Split Cells from the menu. The Split Cells dialog box appears. Choose the Split into Columns option. In the Number of Columns scroll box, specify the number of columns each of the cells in the row should be split into. Then choose OK.

■ *Merge cells.* Click and drag through the cells to be merged, and then choose Table, Merge Cells from the menu.

Inserting a Table Within A Cell

Another method for customizing the layout of information in a table is to insert a table within a table. This gives you the capability to group and lay out one set of data or content within the context of a larger table. Figure 36.27 shows an example of a table within a table layout.

To insert a table within a cell of another table, select the cell and then repeat the steps given in the section "Adding a Table to Your Page."

Customizing Your Table

In addition to merging and splitting the table and the rows, columns, and cells in your table, you can customize a number of other aspects of a table in FrontPage Express. The following list explains the options and techniques you can use to customize your table:

■ *Caption.* You can add a caption to your table in order to provide the user with a quick description of the table's contents. The caption appears centered above the table, and if the table is resized or moved, the caption is automatically moved, too.

To add a caption to your table, click anywhere in the table, and then choose Table, Insert Caption from the menu. The cursor moves to the centered position over the table. Enter the caption.

FIG. 36.27

You can insert a table within another table.

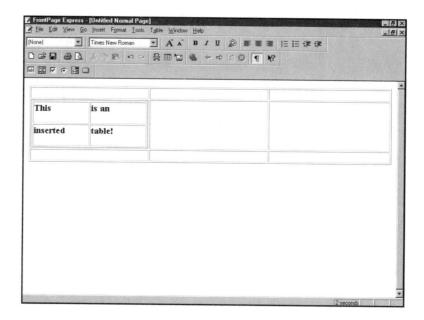

■ *Borders.* You can specify a border for the cells in your table. To do so, first select the table, and then choose Table, Table Properties from the menu. Select a width for the border from the Border Size scroll box. You can also select a color for both the light portion of the shading and the heavy portion of the border shading, as well as for the border itself. Make these selections from the Custom Colors frame at the bottom of the dialog box. Then choose OK.

It is possible to override border settings you've applied to the entire table for just specific cells, columns, or rows. To do that, select the cells whose borders will be customized, and then choose Table, Cell Properties from the menu. Make selections from the Custom Colors frame, and then choose OK.

■ *Background image/color.* You can specify a cell-specific background or image. If you use a background image, the cell must be large enough to accommodate the graphic if you want the user to see all of the graphic.

To specify a background image or color for a cell, select the cell, choose Table, Cell Properties from the menu, and then select either a color or image from the Custom Background Frame.

■ *Alignment.* You can specify the alignment for the contents of any or all of the cells in the table. To do so, select the components of the table for which you want to change the alignment. Choose Table, Cell Properties from the menu. In the Layout frame, specify the Horizontal and Vertical alignments for the selected cells.

■ *Column width/table width.* You can easily specify the width of a particular column or the entire table. You specify the width either in pixels or as a percentage of the entire page.

To specify the width for the table, select the table and then choose Table, Table Properties from the menu. Choose the Specify Width option, and then select either the In Pixels or In Percent option. Enter the desired value, and then choose OK. To do the same for a column(s), choose the column and choose Table, Cell Properties from the menu.

Adding Content to a Table

Now that you have learned how to format and structure a table, here is a quick word on how to enter content. To add text, click in the cell and start typing. All of FrontPage Express's text formatting tools are at your disposal.

As for images, links, and other components, you add these to a table cell by clicking in the cell and continuing as if the new element were standing by itself on the page. The fact that it's in a table makes no difference at all.

Adding Sound and Video

The appeal of a web page can be significantly enhanced by the inclusion of multimedia content, such as sound and video. Many web pages you can browse through today include video clips that you can view online, such as excerpts for upcoming films. Other web sites provide background music as you browse through their pages. Integrating sound and video are simple exercises in FrontPage Express. In this section, you will learn how to integrate video and background music into your web pages.

Adding Video to Your Page

Video is an attractive option for a web page, and adding it to a page is no longer a difficult procedure. New video production hardware and software tools make it easy to develop video at the desktop. Download speeds have increased with new technologies, such as *streaming*, in which the video clip (as well as other multimedia content) is played *as* it is downloaded. Faster modems are also coming into wider use, steadily improving the behavior of multimedia content on the web.

To add video to your web page, follow these steps:

1. From the menu, choose Insert, Video. The Video dialog box appears (see Figure 36.28).
2. Enter the name of the file containing the video content in the From File text box. Use the Browse button if you need help locating the file and/or entering its name and location.
3. Choose OK, and a placeholder appears on the page. This corresponds to the position on the page where the video will be played when the page is opened.
4. To customize how the video will be displayed, right-click on the placeholder and choose Image Properties from the shortcut menu. Then choose the Video tab (see Figure 36.29).

FIG. 36.28

You specify the video you want to add to the page in the Video dialog box.

FIG. 36.29

You can control how often the video runs from the Image Properties dialog box.

5. To specify that you want the video to start immediately when the page is opened, choose the On File Open check box. Alternatively, if you want the video to be started when the user's mouse passes over the video, choose the On Mouse Over option.

   You can choose the number of times the video should repeat by entering a number in the Loop box. To repeat the video as long as the page is open, choose the Forever check box.

6. When you finish specifying your preferences, click OK.

N O T E On File Open works only with Microsoft browsers, which recognize the FrontPage-specific code added to the page by FrontPage Express. ■

Adding a Background Sound to Your Page

You can add a sound to your page and have it played automatically when the page is opened. The sound can be played once, you can specify that it should be played a certain number of times, or you can choose to have it play as long as the page is open.

To specify a background sound for your page, follow these steps:

1. Select File, Page Properties from the menu. In the Page Properties dialog box, choose the Background tab.

2. In the Location text box, enter the name of the file with the background sound. Use the Browse button if you need help locating the file and/or entering its name and location.

3. Specify the number of times the sound should repeat by entering the number in the Loop box. To increment or decrement the value shown in the box, click the up or down button beside the control. To repeat the sound for as long as the page is open, choose the Forever check box.

4. Choose OK.

N O T E If you insert background sound using this technique, it will be heard only by users with Microsoft Internet Explorer browsers version 3 and above. Netscape Navigator users won't hear the sound because Navigator browsers require a Java applet to produce background sound. ▪

Advanced Web Editing Tools

As the web has grown in popularity and complexity, so has the technology surrounding it. This section provides an overview of the more advanced features of FrontPage Express.

Using WebBots

WebBots are prepackaged functions you can add to your web pages. Instead of developing a function from scratch (such as a feature allowing your user to search your web page or site for a specific word or phrase), you can use a WebBot to add that type of feature. FrontPage Express comes with three WebBots: Timestamp, Search, and Include. Each WebBot is described here:

- *Search*. Provides a box on the current page in which the user can enter a word or phrase to search for, as well as one button to start the search and another button to clear the box.

- *Include*. Automatically merges another page on the web into the current page at the position where the WebBot was run. The merged page is updated whenever the page is opened.

- *Timestamp*. Automatically updates a display on the page that shows the last time and date the page was modified.

Knowing that WebBots are designed to save the user work, you would expect that it would be easy to integrate one or more on a web page. Fortunately, this happens to be the case.

To add a WebBot, follow these steps:

1. Click on the location on the page where the WebBot component should be installed.

2. Choose Insert, WebBot Component from the menu. The Insert WebBot Component dialog box appears (see Figure 36.30).

FIG. 36.30
Using WebBots saves you from doing the complicated program-ming work needed for advanced web functions.

3. From the list, select the WebBot Component you want to integrate. Then choose OK.

4. Depending on the WebBot you select, you may need to specify additional options (such as the format of the date and time presented with the Timestamp WebBot). Proceed through the appropriate dialog boxes, choosing Finish at the end.

If you position the mouse pointer over a place on the page where there is a WebBot, the pointer turns into a small robot-like figure. This is the WebBot cursor. Even if you can't see the WebBot itself, the WebBot cursor appears to tell you it's there. If you want to edit the properties of an existing WebBot, double-click while the WebBot cursor is visible, and the properties dialog box for that WebBot will appear.

Adding an ActiveX Control

ActiveX Controls combine the convenience of Java applets with the permanence and functional-ity of Netscape Navigator plug-ins. Like Java applets, ActiveX Controls can be automatically downloaded to a user's system if they are not currently installed or if the installed version isn't the most recent. Like plug-ins, ActiveX Controls remain available to a web browser continu-ously after they are installed. (For more information on Java applets, see the next section.)

ActiveX Controls build on Microsoft's highly successful Object Linking and Embedding (OLE) standard to provide a common framework for extending the capability of web browsers. ActiveX Controls, however, are more than just simple web browser plug-ins or add-ins. Because of the nature of ActiveX Controls, they can be used to extend the functionality of Microsoft browsers and any programming language or application that supports the OLE standard.

To insert an ActiveX Control, do the following:

1. Start FrontPage Express and load a document into the workspace.

2. Choose Insert, Other Components, ActiveX Control to open the ActiveX Control Properties dialog box (see Figure 36.31).

FIG. 36.31

The ActiveX Control Properties dialog box helps you install and configure these controls on your page.

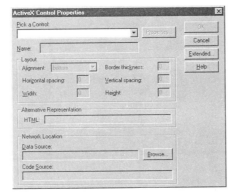

3. Click the Pick a Control drop-down arrow to open the drop-down list of controls that are installed on your system.

4. Choose the control you want. Then click the Properties button and use the properties dialog boxes to customize the control to suit your purposes.

ActiveX Controls can be complicated to use; they all require parameters of one kind or another, and the page designer must know these parameters to make the controls work. Several controls are installed along with FrontPage Express, but at the time of this writing, Microsoft had not made documentation of these controls available.

N O T E The list of controls that appears displays all the ones installed on your system. These will primarily be "run-time" controls that cannot be used at "design time" (like in FrontPage or Visual Basic) without a license. To obtain documentation on a control, you must usually purchase a development license from the company that makes it. Various tools (such as the Object Viewer included with Visual Basic 5) are available that can help you determine a control's properties, methods, and events.

Adding Java Applets

Applets are specialized Java programs especially designed for execution within Internet web pages. To run a Java applet, you need a Java-enabled web browser such as Netscape Navigator 3.x or 4.x or Microsoft's Internet Explorer version 3.x or 4.x. These browsers are capable of recognizing applet tags within an HTML web page and then downloading and executing the specified Java program (or programs) in the context of a Java virtual machine.

Assuming you've created or downloaded an applet, use the Insert, Other Components, Java Applet command to open the Java Applet Properties dialog box shown in Figure 36.32.

FIG. 36.32

To add an applet to a page and configure it quickly, use the Java Applet Properties dialog box.

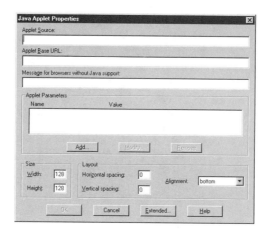

The Applet Source is the name of the source file; this always has a CLASS extension, and the filename is case-sensitive. The Base URL is the URL of the folder containing this file. You must add to it any parameter names and values required by the applet. You can find a selection of ready-made applets to download and experiment with at `http://www.gamelan.com`.

Adding Netscape Plug-Ins

Starting with version 1 of Navigator, Netscape provided ways to enhance its browser with helper applications that support data formats beyond the built-in graphics and HTML. With Netscape Navigator version 2, Navigator began supporting plug-ins, which provided another means of extending the range of data types that can be presented on or with a web page.

FrontPage Express's plug-in insertion command generates the <EMBED> tag, which is recognized by both Navigator and Internet Explorer. Essentially, the <EMBED> tag is a type of link: Objects specified by it are automatically downloaded and displayed when the document is displayed. To insert a plug-in, choose Insert, Other Components, Plug-In to open the Plug-In Properties dialog box (see Figure 36.33).

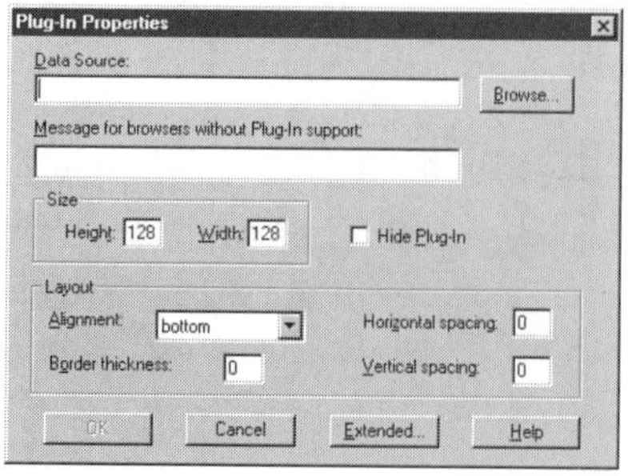

FIG. 36.33

Use the Plug-In Properties dialog box to embed objects in a web page so browsers that support plug-ins can use them.

In the Data Source text box, type the name of the file you want embedded. The MIME type of the embedded file tells a user's browser which plug-in to use. If the browser is Netscape Navigator and it doesn't have the right plug-in, it offers to download one for the user.

Including a PowerPoint Animation

This procedure assumes you have already created a PowerPoint Animation file from a slide presentation. To include it in a web page, choose Insert, Other Components, PowerPoint Animation to open the PowerPoint Animation dialog box (see Figure 36.34).

FIG. 36.34
You can insert a PowerPoint Animation file as either an ActiveX component or a Netscape plug-in.

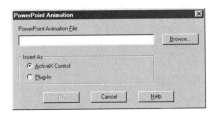

Locate and select the animation file. Then choose one of the dialog box's two radio buttons to indicate whether the file will be inserted into the page as an ActiveX Control or a Netscape plug-in. In order to view the PowerPoint animation, you must first download and install the PowerPoint Animation Player as an ActiveX Control or a Netscape plug-in. You can download the player from www.microsoft.com.

Using Marquees

Marquees are those boxes that have text moving through them. Opinions vary on their best use: Some people keep the text moving, others prefer to slide it into view and then leave it static. Your own design sense will be your best guide here.

> **CAUTION**
> The <MARQUEE> HTML tag is specific to Internet Explorer browsers; it will not work in Netscape browsers. Netscape implements marquees through Java applets.

To insert a marquee, first choose Insert, Marquee to open the Marquee Properties dialog box (see Figure 36.35).

Use the Text box to type the text you want to scroll, and use the other properties in the dialog box to adjust the marquee's onscreen behavior.

Hand-Coding HTML in FrontPage Express

You're bound to run into situations in which you need to modify a page's HTML code directly. To do this, open the page you want to modify. Then choose View, HTML. In the window that opens, you can directly edit the HTML produced by FrontPage Express.

FIG. 36.35

Make scrolling text look the way you want with the Marquee Properties options.

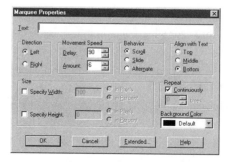

The HTML view provides what is essentially a text editor. The editing tools are fairly basic, but all the essentials are available: Cut, Copy, Paste, Select All, Find, and Replace.

> **CAUTION**
>
> FrontPage Express does some basic syntax checking of any HTML inserted through the HTML view. If it spots what it thinks is a mistake, it will try to correct it, often by inserting <P> tags into and around the offending code. Unfortunately, if you insert valid HTML code that is not recognized by FrontPage Express, the editor will still "correct" the code, even though it's perfectly legal. If this happens to code you insert, you'll have to use the HTML Markup command, as described in the next section.

Using the HTML Markup Command

This is the only safe way to include HTML code that FrontPage Express doesn't directly support. Code inserted with the HTML Markup command is left alone by FrontPage Express, even if the code is incorrect. To use the command, follow these steps:

1. Choose Insert, HTML Markup to open the HTML Markup dialog box.

2. Type the desired HTML into the text box. When you finish, click OK to close the dialog box.

After you close the dialog box, you don't actually see the output of the inserted code; instead, a yellow question mark icon appears in the place where the code was inserted. This icon appears even if the code is recognized by FrontPage Express, and it actually signals the presence of the HTML Markup WebBot. To edit the inserted HTML code, double-click on the question mark icon to open the HTML Markup dialog box again.

 If you don't see the yellow icon, your Format Marks are turned off. Choose View, Format Marks to turn them on.

Publishing Your Pages to a Web Site

When you have created all the pages for your web, you probably will want to publish the pages to a web so that other users can access the pages. Simply saving the pages you've created in FrontPage Express isn't enough, however. You must publish the pages to a specific web so that web server software (which is different from both FrontPage Express and your browser and must be installed separately) can process requests from users for the pages. This web server software (on which a web is created) must reside on a computer that browsers can access. There are two general steps for publishing your pages to the web:

1. Establish or locate a web site on which to publish your web and pages.

2. Publish the pages.

The next two sections cover those steps in detail.

N O T E   Remember that you must have the FrontPage extensions installed on the server and that you also must have appropriate "write" permissions for that server. ▨

Establishing or Creating a Web Site

As you learned earlier in this chapter (in the section, "Using the Personal Home Page Wizard"), many Internet Service Providers host home pages for subscribers. If you plan to provide more than a single page of information, you might want to consider a host site with greater capabilities. A search of the web will turn up dozens of companies interested in hosting your web site for a nominal amount per month—usually less than $50.

If you have access to the server and are interested in learning the technology, Windows NT Server includes the software to host a web site. In addition, Windows NT Workstation and Windows 98 both provide web hosting software perfect for local webs, such as via intranets.

Publishing Your Pages

Windows 98 provides the tools to publish your web via the Web Publishing Wizard. This wizard is available from the Internet Explorer menu, which you access from the Start, Programs menu. If you do not see the Web Publishing Wizard on the menu, it probably has not been installed.

You can install the wizard from either the Windows 98 or Internet Explorer CD, or you can download it from Microsoft's site on the Internet. The wizard walks you through the steps of publishing your pages and creating a starting home page. The steps are easy to follow, and there is no requirement for in-depth web server knowledge.

When You Should Upgrade to FrontPage

As you become more adept at web page development or when your web site development projects grow in complexity, you might consider upgrading to Microsoft FrontPage 98. FrontPage Express is very similar to FrontPage 98's web editor, so you should find it easy to get into the more advanced package. Here are the main differences between FrontPage Express and FrontPage 98:

- FrontPage 98 provides more WebBots than are shipped with the Express version.

- FrontPage 98 includes FrontPage Explorer, which helps to develop and manage entire web sites made up of the pages developed with FrontPage Editor.

- FrontPage 98 provides clip art samples, including video and animated samples, plus support for Dynamic HTML, style sheets, WYSIWYG frame development, a WYSIWYG table drawing tool, and many more enhancements.

- FrontPage 98 gives you a direct link to your web browser, allowing you to view your pages in the browser as you develop them, instead of having to save and load them individually.

CHAPTER 37

Using the Microsoft Personal Web Services

by Dennis Jones

In this chapter

Understanding the Microsoft Personal Web Services

Windows 98 comes with the Microsoft Personal Web Server (PWS), a light-duty World Wide Web server that can sustain up to 10 simultaneous connections. You can use the PWS as the working server for a small intranet and/or as a development environment for such an intranet.

Alternatively, you can install the PWS onto a single, non-networked PC. In this configuration, you would use the PWS for developing and testing web sites and pages that could then be transferred to a more powerful server environment.

▶ **See** "Creating Web Pages with FrontPage Express," **p. 779**

Associated closely with the PWS is the Personal Web Manager. As its name suggests, this is for managing webs that are hosted by the PWS. The Manager also furnishes web publishing facilities, a Home Page Wizard, and configuration tools. Together with the PWS, these facilities make up the Personal Web Services of Windows 98.

The core of these is the Personal Web Server itself. Even if you're not on a network, you can still experiment with the software, because the PWS can be installed and will function on a standalone machine. Of course, if you want to eventually move your pages to a web site that isn't on your PC, you need a connection to the computer where that site is located. On a standalone PC, this link is most likely to be a dial-up connection through a telephone line, to an Internet service provider (ISP). The ISP might also be providing the hardware and software resources needed to host the web site where the pages are to be published.

The PWS is not suitable as a server for a World Wide Web site because it isn't built to handle a lot of traffic. If you need to establish a World Wide Web site, talk with your ISP to find out what facilities they provide for doing this. Often this is a cheaper and easier alternative than purchasing the hardware and software necessary to do an adequate job of WWW hosting. In this situation, the Microsoft PWS can help you out as a development tool, so you can create and test your web prior to sending it on to the ISP.

The most appropriate use of the PWS, other than for development and/or experimental purposes, is to provide the facilities for a small-scale intranet. Most of the Personal Web Services associated with the PWS are best-suited to such a use. The PWS, functioning as an intranet web server, can give you a very effective way to share resources within your organization.

Sharing Resources on an Intranet with the Personal Web Server

Simply put, a typical intranet is an internal network that uses the TCP/IP protocol to provide communications within a single organization. Intranets are essentially private, though they can provide restricted access points for outside users. Where they differ from other types of networks is in the use of a web server, together with related server technologies and web browsers. All of which are linked by the TCP/IP communications protocol and use HTML as the main document-creation language.

The heart of an intranet is its server. Servers come in many configurations and levels of capability. The Microsoft PWS, being at the lower end of the power spectrum, works well for an intranet in an organization of 5–10 workers. If you need more resources than this, you should probably consult with a networking specialist.

Another thing to keep in mind is that PWS for Windows 98 has no built-in user authentication, so it isn't a good choice for information environments where high security is a concern. In addition, the PWS does not provide an FTP service, so you need to install an FTP server from another software source if you want to provide this option on your intranet. However, the PWS does support Active Server Pages (ASPs), so if you need to host or develop ASPs, the PWS can do the job.

Part

VI

Ch

37

N O T E   The earlier versions of the Microsoft PWS (1.0 and 1.0a) did include an FTP service, but this was dropped in the new version. ▪

Installing the Microsoft Personal Web Server

The PWS is not installed in Windows 98 by default, so you have to set it up through the Start/Run dialog box. To carry out a basic installation, excluding any networking configuration, use the following procedure.

▶ **See** the chapters in Part VII, "Windows Network Services," for detailed information about setting up and configuring networks of various types **p. 849**

1. Insert the Windows 98 CD into the CD-ROM drive.
2. Choose Start, Run, to open the Run dialog box.

 The PWS can also be installed via Control Panel, Add/Remove Programs, Windows Setup. Also, note that during a standard Windows 98 installation, a PWS program item is created under the Internet Explorer program group. If you click this PWS item, you are led to the actual installation of the PWS.

3. Assuming your CD-ROM drive letter is D, type **D:\add-ons\pws\setup.exe** into the Open text box. (If the CD-ROM drive is another letter, substitute that for D:). Choose OK.
4. The Microsoft Personal Web Server Setup splash screen opens. This is merely introductory, so choose Next.
5. The next dialog box offers you a choice of Minimum install, Typical install, and Custom install. Choose Typical.

N O T E   The Custom install enables you to set up optional components of the PWS, including additional data access components, the Microsoft Message Queue, additional Transaction Server components, RAD support for Visual Interdev, and various advanced documentation. These components are for advanced web designs and designers, and are well beyond the scope of this chapter. ▪

6. The next dialog box enables you to specify your default web publishing home directory, that is, the folder where your web's home page is stored. The default folder is C:\Inetpub\wwwroot. If you need to change this, either use the Browse button to locate a new default folder, or type the folder's path name directly into the WWW Service text box (see Figure 37.1).

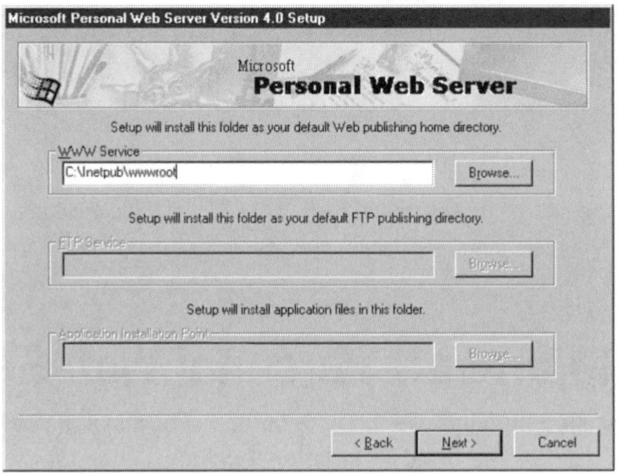

FIG. 37.1

You can specify a new default publishing folder in the Setup dialog box.

7. Choose Next. Setup completes this stage of the installation and opens a final dialog box when it has finished. Choose Finish or press Enter to leave Setup.

8. The Systems Setting Change dialog box appears, asking if you want to restart your computer to put the new settings into effect. You can't use the PWS until you do this; choose Yes to restart and complete the installation.

N O T E A new shortcut icon with the title Publish is on your desktop even before you restart the computer. This is the shortcut to the Personal Web Manager, but you should not use the Manager until you have restarted your computer to complete the PWS installation. ▪

After the computer has restarted, you see a new icon in the System Tray of the Windows 98 status bar. This icon indicates that the PWS is running. Note that the PWS is a system service, and once installed always loads at startup. Although you can't prevent the service from loading when the computer boots, you can start, stop, and pause the server. This is covered later in this chapter.

Testing the Personal Web Server

It's a good idea to test the PWS before continuing. The machine on which you installed the PWS will be either a standalone or a networked machine, so we'll cover these two essential cases.

Testing the PWS on a Standalone Machine

The PWS communicates only through the TCP/IP protocol. Therefore a standalone machine, from the point of view of the PWS, can be either a PC that has no networking connections at all (except possibly a dial-up connection to the Internet) or one that is connected to a network that does not use the TCP/IP protocol.

The PWS requires that TCP/IP services be installed on its host machine, even if the machine is not networked or if its network is using some other protocol. If the services are not installed, you can find out how to install them in Chapter 38, "Configuring Windows Network Components."

▶ **See** the chapters in Part VII, "Windows Network Services."

After the server is installed, you should verify that it's working properly. Begin by starting Internet Explorer. In the browser's Address bar, type the web address http://127.0.0.1; this is a reserved IP address, valid on all computers, for the local machine. The 127.0.0.1 address will always work (assuming the server installation is error-free) even if the machine is not connected to a network or to the Internet.

TIP With IE 3 or later, or Navigator 3 or later, you don't have to type the http:// part. In the example, typing **127.0.0.1** and pressing Enter opens the page.

After you've typed in the address, press Enter. After a brief pause, the default startup page, which was created when you installed the PWS, appears in the browser window (see Figure 37.2).

FIG. 37.2
The PWS's default startup page enables you to test the server installation.

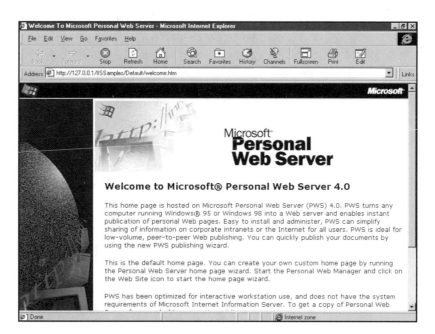

Part
VI

Ch

37

If you look in the Address bar, you'll see that the page location (or URL) is http://127.0.0.1/ IISSamples/Default/welcome.htm. If you want to check this out with Windows Explorer, you will find the file WELCOME.HTM (which is what you're looking at in the browser) stored on your hard drive at C:\Inetpub\iissamples\default\. As you can tell, this isn't the default publishing folder you specified during installation. Instead, it's a special sample folder to help get you started. The default publishing folder (C:\Inetpub\wwwroot) is where you would put the pages of your actual web, assuming you did not change this default during installation.

A more user-friendly address is the actual name of the computer, which you assigned during Windows 98 installation. If you've forgotten it, you can get it from the Personal Web Manager; simply double-click the Publish icon to start the Manager, and you'll see the line Web Publishing is On. Your home page is available at In the Manager's Main Window. Under this line, in blue, is a web address—http:// followed by a name; an example might be http://mypc. To use this name as the web address, simply type http://mypc into the browser Address bar (or just mypc, for recent browsers) and press Enter. The default startup page appears in the browser window.

When you know the server is working, you can close the browser.

N O T E You might be familiar with earlier versions of the Microsoft PWS running on a standalone Windows 95 machine. In the Windows 95 environment, you need a HOSTS file to make the computer name into a valid web address, although the IP address 127.0.0.1 will always work without a HOSTS file. However, the new PWS running on a standalone machine does not need a HOSTS file; the PWS handles the mapping of the computer name to the 127.0.0.1 IP address for you. ■

Testing the PWS on a TCP/IP Networked Machine

This assumes that the TCP/IP network is properly configured to recognize your machine and its name. Network configuration is treated extensively elsewhere in this book and is far too complex to repeat here.

▶ **See** "Configuring Windows Network Components," especially the TCP/IP references in the sections on installing and configuring network protocols **p. 851**

▶ **See** "Setting Up a Simple Windows Network," **p. 917**

The simplest method of testing the PWS is to do it on the local machine. Start a browser and type **http://** followed by the computer name—the name by which the network recognizes the machine—into the Address bar. Then press Enter. The PWS welcome page should appear in the browser window.

T I P You can get the machine name from the Personal Web Manager, as described in the previous section; alternatively, you can obtain it from the Network Neighborhood, Properties, Identification tab.

For a more rigorous test, start a browser on another machine on the same TCP/IP network, and repeat the previous procedure. If the PWS welcome page does not appear, there might be something wrong with the network configuration. For help, refer to the chapters referenced in the previous cross-reference.

Removing or Adding Server Components

After the server has been completely installed, you can remove or add PWS components with the PWS setup program. If you need to do this, begin by inserting the Windows 98 CD into your CD-ROM drive. If the Windows 98 opening screen appears, close it.

After the CD is in the drive, you can start the PWS setup program in two ways. The easiest is to choose Start, Programs, Microsoft Personal Web Server, Personal Web Server Setup. Alternatively, you can use the Add/Remove Programs tool in the Control Panel. Open the Add/Remove Programs dialog box, select the Microsoft Personal Web Server entry, and then choose the Add/Remove button.

Whichever you do, the PWS setup program starts. When the Microsoft Personal Web Server Setup opening screen appears, choose Next. In the next screen, you have two choices (see Figure 37.3).

Part
VI

Ch
37

FIG. 37.3
You can remove the PWS completely, or add and remove components of it.

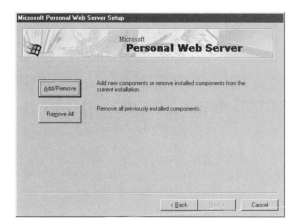

If you want to remove the server completely, choose Remove All and wait until you are instructed to restart the computer. Restarting completes the removal of the PWS.

If you want to remove or add server components, choose Add/Remove. This opens another screen, where you can specify what's to be added or removed (see Figure 37.4).

FIG. 37.4
The Select Components dialog box gives you a complete picture of the PWS components available for addition or removal.

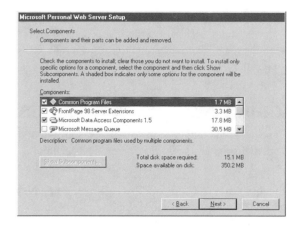

In the Components list box, clear or check the appropriate check boxes to indicate which components you want added or removed. When you have finished, choose Next, and the setup program will modify the PWS installation. Depending on your selections, you might have to restart the computer to complete the setup.

 T I P   The second choice in the Components list box is FrontPage 98 Server Extensions. These are installed by default. However, if you are not going to use FrontPage Express or FrontPage 98 to develop the pages hosted on the PWS, these extensions are not necessary, and you can remove them if you want to. Leaving them installed does no harm, however.

Using the Personal Web Server and Personal Web Manager

The PWS and the Personal Web Manager are tightly integrated. The Manager is the main control point for the PWS and gives you access to the rest of the Personal Web Services. You'll explore these tools and services in the next part of the chapter.

Using the Main Window of the Personal Web Manager

The shortcut icon for the Personal Web Manager, which was installed on the desktop during the setup process, is titled Publish. Double-click this icon to start the Manager. Alternatively, choose Start, Programs, Microsoft Personal Web Server, Personal Web Manager.

The Tip of the Day screen now opens over the main Manager window; if you don't want this to happen every time you start the Manager, clear the Show Tips at Startup check box. To step through all the Tips, choose Next for each new Tip.

When you finish with the Tips window, choose Close. Now you can use the services in the various Manager windows (see Figure 37.5). The Main window of the Manager, which is the default opening window, provides basic start/stop tools, and some usage statistics that may be useful if the PWS is used as an intranet server.

FIG. 37.5
The Personal Web Manager is your base for using Windows 98's Personal Web Services.

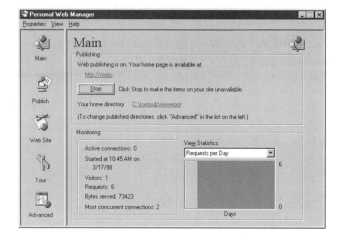

Understanding the Home Page URL (the Web Address)

In the Publishing section of the Main window, you'll see the line Web Publishing Is On. Your Home Page Is Available At. Under this line, in blue, is a web address—http:// followed by a name. This name is actually the one you assigned to your computer when you installed Windows. It is also a name that you can use to access your web; you will remember doing this in the earlier section on testing the PWS.

For example, if you originally named your computer mypc, the blue line is http://mypc. To access the web under this name, type **http://mypc** into the Address bar of a browser, and press Enter to open the page. Upper- or lowercase is not important; either works.

You'll remember that you can also use the local-machine address 127.0.0.1 to open your web provided that the browser is running on the machine that contains the web. However, if the machine is connected to an intranet, the browsers on the other intranet machines can't access the web with that address because it is local-machine only. Those other browsers can instead use the computer name—mypc, in the previous example—to open the web. This assumes that the intranet is properly configured to recognize your machine and its name.

▶ For detailed information about setting up and configuring network hardware and software, refer to the chapters in Part VII, "Windows Network Services," **p. 849**

Starting, Stopping, and Pausing the Server

To stop the server, click the Stop button. This changes the button to a Start button, which you click again to restart the server. You stop the server if you need to make the web site unavailable to users. Note that the Server icon in the system tray remains visible, although it gets a red X on it when it's stopped. Stopping the server, as mentioned earlier, does not unload it from memory.

You can also pause the server. You must do this by right-clicking the Server icon in the system tray (the Manager does not have to be open). This opens a pop-up menu with four choices: Start, Stop, Pause, or Continue. Left-click the one you want.

The functional difference between Stop and Pause is this: If someone tries to access the server when it is stopped, the server does not respond, and the person eventually gets a browser message that it was not possible to connect to the server. If the server is paused, the person's browser gets a message that says, The System Cannot Find the File Specified. This lets the user know that at least the web site exists.

 TIP If you choose Pause, and if the Personal Web Manager window is open, the Start button changes to a Continue button.

Using View Statistics and Monitoring

You can use the View Statistics list box to show requests per day or hour, or visitors per day or hour. The Monitoring box also shows other server performance information:

- The Active Connections entry shows how many connections are transferring data to or from the server at the moment.
- The Started At entry shows when the server was last started, that is, at the boot time of the computer (not when the Start button was last pressed).
- The Visitors entry shows how many unique addresses have connected to the server since it last started.
- The Requests entry shows how many requests were received since the server last started.
- The Bytes Served entry tells how many bytes of information were sent out since the server last started.
- The Most Concurrent Connections entry shows the maximum of simultaneous connections the server handled since it was last started.

Taking the Personal Web Services Tour

The Manager has a short but useful tour built into it. Click the Tour icon in the left pane of the Manager window to view this introduction to the Personal Web Services that are built around the PWS.

Using the Web Site Service

The first time you choose the Web Site service, the Home Page Wizard opens (see Figure 37.6). You need to run this wizard before you can use the Publishing Wizard, which is started when you click the Publish icon.

FIG. 37.6

You can use the Home Page Wizard to create a home page on your Personal Web Server.

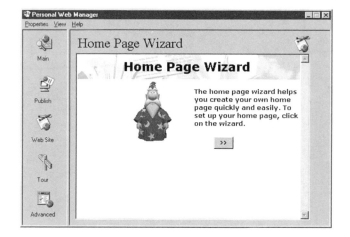

Part

VI

Ch

37

N O T E If you're even moderately experienced at web design and configuration, you might not want to use the home page as produced by the wizard. This is perfectly possible, but might require some minor web reconfiguration. You'll learn how to do this later in the chapter. ■

To create the Home Page, start the wizard as described previously, and follow these steps:

1. In the Home Page Wizard opening window, click the picture of the wizard. A Security Alert opens. Assuming you have no security concerns, choose Yes. Now you can choose among three basic templates for the page appearance. Select any of them (the simplest is Looseleaf) and choose the Forward button, which is marked with a >>. To return to the previous step, choose the button marked with a <<.

2. The Security Alert dialog box appears again. This time, mark the In the Future..." check box to prevent the alert from appearing every time you go to the next step of the wizard. Then choose Yes to move to the next step.

3. Mark the Yes or No option buttons to specify whether you want a guest book. (In the example, all available options are selected). Choose the >> button.

4. Mark the Yes or No option buttons to specify whether you want a drop box. Choose the >> button.

5. At this point, you're told you will get to personalize your home page information. Choose the >> button to continue.

6. The PWS Quick Setup page opens in the browser (see Figure 37.7). This is really a form that you fill out with various kinds of information.

FIG. 37.7

The Quick Setup page enables you to personalize the content of your home page and provides online assistance while you do this.

7. The Hint link at the top of the page leads to a complete help screen for using the setup form. There are various other links on the page that give you help for specific items. Fill in the various heading boxes and text boxes with the appropriate information, referring to the Help links for guidance. You do not have to fill in all the boxes—if you leave a box blank, the wizard ignores that particular entry when it creates the page.

8. You can also specify what links to other web sites will appear on the home page. Locate the URL text box, and type the web address of the site into it. Be sure not to delete the http:// protocol designation.

9. Then, in the Description text box, type the words that are to appear on your page as the link. For example, if the link is to a news site, the URL might read http://www.worldnews.com, and the Description text box might read World News. Then the link on your home page would appear as World News. (If you leave the Description text box blank, the link appears on the page as the full URL). When you're finished, click the Add Link button to place the link on your home page.

10. When you are finished creating the page, click the Enter New Changes button. The wizard generates the new home page and shows it to you. If you need to make changes, you can do so as described next.

Editing an Existing Home Page with the Wizard

After the page is created, you can edit it. Open the Manager if necessary, and click the Web Site icon. The wizard opens again and enables you to edit your page, or view your Guest Book and drop box (see Figure 37.8).

To edit the page, click the Edit Your Home Page Link. This opens the form you used to create the home page. Modify the entries as needed, and click the Enter New Changes button when you are done.

FIG. 37.8

Editing your home page or viewing guest and drop box information is done through the Home Page Wizard.

Part

VI

Ch

37

Using the Guest Book

Including the Guest Book in your home page, either at the time you create the page or if you add the option later, places a link to the Guest Book on the page. This enables visitors to leave you a record of their visit. Visitors can also read the Guest Book entries of other visitors to the site.

When you want to look at this record, open Personal Web Manager, click the Web Site icon, and choose the link to the Guest Book. This displays a query form where you can sort and select the entries you want to see.

To look at all the entries, set the Message Date to Less Than and the date to Today's Date. (This is the default condition, so you may not have to change it). When you click Submit Query, links to all the entries are displayed (see Figure 37.9).

You can also select entries according to date, sender, and subject. Use the query form to specify the values you want, and choose Submit Query. Links to the Guest Book entries are displayed on a scrollable form. Click the one you want to look at, and it displays. After it's displayed, you can use the >> and << buttons to move among the selected Guest Book entries.

 Clicking a column header sorts the display by that header.

To delete a Guest Book entry, open the entry by clicking its link. Then, with the Guest Book entry open, click Delete. You can't restore a deleted entry, so be careful.

FIG. 37.9

Select all or some of the Guest Book entries with this Home Page Wizard form.

When you have finished viewing the entries, you can return to the selection form by clicking the Return to the Guest Book link at the bottom of the page (scroll down if you can't see it). You can also return to the Initial Home Page Wizard screen by clicking the Web Site link at the bottom of the page.

Using the Drop Box

If you add the Drop Box option to your home page at creation time or with a later edit, a visitor can leave you messages by clicking the Drop Box link and filling in a form. The Drop Box differs from the Guest Book entries in that other visitors cannot see the message.

To view your messages, open the Personal Web Manager; then click the Web Site icon. Click the Open Your Drop Box link to display the message links. As with the Guest Book, clicking a column header sorts the display by that header. Click the links to display the message texts, and use the >> and << buttons to move among the messages.

If you need to delete a message, first display it. Then, with the message open, click Delete. Deleting a message cannot be undone.

You can return to the main Drop Box list by clicking the Return to the Drop Box link at the bottom of the page (scroll down if you can't see it). You can also return to the initial Home Page Wizard screen by clicking the Web Site link at the bottom of the page.

Understanding the Home Directory

After the Home Page Wizard has run and the home page has been created, open the Home Directory. This, as you remember, is the folder C:\Inetpub\wwwroot. You can look at it using Windows Explorer, but if you have already opened Personal Web Manager, there's a faster way: in the Main window, click the blue path name next to the words Your Home Directory. This automatically opens Windows Explorer to the home directory.

You can also open your home page quickly, by clicking the blue URL that sits immediately above the Stop button in the Main window.

In the Explorer window, click the wwwroot folder in the left pane, if it isn't already selected. In the right pane, the files and folders contained in wwwroot appear. If you're moderately familiar with web files, you might wonder why you don't see DEFAULT.HTM, the default home page of the web, in this folder. What you do see, instead, is a file named DEFAULT.ASP.

Nevertheless, DEFAULT.ASP is the home page you created with the wizard. ASP stands for Active Server Pages, a Microsoft software technology that (this is very oversimplified) enables the server to combine HTML, scripts, and ActiveX components to do on-the-fly creation of interactive web pages. However, you need to have some knowledge of programming and scripting, as well as HTML, to create Active Server Pages from scratch. That's why the Personal Web Services include a Home Page Wizard—it's so you can set up an interactive home page, with a Guest Book and Drop Box, without knowing anything about Active Server Pages.

At some point, you might want to replace the wizard-produced ASP-type home page with a different page. As mentioned earlier, this might require some minor web reconfiguration and is dealt with later in this chapter.

N O T E   Some non-Microsoft servers require that the default home page be named INDEX.HTM. If you're going to publish your site to a non-Microsoft server, check with the server administrator to see if this is the case. ■

Publishing Documents

After you've created the home page with the Home Page Wizard, you can start using the Publishing Wizard. The Publishing Wizard enables you to easily add documents to your web and automatically adds links to them to your home page. Other people with access to the web— through an intranet, for example—can then access these documents. Making documents available in this way is what is meant by publishing. Documents do not have to be web pages; that is, they do not have to be HTML files.

Of course, you can make documents available without using the Publishing Wizard. This is covered later in this chapter.

Understanding the Publishing Directory

The Publishing directory is a special folder called webpub, located at C:\Inetpub\webpub, and is created during installation of the PWS. It is a read-only directory, which means that documents placed in it cannot be modified. This protects them from being changed by curious, malicious, or meddling visitors to your site—or by you, accidentally.

When you use the wizard to publish a document, a copy—not the original—of the document is made in the Publishing directory. The wizard also maintains a record of the document's original location, so that you can easily update the copy if the original is modified. Deleting a document in the Publishing directory does not delete the original document. Finally, the wizard puts a link to the document on your home page, so that people can get to it after they have your home page open.

Using the Publishing Wizard

To use the wizard, start the Personal Web Manager and click the Publish icon in the sidebar. The Publishing Wizard introductory dialog box opens. Then carry out the following procedure:

1. Click the >> button to move to the next step of the wizard. The Publishing Wizard entry form appears (see Figure 37.10).

FIG. 37.10

The Publishing Wizard form is where you select the documents that will be copied into your webpub Publishing directory.

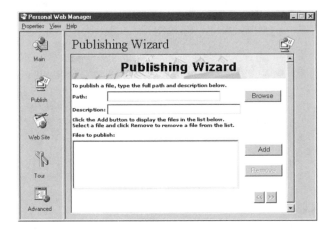

2. Assuming you know the name and full path of the document, type it into the Path text box. (If you don't know it exactly, or you prefer to use Browse, use the procedure described in the next section, "Browsing for Documents with the Publishing Wizard.")

3. Type a description of the document into the Description text box. This description will appear on your page to provide information about the link.

4. Choose Add. This places the document name and description in the Files to Publish list box.

5. If you have other documents to publish, repeat Steps 2 through 4. If you decide not to publish a particular file after all, select its entry in the list box and click the Remove button to delete it from the list. The end result might look like that shown in Figure 37.11.

FIG. 37.11
Here, three documents have been specified for publication and appear in the Files to Publish list box.

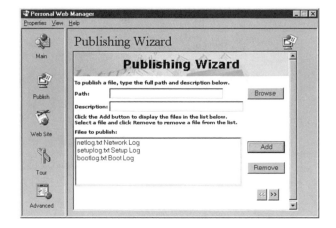

6. After you have selected all the required documents, click the >> button to move to the next step.

7. In the next screen, you are notified that the documents have been added to the webpub folder (also known as the Publishing directory). If you're satisfied with what you've done, you can close the Personal Web Manager or use it to do some other task.

8. However, if you need to make changes to your work, click the << button to go back. You now get the What Do You Want To Do dialog box (see Figure 37.12).

FIG. 37.12
The Publishing Wizard also lets you carry out editing and document maintenance of the contents of the webpub folder.

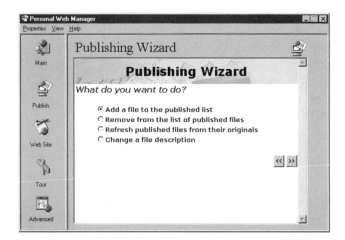

9. To add a file to the published list, mark the top option button and click >>. This takes you to the dialog box where you add documents to the Publishing directory, as in Steps 2 through 7. Follow these steps and, if necessary, go through Step 8 again to return to the What Do You Want To Do dialog box.

10. Assume you're back in the What Do You Want To Do dialog box. To remove a file from the Publishing directory, mark the second option button and choose >>. This opens a dialog box showing all the documents in the Publishing directory (see Figure 37.13).

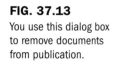

FIG. 37.13

You use this dialog box to remove documents from publication.

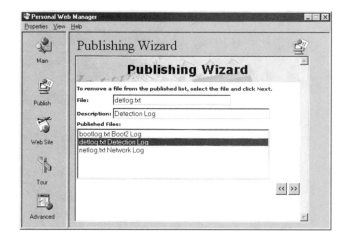

11. To select one document for removal, click its entry in the Published Files list box. To select several documents, hold down the Ctrl key while clicking the document entries. The File and Description list boxes display the filename and description of each selected entry.

12. Choose >>. A Notification dialog box appears, telling you the document was deleted.

13. If you need to make more changes, choose << to return to the What Do You Want To Do dialog box.

14. Assume you're back in the What Do You Want To Do dialog box. To refresh published files with new versions from modified originals, mark the third option button, and choose >>. As before, a dialog box opens to show all the documents in the Publishing directory.

15. Using the Published Files list box, select the files you want refreshed, following the procedure in Step 11. Then choose >>. The Notification dialog box appears again, with the appropriate message. If you need to make more changes, choose << to return to the What Do You Want To Do dialog box.

16. Assume you're back in the What Do You Want To Do dialog box. To change a file description, mark the bottom option button and choose >>. A dialog box opens to show all the documents in the Publishing directory.

17. Using the Published Files list box, select the file whose description you want to change, and type the new description into the Description text box. Choose Update. The entry in the Published Files list box is updated. Choose >> to move to the confirmation dialog box. In the confirmation dialog box, you can again choose <<, if still more changes to the Publishing directory are needed.

After you run the Publishing Wizard for the first time and have placed at least one document in the Publishing directory, the wizard automatically opens with the What Do You Want To Do dialog box when you run it again. Follow the appropriate steps, listed previously, to add, remove, refresh, or redescribe any documents published.

CAUTION

If you accidentally specify an incorrect document path name, the wizard will still add it to the list of documents to be added, removed, or refreshed. You finally get an error message, which asks you to restart the wizard, when you choose the >> button to carry out the operation. If you've just assembled a lengthy list of documents for processing, this can be an annoyance, so be sure all file and path names are correct. Using Browse reduces such errors. Note that this also happens if you try to add a file to the Publishing directory and the file is already there. However, duplicated file descriptions, as distinct from duplicated file names, do not cause an error.

To see the results of the Publishing Wizard, open the home page in your browser. You will see that a link called View My Published Documents has been added to the page. Click this link to view the contents of the Publishing directory. You might see something like the display in Figure 37.14.

FIG. 37.14
Four documents are available in this Publishing directory. Note that they are not all web pages (HTML files)—three of the four are text files.

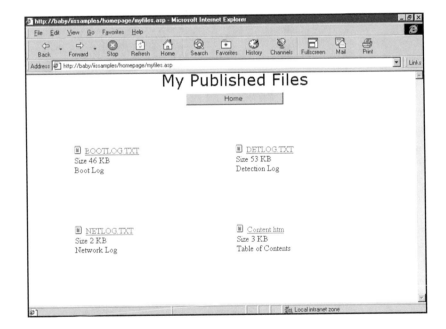

As you've already realized, the Publishing Wizard does not care about the file formats it places in the Publishing directory. A visitor can view a non-HTML file, however, only if his machine has a program that is capable of displaying that kind of file.

Browsing for Documents with the Publishing Wizard

You can select documents to add by using the Publishing Wizard's Browse button, rather than typing the document path names. This is less prone to error, especially when the path names are long and complicated. Do this:

1. In the Personal Web Manager, click the Publish icon to start the wizard, and choose >>. If you don't have any documents in the Publishing directory, you will be taken straight to the screen where you get to add them. If documents already exist in the Publishing directory, you'll be taken to the What Do You Want To Do dialog box. In this case, mark the top option button and choose >> to move to the Publishing dialog box.

2. In the Publishing dialog box, click the Browse button. This opens a browser window to a special page called Server File System, which shows the file structure of the C: hard drive (see Figure 37.15).

FIG. 37.15

The Browse button opens a browser window where you can select files for addition to the Publishing directory.

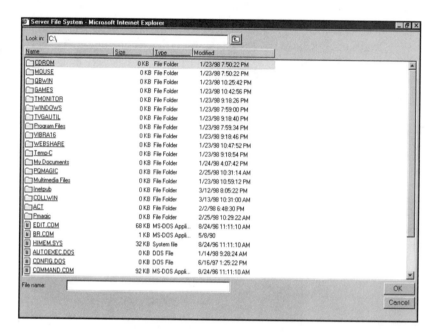

3. Navigation is similar to that used in Windows Explorer. Navigate among the folders until you have located the file you want. Click its entry so that the filename appears in the File Name text box at the bottom of the browser window.

4. Choose OK. The browser closes, and the full path name of the selected file appears in the Path text box of the wizard. Type a description into the Description text box, and choose Add to place the file on the list of documents to be added.

5. Repeat Steps 2 through 4 until all desired files have been added to the list.

6. Choose >> to place the listed documents in the Publishing directory.

N O T E At the time of writing (April, 1998) the Browse tool of the Publishing Wizard had some rough edges. If these persist in the release product, you might need to click a folder icon, wait till a gray selection bar appears, and then click the folder again to open it. Also, you cannot select multiple files in Browse and add them all at once to the wizard. Further, to reference another disk, you have to type its drive designation into the Look In text box, and then click the Up folder icon at the right end of the text box. Finally, the response time of the Browse tool is rather poor. ■

Using Windows Explorer to Add Documents to the Publishing Directory

You can also use Windows Explorer to copy or move an existing document from somewhere in your file system, into the webpub folder. This removes any need to use the Publishing Wizard, and you get some of the wizard's benefits; the very act of placing a file in the webpub folder automatically inserts a link to that file into the home page. You can then use the wizard to edit the link description. The drawback is that you can't refresh the document using the wizard; if you try to, the wizard politely informs you that this is not possible.

Note, however, that placing a document into the home directory of C:\Inetpub\wwwroot does not place a link to this document on the home page. This automatic linking works only with the webpub Publishing directory. Also, if you have a home page other than the one produced by the Home Page Wizard, this automatic linking does not occur.

Part

VI

Ch

37

Adding Documents and Subdirectories to the Home Directory

The simplest way to add documents and subdirectories to the home directory is to use Windows Explorer to create folders and subfolders within the home directory. After the web structure is set up, you can use a Web Page Editor to create, store, and link HTML pages and other types of documents within that structure.

In some cases, however, you may find that virtual directories are a better method of adding content to a web. The use of virtual directories is examined later in this chapter.

▶ **See** "Creating Web Pages with FrontPage Express," **p. 779**

Using Advanced Services to Configure Your Web

The Advanced Service of the Personal Web Manager enables you to reconfigure your web site according to new or changed circumstances. For example, you might need to replace the home page generated by the wizard with a home page of your own design. This is just one possibility of several, all of which will be examined in the next sections.

Replacing the Default Home Page in the PWS Home Directory

Before beginning this task, let's briefly examine how home pages and home directories behave when accessed by a browser. A user accesses a site by using one of two basic methods. If the user uses a path name that ends with a filename (such as http://mypc/reviews/books.htm) then the named page—BOOKS.HTM, in this example—appears in the browser.

However, if the user leaves out the filename and types only the path, such as http://mypc/reviews, the server has to figure out which file to send. Usually there is some sort of default page in the specified directory, and this is the page the server sends to the browser. The default page of the home directory (http://mypc in the example) is the one we usually refer to as the home page of the web. Note, however, that each subdirectory of the home directory can also have its default page; it's sort of a home page for the subdirectory.

As you remember, the default home page created by the Home Page Wizard is C:\Inetpub\wwwroot\default.asp. If you have a different home page you want to use, such as DEFAULT.HTM, you can simply copy it into the wwwroot folder using Windows Explorer.

Then, however, you might need to make a configuration change. Start the Personal Web manager and click the Advanced icon. The Advanced Options dialog box opens (see Figure 37.16).

FIG. 37.16

You use the Advanced Options dialogs to modify the configuration of your web.

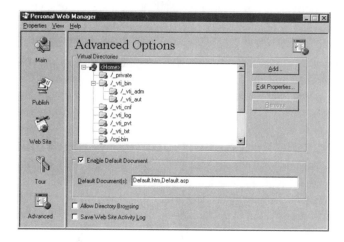

Look at the text box labeled Default Documents(s). As installed, it will have the filenames DEFAULT.HTM and DEFAULT.ASP in it. The entries in this box specify which page the server sends to the browser when the browser first accesses the site.

Let's assume that the name of your PC is mypc, and therefore your web's name is mypc. When a user types http://mypc into the browser, the page first reached is specified by the entries in the Default Document text box, and by their order. DEFAULT.HTM is the first entry, so the server will try to find that file in the home directory, wwwroot. Because you put the file there, the server finds it and sends it to the browser.

As you likely have figured out, if DEFAULT.HTM were not present, the server would search for the next name in the list and find DEFAULT.ASP. DEFAULT.ASP is still in the directory (unless you deleted it,) so the server would send that page to the browser.

You can also delete the existing DEFAULT.ASP and replace it with one of your own design. If you want the server to search for DEFAULT.ASP first and DEFAULT.HTM second, edit the list in the Default Documents text box to reverse the search order. You must put a comma between each file name.

If you want the server to search for only one default filename, edit the list to show only that name.

But what happens if the document is not found? This can result from leaving a comma out of the file list, from naming errors, or because the file is not present. In that case, the server returns an error message saying, Directory Listing Denied. This also happens if you unmark the check box labeled Enable Default Document, unless Directory Browsing is allowed. Directory Browsing is discussed in the section after the next.

Specifying Default Documents in Subdirectories of a Web

You can extend the previous principle to subdirectories. Suppose you wanted to use SUBDEF.HTM as the name of the default file of each subdirectory of your web. First, name the desired subdirectory default pages to SUBDEF.HTM. Then, in the Advanced Options dialog box of the Personal Web Manager, edit the list in the Default Documents text box to read DEFAULT.HTM, SUBDEF.HTM. When a user visits the web and navigates to a subdirectory of it, the server searches for these two names when it opens the subdirectory. It can't find DEFAULT.HTM in the subdirectory, but it does find SUBDEF.HTM. It then sends SUBDEF.HTM to the browser.

Part VI

Ch

37

Allowing Directory Browsing

This is a plain-vanilla way of displaying the documents on your site. You might consider using it if you frequently add to or delete from your site content or if you have a lot of documents in non-HTML format in the site.

To enable Directory Browsing, go to the Advanced Options dialog box of the Personal Web Manager. Unmark the Enable Default Document check box, and mark the Allow Directory Browsing check box. Now, when a visitor enters the site, he or she sees a display like the one in Figure 37.17. To navigate the site, the visitor clicks the various links.

FIG. 37.17
Directory Browsing gives a straightforward list of files and subdirectories within a directory.

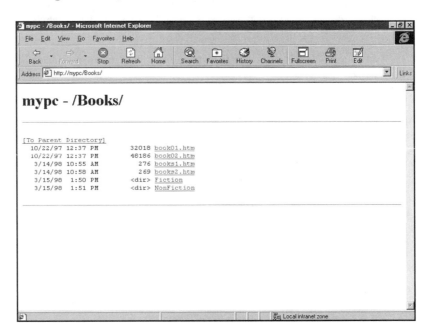

Mixing Default Documents and Directory Browsing

You might find it convenient, for some webs, to mark both the Enable Default Document and Allow Directory Browsing check boxes. With this arrangement, a visitor who enters a directory containing a default document sees that document. However, if you omit a default document from a particular directory, and set up a link to that directory rather than to a page in it, the visitor sees a directory listing after clicking the link. This means you can set up frequently changed directories to use directory browsing, while relatively static directories can have a normal HTML default page.

Changing the Default Home Directory

Before going into this, it would be a good idea to explain briefly the usage of default documents in the context of a web's structure. Every web has a home directory that serves as the primary entry point for visitors; this is where the web's home page is stored. Using our earlier example of a web name, when a visitor types the address http://mypc into the browser, he or she is automatically taken to the home page DEFAULT.ASP of the C:\Inetpub\wwwroot folder (assuming a default installation).

Suppose, however, that you already have an existing web nestled in its own carefully thought-out folder layout, and this is the web you want people to access when they type http://mypc into their browsers. However, you don't want to endure the complications of moving all of the web's folders and files over into the C:\Inetpub\wwwroot structure.

As an example, imagine that this web has a top-level folder called C:\Reviews, and this folder in turn has two subfolders, one called Books, the other called Movies. You want the home page stored in the Reviews folder to be the page that visitors first see when they access your web site. Finally, assume that this home page in the Reviews folder is named DEFAULT.HTM.

To change the default Home Directory from C:\Inetpub\wwwroot to C:\Reviews, follow these steps:

1. Start the Personal Web Manager. Click the Advanced icon in the sidebar to open the Advanced Options dialog box.

2. Click the Home icon at the top of the directory tree. Then choose Edit Properties. The Edit Directory dialog box appears (see Figure 37.18).

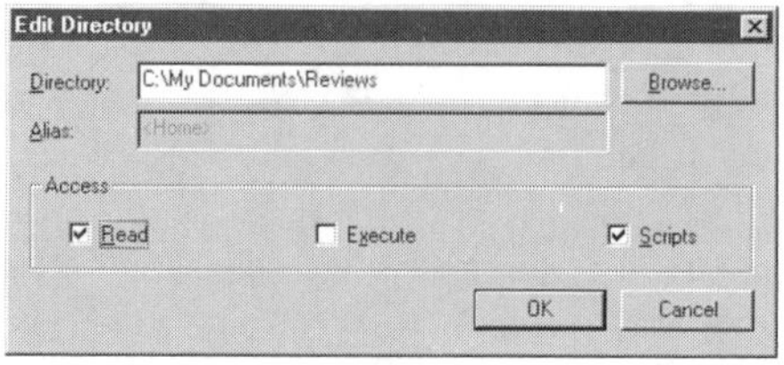

FIG. 37.18
The Edit Directory dialog box enables you to change the Home Directory and modify the permissions associated with it.

3. In the Directory text box, type the path name of the folder that is to be the new home directory. Alternatively, use the Browse button to open a Browse dialog box where you can select the desired folder. When you close the Browse dialog box, the path name of the selected folder appears in the text box.

4. Set the access permissions for the directory by marking or unmarking each check box. You can turn on or off the access for Read, Execute, and Scripts. The details of the access permissions are given in the section immediately following this one.

5. Close the Edit Directory dialog box. The home directory has been changed.

You'll notice that even after the change has taken place, the directory tree shown in the Virtual Directories window shows no visible difference. This is because the window is a display of a virtual directory structure, not a display of a physical directory structure like that of Windows Explorer. All three folders of the Reviews web, in the example, are "contained" in the <Home> folder at the top of the virtual directory tree.

However, if you now open the Reviews web in a browser, your changed home page appears, and its links lead to the other pages and files of that web. You can still use the webpub directory, if you need to. You don't have to physically move it to the home directory of your new web. This is because it's also a virtual directory of the home directory in this display. You'll learn more about virtual directories later in this chapter.

Understanding Directory Access Permissions

You encountered the PWS directory access permissions for the first time in the previous section. As you saw, access permissions come in three flavors: Read, Execute, and Scripts. Each has its own characteristics, as follows:

■ With Read access turned on, visitors can read or download files stored in your home directory and all directories stored in the home directory. If a directory's Read access is turned off, the browser displays an error message. If you turn off Read access for your home directory, then Read access is also turned off for all directories physically contained in the home directory. If you need to set directory access permissions on a directory-by-directory basis, you have to use virtual directories, which will be discussed later in this chapter. Directories containing web content, such as HTML pages, should have Read access. However, you should deny Read access for directories containing Common Gateway Interface (CGI) applications, Internet Server Application Program Interfaces (ISAPI), and dynamic link libraries (DLLs), to prevent curious or malicious users from downloading the application files. All directories created during setup have Read access set to on, by default.

■ Execute access enables an application to run in its owner directory. To enhance security, don't allow Execute access for directories where you have placed web content.

■ With Scripts access turned on, a script engine can run in the directory. This occurs even without having Execute permission set. Use Script access for directories that contain ASP scripts, Internet Database Connector (IDC) scripts, or other scripts. Script access is safer than Execute access because you can limit the applications that can be run in the directory. All directories created during setup have Scripts access set to On, by default.

> **CAUTION**
>
> Even if you don't provide links to certain content in the home directory and in its contained folders, this content can still be viewed by visitors, provided they can discover the file and folder names. Keep only public-access material in the home directory and its contained folders.

Understanding Virtual Directories

A virtual directory is a directory that is not physically contained within the home directory. With the PWS, this home directory (at default) is the folder C:\Inetpub\wwwroot. If you add virtual directories to your web, browsers see these directories as being contained in the home directory, though they are not physically there.

There is a very important security point to be noted about the home directory. It and any subdirectories physically within it are effectively publishing directories, accessible to anyone who visits your site even if you haven't included any links to those subdirectories or to their content. This is because the access permissions applied to the home directory affect both it and the subdirectories physically contained within it; you can't apply permissions on a directory-by-directory basis. So, if you remove Read access from your home directory, nobody can view anything in it, or in its subdirectories. This rather defeats the purpose of your web! Virtual directories provide a way around this.

Additionally, virtual directories make your site more secure because they use an alias. An alias is a name that a browser uses to access a directory, but it is not the real path name to the directory; hence users can't determine where your files are physically located on your PC.

Finally, virtual directories make it easier to modify or reorganize a web site. If your web site uses virtual directories, you can rename and move the real ones as much as you like and simply use the Personal Web Manager to re-map the connection between the virtual directories and the real ones.

Understanding the PWS Virtual Directories

Earlier, you looked briefly at the virtual directory structure provided by the PWS. Now it's time for a more detailed examination; start the Personal Web Manager, and click the Advanced icon. The Advanced Options dialog box appears, with the Virtual Directories Tree displayed (see Figure 37.19)

FIG. 37.19

The Virtual Directories tree helps you organize the "virtual structure" of your web.

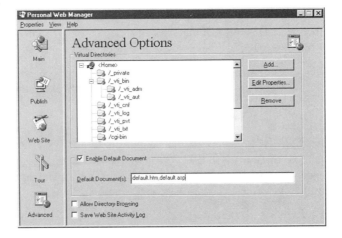

You probably have wondered what all these virtual directories do, especially since they are present even when you change the home directory from the PWS default to a home directory of your own choosing. The essentials are as follows:

- ▓ <Home> contains all the directories that are physically contained in the physical home directory; in other words, the directories as they appear in Windows Explorer.

- ▓ IISADMIN, IISHELP, and IISSAMPLES refer to utility directories used by the PWS. Do not remove these virtual directories.

- ▓ SCRIPTS is a script directory used by the PWS. If you don't need it, you can remove it; however, leaving it alone does no harm.

- ▓ WEBPUB is the special Publishing directory you worked with earlier. You can remove it if you will not be publishing your documents with the PWS-generated Home Page and the Publishing Wizard. Again, leaving it there does no harm.

- ▓ msadc references some system files needed by the PWS. Do not remove this virtual directory.

- ▓ cgi-bin contains Common Gateway Interface scripts for the forms in your web. Do not remove this virtual directory.

The previous list did not include the virtual directories _private, and all the directories beginning with _vti. These directories are associated with the FrontPage server extensions and are needed if the PWS is to run pages you create with FrontPage Express or FrontPage itself. If you aren't going to use FrontPage in either flavor, you don't need these directories. However, you should not simply remove them with the Remove button, as this might cause the PWS to behave unpredictably. You should instead use the PWS Setup program to uninstall the FrontPage Server Extensions.

Including Web Content as Virtual Directories

Using virtual directories can extend the content of your web without requiring drastic changes to your disk's file structure. However, because virtual directories can be a bit confusing at first, let's work with a concrete example. This will be the Reviews web examined in an earlier section of this chapter, on "Changing a Home Directory." This web has a top-level folder called C:\Reviews, and this folder in turn has two subfolders, one called Books, the other called Movies. Within each folder are pages with links to other pages in other folders.

Assume that this web is now the home directory of the PWS. You can verify the identity of a home directory with the following procedure.

Open the Personal Web Manager and click the Advanced icon. In the Virtual Directories tree display, select the <Home> icon, and then choose Edit Properties. The Directory text box tells you that the home directory is indeed C:\Reviews. As mentioned earlier, the virtual directory tree does not show physical subdirectories, such as Movies or Books. This is because they are subsumed under the <Home> virtual directory.

Now assume you have another folder, called C:\Writing, whose content you want to include in your web. You could, of course, physically move or copy this folder into your web's home directory (C:\Reviews in our example). However, it's easier to simply make it into a virtual directory. Then, if you later decide to remove the folder's content from the web, all you need do is remove the virtual directory from the Personal Web Manager's Virtual Directory tree. Doing this has no effect on the real folder called Writing or on its content.

Here's what you do to create a virtual directory that references a physical directory. This example assumes that the virtual directory will be a subdirectory of the home directory.

1. Open the Personal Web Manager and click the Advanced icon to go to the Advanced Options dialog box.

2. Select the <Home> icon at the top of the virtual directory tree. Then choose Add to open the Add Directory dialog box (see Figure 37.20).

FIG. 37.20
You use the Add
Directory dialog box to
add a virtual directory
to the tree.

3. Type the full path name of the physical directory (C:\Writing in our example) into the Directory text box, or use the Browse button to open the Browse dialog box and select the file. When you close the Browse dialog box, the path name appears in the text box.

4. In the Alias text box, type an alias for the directory. This is the fake name that browsers use to access the subdirectory; as a rule, you should make the alias different from the name of the real directory. In the example, it's Novel.

5. Mark the Read, Execute, and Scripts check boxes according to the access you want to allow.

6. Close the Add Directory dialog box. After a pause, the alias you specified (Novel, in the example) appears in the Virtual Directories window. This entry is your new virtual directory.

7. To remove a virtual directory, select it and choose Remove in the Advanced Options dialog box.

Note that a virtual directory can be added as a subdirectory of any higher virtual directory. For example, you could have created Novel as a virtual subdirectory of the /SCRIPTS virtual directory. This gives you enormous flexibility in creating web structures.

Now you can set up links on your other pages to reference the pages in the new virtual directory. However, note that the links that reference the pages of a virtual directory must use the directory's alias in the URL of the link rather than the actual name of the physical directory. For example, if the physical directory is named Writing, and the alias assigned to the virtual directory is Novel, then the URLs of such links must reference Novel, not Writing.

Now, when a user goes to your web and accesses a page in the virtual directory, the visible address (in the example) is http://mypc/novel/. The existence of the Writing folder is hidden.

Part

VI

Ch

37

Managing Link Changes with Virtual Directories

Using virtual directories has one big advantage over using physical directories.

Suppose you have a home page that has a dozen links to pages in a physical (not virtual) directory. The name of this physical directory is Writing. Now suppose you move the physical directory Writing and all its content to somewhere else in your PC's file structure. You then have to manually edit the URL of each link on the home page to reflect the change in the location of Writing. If you don't, the links do not work any more.

This can be a big job if many links are involved. However, if the links are to a virtual directory, the change is simple.

N O T E Web restructuring is one reason why the subdirectories of the home directory are not listed in the virtual directory tree. If you need to move the home directory's subdirectories around, you do so only in Windows Explorer and don't have to repeat the operation in the virtual directory tree.

Now suppose the physical directory is Writing and your web uses a virtual directory to access it, under the alias Novel. Suppose also that the links on the home page reference the virtual directory Novel, instead of the physical directory Writing. Then use the following procedure:

1. Move the physical directory to wherever you like. When you've done so, go to the Advanced Options dialog box of the Personal Web Manager, and use the virtual directory tree to select the name of the virtual directory (Novel, in the example).

2. Choose Edit Properties to open the Edit Directory dialog box, and use the Browse button to locate and select the new location of the physical directory (Writing, in the example).

3. When you've selected the location, close the Browse dialog box. The new path name of the moved physical directory appears in the Directory text box. Do not change its Alias.

4. Choose OK. The virtual structure of your web is now updated. You don't need to edit links that point to Novel, because they are still correct. That is, the PWS has changed the mapping of Novel to the new physical location of Writing, so the links still work.

Managing Permissions with Virtual Directories

Assume now that you create another directory called Programs as a physical subdirectory of C:\Reviews. Into Programs you put some utility programs that you want visitors to be able to run. However, you don't want your visitors to be able to see the program files themselves; in other words, you don't want this directory to have Read access, just Execute access, so the utility programs can run.

However, you soon realize that visitors can indeed see and even download the files containing these utilities. This is because the files are in a physical subdirectory of the home directory and are therefore in a readable directory, because all the subdirectories of a home directory must inherit the home directory's access permissions. What do you do?

You make the Programs directory into a virtual directory and set its access permissions in that directory. Begin by using Windows Explorer to move (not copy) the Programs folder to some other place in your file structure, so it's no longer a subfolder of the Reviews folder.

Then, using the procedure you learned earlier in this chapter, create a virtual directory that references the physical directory; for security, use a different name as the alias. Then unmark the Read and Scripts check boxes, and mark the Execute check box. Now the programs can be run by users, but the users have no other access to them.

Using Activity Logs

If you go to the Advanced Options dialog box of the Manager and mark the check box labeled Save Web Site Activity Log, then the PWS maintains a log of who has visited your site. This can be a useful security check on site activity. The files are stored in the Windows\System folder in a folder named W3svc1. The names begin with NC followed by year, month, and day as numbers. The logs are in NCSA log file format and are viewable in any text editor. ●

Windows Network Services

CHAPTER 38

Configuring Windows Network Components

by James Portanova and Larry Passo

In this chapter

An Administrator's Guide to Windows Networking

Windows 98 includes a comprehensive set of networking tools right out of the box. It supports peer-to-peer and client/server network configurations. Windows 98 preserves and extends Windows 95's strong networking roots and introduces innovations such as Automatic Private IP Addressing and the Microsoft Family Logon.

Private IP Addressing is intended for small, private networks using the popular (and new Windows 98 default) TCP/IP protocol suite, without the need to manually configure IP addresses or a DHCP server.

Microsoft Family Logon lists all users who have accounts on a Windows 98 system and enables those users to simply select their names from a list, instead of having to type it into a logon box.

Virtual Private Networking enables remote workers to reach their office network by tunneling through a public network like the Internet.

> **NOTE** Virtual Private Networking has been available as an add-on for Windows 95 as part of the Dial-Up Networking upgrade v. 1.2. ■

Implementing comprehensive management and security measures still requires the use of Windows NT, Novell NetWare, or IntranetWare Server's management capabilities. However, supervisors of small peer-to-peer networks should be pleased with Windows 98's surprisingly useful additions and improvements to its arsenal of support and administrative utilities.

Windows 98 Network Security

Windows 98 is designed primarily as a client operating system, and as such, shows a dependency upon attachment to a client/server network to realize the full potential of its security features.

To gain tight, but flexible, control of who can access shared resources on your computer, you should use user-level access control. User-level access control enables you to grant access to your shared resources based on accounts maintained by a Windows NT domain or workgroup or a Novell NetWare server. You can control the type of access that each user can have to your resources by assigning passwords to each user instead of your shares, as is the case with share-level access control.

Both user-level and share-level access control protect the network shares on a Windows 98 computer only when they are accessed remotely. Users who bypass the startup password by clicking Cancel at the logon prompt, booting from a floppy disk, or pressing Ctrl during startup to show the Windows 98 Startup menu gain complete access to the local computer's resources. User accounts are maintained with distributed user lists and password lists, which are stored on each individual workstation and are easily compromised.

> **CAUTION**
>
> You use System Policy Editor to force users to log in to access a Windows 98 system. However, a user with an MS-DOS boot floppy can still gain full access to local resources, with the exception of information that is stored on FAT32 partitions.

Windows 98 User Profiles and the Network

Roaming profiles enable users of Windows 98 computers to have their personal user settings follow them from computer to computer by storing the user's profile on a central profile server. Roaming profiles copies the appropriate profile to whichever computer the user logs on to. Any user profile changes are automatically updated to the profile server.

 Roaming profiles are based on the user's account, rather than the particular computer where the user chooses to work.

Part VII
Ch
38

> **CAUTION**
>
> Although Windows 98, Windows NT 3.5x, and Windows NT 4.0 all support roaming user profiles, each of the three operating systems has its own mechanism for the storage of the user profiles on the profile server. If you have users who use computers with more than one of these operating systems, any changes that they make to their user profiles only follow them to another computer with the same operating system.

Through mandatory user profiles, an NT administrator can preconfigure any user's initial environment. Although users with mandatory user profiles can make modifications to their environment, changes made by the user aren't saved to the profile server, and the original preferred desktop reappears the next time that the user logs in to the network. This assures a consistent initial desktop environment across the entire network, easing support time and costs.

 The only way to restrict users from making any undesired changes to their environment is to create a System Policy file with the appropriate restrictions. System Policies are discussed later in this chapter in the section "System Policy Editor."

▶ **See** "Using the System Policy Editor," **p. 378**

Zero Administration

The goal of the Zero Administration Initiative is to lower the total cost of ownership (TCO) in an organization by enabling the organization to

- Lock down desktop configurations and perform centralized management tasks.
- Efficiently install and update software on a networkwide basis.
- Monitor and control software-licensing issues.

Zero Administration specifies the use of several existing, and under-development, non-vendor-specific technologies to create a suite of management tools that achieve the goals stated previously.

Technologies, such as automated software installation, predefined option settings for those installs and configurations, and push updates across the network are all designed with Zero Administration in mind. Following is a list of some of the applications that make up the Zero Administration Initiative:

- The Microsoft Internet Explorer Administration Kit (IEAK) enables administrators to standardize and customize the Active Desktop across an organization or its divisions.

 T I P   You can find full details or obtain a copy of the Internet Administration Kit at **http://
ieak.microsoft.com/Default.asp**.

- The Microsoft Systems Management Server (SMS) handles software and hardware inventory, software distribution and updates, and remote diagnostics on the network.
- The Microsoft Management Console (MMC) hosts enterprise management tools from Microsoft and third-party vendors.

Getting Started with Windows 98 Networking

To get started with Windows 98 networking, you will need the following minimum requirements:

- A null-modem cable (either serial or parallel) for use with direct cable connection software—for low-performance connectivity only
- Network adapter cards for connecting each computer to the network cabling
- Appropriate lengths of the proper cabling and end connectors—enough to wire each workstation to the network
- Possibly a wiring concentrator, popularly referred to as a hub, which centrally attaches each workstation to the network

Network adapter cards should be Plug and Play-compliant to take advantage of Windows 98's automatic hardware configuration features. Token Ring adapters are available in 4Mbps and 16Mbps speeds. Ethernet adapters are offered in 10Mbps and 100Mbps speeds. The newer 100Mbps PCI adapters are all PnP-compliant.

 T I P   It is extremely helpful to keep a reference chart listing usernames, passwords, workgroups, computers, share names, and each of the several other items that come up during the installation of your network.

The rest of this chapter introduces you to the basic steps of setting up a Windows 98 client on a network. It covers the following topics:

- How Windows 98's Plug and Play features detect, install, and configure the basic components of Windows networking, automatically.

- The network adapter card: your computer's connection to the networking infrastructure.

- Protocols: what they do, why they are essential to networking communication, and how to choose and configure them properly.

- Installing and configuring client software: Windows 98 is designed to interoperate with most popular modern and legacy network operating systems.

- Network services: Sharing printers, files, fax modems, and access to the Internet are the main reasons networks were developed. This chapter shows you how your computer and its resources can participate in sharing network services.

- Connecting your local area network to the Internet.

- After your network is up and running, it requires some care and attention. This chapter includes tips and reveals some of the secrets that professional network administrators use to keep their own networks healthier, more secure, and trouble free.

- Even the most skilled and well-informed network administrator occasionally discovers an unwelcome problem adversely affecting the network. This chapter reviews some of the most common network glitches and suggests some proven approaches towards solving them.

Part
VII

Ch
38

Using Plug and Play for Automatic Network Setup

The goal of Plug and Play is computer devices that configure themselves without manual user intervention. Generally, to install an internal Plug and Play device, all you need to do is turn off the machine; install the board; and turn the machine back on.

Windows 98 should then automatically detect the device, install the appropriate device drivers and supporting files, and configure hardware resources, such as the following:

- Interrupt Request Lines (IRQs), hardware lines over which peripherals send requests for service to the CPU.

- Input/Output Ports (I/Os), hardware paths from the hardware bus to the CPU used for communication by peripheral devices.

- Direct Memory Access channels (DMAs), used by intelligent peripherals to directly access system memory without going through the CPU.

To see how your computer's hardware resources are currently allocated, follow these steps:

1. In Control Panel, click the System icon.
2. Select the Device Manager tab.
3. Highlight Computer at the top of the device tree.
4. Click Properties.
5. Toggle between the radio buttons assigned to the various resource listings (see Figure 38.1).

FIG. 38.1

You can view the resources used in your computer, which is useful when installing hardware or trouble-shooting problems.

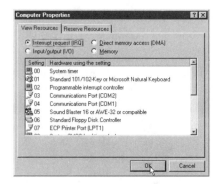

When Windows 98 detects a new device, it arbitrates among the currently installed devices that are vying for use of limited resources. It resolves any conflicts and reassigns resources, to accommodate peripherals that might work with only certain settings.

For example, your network interface card might function properly only while using IRQ 5; your sound card might be able to accept IRQs 5 or 10. If the sound card was occupying IRQ 5 when the network card was installed in the computer, Windows might assign the sound card IRQ 10, freeing up IRQ 5 to be reassigned to the newly installed network card.

Before the development of Plug and Play, each peripheral added to a computer had to be configured in a mostly trial-and-error process. Even today, unless a system is 100 percent Plug and Play equipped, the user might have to do some manual tweaking to install a particular device.

Windows 98's Plug and Play feature is especially useful in the case of network configuration. When a Windows 98 computer comes to life on an existing network connection, the Plug and Play feature performs the following functions:

- Automatically finds and configures the network adapter
- Installs the NDIS (Network Driver Interface Specification) adapter driver
- Installs and binds any protocols that are already in use by other network adapters
- Adds client software
- Activates network services

This configuration is completed transparently during setup when your Windows 98 Welcome Screen comes up for the first time. If you have entered the correct logon password, you are already connected to the network.

Another feature of Windows 98's Plug and Play for networking is the ability to *hot swap* laptop PCMCIA Ethernet cards. When the operating system detects the insertion of a new network adapter, it automatically loads the hardware profile, which includes all the related network device drivers. Conversely, when the card is removed, the alternate profile without network drivers is loaded.

NOTE Some network applications and device drivers can intelligently sense when a computer is disconnected from the network and go into offline mode. For example, a user can continue to print to a network printer while offline, and Windows spools the output to disk. When the printer is available, a prompt notifies the user that output is available to be printed over the network. ■

NOTE To hot swap PCMCIA network adapters and have Windows 98 automatically switch to a network-compliant profile, all running network components, including client software, adapter drivers, and network protocols, must be in full 32-bit protected mode. Real-mode 16-bit drivers are not compatible with hot swapping. ■

Installing and Configuring a Network Adapter

The network adapter is your critical link to the network. It is the physical connection of your computer to the actual network cabling. If your network adapter did not come pre-installed in your computer, here are the steps you can follow to install a Plug and Play-compliant network adapter in your desktop computer:

Part

VII

Ch

38

1. Take the precaution of unplugging the system from the power source, grounding yourself, and so on before working inside the computer case.
2. Find the correct type of expansion slot for the card, usually ISA or PCI. PCI slots are easily recognized by their white coloring.
3. Unscrew the port cover corresponding to the open expansion slot. Be sure not to drop the screw inside the computer case.
4. Carefully insert the network adapter into the slot; apply even pressure across the length of the card until it pushes into place flush against the slot on a level angle.
5. Secure the adapter to the port opening with the screw.
6. Attach the network cabling. If it is 10BaseT, there is a modular jack similar to a modular telephone plug. If it is 10Base2, attach a BNC T connector to the card, and then attach the BNC connector from the coaxial cable to the card. If your node is at the end of the chain, attach a 50-ohm terminator to the free side of the T connector on the card. Otherwise, attach another cable to the T and connect it to the next computer in the network chain.

As already described in the section on Plug and Play devices, after the system is powered back up, Windows 98 detects the new hardware and any preconfigured protocols, installs the NDIS drivers, and configures a Plug and Play network adapter automatically.

CAUTION
Although Windows 98 supports legacy network adapters, you have to make sure that they are properly configured and do not cause conflicts with other devices in your system.

If you install a legacy adapter, which is not Plug and Play, there are some additional steps you need to take to get it to work with your Windows 98 client. First, make a note of what system resources are available to be assigned to your card. To get a resource report, do the following:

1. In Control Panel, click the System icon.

2. Select the Device Manager tab.

3. Highlight Computer at the top of the device tree.

4. Click the Print button on the bottom right of the System Properties dialog box (see Figure 38.2).

5. Select the System Summary radio button.

6. Click OK.

FIG. 38.2

It is a good idea to keep a copy of your system information handy. It can help when troubleshooting problems.

Windows outputs a concise two-page report listing each of your system resource assignments. The important information to notice is the IRQ Summary.

Find out from your adapter's documentation which IRQ assignments are its recommended settings and compare them to the free resources in your current configuration. For example, if the adapter manufacturer recommends IRQ 5 or 11, check your Device Manager report to ensure that the recommended IRQs are not being used by other devices.

N O T E If your adapter is the ISA bus type, it needs exclusive use of an IRQ assignment. If it is a PCI bus type, it probably will be able to dynamically share an assignment with another device already installed in the system because most recent PCI adapters are Plug and Play devices. ■

Configure your legacy, nonPnP, adapter by setting the appropriate hard-wired configuration jumpers or dip switches or by using a disk or CD-ROM based software configuration utility. Then install the adapter in an available expansion slot as described previously.

To configure a legacy adapter with a vendor-supplied utility, boot Windows into a Safe mode command prompt by holding down the Ctrl key during bootup and choosing that option from the Startup menu. After you have configured the card through software, power down the computer and restart it, and then wait for Windows 98 to come up and hopefully detect the addition of the new hardware.

N O T E Windows 98 differs from Windows 95 by its use of the Ctrl key, rather than the F8 key, to boot up into the Startup menu. ■

Allow Windows 98 to attempt to detect your new adapter. Then confirm or change the device it detects in the Add New Hardware dialog box.

If Windows 98 does not detect the new hardware at startup, you can run the Add New Hardware Wizard from Control Panel, and once again, allow Windows to search new hardware. If Windows 98 still cannot detect your hardware, the wizard gives you the option to manually install a device; click Next. Select Network Adapters from the listed hardware types, click Next, and then specify the correct manufacturer and model. Alternatively, if you have a driver on disk, click Have Disk and specify the path to your drivers.

Part

VII

Ch

38

After the legacy adapters are detected or assigned, make sure that the resources Windows assigned match those previously set by jumpers or software-based configuration. If you need to change the resources that Windows 98 uses to communicate with a legacy device, you can do so by going into the Device Manager, selecting the card under Network Adapters on the device tree, clicking Properties, and then clicking the Resources tab.

If you see any entries in the Conflicting Device list, select the resource type; then click Set Configuration Manually and choose the proper setting from the drop-down list. Verify that no further conflicts exist with the new settings in the Conflict Information window. Restart the computer.

N O T E You might need to deselect the Use Automatic Settings check box to access the Change Setting button in the Resources dialog box. ■

CAUTION

Changing the assigned resources in Windows 98 for a hardware component automatically reconfigures only Plug and Play devices. You must change jumpers or use a vendor-supplied utility to reconfigure legacy devices.

After you restart your computer, go back into Device Manager to check that the adapter has been properly configured (see Figure 38.3). If you find a conflict, start Windows 98 Help from your Start menu, click the Contents tab, select Troubleshooting, select Windows 98 Troubleshooting, and then select Hardware Conflict to start the Conflict Resolution Wizard.

FIG. 38.3

Configuring a network adapter's resources in Device Manager.

Installing and Configuring Network Protocols

Protocols define how communication takes place on and between networks. They stipulate the size, timing, and structure of data packets on the network. For network nodes to talk to one another, they must have at least one protocol in common.

Windows 98 includes support for the three protocols that are commonly used to support local area networks (LANs):

- *TCP/IP* is the default protocol suite on Windows 98 networks and is automatically bound to each detected network adapter and client. Due primarily to the popularity of the Internet, TCP/IP has become the standard protocol in modern computer networking.

- *NetBEUI* is a fast, nonroutable, efficient protocol optimized for small- to medium-sized LANs.

- *IPX/SPX-compatible transport* is a routable Novell NetWare-compatible protocol automatically installed with the Microsoft Client for NetWare. Under Windows 98, the IPX/SPX frame type and network address are automatically configured. Nodes running IPX/SPX can communicate with NetWare servers or nodes running File & Print Services for NetWare. They can also become file and print servers under NetWare themselves.

> **CAUTION**
>
> There are several different versions of the IPX protocol, which are commonly referred to as frame types. Computers that are configured with different IPX frame types are not able to communicate with one another. Although Windows 98 attempts to automatically determine and configure your computer to use the IPX frame type that is being used on your network, it is possible that you might need or desire to manually set the IPX frame type.

To manually specify the frame type in Windows 98:

1. Open the Network icon in the Control Panel.

2. From the list of installed network components, select the IPX/SPX-compatible transport for the appropriate adapter and click Properties.

3. In the IPX/SPX-compatible Transport Properties box, select the Advanced tab.

4. From the Property box, select Frame Type.

5. In the Value box, select the desired frame type.

6. Click OK twice, and reboot your computer when prompted.

N O T E In addition to the common LAN protocols, Windows 98 includes support for the following newer protocols:

- *ATM Call Manager*, *ATM Emulated LAN*, and *ATM Emulation Client* for wide area networks (WANs)

- *Fast Infrared Protocol* for connecting laptop computers to one another, as well as compatible peripheral devices (such as printers)

- *Microsoft 32-bit DLC* for connectivity with mainframe computers and network print devices (such as the HP JetDirect devices) ▪

All Windows 98 protocols are 32-bit, protected-mode virtual device drivers (VxDs). Protected-mode drivers are loaded and bound entirely in Windows and therefore do not tie up conventional (the first 640K) RAM on the workstation. In contrast, 16-bit, real-mode drivers, such as those found in earlier versions of network operating systems such as Artisoft's LANtastic, load in DOS prior to booting Windows.

N O T E Protected-mode drivers are generally much faster in execution than real-mode drivers. ▪

For connectivity with LANs, which access or must go across internetworks, Windows 98 offers native support for multiple protocols simultaneously, either on multiple network adapters or all bound to a single network adapter.

N O T E As a rule, it is wise to install and bind only those protocols required for communication across the networks you want to reach in your situation. Extraneous protocols add additional processing overhead to each network transmission and decrease efficiency. For example, you should unbind all but the TCP/IP protocol from a dial-up adapter that accesses the Internet because TCP/IP is the only protocol used on the Internet. ▪

> **CAUTION**
>
> You should disable file and printer sharing from a TCP/IP connection that you use to connect to the Internet. Otherwise, other users on the Internet might be able to access data on your computer.

Computers need only one protocol in common to talk to one another across a network. If an additional protocol is bound to your network adapter, it will be ignored by other computers on that network that do not have that same protocol bound to their adapters.

Choosing a Protocol and Adjusting Bindings

Follow these steps to install a protocol, or protocols, on your Windows 98 computer (see Figure 38.4):

1. In the Control Panel, click the Network icon.
2. On the Configuration tab, click the Add button.
3. In the Select Network Component Type dialog box, select Protocol, and then click the Add button once more.
4. In the Select Network Protocol dialog box (see Figure 38.4), select the manufacturer on the left, in this case, Microsoft, and the protocol on the right. Click OK.
5. When you return to the Configuration tab in the Network dialog box, you can adjust the protocol bindings, which are graphically illustrated in the installed components windows.
6. To deselect a binding, select it and click the Remove button.
7. To add a binding, click the adapter listing, click Properties, choose the Bindings tab, and click the protocol that you want the adapter to use.
8. Click OK to close the Network dialog box, and restart your computer when prompted.

FIG. 38.4

Installing a network protocol.

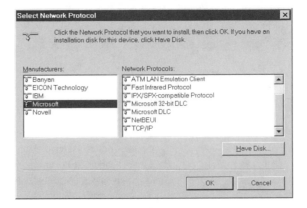

Configuring TCP/IP Addresses

IP addresses need to be unique. In most cases, you can use one of the following methods to obtain a unique IP address:

- Ask your administrator for your address if you are on a corporate network.
- Ask your ISP for your addresses if you have a dedicated connection to the Internet.
- Use DHCP or Windows 98 Automatic Private IP addressing in almost every other case.

Using TCP/IP on a Private Network   On private networks (LANs that will not be accessing the Internet), you can configure your computers with any IP addresses you want. To make configuration of private networks easier, Windows 98 introduces Automatic Private IP Addressing, which automatically assigns a TCP/IP address to each host on the network when a DHCP server is not available.

Windows 98 Automatic Private IP Addressing assigns IP addresses from the class B address range 169.254.X.X, where the first two octets (169.254) are fixed and the last two octets are uniquely assigned to each Windows 98 computer in your network.

Part

VII

Ch

38

> **CAUTION**
>
> Nodes using Automatic Private IP Addressing (APIPA) can communicate only with their private network and cannot be seen or reached from the Internet. APIPA cannot be used on multiple LAN routed configurations, except as a backup.
>
> If you need to be able to communicate with the Internet, you cannot use APIPA unless your network uses a proxy server to provide a connection to the Internet.

When a DHCP server is available, Windows 98 computers that are configured to use Automatic Private IP Addressing act like normal DHCP clients and use whatever dynamically assigned IP address they receive via the DHCP process.

If you specify an IP address (and subnet mask), it will be used instead of APIPA. Otherwise, if a DHCP server is not found when the Windows 98 machine starts up, it checks for a previously assigned default gateway. If the default gateway is found, it keeps the previously leased IP address. If the previously assigned gateway is not found, it assigns itself a random IP address and displays an error message that a DHCP server was not found. Windows 98 then continues to check for a DHCP server every three minutes; if one is found, a status dialog box displays that it is now connected to a DHCP server.

If the Windows 98 machine has no previous IP address and there is no DHCP server, the process is the same except that no error message is displayed (assuming it never had a DHCP server). However, APIPA continues to check for a DHCP server every three minutes.

N O T E   The random IP address assigned by APIPA is based on the time and the hardware address of the network adapter. APIPA also tests to make sure that the selected IP address is not in use before it is activated. ■

To enable Automatic IP Addressing, follow these steps:

1. In Control Panel, open the Network icon.
2. Click the Configuration tab.
3. Select the TCP/IP ==> Network Adapter listing.
4. Click the Properties button to see the dialog box shown in Figure 38.5.
5. Click the Obtain an IP Address Automatically check box.

FIG. 38.5

TCP/IP addressing in Network Neighborhood.

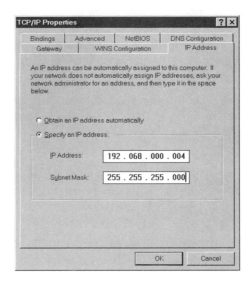

Using DHCP to Automatically Assign IP Addresses   There are two options for assigning TCP/IP addresses over a network: static and dynamic.

With static addressing, each computer is configured with one or more preselected IP addresses. Every time that a computer with a static IP address is moved to a new location in a TCP/IP network, it must be reconfigured with a different IP address that is appropriate for the new network location.

To eliminate the need to manually configure and assign IP addresses across a network, which can become an administrative nightmare on large networks, DHCP (Dynamic Host Configuration Protocol) was developed.

DHCP servers are configured with a range of IP addresses that are appropriate for the various parts of their network. When a computer that has been configured as a DHCP client restarts, it is assigned an IP address by any available DHCP server. Microsoft supplies only a DHCP server capability with Windows NT Server.

N O T E Because DHCP is an industry standard, your network can use a DHCP server that operates on any operating system, including NetWare, UNIX, or OS/2. You also can purchase third-party DHCP server software that runs on Windows 98. ▨

You can use the Windows 98 utility WIN IPCFG to view the IP configuration parameters assigned to your host by the DHCP server (see Figure 38.6). This graphical utility also displays the host name, IP address, subnet mask, and gateway address.

FIG. 38.6
Using WINIPCFG to show IP configuration parameters.

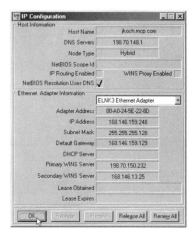

The TCP/IP protocol, using DHCP, is the default in Windows 98. If a DHCP server is not available on the network when the host logs on, it reverts to Automatic Private IP Addressing until a DHCP server comes on the network. DHCP-assigned IP addresses take precedence over automatically configured IP addresses.

Setting Up NetBEUI

There are no configuration options for the NetBEUI protocol.

Setting Up IPX/SPX-Compatible Protocol

To configure the IPX/SPX protocol (assuming that the IPX/SPX-compatible transport protocol has already been installed), follow these steps:

1. In Control Panel, open the Network Icon.
2. Select the IPX/SPX ==> Network Adapter listing in the Network Component window.
3. Click Properties.
4. Click the Advanced tab.
5. Select the property you want to configure.
6. Use the drop-down bar under the Value field to specify the value for that IPX/SPX property.
7. Click OK twice.

N O T E   Under Windows 98, the IPX/SPX frame type and network address are configured automatically. ■

Installing and Configuring Client Software

Before a computer can share its own resources or connect to other computers' resources across a network, compatible client software must first be installed on each of these computers. The basic purpose of client software is the redirection of requests by a local computer to access the shared resources of remote computers and servers on the network. The client software is often referred to as the redirector.

To the user at a computer attached to a network, remote resources (either files or printers) look and behave like locally connected resources. However, it is the client software behind the scenes that redirects file requests over the network to the remote resources. When the client software is configured correctly, this all happens transparently.

The Client for Microsoft Networks is installed automatically by Windows 98 Setup if it finds a previous version during a Windows upgrade, or if a network adapter is found during Setup's hardware detection phase. This client supports the entire Microsoft family of products, including Windows NT, Windows 95, Windows for Workgroups, LAN Manager, and the MS-DOS add-on for WFWG.

Windows 98 can support multiple protected-mode 32-bit clients simultaneously, but only one 16-bit real-mode client at a time.

If you need to manually install the Client for Microsoft Networks, follow these steps:

1. Open the Network icon in Control Panel.
2. Click the Add button.
3. In the Select Network Component Type dialog box, double-click the Client listing and click the Add button.
4. In the Select Network Client dialog box, select Microsoft in the Manufacturers listing and Client for Microsoft Networks in the Network Clients listing.
5. Click OK.

After a client is installed, you can set the Primary Network Logon. In the Network dialog box, open the drop-down list under Primary Network Logon, as shown in Figure 38.7. The choices vary, depending upon which clients are installed.

- Windows Family Logon is appropriate only for household use because it displays a list of all valid users in the logon screen.
- Windows Logon is appropriate for workstations not connected to Windows NT or NetWare networks.
- Client for Microsoft Networks should be chosen for workstations that will log on to and be validated by Windows NT domains or workgroups.

■ Client for NetWare Networks should be chosen for workstations that will log on to and be validated by a Novell NetWare or IntranetWare server.

FIG. 38.7

Selecting the Primary Network Logon.

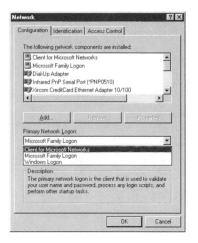

To log on to a Windows NT network, a corresponding user account with user name and password must already exist in the domain for that user. In addition, the Client for Microsoft Networks must specify a logon to a Windows NT domain.

The first time you log on to Windows 98, it presents you with separate logon prompts for each individual network client. If your password for Windows 98 is the same or is made the same as the other client logons, you will be logged automatically onto all the other networks simultaneously each time Windows 98 starts up with just one logon box.

To enable logon validation for Client for Microsoft Networks, follow these steps:

1. In Control Panel, open the Network icon.

2. Select Client for Microsoft Networks and click the Properties button.

3. Select the Logon to Windows NT Domain check box (see Figure 38.8).

4. Enter the domain name where your user account resides in the Domain field.

5. If you would prefer to have each shared network resource, such as remote drives and printers, verified at the time you log on, click the Logon and Restore Network Connections button in the Network Logon Options section. Otherwise, click Quick Logon. The Quick Logon option enables you to log on without connecting to available resources until you actually attempt to access them and, as the name implies, is much faster.

Computers communicating over a network must have unique computer names and at least one protocol in common, bound to the same type of client component. (See the previous section in this chapter titled, "Installing and Configuring Network Protocols.")

Part

VII

Ch

38

FIG. 38.8

Client for Microsoft
Networks Properties in
Network Neighborhood.

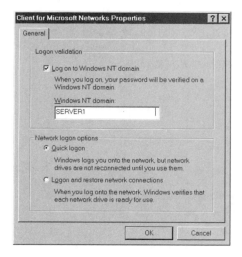

To check the network settings, follow these steps:

1. In Control Panel, open the Network icon.
2. Click the Identification tab.
3. Make sure that the computer name is unique to the network.
4. Make sure the workgroup name specified is identical to the workgroup name used by all other computers in the workgroup.
5. Click OK to return.
6. In the network components display, select the Protocol ==> Network Adapter listing (for example, TCP/IP ==> 3Com EtherLink III) and click Properties.
7. Select the Bindings tab. Click to select the check box next to the client you will use to log on to the network.
8. Click OK twice to close the Network dialog box.

 If you specify the name of the Windows NT domain as the workgroup name under the Identification tab, the names of the Windows NT computers in the domain appear alongside the names of the Windows 98 computers in your workgroup.

Managing a Windows Network

Network management is a very active topic among administrators today. Companies are looking for ways to make their networks more reliable, more efficient, and less costly to support. We have already touched upon several areas of network management in this chapter, such as user profiles, share-level versus user-level resource access, and the Zero Administration Initiative. Although it is outside the scope of this chapter to address every network management issue, we will cover the following remote administration tools included with Windows 98:

- Net Watcher enables network administrators to manage remote resources.
- System Policy Editor creates System Policy files that can enforce settings on the various users and computers in your network.

Net Watcher

Net Watcher enables the administrator of a Windows 98 network to perform the following services on remote computers:

- View current network connections
- Disconnect users from the network or network resources
- Monitor which resources are being shared on the network and by whom
- Activate, deactivate, and modify resource shares

To connect to a remote computer using Net Watcher, the remote computer must have both file and printer sharing services and remote administration services enabled. If your computer is running share-level security, you can connect only to other remote computers running share-level security. If your computer is running user-level security, you can connect to any other remote computers running file and printer sharing services.

There are three views in Net Watcher:

1. By Connections view shows the currently connected users.
2. By Shared Folders view shows shared resources (see Figure 38.9). This view also includes any printer shares on the remote computer.
3. By Open Files view shows open files.

FIG. 38.9
Net Watcher utility
showing shared folders.

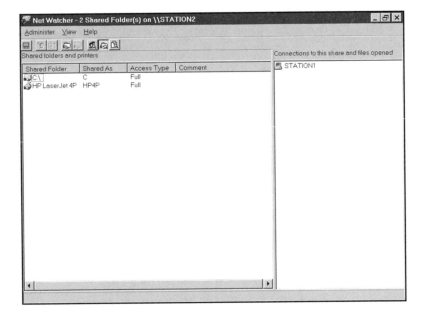

Part VII
Ch 38

To connect to a remote computer using Net Watcher, follow these steps:

1. Select Start Programs, Accessories, System Tools, Net Watcher.
2. From the Administer menu, click Select Server.
3. Enter the name of the Windows 98 system that you want to monitor and click OK.
4. Enter the correct remote administration password for the remote computer.

 T I P You can also run Net Watcher from Network Neighborhood by right-clicking a remote computer, selecting the Tools tab, and clicking the Net Watcher button.

To share a resource on a remote computer while using Net Watcher, follow these steps:

1. Select By Shared Folders from the View menu.
2. Select Add Shared Folder from the Administer menu.
3. Type the resource path of the drive that you want to share in the Enter Path text box.
4. Click OK.

System Policy Editor

The goal of System Policies is centralized administration of all of your network users and computers. Implementation of System Policies requires the use of a centralized Windows NT domain or NetWare Server, and user-level security. A single policy file located on Windows NT Primary Domain Controllers or Novell NetWare Servers controls the System Policies for each user and computer. The System Policy Editor is the tool that is used to create the policy file for a network.

To use System Policy Editor, the Remote Registry Service must be running on the remote computer. To install the Remote Registry Service, follow these steps:

1. In Control Panel, open the Network icon.
2. Click the Add button.
3. Select Service and click the Add button.
4. Click Have Disk and browse to the \tools\reskit\netadmin\remotreg folder on the Windows 98 CD-ROM. Click OK twice.
5. Select Remote Registry Service.
6. Click OK twice to close.
7. Reboot your computer when prompted.

Using the System Policy Editor, an administrator can do the following:

- Modify the desktop
- Remove or restrict access to items such as the Settings folder on the Start menu
- Modify the capabilities of Control Panel applets
- Enable or disable resource sharing

- Hide the Network Neighborhood
- Disable password caching (this would also disable quick logons to resou £es in the Client for Microsoft Networks)
- Prevent modification of the desktop environment

To install the System Policy Editor in Windows 98, follow these steps:

1. In Control Panel, open Add/Remove Programs.
2. Click the Windows Setup tab.
3. Click the Have Disk button.
4. Browse to the \tools\reskit\netadmin\poledit folder on the Windows 98 CD-ROM.
5. Click OK twice and click the check box next to System Policy Editor.
6. Click Install.
7. Click OK to close the Add/Remove Programs Properties box. There is no need to reboot your computer.

Figure 38.10 shows the System Policy Editor displaying a network's default computer properties.

Part

VII

Ch

38

FIG. 38.10
System Policy Editor showing network policies.

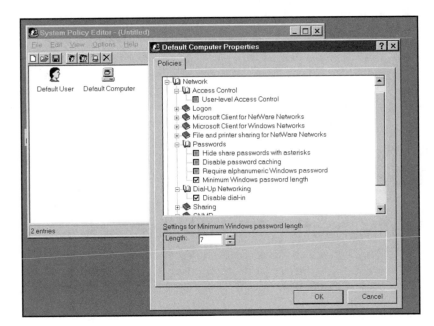

System Policy settings can be applied to groups as well as individuals. Additionally, default policies can be applied to users and computers or to specific computers, groups, and users. To create policies for Internet Explorer and the Active Desktop, use the Internet Explorer Administration Kit.

> **CAUTION**
>
> The System Policies Editor is a very powerful tool and should be used only with knowledge and extreme caution. Each item in the settings tree has three possible states: enabled, disabled, and unchanged. It is possible to make accidental changes to the remote computer's Registry, which can cause unexpected results that cannot be fixed with a complete reinstallation of Windows 98.

Remote Administration Services

Through remote administration, network administrators can manage remote resources, shares and Registries and modify the desktop environment and configuration.

Both user-level security and Remote Administration Services must be enabled on each computer managed by remote administration. The computers must have at least one protocol in common.

To enable remote administration on a Windows 98 computer, follow these steps:

1. In Control Panel, open the Passwords icon.
2. Click the Remote Administration tab.
3. Click the check box next to Enable Remote Administration of This Server.
4. If your system uses user-level security, click the Add button and specify from a browse list which users are authorized to access this computer using Remote Administration Services. If your system uses share-level security, enter and confirm the password that will be used to control access to your system.
5. Click OK.

 When File and Printer Sharing and user-level security are all enabled on a Windows 98-based computer, remote administration is automatically enabled.

Troubleshooting Network Problems

When network problems occur, it is best to start with the more obvious causes of the problem (such as a disconnected cable) and work up to the less obvious ones (such as an incorrect IP address) rather than the other way around.

Try to determine when the problem first occurred and what, if anything, might have changed prior to the first appearance of the problem.

- What specifically is not working now that was working before?
- When did the problem start?
- Is the system plugged in and powered on? Are all components receiving power?
- Does the user who cannot access a network drive or printer have the security permissions to do so?

- Have any exposed network cable segments recently been stepped on, twisted, bent, or relocated? Cable problems are a very common cause of network downtime.

- What might have changed about the system or configuration since the last time it worked properly?

- Was new hardware or software installed recently? Go back and retrace the steps taken during the installation. It could turn out to be an incorrect or outdated software version, or maybe a connector was knocked loose during a component upgrade.

- Was any hardware or operating system error message displayed on the monitor just before the problem occurred?

- Can the problem be reproduced? If so, you might be able to trace the problem back to a misbehaving utility program or incompatible device driver.

- Do the applications related to the problem maintain any kind of activity or error log? If so, the log might contain valuable information that can point to a possible cause of the problem.

Most hardware and software vendors maintain a problem database of some kind on their web sites. Microsoft's Knowledge Base is one of the most comprehensive in the industry. It is available 24 hours a day to anyone with an Internet connection and browser software. You can enter keywords or Boolean search terms to locate technical support documents that relate to your precise problem.

Part
VII

Ch
38

Some Common Network Problems and Proven Solutions

- If you cannot find the computer you are looking for in Network Neighborhood, make sure that you are logged into the correct workgroup. Check the Identification tab in Network Neighborhood to see how you have identified yourself and your workgroup to the network.

- If you can log on to your computer but are not able to connect to the other resources on the network, check your protocol bindings in Network Neighborhood. You can share resources only with computers that have at least one protocol in common with your computer.

You've Lost That Lovin' Password

If you have lost your password on a Windows 98 peer network, you can find a file named *USERNAME*.PWL (where *USERNAME* is your logon name) in the \Windows folder. Erase that file/and restart Windows, and you will be prompted for a new password at startup.

Troubleshooting Network Adapter Problems

If you have difficulty installing your adapter card into Windows 98, or if it seems to be working but you still cannot log on to the network, try these proven troubleshooting ideas to find a solution:

- Open Device Manager and check for any yellow exclamation points or red Xs displayed across device listings. This indicates a resource conflict or a device that has been disabled in the Windows 98 hardware database. From Windows 98 Help, start the Hardware Conflict Troubleshooter Wizard and follow the prompts to resolve the conflict.

- Check to make sure that AC power is being supplied to any 10BaseT hubs.

- Use WINIPCFG or the Network icon in Control Panel to check your network adapter's IP settings for accuracy.

- If you're attempting to log on to a Windows NT Domain, check that your Client for Microsoft Networks is configured to log on to the domain and that the domain name is properly specified in the Client Properties box.

- Legacy adapter cards sometimes cannot be configured under Windows 98 if their hard-coded settings conflict with the resources Windows 98 is attempting to assign to them. See the section "Installing and Configuring a Network Adapter" earlier in this chapter for instructions on how to configure a legacy adapter card under Windows 98.

- Check Thinnet (10Base2) coaxial cabling runs for kinks and sharp bends around corners. Avoid running Thinnet past fluorescent ceiling fixtures because they can cause interference that disturbs network transmissions.

- Check cable lengths between segments and overall network distance according to cable specifications. This is especially a problem with custom cable runs prepared from bulk connectors and wiring.

- Replace the terminators on 10Base2 cable ends. Oxidation and other contaminants can prevent a clean contact between the terminator and its T connector.

- Finally, if all else fails, try a different network adapter in that computer. Some computers have been known to work with one card in a batch and reject a nearly identical card, even from the same manufacturer.

Other Problems

It is an excellent idea to keep a network journal to record all incidences of problems, along with their discovered causes and their solutions.

Maintain up-to-date records that include a schematic of your network with a thorough hardware and software inventory. Record dates and times that software and hardware components are added, removed, and updated, along with a record of users at each workstation. Good records are valuable resources to have when you're trying to track down the possible causes of a problem.

A new feature of Windows 98, the System Configuration Utility, is a useful tool for isolating startup problems. This utility is easier to use and much less prone to error than the old SYSEDIT utility that it replaces.

Through a graphical user interface, you can selectively add and remove individual components of the Windows 98 startup files, including, the AUTOEXEC.BAT, CONFIG.SYS, SYSTEM.INI, and WIN.INI files.

To launch the System Configuration utility, run MSCONFIG from the Start, Run dialog box.

Microsoft System Information provides information on devices, components, and drivers. It keeps a history log of the system and can provide reports showing changes to the system and the dates of same. The System Information Utility is run from the \Accessories\System Tools folder on the Start menu.

Another new tool helpful in tracking down system problems is System File Checker, which automatically checks the Windows 98 system files for corruption. It can be run from the Tools menu inside the System Information Utility.

Scanreg (DOS version) or Scanregw (Windows version) runs automatically each time Windows 98 boots. Such files check and back up the Registry and can also be run from System Information. ●

Part

VII

Ch

38

CHAPTER 39

Connecting to an NT Network

by John West

In this chapter

Choosing Your Primary Network Logon

Windows 98 provides the mechanisms to connect to different types of providers on a network. In this chapter, you learn how to set up your Windows 98 workstation to connect to Microsoft Windows NT servers and workstations and to other Microsoft Windows 98 machines. This connection enables you to access shared files and printers. You also learn how to use some of the services provided by Microsoft, one of which is the capability to secure your shared resources using Windows NT native security account databases.

Because Windows 98 provides connectivity with many different network providers, you may at some point need to select which provider you will connect to first as you log on to your workstation. For example, you may work in a company that uses Microsoft Windows NT servers as a corporate standard. However, your department may have a Novell NetWare server with resources you need to access as well. Or you may have a laptop that you want to log on to Windows NT when you're connected locally, but you may want to bypass the logon when you're on the road. You can choose one provider to be your Primary Network Logon. Common choices include Windows Logon, Windows Family Logon, Client for Microsoft Networks, Client for NetWare Networks, and NetWare Client 32.

Your Primary Network Logon is the first provider you want to get a logon prompt for when you begin working. Logon scripts and other tasks are executed based on your selected Primary Network Logon. The logon script of your selected Primary Network Logon runs last. This arrangement is actually a good thing. A vital function of logon scripts is to provide consistent drive mappings to resources from your network provider. By having your primary provider's script run last, you ensure that the drive mappings for it overwrite any previously assigned mappings from your non-primary providers. The exception to this situation is when you have Client for Microsoft Networks installed. In this case, the Windows NT logon script always runs first.

To select your Primary Network logon, follow these steps:

1. Run Control Panel.
2. Double-click on Network.
3. Choose your Primary Network Logon from the Primary Network Logon drop-down box as shown in Figure 39.1.

Selecting Windows Logon

Windows Logon is the default choice for Primary Network Logon when you have no network connectivity installed, or when you have no network providers to connect to. When Windows Logon is the Primary Network Logon, you are prompted to log on to the workstation with the prompt shown in Figure 39.2.

FIG. 39.1

You can select your Primary Network Logon from any network providers set up on your workstation.

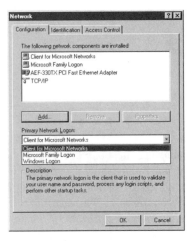

FIG. 39.2

The Windows Logon dialog box.

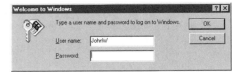

Part

VII

Ch

39

The logon feature provides built-in security for Windows 98. When you log on at the Windows Logon prompt, Microsoft remembers the username and password you provide. Windows 98 enables you to log on and identify yourself to the workstation itself for the following reasons:

- Windows 98 can save each user's settings individually. These settings include Internet favorites, Start Menu items, desktop preferences, and application settings. For instance, if you share your workstation with other members of your household, you probably do not want to use the same desktop settings as your kids use, unless you enjoy staring at Barney all day. See Chapter 20, "Advanced Registry Hacks," for more information.

- Windows 98 employs password caching. Password caching makes it less cumbersome for you to remember your passwords for various services, such as network providers, secure web sites, and custom applications you run. Simply select the Save This Password in Your Password List, as shown in Figure 39.3.

  Windows 98 saves your passwords in an encrypted password cache file named with the username and secured with the password you entered at the Windows Logon dialog box. An example of when this technique is useful is if you log on to Windows NT and NetWare. If your user account with these network providers is the same as your Windows 98 username, you do not have to enter all three passwords. Instead, you enter only the Windows Logon password. When the logon prompts for the other providers are displayed, the password field is already filled in so that you can log on just by clicking OK.

FIG. 39.3

With password caching, Windows 98 can remember passwords to various services you use.

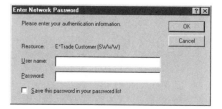

By selecting Windows Logon as your Primary Network Provider, you can prevent Windows 98 from trying to establish connections with your installed network providers. For instance, if you use a laptop, you might want to set up hardware profiles (see Chapter 24, "Setting Up Windows 98 Multimedia") so that your Primary Network Logon will be the Windows Logon when you're on the road. This way, you won't have to attempt to log on to and receive errors regarding a network provider to which you're not connected.

 TIP If you don't want to have to enter a Windows 98 password each time you log on, you can leave the password blank. Of course, your cache file won't be as secure, so you need to balance convenience and security. If you have assigned a password to your Windows 98 username and wish to remove it, you can change it after you log on under the Passwords applet in Control Panel.

TROUBLESHOOTING

If you have any problems with your Windows 98 password cache or simply don't feel comfortable with your passwords being cached, you can delete the cache file. It's located under C:\WINDOWS and is named with your username and the extension .PWL. You don't have to be too concerned about the safety of this file, though. Microsoft uses a 128-bit key to encrypt it. Currently, this level of encryption makes the file virtually impossible to decrypt.

Selecting Windows Family Logon

Windows Family Logon, which is new to Windows 98, extends the concept of the Windows Logon. When you install this client under the Network Control Panel applet and choose this client as your Primary Network Logon, you can choose the Windows 98 username that you want to use to log on. For this approach to work, however, you must have previously established the use of user profiles on your machine (see Chapter 3, "Navigating and Controlling Windows"). To log on with Windows Family Logon as your Primary Network Logon, simply highlight your username and enter your password at the prompt, as shown in Figure 39.4.

FIG. 39.4
The Windows Family
Logon box.

Selecting Client for Microsoft Networks

If Client for Microsoft Networks is your Primary Network Logon, then any system policies and user profiles that network administrators have created will be downloaded to your machine from the Windows NT network. Also, any logon scripts assigned to you on the server or do-main to which you connect will be run.

N O T E   What are system policies and user profiles? *System policies* are settings specific to the workstation from which you're logging on. For example, administrators at your site may have decided to display a dialog box with a legal notice concerning unauthorized use of network resources prior to a user logging on to any workstations on the network. The use of system policies would enable them to distribute the settings for this dialog box over the network.

User profiles are settings specific to a user or group. If you have your PC configured for multiple users, you are using user profiles. However, user profiles that get downloaded from a server overwrite any existing settings you have. For example, you may have a particular graphic you like to use at work for your wallpaper. However, the network administrators might prefer for everyone to use a corporate graphic as wallpaper. If the administrators configure this wallpaper in the network-based user profiles, your PC will be configured for the corporate graphic when you logon. ■

Selecting Client for NetWare Networks

If Client for NetWare Networks is your Primary Network Logon, system policies and user profiles can also be downloaded. They will be retrieved from your preferred server (see the section on configuring Client for NetWare Networks). The NetWare login script will also be run. See Chapter 40, "Connecting to a NetWare Network," for more information on NetWare connectivity.

Joining a Windows Workgroup

Many smaller organizations use a peer-to-peer network to fulfill their file and print-sharing needs. A peer-to-peer network consists of workstations that are used for daily computing tasks by their users, but that have also been configured to make resources available to other users

Part
VII

Ch
39

on a network. With peer-to-peer networks, users' workstations are grouped into logical units called workgroups. Workgroups don't affect whether or not a user can get to a resource on another computer. They affect only what a user sees by default when he or she looks for the resource through Network Neighborhood, Explorer, or other programs in Windows 98 that support network browsing.

Identifying Your Computer

Every computer used in peer-to-peer networking must have a unique computer name. The name can be up to 15 characters long and must not include spaces. Follow these steps to name a computer:

1. Run Control Panel.

2. Double-click on Network.

3. Select the Identification tab, shown in Figure 39.5.

4. Fill in your computer name.

FIG. 39.5

Use the Identification tab to configure your workstation-naming parameters.

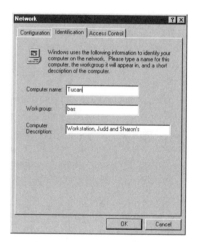

Identifying Your Workgroup

The workgroup name you provide enables you to select which workgroup of computers your computer displays by default when you browse network resources. The name you use is arbitrary as long as any other computers you want to browse use the same name. In other words, if you name the workgroup ABC, for example, you'll see other computers in your default browse list that also gave the name ABC to their workgroup. The workgroup name is not case sensitive.

Adding a Comment to Describe Your PC

While you're at the Identification tab, fill in a comment for your PC. This entry is important when your computer has file and print sharing enabled. Other users browsing for your computer can see this comment if their browse program enables them to view details. Figure 39.6 shows an example of viewing details in Network Neighborhood.

FIG. 39.6
Viewing details in Network Neighborhood enables the user to see comments about the computers in the workgroup or domain.

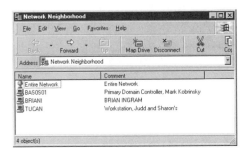

 Include your name in the comment field if your workstation name doesn't already represent your name. This information tells users who need resources located on your computer who to contact if they have problems connecting to your workstation. For example, if your workstation name is Finance and someone has a problem connecting, he or she would know to call you if the description for the workstation is Financial Services – Jane Doe.

Logging On to a Windows NT Network

Windows NT, in both the workstation and server versions, is a more robust network server platform than Windows 98. With Windows NT Server especially, the platform has been designed from the ground up to be a network provider. Windows NT has several advantages over Windows 98 that make Windows NT the better solution for file and print sharing.

- Full 32-bit protected mode operating system. This feature increases performance and reliability.

- Integrated security account database. Users and groups are created and maintained on the Windows NT machine itself. Having an integrated security account database eliminates the need to rely on an external security provider.

- Capability to share an account database. Windows NT servers can be placed in a common logical unit called a domain. When Windows NT servers are made domain controllers in this domain, the security account database can be replicated to all the servers, so they all have the same information.

- Support for file-based security. With the use of a file system called NTFS on the Windows NT machine, user and group security can be assigned individual directories and files, not just shares.

Microsoft Windows NT is gaining more and more market share. Even if your company isn't using Windows NT as its primary network provider, chances are that sooner or later Windows NT will be implemented in some capacity in your environment.

Connecting to a Windows NT Domain

Windows NT servers can be organized into a logical unit called a *domain*. Each domain has one Primary Domain Controller (PDC). The PDC stores the master copy of the security account database for the domain. This database is where users, groups, and their respective settings, such as passwords and the logon script that will be run for the user, are contained. The PDC periodically replicates the changes in the security account database to the Backup Domain Controllers (BDCs). Consequently, resources such as files and printers on any of the servers can be assigned security using the same users and groups. This approach means that you, the user of these resources, do not need a separate user account and password for each server.

Windows NT domains can even be related to each other in a hierarchical fashion by using trust relationships. A *trust relationship* enables the administrator of one domain to assign security rights for resources to users and groups from another domain. This flexibility is important to you because you can log on as a user in one domain and yet access resources in another domain.

Follow these steps to configure your workstation to log on to a Windows NT domain:

1. Run Control Panel.
2. Double-click on Network.
3. Set your Primary Network Logon to Client for Microsoft Networks.
4. Highlight Client for Microsoft Networks in the list of installed network components and click on Properties. See Figure 39.7.

FIG. 39.7

The Client for Microsoft Networks Properties dialog box.

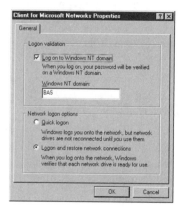

5. Check the Log on to Windows NT Domain check box.

6. Fill in the name of the domain to which you want to log on in the Windows NT Domain: text box. As mentioned previously in regard to trust relationships, the domain you log on to and the domain from which you access resources may be different.

7. Select whether you want to enable Quick Logon or Logon and Restore Connections. Quick Logon displays previously mapped drives (called *persistent drive mappings*) when you browse your computer's drives; however, your workstation does not actually contact the provider of the resource to ensure that it's available until you first attempt to use the drive. Logon and Restore Connections, however, tries to contact the provider as it maps the drives. This option increases your logon time, but at least you know before you begin work that the drives really are ready for use.

 TIP If you're a road warrior, choose Quick Logon to avoid drive mapping errors when you log on to your computer while you're not connected to the network.

After you configure these settings and restart your machine, the logon dialog box shown in Figure 39.8 appears. Then when you successfully enter your username and password for the domain, your logon script runs (if your administrator has assigned you one) and any persistent drive mappings are restored.

Part
VII
Ch
39

FIG. 39.8
Client for Microsoft Networks uses the domain name you specified in the network setup when prompting you to log on.

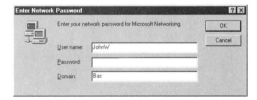

You can also override the domain name shown in the prompt. This approach is useful if you have accounts on more than one domain at your company. To override the default domain name, simply type over it with the name of another domain on your network.

N O T E The workgroup name discussed in the section "Joining a Windows Workgroup" is also useful in a Windows NT domain environment. In this environment, you set the workgroup to the name of the domain that contains most of the resources you use. For instance, if you log on to a domain called Accounts, but you use resources from a trusting domain called Resources (not very original, I know), you are better off setting your workgroup name to Resources. This way, when you browse, you see the servers in the Resources domain first. ■

Connecting to a Windows NT Workstation

A computer with Windows NT Workstation as its operating system stores a security account database on the local machine. (In contrast, Windows 98 has no means to store user account information.) Connecting to a Windows NT workstation is similar to connecting to a Windows

NT server domain. However, instead of entering the domain name at the Windows NT Domain prompt, you should enter the name of the workstation. When you log on, you are prompted for a username and password. If you do not yet have a user account in the security account database on the Windows NT workstation, the administrator of that workstation needs to create one for you before you can log on.

Changing Your Windows NT Password

To change your Windows NT password and your Windows 98 Logon password to the same new password, follow these steps.

1. Run Control Panel.

2. Double-click on Passwords.

3. Click on Change Windows Password.

4. Select any other passwords you want to change. Select Microsoft (see Figure 39.9).

FIG. 39.9
When you change your Windows password, you are prompted to change other provider passwords at the same time.

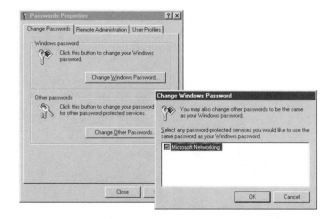

5. Enter your old Windows 98 Logon password and a new password twice for verification.

6. If your current Windows 98 Logon password and your Windows NT password are not the same, you are prompted to enter your current Windows NT password (see Figure 39.10).

FIG. 39.10
If your Windows password and Windows NT password aren't the same, you are prompted to enter your current Windows NT password.

After you enter everything correctly, your Windows and Windows NT passwords will be set to the new password you specified.

 TIP   Keeping your Windows and Windows NT passwords the same means that you won't have to remember two passwords and you won't have to log on twice at startup. See Chapter 44, "Remote Access with Dial-Up Networking," for more details.

If you don't want to keep your two passwords in sync, follow these steps:

1. Run Control Panel.
2. Double-click on Passwords.
3. Click on Change Other Passwords...
4. Select Microsoft Network and click on Change.
5. Enter your old Windows NT password and a new password twice for verification.

Setting Up User-Level Access Control

Windows 98 enables you to share your files and printers with other network users who connect to your machine and access those resources remotely. Of course, you may want to limit the people who can connect to these resources. Therefore, you need some type of security on them. Windows 98 provides two methods. The first method is share-based security. Using this type of security, you specify a password on a resource and whether it allows read-only access, full access, or both, depending on the password entered by the person accessing it. This security method has limitations however. Everyone must use the same password, and you can't limit the access by user. For this reason, Windows 98 provides user-level access.

User-level access enables you to assign rights to resources based on security information kept by a network provider. This section discusses using Windows NT as the provider. Windows NT has a security account database that contains usernames and passwords, as well as other information. User-level access on Windows 98 enables you to leverage these usernames to secure your resources. For instance, to restrict access to a financial package to users in the financial department, you can assign full rights to the package to the LAS0Finance group to which all financial department users belong.

User-level access control enables you to take advantage of security on a per-user or per-group basis without having to administer these users and groups. Your network administrators can worry about that.

To set up user-level access control, follow these steps.

1. Run Control Panel
2. Double-click on Network.
3. If you don't see File and Printer Sharing for Microsoft Networks in the list of networking components, click on File and Print Sharing and make the appropriate selections, depending on whether you want to share files, printers, or both. Close the Control Panel Network applet and reboot.

Part
VII

Ch
39

4. After the reboot, begin at the Control Panel Network applet again. Click on the Access Control tab (see Figure 39.11).

FIG. 39.11

You must specify a domain from which to assign rights to users and groups.

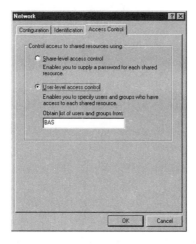

5. Select User-Level Access Control and specify the domain to whose users and groups you will assign rights on your computer.

6. Reboot again.

To see a Windows 98 or Windows NT computer when browsing a workgroup in Network Neighborhood or other such tools, the computer must advertise which workgroup it belongs to on the network.

If a computer isn't sharing any resources, that computer does not need to show up in any workgroup listings. However, if a computer has shared resources, displaying it in a list helps a user on the network choose a resource on the machine to use. Otherwise, you'd have to know the name of the machine ahead of time.

To set up your computer to advertise its existence, go to the Control Panel Network applet, choose File and Print Sharing for Microsoft Networks, and click on Properties. The dialog box shown in Figure 39.12 appears on your screen.

Table 39.1 shows the browse options.

Table 39.1   Browse Options with File and Print Sharing for Microsoft Networks

Option	Description
Browse Master	With a Windows network, the computer that becomes the browse master stores information about all the other computers in the workgroup. Whenever a computer wants to enumerate the other computers in the workgroup, it contacts the browse master for the information. An election process determines which computer becomes the browse master. If you set this option to automatic, it follows a predetermined set of election rules to determine whether it should be the browse master. If you set the option to Enabled, it always acts as a browse master. If you set it to Disabled, it never becomes the browse master.
LM Announce	If you have a LAN Manager domain, you should set this option to Yes. Otherwise, leave the default setting of No.

FIG. 39.12

You need to specify how your computer should advertise its existence on the network.

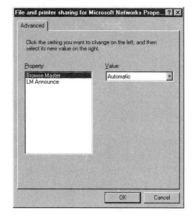

 If your Windows 98 computer is participating in a Windows NT domain, choose the Disabled setting under the Browse Master option. A Windows NT machine should always be the Browse Master. Windows NT has much more robust capabilities to function in this role.

After you set up user-level access control, you can assign rights to the users and groups in the domain you selected when you set up shares on your computer. See Chapter 7, "Advanced File Management Techniques," Chapter 41, "Windows 98 Network Administration," and Chapter 43, "Sharing Network Resources." ●

Connecting to a NetWare Network

by John West

Using NetWare 3.x and 4.x

Two versions of NetWare are in use extensively today, version 3.*x* and version 4.*x*. (The latest version is also referred to as IntranetWare.) A major difference between the two versions is the directory service. Novell version 3.*x* uses a type of directory service called the bindery. The *bindery* uses a flat model for storing account information such as usernames and passwords. Each 3.*x* server has a separate bindery. Therefore, to access resources on more than one 3.*x* server, you must have an account and password for each one. Version 4.*x* improved on this system by using a directory service called NetWare Directory Services (NDS). NDS allows more than one server to share account databases. This technology enables you to use the same account to access all servers to which you have rights. NDS is organized into a logical hierarchical tree.

Both NetWare versions now have full native support under Windows 98 via drivers provided by Microsoft, although there are some limitations. In addition to the NetWare 4.*x* client that Microsoft provides, NetWare also created a client for version 4.*x* called Client 32.

Using Microsoft's Client for NetWare Networks

The Client for NetWare Networks that comes with Windows 98 provides support for 3.*x* servers as well as 4.*x* servers with bindery emulation enabled. Bindery emulation is just what it sounds like. Even though 4.*x* doesn't use a bindery for directory services, Novell added the capability for it to emulate a bindery so that users who have only NetWare 3.*x* software support on their workstations can log on (albeit with limited functionality).

After you have installed the Client for NetWare Networks under the Network Control Panel applet, you need to configure the Client so that you can connect to a server. The following steps explain how:

1. Run Control Panel.
2. Double-click on Network.
3. Set your Primary Network Logon to Client for NetWare Networks.
4. Highlight Client for NetWare Networks in the list of installed network components and click on Properties.

Table 40.1 explains the options.

Table 40.1   Configuring the Client for NetWare Networks Options

Option	Description
Preferred Server	The default server that you are prompted to log on to when you start Windows 98.
First Network Drive	The first drive that is used to map to resources on the NetWare server. By default, it's drive F. If you have devices on your computer that use drive letters beyond drive E, you should adjust this parameter so that NetWare and your devices don't try to use the same drive letters.

Option	Description
Enable Logon Script Processing	This check box determines whether logon scripts execute when you log on to the NetWare server. Administrators create logon scripts to ensure some level of consistency with the configurations of those users that connect to a server. For instance, in your organization drive H may always map to your home directory on the server. You should not turn off this option unless you've contacted the network administrator first.

After you configure everything and start Windows 98, the logon prompt shown in Figure 40.1 appears on your screen. The first time you connect, you need to verify your logon name; after the first time, Windows 98 remembers it. After you enter the correct credentials, your NetWare logon script will run—if you enabled it as described in Table 40.1—and you will be able to use any resources on the server.

FIG. 40.1

To log on to a NetWare 3.*x* server, or a 4.*x* server with bindery emulation, simply specify your user credentials and the name of the NetWare server.

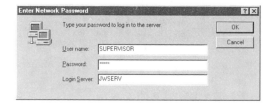

Changing Your Password with Client for NetWare Networks

Microsoft's Client for NetWare Networks does not include functionality to change your password under the Control Panel Password applet. Instead, you must go to a command prompt, change to a drive that is mapped to the System directory on the Novell server, and run the Setpass command. To run it, type **SETPASS** and enter your old and new passwords.

Using Microsoft's Service for NetWare Directory Services

Logging into a 4.*x* server with bindery emulation using the Client for Microsoft Networks has some limitations. For the fullest support of 4.*x* from a Microsoft-supplied client, you'll want to use the Service for NetWare Directory Services. This client enables you to connect to the NDS tree and browse its resources. Also, the logon script in your logon context will run.

To set up your network configuration to allow connectivity to the NDS tree after you've installed Service for NetWare Directory Services (see Chapter 42, "Setting Up a Simple Windows Network") you need to configure the service's parameters. To do so, follow these steps:

1. Run Control Panel.
2. Double-click on Network.

Part
VII
Ch
40

3. Set your Primary Network Logon to Client for NetWare Networks.

4. Highlight Service for NetWare Directory Services in the list of installed network components and click on Properties. Figure 40.2 shows the configuration page.

FIG. 40.2
You need to provide a default tree and context when setting up Service for NetWare Directory Services.

5. Enter your Preferred Tree. This tree is the NDS tree to which you are logging on by default. If you don't specify a Preferred Tree, NDS searches for any existing trees and prompts you to select one when you log on, as shown in Figure 40.3.

FIG. 40.3
When you first log on to NDS, Service for NDS prompts you for a tree if you didn't select one under the Control Panel Network applet.

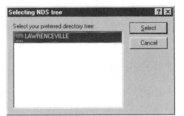

6. Enter the Workstation Default Context. Because NDS is hierarchical, your account may be several levels down from the top of the tree. To make it easier to browse and refer to resources, you can set this parameter so that when you specify resources, it will be assumed they are located under the context specified. For instance, the full distinguished name for your user account may be .CN=JohnD.OU=Research.O=ABCInc. If your Workstation Default Context is .OU=Research.O=ABCInc, then your logon name would be simply JohnD. When you browse, resources under this context will be displayed first.

If other users want to log on to your machine, but their accounts are located under a different context, they can still log on. They need to enter their fully distinguished name at the logon prompt. Their logon script will still run. The only way the Workstation Default Context will affect them is that their default context when browsing and accessing resources will be the one you specified in step 6.

You should also specify a preferred server under Client for NetWare Networks. This designation enables the workstation to make initial contact with a server in the NDS tree without having to search the network for one.

When you log on to NDS using Service for NDS, you are prompted for your username and password. Figure 40.4 shows that you can change your Workstation Default Context and Tree by clicking on the Advanced button.

FIG. 40.4

Logging on to NDS with Service for NDS. Notice that because the default context was set to O=JW, it wasn't necessary to use the fully distinguished name of .CN=Admin.O=JW. Instead all that was required was to simply type **admin**.

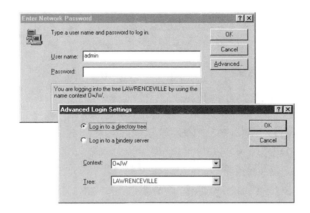

You can use this client to log on to a 3.x server as well; choose Log in to a Bindery Server and specify the server name, as shown in Figure 40.5.

FIG. 40.5

As noted on the logon screen, you will not be able to access the NDS tree when you log in to a bindery server.

Changing Your Password with Service for NDS

You can change your password from the Control Panel Passwords applet with Service for NDS. Follow these steps:

1. Run Control Panel.

2. Double-click on Passwords.

3. Click on Change Other Passwords.

4. Select NDS Tree and click Change.

5. Enter your old password and your new password twice for verification.

Using Novell's Client 32 Software

For the most complete support for NDS, you may want to use Novell's Client 32, which comes with version 4.*x*. In addition to providing support for all NetWare utilities, Client 32 provides granular access to many settings that make it possible to totally optimize and customize the way you interface with NDS under Windows 98.

After you install Client 32 (see Chapter 42), you need to configure it before you can log on to the NDS tree. Follow these steps:

1. Run Control Panel.
2. Double-click on Network.
3. Set your Primary Network Logon to Novell NetWare Client 32.
4. Highlight Novell NetWare Client 32 in the list of installed network components and click on Properties.
5. Fill in the properties on the Client 32 tab and the Login tab. Use the information in Tables 40.2 and 40.3 to fill in the details about these options.

Table 40.2 Setting the Options on the Client 32 Tab

Option	Description
Preferred Server	The server that Client 32 attempts to connect to first. Entering a server name is not necessary if you specify a preferred tree, but it's recommended. Choosing a server eliminates the need to listen for a broadcasting server.
Preferred Tree	The tree to which you are attaching in the NDS hierarchy.
	If you don't specify a preferred server or preferred tree, the client looks for any broadcasting servers on the network and uses the first one that responds.
Name Context	The same as the Workstation Default Context under Microsoft's Service for NDS. It specifies the default context to be used when you log on and when you browse. It does not affect which logon script runs.
First Network Drive	The first drive to which Client 32 connects resources. You should set this drive to a letter after F, the default, if your workstation has devices such as hard drives or CD-ROMs that use these letters.

Table 40.3 Configuring Options on the Login Tab

Option	Description
Display Connection Page	Determines whether the Connection tab gets displayed when you're prompted to logon on during startup. If this option isn't checked, your logon is processed by using the settings set from the Control Panel Network applet.
Log in to Tree	The NDS tree you are prompted to log on to by default.
Log in to Server	You can specify a server if you know of one in the NDS tree you're trying to attach to or if you're making a bindery connection.
Bindery Connection	This option shows that you are connecting to a NetWare 3.*x* server or to a 4.*x* server in bindery emulation mode. If you specify a tree, this option is ignored.
Clear Current Connections	Any current drive mappings you have is deleted when you attach to a different tree or server or change the security context under which you're connected to the resource (that is, attach as a different user).
Login Script	Enables you to specify that a login script other than your user login script should be run. You must have read rights to the login script you specify here.
Profile Script	Enables you to specify that a login script other than your profile login script should be run. Again, you must have read rights
Close Script Results Automatically	By default, you must click close after your login script runs while logging on. This feature gives you the opportunity to view the processing that occurred in the script. However, the display can become annoying. You can have the login script dialog automatically close after it completes by checking this box.
Run Scripts	If you don't want any login scripts to run at all, check this box.
Display Variables Page	
%2-%5	NetWare login scripts can have up to four user-defined parameters passed to them. This entry is where you specify the values for the parameters.
Save Settings When Exiting Login	If you check this box, any changes you make to these settings when you log on will be saved and used each time you log on from that point forward.

Part

VII

Ch

40

When Windows 98 starts, the Client 32 logon prompt as shown in Figure 40.6 appears. The settings you already specified are enumerated in the respective prompts in this dialog box. You can change any of the settings at this time if you specified that the page on which the setting exists should be displayed.

FIG. 40.6

The number of tabs you see on the Client 32 logon dialog box depends on the settings you selected under the Properties page of Client 32 in the Control Panel Network applet.

Changing Your Password with Novell Client 32

To change your password by using Novell Client 32, follow this procedure:

1. Run Control Panel.
2. Double-click on Passwords.
3. Click on Change Other Passwords.
4. Select Novell NetWare and click Change.
5. Enter your old password and your new password twice for verification.
6. Client 32 enables you to synchronize passwords for multiple accounts with which you might be attached. You can change multiple passwords at the same time by selecting the accounts in the NetWare Password Synchronization dialog box shown in Figure 40.7. The caveat is that all the accounts you want to change at the same time must have the same current password.

FIG. 40.7

With Client 32, you can change multiple NetWare account passwords simultaneously.

Configuring NetWare Directory Services

After you configure either Microsoft's Service for NDS or Novell's Client 32, you have support for functionality only NDS provides. You can browse NDS trees by using Network Neighborhood, Explorer, and other third-party browsing tools. You can map drives to NDS volumes. You can install printers in the NDS tree. Figure 40.8 shows an example of browsing the tree. Note that you have context-sensitive options when you right-click an object.

FIG. 40.8
When browsing the
LVLab OU, you can see
the available printers
and volumes.

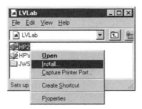

Using NetWare Utilities

Most NetWare 3.*x* applications should run under the 32-bit clients provided by Microsoft and
Novell. The few that won't are utilities that require support that only the VLM or NETX real-
mode clients provide. In most cases, alternative administrative tools are available.

Some NDS applications cannot be used without obtaining the appropriate DLLs from Novell. I
recommend using Novell's Client 32 for maximum compatibility if you expect to run NetWare
utilities such as NDS Manager or NetWare Administrator for Windows 95. Client 32 is provided
with NetWare version 4.*x*.

Setting Up User-Level Access Control

File and Print Sharing for NetWare Networks lets your Windows 98 machine look like a
NetWare server from a user's perspective. You can map to shares and printers, run some
NetWare utilities against it, and assign rights based on users and groups from a real NetWare
server.

Setting up user-level access control with NetWare is very similar to setting it up with NT (see
the previous section "Logging on to a Windows NT Network" for more details). The following
steps show the process.

Part
VII

Ch
40

N O T E NetWare-based user-level security cannot be used with Novell's Client 32 for accessing
files on Windows 98 workstations that are shared with File and Print Sharing for NetWare
Networks or for actually sharing the resources on a machine with Client 32 installed. ■

To set up user-level access control for NetWare, follow these steps.

1. Run Control Panel

2. Double-click on Network.

3. If you don't see File and Printer Sharing for NetWare Networks in the list of networking
   components, click on File and Print Sharing... and make the appropriate selections
   depending on whether you want to share files, printers, or both. Close the Control Panel
   Network applet and reboot to apply your settings. Then start with step 4 at the Control
   Panel Network applet.

4. Click on the Access Control tab.

5. Select User-Level Access Control and specify the NetWare server to whose users and groups you will assign rights on your computer. If you are installing the NetWare client itself for the first time, you are warned that Windows 98 can't confirm that the NetWare server is available, as shown in Figure 40.9.

FIG. 40.9

When you install the NetWare client and File and Print Sharing for NetWare networks at the same time, you get this message because the workstation won't be able to connect to a NetWare server until it reboots.

NOTE If you specify a 4.*x* server, only the users and groups in the bindery context will be listed and available to assign rights to. ■

6. Reboot.

Choosing the Browse Method   After File and Print Sharing is installed, you need to choose how your Windows 98 machine will be located, or browsed, by users. You have two options: workgroup advertising or SAP advertising, as shown in Figure 40.10. Table 40.4 gives details on making this selection.

FIG. 40.10

You can choose to have your Windows 98 machine that is acting as a NetWare server browsed using either workgroup advertising or SAP advertising.

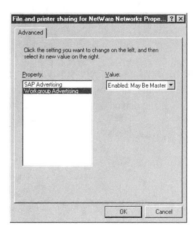

Table 40.4   Choosing Workgroup Advertising or SAP Advertising

Option	Description
Workgroup advertising	Workgroup advertising enables your machine to be browsed by using the standard method any other Windows machine uses to broadcast itself. For example, if all workstations in a workgroup are called ABC, your NetWare server will show up in this workgroup as well. Workgroup advertising is your best option if you're working in an environment with only Windows machines and you don't need to run utilities such as SLIST. It takes up much less bandwidth on a network. You have four settings: *Disabled* means you're not using this type of advertising; *Enabled: May be a Master* means that if no other computers are keeping track of the machines in the workgroup, this one will; *Enabled: Preferred Master* means that this computer will keep track of the machines in the workgroup by default; and *Enabled: Will Not Be Master* means that this computer will never keep track of the other machines in the workgroup. If this workgroup contains NT machines, you should choose *Enabled: Will Not Be Master*.
SAP advertising	SAP advertising is the native method NetWare servers use to make themselves known on the network. If you are using DOS-based clients or you need to run utilities such as SLIST, SYSCON or others against the Windows 98 machines, use SAP. This protocol is known for being bandwidth intensive, so unless you absolutely need it, workgroup advertising is your better choice.

Part
VII

Ch
40

Assigning Permissions to Shares and Printers   File and Print Sharing for NetWare Networks enables you to assign rights to resources on your workstation, using users and groups that have been created on a real NetWare server. As a result, users have to know the username and password of their account only on the actual NetWare server.

When assigning rights, Windows 98 uses two security contexts to enumerate the user and groups from the bindery on the NetWare server. If you're logged on, Windows uses the account with which you're connected to the server to read the bindery information. However, if you're not logged on to the NetWare server, there must be an account called windows_passthru on the server. If the account is missing, Windows 98 does not have the permissions to connect to the server and read the bindery. Instead, you are prompted to log on to the server when you try to assign rights. To assign rights to a folder or printer, right-click on it and choose Sharing (see Figure 40.11).

FIG. 40.11

You need to specify not only the share name for the printer or directory but also who will have what access.

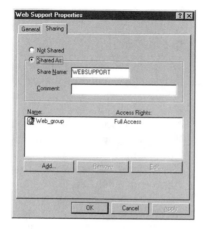

To share a resource, click the Shared As option, assign a Share Name (no spaces), and give the share an optional Comment that will be displayed when a user browses the resources on the machine. Then you need to assign rights to users and groups. For printers, you can grant either Full Access or No Access to users and groups. Folders, however, can have more granular rights. Table 40.5 shows the available rights:

Table 40.5   Assigning Rights to File-Based Resources

Option	Description
Read Only	A user can list the files in the folder and read them, but cannot make any modifications.
Full Access	A user has all possible rights to a folder. This option is not recommended for security reasons. Instead, assign custom rights as needed.
Custom	You can selectively choose to assign any combination of the rights shown in Figure 40.12 when you select Custom. Most of the rights are obvious; however, there are a couple of things to clarify. Write to Files doesn't give a user permission to Delete a file, and List Files only allows a user to see what files are there but doesn't allow him or her to read the files.

CAUTION

The Supervisor account on the NetWare server automatically has full rights to any shares you create on your Windows 98 client using File and Print Sharing for NetWare Networks even if you explicitly specify fewer rights when you assign permissions.

After the resource has been shared, a hand appears under the resource's icon, as shown in Figure 40.13.

FIG. 40.12

The Custom option enables you to assign specific rights.

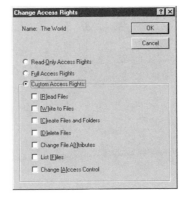

FIG. 40.13

Windows 98 displays a hand under resources that have been shared.

A significant limitation with File and Print Sharing for NetWare Networks is that you can assign rights to users on only one NetWare server. In other words, if you have server JWSERV and server FINANCE, you can't assign users from both servers rights to your WebSupport share. Another limitation is that you can't have File and Print Sharing for Microsoft Networks and File and Print Sharing for NetWare Networks running on the same machine, because they use totally different protocols. Microsoft Networking uses the SMB protocol, whereas NetWare uses the NCP protocol. ●

Part

VII

Ch

40

CHAPTER 41

Windows 98 Network Administration

by Christopher Gagnon

In this chapter

Windows 98 is a good choice for a client operating system in a network. This version of Windows has several built-in features that help ensure consistency of the desktop in a networked environment. Microsoft also provides several methodologies and tools that you can use to install and administer Windows 98.

User Profiles

User profiles define the Windows 98 environment for a particular user. They enable a user to make changes to the system without affecting other users. To accomplish this goal, the user profile consists of several different components. When you enable user profiles on a Windows 98 machine, you have the option of including Start Menu items, Network Neighborhood contents, and Desktop icons in the profile. In addition to these components, user profiles also store wallpaper selections, color schemes, screen saver selections, and sound schemes. This section describes how the system stores a user profile.

Anatomy of User Profiles

When user profiles are activated on a Windows 98 machine, the system stores each user's profiles in the C:\Windows\Profiles folder. Looking through this folder structure for a specific user can help you understand how profiles work. Figure 41.1 shows the basic structure of the profile for user JohnDoe.

FIG. 41.1

A user profile is stored in the Windows folder.

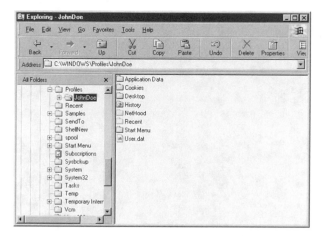

Notice that the profile structure contains many of the folders that you can find under the C:\Windows folder. When you enable user profiles, Windows 98 creates a structure for each user that mimics the standard profile structure. The following folders are created in a user's Profile folder:

■ Application Data

This folder contains specific user information for certain applications such as Internet Explorer.

■ Cookies

This folder stores any cookies downloaded from the Internet.

■ Desktop

The Desktop folder contains any files or shortcuts stored on the user's desktop.

■ History

This folder contains the user's history data.

■ NetHood

This folder stores the current contents of Network Neighborhood.

■ Recent

This folder stores links to the most recently used files on the system.

■ Start Menu

The Start Menu folder stores the user's Start Menu configuration.

N O T E   Depending on the software you install, the program group may be placed in the profile of the user who installed the software or it may be available for all users. Microsoft Office places icons for all users on the system, whereas other programs may not do so. You can make programs available to all users by copying the program group to the All Users profile, which is located in C:\Windows\All Users. ■

Enabling User Profiles

The process for configuring roaming user profiles in Windows 98 is identical to the process used for Windows 95. The first step is to enable user profiles on the machine (see Figure 41.2). To enable user profiles, follow these steps:

1. Open the Control Panel.
2. Double-click on the Passwords icon.
3. Select the User Profiles tab.
4. Select the second box: Users Can Customize Their Preferences and Desktop Settings.
5. Select the user profile settings you want.
6. Click OK.

Roaming User Profiles

Roaming user profiles enable you to define a standard desktop that follows a user from machine to machine. This feature is ideal for users who have to log on to several different machines and want to maintain the same look and feel on each machine. This section describes the process of creating roaming user profiles.

The first step in setting up roaming profiles is to enable user profiles as just described. The second step is to modify the user's account on the Windows NT domain to specify a home directory that resides on a Windows NT server. Windows 98 saves a copy of the user profile on the home directory during the shutdown process. When the user logs on at a different machine, the profile is read from the server.

FIG. 41.2

User profiles are enabled in the Control Panel's Password Properties window.

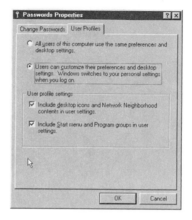

Troubleshooting Roaming User Profiles

One of the most common problems with roaming profiles is an unstable connection to the server where the profile is stored. If a user receives a standard profile when logging on to a system, you should check the following areas:

- Check the User Manager on a Windows NT server machine to verify that the user is mapped to the correct home directory.
- Verify that the user can connect to the server where the home directory resides.
- Verify that user profiles are activated on the Windows 98 machine in question.

Zero Administration Kit

The Zero Administration Kit (ZAK) is a collection of processes and procedures for installing Windows 98 workstations that require little administrative overhead. These processes can be used to automate an install process or even to design an entire connectivity solution for non-power users.

A Note from the Author

Because ZAK is a set of documents and methodologies, this book does not cover the process of creating a Windows 98 load in great detail. The actual process of designing a ZAK installation depends on the requirements of the users. I strongly recommend that you read all the ZAK documents before attempting to design a ZAK solution.

Overview

Microsoft operating systems have traditionally contained procedures for implementing an unattended setup. Although these features have been around for several OS versions, their use has been poorly documented. The ZAK is an attempt to bring these features into the light. ZAK consists of several documents and utilities that distribute and control Windows 95, Windows 98, and Windows NT workstations. As any administrator knows, every business has its own specific IT needs. In addition, every department in the business has specific functions that may not be needed by other departments. Granting levels of access and control to users that do not need them can lead to an administrative nightmare.

Consider the following example:

Two departments found in many medical centers are the fiscal and pharmacology departments. The fiscal department requires both billing and office productivity software. The pharmacology department may require patient records and pharmacology software.

A possible IT solution might include placing a Windows 98 PC on every desk in each department with the required software installed. This solution would meet the needs of each department but can also lead to some user issues. People are naturally curious and will undoubtedly want to explore the system.

ZAK provides procedures that enable you to create a standard Windows 98 load for pharmacology that allows the machine to access the pharmacology software and the patient records database only. You can use the same method to create a standard load for the fiscal department. By restricting access to the required software, you considerably lower the risk of problems on the machine.

Because there is no customization on the desktop, you can replace a bad machine quickly and easily. For example, if someone in the fiscal department is experiencing problems with a machine, you can replace the machine with one that has a fresh load installed. Because there are no individual settings, the user will be ready to start working the minute you boot the new machine.

This solution also saves time for your IT staff members by allowing them to fix a user problem without worrying about a lengthy troubleshooting process.

System Policies and Profiles

System policies and system profiles are two ways of securing a user's environment. *System profiles* define the user's workspace. When you use individual policies, each user that logs on to a particular machine can modify the environment without affecting the environment of other users on the same machine. *System policies* enable the administrator to define a set of security policies that govern how a machine is used by any particular user. For example, you can use system policies to prevent users from running an MS-DOS command prompt. ZAK provides instruction and methodologies for applying system profiles and policies.

> **CAUTION**
>
> System policies edit the Registry of the client machines and can easily cripple a machine to the point of requiring the operation system to be reinstalled. It is a good idea to setup several "crash and burn" systems so that you can test all aspects of the profile before you implement it in a production environment.

Unattended Installation

One of the biggest issues with installing a client operating system at a large site is the installation process. Installing 1,000 Windows 98 machines using the standard installation process can be a grueling and unruly process. Not only do you have to touch every machine, but you also take the risk of accidentally configuring each machine differently. Standardizing your machines greatly reduces troubleshooting time. In addition to the control features, ZAK provides a method for creating an unattended, standardized installation process for your workstations.

ZAK Windows 98 Configuration Options

ZAK defines two specific workstation types that can be used to create an overall solution for a specific IT need. In addition to these two types, you can use ZAK to create an unattended installation of Windows 98 that does not apply policies and profiles. This feature enables you to use ZAK to install Windows 98 in a standard format with no restrictions applied. The three types of ZAK installation types are vanilla, Appstation, and Taskstation.

Vanilla Install   A vanilla install results in a workstation that is virtually identical to a workstation that was installed with the Windows 98 distribution media. You can use this process to speed the installation of Windows 98 on a large number of machines that require no specific access restrictions. This process is similar to cloning machines with products such as Ghost. The process involves configuring a reference machine with all required software, taking a snapshot of the system, and using this snapshot to implement an unattended install of Windows 98. All machines created in this manner are exactly the same, which helps you standardize your site.

Appstation   An *Appstation* is a Windows 98 machine that allows access to certain applications only. At first glance, an Appstation looks like any other Windows 98 machine. The difference is seen when you click on the Start Menu. The Start Menu contains links only to approved applications. The applications reside on a network server and run over the network. All user data is saved to a network location as well. This type of workstation is easily replaced if problems develop because the local machines do not store any data. In addition, users cannot change their settings because the workstations have no link to the Control Panel or to the MS-DOS prompt.

Taskstation   A *Taskstation* takes the control one step further. Some users only need access to one specific task. For example, an order entry clerk only needs to access the order processing database. If you configure the clerk's workstation as a Taskstation, the machine boots to the order processing application and the screen has neither a Taskbar nor a Start Menu. The user has no reason to use anything else on the system. A Taskstation is designed for running one specific task and basically turns Windows 98 into a kiosk.

Internet Explorer Administration Kit

The Internet Explorer Administration Kit (IEAK) is a suite of utilities that enables you to customize the Internet Explorer and web interface settings for Windows 98. Because IE 4.0 is integrated with Windows 98, these tools can be invaluable to the administrator of a Windows 98 network.

Overview

IEAK consists of two utilities that can be used to fully administer the Internet Explorer components of Windows 98. The IEAK Wizard is used to create a custom distribution of Internet Explorer 4 and is not as important when you are administering a Windows 98 network, because IE 4.0 is integrated with the operating system. You can use the IEAK Profile Manager to create profiles to control the clients. As an administrator, you can use these tools to control how your users view the web components of their systems.

IEAK Wizard

The IEAK Wizard creates distribution media for Internet Explorer 4.0. However, this handy tool is unnecessary when your clients are running Windows 98. The IEAK Wizard is used primarily for creating the distribution media for Windows 95 and Windows NT Workstation machines. This tool is less important in a Windows 98 environment and, therefore, is not covered here.

IEAK Profile Manager

The IEAK Profile Manager enables you to create an Internet Explorer profile that you can use to control your clients. You can then use the Windows System Policy Editor to apply the Internet Explorer policies to your users.

Wizard Settings

The Wizard Settings (see Figure 41.3) properties enable you to change some of the basic properties of Internet Explorer. These options are identical to the options in the IEAK Wizard but can be used here to modify the properties with an Internet Explorer policy. The Wizard Settings options are described in this section.

Browser Title   The Browser Title component enables you to customize the browser with your company name. The selections are as follows:

- Title Bar Text

  This text is appended to the title bar in Internet Explorer.
- Toolbar Background Bitmap

  This entry points to a bitmap that Internet Explorer will display on the toolbar.

FIG. 41.3

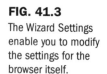

The Wizard Settings enable you to modify the settings for the browser itself.

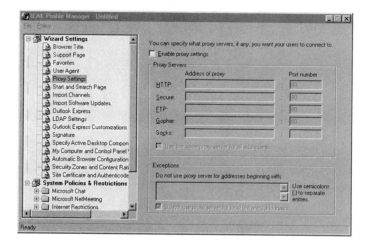

Support Page   The Support Page section enables you to specify the URL that will be accessed when the user chooses Online Support from the Help menu. This feature is handy if you have an internal web site that deals with system support issues.

Favorites   You can use this section to customize the Favorites folder for every client. This way you can have a list of URLs available for every user. The selections are as follows:

- Name

    The name of the site

- URL

    The URL to the site

User Agent   A user agent string is what a web browser uses to identify itself to web servers. You can use this section of the IEAK Profile Manager to add a text string such as your company name to the user agent string. This string generally keeps Internet usage statistics.

Proxy Settings   You can use this setting to define any proxy servers that may be in use on your network. This component is one of the handiest for a network administrator. Because all users on the network use the same proxy servers, controlling this section centrally eliminates the burden of changing this setting on each machine.

Start and Search Page   This section enables you to define both the Home page and the Search page. The Home page is the page that opens when you first launch Internet Explorer. The Search page can be accessed by pressing the Search button on the Internet Explorer button bar. To modify these settings, simply type the desired URL for each page.

Import Channels   The Import Channels section enables you to modify the Channel bar. This section has options for adding, deleting, and importing channels.

Import Software Updates This section is similar to the Import Channels section in that you can customize the Software Distribution Channels. To make changes to this section, you should keep the IEAK Profile Manager open while you make changes to the Software Distribution Channels. Any changes made while the IEAK Profile Manager is open are saved into the profile.

Outlook Express This section enables you to configure the mail settings for Outlook Express. The available options are

- Incoming Mail Server
  The name of the POP3 or IMAP server
- Outgoing Mail Server
  The name of the SMTP server
- Internet News Services
  The address of the Usenet server
- Options
  Settings for default mail, news client status, and SPA status

LDAP Settings This section enables you specify a server that uses LDAP to provide directory access services to your client machines. The options are as follows:

- Friendly Name
- Directory Service
- Home Page
- Search Base
- Service Bitmap

Outlook Express Customizations You can use this section to customize the Outlook Express Info Pane to display the HTML file of your choice. You can also specify a welcome message that will be placed in every user's inbox. The options on this page are as follows:

- URL or Local File
  Defines the information in the Info Pane
- HTML Path
  Specifies the path to the desired welcome message
- Sender
  Identifies the sender of the welcome message to the users
- Reply-to
  Contains the email address of the sender of the welcome message

Signature This section is used to attach a block of text to every email message and Usenet posting sent from Outlook Express. For example, you might want to place a disclaimer at the end of every message for legal purposes. The Signature section has two text boxes so that you can define separate messages for mail and newsgroup messages.

Part

VII

Ch

41

My Computer and Control Panel Web View Customization   You can use this section to add specific web views to both the My Computer and Control Panel windows. This feature can come in especially handy as you can create an HTML file that has instructions on how to complete a task in My Computer and have those instructions displayed as the background of the window. You can also create a file that says Keep Out! for the background of the Control Panel window.

Automatic Browser Configuration   This section defines the INS file that updates Internet Explorer on each client machine. Without this setting, Internet Explorer would have to be reinstalled for the changes to take effect.

Security Zones and Content Ratings Customization   This section enables you to customize the settings for the Security Zones and Content Ratings on each client. You can use this tool to prevent access to sites with questionable content that is against corporate policy. Choosing the Modify Settings button for either option launches the Internet Explorer dialog box for that option.

Site Certificate and Authenticode Settings   You can use this section to modify Site Certificate and Authenticode settings. By modifying these settings, you can prevent your users from accepting and running unauthorized browser plug-ins. Changes here can also prevent the users from designating any software publishers as safe. As in the Security Zones section, choosing Modify Settings launches the Internet Explorer dialog boxes for the settings.

System Policies and Restrictions

The System Policies and Restrictions section contains configuration parameters for the additional components of Internet Explorer such as Outlook Express and Microsoft NetMeeting. It also enables you to set general interface and connection policies (see Figure 41.4).

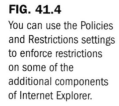

FIG. 41.4
You can use the Policies and Restrictions settings to enforce restrictions on some of the additional components of Internet Explorer.

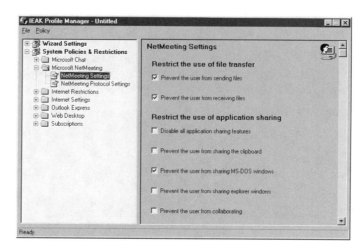

Microsoft Chat   This section enables you to predefine the settings for Microsoft Chat. This application is a utility similar to Internet relay chat (IRC) that combines comiclike graphics with real-time chat. The options for this section are as follows:

■ Server List

The name of the chat server list

■ Default Chat Server

The name of the default chat server

■ Default Chat Room

■ Default Character

Changes the graphic character represented by the user

■ Default Backdrop

Changes the graphic environment for the user

■ User Profile String

Changes the user's profile string

Microsoft NetMeeting   This section restricts usage of Microsoft NetMeeting. The following options are available:

■ Restrict the Use of File Transfer

■ Restrict the Use of Application Sharing

■ Restrict the Use of the Options Dialogue

■ Restrict the Use of Video

■ Default Directory Server

■ Exchange Server Property for NetMeeting Address

■ Preset User Information Category

■ Set the NetMeeting Homepage

■ Set Limit for Audio/Video Throughput

■ Enable Protocols for LiveShare Compatibility

■ Select Enable Set of T120 Protocols

Internet Restrictions   This section enables you to set the options available in the Internet Properties control panel. The settings are as follows:

■ General

■ Security

■ Content

■ Connection

■ Programs

■ Advanced

■ Code Download

■ Channels Settings

Internet Settings   This section enables you to set miscellaneous Internet Explorer default properties. The settings are as follows:

- Colors
- Fonts
- Languages
- Modem Settings
- Advanced Settings

Outlook Express   This section enables you to set up Outlook Express security policies. The options are as follows:

- Mail and News Security Zones
- HTML Mail and News Composition Settings
- Folder and Message Navigational Elements

Web Desktop   This section enables you to restrict access to certain components of the operating system for users that are using the web desktop. The components are as follows:

- Desktop Restrictions
- Active Desktop Items
- Desktop Wallpaper Settings
- Desktop Toolbar Settings
- Start Menu
- Shell
- Printers
- System

Subscriptions   This section enables you to control the amount of information downloaded from channels that your users are subscribed to; that is, to regulate the bandwidth being used. This section has the following options:

- Max KB of Site Subscription
- Max KB of Channel Subscription
- Max Number of Channels
- Max Number of Site Subscriptions
- Max Number of Minutes Between Site Updates
- Beginning of Range to Exclude Updates
- End of Range to Exclude Updates
- Max Site Subscription Crawl Depth

CHAPTER 42

Setting Up a Simple Windows Network

by Theresa Hadden

In this chapter

Understanding Networks

What is a network and why do you need one? A network consists of the components necessary for two or more computers to communicate with one another. These are just some of the advantages of networking:

- *Monetary savings.* Sharing hardware results in saving money. The most common type of hardware that is shared is a printer. Networking enables you to purchase one color printer and give everyone the capability to print to it.

- *Fast access to information.* You can access needed information directly from your PC instead of running around with a floppy disk looking for a particular memo or letter.

- *Easier information management.* By storing commonly needed types of information in a central location, all users of your network will always be able to find what they need. It also allows for the routine backup of important documents and data.

- *Shared access to information.* Customer information can be stored in one database so that all network users can access it.

- *Better communication.* The use of email and group scheduling applications increases productivity.

- *Improved efficiency.* Networking results in improved access to a large variety of information, which means projects will be completed in shorter periods of time.

A networkconsists of two types of components: hardware and software. The hardware components consist of the various pieces of equipment that connect the computers in the network. At a minimum, the required hardware consists of cables and adapter cards. Windows 98 integrates well into a broad variety of network types.

The software required to communicate across a network includes the network operating system, a network client, and one or more network transport protocols. Windows 98 functions as both a networking operating system and a desktop operating system.

N O T E A network client allows your computer to communicate with another computer based on the type of network operating system it is using. A protocol can be thought of as the language that is spoken across your network. If two computers use different protocols, they cannot communicate. Even if both computers use the same protocol, you need to make sure they are both properly configured to communicate with each other. ▦

How Peer-to-Peer Networks Work

Networks are organized in one of two ways: peer-to-peer or server-based. In a peer-to-peer network, each computer acts as both a server and a client. All the information is stored on the various computers. Any computer in the network can function as a server, providing access to such resources as files stored on its local hard drive and peripherals attached to it (such as printers, fax modems, scanners, or CD-ROM drives). Every computer in the network can also function as a client to access resources on the other computers in the network.

Each computer in a peer-to-peer network can share its resources without the need for centralized administration of these resources. Each user in a peer-to-peer network is a network administrator. This alleviates the need for one person to be responsible for various network administrative tasks.

N O T E The main advantage of a peer-to-peer network is that it doesn't require a dedicated network administrator. The main disadvantage of a peer-to-peer network is that it usually lacks a network administrator who can make sure all the network components are running smoothly. For this reason, peer-to-peer networks are suitable only for small networks. ■

Windows 98's built-in networking capabilities make it an excellent choice for implementing a peer-to-peer network. As an operating system, it contains all the elements you need to allow access to local resources or to access resources located on other computers in the network. Its point-and-click interface enables you to browse the network to locate and access available resources. The same interface makes the sharing of resources extremely easy for the user even if he or she is not technically adept at network administration.

How Server-Based Networks Work

You can change a peer-to-peer network to a server-based network by adding a specialized network server. Network servers are typically computers running either the Windows NT Server operating system or a NetWare server. Network servers usually are not out in the open on people's desks; instead they are often locked away in closets or specially equipped "server rooms."

The following list outlines the basic requirements for a server-based network:

- ■ *A centralized user database,* which is used to verify that each user requesting access is actually who he claims to be. This verification process is referred to as *authentication.*
- ■ *A centralized repository of information.* Files can be stored on one or more file servers and can be accessed by all the users on the network. This allows for easier access to saved documents. It also makes creating backups easier because only the file servers need to be backed up, which is easier than backing up each individual computer in the network.
- ■ *Centralized control of resources,* which allows the network administrator to designate which users have access to stored documents and shared peripherals. It also allows for easier configuration of these resources.

In a server-based network, the burden of controlling network administrative tasks is moved from the individual users to one or more persons who are more technically proficient in network administration. This central administrative role allows for more efficient management of the network.

The built-in network components of Windows 98 enable it to work very well in server-based networks by providing the software necessary for user authentication by the network server.

Part

VII

Ch

42

Planning Your Network

When you're planning your network, you need to consider several things. Here are some of the more important decisions you need to make before installing your network:

■ What resources need to be shared? Do you have a small environment and only want to share a single printer, or do you have a larger environment and need to share multiple peripherals as well as many files and/or databases?

■ How fast should your network be? Do you frequently share very large files or print large CAD or graphics files?

■ How large is your network? Are you connecting only two or three computers and one printer, or will hundreds of users be accessing your network?

■ How much distance will your network span? Are you creating a small network that's fully contained in one building, or do you need to connect to computers and other resources located in different cities or countries?

■ Do all your computers run the same operating system, or must you connect various types of computers such as Windows, NetWare, and UNIX-based systems?

■ Is your network small enough that each user will be responsible for his own computer, or will you have one or more individuals responsible for administering your network?

Use the answers to these questions to plan your network. Items that you will need to plan for include its bus topology, what equipment you will use to connect the computers on your network, and what security method you will use. Whether or not you will be creating a peer-to-peer network or a server-based network will influence your choice of operating system.

Wiring Your Network

After determining the size of your network, you will need to decide on the layout and hardware components needed for installing the network. As an example, we will examine a local area network (LAN) situated in a single building because the coverage of larger networks is beyond the scope of this chapter.

Bus Topology

When planning your network, you need to consider which *topology*, or design, is the most appropriate. This is especially important because the largest single cost when installing a new network can be the cost of installing the cable that connects all the computers in the network.

The most basic and easiest type of network topology to install is a bus network, which consists of two or more computers connected by coaxial cabling. Because of their ease of installation, coaxial cable networks have a very low initial cost.

N O T E For many network installations, a major cost is actually the labor charges incurred for the physical installation of the cables that connect the various computers to one another. Pulling cables through ceilings and walls is hard work, and it always seems to take much more time than most people expect. ■

Figure 42.1 illustrates a bus topology. Each computer is connected by coaxial cable using a connector called a T-piece. The coaxial cabling must be properly terminated at each end of the network with 50-ohm terminators.

FIG. 42.1
A diagram of a bus topology network.

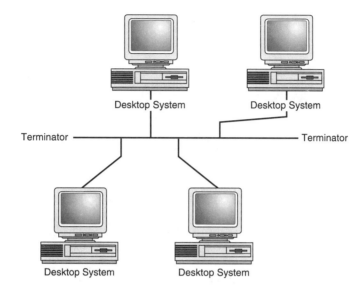

Coaxial cable will support up to 30 computers as long as the total length of the network is no greater than 185 meters. Bus topology lends itself well to installation in areas where running cabling through the ceiling or walls is difficult or impossible. In addition, it is easy to expand a bus network by adding another length of cable and a T-piece.

Although bus networks are easy to install, they can be difficult to troubleshoot if one of the network components malfunctions. A damaged or defective cable or T-piece can disrupt the entire network. Turning off your workstation, however, will not disrupt the function of the network. If you do not want to learn the ins and outs of network troubleshooting, this type of network might end up costing you more in the long run.

 If you have trouble with your network, segment your network by disconnecting the cabling in the middle. Terminate each side of the network to determine which half is not functioning. Then continue subdividing the half that does not work until you have identified the problem component.

Star Topology

The next type of network to consider is a star topology, in which a cable runs from each computer to a central piece of hardware called a *hub*. The capacity of a hub ranges from 4 to 24 computers. Figure 42.2 shows a small star topology.

Part
VII

Ch
42

FIG. 42.2

A cable runs from each computer to the hub to create a star topology.

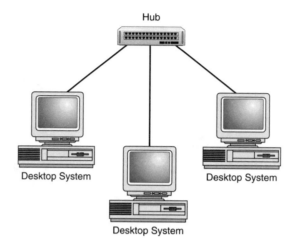

Hub

Desktop System

Desktop System

Desktop System

The twisted-pair wire that is used for this topology resembles telephone wire except that it uses four pairs of wires whereas telephone wire uses only two pairs. The RJ-45 connectors that are used with twisted-pair wires look like a slightly larger version of the connectors that are used on telephone wire. In a star topology, no computer can be more than 100 meters from the hub.

 TIP Twisted-pair wire is categorized by its speed of transmission. If you plan to expand your network, you might want to invest in Category 5 cable, which supports speeds up to 100Mbps. This will prevent you from having to rewire your network later.

Star topology has the advantage of being easy to troubleshoot. A single piece of defective cabling will affect only the computer that it connects to the hub. If the hub malfunctions, however, none of the computers attached to that hub will be able to communicate on the network. This is referred to as a single point of failure.

Initially, this type of network is more expensive than a bus topology because it requires the purchase of additional equipment such as hubs. Expansion of a star topology may require the purchase of an additional hub if no more connections are available on the existing hub. As your network grows, the wiring can become untidy and unwieldy, especially if you are unable to run the wiring through the walls.

 TIP After you decide on the topology for your network, you might want to consider having the cable run by an expert in the field. This initial investment will save you considerable expense later.

Use the following list as a quick reference to the characteristics of different cable types:

Type	Code	Cost	Total Distance	Number of Nodes per Segment
Twisted Pair (UTP)	10BaseT	Least $	100 meters	1
Twisted Pair (STP)	10BaseT		100 meters	1
Thin Coax	10Base2		185 meters	30
Thick Coax	10Base5		500 meters	100
Fiber		Most $	2,000 meters	

Network Adapter Card

After the cabling has been installed, you will need a network adapter card for each computer that will be networked. A network adapter card acts as an interface between your computer and the network. Each card is specific for the bus type of your computer and the type of cabling you have. See the section "Configuring Your Network," later in this chapter, for more details on selecting your network adapter card.

Network Operating System

The network operating system controls how communication takes place. Each computer must have a client operating system installed that allows communication over the network.

Windows 98 is an excellent choice because it serves as both the network operating system and the client operating system. In addition, its graphical user interface allows for ease of use and increased productivity. It supports a wide range of applications and has native support for mobile computing.

Network Transport Protocols

Network transport protocols format data for transmission over a network. Although more than one protocol may be installed on a computer, multiple protocols increase memory demands on computers and can produce excessive network traffic. It is more efficient to use only the protocol or protocols that are necessary to communicate with other computers on your network.

Windows 98 supports three primary transport protocols: NetBEUI, TCP/IP and IPX/SPX. Each of these protocols has advantages and disadvantages:

Part
VII

Ch
42

■ NetBEUI is the smallest and easiest protocol to use because it does not require (or allow) any additional configuration. The disadvantage of this protocol is that it is not routable, which means that it cannot communicate with remote networks via routers. If your network is small, this is usually the best choice because of its ease of implementation.

N O T E A *router* is a device used to connect different networks or network segments. Networks can be subdivided to reduce traffic, improve performance, or increase the distance over which the computers in the network can communicate. ■

■ IPX/SPX is generally used to communicate with a Novell NetWare servers. It is also relatively easy to implement. This network protocol is a good choice if you need to communicate across a router and do not need to access the Internet.

■ TCP/IP is the protocol of choice for the Internet. It is routable, which means that it allows for communication across a large network containing one or more routers. However, it is also the most difficult to configure of the three protocols. If you do not have experience with TCP/IP, this protocol is not a good choice for a small network.

Connecting Two Computers

The easiest and most common small network consists of two computers connected to each other. This setup is commonly used in small offices or home networks for the purpose of sharing a printer and/or sharing files. Three basic configurations can be used to achieve this end:

■ Connection via a coaxial cable

■ Connection via a crossover twisted-pair cable (see the sidebar entitled "Crossover Twisted-Pair Cable")

■ Connection via Direct Cable Connection using a null modem or parallel cable

The first two configurations require that a network adapter card be installed in each computer. The third option connects two computers using a cable attached to a serial or parallel port instead of a network card. The connection is made using either a null modem or parallel cable (not a printer cable).

 T I P Consider using a network connection to transfer information between your laptop and your desktop computer at home. Transferring information between two computers via a network is much easier and faster than carrying floppy disks around in what is commonly referred to as a "sneaker net."

Using a Network Adapter Card

The selection of a network adapter card depends on the type of computer it will be installed in, the type of cabling that will be used, and whether a driver is available for your operating system.

Every PC has one or more types of adapter slots, such as PCI, ISA, EISA, VESA local bus, Microchannel, and PC Card (PCMCIA). The network card you select must be compatible with an available slot in your computer. Refer to your PC's documentation to identify the correct type of adapter for your computer.

 Before installing or upgrading any adapter card in your computer (such as a modem or a video card), you need to know what type of slot is available in order to purchase the correct type of adapter card. If your computer is a Pentium (or newer), it probably has at least one PCI-compatible card slot. PCI cards provide much better performance and are easier to configure than the older ISA standard.

 If you will be purchasing a network card for what will be a heavily used file server, you will gain overall productivity if you use a higher performance card. Check for performance-oriented capabilities such as *bus mastering.*

Network cards generally allow for connection to a network in one or more ways, depending on the type of cable connector on the card. If the network adapter card has more than one type of connector present, it is often referred to as a *combo* or *combination card* and generally is more expensive.

In addition to computer bus and cabling type, other issues include the type of memory the network card uses. Consult the product specifications when selecting the appropriate card for your use.

If you are using coaxial cable, the network card you select must have a BNC adapter. This type of adapter looks like a short metal barrel. The coaxial cable is attached to a T-piece, which is then attached to the network adapter card.

CAUTION
Never attach a coaxial cable directly to the network card. This practice will result in a nonfunctioning network because you will be unable to attach the terminators that are required for the proper function of a coaxial cable-based network.

If you are using twisted-pair cable, select a network adapter card that has an RJ-45 connector, which looks like a larger version of the connector you use to insert your telephone wire into your telephone.

In addition to a network adapter card, your also must have software that allows your computer to communicate with the card. The software you need consists of two components:

- *Network adapter card driver.* This software provides for communication between your computer's operating system and the adapter card.
- *Network transport protocol.* This determines how the data is formatted for transport across the network. Think of it as the language that is spoken on your network.

Part
VII

Ch
42

 Windows 98 uses a Microsoft standard called NDIS to communicate with the network adapter card driver. This standard allows for the use of multiple protocols with a wide variety of network adapter cards.

Before you purchase your network adapter card, make sure that a driver appropriate for your operating system is readily available. Windows 98 includes drivers for most common cards. Check the most recent Hardware Compatibility List (HCL) available with the operating system or from Microsoft to ensure that you have a compatible card.

Connecting Using Coaxial Cable   After the network adapter cards have been installed in each computer, you will need to attach a piece of coaxial cable. This cable must be either RG58U or RG58A/U. Although the type of cable you use for your television looks the same, it will not work.

The cabling is connected using a T-piece connector. Figure 42.3 shows a T-piece. One side of the crossbar is attached to the coaxial cable, and the other is attached to either another cable or to a terminator with a 50-ohm rating. The connector is then attached to the network card. This process is repeated for each computer.

> **CAUTION**
>
> An improperly terminated network or the wrong type of cable can result in network failure. Or even worse, it can lead to intermittent network problems that are extremely difficult to detect and fix.

Connecting Using Twisted-Pair Cabling   Although twisted-pair cabling is ordinarily used with a hub to connect computers, you can connect two computers using a special type of twisted-pair cable called a *crossover cable*. To bypass the need to use a hub, one receive pair and one send pair are crossed at one end of the cable.

Crossover Twisted-Pair Cable

Normally, when attaching the RJ45 connector to a twisted-pair cable, each of the eight wires must be connected to the same groove on each connector. That is, the wire attached to the first groove on one connector should be attached to the first groove on the other cable.

With a crossover cable, the send and receive wires need to be reversed at one end. Figure 42.3 illustrates how to reverse the wires to create a cable that will connect two computers without requiring the use of a hub.

A crossover cable will connect only two computers, however. If you need to connect more than two computers, you will need to use a hub.

After installing the network adapter card, you just plug the crossover cable into each of the network cards in the same manner that you plug in your telephone. If you have wired the crossover cable correctly, the two computers will be able to communicate.

 Instead of making your own cable, you might want to purchase it from a cable supply company. Also, to prevent possible confusion, try to purchase your crossover cables in a different color cable than the cables you use to connect computers to your hubs.

FIG. 42.3

This diagram illustrates how to cross over the wires to create a crossover cable. The numbers on the left refer to the grooves on one connector, and the numbers on the right refer to the grooves on the connector at the other end of the cable.

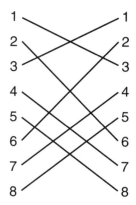

Configuring Your Network   When the physical connections are made, use the Add New Hardware Wizard in Control Panel to detect and install your network adapter card. After you run the hardware wizard, verify that the correct network components are installed. You can examine the network properties either by right-clicking on the Network Neighborhood icon or by opening the Network Applet from the Control Panel.

The following three items need to be installed via the Properties tab of the Network Neighborhood:

Adapter. This is the network card adapter.

Protocol. This is the language that will be used to communicate on your network.

Either Client for Microsoft Networks or Client for NetWare Networks. These components are sometimes referred to as redirectors; they allow you to communicate with other computers on your network.

The adapter should already be listed as the one that was installed using the Add New Hardware Wizard. Thanks to Windows 98 Plug and Play capabilities, no further configuration should be necessary.

 TIP   Use the Device Manager to verify that the network adapter card is functioning properly and that no resource conflicts are present.

The best protocol to install when connecting only two computers is NetBEUI. Its small overhead and the lack of configuration requirements make it the ideal choice. All you need to do is install it.

To install this protocol, open the Network Properties dialog box, select Add, and then select Protocol. The Select Network Protocol dialog box appears (see Figure 42.4). Select Microsoft on the left side of the dialog box, and then select NetBEUI on the right side.

Part

VII

Ch

42

FIG. 42.4

Select Microsoft from the left side of the dialog box. Select NetBEUI from the list of available protocols on the right side.

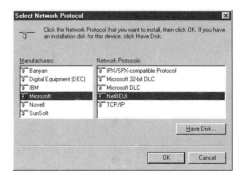

To add the Client for Microsoft Networks, click the Add button on the Configuration tab. Select Client, and then click on the Add button. In the Select Network Client dialog box, select Microsoft on the left side and select Client for Microsoft Networks on the right side (see Figure 42.5).

FIG. 42.5

Select Microsoft on the left side and select Client for Microsoft Networks on the right side.

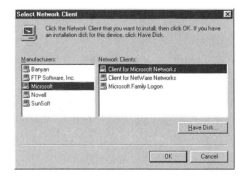

When you return to the Configuration tab of the Network Properties dialog box, be sure that Client for Microsoft Networks is selected in the Primary Network Logon box, as shown in Figure 42.6.

Next, click on File and Print Sharing. Select the appropriate check boxes to allow access to your files and/or to allow others to print to your printer. Then click OK to return to the Configuration tab.

Select the Identification tab to see the options shown in Figure 42.7. Enter a name for your computer and your workgroup, and then click OK.

FIG. 42.6
Notice that Client for Microsoft Networks appears in the Primary Network Logon box.

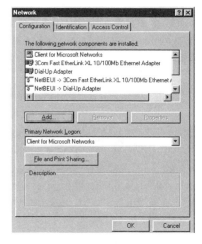

FIG. 42.7
Here the computer name is WhiteStar, and the workgroup name is STARTREK.

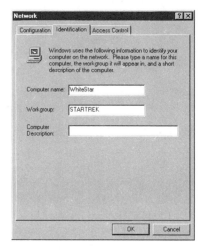

N O T E The name you select for your computer must be a unique name; it is also referred to as the computer's NetBIOS name. This name can contain up to 15 characters but cannot contain spaces or any of these characters:

/ \ * , . " @

You should enter the same workgroup name on each computer. Although you will still be able to communicate if the workgroup names are different, entering the same name on both computers means that both computers will be listed as members of the same workgroup when they're viewed by someone browsing the Network Neighborhood. ■

Part
VII

Ch
42

Using Direct Cable Connection

You can avoid installing a network adapter card by connecting two computers directly using a null modem (serial) or parallel cable attached to a serial (COM) or parallel port on each computer.

To install the Direct Cable Connection capability, run the Add/Remove Programs applet in the Control Panel and click on the Windows Setup tab. In the Components list, select Communications, and then click the Details button. Select Direct Cable Connection and click OK.

After you've installed Direct Cable Connection and connected the two computers with either a serial or parallel cable, open the Start menu and choose Programs, Accessories, Direct Cable Connection. The Direct Cable Connection Wizard runs when you open Direct Cable Connection for the first time. One computer should be designated as a host and the other as a guest, as shown in Figure 42.8.

FIG. 42.8

Configure Direct Cable Connection with the wizard.

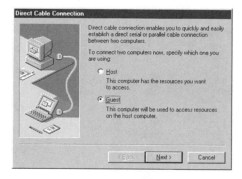

With Direct Cable Connection, you can gain access to shared folders on another computer, even when your computer is not wired to a network. If the other computer is connected to a network, you can also gain access to that network.

 Direct Cable Connection is intended for only light use because it is much slower than a true network connection. For sustained communications between two computers, you would be much better off to buy the appropriate hardware.

Creating a Workgroup

A *workgroup* is an organizational unit. It is a loose association of computers wherein each computer tracks and controls access to local resources. These resources may be folders located on the local hard drive or hardware devices attached directly to the computer (such as a printer). Each individual computer in the workgroup controls how access to these resources occurs.

If your network is small—fewer than 10 computers—a workgroup is an easy way to configure your network and provide access to various resources. It does not require a single individual to be designated as the administrator. Rather, each user is the administrator for his own computer.

The disadvantages associated with a workgroup are related to its advantages. Because each user is his own administrator, there is no centralized control of users or resources. As your network grows, the large number of users can result in a disorganized network. Because there is no centralized location for shared documents and applications, it can become difficult for a user to locate needed information. This can result in lost productivity or the occurrence of duplicate versions of the same document.

Printing is one of the most common tasks performed on a network, and shared printing can lead to problems. Because the computer that is attached to the printer is acting as a print server, the additional load can cause degradation in performance. This can be a significant problem affecting the user working on that computer.

To improve performance of a computer that is extensively used as a file server, use the System option in Control Panel and set the typical role of the computer to Network Server. If the computer is also functioning as a print server, make sure that adequate disk space is available for spooling.

When files and folders are shared, a password is associated with the resource and the level of access that is allowed. Once file sharing has been enabled, various levels of access to a resource can be defined based on passwords. These levels are Read and Full control.

File sharing is enabled through the File and Print Sharing button on the properties sheet for the Network Neighborhood. You can elect to share files, allow others to print to your printer, or both. You must also select Share Level Access Control on the Access Control tab.

To share a folder, right-click on it in Windows Explorer and select Properties. On the Sharing tab, select Share As. Each shared folder must have a name to identify it. A suggested name will be displayed, but you can enter whatever name you want to use as long as it contains no more than 12 characters. The name that you enter here will be displayed to any user browsing your computer across the network. Figure 42.9 shows a shared folder.

Ending the share name with a dollar sign ($) creates a *hidden share*. Hidden shares cannot be seen by users who are browsing your computer across the network and can be accessed only by users who know the share's name.

You can also enter a comment that will be displayed to users as they browse your computer across the network. Use this field to identify the information that is contained in the share, which might make it easier for users to find needed information.

When you name your workgroup on the Identification tab of the Network Properties dialog box, one of two things happens. You either join an existing workgroup or create a new one. If the name you enter is an existing workgroup, the computer you are configuring becomes a member of that workgroup.

Part

VII

Ch

42

FIG. 42.9

The level of access that is granted may be dependent upon what password the user enters to access the resource.

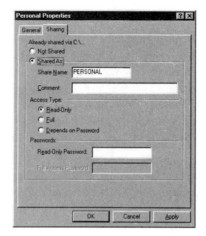

However, if you enter a name that is not the name of an existing workgroup, you create a new workgroup, and that computer becomes its first member. You can then add additional computers to your workgroup simply by entering that workgroup's name on the Identification tab of the Network Properties dialog box of the computer you want to add to the workgroup.

Security

One of the biggest problems in a peer-to-peer network that uses share level access is the number of passwords needed to control access to resources. The more resources that are available to the users, the more passwords that have to be remembered.

If a user has to keep track of multiple passwords, he might forget them or he might write them down. Either one prevents the security policy from doing what it is intended to do—which is to allow access to those you want to have access and deny access to all others.

For that reason, Windows 98 offers a password caching feature that is installed by default. This feature stores passwords in a special file. When you access a password-protected resource for the first time, make sure that Save This Password in Your Password List option is checked. Your password will be encrypted and then stored in a .PWL file in the Windows folder.

> **CAUTION**
> If you delete .PWL files, you will lose all the passwords you have stored. The next time you access a password-protected resource, you will have to retype the password.

If password caching is enabled, you can view the resources listed in the Password List File (.PWL) with the Password List Editor. The editor displays only the .PWL of the user who is logged on. You can disable password caching by using the System Policy Editor.

System Policy Editor

System policies provide a powerful tool for controlling how users interact with their computers and the network. One way to use system policies is to enforce specific password guidelines. These include defining the minimum password length and requiring the use of an alphanumeric logon password. System policies can also be used to disable password caching so that the user must type the password every time she attempts to access a shared resource.

You can use the system policy templates to define your desired policies. You can also create a new template that contains those items you want to control. Besides establishing password requirements, you can also perform the following measures:

- Control access to the Control Panel
- Prevent the use of the Run command from the Start menu
- Customize the desktop
- Configure network settings

To use System Policies, you must install the System Policy Editor and the templates.

Here are some additional policies that you can implement to improve password security:

- Instruct users not to write down passwords.
- Make sure that users know not to use obvious passwords such as the name of a spouse, child, or pet.
- Do not use dictionary words for your password.
- Use a combination of letters and numbers; a password of "good75dog" is harder to crack than "gooddog."
- An easy way to create a password is to combine two short words with a nonalphanumeric character between them, such as "big$meal."

You can improve the security of your network by limiting the total number of shared folders. By keeping those files that require shared access located in a limited number of folders, you decrease the number of passwords a user has to remember.

Disable file and print sharing on those computers that do not contain files requiring sharing. This action not only improves security, it also enhances the performance of the computer.

A Windows 98 network is easy to implement and maintain. This native functionality results in increased efficiency. It also saves you money by allowing all your users to share hardware devices such as printers. ●

CHAPTER 43

Sharing Network Resources

by Paul Sanna and Larry Passo

In this chapter

Understanding Sharing, Windows Shares, and Security

Sharing is a critical part of almost any Windows-based network. Sharing in Windows networks means users can make resources on their computer available to other users. Without sharing, users are forced to copy files and folders to a network server volume if they want others to have access to them. In a more specific scenario, let's say that a coworker is working with a set of files related to a project, and those files are stored in a folder on the coworker's computer. Let's also say that you need to read and possibly edit one of those files. If the person shares the folder where the files are located, you can access any of the files in the folder from your desktop as if the files were stored on your own machine.

Users can also share other resources on their computer, such as printers. Let's say that a coworker has attached a color inkjet printer to her machine, and you have a color presentation you need to print. There is a better method than disconnecting the color inkjet and reattaching it to your computer. The coworker could share the printer, you could attach to it over the network, and then you could print to it as if it were directly attached to your computer.

Understanding Shares and Networks

Sharing is supported on both Windows and NetWare networks, but this chapter focuses primarily on sharing in a Windows network environment. A Windows network is one in which the computers operate on a peer-to-peer basis, and it usually consists of a mix of 16-bit Windows, Windows 95, Windows 98, and Windows NT computers.

Keep in mind that in a peer-to-peer network, any computer that provides resources to other computers is considered a server. Peer-to-peer networks usually have a relatively small number of computers—typically fewer than 10. A network with a dedicated server, which is usually known as a client/server network, is usually used to support networks with more than 10 computers.

Regardless of whether the Windows network is peer-to-peer or client/server, sharing works the same way. Sharing allows users to access such network resources as the following:

- Folders
- Files
- Removable drives (CD-ROM, Jaz, Zip, SyQuest, and so on)
- Printers

When any resource is made available over the network for users on other computers, that resource is known as a *share*. The term share will be used throughout this chapter. When a resource is shared, a hand appears under its icon on the screen (see Figure 43.1).

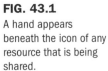

FIG. 43.1
A hand appears
beneath the icon of any
resource that is being
shared.

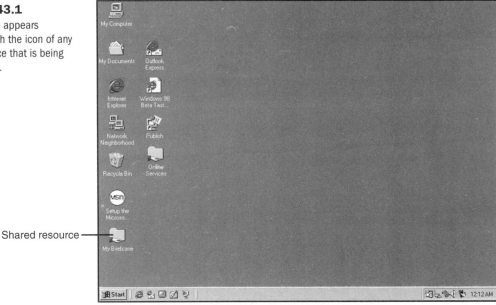

Shared resource ——

N O T E   It's important for you to note that while shares allow files to be accessed from any
computer that is connected to the network, only directories can actually be shared. When a
directory is shared, all files and subdirectories it contains are available for network access. ▓

Understanding Access Types

Before you share any resource over the network, you need to decide what type of access control, or network security, your resources require. You have two choices for access control:

- Share-level access control
- User-level access control

Share-Level Access Control   Share-level security is used to define a common level of security
access to a specific share that applies to all users of that share. In share-level access, the user
defines a share for a resource, gives it a name (such as "Project X Folder"), and optionally
secures the share with a password. The user can also specify whether persons accessing the
share can modify the contents of the shared directory or just read the files that are in the
shared directory.

Users can access the contents of a share, in this case a folder, simply by opening the folder.
Naturally, if the share is secured by a password, the user would have to supply the correct
password to access the contents of the share. The most important point to keep in mind with
share-level access is that all users who know the password that protects the share will have the
same type of access to the share.

Part

VII

Ch

43

User-Level Access Control   User-level access control allows access to be based on who a user is instead of whether he or she knows a password. This allows different users on the network to have individual, unique rights to each share.

User-level security requires that a computer be able to maintain a secure, centralized account database and serve as a security validation server. NetWare Servers, Windows NT Servers, or Windows NT Workstations (in the absence of a Windows NT Server) can all function as security validation servers for Windows 98 computers. Windows NT domains can also act as external security validation agents.

N O T E   The process of using an external security validation server is referred to as *pass-through validation.*

The list of users and groups to which you can give access to your shared resources is maintained by your external security validation server. Any user with an account in the centralized account database can create shares on a Windows 98 system and assign security access to any user or group that has an account on the security validation server. Although you can add users to your own machine, you cannot use those user accounts on any other computer in the domain. Before you can give a user or group access to a share on your computer that is configured for user-level access, that user or group must have an account in the centralized account database on the security validation server.

T I P   Although the account must be created in the centralized account database, you can actually create the necessary account from Windows 98 if you have the proper software on your computer and administrative rights for the domain. Both Windows NT and Novell NetWare supply administrative utilities that allow remote network management from a Windows 98 computer. The Windows NT Server installation CD-ROM includes a copy of User Manager for Domains that can be run on a Windows 98 computer.

Windows NT Domains Versus Workgroups

The two major differences between workgroups and Windows NT domains are their organizational structure and the number of users/computers they can support.

Each computer in a workgroup is responsible for its own administration and security. The various computers in a workgroup might consist of any combination of Windows 98/95, Windows for Workgroups, Windows NT Workstation, or Windows NT Member Server computers. Each user in a workgroup needs to have an account created for him or her on every computer in the network to which he or she needs access. The administrative overhead of creating and maintaining all the multiple user accounts in a workgroup usually limits their size to very small networks, typically fewer than 10 computers.

The central component of a Windows NT domain is a Windows NT Server that has been configured as a Primary Domain Controller (PDC). Every domain must have one PDC and can have one or more Windows NT Server(s) that have been configured as Backup Domain Controllers (BDCs). The PDC maintains a master list of all the valid user accounts in the domain. PDCs also replicate account information to their BDCs. Whenever a user logs on to a domain or requests access to domain resources, the domain's PDC or a BDC authenticates the request. Windows NT domains can be quite large, including up to several thousand users and computers.

N O T E Windows 98 computers cannot join a domain. However, a user working at a Windows 98 computer can be authenticated by a domain controller during network logon and can gain access to domain resources. ▬

Configuring Windows 98 for Resource Sharing

Before user-level or share-level sharing is allowed in Windows 98, you must configure Windows 98 to allow sharing and to share other resources. Follow these steps to configure a Windows 98 machine to allow sharing:

1. Open the Network icon in Control Panel.

2. On the Configuration tab, look for an entry for File and Printer Sharing for Microsoft Networks. If such an entry exists, skip to step 7. Otherwise, continue with step 3.

3. Click the Add button. The Select Network Component Type dialog box appears. Choose Service from the list, and then choose Add. The Select Network Service dialog box appears (see Figure 43.2).

FIG. 43.2

Add the file and printer sharing service.

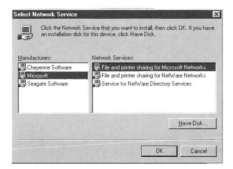

4. Choose Microsoft from the list of Manufacturers, and then choose File and Printer Sharing for Microsoft Networks from the Network Services list.

5. Click OK. When the installation process is complete, you are returned to the Network dialog box.

6. Choose the File and Print Sharing button. The File and Print Sharing dialog box appears (see Figure 43.3).

7. Check the desired options in the dialog box, and then choose OK. Then choose OK in the Network dialog box and restart your computer when prompted.

FIG. 43.3
You can configure
Windows 98 to share
files and printers.

Establishing Share-Level Access to Drive or Folder Resources

Share-level access is the least flexible of options, but it happens to be the easiest to administer. This section covers all the details.

Configuring Windows 98 for Share-Level Security

The first step in creating shares with share-level security is to configure Windows 98 for share-level security. Follow these steps:

1. Open the Network icon in Control Panel.

2. In the Network dialog box, select the Access Control tab (see Figure 43.4).

FIG. 43.4
You must define what
type of access scheme
you will use.

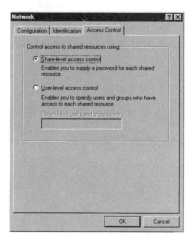

3. Select the Share-Level Access Control option, and then click OK.

4. Click OK and restart your system when prompted.

Reviewing Share-Level Access Types

After you create a share, you must specify what type of access users will have to the resource. You can assign three types of access control to resources in a share-level network:

- *Read-Only* allows users to view resources, such as files, but not to modify them.
- *Full* enforces no restrictions; users can do anything that they want to resources, including deleting files and subdirectories.
- *Depends on Password* gives users either Read-Only or Full access to the contents of the share depending on which of the two share-level passwords they enter.

Providing Share-Level Access to Resources

To create a share with share-level access, follow these steps:

1. Right-click on the resource for which you want to provide user-level access and choose Sharing from the shortcut menu.

TIP You can create the share from wherever you can see the folder or drive, such as My Computer, the desktop, or Windows 98 Explorer.

2. Select the Sharing tab (see Figure 43.5).

FIG. 43.5
The Sharing tab
enables you to define a
share for a resource.

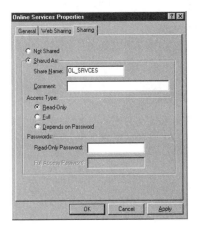

3. Choose the Shared As option, and then enter a name for the share in the Share Name box and an optional Comment. Other users on the network will see the share name and comment when they browse the network and view the resources on your computer.

4. Select one of the three Access Type options: Read-Only, Full, or Depends on Password.

5. If you chose Read-Only or Full, enter and confirm a password if you want to. If you do not specify a password, all users will have access to the share, but their rights will depend on which option you chose.

   If you chose Depends on Password, you must enter a password for both Read-Only and Full.

6. Click OK.

Removing a Share-Level Access

At some point, you might want to stop sharing a resource on the network. To remove a resource's share-level access, right-click on the resource that you want to stop sharing and choose Sharing from the menu that appears. Select the Sharing tab, choose the N<u>o</u>t Shared option, and then click OK. The share will be removed.

> **CAUTION**
>
> Windows 98 will warn you if any network users are currently using a share when you try to remove it. You can then choose to either keep the share or remove it anyway.
>
> To prevent possible data loss, however, you should make sure that no users are using a share before you remove it.

Establishing User-Level Access to Resources

Establishing shares with user-level access requires two steps:

1. Identify the resource you want to share.
2. Specify the users who will have access to the share and the type of access each one will be allowed.

Reviewing User-Level Access Types

When you allow users or groups access to a resource, you must specify what type of access to the resource they have. You assign one of three types of access to the resource:

- *Read-Only* allows users to view resources, such as files, but not to modify them.
- *Full* enforces no restrictions; users can do anything they want to resources, including deleting files and subdirectories.
- *Custom Access Rights* allows the definition of very specific restrictions that can be applied to individuals and groups.

Understanding Custom Access Rights   If you choose the Custom Access Rights option, you can custom-build an access type for a set of users or a group who has access to the resource. When you assign a user or group Custom Access Rights to a resource, you must define which of the following individual access rights the user has to the resource:

- Read Files
- Write to Files
- Create Files and Folders
- Delete Files
- Change File Attributes

- List Files
- Change Access Control

By switching these access rights on and off, you can create a very specialized mode of access to every resource you share. The set of access rights that you assign to a resource is referred to as its *Access Control List* (ACL).

> **CAUTION**
>
> If the ACL for a resource grants permissions to both a user and a group to which a user belongs, the user permissions will completely override the group permissions. This differs from Windows NT, in which user and group permissions are cumulative.

Configuring Windows 98 for User-Level Security

User-level security is not a default option in Windows 98, so you must explicitly configure Windows 98 to use user-level security by performing the following steps:

1. Open the Network icon in Control Panel.
2. When the Network dialog box appears, select the Access Control tab.
3. Select the User-Level Access Control option, and then enter the name of the external security provider that you want to use for pass-through authentication.

N O T E As you learned earlier in this chapter, the external security provider can be a Novell NetWare Server, a Windows NT domain, or a Windows NT Workstation or Member Server. ■

> **CAUTION**
>
> If you are using a Windows NT domain for pass-through authentication, make sure that you enter the domain name—*not* the computer name—of the Primary Domain Controller or of a Backup Domain Controller.

4. Click OK and restart your system when prompted.

N O T E If you change the security context of your Windows 98 computer from share-level access to user-level access (or vice versa), you will have to re-create all the network shares on the system. ■

Providing User-Level Access to a Resource

To create a share with user-level access control, follow these steps:

1. Right-click on the resource to which you want to provide user-level access, and then choose Sharing from the shortcut menu.

TIP You can create the share from any place where you can see the folder or drive, such as My Computer, the desktop, or Windows 98 Explorer.

2. Select the Sharing tab. Notice the dialog box provides an area for adding specific users with rights to the resource you are sharing (see Figure 43.6).

FIG. 43.6

You can give specific users rights to the resource you are sharing.

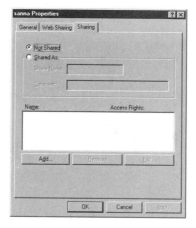

3. Choose the Shared As option, and then enter a name for the share in the Share Name box and an optional Comment . Other users on the network will see the share name and comment as they browse the network and view the resources on your computer.

4. Click Add to begin defining user access to the resource. The Add Users dialog box shown in Figure 43.7 appears. (Notice that the list of users and groups from the computer you specified in the earlier section "Configuring Windows 98 for User-Level Security" fills the Name list box.)

FIG. 43.7

User-level access control gives you access to the list of users from the security validation server.

5. Click on any of the users or groups to whom you want to provide access to this resource. Then click on the Read-Only, Full Access, or Custom button, depending on the level of access you want to grant that particular user or group.

CAUTION

Keep in mind that any access-level rights you provide to a group are granted to all users in that group. Before you grant access to a group, make sure you know the members of the group.

T I P If you are using a Windows NT domain for your external security provider, you can use the Windows NT utility User Manager for Domains to determine the members of any group in a Windows NT domain. A version of the User Manager for Domains utility that will run on Windows 98 comes on the Windows NT Server installation CD-ROM.

If you are using a Windows NT Member Server or Windows NT Workstation for your external security provider, you need to run User Manager on that box to determine the members of a group.

6. Repeat step 5 for every user or group to whom you want to provide access to the resource you are sharing. When you finish, click OK.

7. If you chose Custom Access Rights for any user or group, the Change Access Rights dialog box appears (see Figure 43.8). From this dialog box, you define the specific rights for the users and groups listed at the top of the dialog box. Choose each of the access rights you want to give to the users or groups, and then click OK.

N O T E If you specify Custom Access Rights for more than one user or group, the rights you define in the dialog box at this point apply to each of those users and groups. ▨

FIG. 43.8

If you choose Custom Access Rights, you can grant specific capabilities to certain users and groups.

8. You are returned to the Properties dialog box for the resource you are sharing. Notice that the users and groups to whom you assigned access rights now appear in the Name list (see Figure 43.9). Click OK.

FIG. 43.9

All of the users and groups you created access rights for are listed in the Properties dialog box for the resource you are sharing.

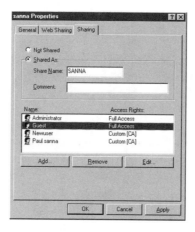

Removing a User's or Group's Rights

You can easily remove an individual user's or group's privileges to a resource you have been sharing with them. Note that this is different than removing a share for a resource, in which case all persons lose access to the resource.

To remove a user's or group's rights to a share, follow these steps:

1. Right-click on the resource whose rights you want to change and choose Sharing from the shortcut menu.

2. Click on the user or group you want to remove from the Name list, and then click the Remove button. If the list contains more than one user or group, a red letter X appears beside the name you select when you click Remove (see Figure 43.10). If only one user has access to the resource, the name is removed from the list as soon as you click Remove.

3. Click OK.

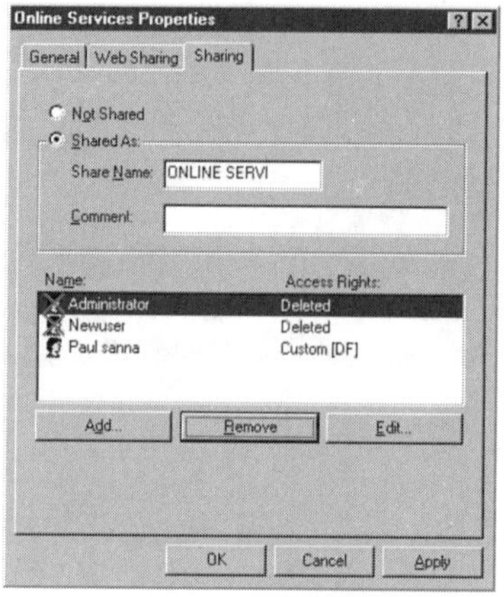

FIG. 43.10

You can see which users and groups you have removed from the share.

Changing User-Level Access Rights

Changing a user's or group's access rights is a simple task. To do so, right-click on the share you want to change, and choose Sharing from the shortcut menu. Click on the user or group in the Name list at the bottom of the dialog box, and then click Edit. The Change Access Rights dialog box appears (see Figure 43.8). Make any changes to the user's or group's rights, and then click OK.

Sharing Printers and Other Resources

So far in this chapter, you have learned about sharing folder and drive resources. Next, you will learn about the process for sharing other resources, such as printers and CD-ROM drives.

Sharing Printers

Sharing a printer is a fairly common task in small organizations. In typical workgroups, not everyone has a printer attached to his computer, but most persons have a printing requirement. In these cases, sharing a printer for the workgroup is the best way to provide everyone with printing capabilities.

To share a printer attached to your computer, you follow the same steps you learned earlier for sharing a file, folder, or drive option. Before you do that, though, you must take the following two steps:

1. Install the printer as you normally would at your workstation. Print a test page to make sure the printer is working properly.

2. Verify that you have allowed printer sharing in your Windows 98 configuration. This is covered in the section "Configuring Windows 98 for Resource Sharing," earlier in this chapter.

In order to enable sharing of the printer, you have to access it from the Printers folder, which you reach by opening the Start menu and choosing Settings, Printers. Note that for user-level access rights, you can define only Full Access for each user or group to whom you provide access (see Figure 43.11). There is no concept of Read-Only or Custom rights when you're sharing a printer.

FIG. 43.11

You can grant only Full Access rights to a printer when you choose user-level access control.

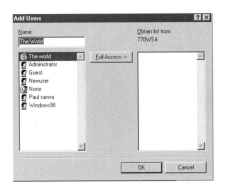

Sharing CD-ROM Drives and Removable Drives

Like sharing a hard drive, sharing a CD-ROM drive is one of the most common uses for sharing. Some users in organizations have not yet upgraded their computers to provide CD capability, but occasions arise when they must access data and programs that are stored on CD-ROM. In these cases, sharing a CD-ROM drive is the best way to solve the problem.

The process for sharing a CD-ROM drive is no different than that for sharing a folder or drive. Here are some tips to help with defining a share to a CD-ROM drive.

- Be mindful of users accessing the CD-ROM drive on your computer. It would be easy to remove the CD from the drive without thinking while a sharing user is accessing the drive.

- Create Read-Only rights to the drive. This keeps the user from attempting to save to the CD, in which case an annoying and difficult-to-clear error message appears.

CAUTION

Keep in mind that CD-ROM drives are much slower than hard disks. If you anticipate that a number of users will simultaneously make use of the data on a shared CD-ROM, you should consider copying the data to a hard disk and then sharing the data from the hard disk.

Using a Shared Printer

You can also use a printer that another user has made available on the network and (presumably) provided you access rights for. The process for adding a network printer simply involves using the Add New Printer Wizard. When the wizard starts, make sure you specify that you are using a network computer. For more information on adding a printer to Windows 98, refer to Chapter 26, "Adding New Hardware." ●

CHAPTER 44

Remote Access with Dial-Up Networking

by Larry Passo, et al.

In this chapter

Connecting to a Remote Access Server

Dial-Up Networking enables clients to connect through Remote Access Servers to remote networks. After this connection is made, the telephone lines become transparent to the client, and users at the remote client can access the same network resources that they could access if they were actually connected directly to the remote network. The only difference that the remote user might notice is a drop in responsiveness because a dial-up connection is much slower than a direct network connection. To achieve this remote connectivity, you must properly configure both sides of the connection.

Installing Dial-Up Networking is simply the first step in connecting to remote resources via a Remote Access Server. To access remote resources, it is also necessary to install the necessary client software and network transport protocols.

By default, Windows 98 can support the following common transport protocols:

- TCP/IP
- NetBEUI
- IPX/SPX Compatible Transport
- DLC

> **CAUTION**
>
> The DLC transport protocol cannot be used for remote access.

Windows 98 also ships with the following networking clients:

- The Microsoft Family Logon (for Internet use)
- The Client for Microsoft Networks
- The Client for NetWare Networks

In addition to the integrated clients and protocols, many third-party client packages are available. A few of these packages follow.

- FTP software www.ftp.com
- Banyan client software www.banyan.com
- Novell's NetWare Client32 www.novell.com
- VAX client Software www.digital.com
- DEC PathWorks client www.digital.com
- Any Telnet client software

The type of network you plan to dial into determines the combination of protocols and clients required for full connectivity. It's always a good idea to ask your network administrator which combination you need.

When you installed Dial-Up Networking, Windows 98 automatically configured your machine with a Dial-Up Adapter, the Microsoft Family logon, and the TCP/IP protocol (see Figure 44.1). These components alone are enough to allow you to connect to the Internet successfully, but are not sufficient to dial into a Windows NT or NetWare network. The following procedure walks you through the installation of additional network clients and protocols.

FIG. 44.1

The Dial-Up Adapter.

1. Determine the network client/protocol combination necessary to successfully communicate on your remote network.

2. Launch your Windows 98 Network Properties either by going to the Control Panel and clicking the Network shortcut or by highlighting the Network Neighborhood shortcut on your desktop and using the right mouse button to launch the drop-down menu and choose Properties from the available values. Either way, the Network applet appears as shown in Figure 44.1.

3. To add clients or protocols, click the Add button to open the Select Network Component Type window (see Figure 44.2).

FIG. 44.2

The Select Network Component Type window.

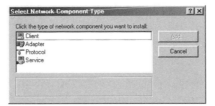

4. To add a client or protocol, highlight the appropriate choice and click Add. Note that the components supported natively under Windows 98 are in the Microsoft category as shown in Figures 44.3 and 44.4.

FIG. 44.3

The Select Network
Protocol window.

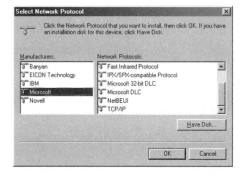

FIG. 44.4

The Select Network
Client window.

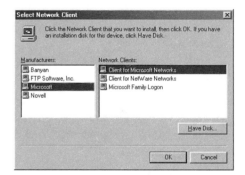

5. After you select the appropriate network component, Windows 98 copies the necessary files to your hard drive. When all components are installed, close the Network configuration applet; Windows prompts you to restart your computer. At this point, you can begin to create and manage dial-up connections.

Configuring Telephony Settings

Windows 98 offers advanced telephony settings for Dial-Up Networking. These settings enable you to create multiple Dial-Up profiles to be used in various situations. For instance, some of the commonly required telephony settings are

■ When at the office, you might be required to dial a 9 before accessing an outside line.

■ At home you might want to disable call waiting.

■ When traveling, you might need to dial the area code to access frequently called numbers back in your home area code.

■ You might also want to automate the use of telephone calling cards.

N O T E The Windows Telephony API (TAPI) provides a standard way for communications applications to control telephony functions for voice and data. TAPI controls all connections between a Windows 98 system and the telephone network. ■

Notice the Dialing From field under the phone number of the ABC Company in Figure 44.5. The Dialing Properties button is next to this field.

FIG. 44.5
Connect to ABC Company.

To manipulate your telephony, or dialing, properties, simply click on the Dialing Properties button to launch the Dialing Properties window, shown in Figure 44.6.

FIG. 44.6
The Dialing Properties window.

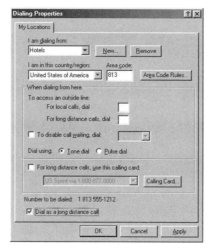

This page enables you to set a number of dial-out variables and save them as different profiles, or locations. The available variables are

- Country or region selection
- Area code selection
- Area code rules
- Outside line access settings
- Long-distance line access settings
- The option to disable call waiting
- The option of pulse or tone dialing
- The option to use a calling card

To create a new location, click the New button next to the I Am Dialing From field. You are told that your new location was created, and all settings from the previous location disappear. Follow these steps to create a new long-distance location for using a calling card from a hotel.

1. Click the <u>N</u>ew button on the top of the form. In the field labeled I Am Dialing From, type **Hotels**.

2. Do not modify the Country/Region or the Area Code settings, but instead select the button labeled Ar<u>e</u>a Code Rules. The Area Code Rules window, shown in Figure 44.7, appears on your screen.

FIG. 44.7

The Dialing Location Area Code Rules page.

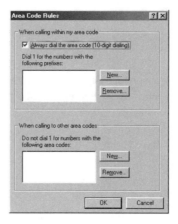

3. At this point you may set some fairly sophisticated rules. However, it is a safe assumption that you won't be staying in too many hotels within your home area code. Simply check the box next to the <u>A</u>lways Dial the Area Code option and click OK to return to the main Dialing Properties window.

4. Focus your attention on the section titled When Dialing from Here. Because many hotels require you to dial a 9 to make local calls and an 8 to make long-distance calls, enter an 8 in the box next to the For Local Calls, Dial option and a 9 in the For Long Distance Calls, Dial option. Or just enter a 9 in both boxes if that is what your hotel requires.

 Some PBXs have a noticeable delay before they supply a dial tone in response to the 8 or 9 that you dial to request a telephone line. If this delay prevents you from being able to establish your connections, simply type one or more commas (,) after either the 8 or the 9 in the appropriate box. Each comma delays the dialing sequence for a couple of seconds. Try adding one comma at a time until you slow down the dialing sequence enough to reliably make your connections.

5. Skip to the section titled For Long Distance Calls, Use This Calling Card and click the Calling Card button. The Calling Card window, in Figure 44.8, appears. Select your Calling Card type from the drop-down list at the top of the page. After you select the correct card type, all default settings are entered into the appropriate fields. In most cases, all you need to enter is your PIN.

TIP If your favorite calling card type isn't listed, you can add it by clicking on the <u>N</u>ew button (see Figure 44.8) and entering the appropriate details.

FIG. 44.8
The Calling Card
configuration window.

Part
VII

Ch
44

6. After your Calling Card settings are configured, click OK at the bottom of the page to return to the main Dialing Properties window.

7. Click OK at the bottom of the page to create your new location. To switch between locations, simply click the down arrow on the drop-down box located on the main dialing window, as shown in Figure 44.8.

You may create as many dialing locations as necessary and use as many calling cards as required. However, each dialing location can be configured to use only one calling card at a time.

TIP The configurations you set up for each connection are stored in the Registry under

    Hkey_Current_User\RemoteAccess\Addresses\My Connection

You can predefine Dial-Up Networking connections for users by including them as part of system policies. If you enable user profiles, different users sharing the same computer can use separate dialing configurations.

Using Resources via Remote Access

When you dial into a Remote Access Server and connect to the network, your workstation is essentially a normal network client with one exception: dialing into your network through a modem is considerably slower than when you're logged on at the office—even at today's modem speeds. Although Dial-Up Networking offers a great deal of functionality, Remote Node connectivity does not enable you to run any sizable applications (such as Office) from the network or to transfer large amounts of data in short time periods. The most effective manner in which to use a dial-up solution is to have all your applications resident on your Windows 98 computer and have any large documents or files on removable media. In this case, when you access your required network resources (such as a standard Word document or a Notes Database), you need to pass only small amounts of data back and forth across the line. Some of the most common uses for Dial-Up Networking clients are

- Access to Microsoft Office documents or databases
- Access to Windows NT, Novell, or UNIX servers
- Access to email such as Exchange or Notes
- Access to a Notes database or an Exchange Public folder
- Access to an intranet
- Access to the Internet (through an Internet service provider)

Dial-Up Networking is very practical for users who need access to centrally located resources or who need to perform remote network administration. Many client/server applications such as SNA Server or Microsoft Exchange work well over remote node connections. With Dial-Up Networking, you can connect to your office's network and map drives, navigate Network Neighborhood, or even connect to the Internet.

Special Considerations for Dial-Up Connections

Many remote users require more than just remote node connectivity, and likewise, many corporations have found value in providing high-performance remote solutions for their mobile work force. Remote control applications and Windows terminal solutions can overcome many of the performance issues seen in remote node connectivity.

Remote Control

Remote control software enables the user to dial in to a network via Dial-Up Networking and take control of a PC on the remote network. The PC that is being managed remotely is referred to as a *host*. After control is taken, the remote control client can manage the host, run applications from it, or even provide technical support for it. Remote control software such as Reach Out, PC Anywhere, Timbuktoo, or Remotely Possible enables you to take control of and manipulate a remote computer by simply passing modifications to the screen across your dial-up connection. For instance, if you take control of a host on your remote network and launch an accounting application, the host does all the processing and the remote control software simply passes information about what is currently on the host's screen to your remote control client. To you, it seems as if you've just launched the application on your own computer. Although remote control performance is slower than performance at the actual workstation, remote performance is acceptable—especially in a situation in which remote control is the only way to access an application.

N O T E In some cases, taking remote control of a remote host and running an application might actually be faster than running the application remotely via Dial-Up Networking. In applications where the host needs to access large amounts of data from either its local hard disk or from a network file server, only the screen updates need to be transmitted over the phone lines.

Windows Terminal Solutions

Remote control software is excellent for many applications; however, it is impractical to provide remote control solutions for a significant number of remote users. Windows terminal solutions, such as Citrix Winframe or Microsoft's Windows Terminal Server(WTS), take remote control one step further. With a Windows terminal solution, a user can dial into a network with Dial-Up Networking and use a Windows terminal client to launch a Windows session from a Citrix or WTS server. This session, which is very much in the vein of a mainframe session, provides the user with a true Windows desktop session, as well as access to almost any application at speeds approaching real-time local computing. A Windows terminal solution does not require a dedicated workstation for every remote user; instead, a single server can provide high-performance remote computing for multiple concurrent users. In addition, a Windows terminal solution enables the network administrator to create and assign profiles to individual users or groups. For instance, the administrator can create a common profile that provides access to all common corporate applications.

For most users, this profile is more than adequate; however, there may be secure applications that other users need to access. For instance, the administrator could create a secure profile for accounting users that offers access to all standard applications, as well as the corporate accounting application. When anyone from the accounting department dials in and launches a Windows terminal client, the user not only sees the standard desktop but also has access to the accounting application. Other dial-in users will not have access to the accounting application. Windows terminal Solutions are evolving rather rapidly and are well worth investigating, particularly in regards to remote employees.

> **CAUTION**
>
> Be careful how you deploy your Windows terminal solutions because they, like other thin clients, require powerful servers to make applications execute quickly on the remote clients.

Maintaining Security over Dial-Up Connections

Whenever you access a remote server over a dial-up phone line, you never really know who might be listening to your communications session. If you care about security, you can configure Dial-Up Networking to use data encryption for your password and data (see Figure 44.9).

NOTE To use encryption, the computer that you are connecting to must support a compatible encryption format. Windows NT Remote Access Servers and many UNIX dial-up servers are compatible with the Windows 98 encryption methods. ■

To configure a preexisting Dial-Up Networking connection to require encryption, as shown in Figure 44.10, follow these steps:

1. Double-click the Dial-Up Networking icon in My Computer.
2. Right-click the appropriate Dial-Up Networking connection and click Properties.

Part
VII

Ch
44

FIG. 44.9
The Communications window.

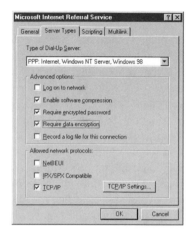

3. Select the Server Types tab, making sure that the Type of Dial-Up Server type is PPP: Internet, Windows NT Server, Windows 98.

4. Select the appropriate encryption settings. You can choose to encrypt just your password or encrypt your entire session.

5. Click OK to save your settings.

Using a Windows 98 PC as a Dial-Up Server

You can use Windows 98 as a dial-up server, much like a Windows NT server or a Windows NT workstation. Unlike Windows 95, where Dial-Up Server was an extra-cost option, Windows 98 includes this feature in the standard package. To install the Windows 98 Dial-up Server component, use the following procedure:

1. Go to the Control Panel and launch the Add/Remove Programs applet.

2. Click on the Windows Setup tab and highlight the Communications option. Select Details to launch the Communications window, as shown in Figure 44.10.

FIG. 44.10
The Communications window.

3. Check the box next the Dial-up Server option and click OK at the bottom of the window. From the Windows Setup page, click OK to tell Windows to copy the appropriate files to your system.

4. Restart your computer for the changes to take effect. The Dial-up Sever component is now installed.

After your computer restarts, configuring it as a dial-up server is simple. Launch the Dial-Up Networking window and go to the Connections menu. Click once for the drop-down menu and choose Dial-up Server to access the Dial-Up Server settings page (Figure 44.11).

FIG. 44.11

The Dial-Up Server Settings page.

Dial-Up Server configuration options are relatively simple:

- You can choose to allow or disallow caller access.

- You can require or change the password that allows dial-up access.

- You can provide a comment for your dial-up server.

- You can view the current status of your dial-up server (either idle or active).

- You can disconnect any currently connected users.

- You can configure your dial-up server as a standard PPP server or as a dial-up server that supports legacy Microsoft clients (see Figure 44.12).

FIG. 44.12

Modifying your Dial-Up Server type.

By default, your Windows 98 computer supports standard PPP connectivity, much like a Windows NT Remote Access Server. Or you can modify your server type on the Server Types page. In most cases, you should retain the default settings.

Using PPTP to Create Virtual Private Networks

Virtual private networking, or VPN, is a relatively new networking technology that enables you to access a remote network across the Internet or a network attached to the Internet via a secure encrypted connection. In Windows 98, VPN uses Point-to-Point Tunneling Protocol (PPTP) to create a secure tunnel to a PPTP or VPN server over Dial-Up Networking.

N O T E   When you use PPTP, your entire communications session, not just your authentication sequence, is automatically encrypted. ■

With PPTP a person can easily avoid expensive long-distance calls when traveling or working from remote locations. If you use a national Internet service provider (ISP), such as MSN or CompuServe, you can access the Internet via local phone numbers from almost anywhere. From a remote location, all you need is a local access number for your ISP. After you dial your ISP, simply launch a VPN connection to connect to your corporate network across the Internet. This connection enables you to access the resources available through traditional Dial-Up Networking.

Although VPN support is native to Windows 98, it is not installed by default. To install VPN support, simply follow these instructions:

1. Launch the Control Panel, open the Add/Remove Programs applet, and go to the Windows Setup page.

2. Highlight the Communications option and select Details. At the bottom of the Communications options, you'll see Virtual Private Networking (see Figure 44.13). Select the check box next to this option and click OK at the bottom of the page.

FIG. 44.13
Communications options.

3. When you return to the Windows Setup page, click OK again. All necessary files are copied.

4. Restart your computer to complete the installation of VPN support.

After VPN is installed on your machine, two new adapters will have been added to your Network properties. Figure 44.14 shows a machine with a standard dial-up adapter (as seen in Figure 44.9), as well as an additional Dial-up adapter to provide VPN support and the Microsoft Virtual Private Networking adapter that serves as the backbone for all VPN connections.

FIG. 44.14
Network properties
with VPN support.

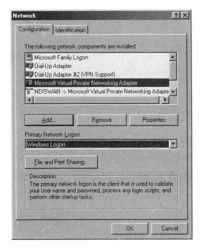

To make a VPN connection over Dial-Up Networking, you must first be attached to the Internet or to a private network that has access to the network you want to attach to. After you make your original connection, you need to make your VPN connection. To create a VPN connection, go to the Dial-Up Networking folder and follow these steps:

1. Launch the Make New Connection Wizard by clicking the Make New Connection shortcut. After the wizard is launched, name your connection appropriately. After naming your connection, move to the Select a Device field and choose Microsoft VPN Adapter from the drop-down list, as shown in Figure 44.15.

FIG. 44.15
Selecting the VPN
adapter.

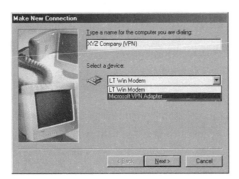

2. Click on <u>N</u>ext to move to the VPN Destination window. When connecting to a remote network via VPN, you connect to a remote server in much the same way as you do when connecting to RAS. However, with VPN you're already connected to a network (or the Internet), so you simply connect to the server via its DNS name or TCP/IP address. On this page, you enter the VPN server's DNS name or IP address, as shown in Figure 44.16.

FIG. 44.16

Entering the VPN destination.

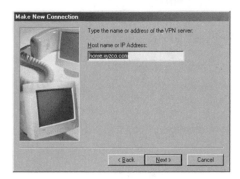

3. Enter the host name or TCP/IP address and then click the <u>N</u>ext button. The next window tells you that you've successfully created your new connection. Click Finish at the bottom of the page to complete the process.

When your VPN connection is complete, you may modify its properties much like any other Dial-Up Networking connection. Go to the Dial-Up Networking window, highlight your VPN connection, and select Properties from the right-click drop-down menu. At this time, you have the option to modify the Host name, to modify the IP address, or to manage the Server Types configuration like a normal Dial-Up Networking. When your VPN connection is completely configured, you're ready to connect.

Using Dial-Up Networking on a Notebook

With the Dial-Up Networking capabilities of Windows 98, you can access other computers, a LAN, or even the Internet and World Wide Web through an ISP. This section covers notebook computer techniques for defining a location, connecting to a remote system, accessing an ISP, and auto dialing.

Defining a Location

Windows 98 provides an easy way to define your current location, which is particularly useful if you're traveling with your notebook computer. Connecting to remote locations while staying in a hotel, for example, can be done quickly by modifying your telephony location setting in the Control Panel.

To modify your location setting, use the following procedure:

1. Open the Telephony object in the Control Panel. The first time you open this object, Windows 98 asks you to select your Country/Region from a list and enter the Area Code of your home base. Then choose Next to display the Dialing Properties sheet (see Figure 44.17).

2. Enter a name for your new location, such as Hotel, in the I Am Dialing From box. Then choose your new Country/Region, Area Code, any codes necessary for accessing an outside line, and your calling card information in this dialog box. Then choose New.

3. Windows 98 tells you that your new location was created.

You can now ready to use your Dial-Up Connections as you normally do.

Part
VII
Ch
44

Connecting to a Remote System

You can use the Dial-Up Networking connection to access remote systems, such as your business's NT Remote Access Server, from any location. Simply double-click on your desktop's My Computer connectoid and choose the Dial-Up Networking connectoid. If you've already set up access to your remote system, it is listed among the Dial-Up Networking connectoids in this window. If you haven't already set up this connection, choose the Make a New Connection object and the wizard walks you through the steps. You end up with a Connect To dialog box similar to the one shown in Figure 44.17.

FIG. 44.17

Verify your remote connection settings before choosing Connect.

Before choosing Connect, verify your username, password, and phone number settings. If you have trouble connecting, confirm these settings with your system administrator. Also double-check your location parameters as described in the preceding procedure. After you establish a connection, you can share files and data as you normally would with the remote computer.

Using a Dial-Up Networking Script

Some ISPs require you to enter your username and password each time you access their service. Fortunately, Windows 98 supplies scripting tools for Dial-Up Networking so that you can automate this process.

You'll find details of the scripting language in a file called Script.doc, located in the directory where Windows 98 was installed (usually C:\Windows). This file contains instructions and examples for building a script that works with your service's logon screens. After you build a script, you need to assign it to a Dial-Up Networking connection.

Assigning a Script to a Dial-Up Networking Connection   After building a script, you need to associate it with the Connectoid that you've already defined. Use the following procedure to assign a script to a Dial-Up Networking Connectoid:

1. Double-click the My Computer icon on your desktop and then click the Dial-Up Networking icon.

2. In the Dial-Up Networking folder, highlight the object to which you want to assign your new script.

3. From the menu of the Dial-Up Networking folder, select File, Properties. Windows 98 displays a Dial-Up Networking properties sheet. Then select the Scripting tab to show the Script Assignment page of this connection. It is similar to the one in Figure 44.18.

FIG. 44.18

Use the scripting tab of a Dial-Up Networking properties sheet to assign a script to a connection.

4. In the Script file box, enter the name and location of your script. Use the Browse button to find the script if you don't remember the exact location.

5. If you want to check each step of the script, put a check in the Step Through Script box.

6. Click OK to complete the process.

Your connectoid now has a script assigned to it that runs each time you activate that Dial-Up Networking connection. ●

P A R T VIII

Appendixes

Installing Windows 98

by Phil Callihan and Keith Underdahl

In this chapter

System Requirements for Windows 98

Windows 98 performance will hinge on the hardware of your computer. The minimum system requirements call for a 486DX2-66 processor with at least 16 MB of RAM. If you choose to install Windows 98 on a system with these specifications, the following recommendations will speed up installation:

■ Run setup from within Windows 95 or Windows 3.x. Try to avoid running the setup from MS-DOS.

■ Remove any disk compression from your hard drive. You might need to temporarily delete some files until after Windows 98 is installed. Generally, Setup will work faster if there is more free space on the hard drive.

■ If you are installing from floppy disks, extract the floppy disks to your hard drive and run setup from the hard drive instead of the floppy disks.

■ If, during setup, you notice that the busy light is flashing on an empty floppy disk drive, insert a blank formatted disk into the drive.

If you have problems during setup, increase the size of your permanent swap file.

No matter what system you are installing Windows 98 on, you should follow these steps as well:

1. Perform a thorough scan of your system for viruses. Ensure that the virus detection software you use has the most current update of virus definitions available. For instance, some Office 97 macro viruses are detectable only by the newest virus scanning programs.

2. Disable all screensavers.

3. Disable all antivirus detection software before proceeding with the Windows 98 installation.

4. Run your CMOS Setup utility and ensure that all virus-protection settings are disabled.

5. Run ScanDisk and fix any problems it finds on your hard drive.

You should also check to ensure that any components installed on your system are on the Windows 98 Hardware Compatibility List (HCL). The Hardware Compatibility List (HCL) contains components that have been tested to work with Windows 98. The most current version of the HCL can be found on the Microsoft web site (http://www.microsoft.com). In general, any devices that worked with Windows 95 should also work with Windows 98.

While installation on a 486 is possible, performance will be poor. A 486 running Windows 98 should be considered only for the most basic operations, such as simple word processing or sending and receiving electronic mail. Users who plan to run more than one application at a time or who often work with large documents should consider a machine with at least the following specifications:

■ A Pentium (or equivalent) CPU

■ More than 16MB of RAM

- At least 110MB of free disk space
- A double-speed CD-ROM drive
- SVGA video capability
- A mouse pointing device

N O T E Before you begin, check the Windows 98 installation CD for the SETUP.TXT file. This file contains last-minute setup information and warnings about possible problems that you may encounter during setup with specific pieces of hardware. ■

Upgrading from Windows 3.x

Windows 3.x users need to take the following steps before upgrading:

1. Back up your CONFIG.SYS and AUTOEXEC.BAT files.
2. Make sure that all of your system components (sound cards and so on) are on the Windows 98 Hardware Compatibility List (HCL).
3. Familiarize yourself with the new Windows 98 interface and basic tasks in Chapter 1.

To begin installation, use File Manager to run SETUP.EXE from the Windows 98 CD-ROM. The menu screens that appear during installation might look slightly different than if you were installing from Windows 95. Your program groups are migrated to the Programs menu of Windows 98. You might need to manually edit your CONFIG.SYS and AUTOEXEC.BAT files to properly configure legacy devices that are not directly supported under Windows 98.

Upgrading from Windows 95

Upgrading from Windows 95 is fairly straightforward. Insert the Windows 98 CD-ROM into your computer and let Autorun begin the installation process. If Autorun is disabled, click Start, Run and browse to SETUP.EXE on the CD-ROM. Click OK to begin installation. All program groups will be migrated during the installation process.

There have been three releases of Windows 95: Windows 95 Build 4.00.950, Windows 95 Build 4.00.950A, and Windows 95 Build 4.00.950B. Windows 98 will upgrade all three releases.

The original release Build 4.00.950 is identical to the product that has been sold commercially since August of 1995. Although service releases have been released since then, no new full installations have been made available to the public. Two OEM releases (4.00.950A and 4.00.950B) have been made available for preinstallation on new personal computers by original equipment manufacturers (OEMs). You can check to see which version you have by clicking on the My Computer icon and selecting Properties. Figure A.1 shows a typical System Properties dialog box.

FIG. A.1
Checking the version
number in Windows 95.

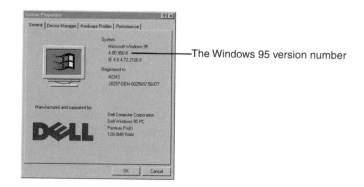

The Windows 95 version number

These OEM releases include many bug fixes and patches to the original Windows 95. Some of these fixes have been made available to previous owners of Windows 95 through the Microsoft web site (http://www.microsoft.com/windows95/info/updates.htm), while others are available only preinstalled on new computers. These releases also include a few interface modifications, in addition to bug fixes. All of these fixes are included in Windows 98. In addition, most devices that were supported under Windows 95 are also supported in Windows 98.

Installing Windows 98 on a Newly Formatted Hard Drive

If you want (or need) to install Windows 98 on a new or freshly formatted hard drive, you must first prepare a System disk according to the following steps. Ideally, you should copy these files from your old hard drive because some of them are not on your Windows 95 or Windows 98 Startup disk. If this is not possible, use the SYS.COM and FDISK.EXE utilities from the Startup disk or a DOS system disk.

Configuring a System Disk

To configure the System disk, follow these steps:

1. Create a new "system" disk. If you are in DOS, format it using the command FORMAT / S. Otherwise, format the disk in Windows Explorer by right-clicking drive A and selecting Format from the shortcut menu. Place a check in the Copy System Files check box and click Start.

2. Copy the Fixed Disk Utility (FDISK.EXE), FORMAT.COM, and SYS.COM files over to the system disk.

3. Copy your CONFIG.SYS and AUTOXEC.BAT files to your system disk, along with any files referenced in those files.

4. Copy any driver files for the CD-ROM drive, including the file MSCDEX.EXE. If you cannot obtain these files from your old hard drive, you should get them from the floppy disks provided by the drive's manufacturer.

Performing a Clean Installation

Once you have created a system disk, you can prepare the hard drive and install Windows 98. Perform the following steps:

1. Boot your machine with the floppy disk, and make sure you can access your CD-ROM drive.

> **CAUTION**
>
> FDISK.EXE erases everything on your hard drive. Make sure you have backed up important data from your hard drive before you using this utility.

2. Run fdisk.exe to remove your partition from your hard drive and create a new one. You should do this even with a brand new hard drive.

3. Format your hard drive by typing **format c: /s** (where c: is your hard drive) at the DOS prompt. The /s switch transfers system files to the hard drive, making it a bootable drive.

4. Copy your CONFIG.SYS and AUTOEXEC.BAT files and your CD-ROM support files to your hard drive.

5. Remove the floppy disk and reboot your machine from your hard drive.

6. Insert the Windows 98 CD-ROM into the drive and change to the CD-ROM directory (probably D:). Run SETUP.EXE to continue with the installation.

How Windows 98 Setup Works

The Windows 98 installation process is driven by an easy to use installation wizard. The wizard guides you through the necessary steps for a successful upgrade.

Basic Setup Steps

To begin the installation of Windows 98 from the CD, follow these steps:

1. Run SETUP.EXE from the Windows 98 CD-ROM. The Windows 98 Installation Wizard appears to guide you through the process of installing Windows 98 (see Figure A.2).

FIG. A.2
The Windows 98 Installation Wizard's welcome screen.

2. Click Continue to proceed.

3. The Microsoft licensing agreement appears (see Figure A.3). After reading through the licensing agreement, select the I Accept the Agreement option. Then click Next to continue.

FIG. A.3

The Microsoft License Agreement screen.

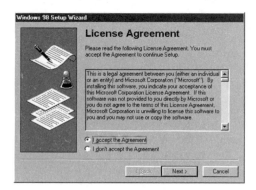

4. The Setup Wizard checks to see if you have enough hard drive space to complete the installation. If you don't have enough disk space, the Setup Wizard displays a screen like the one shown in Figure A.4 to let you know how much disk space you need to free up in order to continue with the installation. Click Next to continue.

FIG. A.4

The Not Enough Disk Space notification screen.

5. If you are upgrading, the Setup Wizard asks if you want to save your old systems files (see Figure A.5). The system files will be saved in a compressed format that takes up approximately 50MB of disk space. You must choose Yes if you ever want to uninstall Windows 98 in the future.

If you choose to save system files, you will be prompted to select a disk drive to which the files will be saved. (These files must be saved to a local hard drive (network drives, floppy drives, and other removable media—such as a ZIP drive—won't work). At this point, you also need to choose your country in order for your Internet Channels to be configured correctly.

FIG. A.5

This is the point of no return if you choose not to save the previous version of your system files.

N O T E You will not be given the option to save your system files if you are installing to a new directory or if you are running a version of MS-DOS earlier than 5.0. ▪

CAUTION

Anytime a new operating system is released, some programs will need to be updated in order to work properly. No matter how sure you are that you do *not* want to go back to Windows 95 or Windows 3.x, you might run into a situation when you have to. (Uninstalling Windows 98 is covered later in this chapter.) Remember, too, that you usually have the option of removing the old system files after you're confident with Windows 98. However, if you convert your hard drive to the FAT32 file system, you might not be able to revert back to your old operating system. See the section on uninstalling Windows 98, later on this appendix.

6. The Windows 98 Setup Wizard begins to automatically detect the hardware that is installed in your computer.

   Next you're prompted to create a Windows 98 startup disk (see Figure A.6). You will not be able to use an old Windows 95 startup disk, so you should create a new one now. Click Next to create the disk.

FIG. A.6

Create a new Emergency Startup Disk during setup.

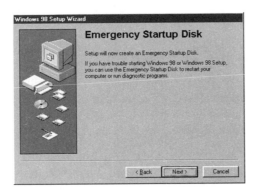

7. When it finishes collecting the necessary information, the Setup Wizard gives you one last chance to change your mind. Click Back if you want to go back and change your selections, or click Next to begin the process of copying files to your hard drive.

As the file copy process progresses, the Setup Wizard keeps you updated on how long setup should take.

Your system goes through a cycle of hardware detection, and your computer reboots a number of times until it has detected all legacy and Plug and Play components.

When the Setup Wizard finishes detecting the hardware on your computer, Windows 98 boots again and displays the Welcome screen shown in Figure A.7. The Welcome screen gives you the opportunity to register Windows 98 with Microsoft, provides a tour of new features, and helps you connect to the Internet or fine-tune your Windows 98 computer.

FIG. A.7

When setup is complete, Windows 98 reboots and displays the Welcome screen.

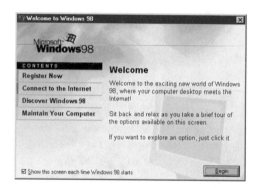

CAUTION

The first time you run the Maintenance Wizard after installation, you will have the option of upgrading your hard disk to FAT32 format. FAT32 optimizes the way in which Windows 98 stores data on your hard drive. If you choose to upgrade to FAT32, only computers running Windows 98, Windows 95 version 4.00.950B, or Windows NT 5.0 will be able to read the data on your hard drive. See Chapter 9 for details on converting your hard drive.

Typical, Portable, Compact, or Custom?

If you are upgrading from a previous version of Windows, Setup will automatically detect the configuration you had before and install Windows 98 in a similar manner. However, if you are installing onto a newly formatted hard drive or are upgrading from DOS, you will need to choose an installation option during Windows 98 Setup. These are the four options:

- *Typical.* Installs the components that most users will find useful; requires 186MB.
- *Portable.* Option that is intended for laptop users; requires 175MB.
- *Compact.* Installs no optional components; requires 159MB.
- *Custom.* Enables you to pick and choose among components; requires up to 285MB.

Which option you choose will depend on your hardware configuration and personal preferences. For instance, if you are installing onto a laptop computer, you will want to select Portable to ensure that portable features (such as PCMCIA bus slots) are supported. The other three options—Typical, Compact, and Custom—are intended for desktop PCs and differ only in which Windows components they install. Whichever one of these three you choose, you can easily make changes using the Windows Setup tab of Add/Remove Programs later. See Chapter 10 for more on adding and removing Windows 98 components.

Advanced Installation Techniques

Windows 98 includes some installation options that most home users will be able to ignore.

Using Custom Setup Mode

Custom setup mode allows you to preselect your setup options. This feature is most beneficial to companies who want to roll out Windows 98 to a large number of machines with a minimum of administrative intervention. By limiting choices, network administrators can automate installation by creating custom setup scripts.

To create a custom setup, follow these steps:

1. Install Windows 98 on a test computer with the configuration you want to replicate.

2. Install the Batch setup from the Windows 98 Resource Kit. (The Resource Kit is located on the Windows 98 CD-ROM in the Tools\reskit\ directory. If you have Windows 98 only on floppy disk, you must download the Resource Kit from the Microsoft web site at http://www.microsoft.com/windows98/.)

3. From the Start menu, run Microsoft Batch 98.

4. Use the Batch program to create an .INF file that will install Windows 98 with options you select.

> **CAUTION**
>
> Microsoft Batch 98 is very involved. Refer to the Windows 98 Resource Kit for specific details regarding custom setup options.

Installing Windows 98 Network Features

Users who will be using Windows 98 in a network environment can install Windows 98 Network components by selecting Start, Settings, Control Panel, Network. Figure A.8 shows the Network dialog box that appears.

> **NOTE** You'll be prompted to install network features if Windows 98 detects a Plug and Play network adapter during setup. ∎

FIG. A.8

The Network dialog box.

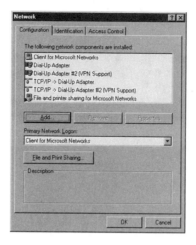

Here you can select options that enable you to connect to Windows NT servers and NetWare servers. You can also configure network protocols like TCP/IP, IPX, and your dial-up adapter. Click Add to add a new network protocol.

 In the Network dialog box, make sure that Client for Microsoft Networks is installed, even if you are not on a network. This will allow the Connect To... dialog box for your Internet connection to save your password.

One nice feature of Windows 98 is the fact that converting your hard drive to FAT32 will not affect its performance on a network. Other network computers using Windows 95, NT, and other FAT16-compatible operating systems will still be able to access resources on a FAT32 hard drive over the network.

The specific options you will need to configure will vary depending on your network. Contact your Network Administrator to find out about options particular to your corporate network.

Using Safe Recovery

Use the Safe Recovery option if your initial installation of Windows 98 fails. If regular installation fails, turn your computer off and then on again. Run setup, and Windows 98 will use Safe Recovery (see Figure A.9) to pass the point at which the original installation failed.

Safe Recovery instructs the Setup Wizard to continue copying files from the point of failure instead of starting over from the beginning. If you don't select Safe Recovery, your system might get caught in a loop, continuously failing at the same point during the installation over and over again.

FIG. A.9

The Safe Recovery option screen.

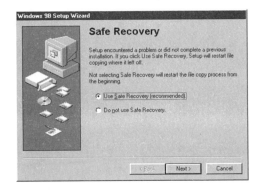

 If Windows setup fails repeatedly even with the Safe Recovery option selected, you will need to begin removing hardware such as game cards, sound cards, and so on. Remove them one at a time to identify the offending piece of equipment. When you have identified it, complete Windows 98 installation and then try to install the hardware using Add/Remove Programs.

Removing Windows 98

If you selected the Save Old System Files option during installation, you might be able to re-move Windows 98. However, if you have converted your hard drive file system to FAT32, you might not be able to revert back to your old operating system. The only operating systems that can be used on a FAT32 hard drive are:

- Windows 98
- Windows NT 5.0 and above
- MS-DOS 7.1 and above
- Windows 95 version 4.00.950B

Be careful not to confuse Windows 95 version 4.00.950B (sometimes called OSR2) with other versions. If, after converting to FAT32, you want to revert back to any operating system other than the ones listed above, you will have to reformat your hard drive and reinstall the old oper-ating system from scratch.

Assuming you *are* able to revert back to the old operating system, follow these steps to remove Windows 98:

1. Click the Start button, select Settings, and click the Control Panel icon.
2. Click the Add/Remove Programs icon to open it.
3. Select the Install/Uninstall tab, select Uninstall Windows 98, and then click Remove. Windows 98 uninstalls itself. When it finishes, you are prompted to reboot your machine, and your previous version of Windows or DOS is restored to your computer.

If you have trouble uninstalling Windows 98 from the Control Panel, you can use your Windows 98 startup disk to perform the removal. To do so, boot your computer using the startup disk and run UNINSTALL from the command line.

Setting Up Windows on a Notebook

During the setup process, Windows 98 asks you to specify the type of installation you want. The choices are Typical, Portable, Compact, and Custom. To install the Windows 98 components that are useful for mobile computer hardware, select the Portable option and click Next.

The Portable installation includes support for PCMCIA devices, power management tools for optimizing battery conservation, docking station compatibility, infrared transmissions, and direct cable connections for communicating with other computers.

> **CAUTION**
>
> If you don't choose the Portable option during your installation, you might have difficulty adding some of these components later on. Specifically, things like PCMCIA, ACPI power management, docking station, and infrared support can be added only through the Add New Hardware icon of the Control Panel—and then only if Windows can detect the hardware.

After you complete setup, you might want to configure a few additional items manually using the following procedure:

1. Open the Start menu and choose Settings, Control Panel.

2. Click on the Add/Remove Programs icon to display the Add/Remove Programs Properties dialog box.

3. Select the Windows Setup tab.

4. Double-click on a component category (such as Accessories) to bring up a list of the components under that heading. Then put a check next to the components that you want installed.

5. Click OK to close the window for the individual category and return to the Add/Remove Programs Properties dialog box. Then click OK again.

Here's a list of the categories that contain useful notebook components that might not already be installed:

Accessibility

Here you'll find the options for modifying your mouse and screen settings to enable better viewing on your notebook. Small icons and fonts can be hard to see on some small LCD monitors, so even though these components were intended for use by people with physical disabilities, they often prove handy for those using notebook computers, too. Mouse cursor options and a screen magnification tool help you find and control your mouse, even on small screens.

Accessories	The large mouse pointers you'll find under this heading let you quickly and easily find your mouse cursor on smaller notebook displays.
Communications	Under this heading, choose the components for Dial-Up Networking, Direct Cable Connection, and Infrared Communications (if available). Dial-Up Networking controls Internet connections via a modem. Direct Cable Connection lets you transfer data from your notebook to another computer over a cable. Infrared Communications lets you send and receive to other computers or devices (such as printers) that have an Infrared (IR) port.
Systems Tools	Use the disk tools in this category to make efficient use of your notebook's hard drive. If your hard drive is smaller than 512MB, you can use DriveSpace3 to make more space available. However, if your hard drive is larger than 512MB, you should consider using the FAT32 Converter to change to a 32-bit file system. FAT32 makes much more efficient use of the space on your hard drive, making compression unnecessary (although disk compression would then be impossible because it cannot be performed on a FAT32 system).

The Windows Update Manager

In the past, tracking down system patches and updated drivers was difficult. However, Microsoft streamlined the process in Windows 98 by including the Windows Update Manager directly on the Start menu. If you have Internet access, you can update your installation of Windows 98 by using the Update Manager, as shown in Figure A.10.

CAUTION

Web sites often change in terms of look and content. It is possible that the Windows Update web site may look differently than what is described here.

From the Start button, select Windows Update. After connecting to the Windows Update site, select Update Wizard. The Update Wizard scans your Windows 98 installation and displays any updates that are available from Microsoft (see to Figure A.10).

FIG. A.10

The Windows 98 Update Manager.

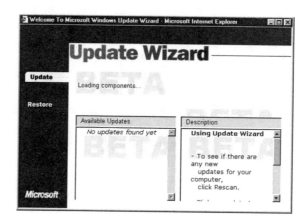

Using Windows Messaging and Microsoft Fax

by Rob Tidrow

In this chapter

Read This First

One of the most popular communications components of Windows 95 is Microsoft Fax. With Windows 98, however, Fax is not an option to install. To use Fax under Windows 98, you must have previously installed Fax under Windows 95. During the Windows 98 Setup process, Fax is left intact. You can then use Fax to send and receive fax messages.

This appendix assumes you want to be able to run Microsoft Fax under Windows 98, but you have not installed Windows 98 yet. You need to work through this appendix before running Windows 98 Setup, as shown in Appendix A, "Installing Windows 98." This appendix also assumes you have Windows 95 running and that Windows Messaging (formerly called Microsoft Exchange in early releases of Windows 95) is installed. If you don't have Windows Messaging installed, refer to your Windows 95 documentation.

> **CAUTION**
>
> If you uninstall Microsoft Fax under Windows 98, you cannot re-install it under Windows 98. You must re-install Windows 95, install Fax, and then upgrade to Windows 98 again.

Identifying the Features of Microsoft Fax

Microsoft Fax enables you to send and receive faxes through your fax modem on your computer. You can use Microsoft Fax on a separate computer to service one user, or connect it to a network to use it as a fax server in a workgroup environment.

Microsoft Fax is part of the Windows Messaging architecture and can replace any fax software you might already have installed on your computer, such as WinFax Pro. Microsoft Fax enables you to create fax messages, add cover pages, and send the messages to another fax machine or fax modem device. Because Fax is a *MAPI (Messaging Application Programming Interface)* compliant application, you can use other applications, such as Microsoft Word for Windows 97, to send faxes. Also, if you use Microsoft Fax to send a fax to a fax modem, you can encrypt it with a password to provide a layer of security for the document.

 Microsoft Fax includes fax printer drivers so you can print to a fax modem from within any Windows application.

You also can use Microsoft Fax to receive fax messages. A message can be faxed to you by the sender calling your fax number and delivering the fax. Or, if you use fax-back services to receive technical support information, sales information, or other data, you can dial the service and have it download the document to your fax modem using Microsoft Fax.

 You can store fax messages in the Windows Messaging Inbox.

A Microsoft Fax message can be sent in one of two ways:

- Binary file
- Hard copy fax

The latter option is the traditional way in which fax messages are sent and received via a fax machine, known as a Group 3 fax machine. The limitation of sending faxes this way is that the recipient cannot edit the document or use it as a binary file, unless the document is scanned or keyed into a file. A *binary file* is simply a file created in an application, such as Word for Windows or Lotus 1-2-3 for Windows. Another frustrating aspect of paper faxes is that they can be difficult or impossible to read.

When you use Microsoft Fax to send a binary file to another fax modem, the recipient can view and edit the fax in the application in which it was created and modify it. This feature is handled by Microsoft Fax's *Binary File Transfer (BFT)* capability. BFT was originally created for Microsoft's At Work program and is now supported by Windows Messaging so that you can create a mail message and attach a binary file to it. Windows for Workgroups 3.11 and other Microsoft At Work enabled platforms also can receive BFT messages.

One way in which you can take advantage of the BFT feature in Microsoft Fax is to use it with other applications, such as Microsoft Word for Windows. You can, for example, create a Word document and send it as a Microsoft Fax message to another user who has Microsoft Fax installed (and Word for Windows). The recipient receives the message and can read it as a Word document.

If the recipient doesn't have a fax modem card and Microsoft Fax and instead has a Group 3 fax machine, Microsoft Fax automatically prints the Word document as a printed fax image. A problem with sending files this way is the transmission speed and compression feature of the recipient fax machine. Fax machines are much slower than fax modems, so a large binary file (such as a 50-page Word document), can take a long time to transmit and print on the recipient's fax machine. Before you send a large attached document to someone's fax machine, you might want to test this feature first.

Fax Modem Requirements of Microsoft Fax

Besides having Windows 98 and Windows Messaging installed, you must have a fax modem installed. Your fax modem must meet the following requirements:

- High-speed fax modem, such as a 14.4 or higher Kbps fax modem
- Phone line
- Minimum requirements of Windows 95, but Pentium-based computer with 16MB of RAM is recommended

App

B

When you install Microsoft Fax on a network, your system must meet the following requirements:

- High-speed fax modem, such as a 14.4, 28.8, or 33.6 Kbps fax modem
- Phone line
- At least an 80486-based computer with 8MB of RAM
- If the computer will be used as a workstation, at least 12MB of RAM

Regardless of the way in which you set up Microsoft Fax, either as a standalone or networked fax service, make sure that your fax modem is compatible with Microsoft Fax.

The following lists and describes the compatible fax modems and fax machines you can use with Microsoft Fax:

- **Class 1 and Class 2.** You need Class 1 or Class 2 fax modems to send BFT messages with attachments. These classes of fax modems also are required to use security features in Microsoft Fax.
- **ITU T.30 standard.** This standard is for Group 3 fax machines, which are traditional fax machines common in many business environments. Microsoft Fax converts any BFT fax messages to a T.30 NSF (nonstandard facilities) transmission to enable compatibility with these types of fax machines. (*ITU* is the *International Telecommunications Union.*)
- **ITU V.17, V.29, V.27ter standards.** These types are used for high-speed faxes up to 33.6 Kbps.
- **Microsoft At Work platforms.** You need Windows 95, Windows for Workgroups 3.11, or another Microsoft At Work compatible platform to use Microsoft Fax. After installed on Windows 95, Fax will work on systems that are subsequently upgraded to Windows 98.

> **CAUTION**
>
> Check the fax modem documentation to ensure that it adheres to the preceding requirements and works with Microsoft Fax. Beware that some fax modems on the market today do not work with Microsoft Fax.

TROUBLESHOOTING

How can I diagnose problems with Microsoft Fax and my modem? One of the ways is to see whether your fax modem is working correctly by selecting Modems from the Control Panel. In the Modem Properties sheet, select the Diagnostics page. In the list of ports, select the port to which your fax modem is connected. Click More Info to run a diagnostic of your fax modem. If everything is okay, you get a report of your modem's properties. If your fax modem is awaiting a call, you receive a message saying that the port is already opened. You need to exit from Windows Messaging and rerun the modem diagnostics to get an accurate reading.

If you still experience problems, you need to open the Modem Properties sheet and change some of the advanced settings. You might have to experiment with these settings before you find one that works for your modem. You also should make sure that you have a Microsoft Fax service set up for Windows Messaging. If not, see the following section, "Installing Microsoft Fax."

Installing Microsoft Fax

To configure Microsoft Fax, you first need to install the Microsoft Fax software onto your system using the Add/Remove Programs Wizard under Windows 95. You need to have your Windows 95 installation disks or CD-ROM to add these files. Use the following steps to do this:

1. Select Start, Settings, Control Panel.

2. Double-click the Add/Remove Programs icon in the Control Panel to display the Add/Remove Programs Properties sheet.

3. Click the Windows Setup page (see Figure B.1).

App
B

FIG. B.1
Make sure that the Windows Setup tab is active.

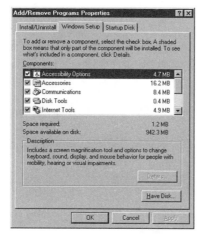

4. Scroll down the Components list box and select Microsoft Fax. Be sure not to click any other component that is already selected, or you will inadvertently remove those programs from your Windows 95 setup.

   If Windows Messaging is not installed, Windows displays a message asking if you want to install it as you install Microsoft Fax. Click Yes.

5. Click OK.

6. When Windows 95 prompts you for a specific Windows 95 Setup disk or CD-ROM, place it in the disk drive. Windows 95 copies the files onto your hard disk and returns you to the desktop when it finishes.

Now that you have Microsoft Fax on your system, you can configure it as a Windows Messaging information service and start sending faxes. You can do this in one of two ways: by using the Control Panel or by using Windows Messaging. Just follow these steps:

1. Select Start, Settings, Control Panel. Double-click the Mail and Fax icon.

   The Windows Messaging Settings Properties sheet appears (see Figure B.2), in which you can configure the Microsoft Fax service.

FIG. B.2

The Windows Messaging Settings Properties sheet contains all the services you configured during Windows 95 setup or when configuring Windows Messaging.

N O T E   If you do not see this sheet, click Show Profiles on the Services page to reveal the Windows Messaging Settings Profiles set up on your system. Select the Windows Messaging Settings profile and click Properties.   ■

   2. Select Microsoft Fax and click the Properties button. The Microsoft Fax Properties sheet displays (see Figure B.3).

FIG. B.3

The Microsoft Fax Properties sheet enables you to configure Microsoft Fax.

   3. Select the User page (see Figure B.4).

   4. Fill out the User sheet with the information you are asked for. For the most part, the text boxes are self-explanatory. The only text box that might need some explanation is the Mailbox (optional) item.

FIG. B.4

Fill out the User page so that your fax recipients know who you are.

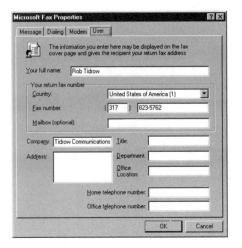

The Mailbox (optional) item in the Your Return Fax Number section pertains to in-house mailboxes that you might have set up to receive fax messages. To fill in this box, type the name your administrator has assigned you, which might be your name, email name, or some other identifier. Otherwise, leave this item blank.

N O T E According to Federal Communications Commission (FCC) regulation Part 68, Section 68.318(c)(3), you must include the following items on all fax transmissions either on the top or bottom margins of all pages or on a cover page:

- Date and time fax is sent
- Identification of the business, "other entity," or the name of the sender
- Telephone number of the sending fax machine ▨

5. After you fill out the User page, click the Modem page to set up your fax modem to work with Microsoft Fax (see Figure B.5). If your fax modem already has been configured for Windows 95 (which it should be if you have an Internet or online service set up), your modem should already appear in the Available Fax Modems list.

   If your modem does not appear in the Available Fax Modems list, click the Add button. From the Add a Fax Modem dialog box, select Fax Modem and click OK. You then are walked through the Install New Modem Wizard.

6. If more than one modem appears in this dialog box, click the modem you want to use as the default fax modem and click the Set As Active Fax Modem button.

App

B

FIG. B.5

You need to assign a fax modem to work with Microsoft Fax from this page.

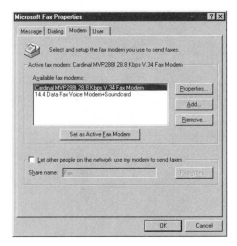

Configuring Fax Modem Options

Microsoft Fax is a sophisticated application that you can set up to answer your phone automatically after so many rings, let you answer it manually, or not answer your phone at all (if you tend to send rather than receive most of your faxes). As part of the configuration process, you need to tell Microsoft Fax how to behave during a call, whether it's a received or delivered call. As in most other Windows components, you do all this by configuring Microsoft Fax's properties.

 TIP You also can configure these options after you've upgraded to Windows 98.

Use the following steps:

1. On the Modem page, select your fax modem in the Available Fax Modems list and click Properties. This displays the Fax Modem Properties dialog box, as shown in Figure B.6.

FIG. B.6

Set the Microsoft Fax properties for your fax modem.

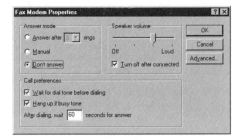

2. Set up each option, as described in the following list:

   - **Answer After.** Set this option to have Microsoft Fax answer a fax call after a certain number of rings. For some reason, you cannot set this value for 1 ring or for more than 10. A good number to set this to is 2 or 3.

- **Manual.** Use this option if you want Microsoft Fax to display a message on-screen when a call comes in. You then answer the call manually. As a recommendation, use this option only if you have one phone line that you use for both voice and fax. Otherwise, select the Answer After option.

- **Don't Answer.** Why have a fax modem if you don't want it to answer incoming faxes? The reason is because you might have to share COM ports with another device. Activate this option if your fax modem shares a port with another device, such as a mouse.

- **Speaker Volume.** It's not a bad idea to set this value to about the middle of the scroll bar so that you can hear when a fax is being received. If it's set too high (such as Loud), your ears might start bleeding when a fax begins transmitting.

- **Turn Off After Connected.** Make sure that a check mark is in this box, unless you enjoy listening to two fax devices talk to each other.

- **Wait For Dial Tone Before Dialing.** For most phone systems, this option needs to be selected to instruct Microsoft Fax to wait until a dial tone is heard before making an outgoing call.

- **Hang Up If Busy Tone.** Leave this option selected so that your fax modem doesn't stay on the line if the number you're calling is busy.

- **After Dialing, Wait x Seconds For Answer.** Many fax machines and fax modems take a few seconds to synchronize after they've been called. This option sets the number of seconds Microsoft Fax waits for the receiving machine to get "in synch" after it answers the call. The default is 60 seconds, which is a good starting number. Increase this number if you notice Microsoft Fax canceling calls too soon.

 TIP Disable the Turn Off After Connected option if you want to hear if your fax transmission is still connected.

After you fill out this screen, click OK to save these configuration settings and to return to the fax modem properties screen.

If you want to configure more advanced fax modem settings, click the Advanced button and read the next section. If not, skip to the "Setting Dialing Properties" section.

 TROUBLESHOOTING

How do I turn off the fax modem speaker? Double-click Mail and Fax in the Control Panel. Click Microsoft Fax on the MS Windows Messaging Settings Properties sheet and click the Properties button. Select the Modems page and click the Properties button. In the Speaker Volume area, move the slider bar to the Off position.

App

B

Configure Advanced Fax Modem Settings

In the Advanced dialog box (see Figure B.7), you have the option of configuring more sophisticated fax modem settings.

FIG. B.7

Use the Advanced dialog box to troubleshoot fax modem problems that you might be experiencing.

These options are detailed in the following list:

- **Disable High Speed Transmission.** High speed transmissions are anything over 9600 bps. If your fax modem is rated for higher speeds, such as 33.6 bps, you might experience transmission errors communicating with other devices. Keep this setting disabled (unchecked) unless your outgoing and incoming faxes are not being handled reliably. Select this option to slow down your transmission speeds.

- **Disable Error Correction Mode.** Fax transmissions demand a great deal of cooperation between the sending fax device and the receiving fax device. You need built-in error-correction procedures to make sure that the fax you send is received properly. This option is used to direct Microsoft Fax to send noneditable faxes, either to a fax machine or as a bitmap file, without using error correction. Keep this option disabled unless you cannot send or receive faxes reliably.

- **Enable MR Compression.** Select this option to compress faxes you send or receive, decreasing the amount of time you're online. This option appears by default and is grayed out if your fax modem does not support MR compression.

> **CAUTION**
>
> Compressed faxes are more susceptible to line noise and interference. If a transmission experiences too much line noise or interference, your fax might become corrupted, or your fax modem connection might be lost.

- **Use Class 2 If Available.** Select this option if you have problems sending or receiving messages using a fax modem that supports Class 1 and Class 2 fax modems. The default is to leave this option disabled.

- **Reject Pages Received With Errors.** Most fax transmissions have some sort of problem occur during sending or receiving. You can set Microsoft Fax to have a high tolerance (more errors can occur during transmission), medium tolerance, low tolerance, and very low tolerance (fewer errors can occur during transmission) for errors before rejecting the page being received. The default is to have a high tolerance for errors.

> **CAUTION**
>
> If you select the Use Class 2 If Available option, you cannot use error-correction, or send or receive editable faxes.

Click OK when these settings are ready. Click OK to return to the Modem Properties dialog box.

Setting Dialing Properties

Now that you have Microsoft Fax set up to work with your fax modem, you need to start setting user-specific information, such as how Microsoft Fax should dial your phone. Click the Dialing page in the Microsoft Fax Properties sheet. To begin, click the Dialing Properties button to display the My Locations page (see Figure B.8).

FIG. B.8

Set your dialing options, such as area code, calling card numbers, and other user-specific options, in the My Locations page.

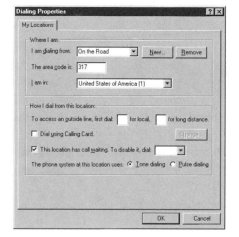

N O T E   The My Locations information might already be filled in if you set up your modem to make an outgoing call or if any of your Windows Messaging services previously dialed online services, such as the Microsoft Network.

Microsoft Fax enables you to use several different configurations depending on where you are when you send a fax. If your computer always stays in one place (such as in your office or home), you generally need only one location configured. If, however, you use a portable PC and travel from work to home and to other places, you can configure several different locations to dial using different configuration settings.

When you are in your office, for instance, you might not need to use a calling card to make a long distance phone call to send a fax. You can set up Microsoft Fax to use a configuration that doesn't require a calling card to be entered first. On the other hand, your office phone system might require you to dial an initial number to get an outside line (such as 9). You can place this in the Microsoft Fax configuration settings that you use from your office.

Another scenario where you use a different dialing procedure is when you stay in hotels. For these calls, you might always place them on a calling card. Set up Microsoft Fax to use your calling card number to place these calls. All your configurations are saved in Windows 95 (and eventually Windows 98 when you upgrade to it) and can be retrieved each time you use Microsoft Fax.

The following steps show you how to create a new dialing location in Microsoft Fax:

1. Click the Dialing tab on the Microsoft Fax Properties sheet.

2. Click the Dialing Properties button and click New. The Create New Location dialog box appears (see Figure B.9).

> **N O T E**   Depending on the version of Windows 95 you have, you might not receive the Create New Location dialog box. Instead, you just enter the new location name in the I Am Dialing From drop-down box.

FIG. B.9
Enter a name for your new location in the Create New Location dialog box.

3. Enter a new name for the location, such as **Office** or **On the Road**. Click OK. You return to the Dialing Properties sheet (refer to Figure B.8).

4. In The Area Code text box, enter the area code from which you are calling. You might need to change or update this if you are not sure of the area code in which you are staying, such as when you are traveling.

   To instruct Windows on which phone numbers in your area code to dial as long distance, click the Dialing Rules button(or Area Code Rules button, in which your dialog box will differ slightly than the one shown in Figure B.10) to display the Dialing Rules dialog box (see Figure B.10). Click the New button and enter the prefix of the phone number Windows should dial as long distance. Click OK. Click OK again to return to the Dialing Properties page.

 T I P   If there are any phone numbers in other area codes that you dial as local numbers, click the New button at the bottom of the Dialing Rules dialog box. Fill out the New Area Code and Prefix dialog box. Click OK twice to return to the Dialing Properties page.

5. Select the country in which you are calling.

6. Enter the number (if any) you need to dial to get an outside line (such as **9**) and to make a long distance call (usually **1**).

7. Click the Dial Using Calling Card For Long Distance option to enter your calling card information. Click the Change button to display the Calling Card dialog box (see Figure B.11). Click the drop-down list and select your card name. Fill out the Calling Card Phone Number and PIN Number fields. Click OK.

FIG. B.10

For phone numbers in your area code that Windows should dial as long distance, fill out the Dialing Rules dialog box.

App

B

TIP Depending on the version of Windows 95 you have, the Calling Card dialog box might display instead of the Change Calling Card dialog box shown in Figure B.11. If the Calling Card dialog box does display, you need to also fill out the PIN field.

FIG. B.11

Microsoft Fax can use calling card numbers to place your fax calls.

N O T E To set up calling scripts for your calling card, click the Long Distance Usage or International Usage buttons to display the Calling Card dialog box. In this dialog box, select an action from the Dial drop-down box, such as Calling Card phone number. Next, select a time or tone action in the Then Wait For drop-down list, such as 10 seconds. Continue selecting actions and times to create your calling script. As you create a script, you might need to walk through the process and write down each step. ■

8. Click the This Location Has Call Waiting. To Disable It, Dial option if your phone line uses call waiting. From the drop-down list, select the code your phone system uses to temporarily turn off call waiting. You need to obtain this code from your local phone company because each system uses a different code. Microsoft Fax provides three common codes in the drop-down list box next to this option: *70, 70#, and 1170. After you finish faxing and your fax modem hangs up, call waiting is turned back on.

N O T E Most hotels use their own phone system to get outside lines, so you need to enter those numbers when you know what they are. ■

9. Select <u>T</u>one Dialing or <u>P</u>ulse Dialing to indicate which type of phone service your phone line uses.

10. Click OK when you have this location set up. You can create as many locations as you need.

Setting Toll Prefixes and Retry Options

Now that you have the locations set up, you need to tell Microsoft Fax which numbers in your local calling area require you to dial as a toll call. To do this, click the T<u>o</u>ll Prefixes button on the Dialing page. In the Toll Prefixes page (see Figure B.12), click all the numbers from the <u>L</u>ocal Phone Numbers list to the Dial 1-*xxx* Fir<u>s</u>t list (*xxx* is your area code) that require you to dial your area code first. Click the <u>A</u>dd button to place numbers from the list on the left to the list on the right. Click OK when you finish with this dialog box.

FIG. B.12

Tell Microsoft Fax which prefixes in your local calling area code are long distance calls.

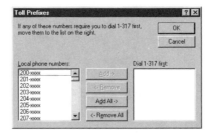

Every time you call a fax number, you're not going to be lucky enough to get through. You'll get busy signals. The fax on the other side of the line won't be ready to accept your call. Or your fax modem and the recipient's fax device won't synchronize properly.

In these cases, you need Microsoft Fax to keep retrying the number you're calling. In the Dialing dialog box, set the <u>N</u>umber of Retries option to the number of times you want Microsoft Fax to dial the number before quitting. The default is three times. You also need to tell Microsoft Fax the amount of time you want it to wait before it tries the number again. In the <u>T</u>ime Between Retries box, set this time in minutes. The default is two minutes.

Now that you've taken care of the dialing options, you are ready to configure the default settings for your fax messages. Click the Message page.

Configuring Message Options

The Message page (see Figure B.13) has three main areas:

- Time to Send
- Message Format
- Default Cover Page

FIG. B.13

Microsoft Fax lets you customize the way your default fax message looks by using settings in the Message page.

The following sections discuss these options in detail.

Setting Time to Send Options   You might not always want to create a fax message and then zip it off to your recipient. You might want to create a message, or several messages, and then send them at specific times, such as when you are going to lunch or when long distance rates are lower. Microsoft Fax enables you to set the time you send fax messages in one of three ways:

- **As Soon As Possible.** This is the default selection; use this option to send faxes immediately after you create one.

- **Discount Rates.** Use this option to send your fax message(s) during predefined hours when long distance tolls are lower. Click the Set button to set the discount rates start and end times. On the Set Discount Rates dialog box, the default discounted rate hours are set between 5 p.m. and 8 a.m. Click OK when you set the appropriate times for your long distance carrier, or keep the default settings.

- **Specific Time.** Set this option to an exact time to send any fax messages you have in the outbox.

Configuring Fax Message Formats   Microsoft Fax can send fax messages in two primary formats: editable formats (as a binary file) and noneditable formats ("hard copy" faxes). Editable fax messages can be manipulated much the same as a word processing document can be changed. A Microsoft Fax editable fax can be received and edited only by a recipient who also has Microsoft Fax installed. A noneditable fax can be received from a "regular" facsimile machine.

In the Message format area, you set the default way in which your messages are sent. Select the Editable, If Possible option when you send faxes to both fax modems and regular fax machines. This is the default selection. If your fax messages always must be edited by the recipient, or if you want to encrypt your fax message with a password, enable the Editable Only option. (See "Setting Up Security" later in this chapter for information on using security options in Microsoft Fax.) This sends all your fax messages as binary faxes. When using this option, if the recipient does not have Microsoft Fax installed, the fax is not sent. Microsoft Fax places a message in your Windows Messaging Inbox folder telling you that the message was not sent.

When you're sure that your recipient doesn't have Microsoft Fax installed, or you don't want your fax to be edited, send it as Not Editable. Even if the receiving device is a fax modem, the fax message is sent as a bitmap image, so the recipient cannot directly edit the message. If, however, the user has an OCR (optical character recognition) program, he or she can export the faxed image or text as a file to edit in another application.

With the first and third options, you also can specify the type of paper used to print your fax message. Click the Paper button to display the Message Format dialog box and adjust paper settings, such as size, image quality, and orientation. For most faxes, the default settings are fine. Click OK when your paper settings are configured.

Configuring Default Cover Pages   You can opt to send a cover page with your fax message. Click the Send Cover Page option to send a cover page with all your fax messages. Microsoft Fax includes four standard cover pages you can use:

- Confidential
- For Your Information!
- Generic
- Urgent

Select a cover page that suits your needs. Generic is the default. As Microsoft Fax creates your fax message and prepares it to be sent, it fills in data fields on the cover page with information, such as recipient name and fax number, your name, and so on.

 TIP   Select a cover page name and click Open to see what a cover page looks like.

The New button is used to create new cover pages by using Microsoft Fax's Cover Page Editor. Also, the Browse button can be used to locate cover page files (denoted as CPE) on your computer.

Finishing Configuring Message Options   One final option on the Message page is Let Me Change the Subject Line of New Faxes I Receive. Use this option to change the subject line of any faxes you receive. Because all incoming faxes are stored in the Windows Messaging Inbox, the subject (if it contains a subject) appears in the subject field there. This option gives you control over what appears in the subject field, enabling you to organize your messages as they come in. On the other hand, you must perform one more action as each fax message is received. The default is to leave this option disabled.

Click OK to save all the Microsoft Fax properties and to return to the MS Windows Messaging Setting Properties dialog box.

Congratulations! You're ready to send a fax using Microsoft Fax.

Configuring a Shared Fax Modem

To reduce the number of fax devices and dedicated phone lines for fax services, many businesses have one centralized fax machine that everyone shares. Because of their convenience and ease of use, most people do not complain too much about walking to a fax machine to send a message or document to another fax machine. Microsoft Fax enables you to extend this sharing of fax devices by letting users in a network environment share a fax modem.

N O T E You must have File and Printer Sharing for Microsoft Networks to share a fax modem across the network. See Chapter 27, "Configuring Hardware," for information on enabling File and Printer Sharing for Microsoft Networks. ▓

The computer that contains the shared fax modem is called the *fax server* and is not required to be a dedicated PC. A fax server can be anyone's computer that is set up in a workgroup of other Windows 98 users. When a fax is received on the fax server, it then is routed to the recipient in the workgroup via Windows Messaging (or by attaching it as an email message using an email application such as cc:Mail).

> **CAUTION**
> Microsoft Fax cannot automatically route fax messages to workgroup recipients. They must be manually delivered to their recipients.

Setting Up a Fax Server

Again, make sure that Windows Messaging is installed and that a fax modem is installed and working on the fax server before completing these steps.

Start Windows Messaging by double-clicking the Inbox icon and then perform the following steps:

1. Choose Tools, Microsoft Fax Tools, Options. The Microsoft Fax Properties sheet appears (refer to Figure B.3).
2. Select the Modem page.
3. Click the Let Other People on the Network Use My Modem to Send Faxes option.
4. If the Select Drive dialog box appears, select the drive that the network fax will use from the drop-down list and click OK.
5. Enter the name of the shared directory in the Share Name text box.
6. Click the Properties button to configure the shared modem's properties. The NetFax dialog box appears, in which you tell Microsoft Fax the name of the shared fax modem folder (see Figure B.14). The NetFax dialog box also enables you to set up passwords for users to connect to the fax server.

FIG. B.14

Use the NetFax dialog box to set the shared fax folder and other settings for sharing a fax modem.

N O T E If the Properties button does not work, switch to Control Panel and double-click the Network icon. Click the File and Print Sharing button on the Configuration page of the Network sheet. Next, select both options in the File and Print Sharing dialog box for the Microsoft network service. You then need to restart Windows 95 (or Windows 98 if you've upgraded to it) for these settings to take effect. These settings enable sharing on your system, so you can share the fax modem with other users in your workgroup. ■

7. In the Share Name field, type the name of the shared folder for the fax server. Microsoft Fax displays the name of the network fax shared directory as the default. When a user in your workgroup wants to use this folder, he or she searches for this folder on your computer on your network.

8. In the Comment field, enter a string that helps users identify the shared fax.

9. In the Access Type section, select the type of access you want users to have to the shared folder. The default is Full. Select Read-Only if you want users to read, but not modify, items in the folder. The Depends on Password option is used if you want to give different people different rights to the shared folder. You can give one password—the Read-Only Password—to users who can have only read rights. You then can give another password—the Full Access Password—to users who can have full access to the folder.

10. Fill out the Passwords section as necessary, based on your selections in step 9.

11. Click OK.

For users in the workgroup to access the fax server, they must know the fax server's full network name. The name is formed by joining the server's computer name (defined in the Network option in Control Panel) with the shared folder name; for example, \\RTIDROW\FAX.

Setting Up a Fax Server Client

Not only must you configure a fax server to share a fax modem, but you also must configure the client's access to the server. The clients are those users who want to share the fax server. Start Windows Messaging on the client machine and then follow these steps:

1. From Windows Messaging, choose Tools, Microsoft Fax Tool, Options.

2. In the Microsoft Fax Properties sheet, click the Modem page.

3. In Modem properties, click the Add button to display the Add a Fax Modem dialog box (see Figure B.15).

FIG. B.15

The Add a Fax Modem dialog box includes the types of fax modems to which you can connect.

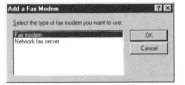

4. In the Add a Fax Modem dialog box, select Network Fax Server and then click OK. The Connect To Network Fax Server dialog box appears, as seen in Figure B.16.

FIG. B.16

To set up a client to use a shared fax server, enter the path of the shared fax server in this dialog box.

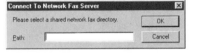

5. In the Connect To Network Fax Server dialog box, type the network name of the fax server, such as **\\RTIDROW\FAX**. If you do not know the network name, ask your network administrator. Click OK.

6. In the Microsoft Fax Properties dialog box, click the server name and then click the Set as Active Fax Modem button.

7. Click OK.

You might have to reboot your computer for the settings to take effect.

Setting Up Security

One of the most discussed topics in the computer industry is security. You hear about security and the Internet. You hear about LAN security. You hear about voice mail security. Microsoft Fax enables you to securely send fax messages using public key encryption developed by one of the leaders in security, RSA Inc. Microsoft Fax also enables you to password encrypt and use digital signatures on your messages with confidence. The security features, of course, extend only to sending digital messages and files, not to printed or hard copy faxes. These types of faxes are still subject to the eyes of anyone who happens to be walking by the fax machine when your transmission comes through.

App

B

N O T E   A *digital signature* is an electronic version of your signature. For most business transactions, such as purchase requests and employee time sheets, a signature is required to
process the request. You can use a secure digital signature to "sign" requests, time sheets, and other
sensitive documents. ◼

One way to secure your fax messages is to password-protect them as you send them. As you
create a fax message and the Send Options for This Message dialog box appears, set the type
of security you want to have for your fax message. Click the Security button to display the
Message Security Options dialog box (see Figure B.17).

FIG. B.17

You can set the type of
security for your fax
message in this dialog
box.

   Share your password so that the recipient can open and read your fax message.

If you have not set up public key encryption, you have to before you can use the Key-
Encrypted option or use a digital signature on your message. You can, however, secure the fax
message with a password by choosing the Password-protected option. Figure B.18 shows you
the Fax Security—Password Protection dialog box that you need to fill out when you want to
send a message with a password.

FIG. B.18

To password-protect
your faxes, enter a
password in this dialog
box.

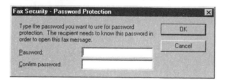

Setting Up Key Encryption

A *key-encrypted message* uses a public key to unlock the message for viewing. This public key is
made available to your fax recipients (who must also have Microsoft Fax installed) so that only
they can open your document.

You must create a public key in Windows Messaging. To do this, choose Tools, Microsoft Fax
Tools, Advanced Security. The Advanced Fax Security dialog box appears (see Figure B.19). In
this dialog box, if this is first time you have created a public key, the only option you can
choose is the last one, New Key Set.

FIG. B.19

Create a public key.

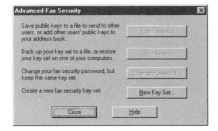

In the Fax Security - New Key Set dialog box, type a password in the Password field and then retype it in the Confirm Password field (see Figure B.20). As you would expect, the password is not displayed; only a string of ***** denotes your password. Don't forget this password; it is now your public key. Click OK to have Windows Messaging create a new public key set on your system. An information box appears, telling you that it might take a few moments to create your key set.

FIG. B.20

You need to enter a new password to create a new public key.

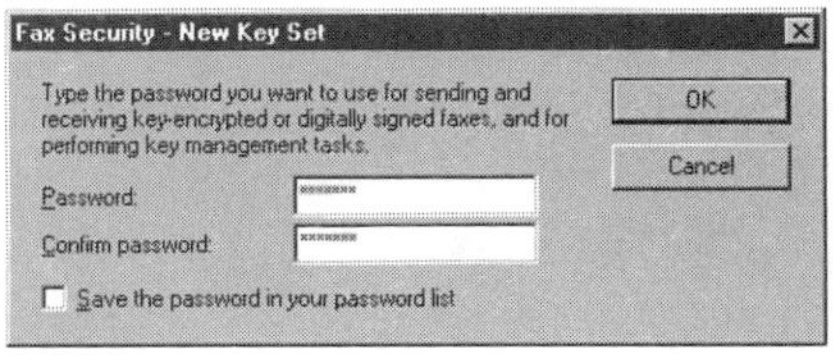

Sharing Public Keys

After you create a public key set, you need to distribute it to your fax recipients for them to read your key-encrypted messages. Do this by clicking the Public Keys button in the Advanced Fax Security dialog box (choose Tools, Microsoft Fax Tools, Advanced Security if you've already closed this dialog box). The Fax Security - Managing Public Keys dialog box appears, from which you need to click Save. This saves your public key to a file so that you can send it to other recipients.

In the Fax Security - Save Public Keys dialog box, click the name or names of the public keys you want to share. As a minimum, you should click your name here. Click OK, and in the resulting window, select a name and folder in which to store the keys. This file has an AWP extension. To finish, you need to send this file to your recipients either via an attachment to a Windows Messaging message or on a floppy disk.

Receiving Public Keys

When you send your public key to a list of recipients, they will need to import the AWP file into Microsoft Fax. Likewise, when you receive a public key from someone, you need to import it into your Microsoft Fax settings and add it to your address book. This enables you to read key-encrypted messages from those users.

After you receive an AWP file from someone, store it on your system and click the Add button in the Fax Security - Managing Public Keys dialog box. Locate the file name that contains the public keys and click Open. Click the key or keys that you want to add. ●

App

B

Using Power Toys

by Christopher Gagnon

Power Toys is a suite of utilities that were originally developed for Windows 95. The suite contains a number of applications and interface extensions that the developers at Microsoft felt should have been included in the Windows 95 interface. Many of these improvements are now integrated into Windows 98, so there's no need to install every utility. However, several components of Power Toys still appeal to the advanced user.

Power Toys for Windows 95 is still an unsupported utility, so if you run into problems, Microsoft will not officially support you. But an updated version of TweakUI is included on the Windows 98 distribution CD, and it addresses some of the new features of Windows 98.

Installing Power Toys

As we mentioned, Power Toys contains several components that are unnecessary because their functionality is already integrated into the Windows 98 interface. Therefore, you should review the individual utilities before starting the installation process. You might decide that you do not want a particular tool on your system.

Contents of POWERTOY.EXE

Before you install Power Toys, you will need to extract the contents of the POWERTOY.EXE file to a clean folder. The following list describes the contents of the POWERTOY.EXE file, sorted by application:

Application	Contents
Autoplay Extender	Aplayext.dll
	Aplayext.inf
	Shellfix.dll
	Shellfix.inf
Cabinet Viewer	Cabview.dll
	Cabview.inf
Round Clock	Clock.exe
Fast Folder Contents	Content.dll
	Content.inf
Deskmenu	Deskmenu.exe
	Deskmenu.inf
DOS From Here	Doshere.inf
Explore From Here	Explore.inf
Find X	Findx.dll
	Findx.inf
Flexi CD	Flexicd.dll
	Flexicd.inf
Install.inf	Installation file that installs all Power Toys components

Quickres	Quickres.exe
	Quickres.inf
Readme.txt	Power Toys Documentation
Send To X	Sendtox.dll
	Sendtox.inf
TapiTNA	Tapitna.exe
Shortcut Target Menu	Target.dll
	Target.inf
TweakUI	Tweakui.cnt
	Tweakui.cpl
	Tweakui.hlp
	Tweakui. inf
Xmouse	Xmouse.exe

Installing the Entire Suite

You use the INSTALL.INF file to install the entire suite of tools. However, because some of the Power Toys have problems with Windows 98, this is not recommended. Specifically, Windows 98 has problems with the AutoPlay Extender and the Cabinet Viewer. You gain no functionality with these tools under Windows 98; it is best to avoid problems altogether by installing each component individually.

Installing Individual Components

Power Toys does not come with an installation utility. Instead, each utility and update has an associated .INF file. To install an individual utility, follow these steps:

1. Extract the Power Toys to a new folder by double-clicking the distribution file.

2. Right-click the .INF file that corresponds to the individual utility you want to install (see the preceding list for descriptions).

3. Select Install from the shortcut menu.

TweakUI

TweakUI is one of the handiest and most popular unsupported utilities you can install. This utility gives you access to features that would otherwise require you to edit the Registry. TweakUI adds an icon to the Control Panel that gives you a central location for making changes.

TweakUI is included on the Windows 98 CD as part of the Resource Kit Sampler and does not require a full installation of Power Toys to function. In fact, Power Toys for Windows 95 contains an older version of TweakUI that does not contain as many features. You will want to be sure that you install TweakUI from the Windows 98 CD to ensure a full set of features. This section discusses how you can use TweakUI to fine-tune some of the advanced features of Windows 98.

Mouse

The Mouse tab allows you to set advanced mouse features (see Figure C.1). The Menu Speed Slider adjusts the speed of the menu animation. For example, if you set the speed to maximum and then maneuver through the Start menu, the menus will fly out much faster than usual. Changing this setting requires that you log off and log back on to put the changes into effect.

FIG. C.1

The Mouse tab allows you to change advanced configuration parameters for your mouse.

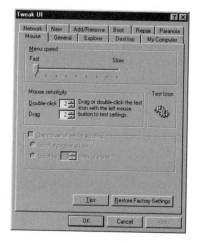

The Mouse Sensitivity section allows you to change the reaction time for double-clicking and dragging icons. If you have a Microsoft IntelliPoint Mouse, you can also make changes to the way your wheel reacts.

The version of TweakUI included on the Windows 98 CD also incorporates the Xmouse utility into the TweakUI interface. If you select this option, the active window will always be the one that your mouse is over; you will no longer have to click on a window to make it active. (Xmouse is discussed in detail later in this chapter.)

General

The General tab (see Figure C.2) controls the advanced features for some of the basic aspects of Windows 98. The Effects section allows you to control the following general effects:

- Window Animation
- Smooth Scrolling
- Beep on Errors
- Menu Animation
- Combo Box Animation

- List Box Animation
- Menu Underlines
- Xmouse AutoRaise
- Mouse Hot Tracking Effects
- Show Windows Version on Desktop

To enable or disable any of these features, simply check the box next to the feature.

The Special Folders section allows you to move the location of any of the required folders. The following folders are considered special folders, which you cannot move using Windows Explorer:

- Desktop
- Common Program Files
- Document Templates
- Favorites
- My Documents
- Program Files
- Programs0
- Recent Documents
- Send To
- Start Menu
- Startup

App
C

FIG. C.2

The General tab allows you to modify advanced features for some of the basic functions of Windows 98.

Explorer

The Explorer tab controls the advanced features for the Windows desktop interface (see Figure C.3). From this tab, you can change the look and feel of some of the desktop elements. For example, you can change the way windows modifies shortcut icons. You can also change the basic startup settings.

FIG. C.3

You can change advanced desktop properties with the Explorer tab.

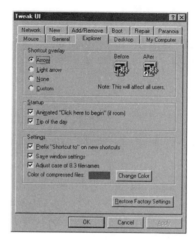

IE4

The IE4 tab gives you control over various settings for Internet Explorer. This includes both the browser and the Active Desktop components. The following options are available:

- *Active Desktop Enabled.* Select this option to activate the Active Desktop. It is the same as activating the Active Desktop by right-clicking the background and setting this option.

- *Add New Documents to Documents on Start Menu.* Disable this option to prevent Windows 98 from displaying previously opened documents in the Documents section of the Start Menu.

- *Allow Changes to Active Desktop.* Use this option to prevent other users from altering your Active Desktop components.

- *Allow Logoff.* Disable this option to remove the Logoff option from the Start menu.

- *Clear Document, Run, Typed URL History on Exit.* Enable this option to have Windows 98 clear the Document and Run sections of the Start menu and the Typed URL section of IE4 at logoff.

- *Detect Accidental Double-Clicks.* Select this option if you want Windows to ignore double-clicks that make no sense. If you choose single-click mode for Windows 98 and you accidentally double-click on a file, Windows will process only the first click.

- *IE4 Enabled.* Disable this feature to return Windows 98 to the Windows 95 Classic interface.
- *Show Documents on Start Menu.* Disable this option to remove the Documents folder from the Start menu.
- *Show Favorites on Start Menu.* Disable this option to remove the Favorites folder from the Start menu.
- *Show Internet Icon on Desktop.* Disable this option to remove the IE icon from the desktop.

Desktop

The Desktop tab (shown in Figure C.4) allows you to place and remove special desktop icons. For example, you might not want the Network Neighborhood icon on your desktop. To remove an icon from your desktop, simply check the box next to the icon you want to remove. You can also use this method to add a listed icon to the desktop.

FIG. C.4
The Desktop tab allows you to add or remove special icons from the desktop.

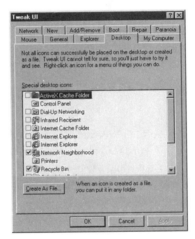

My Computer

With the settings on the My Computer tab, you can prevent a drive letter from being reported in My Computer (see Figure C.5). This tab is similar in functionality to the Desktop tab. To remove a drive from My Computer, simply remove the check mark from the box next to the drive.

N O T E This will not physically disable the drive or prevent the drive letter from being assigned to a drive. It simply hides the drive from My Computer.

FIG. C.5
The My Computer tab
allows you to hide drives
from My Computer.

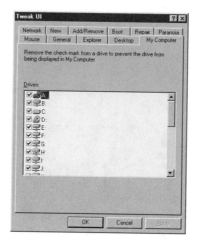

Control Panel

From this section, you can remove unneeded icons from your Control Panel. Unfortunately, you cannot use it to add your own components. Each available component is listed in this section. To disable a particular icon, simply remove the check mark from the box next to the description.

Network

If your computer is on a network, you will probably be prompted to log on when you start Windows 98. The Network tab (shown in Figure C.6) allows you to set a username and password for automatic logon. Enter your username and password, and Windows 98 passes this information on when you start the system. This option gets your computer started faster and keeps you from having to remember your logon credentials.

> **CAUTION**
>
> Setting your system up for automatic logon introduces several security issues. First of all, your password is stored in the Registry and is not encrypted. Therefore, anyone with access to your system can view your password using Regedit. Also, anyone who boots your computer will be automatically logged onto the network with your credentials. Use this option only if you know you are in a low-risk situation.

New

When you right-click on the desktop or in Windows Explorer, one of the options in the shortcut menu is New. That option allows you to create a new item, such as a folder or a text document. The New tab in TweakUI allows you to modify the types of files you can create with the New command (see Figure C.7). To turn off a particular file type, simply remove the check mark from the box next to the name of the file type.

FIG. C.6
From the Network tab, you can configure your system to automatically log on to the network.

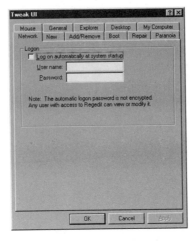

FIG. C.7
The New tab enables you to modify the types of files that can be created with the New command.

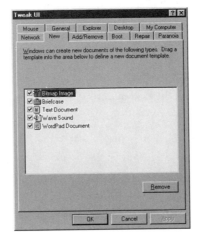

Add/Remove

One of the benefits of Windows 98 is that it contains a section of the Control Panel called Add/Remove Programs. This utility allows you to remove all changes made to your system by a particular program when you uninstall that program. The utility then removes the program from the list of installed programs. As useful as this utility is, it is not flawless. You might find yourself in a situation where a program is listed in the Remove Programs list that is no longer installed on your system.

The Add/Remove tab in TweakUI (see Figure C.8) allows you to remove items from the list of installed programs. To remove a software package from the list of installed software, for example, click on the package and choose the Remove button.

> **N O T E**   Removing an item via the Add/Remove tab of TweakUI does not actually remove the item from the system. It only removes it from the list of installed software. ▪

FIG. C.8
The Add/Remove tab allows you to modify the Installed Software list.

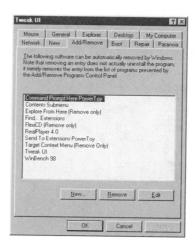

You can also use this utility to add an installed software package to the installed software list. To add a package, follow this procedure:

1. From the Add/Remove tab, click the Add button.

2. Type a description of the package.

3. Type the uninstall command in the dialog box.

> **N O T E**   The uninstall command will differ depending on the software package. Check your documentation for the correct command. ▪

Boot

From the Boot tab (shown in Figure C.9), you can modify the way Windows 98 acts during a system boot. Several options are available. Advanced users will notice that several of these options can be set in the MSDOS.SYS file. This tab gives you a simple interface to make the same modifications. The following options are available:

- ▪ *Function Keys Available for X.* This option allows you to set the amount of time Windows 98 waits for function key input, such as F10 or F4, before booting.

- ▪ *Start GUI Automatically.* This option allows you to boot into command prompt only mode by default.

- ▪ *Display Splash Screen While Loading.* Use this option to suppress the Windows 98 graphic during boot.

- *Allow F4 to Boot Previous Operating System.* If you installed Windows 98 on top of MS-DOS, you can hit F4 at the Starting Windows 98 prompt to boot into MS-DOS. Use this setting to suppress this feature.

- *Autorun Scandisk.* If Windows 98 is not shut down properly, ScanDisk will run automatically at boot. You can modify that behavior by changing this entry.

- *Boot Menu.* This section allows you to force Windows 98 to show the boot menu that is available by pressing F10 every time you reboot. You can also set the amount of time the menu will wait for a selection to be made.

FIG. C.9

You can modify the way Windows 98 boots from the Boot tab.

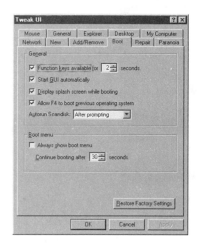

App

C

Repair

The Repair tab allows you to fix some of the problems that can occur when changing system settings (see Figure C.10). This is an important feature of TweakUI, because you can actually cause some of these problems by using Power Toys.

Each of the repair tools is described here:

- *Rebuild Icons.* It is possible for Windows 98 to display the wrong icons for your desktop items if you make the wrong changes. This button rebuilds all the icons and corrects this problem.

- *Repair Font Folder.* The font folder has some special properties that differentiate it from a regular folder. It is possible for the folder to become corrupted. Use this button to rebuild the font folder if it becomes corrupted.

- *Repair System Files.* This button has the same functionality of the System File Checker. It is recommended, however, that you use the System File Checker instead of this utility.

- *Repair Regedit.* It is possible for the Regedit program to stop displaying all the columns in its view. This button resets Regedit and fixes this problem.

■ *Repair Associations.* Windows 98 uses file associations to determine which application to run when a certain file type is selected. The operating system is shipped with several default file associations. Different software packages change the file associations for their related file types. You can use this button to reset all file associations to the Windows 98 defaults.

FIG. C.10

The Repair tab options allow you to fix common problems.

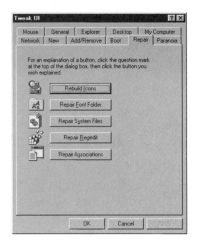

Paranoia

You can use the options on the Paranoia tab, shown in Figure C.11, to remove any signs of what you are doing with the system. For example, you might not want Windows 98 to automatically display the last-used command when you choose Start, Run.

The paranoia options are outlined in the following list:

■ *Clear Document History at Logon* removes entries from the Documents folder in the Start menu.

■ *Clear Find Computer History at Logon* removes previously found computers from the Find utility.

■ *Clear Find Files History at Logon* removes previously found files from the Find utility.

■ *Clear Internet Explorer History at Logon* removes any previously visited URLs from Internet Explorer.

■ *Clear Last User at Logon* instructs Windows 98 not to display the name of the most recent user in the Logon window.

■ *Clear Network Connection History at Logon* deletes the list of previously connected servers from the Map Network Drive dialog box.

■ *Clear Run History at Logon* prevents Windows 98 from displaying the last command run.

■ *Clear Telnet History at Logon* prevents the Telnet application from displaying sites that have been connected to in the past.

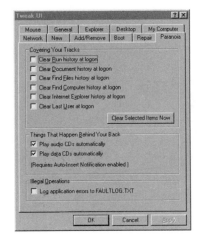

FIG. C.11
You can use the Paranoia tab to keep Windows 98 from displaying certain properties.

Cabfile Viewer

The Cabfile Viewer is a separate utility in Power Toys that allows you to view the contents of the cabinet files on the Windows distribution media. This functionality is already built into Windows 98, so you should not attempt to install this utility.

Deskmenu

The Deskmenu utility places an icon in your system tray that displays the contents of the desktop (see Figure C.12). To use the utility, you simply click on the Desktop Contents icon in the system tray. You can then chose to run any item in the list. This utility has the same functionality as the Desktop Toolbar on the taskbar. (Taskbar toolbars are a new integrated feature of Windows 98 and were covered earlier in this book.) The Deskmenu utility works fine under Windows 98, so if you prefer it to the Desktop Toolbar, feel free to install it.

FIG. C.12
Deskmenu gives you access to your desktop items from the system tray.

DOS Prompt Here

The DOS Prompt Here utility modifies the properties list for every folder on the system and allows you to start a command prompt with the folder set as the active directory. For example, if you are viewing the My Documents folder from Windows Explorer and you need to open a

Command Prompt from that folder, all you need to do is right-click on My Documents and select Command Prompt Here from the list (see Figure C.13). This utility keeps you from having to type a bunch of CD commands when you start the Command Prompt.

FIG. C.13

The Command Prompt Here utility allows you to start a Command Prompt session in any folder.

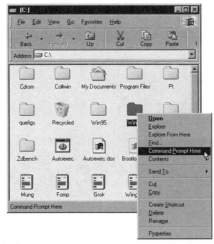

Explore From Here

The Explore From Here utility (see Figure C.14) is similar to the DOS From Here utility in that it modifies the properties list for all folders on the system. The difference is that it opens Windows Explorer with the desired folder active. This is handy if you are searching through My Computer and find that you need the functionality of Windows Explorer for a certain task. Simply right-click the folder and select Explore From Here from the list. This utility keeps you from having to open Explorer and navigate through the directory structure all over again when you already have the folder on the desktop.

 T I P   Explore From Here is especially handy if you are using the Find utility to search for a folder or a computer on the network. After Find displays the desired folder or computer, you can right-click and choose Explore From Here to manage the files in the folder or on the remote system.

FIG. C.14

Explore From Here allows you to start Windows Explorer in any folder.

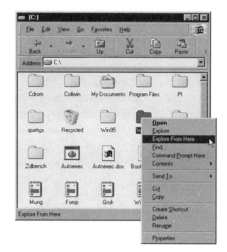

Fast Folder Contents

This utility also modifies the properties list for all folders on the system. It adds an entry called Contents that allows you to view the contents of the folder (see Figure C.15). You can then execute files from this list.

For example, if you right-click the My Documents folder and choose Contents, you will see a list of all documents in the folder. You can then choose the file you want, and Windows 98 launches the associated application. This keeps you from having to launch Windows Explorer to locate a file.

FIG. C.15

Fast Folder Contents allows you to view the contents of a folder by right-clicking the folder.

Find X

Find X is an extension of the Find utility that allows you to create your own Find categories. After installation, you can modify the Find categories by going to Add/Remove Programs in the Control Panel and double-clicking Find Extensions. This launches a small interface that you can use to add the categories. Windows 98 has extended Find support built-in, so this utility is not as useful as it was for Windows 95. However, it does add the ability to add new extensions. You can find different extensions on the World Wide Web.

Flexi CD

Flexi CD is an audio CD player that resides in the system tray. When an audio CD is present in the CD-ROM drive, Flexi CD gives you the ability to control the CD.

This application installs a component called the Autoplay Extender, which seems to have trouble with Windows 98. Installing this application results in an error message at system startup that points to the AUTOPLAY.DLL file. The system seems to run fine after you acknowledge the error, but it is clear that there is an issue here that needs to be resolved by Microsoft before you should install this application.

Quickres

Quickres is a utility that allows you to change your screen resolution and color depth without rebooting the computer. This functionality is integrated into Windows 98, so installing this application is not recommended.

Round Clock

Round Clock is an updated version of the Clock program that came with Windows 3.1 and 3.11. Running this program starts a window with a clock in it. The big difference between this program and the old CLOCK.EXE is that it can actually display a round window (see Figure C.16). To see this, you must choose Analog and No Title from the Settings menu. This displays a round clock with no window around it. The old version of CLOCK.EXE would display a rectangular window with a round clock inside the window.

This utility is really only useful as a demonstration of the Region Windows available in Windows 95 and Windows 98. Both versions of the operating system have support for running a clock in the system tray, so it's not very beneficial to take up room on the desktop with this utility.

FIG. C.16

The enhanced CLOCK.EXE demonstrates how Windows 98 can display nonrectangular windows.

Shortcut Target Menu

If you are familiar with using shortcuts, you should know that choosing Properties after right-clicking on the shortcut will give you the properties for the shortcut itself. The Shortcut Target Menu component adds a menu item called Target that allows you to modify the properties for the program pointed to by the shortcut. You can use the Target menu to copy, open, or view the properties of the target file. Whereas most shortcuts you create on your desktop only point to files that are buried somewhere in the system, this utility gives you easy access to files.

TapiTNA

This utility adds an icon to the system tray that allows you to change your dialing location and launch the dialing properties window (see Figure C.17). This application is especially helpful on a laptop computer, because you're likely to change area codes frequently.

This program is simply an executable and has no installation method. Just copy the TAPITNA.EXE file to your Windows folder and put a shortcut to it in your Startup group. Then, to change your dialing location, you can click on the TapiTNA icon and choose a location from the list. You can also launch the Dialing Properties window or the Phone Dialer by right-clicking the icon and selecting the appropriate entry from the shortcut menu.

FIG. C.17

TapiTNA allows you to quickly change your dialing properties from an icon in the System Tray.

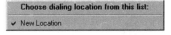

Xmouse

Xmouse is a simple utility that usually appeals to UNIX enthusiasts. It changes the active window to whichever one the mouse is pointing to. To see how this works, launch two occurrences of the command prompt, and then double-click the XMOUSE.EXE icon. Click on the first command prompt window and start typing. While you are typing, move the mouse over the other window, but don't click. When you move the mouse over the second window, whatever you type shows up in that window, even if the first window is in front of it.

This utility is handy if you only have a few windows open. It can get rather confusing as you open more and more windows, though. Xmouse puts an icon in the Control Panel that you can use to adjust settings and deactivate the utility (see Figure C.18).

N O T E   Remember that Xmouse is included in the updated version of TweakUI. You can install this version from your Windows 98 distribution CD.

FIG. C.18

You can modify Xmouse settings by selecting the Xmouse icon in the Control Panel.

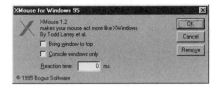

Command-Line Reference

by Christopher Gagnon

In this chapter

How This Appendix Is Structured

This appendix contains the following sections:

- *Command Line Structure.* Here, we'll discuss the basic structure of all commands.
- *Internal Commands.* This section discusses the basic commands that are part of COMMAND.COM.
- *System Commands.* This section covers commands used to change system-level properties.
- *Disk and File Commands.* This section discusses commands used to manipulate disk and file structures.
- *Network Commands.* In this section, we'll discuss the commands used to check and adjust network parameters.

Command Line Structure

The command line structure of Windows 98 is the same as that of MS-DOS and Windows 95 commands. An executable file will end in the extension .EXE, .COM, or .BAT. This is the typical command structure:

C:*command.exe parameter /switch*

Here's how it looks for an actual command:

C:\copy.exe C:\myfile.txt A:\ /V

In this example, the command is FORMAT.EXE, the parameter is C:, and the switch is /s. This command tells Windows 98 to format the C: drive and place the system files on it after the format is complete.

This command structure is consistent throughout Windows 98. Some commands might not have switches or parameters, but those that do will use this structure.

N O T E   Depending on the command, the dash (-) might be substituted for the front slash (/) before a switch. ■

Internal Commands

Several basic Windows 98 commands are loaded into memory at all times. These commands are actually part of the file COMMAND.COM that defines the command line environment. In fact, when you run a Command Prompt in Windows 98, you are actually executing the file COMMAND.COM. These commands are called *internal commands* because they do not exist on the disk. This is opposed to external commands, which are executable files on the hard drive. Table D.1 outlines all the internal commands included with Windows 98.

Table D.1   Windows 98 Internal Commands

Command	Function
BREAK	Activates extended Ctrl+C checking
CD (CHDIR)	Changes the active directory
CHCP	Changes the current Code Page number
CLS	Clears the screen
COPY	Copies files from one location to another
CTTY	Changes the control terminal of the system
DATE	Modifies the system date
DEL (ERASE)	Deletes unwanted files from a disk
DIR	Displays a list of files in the current directory
EXIT	Exits the current command prompt
LH	Loads a program into upper memory
MD (MKDIR)	Creates a directory on a disk
PATH	Sets the PATH system environment variable
PROMPT	Sets the command prompt
RD (RMDIR)	Removes an empty directory from a disk
REN (RENAME)	Renames a file on a disk
SET	Sets and displays the environment variable
TIME	Sets and displays the system time
TYPE	Displays the contents of ASCII files
VER	Displays the current version of Windows on the system
VERIFY	Sets an environment variable that instructs Windows 98 to verify that files are written correctly
VOL	Displays the volume label and serial number for a specified disk

App

D

System Commands

System commands can be used to display and modify the environment settings of the system. The following sections discuss the system commands included with Windows 98. After each command is the location where it is stored on the hard drive.

ACCWIZ

Location: C:\Windows\System\ACCWIZ.EXE

This command starts the Windows Accessibility Settings Wizard. This wizard allows you to change the various accessibility settings that are available via the Accessibility icon in the Control Panel. This application gives you the same controls the Accessibility properties sheet does, but in a wizard format.

DEBUG

Location: C:\Windows\Command\DEBUG.EXE

Debug is an interactive program you can use to test and edit any type of file on the system. To load a program into debug, type the following command:

DEBUG *filename*

Debug loads the file and displays a Debug prompt. The Debug prompt is a dash (-). To display the commands you can use in Debug, type **?** and press Enter. Debug displays the contents of the file in hexadecimal form and allows you to change the values.

Debug is intended for programmers with a knowledge of Assembler and hexadecimal. It is a complicated tool that is not covered in detail here.

> **CAUTION**
>
> Debug will allow you to modify any file on your disk, including Windows system files. Do not make any modifications using Debug unless you are absolutely sure you know what you are doing. You can easily destroy your system files beyond repair using this utility.

DOSKEY

Location: C:\Windows\Command\DOSKEY.COM

Doskey is a program that allows you to create a command buffer in memory. This buffer holds the last several commands you have typed. You can recall these commands by pressing the Up Arrow key on the keyboard. Then you can scroll through the list of commands with the Down Arrow. This command is handy when you need to type the same several commands repeatedly.

DOSKEY takes the following parameters and switches:

/BUFSIZE	Changes the size of the command buffer
/ECHO	Displays or suppresses display of macros
/FILE	Points to a file containing multiple macros
/HISTORY	Shows a list of the commands in the buffer
/INSERT	Inserts new characters while typing

/KEYSIZE	Adjusts keyboard buffer size
/LINE	Adjusts size of line buffer
/MACROS	Displays all macros in use
/OVERSTRIKE	Overwrites any characters on the current line
REINSTALL	Starts a new copy of DOSKEY

EDIT

Location: C:\Windows\Command\EDIT.COM

Edit is a simple text editor that can be used at the command prompt. It is nearly identical to the editor included with Windows 95 and previous versions of MS-DOS. You can use EDIT to create and modify any ASCII file.

EDIT takes the following parameters and switches:

/B	Forces EDIT to display in monochrome
/H	Tells EDIT to display the maximum number of lines that will fit on the screen
/R	Loads files as read-only
/S	Restricts the use of long filenames when saving
/*nnn*	Forces word wrapping at *nnn* characters
filename	Loads the specified file into EDIT.

App

D

KEYB

Location: C:\Windows\Command\KEYB.COM

The KEYB command configures your keyboard for a specific language. To use a keyboard definition file to remap your keyboard, type the following command:

C:\KEYB *filename*

The *filename* parameter is the name of the keyboard map file. This instructs Windows 98 to load the custom keyboard map into memory. This is a handy way of customizing functional keys for a specific application.

KEYB takes the following parameters and switches:

xx	Specifies a two letter keyboard code
yyy	Specifies the code-page used for the character set
/E	Informs Windows that an enhanced keyboard is in use
/ID:*nnn*	Specifies the ID of the keyboard currently in use

MEM

Location: C:\Windows\Command\MEM.EXE

The MEM command displays the amount of memory in your system. It breaks the output into Conventional, Upper, Reserved, Extended, Total, and Free memory.

MEM takes the following parameters and switches:

/C	Lists all programs currently running, classified by memory usage
/D	Displays the status of each memory register, along with driver information
/F	Displays detailed information on the amount of free memory in the system
/M program	Displays memory information for a specific program in memory; must be followed by the name of the program
/P	Pauses after each screen

MODE

Location: C:\Windows\Command\MODE.COM

This command configures system-level devices such as COM and LPT ports. The command syntax changes depending on the task you are trying to complete. You can use this command to set baud and parity rates for your COM ports, for example. This command is rarely used because these settings can be made from the GUI.

MORE

Location: C:\Windows\Command\MORE.COM

More is a program that is used to display output from other commands one page at a time. This command is usually piped onto another command. For example, you can use the following command to force the TYPE command to display a large file one page at a time:

C:\TYPE longfile.txt | MORE

This command prevents the text from scrolling to the end.

The MORE command is handy when another command does not contain a switch that pauses output after each screen is displayed. If MORE is used as the primary command, it displays the contents of the file as if you used the TYPE command. The following command produces the same syntax as the previous command:

C:\MORE longfile.txt

NLSFUNC

Location: C:\Windows\Command\NLSFUNC.EXE

The NLSFUNC command loads country-specific information into the system. Usually, you use this command in conjunction with other country-specific commands, such as KEYB, to convert your system to a specific language.

This command requires a file containing the country-specific information. For example, the following command loads the information from the SPAIN.NFO file:

    C:\NLSFUNC spain.nfo

PROGMAN

Location: C:\Windows\PROGMAN.EXE

PROGMAN launches the classic Windows Program Manager. Although the Explorer interface included with Windows 95 and Windows 98 provides more functionality and ease of use, some people prefer the classic Program Manager interface from Windows 3.1. Running PROGMAN launches that interface.

REGEDIT

Location: C:\Winodws\REGEDIT.EXE

This command launches the Windows 98 Registry Editor. The Registry Editor enables you to modify system settings; it is covered extensively in other sections of this book. It is mentioned here, however, because it is not displayed as an icon by default in the Windows GUI.

App
D

> **CAUTION**
>
> It is possible to cripple your system by making the wrong changes in Registry Editor. Be sure you understand the ramifications of your changes before you make them.

SETVER

Location: C:\Windows\SETVER.EXE

This command sets the version number that Windows 98 reports to a program. This is important when you're running certain applications that run only under a previous version of Windows. The following example of this command sets the reported version of WIN.COM to 3.11:

    C:\SETVER WIN.COM 3.11

After you use this command, when an application requests the version number for this file, it will receive 3.11 instead of 4.1. This fools the application into thinking it is running under Windows for Workgroups.

SETVER takes the following parameters and switches:

FILENAME	Indicates which file's version is to be altered
n.nn	Indicates the new version number to be assigned
/D	Deletes the version table information for the specified file
/Q	Suppresses the warning message displayed when the /D switch is used

START

Location: C:\Windows\Command\START.EXE

This command runs a Windows or DOS program. The reason you would use this command instead of just typing the filename of the program is that it allows you to specify how the program runs initially. To run the GO.BAT file in the background, for example, you would use the following command:

C:\START /m GO.BAT

START takes the following parameters and switches:

/M	Starts the program minimized in the background
/MAX	Starts the program maximized in the foreground
/R	Runs the program restored (foreground)
/W	Prevents the command prompt from returning until the other program exits

WINFILE

Location: C:\Windows\WINFILE.EXE

This command starts the classic Windows File Manager. In Windows 95, this program was replaced by Windows Explorer, but some users prefer to use the File Manager from Windows 3.1. This command was included to give you both options.

WINVER

Location: C:\Windows\WINVER.EXE

This command displays the version of Windows currently running on the system.

Disk and File Commands

Disk and file commands enable you to manipulate files on your system. The following sections cover the Disk and File commands included with Windows 98. After each command is the location where it is stored on the hard drive.

ATTRIB

Location: C:\Windows\Command\ATTRIB.EXE

Use this command to change file attributes from the command line. Each file on the system contains an attribute that Windows 98 uses to protect important files. Those attributes include the following:

- *Archive (A)*. This attribute means the file is an all-purpose file that has no modification restrictions placed on it.
- *System (S)*. The System attribute tells Windows that the file is part of the operating system and should not be directly modified by the user.
- *Read-Only (R)*. The Read-Only attribute protects the file from being modified or deleted. Users can execute and view a Read-Only file, but Windows will not allow users to make any changes to it.
- *Hidden (H)*. The Hidden attribute instructs Windows that the file should not be listed in response to a DIR command. The logic behind this is that a file cannot be corrupted if it is not seen.

To change the attributes of your files with the ATTRIB command, you would use the following command syntax:

ATTRIB [+R | -R] [+A | -A] [+S | -S] [+H | -H] *filename*

The plus and minus sign parameters add or remove the specified attribute. For example, to add the Hidden and Read-Only attributes to a file called TESTDATA.DAT, you would use the following command:

C:\ATTRIB +H +R testdata.dat

You can verify that the attributes have been changed by using the following command:

C:\ATTRIB testdata.dat

When you enter the ATTRIB command followed by the filename only, you see the list of attributes associated with that file.

If you want to change the attribute for all files with a specified path, you can use the /s switch with the command, as shown here:

C;\ATTRIB +r C:\DATA /s

This command adds the Read-Only attribute to all files in the C:\DATA directory.

App
D

CHKDSK

Location: C:\Windows\Command\CHKDSK.EXE

The CHKDSK command runs a quick check of your disk drive and displays a report showing the allocation of space on the disk. CHKDSK is capable of fixing minor problems on a disk, such as file fragmentation. The following command checks a disk and repairs any errors that are found:

C:\CHKDSK C: /F

CHKDSK takes the following parameters and switches:

/F   Tells CHKDSK to fix any errors it finds on the disk

/V   Displays the name and path of every file on a disk

DELTREE

Location: C:\Windows\Command\DELTREE.EXE

The DELTREE command deletes every file in a specified directory and then deletes the folder. This utility is useful for removing unwanted file structures from your drive. For example, to remove a directory called olddata that contains multiple subdirectories, you would use the following command:

C:\DELTREE D:\olddata

CAUTION

This command line utility deletes the specified directory structure without using the Recycle Bin. Be very careful if you use this command.

DELTREE takes the following parameters and switches:

/Y   Tells DELTREE to delete the structure without prompting you for confirmation

path   Specifies the directory you want to delete

DISKCOPY

Location: C:\Windows\Command\DISKCOPY.COM

This command copies the contents of one disk to another. This provides an easy way to duplicate floppy disks. The disadvantage of using DISKCOPY is that both disks must be of the same type. For example, you cannot use DISKCOPY to copy the contents of a 5.25" floppy to a 3.5" floppy. This is because DISKCOPY copies files by tracks. Therefore, both types of media must have the same number of tracks.

To copy the contents of one disk to another using only one disk drive, use the following syntax:

C:\DISKCOPY a: a:

DISKCOPY takes the following parameters and switches:

/1	Forces DISKCOPY to copy only one side of the disk
/V	Verifies the information during transfer
/M	Forces multi-pass copy in memory

EXTRACT

Location: C:\Windows\Command\EXTRACT.EXE

You use the EXTRACT command to extract individual files from *cabinet files*. Microsoft uses cabinet files to store files on distribution media. CAB files can be found on almost every CD or disk that Microsoft distributes. You might use this command, for example, if you wanted to extract a single file from the CD. The syntax of the EXTRACT command is as follows:

C:\EXTRACT *cabfile.cab desiredfile.xxx*

EXTRACT takes the following parameters and switches:

/A	Processes all cabinets starting with the one specified
/C	Copies source file to destination
/D	Displays directory of specified cabinet
/E	Extracts all files
/L	Specifies where to place files after extraction
/Y	Suppresses the confirmation prompt to overwrite existing files

App

D

FC

Location: C:\Windows\Command\FC.EXE

The FC command compares two files and shows the differences between them. To compare the files file1.dat and file2.dat, for example, you would use the following command:

C:\FC file1.dat file2.dat

FC takes the following parameters and switches:

/A	Displays first and last lines of differences only
/B	Forces a binary comparison
/C	Ignores case in letters
/L	Forces ASCII comparison
/LB*n*	Used to set maximum number of mismatches
/N	Displays line number when using an ASCII comparison

/T	Specifies not to treat tabs as spaces
/W	Removes tabs and spaces before comparing the files
/*nn*	Specifies the number of consecutive matching lines required after a mismatch is detected

FDISK

Location: C:\Windows\Command\FDISK.EXE

The FDISK utility enables you to create and delete partitions on a hard drive. FDISK itself is covered earlier in this book. To view partition information from the command line, use the following command:

    C:\FDISK /STATUS

FIND

Location: C:\Windows\Command\FIND.EXE

The FIND command locates a text string in a specified file. For example, to find the word "service" in the file dept.dat, you would use the following command:

    C:\FIND "service" dept.dat

FIND takes the following parameters and switches:

/V	Displays every line in the specified file that does NOT contain the specified text string
/C	Displays only the number of lines containing the string (as opposed to displaying the lines themselves)
/N	Displays line numbers with the lines
/I	Ignores case

FORMAT

Location: C:\Windows\Command\FORMAT.COM

You can use the FORMAT command to format a disk. For example, to format a floppy disk in the A: drive, you would use the following command:

    C:\FORMAT A:

FORMAT takes the following parameters and switches:

/V	Specifies the volume label for the disk
/Q	Forces a quick (erase only) format

/F:*size*	Specifies the size of the disk to be formatted
/B	Allocates space on the disk for system files
/S	Copies the system files to the disk after formatting
/T:*tracks*	Specifies the number of tracks on each side of the disk
/N:*sectors*	Specifies the number of sectors on the track
/1	Formats only one side of a floppy disk
/4	Allows the format of a 360K floppy in a 720K drive
/8	Forces eight sectors per track
/C	Performs a test on any clusters that are marked as bad

LABEL

Location: C:\Windows\Command\LABEL.EXE

The LABEL command allows you to add a volume label to a disk. To add the label HDD1 to your C: drive, for example, you would use the following command:

C:\LABEL C: HDD1

To view the label on your disk, type LABEL or DIR.

MOVE

Location: C:\Windows\Command\MOVE.EXE

The MOVE command enables you to move files from one location to another. It accomplishes this by copying the file to the new location and then deleting the old file. The effect is similar to dragging a file to a new location in Windows Explorer while holding the Shift button.

For example, to move the file EXAM.DAT from C:\data to C:\archive, use the following command:

C:\MOVE C:\data\exam.dat C:\archive\exam.dat

If you want to rename the file to exam.arc while you move it, modify the command as shown here:

C:\MOVE C:\data\exam.dat C:\archive\exam.arc

The MOVE command can also be used to rename a directory without actually moving anything. To rename the data directory to examdata without altering any of the files in it, use the following command:

C:\MOVE C:\data C:\examdata

App
D

SORT

Location: C:\Windows\Command\SORT.EXE

The SORT command sorts input and displays the results. For example, to sort the names in the file NAMES.TXT and write them to the file SORTNAME.TXT, use the following command:

C:\SORT names.txt sortname.txt

You can also pipe other commands through the SORT command in order to sort the output of the primary command. For example, you could type the contents of the AUTOEXEC.BAT file and display each line in alphabetical order with this command:

C:\TYPE autoexec.bat | SORT

SORT takes the following parameters and switches:

/R   Sorts the input in descending order

/+*n*   Sorts the input by the character in column *n*

SUBST

Location: C:\Windows\Command\SUBST.EXE

You can use the SUBST command to associate a path with a drive letter. For example, you would use the following command to associate the path C:\WINDOWS\SYSTEM with the drive letter F:

C:\SUBST F: C:\WINDOWS\SYSTEM

This would allow you to quickly access your system directory without having to type the path repeatedly. Windows 98 will also display a new drive in My Computer and Windows Explorer that corresponds to the specified path. This drive mapping will remain in effect until the system is rebooted or until you use the following command to remove the association:

C:\SUBST F: /D

XCOPY

Location: C:\Windows\Command\XCOPY.EXE

The XCOPY command enables you to copy files and directories from one disk to another. This command is similar to the DISKCOPY command except that XCOPY does not require both disks to be of the same type. Therefore, you can use XCOPY to copy files from a 2GB hard drive to a 6GB hard drive. This is because XCOPY transfers data bit-for-bit instead of copying by tracks.

To copy the contents of drive C: to drive D:, use the following command:

C:\XCOPY C: D:

XCOPY takes the following parameters and switches:

/A	Copies files without changing file attributes
/M	Turns off the Archive attribute when copying files
/D:*date*	Copies only the files that have been modified since the specified date
/P	Prompts before creating each file
/S	Instructs XCOPY not to copy empty directories
/E	Instructs XCOPY to copy empty directories
/W	Prompts for confirmation before copying
/C	Continues copying even if an error occurs
/I	Assumes destination is a directory if it does not exist and multiple files are being copied
/Q	Copies without displaying filenames
/F	Displays full filename while copying
/L	Displays files that will be copied
/H	Copies hidden and system files also
/R	Overwrites read-only files
/T	Creates directory structure without copying the files
/U	Overwrites files that already exist in destination
/K	Copies attributes with files
/Y	Prevents display of a prompt before overwriting existing files
/–Y	Displays a prompt before overwriting existing files
/N	Copies using the short filenames

Network Commands

Network commands can be used to display and modify network settings. The following sections discuss the command line network commands included with Windows 98. After each command is the location where it is stored on the hard drive.

ARP

Location: C:\Windows\ARP.EXE

The ARP command enables you to display and modify the ARP tables used by Address Resolution Protocol to resolve IP addresses to MAC addresses. To display the current ARP tables, type the following command:

    C:\ARP -a

App

D

For example, to add a static entry to the ARP table that associates IP address 172.221.138.14 to MAC address 00-aa-0b-21-c4-02, you would type the following command:

C:\ARP –s 172.221.138.14 00-aa-0b-21-c4-02

Putting this entry in your ARP table effectively ties an IP address to a specific NIC card. Whenever your machine tries to communicate with 172.221.138.14, it ties the specified MAC address into the packet header. You can delete this static ARP table entry with the following command:

C:\ARP –d 172.221.138.14

N O T E   Notice that the switches for this command use the dash (-) instead of the front slash (/). ▪

ARP takes the following parameters and switches:

-A	Displays the current ARP table entries
-N *xxx.xxx.xxx.xxx*	Displays the ARP table of the NIC, specified by IP address; this is handy if you have a multi-homed machine and you need the ARP entries for a specific NIC
-D	Deletes the entry for the specified IP address
-S	Adds an entry to the ARP table

FTP

Location: C:\Windows\FTP.EXE

The FTP command starts the command line File Transfer Protocol utility. This program transfers files with an FTP server. To connect with the FTP server ftp.microsoft.com, for example, you would type the following command:

C:\FTP ftp.microsoft.com

You will be prompted for a username and password. After you enter them, you are returned to the FTP prompt.

Several commands included in the FTP program allow you to navigate through an FTP server. For example, to change to the public directory and download a file called filelist.txt on an FTP server, type the following command:

FTP> cd public
FTP> get filelist.txt

N O T E   Most FTP servers are case sensitive. This is because most FTP servers are running on UNIX systems, and UNIX differentiates between case. If a filename is Filelist.TXT, you must type the name exactly, including case. Typing GET FILELIST.TXT will result in a `file not found` error. ▪

Table D.2 lists the commands you can use to navigate the FTP server.

Table D.2   FTP Command Reference

Command	Description
!	Drops you to a command prompt without exiting FTP. (To return to FTP from the command shell, you must use the exit command.)
?	Displays a list of commands
APPEND	Appends a file to the end of another file
ASCII	Sets the transfer mode to ASCII
BELL	Causes the system to beep when a command is completed
BINARY	Sets the transfer mode to binary
BYE	Disconnects from the remote system and exits FTP
CD	Changes the active directory on the remote system
CLOSE	Disconnects from the remote system
DELETE	Used to delete a file on the remote machine
DEBUG	Activates debug mode
DIR	Displays a list of files in the active directory on the remote system
DISCONNECT	Disconnects from the remote system
GET	Transfers a file from the remote system to the local system
GLOB	Used to expand local filenames
HASH	Prints a pound sign (#) for each buffer transferred. (This is used to monitor file transfer progress.)
HELP	Displays a list of available commands
LCD	Changes the active directory on the local machine
LITERAL	Sends an arbitrary command
LS	Displays the contents of the active directory on the remote machine
MDELETE	Deletes multiple files
MDIR	Displays the contents of multiple directories on the remote machine
MGET	Transfers multiple files from the remote machine to the local machine
MKDIR	Creates a directory on the remote machine
MLS	Displays the contents of multiple directories on the remote machine
MPUT	Transfers multiple files from the local machine to the remote machine
OPEN	Establishes a connection to an FTP server
PROMPT	Forces interactive prompts on any of the multiple-file commands

App

D

continues

Table D.2   Continued

Command	Description
PUT	Transfers files from the local machine to the remote machine
PWD	Shows the contents of the active directory on the local machine
QUIT	Exits FTP
QUOTE	Sends an arbitrary FTP command
RECV	Transfers a file from the remote machine to the local machine
REMOTEHELP	Requests help from the remote server
RENAME	Renames a file
RMDIR	Removes a directory on the remote system
SEND	Transfers a file from the local machine to the remote machine
STATUS	Shows the current environment settings
TRACE	Activates tracing of packets
TYPE	Changes file transfer type
USER	Changes logon credentials without disconnecting from the FTP server
VERBOSE	Activates detailed responses

IPCONFIG

Location: C:\Windows\IPCONFIG.EXE

You can use the IPCONFIG command to display a list of the IP configuration. To display this information, type the following command:

   C:\IPCONFIG

If you are using DHCP, you can use the IPCONFIG command to release and renew your IP address.

IPCONFIG takes the following parameters and switches:

/ALL	Displays detailed information
/BATCH *filename*	Writes the information to a specified filename
RENEW_ALL (DHCP Only)	Renews the IP address for all adapters on the system
RELEASE_ALL (DHCP Only)	Releases all IP addresses on all adapters
RENEW *n*	Renews IP address for the specified adapter
RELEASE *n*	Releases IP address for the specified adapter

N O T E The *n* in the last two switches refers to the LANA number of the card. You can see these numbers by running the IPCONFIG command with no switches. ■

NBTSTAT

Location: C:\Windows\NBTSTAT.EXE

The NBTSTAT command enables you to view current IP connections that are using NetBIOS over TCP/IP. To view the remote machine name table for a machine with an IP address of 169.254.36.201, you would use the following command:

C:\NBTSTAT –A 169.254.36.201

NBTSTAT takes the following parameters and switches:

-a   Displays the remote machine's name table when given its name

-A   Displays the remote machine's name table when given its IP address

-c   Displays the remote name cache

-n   Displays local NetBIOS names

-r   Lists names resolved by broadcast and WINS

-R   Reloads the remote name table

-S   Lists sessions table using IP addresses

-s   Lists sessions table, but resolves IP addresses using the HOSTS file

N O T E Notice that the switches for this command use the dash (-) instead of the front slash (/) and that they are case sensitive. ■

App

D

NET

Location: C:\Windows\NET.EXE

The NET command displays and manages NetBIOS connections to other machines. For example, you can view any network drive mappings by typing the following command:

C:\NET USE

The NET command consists of multiple sections that depend on the first parameter in the command. The following list details the commands available for use with the NET command.

NET CONFIG   The NET CONFIG command displays your current Computer Name, Workgroup name, User Name, and software versions.

NET DIAG   The NET DIAG command enables you to test the connection between two machines on a network. When you run NET DIAG on the first machine, it becomes a network diagnostics server. Subsequent machines will connect to this server when they run NET DIAG.

NET HELP   The NET HELP command provides detailed help on each NET command. You can also use NET HELP to decipher any error number you might receive from a NET command.

NET INIT   You can use the NET INIT command to initialize the network. Basically, it loads the NIC drivers and the protocols, but it doesn't bind them to the Protocol Manager. This command is rarely used anymore because most networking is handled by protected-mode drivers in Windows 98.

NET LOGOFF   This command removes the network bindings from your NIC, which breaks all network connections. This command prevents any network traffic from reaching your system.

NET LOGON   This command allows you to connect to other machines by identifying you as a member of a workgroup. This command is rarely used because you are now given the option of logging on when you start Windows 98.

NET PASSWORD   This command changes your network password stored in the username.PWL file on your system. Changing your password here affects all subsequent logons, including logons on from the GUI at system startup.

NET PRINT   This command allows you to view the printer queues on any network printer you have configured. This command is also rarely used because it is much easier to use the Printers window in the GUI to view print jobs.

NET START   The NET START command allows you to start network services. Note, however, that you cannot start network services from a command prompt. In order to use this command, you must run Windows 98 in MS-DOS mode. This allows you to connect to the network in a fully DOS-compatible environment.

NET STOP   This command stops all network services. Like the NET START command, you cannot stop network services from a command prompt. This command is of value only if you are running in MS-DOS mode.

NET TIME   The NET TIME command enables you to synchronize your system clock with another machine on the network. To synchronize your clock with a computer named TIMESERVER, for example, you would type the following command:

        C:\NET TIME \\TIMSERVER

NET USE   The NET USE command lets you map local drives to network shares. To view a list of drive mappings on your system, type the NET USE command with no parameters. To map your M: drive to the Public share on a computer named HAL9000 from the command prompt, you would use the following command:

        C:\NET USE M: \\HAL9000\PUBLIC

To remove this drive mapping, you would use the following command:

        C:\NET USE M: /DELETE

NET VER   This command displays the type and version of the current redirector.

NET VIEW   The NET VIEW command requests a list of machines on the network from the system designated as the Master Browser. This list is often more up-to-date than what you see in Network Neighborhood because the machine list displayed in Network Neighborhood is received from a backup browser that might not have received the latest update from the Master Browser yet.

NETSTAT

Location: C:\Windows\NETSTAT.EXE

The NETSTAT command displays a list of current IP connections, as well as protocol statistics. This information is useful in troubleshooting connection problems.

The NETSTAT command uses the following switches to modify its output:

-A	Displays all connections
-E	Displays Ethernet statistics
-N	Displays IP addresses and ports numerically
-P *protocol*	Displays connections for only the specified protocol
-R	Displays the routing table
-S	Displays statistics separated by protocol

PING

Location: C:\Windows\PING.EXE

You use PING to measure the stability of a connection by sending ICMP requests to a remote host and measuring the amount of time it takes to receive a response. You can send a ping to either a machine name or an IP address. To ping the IP address 134.16.27.218, you would use the following command:

C:\PING 134.16.27.218

ROUTE

Location: C:\Windows\ROUTE.EXE

The ROUTE command enables you to view and manage the routing table. The routing table is a table of static routes used to direct traffic across the network. Four subcommands are used with the ROUTE command to allow you to perform different functions on your routing tables. These are the four subcommands:

PRINT	Displays information in the routing table
ADD	Adds a route to the routing table
CHANGE	Modifies a route in the routing table
DELETE	Deletes a route from the routing table

App
D

To view the current routing table, type this command:

C:\ROUTE PRINT

To add a static route to the routing table that directs all traffic headed to the 234.0.0.0 subnet through the router 186.124.18.1, you would use the following syntax:

C:\ROUTE ADD 234.0.0.0 255.255.255.0 186.124.18.1

To change this route to point to the router 186.124.18.2, you would use the following command:

C:\ROUTE CHANGE 234.0.0.0 255.255.255.0 186.124.18.2

Finally, to delete this route from the routing table, use the following command:

C:\ROUTE DELETE 234.0.0.0

TRACERT

Location: C:\Windows\TRACERT.EXE

TRACERT enables you to trace the route to a remote machine. For example, you might want to see how many routers you go through when you connect to www.microsoft.com. You could then use this information to help troubleshoot where connection problems exist. To trace a route to www.microsoft.com, use the following command:

C:\TRACERT www.microsoft.com

TRACERT takes the following switches:

-D	Suppresses name resolution
-H *nn*	Indicates the maximum number of hops TRACERT will allow before failure
-W *nn*	Specifies the amount of time to wait for each hop before timeout

Special Features for Notebook Users

by Dean Andrews and Larry Passo

In this chapter

Configuring a Notebook Docking Station

Docking Stations provide an expandable platform for notebook computers. For travel, an un-docked notebook contains the bare minimum of components needed to get the job done—thus keeping weight down. But a docking station brings a notebook's flexibility up to that of a desktop computer by adding additional card slots, drives, and devices such as network and/or video adapters.

Windows 98 supports *hot-docking*, which means you can dock or un-dock a notebook without worrying about whether the notebook's power is on or off. The operating system automatically recognizes the added components of the docking station and configures the necessary software components, including drivers, to support them.

To un-dock a notebook while Windows 98 is running, open the Start menu and choose Eject PC. Windows 98 resets the configuration parameters of the notebook and then asks you to remove the notebook from the docking station.

Creating and Modifying Hardware Profiles

Windows 98 lets you set up multiple hardware profiles for different hardware configurations of your computer. When you install the operating system on a notebook, Windows 98 sets up one hardware profile automatically for you. Then when Windows 98 detects a major change in hardware, such as when you dock the notebook, it creates a second hardware profile for you.

If you want to modify a hardware profile or create a new one, use the following procedure:

1. Open the Start menu and choose Settings, Control Panel.
2. Double-click the System icon to display the System Properties dialog box.
3. Click the Hardware Profiles tab to display the Hardware Profiles page.
4. Select the hardware profile you want to use as the basis for your new profile, and then click Copy. Windows 98 displays a Copy Profile dialog box in which you can edit the name for your new hardware profile (see Figure E.1).
5. Enter a name for your new hardware profile, and then click OK. The new hardware profile appears in the Hardware Profile list.

FIG. E.1

Edit the name for your new hardware profile.

In some cases, you might want to modify a hardware profile—if Windows 98 fails to properly detect your hardware configuration, for example. You can manually adjust the hardware profile.

To modify a hardware profile, use the following procedure:

1. Open the Control Panel and double-click on the System icon. Then click the Device Manager tab to display the Device Manager page.

2. Select the hardware device that you want to add or remove from a particular profile. Then choose Properties to display the General page of the appropriate properties sheet.

3. At the bottom of the device's General page is a Device Usage list that defines which profiles should use this device (see Figure E.2). To remove the device from the current profile, check Disable In This Hardware Profile. To add the device to the current hardware profile, make sure this box is not checked.

4. Click OK to apply the changes.

FIG. E.2

Use the Device Manager Usage list to add or remove hardware from a profile.

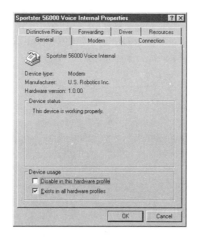

N O T E When you power on the system, Windows 98 automatically detects the hardware profile you previously selected and whether your computer is undocked or docked, and it applies the appropriate hardware profile. If your hardware profiles are so similar that Windows 98 cannot determine which should be used, Windows 98 displays a menu containing a list of available profiles and prompts you to select the profile you want to use. ▪

Working with Different Configurations In Windows 98, you can store different configurations for the same set of hardware devices. You could, for example, run your notebook's video graphics adapter at 640×480 resolution when you don't have an external monitor attached, but set up a profile for using 800×600 resolution when you do have the monitor attached.

To configure a new profile with the same hardware set, first start Windows 98 using the hardware profile in which you want to make changes. To change the resolution for use with an external monitor, for example, select the hardware profile you use when you have the monitor attached. Then change the settings for your new resolution. These changes will be saved in the current hardware profile only; the other hardware profiles are unaffected.

Using PC Card Devices

Almost all notebook computers now come with credit card-sized PC Card slots for quickly adding or removing devices. A wide variety of devices can be found on PC Cards including network adapters, hard drives, SCSI adapters, modems, sound cards, video capture cards, and so forth. PC Card devices allow you to quickly expand the capability of your notebook, yet still maintain the small size and travel weight of the base notebook platform. Windows 98 works with the PC Card controller on-board your notebook to activate these devices.

N O T E As with docking stations, Windows 98 lets you insert and remove PC Cards on-the-fly (called *hot-swapping*) without re-booting the PC.

Notebooks only come with two or three PC Card slots, so sometimes PC Card manufacturers put two or more functions on one PC Card (such as a modem and a network adapter). Windows 98 improves over Windows 95 in the handling of multifunction PC Cards by automatically recognizing the individual functions of these types of cards. Windows 98 lets you configure and enable the functions separately.

N O T E In the past, the PC Card data path was limited to 16 bits. Newer PC Card controllers support PC Card32 (Cardbus), which expands the data path for PC Cards to 32 bits. Windows 98 supports PC Card32, which allows for high-bandwidth data transfer to and from PC Card devices. PC Card devices that require this amount of bandwidth include video capture cards and 10/100Mbs networking cards.

Real-Mode Versus Protected-Mode PC Card Drivers

If your computer has PC Card slots, Windows 98 automatically recognizes and loads the PC Card components of the operating system during the operating system installation. During the installation, Windows 98 preserves any existing PC Card support software so as not to accidentally disable any PC Card devices. It's possible that your pre-Windows 98 PC Cards uses real-mode drivers, but Windows 98 requires a 32-bit protected-mode driver for any card that will be supported via the Plug and Play architecture. Plug and Play PC Card support allows Windows 98 to maximize performance, dynamically load drivers, and stay aware of the insertion and removal of PC Card devices. Fortunately Windows 98 provides two tools that help you transition from real-mode to protected-mode drivers: PC Card Wizard and the PC Card Troubleshooter.

To enable 32-bit PC Card support, activate the PC Card Wizard. To start the PC Card Wizard use the following procedure:

1. Open the Start menu and choose Settings, Control Panel.
2. Double-click on the PC Card (PCMCIA) icon. The first time you do this, Windows 98 displays the PC Card (PCMCIA) Wizard.
3. Choose No and then Next to inform the wizard that you are not setting up Windows 98 from a network server. (If your Windows 98 installation disk is on a network server or a CD-ROM device connected through a PC Card adapter, choose Yes and then Next.)
4. If Windows 98 detects any existing real-mode PC Card drivers, it displays a dialog box asking whether you want to review the changes before Windows disables the drivers. If

you want the wizard to automatically remove the drivers, choose <u>N</u>o and click Next. If you want to view and verify the deletion of the real-mode drivers, choose <u>Y</u>es and click Next.

5. If you selected Yes in step 4, the wizard displays a set of dialog boxes that show the device entries for CONFIG.SYS, AUTOEXEC.BAT, and SYSTEM.INI that it will delete. If you want to save any of these entries, click on it to deselect it, and then click Next.

6. After removing the real-mode drivers (if any), the wizard displays the final dialog box and asks you to click Finish to complete the process and enable 32-bit PC Card Support. Click Finish, and Windows 98 restarts so that the changes can take effect.

If you're having any difficulty getting a particular PC Card to work, invoke the PC Card Troubleshooter. The PC Card Troubleshooter asks you questions about your problem and makes suggestions on possible fixes.

To activate the PC Card Troubleshooter, use the following procedure:

1. Open the Start menu and choose <u>H</u>elp to display the Windows Help screen.

2. On the <u>C</u>ontents tab, click Troubleshooting. Then choose Windows 98 Troubleshooters from the expanded list of troubleshooters.

3. Click on PC Card to activate the PC Card Troubleshooter (see Figure E.3).

FIG. E.3
Use the PC Card
Troubleshooter for help
with PC Card devices.

App

E

Installing PC Card Devices

After you have enabled 32-bit PC Card support, Windows 98 can usually install PC Card devices automatically. When you insert a modem card, for example, Windows 98 detects the new card and automatically installs the new drivers for it. If your PC Card is not recognized automatically, you must manually install support for it.

To manually install a PC Card device other than a modem or network adapter, use the following procedure:

1. Insert the new PC Card into an appropriate slot. (Read the card's documentation and your system's documentation to determine if a particular slot is required.)

2. Open the Control Panel and choose the Add New Hardware object to start the Add New Hardware Wizard. Then choose Next.

3. Choose Yes and then Next to enable the wizard to automatically detect your new PC Card device.

4. If it is unable to detect the new device, the wizard displays a hardware selection dialog box. Choose the type of device you are installing and click Next.

5. Answer the questions regarding your problem and choose Next to continue with the troubleshooting session.

6. Select the Manufacturer of the device you are installing from the Manufacturer's list. Then choose the model of the device from the Model list on the right. If you cannot find your particular device or if your device includes a driver disk, click Have Disk and then follow the onscreen instructions for installing the driver.

7. Click OK to complete the new hardware installation process.

Proper Technique for Removing or Inserting PC Card devices

Before you remove a PC Card device, you should shut it down. Choose the PC Card object in the Control Panel to display Windows 98's PC Card Properties dialog box. There you'll find the list of active PC Cards and their sockets.

To shut down a device, select the device from the list on the Socket Status page and click on Stop. Windows 98 shuts down the device and lists the socket as empty. Then you can physically remove the card from the PC Card slot.

 TIP   If you frequently need to shut down your PC Cards, make it simple by checking the Show Control on Taskbar check box on the PC Card Devices properties sheet. After you install the control on the taskbar, you can double-click on it to open the PC Card Devices Properties sheet.

To insert a new device, you don't need to follow any procedure. Simply insert the device into an appropriate PC Card slot, and Windows 98 automatically starts services for it.

Sharing Resources via a Direct Cable Connection

With Direct Cable Connection, Windows 98 allows you to share files and resources (like a printer) with another computer through either a cable or wireless Infrared ports connecting the two systems. If both PCs do not feature Infrared ports, you must, of course, provide your own serial or parallel cable to attach one PC to another. Once connected, you can quickly access or transfer files back and forth.

Under Direct Cable connection, one PC acts as the host (or server), while the other PC assumes the role of guest (or client). The host PC is the gateway that enables the guest PC to access a network to which the host is attached. In Windows 98, the host can act as a gateway for NetBEUI and IPX/SPX network protocols, as well as for TCP/IP networks.

> **T I P** Because Direct Cable Connection establishes a network connection between the two computers, the guest can access only resources on the host that have been shared for network access.

Setting Up the Direct Cable Connection

Windows 98 automatically installs the Direct Cable Connection components unless you tell it not to with a custom installation. If, for some reason, you do not have Direct Cable Connection installed on your PC, you can go back to the Windows 98 installation disc and install it. Use the following procedure to install Direct Cable Connection from the installation disc:

1. Open the Start menu and choose Settings, Control Panel.
2. Choose the Add/Remove Programs object, and then select the Windows Setup tab.
3. In the Components list, double-click on Communications component to display the communications tools of Windows 98.
4. Click to put a check mark in the Direct Cable Connection box. (If there is already a check there, this utility is already installed on your PC.)
5. Click OK, and Windows installs Direct Cable Connection.

Next you must attach the two computers with a cable or use Infrared ports. Check the documentation of both PCs to determine if they have Infrared ports. Otherwise, locate either a serial or parallel port cable and use it to connect the two systems.

For best performance results, use a parallel port cable. Modern parallel ports can be set to different modes via a computer's BIOS. These settings are usually classified as standard bidirectional, EPP (Enhanced Parallel Port), and ECP (Enhanced Capabilities Port). For fastest data transfer, set both computers to use either EPP or ECP mode for the parallel ports.

The final step involves setting one of the computers as the host and the other as the guest. Those procedures are outlined in the next two sections.

Setting Up the Host

Again in Direct Cable Connection, you need to set up one computer as the host and the other as the guest. First, set up the host computer. To do so, use the following procedure:

1. Open the Start menu and choose Programs, Accessories, Communications, Direct Cable Connection. Windows 98 displays a dialog box asking you if you're setting up the host or the guest.
2. Select the Host option, and then choose Next. Windows 98 displays a dialog box that asks you to choose the port you'll be using for Direct Cable Connection.
3. Choose the port you want to use for your connection. If you are planning to use an Infrared port, choose Install New Ports and follow the instructions for selecting your Infrared device. Otherwise, choose Next.
4. Windows 98 then asks if you want to enable file and print sharing with the guest. If so, choose File and Print Sharing and follow the instructions. Otherwise, choose Next.

App
E

5. Windows 98 asks if you want to password-protect the host in order to prevent unauthorized access. To enable password protection, put a check mark next to Use Password Protection (as shown in Figure E.4). Then choose Set Password to enter the password the guest computer must use to access the host.

6. Choose Finish to complete the setup.

FIG. E.4

Check Use Password Protection if you want to restrict access to the host.

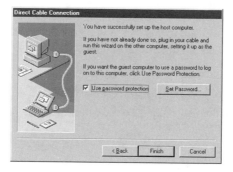

Setting Up the Guest

After you've configured the host, use the following procedure to set up the guest:

1. Open the Start menu and choose Programs, Accessories, Communications, Direct Cable Connection.

2. In the Direct Cable Connection dialog box, choose Guest and then Next.

3. Choose the port for the guest, and then choose Next.

4. Choose Finish to complete the setup.

Using the Direct Cable Connection

After setup, you need to start the Direct Cable Connection software on both the host and guest computers before you can begin sharing resources. First, start the host computer by opening the Start menu and choosing Accessories, Communications, Direct Cable Connection. If the settings in the resulting dialog box are correct, choose Listen to set the host mode. If you want to change any of the settings, choose Change and make your changes.

Then start the Direct Cable Connection on the guest computer. To do so, open the Start menu and choose Accessories, Communications, Direct Cable Connection. The dialog box that appears will look similar to the one you saw when you started the host, except that the Listen button will be a Connect button. Choose Connect to activate the Direct Cable Connection so you can begin sharing resources.

Using the Briefcase to Keep Files in Sync

Most notebook PC users work on a desktop system as well. Many times, users need to transfer files back and forth between their notebook computers and their desktop computers. Someone who takes a notebook while traveling, for example, often finds the need to keep these two sets of files synchronized so that he or she doesn't lose valuable work. Windows 98 supplies a Briefcase feature to help users track and synchronize files shared between PCs.

Here is a typical scenario using Briefcase:

1. You create a Briefcase on your notebook PC.

2. Using Direct Cable Connection, you copy one or more files to the Briefcase over a network or from a desktop.

3. You modify and update the Briefcase files while traveling with your notebook.

4. While you are away from your office, a colleague modifies the same files on your desktop system.

5. When you return to the office you reconnect the notebook and desktop via a network connection or Direct Cable Connection. Then you open the Briefcase on your notebook.

6. You use the Briefcase to determine which files have been modified and which are the most current versions. You can also use the Briefcase to transfer updated files back and forth between the systems.

In essence, the Briefcase is an ordinary folder that has shell extensions and hidden database files that track file changes to the files within the Briefcase folder. Windows 98 creates one Briefcase folder on your desktop during the installation process. However, you might find that creating several small Briefcases where you need them might be more manageable. Additionally, using Briefcases on floppy disks isn't really recommended—even though the Windows documentation says you can—due to the limited space available on floppies.

Creating a Briefcase

Again, Windows 98 automatically creates a Briefcase called My Briefcase on your desktop during installation. But you might find it more effective to create new Briefcases that relate to individual projects. To create a Briefcase, use the following procedure:

App
E

1. Determine where you want to create your new Briefcase. You can specify the desktop or a folder on any available drive.

2. To create a new Briefcase on the desktop, simply right-click on the desktop, choose New, and then choose Briefcase. To create a new Briefcase on your hard drive, start the Windows Explorer, select the folder where you want to store the new Briefcase, and then choose File, New, Briefcase from the Explorer menu. Windows 98 adds a New Briefcase object to the location you have specified.

3. To change the name of the new Briefcase folder, right-click on the folder and choose Rename. Enter the new name for your Briefcase and press Enter.

Adding Files and Folders to a Briefcase

You can use standard file Move and Copy techniques to add files to a Briefcase. Simply open the folder (through My Computer, for example) where the files reside and drag them into the Briefcase folder. If you hold down the Ctrl key while dragging, the files will be copied. If you hold down the Shift key, the files will be moved.

You can also use the Windows Explorer to copy or move files to a Briefcase. By right-clicking on a file, you can send it to a Briefcase. Specifically, you right-click on the file or files you want to send and choose Send To. From the list of files that appears, choose your Briefcase folder. Windows 98 then copies the files you specified.

TIP If you right-drag a file to a Briefcase folder, a menu displays your options. Choose Move Here to move the file or choose Make Sync Copy to copy the file.

Synchronizing Files

Synchronizing files is the key feature of the Briefcase. After you work with shared files remotely on your notebook, save them back to the Briefcase folder.

To do so, reconnect the two computers that you're sharing files between, open the Briefcase, and choose Update All from the controls at the top of the window. Windows 98 displays a dialog box similar to the one shown in Figure E.5.

FIG. E.5
Briefcase displays how the files have been modified.

The Briefcase dialog box shows you when the files were last updated on each of the two machines and which is the more recent version. If the actions suggested in the dialog box are appropriate, choose Update, and Briefcase performs those actions. If an action is not appropriate, right-click on the action to change it. Windows 98 displays the action options from which you can choose. If you just want to check the status but do not need to synchronize the files, choose Cancel in this window.

If you prefer to update individual files, select each file by clicking on it (or hold down the Ctrl key and click on a group of files). Then choose Update Selection from the controls at the top of the Briefcase menu. Only the files you selected will appear in the update list.

For the most effective use of Briefcase, update files across a network or Direct Cable Connection. Using a floppy disk is usually incredibly slow.

Splitting Sync Copies from Originals

In some cases, you may want to disassociate a Briefcase file from the original file. For example, you might need to generate two different reports from the same base file. If you do, you'll need to "split" the file in the Briefcase (the sync copy) from the original file. To do so, highlight the file within the Briefcase and choose Briefcase, Split from Original. Windows 98 changes the entry for that file in the status column to "orphan."

Another way to split a sync copy from an original file is by using the file's properties sheet. Right-click on the Briefcase file you want to split and choose Properties to display the file's properties sheet. Choose the Update Status tab to see the file's synchronization status. You'll see a dialog box similar to the one shown in Figure E.6. Click Split From Original to remove the link between the files.

FIG. E.6

You can also split a sync copy from an original via the file's properties sheet.

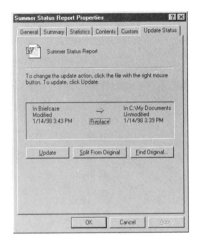

Using Infrared Connections

Infrared light is below the spectrum of red light and is not visible to the human eye. Recently, the use of this light spectrum has moved beyond the world of television and VCR remote controls and into the realm of computers. New Infrared (IR) ports on computers allow wireless connections between computers and devices. Windows 98 supplies software supporting IR ports on notebooks and desktops. Although Infrared ports are still not a common communication medium for computers and computer peripherals, the very latest computers do ship with these IR ports. On a computer with an IR port, Windows 98 lets you share files and resources, communicate to networks, and even print to other computers and peripherals with IR ports.

Unless Windows 98 finds an IR port on your PC during the installation process, it will not install the IR component of the operating system. If, for some reason, your computer features an IR port but Windows 98 did not install the IR software, you can load the software manually from the installation disc.

Use the following procedure to install the Infrared component of Windows 98:

1. Open the Start menu and choose Settings, Control Panel.

2. Choose Add/Remove Programs, and then choose the Windows Setup tab of the Add/Remove Programs Properties dialog box.

3. From the Components list, choose Communications, and then choose Details. Put a check next to the Infrared component and click OK. If the Infrared check box is already checked, the IR software is already installed on your computer.

Setting Up an Infrared Port

Once you've installed the software, you must set up your IR port. Windows 98 provides a wizard to help you through the process. To set up an IR port, use the following procedure:

1. Open the Start menu and choose Settings, Control Panel.

2. Choose the Infrared object in the Control Panel. Windows 98 displays the Add Infrared Device Wizard, shown in Figure E.7.

FIG. E.7
Use the Add Infrared Device Wizard to set up an Infrared port.

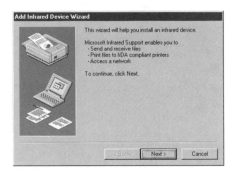

3. Choose Next to display the manufacturer's list of IR devices.

4. If you have driver software for your IR port that arrived with your computer, choose Have Disk. Otherwise, pick the manufacturer's name from the list on the left, and then choose the model name of your IR device.

5. Windows 98 asks you to verify your selection. If it's correct, choose Next. Otherwise, choose Back to go back to the previous screen.

6. The next dialog asks you to confirm the port to which your IR device is attached. If that information is correct, choose Next. Otherwise, choose Back to go back to the previous screen.

7. Choose Finish to complete your IR port setup.

After your IR port is installed, you can use it in place of a serial and parallel cable for a Direct Cable Connection. Read that section of this chapter to find the instructions for setting an IR port for Direct Cable Connection. ●

Index

B

back slashes (\\), in URLs, 606

backgrounds
colors (Windows Paint toolbox), 280
inserting in web pages, 803
web pages as, 679

Backup Domain Controllers (BDCs), 884, 939

Backup Job Options dialog box, 348, 368

backups
Backup utility, 13, 338-340
changing settings, 349
formatting tapes, 345
full system, 345-347
installing tape drives, 344-345
partial, 348
Registry, 347-348, 366
copying, 367-368
creating startup disks, 367
ERU (Emergency Repair Utility), 369
exporting, 368
tape drives, 368
restoring, 350-351
running backup jobs, 349
schedules for, 342, 349
selecting
files for, 342-343
hardware for, 343-344
storage, 340
strategy for, 341
types of, 341-342
verifying, 339

batch files (WordPad), 266-267

batteries (power management), 559

BBSs (bulletin board systems), file exchange, 253

BDCs (Backup Domain Controllers), 884, 939

BELL FTP command, 1037

bfff series (Fatal Exception errors), 300

BFT (Binary File Transfer), 983

Binary data (Registry), 356

binary files
faxing, 983
opening with Notepad, 263
uploading with HyperTerminal, 255-256

BINARY FTP command, 1037

Bindery Connection option (Client 32 Login tab), 897

bindings (protocols), adjusting, 862

BIOS (basic input/output system)
CD-ROM disk drives, support, 138
Plug and Play compliant, 542

bit depth (WAV files), 506

bitmap fonts, 456-458

Bitstream Font Navigator, 464

Bitstream TrueDoc fonts, 464

BMP (Windows bitmap files), in Thumbnail view, 82

Bookmark dialog box (FrontPage Express), 799

bookmarks, inserting in web pages, 799-800

boot process
Plug and Play, 543-544
see also startup disks

Boot tab (TweakUI), 1012-1013

bootable hard disk drives, 147-148

borders around tables in web pages, 808

BREAK command, 1023

Briefcase, 1050-1051
adding files to, 1051-1052
creating, 1051
splitting sync files from originals, 1053
synchronizing files, 1052

Browse dialog box, 173, 177

browse methods (user-level access), NetWare networks, 900-901

Browser Title, Wizard Settings (IEAK), 911

browsers (Internet Explorer)
accessibility options, 625
add-ins and plug-ins, 617-618
Address bar, 605-606
AutoComplete feature, 606-607
browsing options, 625-627
offline, 644-645
without graphics, 621-623
cache management, 623
default mail/news clients, 620
displaying web pages, 603-610
fonts/colors, changing, 615-616
foreign language web pages, viewing, 616-617
frame-based pages, 607-609
hiding toolbars and status bar, 613
home page, setting, 613
HTTP 1.1 options, 632
hyperlinks, 603-605
image maps, 610
increasing
browser window size, 613-614
speed of downloads, 621-624
Java VM options, 630
Links toolbar, 637-638
multimedia options, 627-628
navigating
with keyboard, 609-610
with mouse, 607
overview, 600
printing options, 631
frames, 234
web pages, 645-647
refreshing web pages, 612
revisiting sites with History Bar, 643-644
saving and editing web pages, 648
searching options, 631
with Find, 642
search engines, 639-642
security options, 628-630
starting, 605
status bar, 611-612
stopping web page downloads, 612
streaming media players, 619-620
toolbar options, 632
URLs (Uniform Resource Locators), 600-602
viewing cached files, 624